SECOND

THE
PROGRESSIVE
ENGLISH
DICTIONARY

A S Hornby and E C Parnwell

OXFORD UNIVERSITY PRESS

Oxford University Press, Walton Street, Oxford OX2 6DP

GLASGOW NEW YORK TORONTO MELBOURNE WELLINGTON
CAPE TOWN IBADAN NAIROBI DAR ES SALAAM
DELHI BOMBAY CALCUTTA MADRAS KARACHI
KUALA LUMPUR SINGAPORE JAKARTA HONG KONG TOKYO

Set in Monotype Univers and Plantin and
printed in Great Britain by Richard Clay
(The Chaucer Press) Ltd, Bungay, Suffolk

PREFACE TO THE SECOND EDITION

The Progressive English Dictionary is one of three Oxford dictionaries that have been specially compiled for learners of the English language, under the general editorship of A S Hornby. The common purpose of these dictionaries is to provide definitions of words in the simplest terms consistent with accuracy.

This second edition has been carefully revised to offer a unique pocket guide to the meanings, structure, and usage of current English. It includes a vocabulary likely to be met in general conversation and reading and, as the spoken word becomes more important with the advance of mass communications through newspapers, radio, films, and TV, more attention has been paid to colloquialisms and contemporary words and phrases, which these media now bring into homes everywhere.

Features of the first edition such as stress patterns, parts of speech, and stylistic values (legal, commerce, etc) have been retained and revised. Information on irregular plurals and conjugations, comparatives and superlatives, and the doubling of consonants has been re-examined and expanded. Where necessary, definitions are supported by pictures and numerous illustrative phrases and sentences. A full set of Appendices and Exercises on how to use the dictionary are included for the first time.

Those who become familiar with the use of this pocket dictionary will be fully prepared for using the larger *An English-Reader's Dictionary* and later *The Advanced Learner's Dictionary of Current English*.

London 1972

A S H
E C P

HOW TO USE THIS DICTIONARY

A dictionary, used properly, can tell you much more than how to spell words. It can extend and improve your knowledge of English far beyond the range of any text-book. Below is a detailed explanation of the information available to you in this dictionary. Numbers in brackets refer to the short extracts opposite which give you an example of each feature mentioned.

The headword is printed in **bold** type (1) with stress marks, ' for the main stress in words of more than one syllable (1) and ₁ for a secondary stress, as in the word ₁ado'lescent. Where a word is spelt the same but has two or more unrelated meanings, the word is listed a second or third time and numbered ¹, ² etc (1).

Derivatives (2) and idiomatic usage (3) are also shown in **bold** type. Parts of speech (4) are in *italicized* abbreviations (⇨ the list opposite).

Definitions are in simple English and numbered with **bold** figures in the articles. Example phrases and sentences, in *italics*, are included (5) and prepositions that always follow the headword in a particular usage are also shown in *italics* (11). A number in brackets (⇨ the entries at **affect**, **age**) refers to the **bold** definition number in the article of the preceding word.

Comparatives and superlatives of adjectives are included for all the irregular examples (**bad**, worse, worst) and the common -r, -st (6) varieties (or -er, -est; -ier, -iest, etc). The doubling of the final consonants of certain verbs is indicated (7) and irregular conjugations (10) are also included. ⇨ p 329.

Irregular plurals of nouns are given (8); where the stress or the spelling of the headword changes, the plural form is printed in full (a), in other cases, only the plural ending is given (b). Special meanings and usage in particular contexts (law, maths, old use, etc) are shown (12) (⇨ the list on the next page). Cross-references are always preceded by an arrow (9); when the reference is to a picture, a page number is given (a), and when it is to another article, the other head-word is printed (b). Where — or — appears in an article it replaces the headword of that article (5).

⇨ p 340 for Exercises on how to use this dictionary.

EXTRACTS

'absent¹ *adj* not here; not present.
  'absent-'minded *adj* not thinking of what one is doing. **,absen-**
  'tee *n* one who is —. **'absence** *n*.
ab'sent² *v* — oneself from, not be
  present at.

— 2
— 3
} 1

a'cross *prep* **1** from side to side of:
run — the road. **2** on the other side
of: *the house — the street.* **3** so as to
cross or form a cross: *She lay with
her arms — her breast.* *adv*: *The
river is a mile —*, a mile wide.

— 4
} 5

a'cute *adj* (-r, -st) **1** (of pain)
sharp. **2** (of the senses, mind, etc)
keen. **3** clever; responding quickly
4 (of an illness) coming quickly to
a turning-point. **5** an — angle,
one of less than 90°.

— 6
— 3

an'nul *v* (-ll-) put an end to (a law,
agreement, etc).

— 7

appendix *n* **1** (*pl* ap'pendices)
sth added, esp at the end of a book.
2 (*pl* -es) small tube attached
to the large intestine. ⇨ p 30.

— a
— b
} 8

are, aren't ⇨ be.

— a
— b
} 9

a'rise *v* (*pt* a'rose, *pp* a'risen)
1 come into existence; come to
notice. **2** result (*from*). **3** (old use)
stand up, get up.

— 10
— 11 — 12

ABBREVIATIONS

The following abbreviations, in *italics*, give the parts
of speech after each headword and subsidiary headword:

adj	adjective	*pp*	past participle
adv	adverb	*prep*	preposition
conj	conjunction	*pron*	pronoun
int	interjection	*pt*	past tense
n	noun	*sing*	singular
pl	plural	*v*	verb

Other abbreviations used in the text are:

attrib	attributive	liter	literary style
cf	compare	neg	negative
colloq	colloquial	opp	opposite
eg	for example	p	page
esp	especially	sb	somebody
etc	et cetera	sth	something
fig	figurative	USA	American usage
Gt Brit	British usage	usu	usually

▷ p 247 means *look at page 247.*
▷ foot means *look at the entry at 'foot'.*
See also Common Abbreviations, p 323.

Comparatives and superlatives are shown as follows:

well ('better, best)　　　　**full** (-er, -est)
fine (-r, -st)　　　　**'angry** (-ier, -iest)

The doubling of consonants is shown as follows:

fit (-tt-)　　　**hem** (-mm-)　　　**pre'fer** (-rr-)
ban (-nn-)　　　**mop** (-pp-)　　　**shrug** (-gg-)

Irregular plural forms of nouns are shown as follows:

'mango (*pl* 'mangoes)　　　　**'radius** (*pl* 'radii)

or the plural ending is given:

,appa'ratus (*pl* -es)　　　　**'body** (*pl* -ies)

Words beginning with **ch-** which are pronounced as if they begin **k-** are shown as follows:

'cholera (k-)　　**chord** (k-)　　**'Christian** (k-)　　**choir** (kw-)

Many words have special meanings in particular contexts. These contexts are given in brackets.
See the following entries for examples:

corporal	(army)	pitch	(music)
ark	(Bible)	rating	(navy)
credit	(book-keeping)	brethren	(old use)
petty cash	(business)	density	(physics)
salt	(chemistry)	left	(political)
advise	(commerce)	compose	(printing)
century	(cricket)	loch	(Scotland)
noun	(grammar)	genus	(science)
herald	(historical)	transplant	(surgery)
damage	(law)	billion	(Gt Britain)
apparel	(literary)	analyst	(USA)
congruent	(maths)	bloody	(vulgar)
genteel	(modern use)	front	(war)

A

a, an (*indefinite article*) **1** one; any. **2** each, every: *twice a day*; *twenty miles an hour*.

a'back *adv* **taken —**, surprised.

a'bandon *v* **1** leave, go away from (not intending to return to). **2** give up. **— oneself to**, give oneself up to; cease to control (one's feelings). **—ed** *adj* (of a person) given up to bad ways.

a'base *v* bring or make lower (in rank, honour, or self-respect).

a'bashed *adj* embarrassed; confused.

a'bate *v* **1** make or become less. **2** (law) put a stop to.

'abbess *n* woman at the head of a nunnery; Mother Superior.

'abbey *n* (*pl* —s) **1** society of men (monks) living apart from others in the service of God. **2** building(s) in which they live(d). **3** the church of an —.

an abbey   an abbot

'abbot *n* man at the head of a monastery; Father Superior.

ab'breviate *v* make (a word, story, etc) shorter. **ab,brevi'ation** *n* shortening; short form.

'abdicate *v* give up (a throne, right, position of authority). **,abdi'cation** *n*.

'abdomen, ab'domen *n* belly; lower front part of the body including the stomach and bowels. ⇨ p 29.

a'bet *v* (-tt-) **aid and —**, help and encourage (to do wrong).

a'beyance *n* **in —**, condition of not being in force or in use for a time.

ab'hor *v* (-rr-) feel hatred or disgust for. **—rence** *n* extreme hatred or disgust; sth for which hatred or disgust is felt.

a'bide *v* (*pt & pp* a'bode) **1 — by**, be true and faithful to (a promise, etc). **2** bear; put up with.

a'bility *n* **1** power (esp of mind) to do things. **2** (*pl*) cleverness of mind.

'abject *adj* **1** unreserved; without self-respect: *an — apology*. **2** (of behaviour) deserving contempt. **3** (of conditions) wretched. **'ably** *adv*.

a'blaze *adv & adj* on fire; bright as if on fire.

'able *adj* **1 be — to do sth**, have the time, power, money, etc. ⇨ can, could. **2** clever; showing or having skill and knowledge. **'ably** *adv*.

ab'normal *adj* not normal; different from what is usual, ordinary, or expected. **,abnor'mality** *n* being —; sth —.

a'board *adv & prep* on(to) or in(to) a ship or aircraft.

a'bode *n* (old use) house; living-place. *v* ⇨ abide.

a'bolish *v* put an end to; stop altogether (eg war or slavery). **,abo'lition** *n* act of —ing; being —ed.

a'bominable *adj* causing horror and disgust; (colloq) very bad.

,abo'riginal *adj* existing (in a place, country, etc) from the beginning. *n* — person, plant, etc. **,abo'rigines** *n pl* earliest known inhabitants of a country (esp Australia).

a'bound *v* **1** be plentiful. **2 — in (with)**, have in great numbers or amounts.

a'bout *prep* **1** in various directions; to or in various places. **2** somewhere near: *The town is — here on the map.* **3** having to do with; concerning. *adv* **1** a little more or less: *— a half*; a little before or after: *— 10 o'clock.* **2** here and there; to or in various places.

a'bove *prep* **1** higher than: *Your name comes — mine on the list.* **2** greater in number, price, weight. **3** more than: *A good soldier values* *honour — life.* **— all,** more than anything else. *adv* **1** *Seen from —, the land looks flat.* **2** (in a book, etc) earlier: *I must repeat what I said —.* **'above-'board** *adj & adv* straightforward(ly).

a'breast *adv* (of persons, ships, etc) (moving) side by side (in the same direction). **— of,** level with; informed about.

a'bridge *v* make shorter, esp by using fewer words; cut short an interview (the time a thing lasts). **—ment** *n* making shorter; sth (esp a book or play) made shorter.

a'broad *adv* **1** to or in other countries. **2** everywhere; in all directions.

a'brupt *adj* **1** sudden; unexpected. **2** (of speech, writing, behaviour) sudden; rough.

'abscess *n* collection of thick yellowish-white liquid (called *pus*) or other poisonous matter in a hollow place in the body.

ab'scond *v* go away (*with* sth) suddenly, secretly, and aware of doing wrong.

'absent¹ *adj* not here; not present. **'absent-'minded** *adj* not thinking of what one is doing. **,absen-'tee** *n* one who is —. **'absence** *n.*

ab'sent² *v* — oneself from, not be present at.

'absolute *adj* **1** complete; perfect. **2** unlimited; having complete power. **,abso'lutely** *adv.*

ab'solve *v* set or declare free from (blame, guilt, a promise, duty, or the consequences of past sin). **,abso'lution** *n* forgiveness (by a religious act) for past wrongdoing.

ab'sorb *v* **1** take in or up; soak up. **2** take up or occupy (attention, time). **—ent** *adj* able to —. **—ing** *adj* taking up the thoughts, attention, etc, completely.

ab'stain *v* do without (esp alcoholic drinks); hold oneself back (*from*). **—er** *n* sb who —s.

ab'stemious *adj* sparing or moderate in the use of enjoyable things (esp good food and drink).

'abstinence *n* abstaining (*from* food, drink, enjoyment). **total —,** abstaining completely from alcoholic drinks.

'abstract *adj* opposite to what is material or concrete. **— painting,** one with shapes and designs that do not represent the actual image of its subject(2). *n* short account (of the chief ideas in a book, speech, etc). **ab'stract** *v* take away; separate from. **ab'stracted** *adj* not paying attention. **ab'straction** *n* state of being —ed or lost in thought; idea not concerned with material things, eg *truth, whiteness.*

ab'struse *adj* whose meaning or answer is hidden or obscure.

ab'surd *adj* foolish; causing laughter; unreasonable. **—ity** *n* state of being —; — idea or thing.

a'bundance *n* **1** great plenty. **2** number or quantity that is more than enough. **a'bundant** *adj* more than enough; plentiful; rich (*in*).

a'buse *n* **1** wrong, rough, or harmful treatment. **2** angry complaint. **3** wrong or unjust custom or practice. **4** wrong use. *v* make wrong use of; treat badly; say severe and harsh things to or about. **a'busive** *adj* containing or using —.

a'byss *n* great hole so deep as to appear bottomless. **a'bysmal** *adj* bottomless; extreme.

,aca'demic *adj* of schools, colleges, learning, or teaching; concerned with theory rather than with practice.

a'cademy *n* **1** school for higher learning, usu for a special subject or purpose: *a military —.* **2** society of learned men.

ac'cede *v* **1** agree (*to* a proposal, etc). **2** succeed (*to* a position of authority).

ac'celerate *v* increase the speed of; become quicker; make sth happen sooner. **ac'celerator** *n* (esp) that part of a machine (eg a pedal in a motor vehicle) that controls its speed.

'accent *n* **1** (in speaking) extra force or stress given to one part of a word of more than one syllable, or to certain words in a sentence. **2** printed mark above or below a letter. **3** particular way of speaking or pronouncing a language. **ac'cent** *v* add stress to; mark with a written or printed —.

ac'centuate *v* give more force or importance to. **ac,centu'ation** *n.*

ac'cept *v* (agree to) take what is

offered. **—able** adj pleasing; welcome. **—ance** n.

'access n 1 way (in)to a place. **easy of —,** easy to get at, in(to). 2 right of reaching, using, speaking (to). **ac'cessible** adj easy to reach or approach.

ac'cession n 1 coming to or reaching power or a position: the Queen's — to the throne. 2 addition; increase.

ac'cessory n sth extra, helpful, and useful, but not a necessary part.

'accident n chance happening; disastrous event: a railway —. **by —,** by chance. **,acci'dental** adj happening by chance.

ac'claim v 1 welcome (with shouts of approval). 2 make (sb) ruler with loud cries.

ac'climatize v get (oneself, an animal or a plant) used to a new climate.

ac'commodate v 1 have or provide room(s) for. 2 adjust (to). **ac'commodating** adj willing to fit in with the wishes of others. **ac,commo'dation** n room(s), etc, provided for visitors.

ac'company v 1 go with; happen or do at the same time as. 2 play music to support a singer or other performer. **ac'companiment** n sth that accompanies, esp music on or for a piano to support a voice or solo instrument.

ac'complice n helper or companion in wrongdoing.

ac'complish v finish successfully. **—ed** adj skilled (esp in social arts such as music, painting). **—ment** n 1 finishing. 2 sth well done; sth one can do well (eg in social arts).

ac'cord n agreement (eg between two countries). **of one's own —,** without being asked or forced. v give (a welcome) (to); be in harmony (with). **—ance** n agreement. **—ing to** prep as stated by; in a way that is fitting. **—ingly** adv for that reason.

ac'cordion n portable musical instrument with a keyboard. ⇨ p 180.

ac'cost v speak to (usu a stranger).

ac'count v 1 — for, explain satisfactorily; give reasons for; keep or, give written statements about

(money or goods). 2 consider. n 1 written statement(s) with details (esp of money received and paid, articles bought and sold, etc). **on —,** in part payment. 2 story or description. 3 reason; cause. **on no (not on any) —,** for no reason. **on this —,** for this reason. 4 use; profit; importance. **of no —,** useless; worthless. **take into —,** consider. **take no — of,** pay no attention to. **on one's own —,** by and for oneself. **—able** adj expected to give an explanation (for). **—ancy** n work of keeping **—s(1).** **—ant** n person who keeps **—s(1).**

ac'cumulate v come or gather together; become (cause to become) greater in number or amount. **ac,cumu'lation** n.

'accurate adj careful and exact (in doing things); free from error. **'accuracy** n.

ac'cuse v say (a person) is guilty (of). **the —d,** the —d person in a law court. **,accu'sation** n.

ac'custom v get (sb) used to (sth). **—ed** adj usual.

ace n 1 playing card with the value 'one' mark on it. **within an ace of,** very near to. 2 champion airman or racing-driver.

ache n continuous pain. v have an —.

a'chieve v finish; reach; carry out successfully. **—ment** n achieving; sth —d.

'acid n 1 strong, sour liquid. 2 (chemistry) one of a class of substances containing hydrogen, that combine with alkalis to form salts. adj with the properties of an —; sour; sharp-tasting. **a'cidity** n.

ac'knowledge v 1 admit (that sth is true). 2 send news that one has received sth. 3 regard (as). **—ment** n act of acknowledging; letter given or sent that **—s** sth received.

'acme n highest point: the — of good behaviour.

a'coustic adj of the sense of hearing. **—s** n the science of sound; the — properties (eg of a hall).

ac'quaint v make aware; make familiar (with). **be —ed with,** have personal knowledge of (sb or sth). **—ance** n 1 slight personal knowledge. 2 person whom one has met a few times.

,acqui'esce v agree without protest (in). ,acqui'escence n
,acqui'escent adj willing to —.

ac'quire v become the owner of;
gain by skill, cash, ability, or
experience. an —d taste, one that
is not natural (3). —ment n acquiring; sth —d. ,acqui'sition n
—ment. ac'quisitive adj eager to
—; in the habit of acquiring.

ac'quit v (-tt-) 1 say that (sb) has
not done wrong, is not guilty (of
a crime). 2 — oneself (well, etc),
do one's work or duty (well, etc).
—tal n.

'acre n measure of land area (4,840
square yards or about 4,000 square
metres).

'acrid adj (of smell or taste) sharp;
bitter.

'acrobat n person who can do clever
tricks with his body, such as
balancing on a rope. ,acro'batic
adj.

a'cross prep 1 from side to side of:
run — the road. 2 on the other side
of: the house — the street. 3 so as to
cross or form a cross: She lay with
her arms — her breast. adv: The
river is a mile —, a mile wide.

act v 1 do sth. 2 take a part in a play
on stage, a film, etc. act as, serve
as; do the work of. act upon, have
an effect on; (advice, etc), do (what
is advised, etc). n 1 thing done. in
the act of, while doing. 2 law
passed by Parliament. 'acting
adj doing work usually done by
another.

'action n 1 movement; doing; using
energy, influence, etc. out of —,
not fit to work, to be used, etc.
2 effect. 3 thing done. 4 fighting;
a battle. 5 (law) bring an —
(against), seek judgement
(against) in a law court.

'active adj 1 working; at work;
in the habit of moving quickly.
2 practical; effective. on — service, (of a soldier) engaged in
fighting. ac'tivity n being —;
purpose about which a person
is —.

'actor n man who acts in plays and
films. 'actress n woman actor.

'actual adj real; not imagined; present. —ly adv really; in truth; for
the time being.

a'cute adj (-r, -st) 1 (of pain)
sharp. 2 (of the senses, mind, etc)

keen. 3 clever; responding quickly.
4 (of an illness) coming quickly to
a turning-point. 5 an — angle,
one of less than 90°.

a'dapt v change in order to make
suitable for (a new purpose).
—able adj able to — or be —ed.
,adap'tation n —ing; result of
—ing. a'daptor n attachment that
enables sth (esp electrical apparatus) to be used for a new
purpose.

add v 1 find the total of (two or
more numbers). 2 join (one thing
to another). 3 say sth more.

ad'dendum n (pl ad'denda) thing
(omitted) that ought to be added.

'adder n small poisonous snake.

ad'dict v —ed to, (of a person) in
the habit of devoting himself to;
given up to. 'addict n person
—ed to (drugs, etc).

ad'dition n adding; thing (to be)
added. in — (to), further; besides.
—al adj extra.

ad'dress v 1 direct (send) a written
or spoken message; make a speech
to. 2 — oneself to (a piece of work,
etc), be busy with; work at. n 1
particulars of the town, street, etc,
where a person can be found.
2 speech to an audience. 3 way of
speaking or behaving. 4 pay one's
—es to, show by words, etc that
one wants the favour of.

'adept n & adj (one who is) skilled
(in, at).

'adequate adj enough; having the
qualities needed.

ad'here v become or stay stuck fast
to (eg with glue); give support (to
a party, etc); hold or be faithful
(to opinions, etc). —nce n. —nt n
supporter.

ad'hesive adj sticky. n glue.

a'dieu int good-bye.

ad'jacent adj near; next (to) but
not necessarily touching.

'adjective n word that names a
quality: large, red, beautiful.
,adjec'tival adj.

ad'join v be next or nearest to.

ad'journ v 1 break off (a meeting,
etc) until later. 2 (of a group) stop
doing sth, and separate or go to
another place. —ment n.

'adjunct n sth joined to a more
important thing.

ad'just v put in order or agreement; make suitable or convenient.

—able *adj.* —ment *n* —ing or being —ed; thing used for —ing.

ad'minister *v* 1 control; manage; look after (*business affairs*, etc). 2 put (*laws*, etc) into operation; give (*justice, punishment*). 3 cause (sb) to take (*medicine, an oath*). ad,minis'tration *n* 1 management (*of business affairs*, etc). 2 government of a country. 3 the Administration, the officials who govern. 4 giving (*of relief, justice*, etc). ad'ministrative *adj.* ad-'ministrator *n.*

'admirable *adj* excellent.

'admiral *n* naval officer of highest rank; officer commanding a fleet of warships. 'Admiralty *n* branch of government controlling the Navy.

ad'mire *v* look at with pleasure or respect; have a high opinion of. ,admi'ration *n* feeling of pleasure, satisfaction, and respect (*for*).

ad'mit *v* (-tt-) 1 allow to enter. 2 say unwillingly; confess; agree (that sth is true). 3 — of, leave room for (*doubt*, etc). ad'mission *n* —ting(1) (2) or being —ted(1) (2); statement —ting(2) sth. ad'missible *adj* that may be allowed or considered. —tance *n* —ting(1) or being —ted(1).

ad'monish *v* advise to do right; warn against wrongdoing. ,admo'nition *n.*

a'do *n* activity, usu causing excitement.

,ado'lescent *n & adj* (boy or girl) growing up (between the ages of about 13 and 20). ,ado'lescence *n.*

a'dopt *v* 1 take (sb) into one's family legally as one's own child. 2 follow or use (*a method*, etc). —ion *n* act of —ing.

a'dore *v* worship (God); love (sb) deeply and respect highly; (colloq) be fond of. a'dorable *adj* fit to be —d. ,ado'ration *n.*

a'dorn *v* add beauty or ornaments to. —ment *n* —ing; sth used for —ing.

a'drift *adv & adj* (of ships and boats) driven by wind and water and not under control. turn —, send away (from home or employment).

a'droit *adj* clever; skilful.

adu'lation *n* too much praise or respect (esp to win favour).

'adult *n & adj* (person or animal) grown to full size and strength.

a'dulterate *v* make impure or poorer in quality by adding sth of less value. a,dulte'ration *n.*

a'dultery *n* (of a husband or wife) act which breaks the marriage vow of faithfulness. a'dulterer *n*, a'dulteress *n* man, woman, guilty of —.

ad'vance *v* 1 come, go, put or keep, forward. 2 (of prices) make or become higher. 3 pay (money) before it is due; lend (money). *n* 1 forward movement. in — (of), in front (of); sooner. 2 rise in price of value. 3 sum of monty asked for, paid or given before it is due. 3 (*pl*) attempts to become a friend or lover. —d *adj* leading others (in ideas, etc). —ment *n* progress.

ad'vantage *n* better position; profit; sth likely to bring success. take — of, make (fair or unfair) use of. ,advan'tageous *adj* helpful; useful; profitable.

'advent *n* coming or arrival (of an important person or event). A—, season (with four Sundays) before Christmas; the coming of Christ.

ad'venture *n* unusual, exciting, or dangerous journey or activity. —r *n* person who seeks —; person ready to make a living in dangerous (and often dishonest) ways. ad'venturous *adj* fond of, ready for, —; full of danger and excitement.

'adverb *n* word which answers questions beginning *How? When? Where?* ad'verbial *adj* of or like an —.

'adversary *n* enemy.

'adverse *adj* unfavourable; against one's interests. ad'versity *n* trouble; misfortune.

'advertise *v* make known to people by printed notices (in newspapers, etc), or by other methods, usu for the purpose of trade; ask (*for*) by a public notice. —r *n.* ad'vertisement *n* advertising; statement or other thing which —s.

ad'vice *n* opinion given about what to do or how to act.

ad'vise *v* give advice to; (commerce) inform. ill-advised, unwise. well-advised, wise. ad'visable *adj* to be —d; wise.

'advocate *n* sb who speaks in favour of a person or cause (esp in a law court). *v* speak in favour of (ideas, causes).

'aerial *n* wire(s) for receiving or sending radio waves. *adj* of or in the air; imaginary.

'aero- *prefix* of air and flying. **—drome** *n* landing-ground. **—plane** *n* flying-machine.

aes'thetic *adj* of beauty in nature, art, literature, music, etc.

a'far *adv* far off.

'affable *adj* friendly; good-humoured; easy to talk to. ,affa'bility *n*, **'affably** *adv*.

af'fair *n* 1 sth done or thought about; business matter. 2 (*pl*) business; events. 3 event; happening.

af'fect *v* 1 have a result or effect on; arouse the feelings of. 2 pretend to have, do, or be. **—ed** *adj* not natural (3). ,affec'tation *n* behaviour, show of feeling, that is not natural or genuine.

af'fection *n* 1 love; kindly feeling. 2 illness; disease. **—ate** *adj* loving; showing a feeling of love.

,affi'davit *n* written statement made on one's oath.

af'filiate *v* accept as a member or branch of a society; become connected (*with*). af,fili'ation *n*.

af'finity *n* 1 close connection, eg between animals, languages, etc. 2 attraction.

af'firm *v* declare firmly. ,affir'mation *n* **—ing**; sth **—ed**, esp (law) a solemn declaration made by a person not wishing to take an oath. **af'firmative** *adj & n* (answering) 'yes'.

'affix *n* suffix or prefix. **af'fix** *v* fix or fasten (sth *to* or *on*); put on (*a stamp*, etc).

af'flict *v* cause pain, suffering, or trouble to. **—ion** *n* (cause of) suffering.

af'fluence *n* being wealthy. **in —**, having plenty of money for one's needs. **'affluent** *adj* wealthy; well off.

af'ford *v* spare or find enough time or money for; (of things) provide; give.

af'front *v* hurt sb's feelings or self-respect, esp in public. *n* public insult.

a'field *adv* to or at a distance.

a'fire *adv & adj* aflame.

a'flame *adv & adj* burning.

a'float *adv & adj* 1 resting on the surface of. 2 at sea. 3 (of a business) started. 4 (of rumours) spreading about.

a'fraid *adj* 1 frightened; feeling fear. 2 *I'm — I can't come*, polite way of giving information that will not be welcome.

a'fresh *adv* again; in a new way.

aft *adv* at or towards the rear (stern) of a ship.

'after *prep* 1 following in time; later than. **— that,** then. 2 next in order; following: *Wednesday comes — Tuesday.* 3 one — another, in turn, in succession. 4 in search of: *The police are — the men who robbed the bank. adv* later in time. *conj* at or during a time later than: *He came — I had left.*

'aftermath *n* (fig) what follows; the outcome (of an event).

,after'noon *n* period between morning and evening.

'afterthought *n* thought or explanation that comes to mind after sth has happened.

'afterwards *adv* following in time or position; after; later: *I did not realize what had happened till —.*

a'gain *adv* 1 once more; a second time. **now and —,** occasionally. **— and —,** very often. 2 as before: *She will soon be well —.*

a'gainst *prep* 1 in opposition to: *The majority voted — the scheme. John ran — Paul in the first race.* 2 in the opposite direction to: *We sailed — the current.* 3 close to, alongside and touching: *He left the ladder leaning — the wall.*

age *n* 1 length of time a person has lived or sth has been in existence. **of age,** (in Gt Brit) 18 years old. 2 a stage or period in life: *old age; middle age.* 3 long period of time, esp one in history: *the Middle Ages* (in Europe, A.D. 600 to 1450). 4 (colloq) a long time. *v* (cause to) grow old; begin to look old. *adj* 1 **aged** of the age of. 2 **'aged** having lived long. **'ageless** *adj* never fading. **'age 'long** *adj* going on for an age (4).

'agency *n* business, work, or office of an agent.

a'genda *n* (list of) things to be talked about (at a meeting).

'agent *n* **1** person who acts for, or manages the business affairs of, another. **2** person or thing producing an effect.

'aggravate *v* make more serious; (colloq) annoy.

'aggregate *n & adj* total. **in the —**, taken as a whole.

ag'gression *n* act of attacking; attack made without just cause. **ag'gressive** *adj* **1** fond of attacking; likely to attack without good cause. **2** of or for the purpose of attack. **ag'gressor** *n*.

ag'grieved *adj* hurt in the feelings; conscious of unjust treatment.

a'ghast *adj* filled with sudden terror or great surprise.

'agile *adj* (of living things) quick-moving; active. **a'gility** *n*.

'agitate *v* **1** move or shake (liquids). **2** disturb, cause anxiety to (a person, his feelings). **3** — for, keep on trying to get (*a change in conditions*, etc). **,agi'tation** *n*. **'agitator** *n*.

a'glow *adv & adj* showing warmth from exercise or excitement; giving out light and heat.

ag'nostic *n* one who believes that nothing can be known about God. *adj* connected with this belief.

a'go *adv* before a certain time; in the past. **long ago**, in the distant past.

a'gog *adv & adj* excited; eager; full of interest.

'agony *n* great pain or suffering (of mind or body). **'agonizing** *adj* causing —.

a'gree *v* **1** say 'yes'; consent. **2** have the same opinion. **—able** *adj* pleasing; ready to —. **—ment** *n*.

'agriculture *n* science or practice of farming. **,agri'cultural** *adj*.

a'ground *adv & adj* (of ships) touching the bottom in shallow water.

a'head *adv* in front (of); (of ships in line) sailing one in front of another.

a'hoy *int* seamen's greeting or cry of warning.

aid *n* help; sth that gives help. **in aid of**, for the help of. **first aid**, urgent treatment given to a sick or injured person. *v* help.

ail *v* trouble; afflict; be ill. **'ailment** *n* illness; sickness.

aim *v* **1** point (*a gun*, etc) (*at*).

2 send (*a blow, object*, etc) towards. **3** have in view as a purpose or design. *n* act of aiming; purpose. **'aimless** *adj* without aim (3).

air *n* **1** mixture of gases that we breathe. **air force**, all the aircraft owned by a country for use in war. **by air**, in an aeroplane. **(be) on the air**, (be) broadcasting. **2** (music) tune; melody; song. **3** appearance; way of behaving. **put on (give oneself) airs**, behave immaturely in order to impress. *v* **1** put (*clothing*, etc) into the open or warm air to dry. **2** let air come into. **3** cause others to know (*one's views*, etc).

air- *prefix*: **'airborne** *adj* above the ground; carried by air. **'air-con'ditioned** *adj* supplied with pure air at a comfortable temperature. **'aircraft** *n* aeroplane(s). **'airline** *n* air transport system or company. **'airliner** *n* passenger carrying aircraft. **'airmail** *n* letters and parcels carried by air. **'airman** *n* man who flies an aircraft. **'airport** *n* public flying-ground for commercial use. **'airway** *n* airline.

'airy *adj* with air entering freely; of or like air; not serious. **'airily** *adv*.

aisle *n* passage separating blocks of seats (esp in a church).

a'jar *adv* (of doors) slightly open.

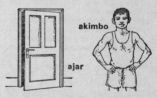

akimbo

ajar

a'kimbo *adv* with arms —, ⇨ the picture.

a'kin *adj* belonging to the same family. **— to**, like.

a'lacrity *n* quick and willing eagerness.

a'larm *n* **1** sound or signal giving a warning of danger. **— clock**, one that rings a bell at a fixed time to wake a sleeping person. **2** fear and excitement. *v* give a warning or feeling of danger to.

a'las *int* cry of sorrow or anxiety.

album *n* book in which photographs, postage stamps, etc, are (to be) kept.

alcohol *n* (colourless, intoxicating liquid present in) beer, wine etc. **alco'holic** *adj* containing —. *n* person in a diseased condition caused by drinking —.

alcove *n* small space formed by a break in the line of a wall, etc, often occupied by a bed or seat(s).

ale *n* pale beer.

a'lert *adj* watchful; fully awake. *n* on the —, on guard, watchful.

algebra *n* branch of mathematics using signs and letters to represent numbers.

alias *n* name which sb uses instead of (usu to hide) his real name.

alibi *n* argument or proof that (when a crime took place, etc) one was in another place.

alien *adj* 1 of another race, country, or nation. 2 — to, out of harmony with. *n* foreigner.

alienate *v* 1 turn away the love or affection of. 2 (law) transfer to the ownership of another. **alie-'nation** *n*.

a'light¹ *adj* burning; lit up.

a'light² *v* get down from or off (a bus, etc); come down to rest from the air.

a'lign *v* put, bring three or more things or persons (eg *soldiers*) into a straight line.

a'like *adj* like one another. *adv* in the same way.

ali'mentary *adj* of digestion. — **canal**, tube in the body, in which food is received and digested.

a'live *adj* 1 having life. 2 in force; in existence. —**to**, fully aware of.

alkali *n* one of a group of chemical substances that combine with acids to form salts. **'alkaline** *adj*.

all *n* everything. *adj* (with *pl n*) the whole number of: *All the students passed the examination*; (with *sing n*) the full extent or amount of: *He spent all his life in India. pron* everything; everyone. **above all**, more than anything else. **once and for all**, for the last or the only time. **all in**, exhausted. **all together**, united and at the same time. *adv* entirely: *They were dressed all in black.* **all over**, (a) in every part of: *all over the world.* (b) at an end: *The party is all over.*

all right, alright (colloq but incorrect), (a) well; acceptable; (b) (in answer to a question) yes, I agree.

al'lay *v* make (*pain, fears*, etc) less.

al'lege *v* put forward (a statement) as a fact (*that*). **,alle'gation** *n*.

al'legiance *n* support, duty, loyalty, that is due (*to a ruler, government*, etc).

'allegory *n* story in which virtues (*Patience, Purity, Truth*, etc) appear as living characters. **,alle-'gorical** *adj*.

al'leviate *v* make (pain or suffering) less or easier to bear. **al,levi-'ation** *n*.

'alley *n* narrow passage between buildings. **blind** —, path with a closed end.

al'liance *n* union of persons, parties, or states. **in — (with)**, united (with).

al'lied *adj* joined by agreement; related; connected.

'alligator *n* crocodile-like reptile living in lakes and rivers in America. ⇨ p 233.

al'locate *v* (decide to) put (*money, supplies*, etc) to a (particular) purpose. **,allo'cation** *n*.

al'lot *v* (-tt-) decide a person's share of; make a distribution. —**ment** *n* that which is —ted; ground rented for growing vegetables.

al'low *v* 1 permit. 2 — **sb to have**, agree to give. 3 — **for**, take into account; leave enough space for. —**ance** *n* amount (*of money*, etc) given or paid to sb regularly. **make** —**ances for**, not be too severe in judging.

'alloy *n* mixture of two or more metals. **al'loy** *v* mix (metals).

al'lude *v* — **to**, speak or write of indirectly; refer to; hint at. **al'lusion** *n*.

al'lure *v* attract; charm; tempt. —**ment** *n* that which —s.

al'luvial *adj* made up of sand, earth, etc, washed down by rivers.

al'ly *v* join; unite (for a special purpose). **be allied (to)**, be closely connected (to). **'ally** *n* person or country allied to another.

'almanac *n* book or calendar with notes of coming events, information about the sun, moon, tides.

al'mighty *adj* powerful beyond measure; **the A—**, God.

'**almost** *adv* 1 nearly: *Dinner is ≈ ready.* 2 (with *no, none, nothing, never*): *The speaker said — nothing,* a few words of little importance.

alms *n* money, clothes, etc, given to poor people. '**—house** *n* charitable house in which poor or old people may live.

a'**loft** *adv & adj* high up overhead.

a'**lone** *adv* 1 without anyone else present; without help. 2 with no other(s) near: *The house stood — on the hillside.* 3 let (sb or sth) —, not touch or interfere (with him, it).

a'**long** *prep* .from one end to the other end of; through any part of the length of. *adv* Run —! Go away!

a'**longside** *adv & prep* against the side of (*a ship*, etc); parallel to.

a'**loof** *adv & adj* away; at a distance. **stand (keep, hold)** —, not take part in conversation, activities.

a'**loud** *adv* so as to be heard; not in a whisper.

'**alphabet** *n* the letters of a language. ,**alpha'betic(al)** *adj* in the order of the —.

al'**ready** *adv* by (this) that time; before now: *I've been there — so I don't want to go again.*

'**also** *adv* too; besides; as well.

'**altar** *n* raised place (table or platform) on which offerings are made to a god; (in a Christian church) Communion table.

'**alter** *v* make or become different. ,**alte'ration** *n*.

,**alter'cation** *n* quarrel; noisy argument.

al'**ternate** *adj* (of two things or two kinds) in turn, first one and then the other. '**alternate** *v* 1 (of things of two kinds) do, put, by turns; replace (one thing) with (the other). **alternating current**, electric current which travels first one way and then the opposite way along a wire. 2 (of two things) keep coming one after the other in turn. ,**alter'nation** *n*. al'**ternative** *adj* offering the choice between two things. *n* a second or later choice that can be made other than one's first choice.

al'**though** *conj* ⇨ though.

'**altitude** *n* height (esp height above sea-level).

,**alto'gether** *adv* entirely; com-

pletely: *It's '— wrong to hurt animals.*

,**alu'minium** *n* very light silver-white metal.

'**always** *adv* 1 at all times; with no exception. 2 repeatedly: *He — finds me out.*

am (I'm = I am) ⇨ be.

a'**malgam** *n* 1 mixture of mercury and another metal. 2 any soft mixture.

a'**malgamate** *v* join together; mix. a,**malga'mation** *n*.

a'**mass** *v* heap up (or together) a great amount of (esp riches).

'**amateur** *n* person who works (*painting pictures, playing music,* etc) or plays a game, for the love of it and not for money. ,**ama'teurish** *adj* in the manner of an —; not expert.

a'**maze** *v* fill with great surprise or wonder. **—ment** *n*.

am'**bassador** *n* 1 political representative of the government of one country who conducts its business with the government of another. 2 messenger, representative.

'**amber** *n* clear, hard, yellow substance used for making ornaments; its colour.

,**ambi'guity** *n* (word, phrase, etc) having more than one possible meaning. am'**biguous** *adj* of doubtful meaning or nature.

am'**bition** *n* 1 strong desire to be successful, etc, or to do a particular thing. 2 that which one desires to do or be. am'**bitious** *adj*.

'**amble** *v* move along without hurrying,

'**ambulance** *n* closed motor-vehicle for carrying wounded, injured, or sick persons.

'**ambush** *n* (the placing of men in hiding for making a) surprise attack. *v* wait in — for; place (men) in —; attack from a position or place of —.

a'**men** *n, int* word used at the end of a prayer or hymn, meaning 'May it be so'.

a'**menable** *adj* — to, willing to be guided or persuaded by; able to be tested by.

a'**mend** *v* 1 improve; correct; make free from faults. 2 make changes in (a law or rule). **—s** *n pl* compensation. **—ment** *n*.

a'menity *n* pleasantness; sth that makes life pleasant.

'amiable *adj* friendly; kind-hearted.

'amicable *adj* friendly; showing good feeling.

a'mid(st) *prep* in(to) the middle of. a'midships *adv* half-way along the length of a ship.

a'miss *adj & adv* wrong(ly); out of order. take sth —, feel offended at.

'amity *n* friendship; friendly behaviour.

am'monia *n* colourless gas with a strong, sharp smell; this gas dissolved in water, used for cleaning.

,ammu'nition *n* military stores, esp shells, etc, to be used against the enemy in battle.

'amnesty *n* general pardon of those who have committed a crime (esp in a rising against the government).

a'mok ⇨ amuck.

a'mong(st) *prep* 1 surrounded by; in the middle of. 2 (with a superlative) one of: *The Nile is — the longest rivers in the world.* 3 (indicating a sharing of possessions, activity, etc): *He divided his fortune — his four sons.*

'amorous *adj* easily moved to love; showing love.

a'mount *v* add up (*to*); be equal (*to*). *n* 1 the whole or total. 2 quantity.

'ampere *n* measured unit of electric current.

am'phibian *n* animal able to live on land and under water: *frog.* am'phibious *adj.*

'amphi,theatre *n* 1 round or oval building with rows of seats rising behind and above one another around an open space, used for games and amusements. 2 part of a theatre with rows of seats similarly arranged in half-circles.

'ample *adj* (-r, -st) 1 roomy; with plenty of space. 2 more than enough. 'amply *adv.*

'amplify *v* give more details or fuller information about; increase the strength of (*radio signals*, etc). 'amplifier *n.* ,amplifi'cation *n.*

'amputate *v* cut off (eg *a leg or arm*). ,ampu'tation *n.*

a'muck *adv* run —, run about wildly with a desire to kill people.

'amulet *n* thing worn on the body in the belief that it will protect against diseases or evil powers.

a'muse *v* cause time to pass pleasantly; cause smiles or laughter. —ment *n.*

an ⇨ a.

a'nachronism *n* (description of a) thing or event that could not have existed or occurred at the time stated: *Napoleon telephoned to Paris.*

,anaes'thetic *n* substance that makes persons unable to feel pain, used in surgery.

a'nalogy *n* partial likeness to or partial agreement with another thing or between two things.

'analyse *v* examine (sth) in order to learn what the separate parts are. a'nalysis *n* process of analysing; statement of the result of this. 'analyst *n* sb who —s; (USA) psychiatrist. ,ana'lytical *adj.*

'anarchy *n* absence of government or control; disorder. 'anarchism *n.* political theory that government is undesirable. 'anarchist *n* one who favours —.

a'natomy *n* study of how the animal body is built; the cutting up of animal bodies and separation into parts for this purpose. ,ana'tomical *adj.* a'natomist *n.*

'ancestor *n* any one of those persons from whom one's father or mother is descended.. an'cestral *adj.* 'ancestry *n* all one's —s.

'anchor *n* iron hook lowered to the sea bottom to keep a ship at rest. *v* lower an —. —age *n* place where ships —.

'ancient *adj* 1 belonging to times long past; not modern. 2 very old.

and *conj* 1 *Jack and Jill went up the hill.* 2 (colloq) in order to: *If you want it, come and get it.*

'anecdote *n* short, usu amusing story about some person or event.

a'new *adv* again; in a new way.

'angel *n* (in Christian belief) messenger from God. an'gelic *adj* good, pure, and beautiful.

'anger *n* feeling (after one has been wronged, insulted, etc, or when one has seen injustice, cruelty, etc) that makes one want to quarrel or fight. 'angry (-ier, -iest) *adj.* 'angrily *adv.*

'angle¹ *n* space between two lines or surfaces that meet.

'angle² *v* try to catch fish with a rod, line, hook, and bait. 'angler *n.*

'**Anglican** *n & adj* (member) of the Church of England.

'**Anglo-** *prefix* English: **Anglo-American**, of England and America.

'**anguish** *n* severe pain or suffering (of mind).

'**angular** *adj* **1** having angles or sharp corners. **2** (of a person) thin; bony.

'**animal** *n* **1** living thing that is not a plant. **2** — other than man. **3** four-footed —. ⇨ pp 12, 84, 233, 247, 317.

'**animate** *v* make bright and full of life. ,ani'mation *n*. 'animated *adj*.

,ani'mosity *n* active and bitter dislike or hate.

'**ankle** *n* joint and thin part of the human leg above the foot. ⇨ p 29.

an'**nex** *v* add or join to (a larger thing); take possession of (a country). '**annexe**, an'nex *n* smaller building(s) added to or situated near to a larger one. ,annex'ation *n*.

an'**nihilate** *v* destroy completely. an,nihi'lation *n*.

,anni'versary *n* yearly return of the date on which sth happened.

'**annotate** *v* add notes (explaining difficulties or giving opinions).

an'**nounce** *v* make known (*news, the name of a guest, speaker*, etc); give or be a sign of. —r *n* (esp) sb who —s radio and TV programmes. —ment *n*.

an'**noy** *v* give trouble to; make rather angry. —ance *n*.

'**annual** *adj* **1** coming or happening every year. **2** lasting for a year. *n* **1** plant that lives for a year only. **2** book, etc, that appears under the same title but with different contents every year. —ly *adv*.

an'**nuity** *n* fixed sum of money paid to sb yearly as income during his lifetime.

an'**nul** *v* (-ll-) put an end to (a law, agreement, etc).

a'**noint** *v* pour oil on (the head or body), esp at a religious ceremony. —ing *n*.

a'**nonymous** *adj* without a name; with a name that is not made known.

a'**nother** *adj & pron* different (one); one more of the same kind. **one** —, each to each: *He and she give one — presents at Christmas*.

'**answer** *n* sth said, written, or done in return. *v* give an — to. —**back**, give an impolite — when being corrected. — **a purpose**, be suitable or sufficient. — **for**, be responsible for. — **to**, correspond to. '—**able** *adj* responsible (*to* sb *for* sth).

ant *n* small insect well known for its highly developed social behaviour. ⇨ p 144.

an'**tagonize** *v* make an enemy of. an'tagonist *n*. an,tago'nistic *adj*. an'tagonism *n*.

ant'**arctic** *adj* of or near the South Pole.

'**ante-** *prefix* before. '**ante-'natal** *adj* before birth.

'**antelope** *n* animal like a deer. ⇨ p 317.

an'**tenna** *n* (*pl* an'tennae) **1** one of the two feelers on the head of an insect, etc. ⇨ p 144. **2** aerial for a radio.

'**anthem** *n* piece of sacred music (usu for a choir) sung in churches. **national** —, song of a country.

an'**thology** *n* collection of poems, etc, by different writers, or selections from one writer's works.

,anthro'pology *n* science of man, esp of the beginnings, development, beliefs, and customs of man. ,anthro'pologist *n*.

'**anti-** *prefix* against: *anti-aircraft guns*.

an'**ticipate** *v* **1** do or make use of before the right or natural time. **2** do sth before sb else does it. **3** see what needs doing and do it in advance. **4** look forward to. an,tici'pation *n*.

,anti'climax *n* weak or disappointing end to a situation in which there were high hopes or important possibilities.

'**antics** *n pl* playful, jumping movements, often amusing; light-hearted or care-free behaviour.

'**antidote** *n* medicine used to prevent poison or disease from having an effect.

an'**tipathy** *n* fixed feeling of dislike.

,anti'quarian ⇨ antiquity.

'**antiquated** *adj* no longer in use; out of date; (of a person) having old-fashioned ways and ideas.

an'**tique** *adj* belonging to the distant past; in the style of past times. *n* relic or work of art of the past.

an'**tiquity** *n* **1** the distant past;

some small animals

badger

rabbit

otter

beaver

mouse

rat

guinea-pig

squirrel

mole

hare

early times in history. 2 (*pl*) buildings, ruins, works of art, etc, remaining from early times. ˌanti-'quarian *adj* of the study of antiquities; antiquary. 'antiquary *n* one who studies, collects, or sells antiquities.

ˌanti'septic *n & adj* (substance for) destroying germs.

ˌanti'social *adj* opposed to social order; unsociable.

'antler *n* branched horn of a stag or other deer. ⇨ p 317.

'antonym *n* word opposite in meaning to another.

'anvil *n* block of iron on which heated metal is hammered into shape.

an'xiety *n* 1 feeling of uncertainty and fear. 2 eager desire. 'anxious *adj*.

any *pron & adj* one, a, an, some; no matter which. 'anybody, 'anyone *n* no matter which person; all people. 'anything *n* (cf *something*) no matter what object, animal, plant, idea, etc. 'anyhow, 'anyway *adv* in no matter which order or way. 'anywhere *adv* in or to no matter which place or position.

a'pace *adv* quickly.

a'part *adv* on one side; separately.

a'partheid *n* (South African) policy of separate development of Europeans and non-Europeans.

a'partment *n* 1 (usu flat(3) in Gt Brit) set of rooms for living in (usu in a building with other —s). 2 single room for living in.

'apathy *n* lack of feeling, sympathy, or interest. ˌapa'thetic *adj*.

ape *n* large tailless monkey. *v* imitate foolishly.

'aperture *n* (usu small or narrow) opening, esp one that admits light into a scientific instrument.

'apex *n* pointed top; highest point.

a'piece *adv* to, for, or by each one of a group.

a'pology *n* statement of regret for doing wrong or for hurting a person's feelings. a'pologize *v* make an — for. aˌpolo'getic *adj*.

'apoplexy *n* loss of power to feel, move, or think, usu caused by injury to the brain. ˌapo'plectic *adj* suffering from —; easily made angry.

a'postle *n* 1 A—, one of the twelve men sent out by Christ to spread his teaching, also Barnabas and Paul. 2 leader or teacher of a faith or movement. ˌapos'tolic *adj*.

a'postrophe *n* the sign '.

ap'pal (-ll-) *v* fill with fear or terror.

appa'ratus *n* (*pl* -es) set of tools, of instruments, of parts of the body, constructed for a special purpose.

ap'parel *n* (liter) dress; clothing.

ap'parent *adj* 1 clearly seen or understood. 2 seeming. —ly *adv*.

ˌappa'rition *n* coming into view, esp of a ghost or spirit; ghost.

ap'peal *v* 1 ask earnestly (*for*). 2 refer a question or decision (*to* a higher authority). 3 — to, attract, interest. *n* act of —ing; interest; (power of) attraction. —ing *adj* attractive.

ap'pear *v* 1 come into view; arrive. 2 seem. 3 (*of an actor, book,* etc) come before the public. —ance *n* 1 act of —ing. 2 that which shows; what sth or sb seems to be.

ap'pease *v* make calm or quiet; satisfy (by giving what is wanted). —ment *n*.

ap'pendix *n* 1 (*pl* ap'pendices) sth added, esp at the end of a book. 2 (*pl* -es) small tube attached to the large intestine. ⇨ p 30. apˌpendi'citis *n* disease of the —.

'appetite *n* desire (esp for food). 'appetizing *adj* pleasing or exciting the —.

ap'plaud *v* show approval by clapping the hands or by other loud sounds. ap'plause *n*.

'apple *n* (tree with) round fruit with a firm, juicy flesh. ⇨ p 115.

ap'pliance *n* instrument, tool, or apparatus.

'applicable *adj* fitting; suitable to be applied.

'applicant *n* one who applies (*for* .sth).

ˌappli'cation *n* 1 act of applying; letter applying; request. 2 that which is applied(2). 3 industry, effort, or attention.

ap'ply *v* 1 — for, ask to be given. 2 put sth into position. 3 put into use. — oneself to, give one's efforts and attention to. 4 have reference (*to*). ap'plied *adj* put to practical use.

ap'point *v* 1 fix or decide (a time or place for). 2 choose and name (sb for a position). —ment *n*.

ap'preciable adj that can be seen or felt. ap'preciably adv.

ap'preciate v 1 understand, judge, enjoy rightly. 2 put a high value on. 3 become higher in value. ap,preci'ation n. ap'preciative adj.

,appre'hend v 1 understand. 2 fear; be anxious about. 3 seize, arrest. ,appre'hension n. ,appre'hensive adj.

ap'prentice n learner of a trade who has agreed to work for a number of years in return for being taught. v employ (sb) as an —.

ap'proach v 1 come near or nearer to. 2 go to (sb) with a request or offer. n 1 act of —ing. 2 way to a place, person, or thing, esp one not easily reached.

,appro'bation n approval.

ap'propriate adj right or suitable (for a purpose, on an occasion). v take and use as one's own; put on one side (for a purpose). ap,propri'ation n.

ap'proval n feeling, saying, or showing that one is satisfied. ap'prove v give — to.

ap'proximate adj very near to; almost right. v bring or come near (to). ap,proxi'mation n.

'April n fourth month of the year. ⇨ fool.

'apron n loose garment tied over the front of clothing to protect it.

,apro'pos adj & adv to the purpose; well suited. — of, with reference to.

apt adj (-er, -est) 1 quick at learning. 2 suitable. 3 apt to, having a tendency to; likely to.

'aptitude n natural talent.

a'quarium n place for keeping and showing living fish and water plants.

a'quatic adj growing or living in or near water; done in or on water.

'arable adj (of land) suitable for ploughing.

'arbitrary adj based on opinion rather than reason.

'arbitrate v judge between one party and another. ,arbi'tration n. 'arbitrator n.

'arbour n shady place, often with a seat, in a garden.

arc n part of a circle; a curve.

ar'cade n covered passage, usu with arches, esp one with shops.

arch n curved structure supporting the weight of what is above it. v form into, be like, an —.

an arch

an arena

arch- prefix chief: —angel; —bishop.

,archae'ology n study (and often digging up) of ancient things, esp of earliest times. ,archaeo'logical adj.

ar'chaic adj of ancient times; (of language) not now used.

'archer n one who shoots with a bow and arrow. —y n.

,archi'pelago n sea with many small islands; group of small islands.

'architect n designer of buildings, etc. —ure n art and science of building; design or style of building(s). ,archi'tectural adj.

'archives n pl (place for keeping) government or public records; other historical records.

'arctic adj of or near the North Pole.

'ardour n enthusiasm; earnestness; warmth of feeling. 'ardent adj full of ardour.

'arduous adj needing and using up much energy.

are, aren't ⇨ be.

'area n measure; extent of surface; region.

a'rena n central part, for games, entertainment and fights, of an amphitheatre.

'argue v give reasons (for and against plans, opinions, etc); discuss earnestly. 'argument n.

'arid adj dry; barren. a'ridity n.

a'rise v (pt a'rose, pp a'risen) 1 come into existence; come to notice. 2 result (from). 3 (old use) stand up, get up.

,aris'tocracy n 1 (country with a) government by persons of the highest rank. 2 nobles or other persons of high rank. 'aristocrat n person of high birth or rank. ,aristo'cratic adj.

a'rithmetic n science of, working with, numbers.

ark n (Bible) covered ship in which

Noah, his family and the animals were saved from the Flood.

arm n 1 either of two parts of the body from the shoulder to the hand. ⊏⊐ p 29. **'arm-'chair** n chair with supports for one's arms. 2 (usu pl) weapon(s). **in arms**, having weapons, ready to fight. 3 division of military forces: the air arm. **arm of the law**, its authority and power. 4 **coat of arms**, pictorial design used by a noble family, town, etc. v supply with arms or armour; get ready for war.

'armament n 1 military forces; preparation for war. 2 (usu pl) guns on a ship, tank, etc.

'armistice n agreement during a war to stop fighting for a time.

'armour n 1 metal covering for the body, ships, tanks, etc. 2 fighting vehicles protected with —. **'armoury** n place where arms(2) are kept.

'army n 1 military forces of a country; large body of organized persons. 2 large number: an — of ants (workmen).

a'roma n sweet smell.

a'rose ⊏⊐ arise.

a'round adv & prep 1 on all sides; enveloping. 2 about: — a pound; here and there.

a'rouse v awaken; stir to activity.

ar'range v put in order; make plans. **—ment** n.

ar'ray v place (soldiers) in order for battle. n (pl -s) order or arrangement (for fighting); display.

ar'rears n pl overdue payments; work waiting for attention. **in —** (**with**), behindhand (with).

ar'rest v 1 put a stop to (a process, etc). 2 catch (sb's attention). 3 make (sb) a prisoner by the authority of the law. n act of —ing. **under —**, held prisoner.

ar'rive v 1 come to a place; reach the end of a journey. 2 (of time) come. **ar'rival** n (esp) sth or sb that —s.

'arrogant adj behaving in a proud, superior manner. **'arrogance** n.

'arrow n thin, pointed stick to be shot from a bow; the mark or sign ⟶, ⊏⊐, etc.

'arsenal n building(s) where arms and ammunition are made or stored.

'arsenic n strong poison.

'arson n act of setting sth on fire unlawfully.

art n 1 work of man, not of nature. 2 study and creation of things giving pleasure to the mind through the senses: a work of art (eg a painting). **the (Fine) Arts**, drawing, painting, sculpture, architecture, music, ballet, etc. 3 branch of learning including history, languages, and literature, studied at universities: Bachelor (Master) of Arts (cf the sciences). 4 cunning behaviour; tricks. **'artful** adj cunning. **'artless** adj simple; innocent.

'artery n 1 one of the tubes carrying blood from the heart. 2 main road or river, esp one used for carrying supplies.

ar'tesian 'well n deep narrow well producing a stream of water.

article n 1 thing. 2 piece of writing 3 one of the separate items of an Agreement. 4 (in grammar) each of the words the, a, an.

ar'ticulate v say clearly and distinctly. **ar,ticu'lation** n.

'artifice n skilful way of doing sth.

,arti'ficial adj not natural; made by man in imitation of a natural object; insincere, unnatural in behaviour.

ar'tillery n big guns, usu those on wheels; branch of an army managing such guns.

,arti'san n skilled workman in industry or trade.

'artist n person who practises one of the arts, esp painting. **ar'tistic** adj of art; showing, done with, good taste.

ar'tiste n professional performer on the radio, TV, stage, etc.

as conj while, when: He waved as the train left the station; since: As he wasn't ready, we left without him. **as . . . as**, equal: as easy as ABC. **as far as**, to the extent that; up to a certain point. **as well as**, also. **as if (though)**: It lóoks as if he'll win the race, seems he'll win. **as long as**, (a) while. (b) on condition that: I'll come as long as she'll be there.

as'bestos n soft mineral substance made into a material that does not burn.

as'cend v go or come up (a river,

a mountain). **the As'cension** n the departure of Jesus from the earth. **as'cent** n act of —ing.

,ascer'tain v find out. —able adj that can be —ed.

'as'cribe v — to, consider to be the cause, author, origin, etc, of.

ash n powder left after sth has burnt.

a'shamed adj feeling shame.

a'shore adv on, to, on to, the shore.

a'side adv on, or to, one side; away.

ask v seek an answer (to), request; invite. ask after, inquire about (the health of sb).

as'kance adv look — at, look at with suspicion.

a'sleep adv & adj sleeping; in a state of total relaxation as regularly when in bed.

'aspect n 1 appearance. 2 direction in which a building faces.

'asphalt n black, sticky, water-proof substance used for road surfaces.

as'pire v be filled with high ambition (for sth, to do or be sth). ,aspi'ration n.

'aspirin n medicine used to relieve pain and reduce fever.

ass n 1 animal like a donkey. ⇨ p 84. 2 (colloq) stupid person.

as'sail v make an attack on. —ant n.

as'sassinate v kill violently, esp for political reasons. as'sassin n person who —s. as,sassi'nation n.

as'sault v & n (make a) violent and sudden attack.

as'semble v gather together; put (parts) together. as'sembly n meeting of a group of people for a special purpose.

as'sent v & n (give one's) agreement.

as'sert v declare; make a claim to (one's rights, etc). — oneself, insist on one's rights. as'sertion n.

as'sess v decide or fix (a value or amount, esp for payment). —ment n.

'asset n 1 (usu pl) anything owned by a person, company, etc, which may be used to pay debts. 2 valuable or useful quality or skill.

as'siduous adj hard-working; persevering. ,assi'duity n.

as'sign v 1 give (to sb) for use or enjoyment, or as a share of duty, work, etc. 2 name or put forward as a place, a reason, etc. —ment n.

as'similate v (cause food to) become part of the body; (cause people to) become part of another social group or state; absorb (ideas, knowledge). as,simi'lation n.

as'sist n & v help. —ance n.

as'sociate v 1 join (persons or things, one with another); connect (people, etc) in one's mind; get or come together (for a common purpose). 2 (with) be often in the company of. n & adj (person) associating with another or others (in work or business). as,soci'ation n.

as'sorted adj of various sorts; mixed. as'sortment n (esp) — collection of differing examples or articles of one class or several classes.

as'sume v 1 suppose; take as true. 2 take up (office). 3 take for one's own (a new name, etc). as'suming adj claiming greater importance than one has the right to. as'sumption n the act of assuming; sth —d.

as'sure v 1 tell with confidence. 2 make (sb) certain. 3 insure (esp one's life). —dly adv without doubt. as'surance n 1 assuring or being —d. 2 feeling of certainty about oneself, one's abilities, etc. 3 insurance.

'asterisk n the sign *.

a'stern adv in, at, or towards the stern (back end) of a ship; behind; backwards.

a'stir adv & adj in motion; excited.

a'stonish v surprise greatly. —ment n.

a'stound v overcome with surprise.

a'stray adv & adj away from the right path, esp in wrongdoing.

a'stride adv & prep with one leg on each side (of): — a horse.

a'strology n observation of the positions of the stars in the belief that they influence human affairs.

'astronaut n traveller in a spacecraft.

as'tronomy n science of the sun, moon, planets, and stars. as'tronomer n. ,astro'nomical adj.

as'tute adj quick at seeing how to gain an advantage.

a'sunder adv apart; in pieces.

a'sylum n 1 (formerly an) institution for the care of people considered to be mad (now called a *mental home*). **2** (place of) refuge, safety or sanctuary. ⇨ **political**.

at *prep* **1** (place): *at his office*; *at the station* (cf in (1)); (direction): *look at sb*; *shoot at the enemy*; *laugh at John*. **2** (time): *at 2 o'clock*; *at any moment*; (of age): *He left school at (the age of) 15*; (indicating order): *at the third attempt*; *at last*; *at first*. **3** (indicating occupation): *at work (play)*; (after an *adj*): *good at swimming*; (manner): *at a gallop*. **4** (rate): *at full speed*; *buy sth at 5 cents and sell it at 10 cents*; (with superlatives): *at least*; *at its (his, her, their) best*. **5** (cause, after a *v*): *He laughed at the actors*; (cause, after an *adj* or a *pp*): *delighted at the idea*.

ate ⇨ **eat**.

'atheism *n* belief that there is no God. **'atheist** *n*.

ath'letic *adj* **1** of outdoor games and sports. **2** fond of these. **—s** *n pl* outdoor sports, esp competitions in running, jumping, etc. **'athlete** *n* person trained for **—s**.

'atlas *n* book of maps.

'atmosphere *n* **1** mixture of gases surrounding the earth. **2** the air in a particular place. **3** feeling (of good, evil, etc) which the mind receives from a place, conditions, etc. **,atmos'pheric** *adj*.

'atom *n* smallest unit of an element(1) divisible by electrical force but not by chemical means. **a'tomic** *adj*.

a'tone *v* do sth to put right or compensate for doing wrong.

a'trocious *adj* wicked; very bad. **a'trocity** *n* cruel or wicked act.

at'tach *v* fasten (*to*); join (*to*); connect (*with*). **be —ed to**, be fond of. **—ment** *n* (esp) sth **—ed**.

at'tack *v* begin violent action or speech (against). *n* **1** violent action; adverse criticism. **2** start of a pain, disease, etc. **—er** *n* sb who **—s**.

at'tain *v* reach; arrive at; succeed in doing or getting. **—able** *adj*. **—ment** *n* (esp) skill in some branch of knowledge.

at'tempt *n & v* try.

at'tend *v* **1** give thought and care (*to*). **2** be present at. **3** (be waiting to) serve (sb). **—ance** *n*. **—ant** *n* servant; companion.

at'tention *n* **1** act of attending(1)

to. **2** (often *pl*) kind or polite acts. **3 come to (stand at) —, A—!** stand erect and still. **at'tentive** *adj* giving, paying, **—**.

'attic *n* room within the roof of a house.

at'tire *v & n* dress.

'attitude *n* **1** manner of placing or holding the body. **2** way of feeling, thinking, or behaving.

at'torney *n* person who has legal authority to act for another in business or law.

at'tract *v* **1** pull towards (by unseen force). **2** arouse interest and pleasure in; get the attention of. **—ion** *n*. **—ive** *adj*.

'attribute *n* **1** quality, sign, or mark that is characteristic of sth or sb. **2** special sign (of sth or sb). **at'tribute** *v* **— to**, consider as belonging to, caused by, owing to, sb or sth. **at'tributive** *adj* (grammar) naming an **—**. In 'the old man', *old* is an attributive adj.

'auburn *adj* reddish-brown.

'auction *n* public sale at which goods are sold to the person(s) offering the highest price. *v* sell by **—**. **,auctio'neer** *n*.

au'dacious *adj* bold; impudent. **au'dacity** *n*.

'audible *adj* loud enough to be heard.

'audience *n* **1** (group of) people listening. **2** interview given by a ruler.

'audit *v* examine (business accounts) to see that they are in order. *n* examination of this kind. **—or** *n*.

,audi'torium *n* building, or part of a building, for an audience.

aught *n* (liter) anything.

aug'ment *v* make or become bigger.

'August *n* eighth month of the year.

aunt *n* sister of one's father or mother; wife of one's uncle.

aus'picious *adj* showing signs of future success.

aus'tere *adj* **1** severely moral and strict. **2** simple and plain; without ornament. **aus'terity** *n*.

au'thentic *adj* genuine; known to be true.

'author(ess) *n* man (woman) who writes books, stories, etc.

au'thority *n* **1** power or right to give orders. **2** person(s) having such powers or rights. **3** person with special knowledge; books, etc, giving information, proof, etc. **au'thoritative** adj. **'authorize** v give — to.

autobi'ography n story of a person's life, written by himself.

'autocrat n person who rules with unlimited powers. **auto'cratic** adj.

'autograph n person's own handwriting, esp his signature.

auto'matic adj **1** (of machines) acting or working without outside control; self operating. **2** done without thought.

auto'mation n use of methods and machines to make manufacturing, etc, as automatic as possible.

'automobile n motor-car.

'autumn n season of the year between summer and winter. **au'tumnal** adj.

au'xiliary adj supporting; helpful. n sth or sb that gives help.

a'vail v & n (be of) use or help (to). —**able** adj that may be obtained or used. **a,vaila'bility** n.

'avalanche n mass of snow, stones, etc, falling down a mountainside.

'avarice n greed (for possessions). **ava'ricious** adj.

a'venge v get or take revenge for.

'avenue n road with trees on each side; wide street; way of reaching.

a'ver v (-rr-) say (that sth is so).

'average n **1** the result of adding several quantities together and dividing the total by the number of such quantities. **2** normal standard or level. adj found by making an —; of the ordinary or usual standard. v find the — of; come to as an —.

a'verse adj — to. opposed; not inclined (to or from). **a'version** n strong dislike (to, from); sth or sb that is disliked.

a'vert v **1** turn away (one's eyes, etc) (from). **2** avoid.

avi'ation n (art and science of) flying. **'aviator** n airman.

a'void v keep away from; get or keep out of the way of. —**able** adj. —**ance** n.

avoirdu'pois n British system of weights (1 pound = 16 ounces), used for all goods except gold, silver, jewels, and medicines.

a'vow v confess. —**al** n.

a'wait v be waiting for.

a'wake adj not sleeping, conscious(2). **'wide-a'wake** fully conscious, alert.

a'waken v (pt **a'woke**, pp **a'wakened**) stop sleeping; become active, aware; wake sb up.

a'ward n decision made by a judge; sth given as the result, esp a prize in a competition. v give as an —.

a'ware adj having knowledge or realization (of sth, that . . .).

a'way adv **1** to or at a distance (from the place, person, etc, in question): two miles —. **2** (indicating loss, lessening, etc): The water has boiled —. **right (straight)** —, immediately.

awe n respect combined with fear or reverence. v fill with —. **'awful** adj. **1** terrible; dreadful. **2** very bad. **'awfully** adv (colloq) extremely: That's awfully kind!

a'while adv for a short time.

'awkward adj **1** not well designed for use. **2** clumsy; having little skill. **3** causing trouble or inconvenience. —**ness** n.

awl n tool for making holes in leather. ⇨ p 293.

'awning n canvas overhead covering (on ship's deck, etc) against sun or rain.

a'woke ⇨ awake.

a'wry adj & adv crooked(ly); wrong(ly).

axe n tool for chopping wood. ⇨ p 293.

'axiom n statement accepted as true without proof or argument. **,axio'matic** adj.

'axis n (pl **'axes**) imaginary line around which a turning object spins.

'axle n rod around which a wheel or pair of wheels turn(s).

ay(e) int yes.

'azure adj & n sky-blue.

B

baa n cry of a sheep or lamb.

'babble v make sounds like a baby; talk foolishly; tell a secret.

babe n baby.

ba'boon n large monkey with a dog-like face. ⇨ p 317

'baby n child (before the age when it can walk). **—hood** n period of being a —. **—ish** adj immature.

'bachelor n 1 unmarried man. 2 person who has a first university degree.

back n 1 part of anything that is behind or farthest from the front (esp the body from the neck to the buttocks. ⇨ p 29). 2 part of anything that is less used or less important. **'—bone** n line of bones in an animal's —. ⇨ p 30. adv to or at the rear; in(to) an earlier position: *Put the book — when you have finished reading it.* v 1 go (cause to go). **— down**, give up a claim or position. **— out** (of), escape from, withdraw from, a promise. **— a horse**, bet (money on its winning a race). **'—er** n supporter; person who bets. **'—ground** n 1 that part of a view farthest away. 2 past experience, education, etc. **'—'side** n (colloq) buttocks. **'—ward** adj (esp) slow to learn. **'—wards** adv in a direction opposite to the usual one. **'—wash** n rush of water behind a steamer, etc. **'—,water** n part of a river not reached by its current. **'—woods** n wild forest land far from towns.

'bacon n salted or smoked meat from the sides or back of a pig.

bac'teria n pl smallest and simplest forms of plant life, existing in air, water, soil, and in living and dead creatures, sometimes a cause of disease. **'bacteri'ology** n.

bad adj (worse, worst) 1 evil, wicked. 2 unfit for use (esp food and drink). 3 unpleasant (weather, news). 4 painful; diseased: *a bad leg*. **badly** adv.

bade ⇨ bid.

badge n sth worn (usu a small design in cloth or metal) to show rank, position, etc.

'badger n small, grey animal living in holes in the ground. ⇨ p 12. v worry (sb) with troublesome requests, etc.

'baffle v prevent from doing sth, cause to be uncertain.

bag n container (made of cloth, leather, paper, etc) in which things are carried, stored, etc. v (-gg-) 1 put in a bag. 2 hang loosely. **'baggy** adj: *baggy trousers*.

'baggage n traveller's belongings.

bail¹ v — sb out, secure the freedom of an accused person (till he is called for trial, by lodging with the law court money to be kept if he does not attend). n the money so demanded by the court. **go — for sb**, — him out.

bail² v — out, throw water out of (*a boat*); empty out (water).

'bailiff n law officer who helps a sheriff; agent or manager for a landowner.

bait n food, or imitation of food, put on a hook or in a trap, etc, to catch fish or animals. v put — on (a hook, etc); worry or annoy in order to make angry.

baize n thick (usu coarse, green) woollen cloth.

bake v cook, be cooked, by dry heat in an oven; make or become hard by heating. **—r** n. **—ry** n place where bread is —d for many people.

'balance n 1 apparatus for weighing. **in the —**, (of a result) still uncertain. 2 condition of being steady; condition existing when opposite forces, amounts, etc, are equal. **keep (lose) one's —**, remain (fail to remain) upright. 3 difference between two columns of an account. 4 apparatus in a watch regulating the speed. v 1 be, put, keep, in a state of —. 2 weigh or compare two things, plans, etc.

'balcony n 1 platform (with a wall or rails) built on the outside wall of a building, reached from upstairs room(s). 2 rows of seats rising one above the other, and above the floor level of a theatre, etc.

bald adj 1 having no or not much hair, not many feathers, trees, or leaves. 2 plain; without ornament. **'—ly** adv. **'—ness** n.

bale n bundle of goods, packed (usu in canvas), ready for transport. v — out, jump from an aircraft with a parachute.

balk v 1 prevent; get in the way of (on purpose). 2 (of a horse) refuse to go forward.

bags

ball¹ *n* **1** round solid or hollow object used in games, sport. **2** anything having the shape of a —(1).
'ball-point (pen) *n* pen that writes with a tiny ball at the end of a narrow tube of ink, often called a *Biro.*

ball² *n* social gathering for dancing. **'—room** *n* place for a —².

'ballad *n* simple song or poem, esp one that tells a story.

'ballast *n* heavy material loaded in a ship to keep it steady.

'ballet *n* **1** musical play without dialogue or songs, performed by a group of dancers in a theatre. **2** the dancers. **3** the —, stage dancing as an art.

bal'loon *n* bag filled with air or gas lighter than air, esp one sent up into the sky.

'ballot *n* **1** secret voting (by marking a paper). **2** paper used in voting. *v* give a secret vote.

balm *n* sweet-smelling oil or ointment; (fig) that which gives peace of mind. **'—y** *adj* (of air) warm.

bam'boo *n* tall plant, with hard, hollow stems; its wood.

ban *v* (-nn-) order that sth must not be done, said, etc. *n* order banning sth.

ba'nana *n* (tropical tree with) long, yellow-skinned fruit. ⇨ p 115.

band *n* **1** flat, thin strip of material, esp for fastening things together, or for putting round sth to strengthen it. **2** strip or line, different in colour or design, on sth. **3** group of persons (esp musicians) acting together under a leader and with a common purpose. *v* (of people) join, bring, or come, together. **'—age** *n* — of material for putting round wounds. *v* put a —age on.

'bandit *n* robber (esp one of an armed band living in mountains or forests).

'bandy¹ *v* pass or send backwards and forwards; exchange (words, blows).

'bandy² *adj* (-ier, -iest) (of the legs) curving outwards at the knees.

bang *n* **1** violent blow. **2** loud, sudden noise. *v* make a —; give a — to.

'bangle *n* ornament worn round the arm or ankle.

'banish *v* send (sb) away, esp out of the country, as a punishment; (fig) put away from or out of (the mind). **—ment** *n*.

'banjo *n* musical instrument played by plucking the strings. ⇨ p 180.

bank¹ *n* **1** sloping land or earth, often a dividing line; land along each side of a river or canal. **2** large, usu flat, mass (of sand, snow, clouds, etc), esp one formed by wind or water. *v* **1** make or form into —s. **2** (of an aircraft) fly with one side higher than the other, when turning. **— up**, *(a fire)* make a mass (*of coal*, etc) for slow burning.

bank² *n* establishment for keeping money, etc, safely, and for lending and exchanging money. **bank-'holiday** *n* day when banks, offices, and most shops are closed. **'bank-note** *n* piece of paper money. *v* place or keep (money) in a —. **'—er** *n* person managing the business of a —.

'bankrupt *n & adj* (person) judged by a law court to be unable to pay his debts in full. **— in (of)**, (fig) completely without. **—cy** *n*.

'banner *n* flag carried on one or two poles.

banns *n pl* public announcement that two people are to be married in church.

'banquet *n* feast, esp an official dinner for a special event.

'banter *v* tease in a playful way (by talking and joking). *n* teasing of this sort.

'baptism *n* ceremony of sprinkling (a person) with or bathing (him) in water in accepting (him) as a member of the Christian church and giving (him) a Christian name. **bap'tize** *v* give — to.

bar *n* **1** long, stiff piece (*of metal, wood, soap,* etc). **2** rail or rod across a door, etc, to prevent its being opened or to stop passage; (fig) sth that stops or hinders progress. **3** bank of mud or sand at a river-mouth, etc. **4** narrow band or strip (*of colour*, etc). **5** the place in a law court where the prisoner stands before the judge. **6** the Bar, the profession of barrister; all those lawyers who are barristers. **7** (room in a hotel, etc with a) counter where drinks are sold and drunk. **8** (music)

upright line marking divisions equal in time-value; one such division with its notes. *v* (-rr-) put bars across; prevent (sb from doing sth). *prep* (also 'barring) except.
'barmaid, 'barman *n* woman, man, serving drinks in a bar.

barb *n* back-turned point of an arrow, spear, fish-hook, etc. '—ed 'wire *n* wire with sharp points at intervals, used for fencing, etc.

bar'barian *n* uncivilized person. bar'baric *adj* in the manner of uncivilized people. 'barbarous *adj* very cruel. 'barbarism *n* state of being uncivilized. bar'barity *n* (esp) savage cruelty.

'barber *n* one whose trade is shaving and cutting men's hair.

bare *adj* (-r, -st) 1 not covered or clothed or decorated. 2 mere: *a — possibility*. *v* make —; uncover. '—ly *adv* 1 in a — way. 2 hardly; scarcely.

'bargain *n* 1 agreement about buying and selling or exchanging. 2 sth got as the result of a —. into the —, in addition. 3 sth bought, sold, or offered cheap. *v* try to make a —. not — for, not expect, not be ready for.

barge *n* flat-bottomed boat for carrying goods on canals, etc.

'baritone *n* male voice between tenor and bass.

bark¹ *n* outer covering or skin on the trunk and branches of trees. *v* take the — off.

bark² *n & v* (make the) cry of a dog or fox.

'barley *n* grass-like plant and its grain, used as food and for making beer.

barn *n* farm building for storing hay, grain, etc.

ba'rometer *n* instrument for measuring the pressure of the air, used to get information about weather and height above sea level.

'baron *n* (in Gt Brit) nobleman of the lowest rank; (in other countries) nobleman. —ess *n*. —y *n* rank of —. —et *n* person lower in rank than a noble, with the title *Sir* which is carried on from father to son.

'barrack *n* (usu *pl*) large building(s) for soldiers to live in.

'barrage *n* 1 dam built across a river. 2 heavy continuous gunfire.

'barrel *n* 1 round container, eg of wood, with flat ends and curved sides held together with strips of iron, etc. 2 metal tube of a gun, revolver, etc.

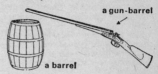

a gun-barrel

a barrel

'barren *adj* unable to produce crops, fruit or young.

,barri'cade *v & n* (put up a) wall of objects (eg carts, barrels) across or in front of sth as a defence or obstruction.

'barrier *n* sth that stops, hinders, or controls progress and movement.

'barring ⇨ bar.

'barrister *n* lawyer with the right to speak and argue in higher courts.

'barrow *n* small cart with one or two wheels, usu pushed or pulled by hand.

'barter *v & n* (make an) exchange of goods or property without using money.

base¹ *n* (*pl* 'bases) 1 lowest part of anything, esp the part on which sth is supported. 2 place at which armed forces, expeditions, etc, keep stores. 3 starting-point for runners in games. 4 substance into which other things are mixed. *v* — on, build or place on. '—less *adj* without cause. '—ment *n* part of a building wholly or partly below ground level.

base²; *adj* (-r, -st) 1 (of persons, their acts, etc) selfish; dishonourable. 2 (of metals) low in value.

'bases ⇨ base, 'basis.

ba'sh *v* (colloq) strike violently.

'bashful *adj* shy.

'basic *adj* of, at, or forming a base¹(1); fundamental.

'basin *n* 1 round, open, wide bowl for holding liquids. 2 place where water collects. 3 deep harbour surrounded by land. 4 area of land from which water is carried away by a river.

'basis *n* (*pl* 'bases) 1 = base¹ (4). 2 (esp) facts, etc, on which an argument is built up.

bask v enjoy warmth and light: —ing in the sunshine.

'basket n container, usu made of materials that can be twisted or woven.

bass¹ n ('double-'bass), largest stringed musical instrument. ⇨ p 180.

'bass² adj low in tone; deep-sounding. n lowest part in music; (male singer with the' lowest voice.

'bastard n child of unmarried parents. .

bat¹ n shaped wooden object for hitting the ball in cricket, etc. v (-tt-) use a bat. **'batsman,** **'batter** n.

bat² n small, winged, four-footed animal that usu flies at night.

batch n number of things or persons receiving attention as a group.

'bated adj with — breath, with the voice lowered to a whisper.

bath n 1 a washing of the whole body. 2 (**bath-tub**), large vessel in which to have a —. v give a —; have a —.

bathe v 1 go into the sea, a river, etc, for swimming. 2 wash. 3 (of light) make bright all over. n act of bathing, esp to swim.

bat'talion n army unit of (about 1,000) soldiers.

'batter¹ v strike violently (at or on) so as to break or crush.

'batter² n beaten mixture of flour and eggs for baking.

'battery n 1 number of big guns, with the officers and men who work them. 2 group of connected cells from which electric current will flow.

'battle n fight (between armies, etc).

'battlement n (usu pl) wall round the flat roof of a tower or castle with openings for shooting through.

bawl v shout; cry loudly.

bay¹ n part of a sea within a deep curve of the coastline.

bay² n division of a wall or building between columns or pillars; part of a room built out beyond the line of an outside wall.

bay³ n the deep bark of large dogs, esp when hunting. **at bay,** forced to turn and attack. **hold (keep) at bay,** keep (attackers, enemies) off. v (of large dogs) bark.

'bayonet n short knife fixed to a rifle. v kill or wound with a —.

ba'zaar n 1 shopping centre in the East. 2 shop selling small cheap articles. 3 sale to raise money for charity.

be v (present tense am, is, are; pt was, were; pp been) exist; live; occur. **been to,** visited. **the . . . -to-be,** the future . . .: the mother-to-be.

be-. prefix all over. **be-grimed,** dirty all over.

beach n sandy or stony stretch at the edge of the sea, covered at high tide. v get (a boat) up on the —.

'beacon n 1 warning light at sea, or on mountains, etc (for aircraft).

bead n 1 small ball of wood, glass, etc, with a hole through, for putting it on string or wire. 2 small drop (of sweat, etc). **'—y** adj small and bright.

beak n hard, horny part of a bird's mouth. ⇨ p 26.

'beaker n open glass or plastic vessel, usu with a lip.

beam n 1 long, thick, usu heavy, bar of wood, esp one used in building (to support a roof) or in a ship. 2 breadth, side, of a ship. **on her — ends,** on her sides. 3 cross-bar of a balance. 4 (**sun—**), ray of light; directed radio wave; (fig) smile. v' send out (light, warmth, radio signals); look smilingly (at).

bean n plant with seeds growing in pods, used as food; the seed ⇨ p 306; bean-like seeds of other plants: coffee —s.

bear¹ v (pt bore, pp borne) 1 carry, hold up (weight). — **arms,** be a soldier; carry weapons. 2 (pp born) produce (fruit, young); give birth to. 3 stand up to; put up with, endure (suffering, etc). 4 show (signs, evidence, likeness, love, etc). 5 — **sb** company, be or go with sb. — **up,** be brave (against), not show weakness. — **down on,** attack, press heavily on. — **on,** influence, refer to. — **out,** agree with, support (an opinion, etc). — **in mind,** remember. — **oneself** (well, like a man, etc); behave. — **straight on, to the right,** etc, move or go (straight on, etc). **'—able** adj that can be borne or endured. **'—er** n 1 person who carries (a coffin, message, *news*, etc). **2** person presenting a cheque at a bank for payment. **3** house-servant, porter, in the East.

bear² *n* **1** large, heavy animal with rough hair. ⇨ p 317. **Great B—, Little B—**, two groups of stars in the northern sky. **2** rough and clumsy person.

beard *n* growth of hair on the chin and cheeks (not lips). **'—ed** *adj*. **'—less** *adj*.

'bearing *n* **1** connection between one thing and others. **2** part of a machine which supports other moving parts. **ball —s**, fittings with small balls for reducing friction. **3** direction of a place in relation to another. **lose one's —s**, be doubtful about one's position. **find (get) one's —s**. **4** way of behaving, walking, etc: *a soldierly —*.

beast *n* **1** animal. **2** disgusting person. **'—ly** *adj* (colloq) nasty.

beat *v* (*pt* beat, *pp* 'beaten) **1** hit or strike (with the hand, a stick, etc); (of sun, light, rain, etc) come down (upon); punish by hitting. **2** win a victory over; do better than. **3** (of the heart, a bird's wings, etc) move regularly. **— time**, make regular movements to show time in music. *n* **1** regularly repeated stroke or its sound. **2** a unit of time in music. **3** path or course regularly used or taken. **'—ing** *n* (esp) defeat; punishment by —ing.

'beauty *n* combination of qualities that please. **'beauty-spot** *n* particularly pleasing area of the countryside. **'beautiful** *adj*. **'beautifully** *adv*.

'beaver *n* fur-covered animal living on land and in water; its soft brown fur. ⇨ p 12.

be'calmed *adj* (of a sailing-ship) stopped because there is no wind.

be'came ⇨ become.

be'cause *conj* for the reason that. **— (of)**, as a result (of).

'beckon *v* make a sign (to sb asking him to come).

be'come *v* (*pt* be'came, *pp* be'come) **1** come or grow to be. **2** — of, happen to. **3** be suitable for; (of clothing) look well on.

bed *n* **1** piece of furniture for sleeping on (or in). **2** base or foundation on which sth rests. **3** layer (*of clay, rock,* etc). **4** ground under-

neath a sea, river, lake: *the sea-bed*; *a river-bed*. **5** piece of ground for plants in a garden. *v* (-dd-) provide with, put into, a bed. **'bed-clothes** *n pl* sheets, blankets, etc. **'bedroom** *n* room for sleeping in. **'bedtime** *n* time for going to bed.

'bedlam *n* state of noisy confusion.

'Bedouin *n* Arab, esp one living in the deserts of N. Africa, Syria, or Arabia.

bee *n* small, winged insect that makes honey. ⇨ p 144. **make a bee-line for**, go the shortest way to. **beehive** *n* structure in which bees are kept.

beef *n* meat from an ox, a cow or a bull, used as food.

been ⇨ be.

beer *n* bitter drink made from barley and hops.

'beetle *n* insect with hard, shiny wing-covers. ⇨ p 144.

be'fall *v* (*pt* be'fell, *pp* be'fallen) happen (to).

be'fore *prep, adv, & conj* earlier than; in front (of).

be'forehand *adv & adj* in readiness; in plenty of time.

be'friend *v* act as a friend to.

beg *v* (-gg-) ask for (money, food, clothes, etc); ask earnestly for or with great feeling. **I beg your pardon**, (a) I'm sorry, (b) Please say that again. **go begging**, be unwanted. **beg off**, ask to be excused (from doing sth).

be'gan ⇨ begin.

be'get *v* (*pt* be'got, *pp* be'gotten) **1** (old use) give existence to (as father). **2** be the cause of: *War —s misery and ruin.*

'beggar *n* person who begs. *v* make poor; ruin. **—ly** *adj* fit for a beggar.

be'gin *v* (*pt* be'gan, *pp* be'gun) start doing (or *to* do): *It's time to — work*; open(1). **—ning** *n* start; opening(1).

be'grudge *v* = grudge.

be'guile *v* **1** cause (sb to do sth) by guile (deceit or tricks). **2** cause (time) to pass pleasantly.

begun ⇨ begin.

be'half *n* **on (in) — of**, for, in the interest of. **on (in) his (her,** etc) **—**, for him (her, etc).

be'have *v* act(1). **be'haviour** *n* way in which one —s.

be'head *v* cut off the head of.

be'held ⇨ behold.

be'hind prep & adv in, at or to the rear (of).

be'hindhand adv late; slow; after others.

be'hold v (pt & pp be'held) see (esp sth unusual); take notice.

'being n state of existing; human creature. the Supreme B—, God.

be'lated adj coming too late or very late; overtaken by darkness.

belch v send out (air, smoke, gas, etc) with force. n act or sound of —ing.

'belfry n (part of a) tower, esp in a church, for bell(s).

be'lief n believing; sth believed. to the best of my —, so far as my knowledge goes.

be'lieve v feel sure that sth said is true, that sb is saying what is true: I — that statement. I — you. — in, (a) have trust (in); (b) feel sure of the good, value, of; (c) feel sure of the existence of.

bell n hollow, metal instrument that sounds when struck. one — to eight —s half-hour divisions of four-hour periods of duty in a ship, marked by strokes on the ship's —.

bel'ligerent n country or party that is at war. adj threatening, violent; warlike.

'bellow n loud cry of anger or pain; cry of a cow or bull. v make such a noise.

'bellows n apparatus for blowing air into a fire or a church organ.

'belly n abdomen; stomach.

be'long v 1 — to, be the property of; be a member of. 2 have as a right or proper place. —ings n pl personal possessions (not including land, business, etc).

be'loved n & adj (one who is) much loved (by, of, sb).

be'low adv & prep under (and not necessarily touching).

belt n 1 strip of material tied round the waist. 2 wide strip or band; endless leather band used to connect wheels and drive machinery. v fasten on with a —.

bench n 1 long, hard seat. 2 work-table. 3 the B—, judge's or magistrate's seat. raised to the —, made a judge or a bishop.

bend v (pt & pp bent) 1 (cause to) become curved or at an angle;

force out of a straight line. 2 turn; cause (the mind, attention, etc) to turn (towards). bent on, having the mind set on, having as a fixed purpose. n curve, turn, or angle.

be'neath prep & adv below; lower than.

,bene'diction n blessing.

'benefactor n one who gives kindly help (esp money) to a school, hospital, etc).

,bene'ficial adj having good effect.

'benefit n help, advantage, improvement; good done to or got from sb or sth. v do good to; be helped (by).

be'nevolent adj kind and helpful; doing good. be'nevolence n.

be'nign adj kind and gentle; mild; (of diseases) not serious or dangerous.

bent n natural tendency; inclination (of the mind). ⇨ bend.

be'queath v (arrange to) give (property, etc) at death. be'quest n —ing; sth —ed.

be'reaved adj having had (sb) taken away by death; made unhappy by the loss (esp death) of. be'reavement n. be'reft adj — of, having lost.

'berry n small, juicy fruit with many seeds: strawberries.

berth n 1 sleeping-place in a train or ship. 2 place for a ship in a river or harbour. 3 (colloq) work; position.

be'seech v (pt & pp be'sought) ask earnestly or urgently.

be'set v (-tt-) (pt & pp be'set) attack from all sides; be on all sides.

be'side prep at the side of. — the point, having nothing to do with the point(7). —s prep & adv as well (as); in addition (to).

be'siege v 1 close in upon, attack (a town, etc), from all sides. 2 — with (questions, etc), put forward a large number of.

be'sought ⇨ beseech.

best adj & adv ⇨ good.

'bestial adj of, like a beast; brutal.

be'stir v (-rr-) — oneself, move quickly; get busy.

be'stow v — sth on sb, give.

be'stride v (pt be'strode, pp be'stridden) put, sit or stand, with one leg on each side of.

bet v (-tt-) (pt & pp bet) risk

money, etc, on the result of a race or some other event. *n* offer of this kind; the money, etc, offered.

be'tray *v* 1 be false or unfaithful to. 2 allow (a secret) to become known. 3 be or give a sign of. —al *n*.

be'troth *v* (usu in *pp*) be —ed, promised in marriage.

'better *adj & adv* ⇨ good. **get the — of**, beat, conquer. **— off**, more prosperous, comfortable. *v* improve.

be'tween *prep* (separating (usu) two objects, places, ideas, etc) 1 (of place): *The letter B comes — A and C.* 2 (of time): — 1 *o'clock and* 2 *o'clock.* 3 (of distance, amount, etc): — *five and six miles*; — *twenty and twenty-five degrees.* 4 to and from: *This ship sails — Lagos and Tema.* 5 (to show sharing; used of two only): *Divide (share) the money — you.* 6 (showing relationship): *quarrels — nations; distinction — right and wrong. adv* in(to) a place or time that is —: *We worked in the morning and played football later, with a quick lunch —.* **in —**, spaced out among.

'bevel *n* sloping surface at an edge. *v* (-ll-) give a — to.

'beverage *n* kind of drink (eg *coffee, tea,* etc).

be'ware *v* be on guard; be careful (*of*); keep away.

be'wilder *v* puzzle; confuse greatly. **—ment** *n*.

be'witch *v* 1 work magic on. 2 attract or charm greatly.

be'yond *adv & prep* at, on, or to the further side of; farther on; exceeding: *That's — a joke.*

bi- *prefix* twice; having two; coming once in every two.

'bias *n* 1 prejudiced opinion. 2 **cut on the —**, cut diagonally. *v* (*pt & pp* 'biased or 'biassed) give a —(1) to; be —(s)ed(1).

bib *n* cloth placed under a child's chin; upper part of an apron.

'Bible *n*, sacred writings of the Jews and the Christian church. **'biblical** *adj*.

,bibli'ography *n* list of books and writings by one author or on one subject.

'biceps *n* large muscle at the front part of the upper arm.

'bicycle (colloq **bike**) *n* two-wheeled vehicle for riding driven by pedalling. **'motor-bike** *n* similar vehicle driven by an engine.

bicycles

bid *v* (-dd-) (*pt & pp* bid) offer. to pay a stated sum for. *n*.offer of a price. **make a bid for**, try to obtain.

bide *v* **— one's time**, wait for an opportunity.

bier *n* wooden stand for a coffin or a dead body.

big *adj* ('bigger, 'biggest) large in size; of great importance.

'bigamy *n* having two wives or husbands living. **'bigamous** *adj*: *a bigamous marriage.* **'bigamist** *n*.

'bigoted *adj* strict and obstinate beyond reason in holding to a belief or opinion.

bike *n* ⇨ bicycle.

bi'lingual *adj* speaking, written in, two languages.

'bilious *adj* subject to sickness; feeling sick owing to poor digestion.

bill[1] *n* horny part of a bird's mouth; beak.

bill[2] *n* 1 statement of money owing for goods or services. 2 written or printed notice, handed out or stuck on a wall, etc. 3 proposed law, to be discussed by a parliament. 4 **B— of Exchange**, written order to a bank, etc, to pay money to sb on a certain date. *v* make known by means of —s(2).

'billet *n* place (usu a private house) where a soldier is lodged. *v* — on, lodge (eg a soldier) with.

'billion *n* (*pl* 'billion) (Gt Brit) one million millions; (USA) one thousand millions.

'billow *n* great sea-wave; (*pl*) the sea. *v* rise or roll like great waves.

bin *n* large container with a wide lid for storing coal, grain or rubbish.

bind *v* (*pt & pp* bound) 1 tie or

fasten together (with rope, etc); put (one thing) round (another). 2 fasten together; put (sheets of paper, etc) into a cover. 3 — oneself (*to do sth*), promise or guarantee. — sb (over) to keep the peace, order that he shall appear before the judge again if he makes more trouble. (⏵ bound for special uses of the *pp*). '—er *n* person, thing, machine, that —s. '—ing *n* book cover.

bi'noculars *n pl* instrument with lenses looked through with both eyes for making distant objects seem nearer.

bi'ography *n* person's life-history written by another.

bi'ology *n* science of life, of animals, and plants. ,bio'logical *adj*. bi'ologist *n*.

bird *n* winged, feathered animal(1) that lays eggs. ⏵ below.

birth *n* act of being born. 'birth-control *n* way(s) of avoiding unwanted —s. '—day *n* annual remembrance of the day sb was born. 'birth-rate *n* number of —s each year.

'biscuit *n* kind of thin, crisp, flat cake.

bi'sect *v* cut or divide into two.

some birds

—ion *n* division into two equal parts.

'bishop *n* clergyman of high rank who organizes the work of the Christian Church in a city or district. **—ric** *n* district under a —.

'bison *n* wild ox; American buffalo.

bit¹ *n* very small piece. **bit by bit**, gradually. **a bit** (*better*, etc), rather (*better*, etc).

bit² *n* **1** steel bar placed in a horse's mouth to control it. **2** the biting or cutting part of certain tools.

bite *v* (*pt* bit, *pp* 'bitten) cut into with the teeth. *n* injury caused by biting.

'bitter *adj* **1** tasting like beer or vinegar; opposite to sweet. **2** causing sorrow; filled with, showing or caused by, anger, envy, or hate.

black *adj & n* (having the) colour of this printing ink. **give sb a — look, look — at sb**, look at with anger. **— sheep**, person of bad character. **be in sb's — books**, be quite out of his favour. **— flag**, one used by sea-robbers. **— art**, evil magic. **'—berry** *n* (*pl* **-ies**) (bush with) small, sweet — berries. ⇨ p 115. **'—en** *v* make or become —. **'—guard** *n* person quite without honour; scoundrel. **'—leg** *n* person who offers to work for an employer whose men are on strike (⇨ strike). **'—list** *v & n* (put on a) list of persons who are considered dangerous or wrongdoers. **'—mail** *v* (try to) make (sb) pay money by threatening to tell sth against him. *n* such a threat. **'—smith** *n* iron-worker, esp one who repairs tools and makes horseshoes.

'bladder *n* **1** skin bag in the body in which urine collects. **2** rubber bag in a football.

blade *n* **1** sharpened part of a knife, sword, razor, etc. **2** flat narrow leaf (eg of grass). **3** wide part of an oar. **4** ⇨ shoulder.

blame *v* find fault with; say that (sb or sth) is the cause of what is wrong. *n* blaming; responsibility for failure. **'—less** *adj*.

blanch *v* (cause to) become white.

bland *adj* **1** gentle or polite in manner. **2** having little taste.

'blandishment *n* (often *pl*) soft, gentle words or ways used to make sb do sth.

blank *adj* **1** (of paper) with nothing drawn, written, or printed on it. **2** (of sb's face) puzzled, without interest or expression. **3 — wall**, without doors or windows. **—cartridge**, with powder but no shot(3). **— verse**, without rhyme. *n* — space (in writing or print); emptiness. **'—ly** *adv*. **'—ness** *n*.

'blanket *n* thick (usu) woollen cloth used as a bed covering, etc.

blare *n* loud sound or noise (of a horn or trumpet) (cf blast) *v* make such sounds.

blas'pheme *v* cry out against God; speak rudely and without respect (of sacred things). **'blasphemous** *adj*. **'blasphemy** *n*.

blast *n* **1** strong, sudden rush of wind or air. **2** sound made by a wind-instrument such as a horn or trumpet. **3** shot(1) from a gun. *v* break up or destroy by explosion; bring (hopes, plans, etc) to nothing. **'blast-,furnace** *n* one for melting iron ore by forcing heated air into it.

'blatant *adj* noisy; trying to attract attention in a vulgar way.

blaze *n* **1** bright fire, flame, or light; bright display or glow. **2** violent outburst (of feeling): *v* **1** burn with bright flames; shine brightly and with warmth. **2** burst out with strong feeling. **3** fire (guns).

bleach *v* make or become white (by chemical process or sunlight).

bleak *adj* (of weather) cold; (of a place) bare, windy; (of an outlook) unhopeful.

bleat *n & v* (make the) cry of a sheep, goat or calf.

bleed *v* (*pt & pp* bled) lose blood; cause blood to flow from.

'blemish *v & n* (make a) mark, etc, which spoils the beauty or perfection of sb or sth.

blench *v* jump suddenly back, close the eyes quickly, in fear.

blend *v* **1** mix (tea, tobacco); become mixed (so as to make a desired mixture). **2** (of colours) go well together; have no sharp contrast. *n* mixture made by **—ing**.

bless *v* **1** ask God's favour for. **2** wish good to; make happy. **3** make, call (God), sacred or holy. **4 be —ed with**, be fortunate in having. **'—ed** *adj* holy; sacred.

'**—ing** n favour; sth that brings happiness.

blew ⇨ **blow**.

blight n p'ant disease; evil influence which spoils hopes, pleasures, etc. v be a —to.

blind[1] adj 1 unable to see. 2 not controlled by reason or purpose: in — haste. 3 — wall, without doors or windows. — turning, difficult to see past. v make —. '**—ness** n. '**—fold** v cover a person's eyes (with a band of cloth, etc). adv with the eyes so covered.

'**blind**[2] n roll (of cloth) fixed above a window and unrolled to cover it.

blink v 1 shut and open the eyes quickly. 2 (of lights) come and go; shine in an unsteady way.

bliss n perfect happiness. '**—ful** adj.

'**blister** n small, watery swelling under the skin; similar swelling, air-filled, under paint. v cause, get, —s on.

'**blizzard** n severe snowstorm with violent wind.

block n 1 large, solid piece of stone, wood, etc. 2 piece of wood or metal with designs, etc, cut (engraved) on its surface for printing. 3 number of large buildings joined together, often with streets on all four sides; a division of seats (in a theatre, etc). 4 — and tackle, apparatus (a pulley in a — of wood) for lifting and pulling. 5 sth that stops movement, eg a number of cars, buses, etc, held up in a street. v make movement difficult or impossible by getting or putting sth in the way: roads —ed by snow. '**—age** n state of being —ed; sth —ing.

block'ade n the enclosing or surrounding of a place, eg by warships or armies, to keep people and goods in or out. v make a — of.

blonde n & adj (person, usu female) having light-coloured hair.

blood n red liquid flowing throughout the body of man and higher animals. in cold —, not in the heat of anger. make bad — (between), cause ill-feeling. His — was up, he was very angry. '**—hound** n large dog able to trace a person by smell. '**—shed** n killing; putting to death. '**—shot** adj (of the whites of the eyes) red. '**—thirsty** adj eager

to take life. '**blood-,vessel** n vein or artery. '**—y** adj 1 covered with —; very much —shed. 2 (colloq, vulgar) extremely; damnably.

bloom n any flower or blossom. v be in flower.

'**blossom** n flower; mass of flowers, esp on fruit-tree. v open into flowers.

blot n 1 mark caused by ink spilt on paper. 2 sth that takes away from the value, beauty, or goodness of: a — on his character. v (-tt-) 1 make a — or —s on. 2 dry wet ink marks with a kind of paper, called '—ting paper. 3 — out, rub off; hide completely.

blotch n large discoloured mark (eg on the skin); dirty ink mark. v mark with —es.

blouse n outer garment from neck to waist, usu with sleeves.

blow[1] v (pt blew, pp blown) 1 (of air) be moving or flowing. 2 (of things) be moved or carried by the wind; (of the wind, etc) cause to move. 3 force air upon, through or into: — the dust from a book. — up, (a) fill with air: — up a tyre. (b) destroy by explosion: — up a bridge. (c) enlarge: — up a photograph. 4 (of a whistle, etc) give out, cause to give out, sounds. 5 breathe hard and quickly. 6 give shape to (glass) by —ing. n have (go for) a —, go outdoors for fresh air. '**—er** n apparatus for forcing air into or through sth (eg a fire); sb who —s or pumps air.

blow[2] n 1 sudden stroke (given with the hand, etc). come to —s, begin fighting. 2 shock; sudden loss or misfortune causing unhappiness.

blue adj & n (having the) colour like that of a cloudless sky during the day, '**blue-'blooded**, of aristocratic birth. a bolt from the —, (sth) out of the — (sth) unexpected. '**—print** n photographic print, with a white design on a blue background, usu for building-plans. '**blue-book** n government report.

bluff[1] v deceive by pretending to be stronger, etc, than one really is. n deception of this kind.

bluff[2] adj rough and noisy but honest and kindly.

'**blunder** n foolish or careless mistake. v make a —; move about uncertainly, as if unable to see.

blunt adj **1** without a point or sharp edge. **2** (of a person, his speech) not showing polite consideration. v make —. '**—ly** adv. '**—ness** n.

blur v (-rr-) (cause to) become unclear; (cause to) become confused in shape or appearance. n dirty spot or mark; sth seen only in indistinct outline.

blurt v — sth out, say or tell sth (esp a secret) suddenly, often without thinking.

blush v become red in the face (from shame or confusion). n red colour spreading over the face.

'**bluster** v be rough or violent. n (esp) noisy, threatening talk and behaviour.

boar n male pig.

board n **1** long, thin, flat piece of wood with squared edges, used in building walls, floors, boats, ships' decks, etc. on —, in(to) a ship. **2** flat piece of wood for a special purpose: '**black—**, '**notice-board**. **3** table; group of persons controlling a business or government department: the B— of Governors; the B— of Trade. **4** the supply of meals by the week or month: — and lodging, £10 weekly. **5** thick, stiff card used for book covers. v **1** make or cover with —s. **2** get, supply with, —(4). **3** go on (a ship, tram, etc). '**—er** n person who —s(2) at sb's house; child who lives at school. '**—ing-house**, '**—ing-school** n one which provides —(4) and lodging.

boast n **1** proud words used in praise of oneself, one's acts, belongings, etc. **2** cause for self-satisfaction. v make —s; possess (sth) with pride. '**—ful** adj. '**—fully** adv.

boat n small open vessel for travelling on water; any ship. be all in the same —, have the same dangers to face; be in the same condition. burn one's —s, do sth that makes a change of plans impossible. '**—man** n man who takes people in a — for pay.

bob¹ v (-bb-) & n (make a) quick, short down-and-up movement.

bob² n (colloq) shilling.

'**bobbin** n small roller for thread or yard as in a sewing-machine.

bode v — well (ill), be a sign of good (evil) in the future.

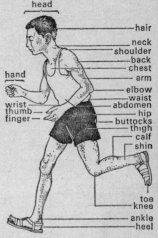

the human body 1

head — hair
neck
shoulder
back
chest
hand — arm
elbow
waist
abdomen
wrist — hip
thumb — buttocks
finger — thigh
calf
shin
toe
knee
ankle
heel

'**body** n (pl -ies) **1** the whole physical structure of a man or animal. ⇨ above and p 30; —without the head, arms, and legs. **3** the main part of a structure: the — of a motor-car; the — of a hall (the central part where the seats are). **4** group of persons: a large — of troops. in a —, all together. **5** collection (of facts, information, etc). **6** substance; piece of matter. the heavenly bodies, the stars and planets. **7** person: any—, no—, etc. '**bodily** adj of, in, the —. adv as a whole; completely. '**—guard** n man, group of men, guarding an important person.

bog n wet, soft ground. '**boggy** adj.

boil¹ v **1** (of water, etc) reach, cause to reach, the temperature at which change into vapour occurs. **2** cook, cause to be cooked, by —ing. **3** be excited or angry. n —ing-point: to bring sth to the —. '**—er** n metal container for heating or —ing liquids.

boil² n hard (usu red) poisoned swelling under the skin which bursts when ripe.

'**boisterous** adj rough; violent; (of a person) noisy and cheerful.

the human body 2

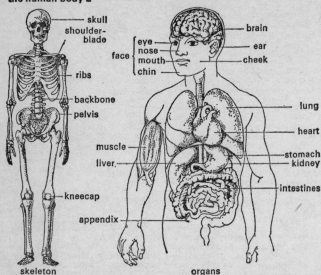

skull
shoulder-blade
ribs
backbone
pelvis
muscle
liver
kneecap
appendix

brain
face — eye, nose, mouth, chin
ear
cheek
lung
heart
stomach
kidney
intestines

skeleton   organs

bold *adj* (-er, -est) **1** without fear. **2** without feelings of shame. **3** well marked. **'—ly** *adv.* **'—ness** *n.*

'bolster *n* long under-pillow for the head of a bed. *v* **— up**, give support to; encourage.

bolt¹ *n* **1** metal fastening for a door or window. **2** metal pin for joining machine parts, usu with a

bolts

thread(3) at one end for a nut. *v* fasten or join with a **—** or **—s.**

bolt² *v* **1** run away suddenly and unexpectedly. **2** swallow (food) quickly.

bolt³ *adv* **— upright**, quite upright.

bomb *n* hollow metal ball or shell filled with explosive. *v* drop **—s** on; throw **—s** at. **'—shell** *n* (fig) great surprise. **'—er** *n* aircraft carrying **—s**; soldier who throws **—s.**

bom'bard *v* attack with gunfire, bombs, questions, etc. **—ment** *n.*

bond *n* **1** written agreement or promise. **2** printed paper saying that money has been received and will be paid back with interest. **3** sth that unites or joins. **4** (of goods) **in —**, in a customs warehouse (until duties(3) are paid). **5** (*pl*) chains. **in —s**, in prison or slavery. **'—ed** *adj* (of goods) placed or held in **—(4)**. **'—age** *n* slavery.

bone *n* **1** any one of the parts of the hard framework of the animal body. **2** the material of **—s**. **'bone-'dry** *adj* completely dry. **'bone-'idle** (**'lazy**) *adj* thoroughly idle. **feel in one's —s**, feel certain about sth without proof. *v* remove the **—s** from (esp in cooking). **'bony** *adj* with little flesh.

'bonfire *n* fire made in the open air (eg to burn garden rubbish).

'bonnet *n* **1** small, round hat, usu tied under the chin, worn by women and children and some soldiers. **2** cover of a motor-car engine.

'bonny, 'bonnie *adj* healthy-looking.

'bonus *n* extra payment beyond the agreed amount.

boo(h) *v & int* (make a) sound showing contempt or disapproval.

'booby *n* foolish person.

book *n* 1 sheets of paper fastened together for reading or writing purposes. 2 division or part of a long poem or of the Bible. **bring sb to —**, require him to explain his conduct. **in sb's good (black, bad) —s**, having (not having) his favour and approval. *v* 1 give, send or record (orders, etc) in a note —. 2 give or receive an order for (tickets for a journey, seats at a theatre, etc). **'—case** *n* piece of furniture with shelves for —s. **'—ing-clerk** *n* clerk who sells tickets. **'—ing-office** *n* one where tickets for travelling are sold. **'book-keeper** *n* person who keeps business accounts. **'—let** *n* small —, usu in paper covers. **'—maker** *n* man whose business is taking bets on races. **'—stall** *n* stall (booth) where newspapers, magazines, and —s are sold.

boom¹ *n* long pole used to keep the bottom of a sail stretched out.

boom² *n* sudden increase in trade activity, esp a time when traders are prosperous. *v* have a —; advertise in order to have a —.

boom³ *v* speak in a deep, loud voice.

boon¹ *n* advantage; blessing; gift.

boon² *adj* — companion, pleasant and merry companion.

boot *n* 1 outer covering for the foot and ankle. 2 separate place for luggage in a car or coach.

booth *n* 1 shelter of wood or canvas used as a shop. 2 place used for voting.

'booty *n* things taken by robbers of captured from enemies in war.

'border *n* 1 edge; part near the edge. 2 (land near the) line dividing two countries. *v* put a — on; be a — (on, upon); be next to.

bore¹ *v* make a narrow, round, deep hole in, eg by turning a pointed instrument. *n* 1 hole made by boring. 2 the hollow inside of a gun barrel.

bore² *v* make (sb) tired by dull

uninteresting talk or work. *n* person or thing that —s. **'—dom** *n*.

bore³ ⇨ bear¹.

born ⇨ bear¹(2) **be —**, come into the world by birth. **a — poet**, poet by natural ability.

borne ⇨ bear¹.

'borough *n* (in England) town, part of a town, sending one or more members to Parliament; part of a town with a mayor and councillors for local government.

'borrow *v* get sth, or the use of sth, after promising to return it.

'bosom *n* 1 centre or inmost part where one feels joy or sorrow. 2 person's breast.

boss *n* (colloq) man who controls or gives orders to workmen. *v* give orders to; control.

'botany *n* science of the structure of plants. **bo'tanical** *adj*. **'botanist** *n*.

both *adj, n, & pron.* the one and the other; not only . . . but also.

'bother *v & n* (cause, be a) trouble (to).

'bottle *n* narrow-necked container for liquid (usu made of glass).

'bottom *n* 1 lowest part: — *of the sea.* 2 (colloq) buttocks. **'—less** *adj* (fig) very deep.

bough *n* large branch coming from tree trunk.

bought ⇨ buy.

'boulder *n* large piece of rock, or large stone, rounded by weather or water.

bounce *v* 1 (of a ball, etc) (cause to) spring or jump back when sent against sth hard. 2 move, cause to move, violently: *to — into a room*; throw, be thrown, about.

bound¹ *n* (usu *pl*) limit. **in (out of) —s**, within (outside) a permitted area. *v* form the —s of; put —s to. **'—ary** *n* dividing line. **'—less** *adj* without —s.

bound² *v* jump; move or run in jumps. *n* jump up or forward. **by leaps and —s**, very quickly.

bound³ *adj* about to start (*for*); on the way to.

bound⁴ ⇨ bind. **— to**, obliged or compelled to; certain to. **— up in**, much interested in; very fond of; busy with.

'bounty *n* 1 generosity. 2 sth given freely out of kindness. 3 payment offered by government to farmers, traders, etc, to encourage production, etc. 'bounteous adj generous; plentiful. 'bountiful adj.

bou'quet n bunch of flowers for carrying in the hand.

'bourgeois n & adj (person) of the middle class of society.

bout n period of exercise or work; attack (of illness).

bow¹ n 1 curved piece of wood with string, for shooting arrows. 2 piece of wood with horsehairs stretched from end to end for playing the violin, etc. 3 curve like a bow(1). 4 knot with a loop or loops (eg shoe laces tied in a bow; a bow tie).

bow² v 1 bend the head or body forward (as a greeting or in respect). 2 bend; (fig) give way (to). n act of bowing.

bow³ n front end of a boat or ship.

'bowel n (usu pl) the long tube into which food passes from the stomach; the innermost part.

bowl¹ n 1 deep, round, hollow dish; part of a pipe in which tobacco is placed.

bowl² v 1 (cricket) send a ball to the batsman; defeat the batsman by hitting the wicket with the ball. 2 move quickly and smoothly (along a road), on wheels. '—er n 1 one who —s (in cricket). 2 a hard, rounded, black hat.

box¹ n 1 container made of wood, cardboard, metal, etc for holding solids. 2 'Christmas box, present given at Christmas. 'Boxing Day, 26 December. 3 separate compartment, with seats for several persons, in a theatre or for a witness at a trial(3). 'box-'office, place where tickets are sold in a theatre, concert-hall, etc.

box² n blow with the open hand on the ear(s). v 1 box sb's ear(s), give him a blow or blows on the ear(s). 2 fight with the fists, usu with thick gloves, for sport. 'boxer n person who fights in this way. 'boxing n fighting with gloves.

boy n male child till about 17 years old. 'boyhood n period of being a boy.

'boycott v (join with others and) refuse to have anything to do with, to trade with, etc. n —ing.

bra n (colloq) pair of brassières.

brace¹ n 1 piece of wood or iron

used as a support or to hold things together. 2 — and bit, tool used for making holes in wood. ⇨ bit²2. v support; give firmness or strength to. —oneself up, strengthen oneself in readiness.

brace² n pair (of dogs, birds).

'bracelet n band or chain (of metal, etc) worn on the arm or wrist as an ornament.

'braces n pl straps passing over the shoulders to keep trousers up.

'bracket n 1 wood or metal support (eg for a shelf or lamp). 2 marks (), [], {} used in writing and printing. v put inside, join with, —s.

brag v (-gg-) & n boast. '—gart n boasting person.

braid n 1 band made by twisting together two or more strands of silk, hair, etc. 2 such bands, used for binding edges of cloth or (if of silver or gold) for decoration.

braille n system of printing for the blind, to enable them to read by touch.

brain n (often pl) the mass of soft grey matter in the head, centre of the nervous system; the centre of thought. ⇨ p 30. v kill by a hard blow on the head. —less adj stupid. —y adj (-ier, -iest) clever.

brake n apparatus that can be pressed or rubbed against a wheel to reduce the speed. v put on the —(s).

'bramble n thorn-covered shrub.

bran n outer covering of grains (eg wheat) separated from flour after grinding.

branch n 1 arm-like part of a tree growing out from the trunk of a bough. 2 anything like a —, going out from or managed from the central part: a — railway (road, office). v send out, divide into, —es. — out, become active in a new direction.

brand n piece of burning wood; red-hot iron used for marking (cattle, etc); mark or design made in this way; trade mark. v mark with a —. 'brand-'new adj quite new.

'brandish v wave about.

'brandy n strong alcoholic drink made from wine.

brass n bright yellow alloy made

by mixing copper and zinc; things made of this.

'brassière(s) n woman's close-fitting support for the breast.

bra'vado n display of (usu foolish) daring or boldness.

brave v & adj (-r, -st) (be) ready to face danger, pain; courageous. **'—ly** adv. **'—ry** n.

bra'vo int Well done!

brawl n noisy quarrel or fight. v have, take part in, a —.

brawn n 1 strength; muscle. 2 pickled pig-meat. **'—y** adj (-ier, -iest) with strong muscles.

bray v & n (make the) cry of an ass; sound of a trumpet.

'brazen adj 1 made of brass; like brass. 2 shameless.

'brazier n open metal framework (like a basket), usu on legs, for holding burning coals.

breach n 1 act of breaking (a law, duty, promise, etc). **— of the peace**, unlawful fighting in a public place. 2 opening made in a wall, etc, esp one made by enemy forces. v make a — in.

bread n food made by baking flour with water and yeast.

breadth n distance from side to side. **to a hair's —**, exactly.

break v (pt broke, pp 'broken) 1 (cause a whole thing to) divide into two or more pieces (as the result of a blow or other force, not by cutting, etc): to — a cup; to — to pieces; to — a branch off (a tree); to — up a box. 2 stop, interrupt, for a time (eg a journey, silence). **—down**, (of machinery, a system, etc) fail to work; (of a person) start to cry, lose one's mental control. **— up**, (a meeting, etc) end. 3 become parted: the clouds broke; make a way through: the moon broke through the clouds; force a way through or into: disease (fire, war) broke out. The prisoners broke out (ie escaped). Robbers broke into the bank. 4 lessen the force of (the wind, a fall, bad news). **— in**, (eg a horse) tame. 5 fail to keep (a law, promise, etc). 6 **— a record**, create a new record(3). n 1 (place of) —ing; space between. **without a —**, continuously. 2 (colloq) change of circumstances: a lucky —. **'—able** adj sth that can be broken(1).

'breakage n 1 action of breaking. 2 (usu pl) damage by breaking.

'breakdown n 1 failure (of machine, motor, etc): a — on the railway. 2 failure of mind or body: a nervous —.

'breaker n large wave ready to fall and break (on the beach).

'breakfast n first meal of the day.

'breakneck adj at (a) — speed, at a speed likely to cause an accident.

'break,water n wall built (eg in a harbour) to break the force of the waves.

breast n 1 milk-producing part of a woman. 2 upper front part of the human body and part of a garment covering this; part of an animal's body in a similar position. 3 the feelings. **make a clean — of**, confess (wrongdoing, etc).

breath n 1 air used in the act of breathing. 2 single act of taking in and sending out air. **catch one's —**, stop taking in — for a moment (from excitement, etc). **under one's —**, in a whisper. **out of —**, needing to breathe more quickly than usual. **'—less** adj out of —.

breathe v 1 take air into the body and send it out. 2 say in a whisper.

bred ⇨ breed.

'breeches n pl short trousers fitting closely below the knees.

breed v (pt & pp bred) 1 give birth to young; reproduce. 2 keep (animals, etc) for the purpose of having young. 3 train; educate: well-bred boys. 4 be the cause of. n kind of animal, etc; group of animals, with the same qualities. **'—er** n one who —s(2) animals. **'—ing** n (esp) behaviour; training.

breeze n wind. **'breezy** adj windy.

'brethren n pl (old use) brothers.

'brevity n shortness, esp in speaking and writing.

brew v prepare (drinks such as tea, beer) by soaking or boiling leaves, grain, etc, in liquid; (fig) set working (usu for evil purposes). n result of —ing. **'—er** n maker of beer. **'—ery** n place where beer is —ed.

bribe n sth given or offered to sb to influence or persuade him to do sth wrong, or sth he hesitates to do. v offer, give a — to. **'—ry** n giving or taking of —s.

brick *n* rectangular block of baked clay used for building.

bride *n* woman on her wedding-day; newly married woman. **'—groom** *n* man on his wedding-day. **'—smaid** *n* girl or young unmarried woman attending a —. **'bridal** *adj* of a — or a wedding.

bridge *n* **1** construction (over a river, road, railway line) providing a way from one side to the other. **2** high platform over and across a ship's deck, from which orders are given by the ship's officers. *v* build a — over.

'bridle *v & n* (put on a) set of leather straps with a metal bit for the mouth, for controlling a horse.

brief *adj* (-er, -est) (of time, writing, speaking, etc) short; lasting only a short time. **In —,** in a few words. **'—ly** *adv.* **—s** *n* short knickers.

bri'gade *n* **1** army unit of usu two, three, or four battalions. **2** organized and uniformed body of persons with special work: *the fire —.*

'brigand *n* 'robber, esp one of a band attacking travellers in forests or mountains.

bright *adj* (-er, -est) **1** full of colour, light, etc. **2** quick at learning, intelligent. **3** cheerful. **'—en** *v* make —(er). **'—ly** *adv.* **'—ness** *n.*

'brilliant *adj* very bright; very clever; splendid. **'brilliance** *n.*

brim *n* **1** edge (of a cup, bowl, etc). **2** out-turned edge of a hat (giving shade). **'—ful(l)** *adj* full to the —.

brine *n* salt water.

bring *v* (*pt & pp* brought) **1** cause to come, have, with oneself: *I will — you the book tomorrow. B— the chairs in from the garden.* **2** carry, lead, drive, to or towards (the place where the speaker is or will be): *B— your sister with you next time.* **3** cause; cause to become. **— about,** — to pass, cause to happen. **— back,** cause to remember. **— down,** cause (eg prices) to be lower. **— forward, up,** cause to be considered. **— off,** succeed in an attempt. **— on,** be the cause of; lead to. **— out,** cause to appear clearly; publish (a book). **— sb round,** cause him to be conscious after fainting. **4 — sb through,** (an illness, etc), care for until he is well again. **— up,**

(children) educate, train. **— forth,** produce (young, fruit).

brink *n* edge of sth unknown, dangerous, or exciting; upper end of a steep place.

brisk *adj* quick-moving.

'bristle *n* short, stiff hair. *v* (of hair) stand up on end (with fear, etc); (of an animal) have the hair on end. **— with,** have (difficulties, etc) in large numbers.

'British *adj* of Great Britain.

'brittle *adj* hard but easily broken (eg coal, glass).

broach *v* open (a barrel); (fig) begin to discuss (a problem).

broad *adj* (-er, -est) **1** wide. **It's as — as it's long,** whichever way sth is viewed, it is the same (esp differences in an argument). **.2** (of the mind, ideas, etc) not limited. **3** full and complete: *— daylight.* **4** strongly marked: *a — hint.* **'—ly** *adv* generally: *—ly speaking.* **'—en** *v.*

'broadcast *v* (*pt & pp* 'broadcast) send out everywhere, esp by radio. *n* sth — by radio.

bro'cade *n* fine cloth with raised designs (eg in silver thread) worked on it.

broke, broken ⇨ break.

'broker *n* one who brings together buyers and sellers (esp of shares, bonds).

bronze *n* mixture of copper and tin; work of art made of —; the colour of — (reddish-brown). **—d** *adj* sun-tanned.

brooch *n* ornamental pin for fastening (on) a dress (esp at the neck).

brood *n* all the young birds hatched at one time in a nest. *v* (of a bird) sit on eggs; (fig) think about (troubles, etc) for a long time.

brook *n* small stream.

broom *n* brush on a long handle for sweeping floors.

broth *n* meat soup.

'brother *n* **1** son of the same parents as sb else. **2** person in the same profession, religious society, etc, as another. **'brother-in-law** *n* — of one's husband or wife; husband of one's sister. **'—ly** *adj* friendly, affectionate. **'—hood** *n* group of men with common aims and interests, esp a religious society.

brought ⇨ bring.

brow *n* **1** part of the face over the eyes. **2** (usu *pl*) (also **'eye—**) arch of hair above the eye. **3** top of a slope. **'—beat** v frighten by shouting at or treating roughly.

brown adj & n (having the) colour of chocolate.

browse v eat, crop (grass, etc); (fig) read here and there in a book or newspaper.

bruise v & n (give or receive) injury to the flesh of the body without breaking the skin.

bru'nette n woman of European race with dark-brown or black hair and eyes.

brunt n bear the —(of an attack), bear the main force, the weight.

brush n implement of bristles, wire, nylon, etc, fastened in wood used for scrubbing, etc. v use a —.

brusque adj rough, abrupt (in behaviour or speech).

brute n **1** animal (except man). **2** stupid and cruel man. adj unreasoning; animal-like. **'brutal** adj savage; inhuman. **'brutalize** v make brutal. **bru'tality** n cruelty.

'bubble n (in air) floating ball formed of liquid and containing air or gas; (in liquid) ball of air or gas rising to the surface. v send up —s; rise in —s.

buck n male of a deer, hare, or rabbit.

'bucket n deep, hollow container with a handle for holding liquids. ⇨ pail.

'buckle n metal fastener for belt or strap. v **1** fasten with a —. **2** (of metal work, etc) bend, become twisted (because of strain at the ends, or from heat).

bud n leaf, flower, or branch at the beginning of its growth. v (-dd-) put out —s.

Buddhism n religion founded by 'Buddha. **'Buddhist** n.

budge v (usu neg or interr) move sth heavy or stiff.

'budget n statement of income and estimate of probable future payments. v — **for**, plan for in a —.

buff n thick, strong, soft leather; its colour, a brownish-yellow.

'buffalo n ('water-,buffalo) (pl -es) kind of wild ox. ⇨ p 317.

!buffer(s) n apparatus (usu with springs) for lessening the force of a blow, esp on or of a train.

'buffet v & n (give a) blow (to) (esp with the hand); sideboard,

table, from which food and drink are served (in a hotel).

bug n small, bad-smelling insect that sucks blood.

'bugle n musical wind instrument of brass or copper, used in the army. ⇨ p 180.

build v construct (a house, bridge, etc); amass in order: — a library (of books). — **up**, make bigger or stronger (a business, one's health). — **upon**, use as a foundation; (fig) allow to rest on. n general shape: a man of slight —. **'—ing** n house, church, office, etc (but not a bridge, wall, etc). **'—ing-estate**, planned area of land for houses, shops, etc.

bulb n **1** thick, round part, in the ground, of such plants as lilies and onions. **2** bulb-shaped object (eg an electric lamp).

bulbs

bulge v (cause to) swell beyond proper size; curve out. n place where a swelling or curve shows.

bulk n **1** quantity or volume, esp when great. **in** —, loose or in large amounts. **2** the greater part or number (of). **'—y** adj (-ier, -iest) taking up much space.

bull[1] n uncastrated male of any animal of the ox family and of some other large animals. ⇨ p 84.

bull[2] n written order from the Pope.

'bulldozer n machine for shifting large quantities of earth, levelling road surfaces, etc.

'bullet n shaped piece of lead coated with copper, etc, fired from a rifle or revolver.

'bulletin n official statement of news.

'bullion n gold or silver in bulk, before manufacture.

'bullock n castrated bull.

'bully n person who uses his strength or power to frighten or hurt those who are weaker. v use strength, etc, in this way: to — sb into doing sth.

bulwark n wall, esp one built of earth against attack; (fig) defence.

bump n blow or knock (as when two things come together with force); swelling of, lump on, the flesh caused by this, or made on a road surface by traffic. v knock against; move (along) over —s. '—y adj (-ier, -iest) full of —s.

bumper n 1 bar on a motor-car to prevent damage from a slight collision, etc. 2 (as adj) (of crops, etc) unusually large.

bun n small, round, sweet cake.

bunch n number of small, similar things naturally growing together (a — of grapes) or gathered together (a — of keys). v come or bring together in a —.

bundle n number of articles wrapped or tied up together: a — of old clothes (books, sticks). v make into a —; put away without order; go or send (off) in a hurry.

bungalow n house with only one storey.

bungle v do (a piece of work) badly. n —d piece of work.

bunk n sleeping-place fixed on the wall (eg in a ship or train).

buoy v & n (mark positions on the water with a) floating, fixed object. — up, prevent from sinking; keep up (hopes, etc). '—ant adj able to float or keep things floating; (fig) full of hope; light-hearted.

burden n load, esp a heavy load carried on the back; anything difficult to bear. v put a — on. —some adj hard to bear.

bureau n 1 office, esp for public information. 2 writing desk. —crat n government official, esp one who does not lose his position when another political group comes into power. ,bureau-'cratic adj. bu'reaucracy n.

burglar n person who breaks into a house, shop, etc, by night, to steal. —y n.

burial ⇨ bury.

burly (-ier, -iest) adj (of a person) big and strong.

burn v 1 be in flames; be hot enough to hurt. 2 destroy, damage by fire. 3 use for the purpose of lighting, heating, or driving: — oil. — the candle at both ends, stay up late and get up early. ⇨ sunburn. n (esp) mark or scar caused by —ing.

burnish v polish.

burrow v & n (make a) deep hole in the ground (esp as dug by rabbits and foxes).

burst v 1 fly into pieces; (cause to) break open; explode. 2 make a way (out, through, into). —ing with, full of. n 1 a —ing; hole, crack, made by —ing. 2 short, violent effort.

bury v 1 put (a dead body) in the ground, in a grave, in the sea, etc. 2 cover with earth, hide from view. 'burial n act of —ing.

bus n (pl 'buses) (formerly 'omnibus) large motor-car carrying passengers for fixed payments along a fixed route.

buses

bush n 1 plant with many woody stems coming from the trunk. 2 the —, wild, uncultivated country (esp in Africa and Australia). '—y adj 1 covered with —es. 2 looking wild and rough: —y eyebrows.

bushel n measure for grain and fruit; 8 gallons.

business n 1 work, employment. 2 buying and selling. —man n sb who works in trade or commerce. 'business-like adj careful, systematic.

bust n 1 head and shoulders of a person, cut in stone, cast in bronze, etc. 2 upper front of a woman's body; measurement of a woman's body round the chest and back.

bustle v move about quickly and excitedly. n such movement(s).

busy adj (-ier, -iest) having much to do; full of activity. **busily** adv.

but conj: John did not come but Jim did. I cannot help but think of you.

prep except. **next (last) but one:**
*Take the next (last) but one (the
second, the one before the last)
turning.*

'**butcher** *n* person who kills, cuts
up, and sells animals for food. *v*
kill violently, esp with a knife.

'**butler** *n* head man-servant (in
charge of the wine-cellar, etc).

'**butter** *n* fatty food (yellow or
yellowish-white) made from cream.
v put — on.

'**butterfly** *n* insect with large,
coloured wings. ⇨ p 144.

'**button** *n* **1** small, usu round, piece
of plastic, metal, etc, for fastening
articles of clothing. **2** button-like
object, pushed or pressed (eg to
ring an electric bell). *v* fasten, be
fastened, with —s.

'**buttress** *v & n* (strengthen, hold
up with) support built against a wall.

buy *v* (*pt & pp* bought) obtain
(sth) by paying a price.

buzz *n* sound made by bees when
flying, by machinery, by many
people talking. *v* make a —; be
filled with a —ing noise.

by *prep* **1** near; at or to the side of.
by oneself, alone. **2** (of time)
during: *by day (night)*; not later
than: *Be here by 4 o'clock.* **3** (showing direction of movement)
through; along; across; over: *We
came by the shortest route.* **4** by
means of: *This house is lit by
electricity.* **4** according to: *It's
6 o'clock by my watch.* *adv* **1** near:
Be by my side this evening. **2** past:
He hurried by. **3** aside: *He put his
money by for use later.* **by and by**,
later on. **by(e)-** *prefix* **1** less
important: '**by-road**, '**by-way**.
2 made or obtained during the
manufacture of sth else: '**by-
products.** **3** = *by adv*: '**bygone**,
belonging to the past. **bygones**
n pl past offences: *Let bygones
be bygones.* '**by,stander**, person
standing near and looking on.
4 '**by-e,lection**, one made necessary by the death or resignation of
a member during the life of Parliament. '**by(e)-law**, rule made by
a local authority (eg a town
council). '**bypass**, road taking
traffic round (the busy areas of)
a town. '**by-word**, person, place,
etc, considered as a type and usu
deserving contempt.

C

cab *n* **1** horse-carriage or motor-
car which may be hired for short
distances. **2** part of a railway
engine or lorry for the driver.

'**cabbage** *n* plant with a round head
of thick green leaves used as a
vegetable. ⇨ p 306.

'**cabin** *n* **1** small, roughly built
house (eg of logs). **2** small room
(esp for sleeping in) in a ship.

'**cabinet** *n* **1** piece of furniture with
shelves and drawers. **2 the C—,**
group of men (*Ministers of State*)
who are responsible for government departments and affairs.

'**cable** *n* **1** thick strong rope or wire.
2 line of wires (for sending messages by telegram or telephone);
message so carried. *v* send by —.
—gram *n* —d telegram.

'**cackle** *v & n* (make a) noise made
by a hen after laying an egg;
foolish talk or laughter.

'**cactus** *n* (*pl* 'cacti, -es) plant (usu
in a hot, dry climate) with thick,
fleshy stem, covered with prickles.

ca'det *n* **1** student at a naval or
military college. **2** young man
training for a profession: *police-
cadet.*

'**café** *n* small restaurant.

cage *n* **1** enclosed place in which
birds or animals are kept. **2** cage-
like part of a lift(2) used in coal-
mines, etc. *v* put in a —.

ca'jole *v* use flattery or deceit to
persuade sb to do sth.

cake *n* **1** sweet mixture of flour,
eggs, etc, baked in an oven;
mixture of other kinds of food.
2 shaped lump of any substance:
a — of soap. *v* form into a thick
mass. **—d with**, covered with a
thick mass: *shoes —d with mud.*

'**calabash** *n* hard, outer skin or shell
of a gourd, used for holding liquids,
etc.

ca'lamity *n* great and serious misfortune or disaster. **ca'lamitous**
adj.

'**calculate** *v* **1** find out by working
with numbers. **2** plan; intend;
arrange. **— on**, rely on; be sure of.
,**calcu'lation**, *n.*

'**calendar** *n* list of the days, weeks,
months, etc, of a particular year.

calf[1] *n* (*pl* calves) the young of the
cow and some other animals.

calf² n (pl calves) the fleshy part of the back of the leg, between the knee and the ankle. ⇨ p 29.

'calibre n inside measurement across (the diameter of) a gun-barrel or other tube, or of a bullet, shell, etc; (fig) quality of mind or character.

call v 1 give (a name) to. 2 consider; think. 3 (often — out), cry; shout. 4 pay a short visit to. 5 ask for the presence or attention of: — sb (up) by telephone. 6 — sth off, give orders, decide, to stop sth. — up, — to mind, (cause to) remember. — up, summon sb to serve in the military forces. — attention to, point out. n 1 shout. 2 message: telephone-call. 3 short stay or visit. 4 claim. 5 need. '-er n. '-ing n (esp) occupation; trade.

'callous adj (of the skin) hard; (of a person) disregarding the feelings of other people.

calm adj (-er, -est) quiet; untroubled. v make or become —. n period when all is —. '-ly adv. '-ness n.

'calorie n unit of heat; unit of energy supplied by food.

'calumny n slander; untrue and damaging statement about sb.

came ⇨ come.

'camel n long-necked animal with either one or two humps on its back, much used in desert countries for riding, etc. ⇨ p 317.

'camera n apparatus for taking photographs.

'camouflage v & n (use a) system of hiding or disguising the real nature of things, esp (in war) by the use of paint, netting, etc, to deceive the enemy.

camp n place where people (esp soldiers) live for a time in tents or huts. v make a —; live in a —; go —ing, spend a holiday living in tent(s).

cam'paign n 1 group of military operations with a set purpose or objective, usu in one area. 2 planned activities to gain a special object, esp political. v take part in a —; go on a —.

'campus n grounds of a college or university.

can¹ v (pt could) 1 be able to; know how to: I can swim (cf

may). 2 indicating possibility: How can that be true? 3 indicating a right: You can go into that private garden. 4 indicating permission: They asked if they could go swimming.

can² n metal container for liquids, etc; tin: oil-can; milk-can. v (-nn-) put into a can or cans. 'cannery n (USA) factory where food, etc, is canned.

ca'nal n channel cut through land for use of ships (eg the Suez C—) or for irrigation; tube in an animal's body for conducting food, etc.

ca'nary n small songbird, usu kept in a cage; its colour, light yellow.

'cancel v (-ll-) 1 cross out; draw a line through (words, figures); make marks on to prevent re-use: to — a stamp. 2 say that sth already arranged will not be done or take place. ,cancel'lation n.

'cancer n diseased growth destroying part of the body, often causing death. —ous adj.

'candid adj frank. —ly adv.

'candidate n person wishing, or put forward by sb, to take an office or position; person taking an examination.

'candle n round stick of wax with thread (called a wick) through it for giving light, heat, etc.

'candour n quality of being frank, saying openly what one thinks.

'candy n sugar made hard by repeated boiling; (USA) sweet things made of sugar, etc. v preserve (fruit, etc) by boiling in sugar.

cane n long, hollow, jointed stem of plants (eg bamboo, sugar-cane). v make or repair with —(s); punish with a —.

'canine adj of dogs.

'canker n disease which destroys the wood of trees; (fig) evil influence or tendency causing decay.

canned, 'cannery ⇨ can².

'cannibal n person who eats human flesh; animal that eats its own kind.

'cannon n 1 large gun, fixed to the ground or to a gun-carriage. 2 shell-firing gun used on aircraft. 'cannon-ball n ball fired from old-style cannon.

'cannot = can not. ⇨ can¹.

'canny adj cautious; not prepared to take unknown risks.

ca'noe n long, narrow boat. paddle one's own —, act without assistance. v travel by —.

a canoe

canon n 1 church law. 2 general standard by which sth is judged. 3 priest with duties in a cathedral. 4 list of saints. ca'nonical adj according to church laws. —ize v place in the list of saints.

canon ⇨ canyon.

canopy n covering over the head of a bed, a throne, etc; any similarly placed covering.

cant n 1 insincere talk. 2 special talk used by thieves.

can't = cannot.

can'teen n place where meals, etc, are supplied (eg in army barracks, factories).

canter v & n (cause a horse to go at a) slow or easy gallop.

canvas n strong, coarse cloth used for sails, bags, tents, etc. under —, (a) in tents, (b) with sails spread.

canvass v ask (people) for support, votes, orders for goods, etc.

canyon n deep gorge (usu with a river flowing through it).

cap n 1 soft head-covering worn by boys and men, usu with a peak but no brim. 2 small object fitted over the opening of a tube, bottle, etc. v (colloq) — that! Beat that!

capable adj able. — of, having the power or inclination for. ,capa'bility n.

ca'pacity n ability to hold or get hold of (knowledge, ideas, etc); amount or number that can be held or contained. in the — of, in the position of. ca'pacious adj able to hold much.

cape¹ n loose outer garment, without sleeves, worn over the shoulders.

cape² n high point of land going out into the sea.

caper v jump about playfully. n cut —s, jump about merrily.

capital n 1 chief city of a country. 2 (of letters): A, B, C, etc. 3 wealth (money and property) used for producing more wealth. 4 — punishment, by death. adj (colloq) excellent. —ist n person owning and controlling much —. —ism n economic system in which trade and industry are controlled by —ists.

ca'pitulate v surrender. ca,pitu-'lation n.

ca'price n sudden change of mind or behaviour without apparent cause. ca'pricious adj.

cap'size v (of a boat) overturn; (of sb) cause or be in a —d boat.

'capsule n 1 seed-case on a plant; small, soft container for a dose of medicine. 2 part of a spacecraft that can be ejected for independent travel.

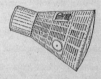

a capsule

'captain n 1 leader or commander. 2 army officer between a lieutenant and a major; naval officer of a rank next above commander. v act as — of.

'caption n short title or heading of an article, an illustration, photograph, etc.

'captivate v capture the fancy of; charm.

'captive n prisoner. be taken —, be captured. cap'tivity n state of being held —.

'capture v make a prisoner of; take (by force, skill, trickery, etc). n act of capturing; person or thing —d. 'captor n sb who —s.

car n 1 motor-car or tram-car. 2 (on a railway train) coach: 'sleeping-car; 'dining-car.

'caramel n burnt sugar used for colouring and flavouring; sticky sweet.

'carat n unit of weight for jewels and for the quality of gold.

'caravan n 1 company of people (esp travellers, merchants) making a journey together (across desert or dangerous country). 2 covered car or wagon used for living in.

car'bolic 'acid n acid made from coal-tar, used as a disinfectant and germ-killer.

'carbon n chemical substance present in diamonds, coal, charcoal, etc. — paper, thin paper coated with coloured matter, used between sheets of writing paper for taking copies of letters, etc.

,carbu'rettor n part of an engine in which petrol vapour and air are mixed.

'carcass, 'carcase n dead body of an animal.

card n thick, stiff paper, esp an oblong piece of this, as used for a special purpose. 'post— (for sending by post); a visiting — (giving a person's name, etc). 'Christmas —s; 'playing-cards. '—board n thick — used in making boxes, etc.

'cardigan n knitted woollen garment, with sleeves and open at the front.

'cardinal adj chief: the — points of the compass (N, S, E, W); — numbers (one, two, three, etc). ⇨ p 333. n one of the seventy members of the Sacred College which elects the Pope.

care n 1 serious attention. take —, pay attention; be on the watch. take — of, look after; see to the safety or welfare of. in (under) the — of, looked after by; (address) — of, (us written C/o): John Smith, C/o William Brown. 2 troubled state caused by doubt or fear; (cause of) sorrow or anxiety. v 1 feel interest, anxiety, sorrow. 2 — for, have a liking for; look after. — to, be willing to. '—ful adj taking —; done with —. '—less adj taking no —; done without —. '—,taker n person taking — of a building while the owners are away.

ca'reer n 1 progress through life; (person's) life history. 2 way of earning a living; occupation. 3 quick or violent movement: in full —. v rush: — along; — about (over, etc) a place.

ca'ress v & n (give a) loving touch (to); kiss.

'cargo n (pl -es) goods carried in a ship or aircraft.

'caricature n picture of sb or sth, imitation of sb's voice, behaviour, etc, stressing features to cause amusement or ridicule. v make a — of.

'carnage n killing of many people.

'carnal adj of the body or flesh; sensual (cf spiritual): — desires.

'carnival n public merry-making and feasting, eg during the week before Lent in RC countries.

car'nivorous adj flesh-eating.

'carol n song of joy or praise, esp a happy Christmas hymn. v (-ll-) sing happily.

carp v complain; make unnecessary trouble about.

'carpenter n workman who makes the wooden parts of buildings. 'carpentry n work of a —.

'carpet n large, thick floor-covering of wool, hair, etc. v cover with a —.

'carriage n 1 vehicle, esp one with four wheels pulled by a horse, for carrying people. 2 division of a railway coach. 3 (the cost of) carrying goods from place to place. — forward, cost to be paid by the receiver. 4 moving part of a machine changing the position of other part(s). 5 manner of holding the head or the body.

'carried ⇨ carry.

'carrier ⇨ carry.

'carrion n dead and decaying flesh.

'carrot n vegetable with yellow or orange-red root. ⇨ p 306.

'carry v (pt & pp 'carried) 1 hold off the ground and move (sb or sth) from one place to another. be carried away, (fig) lose self-control (through strong feeling, etc). — forward, take (figures, etc) to the next page or column. 2 support (the weight of). 3 have with oneself. 4 make longer; continue. — out (a plan, etc), put into practice; get done. 5 keep (the head or body) in a certain way: — oneself like a soldier. 6 (of sounds, etc) be heard. 7 win; persuade; overcome resistance: to — one's point (the day). 'carrier n 1 person or company carrying goods for payment. 2 support for parcels, boxes, etc, fixed to a bicycle, motor-car, etc. 3 ship built to — aircraft.

cart n strong (usu two-wheeled) vehicle pulled by an animal, for carrying goods. v carry in a —. '—age n (cost of) —ing. '—er n man in charge of a —.

'carton *n* cardboard box.

car'toon *n* 1 drawing eg dealing with current events (esp politics) in an amusing way. 2 cinema film made by photographing a series of drawings.

'cartridge *n* case containing powder and bullet (or shot) for firing from a fire-arm.

carve *v* 1 cut up (cooked meat) into slices or pieces. 2 make (a shape, design, etc) by cutting: *to — a statue out of wood.* '—r *n* 1 sb who —s. 2 knife used in —ing (esp meat). 'carving *n* piece of wood, etc, shaped by cutting or with a design cut on it.

cas'cade *n* small waterfall.

case¹ *n* 1 in this (that) —, if this (that) happens. 2 person suffering from a disease. 3 question to be judged in a law court; evidence and arguments used.

case² *n* box, bag, container or covering: *'packing-case*; *'suit-case.*

cash *n* money in coin or notes. 'cash-,register *n* machine for recording and storing — received. *v* give or get — for. ca'shier *n* person receiving and paying out money in a bank, shop, etc.

'casing *n* protective covering: *copper wire with a — of rubber.*

cask *n* barrel (for wine, etc).

'casket *n* small box (for jewels).

cas'sava *n* (tropical) root, like a potato, eaten as a vegetable. ⇨ p 306.

'casserole *n* & *v* (dish for) cooking stews in an oven.

'cassock *n* long, close-fitting garment, usu black, worn by some priests.

cast *v* (*pt* & *pp* cast) 1 throw (a net, etc); allow to fall: — *anchor.* cast-off clothes, clothes which their owner does not wish to wear again. 2 send or turn in a certain direction: — *an eye on.* 3 pour (liquid metal, etc) into a mould(1): — *iron.* 4 — up, add. 5 be — down, be sad. 6 — off (on), finish off (begin) knitting. *n* 1 sth made by —ing(3): *plaster —s.* 2 act of —ing(1) (eg a net or fishing-line). 3 actors in a play. '—away *n* person reaching a strange land after escaping from a wrecked ship. '—ing *n* (esp) metal part for a machine, etc, made by —ing(3).

caste *n* one of the fixed social classes among the Hindus; the system of dividing people into such classes; any exclusive social class.

'castle *n* fortified stone building used before gunpowder was invented. —(s) in the air (in Spain), day-dreams; imagined adventures and hopes.

'castor *n* small wheel for the foot of a piece of furniture, to make it easy to move.

cas'trate *v* remove or make useless (for breeding) the sex organs of (a male animal).

'casual *adj* 1 happening by chance. 2 careless; without special purpose. 3 not continuous: — *labour.* —ly *adv.* —ty *n* person killed, wounded, or injured (in war, an accident, etc).

cat *n* 1 small furry domestic animal that chases mice. ⇨ p 84. let the cat out of the bag, allow a secret to become known. wait for the cat to jump, wait to see what others think or do before giving an opinion or taking action. 2 class of animals including leopard, lion, tiger, cat(1), etc. 'catnap *n* short, light sleep. 'catty *adj* (colloq) spiteful, quarrelsome.

'cataclysm *n* sudden and violent change, esp in nature.

'catalogue *v* & *n* (make a) list (of names, places, goods, etc) in a special order.

'catapult *n* Y-shaped stick with a piece of elastic, for shooting stones, etc.

'cataract *n* 1 large waterfall. 2 eye disease causing partial blindness.

ca'tarrh *n* disease of the nose and throat causing a flow of liquid, as when one has a cold.

ca'tastrophe *n* sudden happening that causes great suffering (eg a flood, fire, or earthquake). ,cata'strophic *adj.*

catch *v* (*pt* & *pp* caught) 1 stop sth moving (through the air, etc), eg by grasping it, holding out sth into which it falls, etc. 2 be in time for; be able to use, meet, etc: *to — a train* (*the post*). — sb up, — up with sb, come up to sb going in the same direction. 3 come unexpectedly upon sb doing sth: *to — sb stealing flowers from your garden.* 4 get; receive: — *cold;* —

fire (begin to burn); — *sb's meaning*; — *sight of* (see); — *sb's eye* (get his attention). **5** (cause to) become fixed: *The nail caught her dress. Her dress caught on a nail.* **6** — *one's breath*, take a short, sudden breath. — *hold of*, seize. — *at*, try to seize. — *up*, seize quickly. *n* **1** act of —ing. **2** sth or sb caught, or much wanted. **3** part of a lock, fastener, etc, by which sth is kept shut· or safe. **4** sth intended to deceive; a cunning question. '**—ing** *adj* (of a disease) that can be spread from person to person.

'**catechism** *n* set of questions and answers (esp about religious teaching). '**catechize** *v* teach or examine by means of a —.

'**category** *n* division; class. ,**cate**-'**gorical** *adj* unconditional.

'**cater** *v* — *for*, undertake to provide (food, amusements, etc) for. —**er** *n*.

'**caterpillar** *n* **1** moth or butterfly larva. **2** endless belt passing over the toothed wheels of tanks (3), etc.

ca'**thedral** *n* chief church of a diocese (bishop's district).

'**catholic** *adj* **1** liberal; including much or all: — *tastes and interests.* **2 Roman C—**, of the Church of Rome. *n* member of the Church of Rome. ,**Roman Ca'tholicism** *n* teaching, etc, of the Church of Rome.

'**cattle** *n pl* oxen (*bulls, bullocks, cows*).

'**caught** ⇨ catch.

'**cauldron** *n* large hanging pot for cooking, etc.

'**cauliflower** *n* (cabbage-like plant with a) large white flower-head used as a vegetable. ⇨ p 306.

'**cause** *n* **1** that which produces an effect: *the —s of war.* **2** reason. **3** purpose for which efforts are being made: *working for a good —.* *v* be the — of.

'**causeway** *n* raised path or road, esp across wet land.

'**caustic** *adj* **1** able to burn away by chemical action. **2** bitter; sarcastic.

'**cauterize** *v* burn (a snake-bite, etc) with a hot iron or caustic substance.

'**caution** *n* **1** taking care; paying attention (to avoid danger or mistakes). **2** warning words. ·*v* give a — to. '**cautious** *adj* having or showing —.

'**cavalry** *n* soldiers who fight on horseback.

cave *n* hollow place in the side of a cliff or hill; large natural hole underground. '**—rn** *n* large cave.

'**cavity** *n* hole; hollow space.

cease *v* come to a stop or end. *n* end. '**—less** *adj* never ending.

'**cedar** *n* (hard, red, sweet-smelling wood of an) evergreen tree.

cede *v* give up (rights, land, etc) (to another person, state, etc).

'**ceiling** *n* **1** under-surface of the top of a room. **2** maximum: *price* (*wage*) —.

'**celebrate** *v* **1** do sth to show that a day or an event is important or for rejoicing: *to — Christmas* (*one's birthday*). **2** praise and honour. '**cele,brated** *adj* famous. ,**cele**-'**bration** *n.* **ce'lebrity** *n* being famous; famous person.

ce'**lerity** *n* quickness.

ce'**lestial** *adj* of the sky; heavenly; perfect.

'**celibacy** *n* state of living unmarried. '**celibate** *n & adj* (sb, usu a priest) having taken a vow of —.

cell *n* **1** small room for one person (esp in a prison or monastery). **2** small structure of a larger structure: *—s in a honeycomb.* **3** unit of living matter. **4** unit of apparatus for producing electric current. '**—ular** *adj* formed of —s (3); (of material) loosely woven.

'**cellar** *n* underground room for storing coal, wine, etc.

'**cello** *n* (rarely ,**violon'cello**) large stringed musical instrument. ⇨ p 180.

'**cellophane** *n* transparent substance used like paper for wrapping food, etc.

ce'**ment** *n* **1** grey powder (used in building, etc) which, after being wetted, becomes hard like stone. **2** any similar soft, hard-setting substance used for filling holes (e g in teeth), joining things together, etc. *v* put — on; join with —; (fig) strengthen; unite.

'**cemetery** *n* area of ground, not a churchyard, for burying the dead.

'**censor** *n* official with the power to examine letters, books, plays, films, etc, and to cut out anything regarded as immoral, or, in time of war, helpful to the enemy. *v* examine, cut (parts) out, as a —. **-ship** *n* office, duties, etc, of a —. **cen'sorious** *adj* fault-finding.

'censure *v & n* (express) blame or disapproval (of).

'census *n* official counting of all the people in a country, etc.

cent *n* (c) the 100th part of a dollar, franc, etc. **per —** (often %), in, by, for, every 100.

'centaur *n* (in old Greek stories) creature half man, half horse.

cen'tenary *adj & n* (having to do with a) period of 100 years; 100th anniversary.

'centigrade *adj* in, of, the temperature scale which has 100 degrees between freezing-point and the boiling-point of water. p 336.

'centimetre *n* the 100th part of a metre.

'centipede *n* small, long, wingless creature with many jointed sections and a pair of feet at each joint.

'centre *n* 1 middle part or point. 2 place of great activity. 3 person or thing attracting (notice, interest). *v* place in, bring to, the —; have as —. **'central** *adj* of, at, or near the —; chief. **'centralize** *v* bring to the —; put, come, under central control.

'century *n* 1 100 years. 2 one of the periods of 100 years before or after the birth of Christ. 3 (cricket) 100 runs.

'cereal *adj & n* (of) any kind of grain used for food (eg *rice, wheat, maize*).

'ceremony *n* 1 special act(s), religious service, on an occasion such as a wedding, the opening of a new public building. 2 behaviour required by social custom, esp among people of high class, officials, etc. **stand on —**, pay great attention to rules of behaviour. **,cere'monial** *adj* formal, as for ceremonies.

'certain *adj* 1 proved or known beyond doubt; having or feeling no doubt. **make —**, inquire in order to be sure. 2 not named or described, although known: *under — conditions.* 3 some, but not much. **—ly** *adv* without doubt;

willingly. **—ty** *n* being —; sth that is —.

cer'tificate *n* written or printed statement which may be used as proof, made by sb in authority: *marriage —.* **cer'tificated** *adj* having the right to do sth (eg teach) as the result of obtaining a —.

'certify *v* declare (usu by giving a certificate) that sth is true: *certified insane.*

'certitude *n* state of being certain.

ces'sation *n* ceasing; a stop or pause.

'cession *n* act of giving up (a right, etc); sth ceded.

'cesspool *n* hole or pit into which house-drains empty.

chafe *v* 1 rub (the skin, etc) for warmth. 2 make, become rough or sore by rubbing, (fig) make, become impatient or irritated.

chaff[1] *n* 1 outer covering of grain, removed before it is used as food. 2 hay or straw cut up as cattle food.

chaff[2] *n* good-humoured teasing or joking. *v* tease.

chagrin *n* feeling of shame or annoyance (at failure, making a mistake, etc).

chain *n* 1 number of (usu metal) rings or links going through one another to make a line. **in —s**, kept as a prisoner. 2 number of connected things, events, etc. **'chain-store**, store(5) with many branches(2). *v* fasten with a —.

chair *n* 1 movable seat with a back for one person. 2 post or position held by a professor at a university; seat, authority, of a person presiding at a meeting. **take the —**, preside. **'—man** *n* man or woman who presides at a meeting.

chairs

chalk *v & n* (use a) soft substance (white or coloured) for writing, drawing, etc.

'challenge *n* 1 invitation to fight, play a game, run a race, etc, to see who is stronger, etc. 2 order given by a sentry to stop and explain who one is, etc. *v* give a — to; ask for reasons in support of a statement.

'chamber *n* 1 (old use) room, esp bedroom. **—maid** woman servant keeping bedrooms in order. 2 body of persons making laws; the place where they meet. **C— of Commerce,** group of persons organized to develop trade, etc. 3 hollow space in a gun where a shell (cartridge) is laid.

cha'meleon *n* (k-) small reptile able to change its colour to suit its background. ⇨ p 233.

'chamois *n* soft leather from a goat-like animal living in mountains.

'champion *n* 1 one who fights for, supports the cause of, another person. 2 person, team, animal, taking first place in a competition, etc. *v* support.

chance *n* 1 accident; luck; happening which has no known cause or intention. **take one's —,** trust to luck; take whatever comes. **game of —,** one which luck, not skill, decides. 2 possibility. **on the —** (*that*), in view of the possibility. 3 opportunity; occasion when success seems certain: *the — of a life-time.* 4 (*attrib*) coming or happening by —. *v* 1 happen by —. 2 — **upon,** happen to find or meet. 3 take a risk.

'chancel *n* eastern end of a church, used by the priests and the choir.

'chancellor *n* (in some countries) chief minister of state; (of some universities) head; (in Gt Brit) **C— of the Exchequer,** chief finance minister. **Lord C—,** highest judge.

change *v* 1 take or put one thing in place of another. **— one's mind,** make different plans; reach a different opinion. **— trains (buses),** leave one and get into another during a journey. 2 (= exchange) give sth to sb and receive sth else of equal value in return; give or get money in smaller coins or notes for a larger coin or note. 3 make or become different. *n* 1 changing; being or becoming different; sth taken or used in place of another thing. 2 coins of low value: *— for a £1 note;* difference between the cost of what is bought and the amount of money offered

in payment. **'—able** *adj* likely to —; able to be —d; often changing.

'channel *n* 1 stretch of water joining two seas. 2 bed of a river, etc; the part of a waterway deep enough for ships. 3 passage along which a liquid may flow; (fig) way by which news, ideas, etc, may travel.

chant *n* tune to which some Psalms and Prayer Book hymns are fitted, often with several words on one note. *v* sing a —; use a singing tone (eg for a prayer in church).

'chaos *n* (-k-) complete absence of order; confusion.

chap[1] *v* (-pp-) (of the skin) become rough and cracked; (of the wind) cause (the skin) to —.

chap[2] *n* (colloq) man; boy.

'chapel *n* 1 place used for Christian worship, eg in a school, prison, private house, etc. 2 small place for private prayer within a church.

'chaperon *n* married or elderly person, usu a woman, who sometimes accompanies a girl to parties, etc.

'chaplain *n* priest or clergyman, esp in the armed forces or in charge of a private chapel.

'chapter *n* division of a book.

char[1] *v* (-rr-) make or become black by burning: **—red wood.**

char[2] *v* (-rr-) & *n* (do) odd job(s); clean (houses, offices, etc) with payment by the hour or day. **'—,woman** *n* woman who —s.

'character *n* (k-) 1 mental or moral qualities; moral strength; name or reputation; description of sb's qualities (for use in getting work). 2 person who does sth unusual; person in a novel, play, etc. 3 those special qualities which make sth what it is: *the — of the Sahara Desert* (eg sandy and hot). 4 letter, figure, or sign used in writing or printing: *Chinese —s.* **,characte-'ristic** *adj* forming part of, showing, the — of sb or sth. *n* special mark or quality. **—ize** *v* show the — of; give — to; mark in a special way.

'charcoal *n* black substance made from wood by burning it slowly, used as a fuel and for drawing; its colour.

charge *n* 1 accusation; statement that a person has done wrong: *bring a — of murder against sb.*

2 sudden attack (by rushing towards the enemy, etc). 3 price asked for sth, or for doing sth. 4 amount of powder needed for firing a gun, causing an explosion, or of electricity put into an accumulator. 5 work given to sb as a duty; thing or person given to sb to be taken care of. in — of, taking care of; being cared for by: *Mary was in — of the baby. The baby was in Mary's —.* take — of, be responsible for. give sb in —, give him up to the police. v 1 — sb with sth, say that he has done sth (wrong); accuse him of sth. 2 rush or run against (and attack). 3 ask as a price; ask in payment. 4 put a — of powder, electricity, into. 5 give orders or instructions to; give as a task or duty.

'chariot n two-wheeled car, pulled by horses, used in ancient times in races and in war.

'charity n 1 kindness in giving help, esp to poor or suffering people; neighbourly love. 2 organization for giving such help. 'charitable adj having or showing —.

charm n 1 quality or power of attracting, giving pleasure. 2 sth believed to have magic power, good or bad. v 1 attract; give pleasure to. 2 use magic on; influence or protect as if by magic. '—ing adj giving pleasure (eg by appearance or actions); full of —(1).

chart n 1 map of the sea, used by sailors. 2 sheet of paper, etc, with information, in the form of curves, diagrams, etc, about facts (such as the weather, prices, sales, etc). v make a — of; show on a —.

'charter n (written statement of) right, permission, to do sth (eg form a business company), esp from a ruler or government. v 1 give a — to. 2 pay money to use (a ship, aircraft, etc) for an agreed purpose or period of time.

'chary adj — of, cautious or shy of.

chase v run after (to capture or kill or to drive away). n the act of chasing. give —, try to catch. the —, hunting as a sport.

'chasm n (k-) deep opening or crack in the ground; (fig) wide difference (of feeling, interests, etc, between groups, nations).

chaste adj pure in thought, word, and acts. 'chastity n.

'chasten v correct (sb) by giving punishment or pain.

chas'tise v punish severely. 'chastisement n.

'chastity ⇨ chaste.

chat v (-tt-) & n (have a) friendly talk (usu about unimportant things). '—ty adj fond of —ting.

'chattel n piece of movable property (eg a chair, motor-car).

'chatter v 1 talk quickly or foolishly; talk fast. 2 make quick, indistinct sounds (eg the cries of some birds, of monkeys, the sound of upper and lower teeth striking together, of typewriter keys). n sounds of the kind noted above. —box n person who —s(1).

'chauffeur n man paid to drive a privately owned motor-car.

cheap adj (-er, -est) 1 costing little money; worth more than the price. 2 poor in quality. 3 easily obtained and of little value. adv at a low price. '—ly adv. '—ness n. '—en v make —(er); lower the value of.

cheat v try to win an advantage by doing sth dishonest. n person who —s; dishonest trick.

check v 1 examine in order to learn whether sth is correct. 2 hold back; cause to go slow or stop. n 1 —ing; person who —s. keep a — on, keep in —, control. 2 receipt (eg a piece of paper, bit of metal, etc) showing that a person has a right to sth (eg luggage sent by train or left in a railway station to be collected later). 3 pattern of crossed lines forming squares; cloth made with this pattern. 4 (USA) cheque. '—'mate v obstruct or defeat (a person or his or her plan(s)).

cheek n 1 each side of the face below the eye. ⇨ p 30. 2 impudence. '—y adj impudent. '—ily adv.

cheer v 1 make (sb) feel happier. — up, become happier. — sb up, make him happier. 2 give shouts of joy, approval, encouragement. n 1 state of hope or gladness. 2 shout of joy, encouragement, etc. '—ful adj happy; bringing happiness. '—less adj without joy or comfort. '—ily adv.

cheese n solid food made from milk curds.

chef *n* head male cook in a hotel, restaurant, etc.

'chemist *n* (k-) **1** person with knowledge of —ry. **2** person who prepares and sells medical goods, toilet articles.

'chemistry *n* (k-) branch of science dealing with the elements(1) and how they combine. **'chemical** *adj* of, made by, —. *n* substance used in — or made by —.

cheque *n* written order (usu on a printed form) to a bank to pay money. **'cheque-book** *n* number of —s fastened together.

'cherish *v* care for tenderly; keep alive (hope, etc) in one's heart.

'cherry *n* (tree with) small, round, red, yellow, or black fruit with a stone in the middle. ⇨ p 115. *adj* of the colour of ripe, red cherries.

chess *n* game for 2 players with 16 pieces each, on a board marked with 64 squares.

chest *n* **1** upper front part of the human body, containing the heart and lungs. ⇨ p 29. **2** large, strong, wooden box for a special purpose: *medicine* —; *linen* —; *tea-chest*; — *of drawers* (piece of furniture with drawers).

'chestnut *n* (wood of a) tree with shiny brown nuts; colour of these.

chew *v* work (food, etc) about between the teeth in order to crush it. **'—ing-gum** *n* flavoured gum for —ing.

'chicken *n* a fowl. ⇨ p 211; young bird; meat of a —.

chide *v* (*pt & pp* chid or 'chided) scold; speak angrily to.

chief *n* leader or ruler; head of a tribe. *adj* principal; most important. **'—ly** *adv*. **'—tain** *n* —.

child *n* (*pl* 'children) **1** person between babyhood and adolescence; infant. **2** son or daughter (of an age). **'—ish** *adj* immature. **'—like** *adj* simple; innocent. **'—hood** *n* period of being a —.

chill *n* unpleasant cold feeling; illness caused by cold or damp. *adj* unpleasantly cold. *v* make or become cool or cold. **'—y** *adj* (of weather, behaviour) rather cool.

chime *n* (series of notes sounded by a) tuned set of bells. *v* (of bells or a clock) make bell-like sounds; give out bell-tones. — **in**, break in (on the talk of others).

'chimney *n* structure through which smoke from a fire is carried away from a room through the roof.

,chimpan'zee *n* African ape, smaller than a gorilla. ⇨ p 317.

chin *n* part of the face under the mouth. ⇨ p 30.

china *n* baked fine white clay; plates, cups, etc, made from this.

chink¹ *n* break or crack through which one can see.

chink² *v & n* (make a) sound as of money, glasses, etc, striking together.

chip *n* **1** small piece cut or broken off (from wood, stone, china, etc). — *of(f) the old block*, son very like his father. **2** oblong piece of potato; slice of apple, etc. **3** rough place from which a —(1) has come. *v* (-pp-) **1** cut or knock —s(1) from. **2** make into —s(2).

,chipo'lata *n* small, thin sausage.

chirp *v & n* (make) the short, sharp sound of some birds (eg sparrows) and insects (eg crickets).

'chisel *n* steel tool with a squared, sharpened end for cutting or shaping wood, stone, or metal. *v* (-ll-) cut or shape with a —.

'chivalry *n* **1** laws and customs of knights in the Middle Ages. **2** the qualities of knights: courage, honour, loyalty, kindness to women, children and the weak. **'chivalrous** *adj*.

'chloroform *n* (k-) vapour used to make a person unconscious. *v* make unconscious with —.

'chocolate *n* sweet food substance made from crushed cocoa beans; drink made with cocoa powder; the colour of —, dark brown.

choice *n* **1** act of choosing; right or possibility of choosing. **for** —, if one has to choose. **2** person or thing chosen; number of things from which to choose. *adj* carefully chosen; uncommonly good.

choir *n* (kw-) company of persons trained to sing together, esp to lead the singing in church; part of a church occupied by a —.

choke *v* **1** be unable to breathe because of sth in the windpipe: *His voice was* —*d with anger.* — *back*, hold or keep back: *He* —*d back his tears.* **2** stop sb's breathing by pressing the windpipe from the outside. **3** fill (partly or completely) a passage, opening, etc, which is usually clear. *n* valve in a motor engine that controls the flow of air into the carburettor.

'cholera *n* (k-) disease, common in hot countries, which attacks the bowels and may cause death.

choose *v* (*pt* chose, *pp* 'chosen) 1 pick out from two or more. 2 decide between one and another.

chop *v* (-pp-) cut by giving blows to (eg with an axe). — and change, keep on changing. *n* —ping blow; sth —ped off, esp a thick piece of meat with a bone in it, cooked for one person. '—per *n* heavy tool for —ping firewood, etc.

'choppy *adj* (of the sea) having short, rough waves.

'chopsticks *n pl* (pair of) sticks used by the Chinese and Japanese for lifting food to the mouth.

'choral *adj* (k-) of, for, sung by or together with, a choir.

chord *n* (k-) 1 straight line joining two points on a circle. 2 (music) combination of three or more notes sounded together. 3 (also cord) part of the body that looks like string: *the vocal* —*s* (in the throat).

'chorus *n* (k-) 1 (music for a) group of singers (esp on stage). 2 (part of a) song for all to sing (after solo verses). 3 sth said or cried by many people together: *a* — *of praise*. in —, all together.

chose, 'chosen ⇨ choose.

'christen *v* (k-) receive (an infant) into the Christian Church by baptizing; give a name to at baptism.

'Christian *adj* (k-) of Jesus Christ and his teaching; of the religion, Church, etc, based on this teaching. — name, first name, given at baptism. *n* — person. ˌChristi-'anity *n* the — religion.

'Christmas Day *n* (k-) yearly celebration of the birth of Jesus Christ, 25 December.

'chronic *adj* (k-) (of illness, pain) continual; lasting a long time: — *invalid*, person with a — illness.

'chronicle *n* (k-) record of events in the order of their happening.

chro'nology *n* (k-) science of fixing dates; arrangement of events with dates; list showing this. ˌchrono'logical *adj*.

'chrysalis *n* (k-) stage of an insect's growth between creeping and flying; the case which covers it during this time.

chuck *v* 1 (colloq) throw: — *sth away*. 2 stop (doing sth); give up: — *up one's job*.

'chuckle *v & n* (give a) low, quiet laugh (of satisfaction, triumph, or amusement).

chum *n* close friend. *v* (-mm-) — up (with), become friendly (with).

church *n* 1 building for Christian public worship; service in a —. 2 body or division of Christians with the same beliefs, same forms of worship, etc: *the C— of England*; *the Methodist C—*. enter the C—, become a priest or minister of religion. '—ˌyard *n* walled ground round a —, often used as a burial place.

'churlish *adj* bad-tempered.

churn *n* container in which cream is shaken or beaten to make butter; very large milk-can. *v* beat and shake in a —; (of any liquid, the sea, etc) move, be moved, about violently.

'cider *n* drink made from apples.

ci'gar *n* roll of tobacco leaves for smoking. ˌciga'rette *n* shredded tobacco rolled in thin paper for smoking.

'cinder *n* piece of wood or coal partly burnt, not yet ash.

'cinema *n* theatre for showing films. ˌcine'camera *n* one for taking moving pictures.

'cipher *n* 1 the figure o, zero. 2 person or thing of no importance. 3 (system of) secret writing; key to such a system. *v* put into a —(3); do arithmetic.

'circle *n* 1 (outline of a) perfectly round, flat figure ⇨ p 253; sth round, like a —: *a* — *of trees*. 2 block of seats in a theatre or hall, above floor level. 3 group of persons with common interests. move in a —, go round in a group.

'circuit *n* 1 journey round, beginning and ending at one place. 2 continuous path of an electric current. cir'cuitous *adj* indirect; roundabout.

'circular *adj* in the shape of a circle. — tour, one ending at the starting-point without going to the same place more than once. *n* printed letter, advertisement, etc, sent to a number of people. —ize v send —s to.

'circulate v go round continuously; move or send freely from place to place, person to person; move or pass round. ,circu'lation n circulating or being —d (esp of the blood); total number of each issue of a newspaper, etc, sold to the public.

cir'cumference n outline of a circle; its length.

,circum'navigate v sail round (esp the world).

'circumscribe v draw a line round; mark the limit(s) of.

'circumspect adj paying careful attention to everything before deciding on an action; cautious.

'circumstance n 1 (usu pl) conditions, facts, etc, connected with an event or person. in (under) the —s, the —s being so. under no —s, never, whatever may happen. 2 fact; detail. ,circum'stantial adj giving full details; based on details which do not give direct proof but which suggest sth.

,circum'vent v prevent (sb) from doing sth; prevent (a plan, etc) from being carried out.

'circus n 1 (round or oval space with seats all round, for a) show of performing animals, horse-riding, etc; the persons and animals giving such a show. 2 circular place where several streets meet: Piccadilly C—.

'cistern n water-tank, esp for storing water in a building.

'citadel n fortress for protecting a town; place of refuge or safety.

cite v give as an example; quote (from a book); mention (a soldier) for bravery.

'citizen n person who lives in a town, not in the countryside; person having full rights in a country, either by birth or by gaining such rights (cf. British subject; American citizen). —ship n being a —; rights and duties of a —.

'citron n (tree with) pale-yellow fruit similar to a lemon. 'citrus adj of such fruits as lemons, citrons, and oranges.

'city n large important town. the C—, the oldest part of central London; its banking and civic centre.

'civic adj of the official life and affairs of a town. —s n pl study of city government, rights and duties of citizens, etc.

'civil adj 1 of human society; of citizens. — war, war between two parties belonging to the same state. — law, law dealing with private rights, not crime. — engineering, building of roads, railways, canals, docks, etc. — marriage, one without a religious ceremony. 2 not of the armed forces. the C— Service, all government departments except the armed forces. C— servant, official in the C— Service. 3 politely helpful. ci'vility n politeness; polite act. ci'vilian n & adj (person) not serving with the armed forces.

'civilize v bring from a savage or ignorant condition to a higher one (by giving teaching in art, science, methods of government, morals, etc). ,civili'zation n making, becoming, —d; a system or stage of civilization; all —d states.

claim v 1 say firmly that one is, or owns, or has a right to. 2 say that sth is a fact. 3 (of things) need; deserve. n 1 act of —ing. lay — to, say that one owns or ought to own. 2 right to demand. 3 that which is —ed.

'clamber v climb with some difficulty, esp using the hands.

'clammy adj (-ier, -iest) damp, usu cold, to the touch.

'clamour n loud, confused noise; angry request, complaint, etc. v make a —. 'clamorous adj.

clamp n 1 appliance for holding things together tightly by means of a screw. 2 iron band for strengthening or making tight. v put in a —; put —s on.

clan n large family group (smaller than a tribe): Scottish —s.

clang v & n (make a) loud, ringing sound (like that of a heavy bell).

clank v & n (make a) loud sound (like that heard when chains or swords strike together).

clap v (-pp-) 1 — one's hands, strike (the hands) sharply together, esp to show approval. 2 strike or slap lightly with the open hand: — sb on the back. — eyes on, notice. n sharp, loud noise: a — of thunder.

'claret n kind of red wine.

'clarify v make or become clear. **'clarity** n clearness.

'clarinet n wooden musical instrument with keys, played by blowing. ⇨ p 180.

clash v & n 1 (make a) loud confused noise (as when metal objects strike together). 2 (be in) disagreement or conflict: a — of colours (ideas).

clasp n 1 device for keeping two things or parts (eg the ends of a necklace) fastened. 2 firm hold (with the fingers, arms). v 1 fasten with a —. 2 hold tightly.

class n 1 group having the same qualities: lemons are in the — of citrus fruits; kind, sort, division, esp of society. 2 group of persons taught together. v put in the correct group.

'classic adj 1 excellent; of the highest quality. 2 of the standard of ancient Greek and Latin writers, art and culture. 3 well-known because of a long history. n writer, painter, book, painting, etc, of the highest class. **the C—s**, — Greek and Latin literature. **—al** adj of the C—s; of the highest class; simple and restrained.

'classify v put into classes or groups. **,classifi'cation** n.

'clatter v & n (make a) loud confused noise (as of hard things falling or knocking together, or of noisy talk).

clause n 1 one complete paragraph in an agreement, law, etc. 2 component part of a (complex) sentence, with its own subject and predicate, doing the work of a noun, adjective, or adverb.

claw n one of the long, pointed nails on the feet of some animals and birds; thing or instrument like, or used like, a —. v get hold of with the —s or finger-nails; pull roughly with the —s.

clay n soft, sticky earth which becomes hard when baked; material from which bricks, pots, etc, are made.

clean adj (-er, -est) 1 free from dirt, marks, etc. 2 not having rough or irregular lines: a — cut. v make —(1) by washing, sweeping, etc. — out, get dirt, rubbish, etc, from the inside of. — up, make tidy; put in order. adv completely. n act of —ing. adv completely. **'—ly** adv in a — way. adj having — habits. **'—liness** n.

cleanse v make clean or pure.

clear adj (-er, -est) 1 easy to see through; easily seen, heard, or understood; (of the sky) without cloud; bright. 2 easy or safe to pass along; free from danger or obstacles. **keep — of**, keep out of the way of. 3 complete: two — days; a — profit of £5. v 1 remove obstacles; empty: — one's throat. — **the table**, take away things after a meal. **C—off! (out!)** Go away! 2 get past or over (eg a gate) without touching. adv completely: to get — away. 3 show proof of sb's innocence. **'clear-'cut** adj with distinct outlines. **'—ly** adv distinctly; obviously. **'—ance** n making —; space between one thing moving past another; free space. **'—ing** n (esp) land made — of trees.

cleave v (pt clove or cleft, pp cleft or 'cloven) cut in two with a blow from a heavy knife, axe, etc.

'clement adj (of weather) mild; (of a person) showing mercy. **'clemency** n.

clench v (of teeth, fingers, or fist) close, hold tightly.

'clergy n the —, the ministers of the Christian Church. **—man** n one of these.

'clerical adj 1 of the clergy: — dress. 2 of the work of a clerk; of writing and copying.

clerk n office worker who writes letters, keeps accounts, etc.

'clever adj (-er, -est) quick to learn and understand; showing skill and ability. **—ly** adj. **—ness** n.

click v & n (make a) short sound (like that of a key turning in a lock).

'client n person receiving the help of a lawyer, etc.

cliff n high, steep face of rock.

'climate n weather conditions (of a place). **cli'matic** adj.

'climax n event, point, of greatest interest or importance.

climb v go up a tree, rope (stairs, mountain); go higher. — down, get down (from a tree, etc) with some difficulty. n act of —ing; place to be —ed. **'—er** n.

cling v (pt & pp clung) hold tight

(to); (of clothes) fit closely to the skin.

'clinic n (part of a) hospital, etc, where medical advice and treatment are given: *an eye —.*

clink v & n (make the) sound of small pieces of metal (eg coins or keys), glass, etc, knocking together.

clip¹ n wire or metal fastener for papers, etc. v (-pp-) put or keep together with a —.

clip² v (-pp-) cut (with scissors, shears, etc); make short or neat: *to — sheep* (cut the wool off). **'—pers** n pl instrument for —ing hair, nails, etc. **'—ping** n sth —ped out (esp from a newspaper).

cloak n loose outer garment without sleeves; (fig) anything that hides or covers. v (fig) hide; cover. **'—room** n place where coats, parcels, etc, may be left for a short time.

clock n instrument (not worn like a watch) for telling the time. **'clock-wise** adj & adv moving in the direction taken by the hands of a —. **'—work** n & adj (machine) having wheels, springs, etc, like a —. **like —work,** regularly; without trouble.

clod n lump of earth.

clog v (-gg-) be, cause to be, become blocked with dirt, etc, so that movement is made difficult.

'cloister n 1 covered walk, usu on the sides of an open square within a convent, cathedral, or college building. 2 convent or monastery. v put in, live in, a convent or monastery.

close¹ v 1 shut. 2 come near or together. **— in (upon),** come nearer, surround, esp to attack. **— with an offer,** accept it. 3 end. end(ing). **draw (bring) to a —,** end.

close² adj (-r, -st) 1 near. *a — friend,* a dear friend. 2 (of the air, the weather) not fresh; uncomfortably warm. 3 receiving care; thorough; with every step clearly shown: *— attention; a — translation (argument).* 4 secret; keeping things secret. **lie —,** hide. **keep sth —,** say nothing about it. 5 **— season,** period when certain wild birds, animals, etc, must not be killed. 6 with very little space or freedom: *a — prisoner; in — confinement; at — quarters.* adv

near. **'—ly** adv. **'—ness** n. **'close-up** n picture taken with a camera — to an object or a person.

'closet n 1 small room; cupboard; (USA) storeroom. 2 (short for) water-closet.

clot n half-solid lump formed from liquid, esp blood. v (-tt-) form into —s.

cloth n 1 material made by weaving (cotton, wool, nylon, etc) thread. 2 piece of this for a special purpose (eg a table-cloth).

clothe v (pt & pp clothed, old pp clad) 1 put —s on; give —s to. 2 (fig) *to — thoughts in words.*

clothes n pl 1 dress; coverings for the body. 2 **'bed-clothes,** coverings used on a bed. **'clothes-line,** one of which — are hung to dry. **'clothes-peg,** for fastening garments to a clothes-line.

'clothing n = clothes.

cloud n 1 mass of visible water vapour in the sky. **in the —s,** daydreaming, not paying attention. **'—burst** n sudden downpour. 2 mass of things like a —; *a — of arrows (mosquitoes).* 3 state of unhappiness or fear: *a — of grief; the — of war.* **under a —,** in disgrace or disfavour. v make or become dark with —s. **'—less** adj. **'—y** adj (-ier, -iest) covered with —s; (of a liquid) not clear.

a clown

clouds

clout n blow; knock. v give a blow to; strike.

clove¹ n dried, unopened flower-bud of a tropical tree, used to flavour food, etc.

clove² n one of the small bulbs making up a compound bulb: *a — of garlic.*

clove(n) ⇨ cleave.

'clover n low-growing plant with three leaves on each stalk, grown as food for cattle. (fig) **in —,** in great comfort.

clown n man who makes a living by amusing people (esp in a circus) with foolish tricks and behaviour; person who acts like a —; rude, clumsy man. v behave like a —. '-ish adj.

cloy v make distasteful; become weary of sth (by having too much of it, by its being too sweet, etc).

club¹ n heavy stick with a thick end used as a weapon, or for hitting the ball in some games (eg golf). v (-bb-) hit with a —.

club² n group of persons who subscribe money to provide themselves with sport, social entertainment, etc, sometimes in their own grounds and buildings where meals, etc, may be had; the rooms or building(s) used by such a group. v (-bb-) join (together) to raise money, etc.

club³ n black clover-leaf design on some playing-cards: ♣.

cluck v & n (make the) sound of a hen (eg when calling her chickens).

clue n fact, idea, etc, that suggests a possible answer to a problem, esp a crime mystery or a crossword puzzle.

clump n group (of trees).

'**clumsy** adj (-ier, -iest) heavy and ungraceful in movement or con- struction; not well designed for a purpose. '**clumsily** adv. '**clumsiness** n.

clung ⇨ cling.

'**cluster** n number of things of the same sort growing closely together (a — of flowers, curls) or in a group close together (a — of bees, houses). v be, gather, in a —.

clutch v seize(2) (eg in fear or anxiety). n 1 the act of —ing; a strong hold. **in the —es of**, in the power of. 2 device in a machine for connecting and disconnecting the working parts.

co- prefix together with (another or others). **co-education**, education of boys and girls together.

coach¹ n 1 four-wheeled carriage pulled by four or more horses.

2 railway carriage; long-distance motor-bus. '—man n driver of a —(1).

coach² n teacher, esp one who gives private lessons to prepare students for examinations; person who trains athletes for games. v teach; train.

coal n hard black mineral that is burnt to supply heat, raise steam, make coal-gas, etc. v put — into (a ship); take in —.

coa'lition n union of (esp political) parties for a special purpose.

coarse adj (-r, -st) 1 rough; of poor quality. 2 not fine or small: — hair; — sand. 3 rude(1); unrefined. — language (speech).

coast n land near or by the edge of the sea. v go in, sail, a ship along the —. '—guard n officer on police duty on the —. '—al adj of the coast. '—wise adj & adv along the coast.

coat n 1 outer garment with sleeves and opening in the front. 2 animal's covering of hair, etc. 3 covering of paint, varnish, etc. '— of 'arms n ⇨ arm(4). v cover with a —(3). '—ing n covering: a —ing of paint.

coax v get, by kindness or patience, sb or sth to do sth.

'**cobble** v mend or patch roughly (eg shoes, boots). **—r** n.

'**cobweb** n fine network or single thread made by a spider.

cock¹ n male bird of the farmyard fowl. '—crow n daylight. '—y, '—sure adj full of confidence; conceited.

cock² n 1 tap and spout for controlling flow of liquid. 2 lever in a gun. **at half (full) —**, half-ready (ready) to be fired. '**cock-pit**, compartment in a small aircraft for the pilot. v 1 turn upwards (showing attention, defiance, etc): to — the ears; — an eye at (sth or sb). 2 raise (the — of a gun) ready for firing.

'**cockney** adj & n (of a) native of central London.

'**cockroach** n large dark-brown or black insect which comes out at night in kitchens and places where food is kept. ⇨ p 144.

'**cocktail** n mixed alcoholic drink, usu taken before meals.

'**cocoa** n tree with dark-brown

a coach

seeds; these seeds crushed to a powder; drink made from this with hot water or milk.

'coco(nut) *n* large hard-shelled seed of the coco palm with an edible white lining. 'coconut-'matting, floor covering made from the outer covering of the —.

co'coon *n* silky covering made by a caterpillar for use while it is a chrysalis.

cod *n* large sea-fish.

code *n* 1 collection of laws. 2 set of rules, principles, etc; system of morals. 3 system of signs, of secret writing; system of sending messages: *a telegraphic* —; *the Morse* —. *v* put into — signs. 'codify *v* put into the form of a —.

co'erce *v* force (sb into doing sth). co'ercion *n*. co'ercive *adj*.

'coffee *n* bush or shrub with seeds which, when roasted and powdered, are used for making a drink; the seeds; the powder; the drink. 'coffee-bean (-berry), — seed.

'coffer *n* large strong box for money or jewels.

'coffin *n* box to hold a dead person.

cog *n* one of a number of teeth on a wheel or rod.

coil *v* wind or twist into rings one above the other; curl (sth) round and round (sth else). *n* sth —ed: *a* — *of rope*; a single turn of sth —ed.

coin *n* piece of metal money. *v* make (metal) into —s. be —ing money, be getting rich. — a word, make up a new word. '—age *n* making —s; —s so made; system of —s: *a decimal —age*.

,coin'cide *v* 1 (of two or more objects) correspond in area or outline. 2 (of events) happen at the same time. 3 (of ideas, etc) be in harmony (*with*). co'incidence *n* (esp) chance coinciding of events, circumstances, etc.

coke *n* substance remaining when gas has been taken out of coal by heating in an oven.

'colander *n* bowl with small holes, for draining off water from rice, vegetables, etc.

cold *adj* (-er, -est) 1 with little heat, esp when compared with the human body. in — blood, when one is not angry or excited. throw — water on, (try to) discourage.

give sb the — shoulder, treat him in an unfriendly way. 2 (fig) not easily excited; not friendly or cheerful: 'cold-'hearted; 'cold-'blooded. *n* 1 low temperature (esp in the atmosphere). 2 (often the common —) illness marked by a flow of liquid from the nose, sneezing: *to catch (a)* —. '—ly *adv*. '—ness *n*.

col'laborate *v* work together with another or others (esp in writing, in art). col,labo'ration *n*.

col'lapse *v* 1 fall down or in; come or break to pieces. 2 lose (health, courage, mental powers, etc) completely. *n* complete breakdown, failure, loss of these kinds. col'lapsable, -ible *adj* made so as to fold up for packing or transport: *a collapsible chair*.

'collar *n* 1 part of a garment that fits round the neck. 2 separate piece of linen, lace, etc, worn round the neck and fastened to a shirt. 3 band of leather, etc, put round the neck of a horse, dog, or other animal. 4 metal band joining two pipes or rods. *v* seize by the —; take hold of roughly.

'colleague *n* one of two or more persons working together and (usu) having similar rank and duties.

col'lect *v* bring or gather together; get from a number of people or places. —ed *adj* with one's feelings under control. —ion *n* —ing; number of things which have been —ed or which have come together; money —ed at a meeting (esp at church). —ive *adj* of a group or society as a whole: —*ive ownership*; —*ive farms*. —or *n* person who —s.

'college *n* school for higher (or professional) education; body of students and teachers forming part of a university. col'legiate *n & adj* (member) of a —.

col'lide *v* come together violently; be opposed. col'lision *n*.

'collier *n* coal-miner; ship carrying a cargo of coal. —y *n* coalmine.

col'loquial *adj* (of words) used in ordinary conversation but not considered suitable for formal writing or speech.

col'lusion *n* secret agreement for a wrong purpose.

'colon[1] *n* the mark : in writing and printing.

'colon² n lower part of the intestines.

'colonel n army officer, above a major, commanding a regiment.

,colon'nade n row of columns(1).

'colony n 1 land which has been developed by people from another country and which is still, fully or partly, controlled from the mother country. 2 group of people from another country, or with the same occupation, living together: *the Italian — in London; a — of artists.* **co'lonial** adj of a —. n person from overseas who has become resident in a —. **'colonist** n person who settles in a new —. **'colonize** v form a — in; send colonists to. **,coloni'zation** n.

co'lossal adj immense.

'colour n 1 *red, yellow, brown,* etc are all —s. 2 (usu pl) material used by artists: *water-colours.* 3 (of events, descriptions) appearance of truth or reality. **give (lend) — to,** make (sth) seem reasonable. **local —,** (in writing) details which make a description more real. 4 (pl) flag. **stick to one's —s,** refuse to change (ideas, etc). **come off with flying —s,** be successful. v put — on; become —ed; blush. **'colour-blind** adj unable to see the difference between certain —s.

colt n young horse (up to 4 or 5 years old).

'column n 1 tall, upright pillar, either supporting or decorating part of a building, or standing alone as a monument. 2 sth shaped like a —: *a — of smoke (figures, marching soldiers).* 3 upright division of a page of an account book, newspaper, etc.

a column   a comet

comb n 1 instrument with teeth for making the hair tidy, holding it in place, etc. 2 similar instrument, often part of a machine, for preparing wool, cotton, etc, for manufacture. 3 ⇨ honey. v 1 use a — on (the hair, etc). 2 search

thoroughly. **— out,** (esp) take out after searching for.

'combat n & v fight; struggle. **—ant** adj & n fighting (man).

com'bine v (cause to) join together; have at the same time. **'combine** n group of persons or parties, esp for trade, controlling prices, etc. **,combi'nation** n joining or putting together; number of persons or things joined or joining together, for a purpose.

com'bustible n & adj (substance) catching fire and burning easily.

com'bustion n destruction by fire; process of burning.

come v (pt came, pp come) move towards the speaker or a point in time, space, etc; arrive (special combinations only). **— by (sth),** get possession of. **— to, — round, — to one's senses,** become conscious (after fainting); become sensible (after being foolish). **— into** (*a fortune*), inherit; get (when sb dies). **— out,** (of a book) be published; (of facts) become known. **— off,** have the result hoped for; take place. **— of age,** reach the age of 18 (in Gt Brit). **— to blows,** begin fighting. **— about,** happen. **— across, — upon,** find by accident. **— true,** become real, become a fact. **— of,** have as a result: *What came of the discussion?* (What happened afterwards? What was the result?). **— to,** (inf) happen to: *How did you — to hear of it?* **in years to —,** in future years. **'come-back** n return to one's earlier powers or position. **'come-down** n change for the worse in one's circumstances.

'comedy n play for the theatre, usu dealing with ordinary life in an amusing way. **co'median** n actor in comedies; person whose aim is to make people laugh.

'comely adj (-ier, -iest) (of persons) pleasant to look at.

'comet n heavenly body looking like a star with a tail of light (moving round the sun).

'comfort n 1 help or kindness to sb who is suffering; relief from pain or anxiety; sth that brings such relief. 2 being free from worry; contentment. v give — to. **—able** adj giving — to the body;

free from pain or trouble: *feeling —able*. **—ably** *adv.* **—less** *adj.* **—er** *n.*

'**comic** *n* pictorial newspaper with amusing stories. *adj* causing people to laugh. **—al** *adj* amusing.

'**comma** *n* the mark , used in writing and printing.

com'**mand** *v* **1** give order(s) to; have power or authority over; control (oneself, one's temper, etc). **2** be in a position to use; deserve to have. **3** (of a place) overlook (and control): *a fort —ing the valley*. *n* order; authority; (power to) control. **—er** *n* person in —; (navy) officer of rank between lieutenant and captain. **—ment** *n* (esp) one of the ten laws given by God to Moses.

com'**memorate** *v* keep or honour the memory of (a person or event); (of things) be in memory of. com,memo'ration *n.*

com'**mence** *v* begin. **—ment** *n.*

com'**mend** *v* praise; approve. **—able** *adj* deserving praise. ,commen'dation *n* praise; approval.

'**comment** *v & n* (give) opinion(s), (make) remark(s) (*on* events, difficulties in books, etc). **—ary** *n* book of —s or explanations (eg of difficulties in the Bible); number of —s on an event (eg a football game): *a running* (ie continuous) *—ary*.

'**commerce** *n* trade (esp between countries); the buying, selling, and distribution of goods. com'**mercial** *adj* of —. commercial traveller, person who travels with samples of goods to obtain orders. commercial TV (radio), TV (radio) service paid for by advertisers. *n* advertisement (esp on TV).

com'**mission** *n* **1** the giving of authority to sb to act for another; the work he does. **2** the performance of sth, esp a crime. **3** payment made to sb for selling goods, etc, in proportion to the results obtained: *to sell goods on —*. **4** official paper giving a person authority, esp (in Gt Brit) one signed by the Sovereign appointing officers in the armed forces. **5** body of persons given the duty of making an inquiry and writing a report. *v* give a — to.

com'**mit** *v* (-tt-) **1** perform (a crime, a foolish act): *to — murder (suicide, a blunder)*. **2** send, hand over, give up, for safe keeping or treatment: *to — a man to prison (a prisoner for trial)*. **— to memory**, (learn by heart). **3 — oneself**, make oneself, admit that one is, responsible; promise. **—ment** *n* promise or undertaking.

com'**mittee** *n* group of persons appointed (usu by a larger group) to discuss or do special work.

com'**modious** *adj* having plenty of space for what is needed: *a — house (cupboard)*.

com'**modity** *n* useful article of trade.

'**common** *adj* (-er, -est) **1** belonging to, used by, coming from, done by, all members of a group or society: *— property*. **2** usual or ordinary; happening or found often or in many places. **—sense**, practical, good sense coming from experience of life. **— knowledge**, what is known to most persons, esp in a group. **3** (of persons, their behaviour) vulgar; rude. *n* **1** (in English villages) area of grassland for all to use. **2 House of Commons**, lower house of Parliament, of persons elected by the — people. **3 in —**, used by all (members of a group). **have in —** (*with*), share with. **out of the —**, unusual. '**—ly** *adv.* **—place** *n & adj* (remark, event, etc, which is) ordinary, usual. **—wealth** *n* State; group of States (esp *the C—wealth of Australia*) associating politically, etc for their —(2) good. The '**C—wealth**, that of Britain and former British colonies, dominions, protectorates, etc.

com'**motion** *n* noisy confusion.

'**communal** *adj* of or for a community; for the common use.

com'**mune** *v·* feel in close touch with; talk in an intimate way (*with*).

com'**municate** *v* **1** pass on (news, heat, motion, a disease, etc) (to sb). **2** share or exchange (news, etc) (*with* sb). **3** (of rooms, roads, etc) be connected (*with* others, by means of doors, gates, etc). **4** take Holy Communion. com,muni'cation *n* (esp) road, railway, telegraph, etc, which connects places. **in communication with**, exchanging letters, news, etc with.

com'munion n 1 sharing. 2 group of persons with the same religious beliefs. 3 exchange of thoughts, feelings, etc. 4 Holy C—, (in Christian churches) celebration of the Lord's Supper. **com'municant** n one who receives Holy C—.

'communism n 1 (belief in a) social system in which property is to be owned by the community and used for the good of all its members. 2 political system in which all power is held by the highest members of the Communist Party, which controls the land and its resources, the means of production, etc, and directs the activities of the people. **'communist** n believer in, supporter of, —.

com'munity n 1 the —, the people living in one place or district. 2 group of persons with the same religion, race, occupation, etc, living in one place or district. 3 condition of sharing or being similar, of doing the same thing.

com'mute v 1 exchange; change (one form of punishment for another, less severe). 2 travel (daily) to and from a town on business. **—r** n sb who —s(2).

'compact¹ n agreement.

com'pact² adj neatly fitted, closely packed, together. **'compact** n small flat box of face-powder carried in a handbag.

com'panion n 1 person who goes with, or is often or always with, another or others. 2 person (usu a woman) paid to live with another person (as a friend and helper). **—ship** n.

'company n 1 being with another or others: to keep sb —; in — with a friend (ie with him). 2 number of persons working together: a — of actors; group of persons united in business or commerce. 3 subdivision of an infantry battalion commanded by a captain or major.

com'parative adj 1 of comparison or comparing. 2 measured or judged by comparing: living in — comfort. 3 (grammar) form of adjectives and adverbs expressing 'more'. **—ly** adv.

com'pare v 1 say, judge, how far things are similar or not similar. 2 — (sth) to, point out the likeness or relation between: to — death to

sleep. 3 (grammar) form the comparative and superlative degrees (of an adj or adv) (eg by adding -er, -est, more, most). **'comparable** adj that can be —d (to).

com'parison n comparing; statement that compares. **in — with**, when compared with. **stand (bear) — with**, be able to be compared favourably with.

com'partment n one of several separate divisions of a structure, esp of a railway coach: a third-class —.

'compass n 1 instrument with a needle that points north. 2 (pl) instrument for drawing circles. 3 range; extent.

a compass

a pair of compasses

com'passion n pity (for sb or sth). **—ate** adj having —.

com'patible adj (of ideas, principles) agreeing with each other. **com,pati'bility** n.

com'patriot n person born in or citizen of the same country as another person mentioned.

com'pel v (-ll-) force (sb to do sth); obtain (a result) by using force.

'compensate v make suitable payment, give sth, to make up (for loss or injury). **,compen'sation** n (esp) sth given to — sb.

com'pete v take part in a race, or an examination, etc. **,compe'tition** n competing; any activity in which persons (schools, etc) —. **com'petitive** adj. **,com'petitor** n one who —s.

'competent adj having the necessary qualities or abilities to do what is needed. **'competence** n.

com'pile v collect (information) and arrange (in a book, etc). **,compi'lation** n.

com'placent adj satisfied with oneself. **com'placency** n.

com'plain v say that one is not satisfied, that one is suffering in some way. **—t** n 1 —ing; cause of dissatisfaction. 2 illness or disease.

com'plaisant *adj* ready and willing to please or oblige others.

'complement *n* that which makes sth complete; the full number or quantity needed.

com'plete *adj* 1 whole; having all its parts. 2 finished. 3 in every way; thorough: *a — surprise*. *v* finish; make perfect. com'pletion *n* completing; being —.

com'plex *adj* made up of many parts; difficult to explain. —ity *n*.

com'plexion *n* 1 natural colour, appearance, etc, of the skin, esp the face. 2 general character or appearance (of events, etc).

com'pliance *n*. in — with, in obedience to; according to (a person's wishes, request, etc). com'pliant *adj* ready and willing to comply.

'complicate *v* make complex; make (sth) difficult to do or understand. —d *adj* (esp) made up of many parts. ˌcompli'cation *n* state of being —d; that which makes an illness or other trouble more serious.

com'plicity *n* taking part with another person (in wrongdoing).

'compliment *n* 1 expression of admiration or approval. 2 (*pl*) greetings. *v* pay a — (*to sb*, *on sth*). ˌcompli'mentary *adj* expressing a —: *complimentary tickets*, tickets (for a concert, etc) given free.

com'ply *v* — with (*a request*, etc), do (what is asked).

'component *adj* helping to form (a complete thing). *n* — part.

com'port *v* — oneself, behave.

com'pose *v* 1 (usu in the passive) be —d of, be made up of (parts). 2 put together (words, ideas, musical notes) in literary, musical, etc, form: *to — a letter* (*a sentence*, *a song*). 3 (printing) set up (type) to form words, pages, etc. 4 get under control; settle: *to — oneself*; *to — a quarrel*. —d *adj* calm. —r *n* (esp) one who —s music. com'positor *n* one who —s type.

ˌcompo'sition *n* 1 act of composing. 2 that which is written (eg a poem, a book or music). 3 nature of the parts of which sth is composed.

'compost *n* manure made from decayed vegetable stuff. *v* make into —; treat (the soil) with —.

com'posure *n* condition of being calm (in mind or behaviour).

'compound¹ *n & adj* (sth) made up of two or more parts (eg a word, a chemical substance). —interest, interest reckoned on the capital sum and on the interest already accumulated. com'pound *v* mix together (to make sth different): *to — a medicine*.

'compound² *n* enclosed area with buildings, etc, eg one used as a trading or commercial centre(a house and its gardens, a school and its grounds, etc.

ˌcompre'hend *v* 1 understand fully. 2 include. ˌcompre'hensible *adj* that can be —ed(1). ˌcompre-'hension *n* power of —ing. ˌcompre'hensive *adj* that —s(2) much.

com'press *v* 1 press together; get into a small(er) space. 2 (of writings, ideas) get into fewer words. —ion *n*. 'compress *n* pad of cloth pressed on part of the body (eg to stop bleeding, reduce fever).

com'prise *v* include; have as parts.

'compromise *n* settlement of a disagreement by which each side gives up sth it has asked for. *v* 1 settle (a dispute, etc) by making a —. 2 bring (sb) under suspicion by unwise behaviour.

com'pulsion *n* compelling or being compelled. under (upon) —, because one must. com'pulsory *adj* that must be done, etc.

com'punction *n* feeling of doubt or regret (about one's action).

com'pute *v* calculate; reckon. —r *n* calculating machine; machine for storing and analysing information.

'comrade *n* trusted companion; loyal friend (with whom one works, plays, etc). —s in arms, soldiers who have served together. —ship *n*.

con¹ *v* (-nn-) — (over) (*one's lessons*) learn by heart; study.

con² *n & adv* pro(s) and con(s), (arguments) for and against.

'con'cave *adj* curved inwards like the inside of a ball or circle.

concave

convex

con'ceal v hide; keep secret. **—ment** n.

con'cede v 1 admit or allow (that sth is true). 2 allow (sb) to have (a right, privilege, etc). **con'cession** n conceding; sth that is —d.

con'ceit n too high an opinion of, too much pride in, oneself, what one has or does. **—ed** adj full of —.

con'ceive v 1 form (an idea, plan, etc) in the mind. 2 (of a woman) become pregnant. **con'ceivable** adj that can be —d or believed.

'concentrate v bring or come together to one point: — your attention on your work. —d liquid. —d adj (of liquid) boiled so as to reduce the quantity of water in relation to the other substance(s). **,concen'tration** n concentrating or being —d; that which is —d; power of concentrating.

con'centric adj having a common centre (with another circle, etc).

'concept n general idea; idea underlying a class of things. **con'ception** n 1 (the act of forming an) idea or plan. 2 conceiving(2).

con'cern v 1 have relation to; be of importance to. **be —ed** (in an event), have some part in it. 2 — oneself with, be busy with; take a share or interest in. 3 to be —ed at (or about), made unhappy or troubled: —ed at the news; —ed about one's health. n 1 connection; reference; sth in which one is interested or which is important to one. 2 business or undertaking: a shipping —. 3 anxiety: filled with —. **—ing** prep about.

'concert n 1 musical entertainment, esp one given in public by players or singers. 2 in — (with), together (with); in agreement (with). **con'certed** adj planned, performed (by two or more persons together).

,concer'tina n musical wind instrument.

con'certo n musical composition for one or more solo instruments (eg a piano) supported by an orchestra.

con'cession n ⇨ concede.

con'ciliate v calm sb's anger; win the friendly feelings of. **con'ciliation** n.

con'cise adj (of a person, his speech or style; of writings) giving much information in few words.

con'clude v 1 come or bring to an end. 2 bring about; arrange: to — a treaty. 3 arrive at a belief or opinion: to —, from a pupil's work, that he is stupid. **con'clusion** n 1 end. **in conclusion**, lastly. 2 belief or opinion that is the result of thought, study, etc. 3 decision; settling (of sth).

con'coct v invent (an excuse, story, etc); prepare by mixing.

'concord n agreement; harmony.

'concrete adj of material (not abstract) things. **— noun**, name of a thing, not of a quality. n building substance made by mixing cement with sand, gravel, etc: — walls.

con'cur v (-rr-) agree in opinion (with sb).

con'cussion n (injury to the brain caused by a) violent shock, blow, or fall.

con'demn v 1 say that sb is, or has done, wrong; (law) give judgement against. 2 say that sth is faulty or unfit for use: to — bad meat. 3 send, appoint (to sth painful or unhappy in the future). **,condem'nation** n.

con'dense v 1 (cause to) increase in density or strength; (of a gas or vapour, eg steam) (cause to) become liquid; (of a liquid) (cause to) become thicker: —d milk. 2 put (an account, description, etc) into fewer words. **,conden'sation** n drops of liquid formed when vapour —s(1) (dew, clouds, mist, etc).

,conde'scend v 1 behave towards sb more humbly than one's ability, position, etc, would justify. 2 stoop(2) to unworthy behaviour. **,conde'scension** n.

con'dition n 1 sth needed before sth else is possible; sth on which another thing depends. **on — that**, only if; provided that. **on this —**, if this is true; if this is done, etc. 2 the present state of being; nature or character of sb or sth: the — of a person's health; goods which arrived in good —. 3 (pl) circumstances: under existing —s, while things are as they are now. 4 position in society. v determine; place —s(1) upon; control. **—al** adj depending upon, containing, a —(1).

con'dole v express sympathy (with

con'dolence n expression of sympathy.

con'done v (of a person) overlook or forgive (an offence); (of an act) atone for: *Nothing can — his failure to help his old parents.*

con'duce v — to, help to produce.

'conduct n 1 behaviour (esp moral behaviour). 2 way of managing or directing (affairs, a business, etc). **con'duct** v 1 lead; guide. 2 control; direct; manage. 3 —oneself (*well*, etc), behave. 4 (of substances) allow (*heat, electric current*) to pass along or through. **con'ductor** n 1 person on a bus, tram, etc, who sells tickets, etc. 2 person who —s an orchestra. 3 substance which —s(4) heat or electricity.

cone n 1 solid figure which narrows to a point from a round, flat base. ⇨ p 253. 2 sth of this shape, whether hollow or solid. 3 fruit of certain evergreen trees: *pine, fir, cedar —s.*

con'fectioner n person who makes or sells cakes, sweets, pastries, etc. **—y** n the things he makes or sells.

con'federate adj joined together by an agreement. n person who joins with another (esp for wrongdoing). **con,fede'ration** n uniting or being united; alliance.

con'fer v (-rr-) 1 give or grant (a right, title, favour). 2 consult, discuss (*with* sb). **'conference** n (meeting for) discussion, consultation.

con'fess v 1 admit (that one has done wrong). 2 tell one's sins or faults to a priest (esp in the Roman Catholic Church); (of a priest) listen to sb doing this. **—ion** n —ing; that which is —ed: *a —ion of guilt.* **—or** n (esp) priest who hears a —ion.

con'fide v 1 tell (a secret *to*); give (sb or sth) to sb to be looked after; give (a task or duty to sb). 2 — in, have trust or faith in. **'confidence** n 1 act of confiding: *tell sth in confidence* (ie as a secret). 2 sth —d; a secret: *The girls exchanged confidences about the young men they knew.* 3 belief in oneself or others: *to answer questions with confidence; have confidence in your teachers.* **'con-**fident** adj having or showing confidence. **,confi'dential** adj 1 (to be kept) secret; given in confidence. 2 having the confidence of another: *my confidential secretary.*

con'fine v restrict within limits; keep shut up or as a prisoner. n (usu pl) limit; edge. **—d** adj (esp) in bed giving birth to a baby. **—ment** n being —d; imprisonment.

con'firm v 1 make firm(er) or strong(er). 2 agree definitely to (an appointment, etc). 3 admit to full membership of the Christian Church. **—ed** adj (esp) unlikely to change. **,confir'mation** n —ing or being —ed.

'confiscate v (as punishment or in enforcing authority) take possession of (the private property of sb). **,confis'cation** n.

,confla'gration n great destructive fire.

'conflict n 1 fight(ing); struggle; quarrel. 2 (of opinions, etc) disagreement. **con'flict** v be in disagreement; be opposed or against.

con'form v — to, make or be in agreement with; comply. **—ity** n agreement; doing what is asked or wished.

con'found v 1 fill with, throw into, confusion. 2 mix up; overthrow (enemies, plans, etc).

con'front v be, come, bring, face to face (*with*); be opposite to.

con'fuse v put into disorder; upset; mistake one thing for another. **con'fusion** n.

con'fute v prove (sb) to be wrong; show (an argument) to be false.

con'geal v make or become stiff or solid (esp because of the effect of cold or air): *—ed blood.*

con'genial adj 1 (of persons) having the same or a similar nature and common interests. 2 (of things) agreeable; satisfying one's taste, interests, etc: *— work.*

con'gested adj overcrowded; too full; (of parts of the body, eg the brain, lungs) having too much blood. **con'gestion** n.

con'gratulate v 1 tell (sb) that one is pleased about sth good or fortunate that has come to him: *to — a man on his success.* 2 **—oneself**, consider oneself fortunate.

con,gratu'lation *n* (often *pl*) words which — sb.

'congregate *v* come or bring together. **,congre'gation** *n* (esp) persons —d for a church service.

'congress *n* **1** meeting(s) of persons who represent societies, etc, for discussions: *a medical* —. **2** C—, law-making body in some countries (eg USA); political party in India. **con'gressional** *adj* of a —: *congressional debates.*

'congruent *adj* (maths) (esp) having the same size and shape: — *triangles.*

'conical *adj* cone(1)-shaped.

con'jecture *v & n* (make a) guess; (put forward an) opinion formed without facts to prove it.

'conjugal *adj* of marriage; of wedded life; of husband and wife.

'conjugate *v* give the forms of a verb (eg *am, is, are, was, were,* of the verb *to be*). **,conju'gation** *n*.

con'junction *n* **1** (grammar) word that joins other words, clauses, etc (eg *and, or, but*). **2** state of being joined. **in — with,** together with.

'conjure *v* **1** do clever tricks by quick movements: *to — a rabbit out of* (what seems to be) *an empty hat.* **2 — up,** cause to appear as a picture in the mind.

con'nect *v* **1** join; be joined. **2** think of (different things) as being related to each other. **—ion, con'nexion** *n* **1** —ing or being —ed; sth which —s. **in —ion with,** —ed with. **2** train, boat, etc, timed to leave a station, port, etc, soon after the arrival of another, enabling passengers to change from one to the other. **3** number of persons who do business with sb or who go to a professional man: *a dressmaker with a good —ion* (ie many good customers). **—ive** *n & adj* (word) that —s.

con'nive *v* — **at,** pretend not to know about (what is wrong, sth that ought to be stopped). **con'nivance** *n*.

,connois'seur *n* person with good judgement in matters of taste: *a — of antique furniture, wines, etc.*

'conquer *v* **1** defeat or overcome (enemies, bad habits, etc). **2** take possession of (land, etc) by force, esp in war. **—or** *n*. **'conquest** *n*

—ing; sth got by —ing: *the Roman conquests in Africa.*

'conscience *n* awareness of the choice one ought to make between sth right and sth wrong. **have a clear (guilty) —,** know that one has done nothing (sth) wrong. **,consci'entious** *adj* (of a person) guided by —; (of work, etc) done as — directs; done carefully and honestly.

'conscious *adj* **1** aware; awake; knowing (from experience, not from study): — *of one's failure* (that one has failed). **2** knowing things because one is using bodily senses and mental powers. **3** (of actions) realized by oneself: *to make a — effort.* **—ness** *n* **1** being —. **2** all the ideas, thoughts, and feelings of a person.

con'script *v* compel (sb) by law to serve in the navy, army, or air force. **'conscript** *n* person compelled to serve in this way. **con'scription** *n*.

'consecrate *v* make sacred; set on one side as sacred, or for a special purpose. **,conse'cration** *n*.

con'secutive *adj* following, coming one after the other; continuously, in regular order.

con'sent *v & n* (give) agreement or permission.

'consequence *n* **1** that which follows or is brought about, as the result or effect of sth. **in — (of),** as a result (of). **2** importance. **'consequent** *adj* following as a —.

,conser'vation *n* keeping in good condition; prevention of loss, waste, damage, etc.

con'servative *n & adj* **1** (sb who is) moderate, cautious, opposed to sudden change. **2** C—, (member or policy) of the C— and Unionist political party in Britain. **con'servatism** *n* principle of being —(1) (esp in politics).

con'servatory *n* building or part of a building with glass walls and roof in which plants are protected from cold.

con'serve *v* keep from change, loss, or destruction. *n* (usu *pl*) preserved fruit; jam.

con'sider *v* **1** think about. **2** make allowances for: — *his youth.* **3** be of the opinion; regard (as). **—able** *adj* deserving to be —ed; great;

60 consign | consume

much. **—ably** adv much; a good deal. **—ate** adj thoughtful (of the needs, etc, of others). **con,side-'ration** n 1 quality of being —ate. **under consideration,** being —ed(2). 2 sth which must be —ed(1). 3 reward or payment. **—ing** prep in view of; having regard to.

con'sign v 1 send (goods, etc, by rail, etc, to sb). 2 hand over; give up to. **,consign'ee** n person to whom sth is —ed. **—ment** n —ing; goods —ed.

con'sist v 1 — of, be made up of. 2 — in, have as the chief (or only) element: *Does happiness — in wanting little?* **—ence, —ency** n 1 (always —ency) state of being always the same in thought, behaviour, etc. 2 degree of thickness, firmness, or solidity of (esp a thick liquid). **—ent** adj 1 (of a person, his behaviour) regular; conforming to a regular pattern or style. 2 in agreement (*with*).

con'sole v give comfort or sympathy to. **,conso'lation** n consoling or being —d; sth that —s: *consolation prize.*

con'solidate v 1 make or become solid or strong. 2 unite or combine (debts, business firms, etc) into one. **con,soli'dation** n.

'consonant n speech sound which is not a vowel sound; letter or symbol representing such a sound.

'consort[1] n husband or wife, esp of a ruler. **prince —,** reigning queen's husband.

con'sort[2] v — with, pass much time in the company of; be in harmony with.

con'spicuous adj easily seen; remarkable; attracting attention.

con'spire v 1 make secret plans (esp to do wrong) with others. 2 unite (to have an effect). **con-'spirator** n. **con'spiracy** n.

'constable n policeman. **con-'stabulary** n the police force.

'constancy n quality of being firm and unchanging.

'constant adj 1 going on all the time; never-ending. 2 firm; faithful; unchangeable. **—ly** adv.

,constel'lation n group of stars; (fig) group of celebrities.

,conster'nation n surprise and fear.

,consti'pation n difficulty in emptying the bowels. **'constipate** v cause —.

con'stituency n (persons living in a) town or district sending a representative to Parliament.

con'stituent adj 1 having the power to make or alter a political constitution. 2 forming or helping to make a whole. n person having a parliamentary vote.

'constitute v 1 give (sb) authority to hold (a position). 2 establish; give legal authority to. 3 amount to; make up.

,consti'tution n 1 laws and principles according to which a state is governed. 2 general structure of a thing, of a person's body: *a man with a sound —* (ie with a strong and healthy body). **—al** adj of a —: *—al government* (cf despotism); *a —al weakness* (ie of the body).

con'strain v make (sb) do sth by using force or strong persuasion. **—ed** adj (of voice, manner, etc) not natural; uneasy. **—t** n.

con'strict v cause (eg a vein or muscle) to become tight or smaller; make tighter or smaller. **—ion** n.

con'struct v build; put together. **—ion** n 1 act or manner of —ing; being —ed; sth —ed. 2 sense in which words, actions, etc, are understood: *to put a wrong —ion on what sb says or does.* **—ive** adj helping to —.

con'strue v translate or explain the meaning of (words, remarks, etc).

'consul n 1 State's agent living in a foreign town to help and protect his countrymen there. 2 (ancient Rome) one of the two heads of the State before Rome became an empire. **—ar** adj. **—ate** n position, office, of a —(1).

con'sult v go to (a person, book, etc) for information or advice. **—ant** n expert —ed for his professional advice. **,consul'tation** n —ing; meeting for —ing.

con'sume v 1 eat or drink. 2 use up; get to the end of. 3 destroy (by fire, wasting). 4 be —d with (*desire, curiosity*), be filled with. **—r** n person who uses goods (opp to producer). **con'sumption** n 1 consuming (of food, energy, etc); the amount —d. 2 tuberculosis.

con'sumptive *n & adj* (person) suffering from consumption (2).

'contact *n* (state of) touching. in — with, in communication with. con'tact *v* make — with.

con'tagious *adj* (of disease) spreading by touch; (fig) spreading by example: — *laughter*.

con'tain *v* 1 have or hold within itself: *The bag* —*s 5 lb of potatoes. Whisky* —*s alcohol.* 2 keep (feelings, an enemy force) under control. —er *n* box, bottle, etc, made to — sth.

con'taminate *v* make dirty, impure, or diseased: *food* —*d by flies.* con,tami'nation *n*.

'contemplate *v* look at (with the eyes or the mind); have in view as a purpose, etc. ,contem'plation *n*.

con'temporary *adj* of a time or period referred to; (esp) of the present time. *n* person — with another.

con'tempt *n* 1 scorn; way of looking down on something which should not be respected, admired, or feared: *to feel — for a liar; to show one's — of danger.* 2 condition of being looked down upon: *to fall into —.* 3 — of court, disobedience to, disrespect ,shown to, a judge. —ible *adj* deserving —. —uous *adj* showing —.

con'tend *v* struggle or compete (*with sb, for* sth); argue (*that*). con'tention *n* —ing; argument used in —ing.

con'tent¹ *adj* 1 not wanting more; satisfied with what one has. 2 — to, willing or ready to. *v* make —. —ed *adj* satisfied. —ment *n* state of being —.

'content² *n* 1 (usu *pl*) that which is contained in sth. 2 amount which can be contained (in a cask, barrel, etc).

con'test *v* 1 take part in a struggle or competition (*for*). 2 argue against. 'contest *n* struggle; competition. con'testant *n* person taking part in a —.

'context *n* what comes before and after (a word, phrase, statement, etc), helping to fix the meaning.

'continent *n* one of the main land masses (*Europe, Asia, Africa,* etc). ,conti'nental *adj* of a —; (esp) of Europe.

con'tinue *v* go on (doing sth); go on (to do sth else); start again after stopping. con'tinual *adj* going on all the time without stopping or with only short breaks. con,tinu'ation *n* continuing; part, etc, by which sth is —d. con'tinuous *adj* (of space or time) going on without a break.

con'tort *v* force or twist out of the usual shape or appearance. —ion *n*. —ionist *n* person clever at —ing his body.

'contour *n* outline (of a coast, mountain, etc). 'contour-line, line (on a map) joining points representing places that are at the same height above or depth below sea level.

'contra- *prefix* against.

'contraband *n* the bringing into, taking out of, a country of certain goods that are forbidden by law; (trade in) such goods.

'contract¹ *n* agreement (between persons, groups, or states); (esp) business agreement to supply goods, do work, etc, at a fixed price. con'tract *v* 1 make a —: *to* — *to build a railway.* 2 form; get: *to* — *bad habits.* 3 catch: *to* — *a disease.* —or *n* person who makes —s.

con'tract² *v* make or become smaller or shorter, tighter or narrower. —ion *n* —ing or being —ed; sth —ed: '*Can't' is a* —*ion of 'can not'.*

,contra'dict *v* 1 deny that sth (read or written) is true. 2 (of facts, statements, etc) be contrary to. —ion *n*. —ory *adj*.

con'tralto *n* lowest female voice; woman with such a voice; musical part to be sung by her.

'contrary *adj* 1 opposite (in nature or quality); (of the wind) unfavourable (for sailing). 2 con'trary (colloq) self-willed; doing the—of what is wanted. *adv* against. *n* the —, the opposite (of sth). on the —, to the opposite effect.

con'trast *v* compare (one thing *with* another) so that the difference is clear; show a difference when compared. 'contrast *n* the act of —ing; difference which is clearly seen when unlike things or persons are put together; sth showing such difference (*to*).

,contra'vene v go against (a law, custom); dispute (a statement). ,contra'vention n.

con'tribute v 1 join with others in giving (money, help, ideas, suggestions, etc) (to). 2 — to, help towards. 3 write (articles, etc) and send in (to a newspaper, etc). ,contri'bution n (esp) sth —d. con'tributor n.

'contrite adj filled with, showing, deep sorrow for wrongdoing. con'trition n.

con'trive v invent; design; find a way ,(to do sth, cause sth to happen). con'trivance n.

con'trol n 1 power to rule, guide, or keep order: to have one's feelings under —; to lose — of one's bicycle. 2 means of regulating or directing: traffic —; government —s of trade and industry. 3 (often pl) apparatus, etc, by which machines are operated: sitting at the —s of an aircraft. v (-ll-) have — of. —ler n person who —s.

'controversy n prolonged argument. ,contro'versial adj.

,conva'lescent n & adj (person who is) recovering from an illness. ,conva'lescence n.

con'vene v call (persons, usu members of a society, etc) together (for a meeting); come together for a meeting.

con'venient adj suitable; not causing trouble or difficulty. con'venience n being —; sth that is helpful and —.

'convent n 1 society of women (called nuns) living apart from others in the service of God. 2 building(s) in which they live and work.

con'vention n 1 general conference of members of societies, etc. 2 agreement (between states, etc). 3 way(s) of behaviour, customs, followed by most people in a community(1). —al adj based on —(3).

con'verge v (of lines, moving objects, opinions) come (cause to come) towards each other and meet at a point; show a tendency to do this.

con'versant adj — with, having a knowledge of.

,conver'sation n talk(ing). con'verse v have a talk (with).

'converse n & adj (idea, statement, that is) opposite. —ly adv.

con'vert v 1 change (from one state, use, etc, into another). 2 cause (a person) to change his beliefs: to — a man to Christianity. 'convert n person who is —ed(2). —ible adj that can be —ed(1). con'version n —ing or being —ed.

'convex adj with the surface curved like the outside of a ball. ⇨ p 56.

con'vey v 1 carry from one place to another; make known (news, feelings, etc) to another person. 2 (law) give full legal rights in (property). —ance n —ing; sth that —s; a carriage, car, etc.

con'vict v 1 make (sb) feel sure that he has done wrong. 2 (of a jury or judge) declare in a law court that (sb) is guilty of crime. 'convict n person —ed of crime and under punishment.

con'viction n 1 the convicting of a person of crime. 2 the act of convincing. 3 firm belief.

con'vince v make (sb) feel certain (of sth, or that . . .); cause (sb) to realize. con'vincing adj.

con'vivial adj gay; (esp) fond of drinking and merry-making; marked by this.

con'voke v call together (to a meeting). ,convo'cation n meeting (esp for church or university business).

con'voy v go with in order to protect. 'convoy n —ing; protecting force (of warships, soldiers, etc); ships sailing together for safety.

con'vulse v cause violent movements or disturbances. con'vulsion n violent disturbance; uncontrolled physical movements (through pain, laughter). con'vulsive adj.

cook n & v (sb who can) prepare (raw) food by heating (boiling, frying, roasting, etc). —er n sth in which to —: a gas —er.

cool adj (-er, -est) 1 between warm and cold: a — day. 2 calm; unexcited. 3 impudent in a calm way. 4 (of behaviour) not showing interest or liking.

'coolie n (in the Far East) unskilled workman or porter.

coop n small cage for hens. v — up, keep in a small space.

co-'operate v work or act together to bring about a result. **co-,ope'ration** n. **co-'operative** adj **co-operative society,** group of persons who —, eg to buy machines and services for all to share; to produce, buy, and sell goods amongst themselves for mutual benefit; to save and lend money as a group.

co-'opt v add (sb) as a member (of a committee) by the votes of those who are already members.

cope v — **with,** manage to deal with or keep under control.

'copious adj plentiful; (of a writer) writing much.

'copper n **1** common reddish-brown metal. **2** coin made of — or bronze. **3** large vessel used for boiling clothes, etc. v cover with a coating of —.

'copra n dried kernel of coconut, used in soap-making, etc.

'copy n **1** thing made to be like another. **2** one example of a book, newspaper, etc, of which many have been made. v make a — of; (try to) do the same as.

'coral n hard red, pink or white substance built up on the sea-bed by small sea-creatures, forming reefs and islands as it reaches the surface. adj pink or red.

cord n **1** length of twisted threads, thicker than string, thinner than rope. **2** ⇨ chord(3). v put a — or —s round.

'cordial adj warm and sincere (in feeling, words, behaviour). n sweetened and concentrated fruit juice. **—ly** adv. **,cordi'ality** n.

'cordon n line, ring, of police, soldiers, etc, acting as guards.

'cordu'roy n thick, coarse, strong cotton cloth with raised lines on its surface: (pl) trousers made of this cloth.

core n **1** hard middle part with seeds, of apples and pears. ⇨ p 115. **2** central or most important part: to get to the — of the question.

cork n light, tough material forming the thick outer bark of some trees; piece of this used as a stopper for a bottle. **'cork-screw,** tool for removing —s from bottles. v put a — in.

corn[1] n seed of various grain plants, chiefly wheat, barley, oats, rye, and maize.

corn[2] n (often painful) area of hardened skin on a toe, etc.

'corner n **1** place where two walls, sides, roads, etc, meet. **turn the —,** (fig) pass a crisis (eg in illness) safely. **2** (commerce) **make a — in** (wheat, etc), buy up all available supplies in order to control the price. v drive, get, (sb) into a —. **'corner,stone** n foundation.

,coro'nation n ceremony of crowning a king or queen.

'coroner n official who inquires into any violent or unnatural death. **—'s inquest,** such an inquiry.

'coronet n small crown worn by a noble at state(2) ceremonies.

'corporal[1] adj of the body: — **punishment,** (whipping or beating).

'corporal[2] n (army) non-commissioned officer (below a sergeant).

,corpo'ration n **1** group of persons elected to govern a town. **2** group of persons allowed by law to act, for business purposes, as one person. **'corporate** adj of a —.

corps n **1** one of the technical branches of an army: Royal Army Medical Corps. **2** military force made up of two or more Divisions.

corpse n dead body (usu of a human being).

'corpulent adj (of a person's body) fat and heavy. **'corpulence** n.

cor'rect adj true; right. v make —; take out mistakes from; point out faults; punish. **—ion** n **—ing;** sth — put in place of an error.

,corres'pond v **1** be in harmony (with). **2** be equal (to); be similar (to). **3** exchange letters (with). **—ence** n **1** agreement; similarity. **2** letter-writing; letters. **—ent** n **1** person with whom one exchanges letters. **2** person regularly contributing local news or special articles to a newspaper.

'corridor n long, narrow passage from which doors open into rooms.

cor'rode v wear away, destroy slowly, by chemical action or disease; be worn away in this way. **cor'rosion** n.

'corrugated adj shaped into narrow folds or with a wave-like surface: —iron (used for roofs); —cardboard (used for packing).

cor'rupt adj 1 (of persons, their actions) dishonest (esp through taking bribes). 2 impure. v make —. —ible adj that can be —ed by bribes. —ion n.

'corset n tight-fitting undergarment supporting or shaping the waist and hips.

cos'metic n substance used to make the skin or hair more beautiful.

'cosmic adj of the whole universe.

'cosmonaut n astronaut.

,cosmo'politan adj of or from all, or many different, parts of the world; resulting from wide experience of the world: — views (interests). n — person.

cost v (pt & pp cost) 1 be obtainable at the price of; result in the loss or disadvantage of. 2 (commerce) estimate the price to be charged for an article. n 1 price (to be) paid; that which is needed in order to obtain. at all —s, however much expense, trouble, etc, may be needed. to one's —, to one's loss or disadvantage. 2 (law, pl) expenses of having sth decided in a law court. '—ly adj. —ing much.

'costume n 1 style of dress. 2 a woman's short coat and skirt.

'cosy adj (-ier, -iest) warm and comfortable. 'cosily adv.

cot n bed for a baby with sides to prevent him from falling out.

'cottage n small house, esp in the country.

'cotton n white, woolly substance from the seeds of the — plant; thread made from this. cotton-wool, cleaned natural — as used for padding, bandaging, etc.

couch n long, bed-like seat for sitting or lying on during the day. v (of animals) lie flat, either to hide or in readiness for a jump.

cough v send out air from the lungs violently and noisily. n act or sound of —ing; illness causing a person to — often.

could ⇨ can.

'council n group of persons appointed or elected to give advice, make rules, carry out plans, manage affairs, etc: the town —. —lor n member of a —.

'counsel n 1 advice; opinions; suggestions: to take — with a friend

(consult him). 2 (pl unchanged) barrister(s) giving advice in a lawsuit. v (-ll-) give advice to. —lor n adviser.

count¹ v 1 add up; say the numbers. 2 include: fifty, not —ing those that are broken. 3 — (up)on, rely upon; consider as certain. — for much (nothing, etc), be of much (no, etc) importance. to —, oneself (fortunate, etc), to consider oneself (fortunate, etc). n 1 act of —ing(1). 2 account; notice. to take no — of, to pay no attention to. 3 one of several things of which a prisoner has been accused: guilty on all —s. '—less adj too many to be —ed.

count² n title of nobility in some countries (but not Gt Brit). '—ess n wife or widow of an earl or —; woman with rank equal to that of an earl.

'countenance n 1 face, including its appearance and expression. keep one's —, hide one's feelings (esp of amusement). 2 support; approval: give — to a proposal. v give —(2) to.

'counter¹ n long table on which goods are shown, customers are served, in a shop or bank.

'counter² adv against.

'counter- prefix 1 opposite in direction: ,counter-at'traction. 2 made in answer to; against: 'counter-attack.

,counte'ract v act against and make (action, force) of less or no effect. —ion n.

,counter'balance n weight, force, etc, equal to and balancing another.

'counterfeit n & adj (sth) false; (sth) made in imitation of another thing in order to deceive: — money. v make a — of.

'counterfoil n part of a cheque, receipt, etc, kept by the sender as a record.

,counter'mand v take back, cancel, a command already given.

'counterpart n person or thing exactly like, or corresponding closely to, another.

'countersign n secret word(s) to be given, on demand, to a sentry as proof that one is not an enemy.

'country n 1 large area in which people share a government, monetary system, etc, eg Britain, France.

2 land outside urban areas: —side. **'countrified** adj with the habits and ways of the —, not of towns. —**man** n **1** man of the —(2), not of a town. **2** man of the same —(1) as another.

'county n division of Gt Brit, the largest unit of local government.

'couple n **1** two persons or things seen or associated together. **2** two persons married or to be married to one another. v join (two things) together; associate (two things) in the mind. **'coupling** n (esp) link, etc, that joins two railway coaches or other vehicles.

'coupon n ticket, part of a paper, document, etc, that gives the holder the right to receive sth or do sth.

'courage n bravery. **cou'rageous** adj brave.

course n **1** forward movement in space or time. **in (the)** — **of**, during: in — of construction (etc) being constructed (etc). **in due** —, in the proper or natural order. **2** direction taken by sth; line along which sth moves: The ship changed —. **a matter of** —, sth natural and expected. **of** —, naturally. **3** ground for playing golf; place for (esp horse-) races: a race-course. **4** series (of talks, treatments, etc): a — of lectures. **5** one of the separate parts of a meal (eg soup, meat, dessert).

court n **1** place where lawsuits are heard; the judges and other officers who hear such cases. **2** great ruler (king, emperor), his family, councillors, etc; reception given by such a ruler. **3** space marked out for certain games: a **'tennis-court**. **4** (also —**yard**) space with buildings or walls round it; the houses round such a space. **5** attentive and polite behaviour: to pay — to a woman (eg when hoping to marry her). v **1** pay one's —(5) to; try to win (support, approval, etc). **2** take action that may lead to: to — defeat (danger). **'—ier** n person belonging to the —(2) of a ruler. **'—ly** adj polite and dignified. **'—'martial** n (trial by a) —(1) for offences against military law. **'—ship** n (time of) paying —(5) to a woman.

'courteous adj having, showing,

good manners; polite. **'courtesy** n — behaviour; a — act.

'cousin n child of one's uncle or aunt.

cove n small bay(1).

'covenant v & n (make a) solemn agreement.

'cover v **1** put (sth) over or in front of (sth else). **2** travel (a distance). **3** aim at (with a gun, etc). **4** protect; provide with insurance (against): to be —ed against loss by fire. **5** (of a sum of money) be enough for (one's needs). n **1** that which —s (1): bed-cover, book-cover, etc. **2** place giving shelter or protection: to take —; to get under —. **3** sb who acts as an alibi for sb else. —**ing** n sth that —s or protects.

'covet v desire eagerly. —**ous** adj.

cow[1] n full-grown female of any animal of the ox family, kept for milk. ⇨ p 84.

cow[2] v frighten (sb) into doing what one wants, etc.

'coward n person unable to control his fear; one who runs away from danger. —**ly** adj not brave; contemptible. —**ice** n feeling, behaviour, of a —.

'cower v lower the body, be in a bent or crouching position (from cold, fear, or shame).

'cowrie n small shell formerly used as money in parts of Africa and Asia.

cox, 'coxswain n person who steers a rowing-boat.

coy adj (eg of a girl) shy; modest.

crab n ten-legged shell-fish; its meat as food. ⇨ p 247.

'crabbed adj **1** bad-tempered. **2** (of handwriting) difficult to read.

crack n **1** line of division where sth is broken but not into separate parts. **2** sudden, sharp noise (of a gun, whip, etc). **3** sharp blow which can be heard. v **1** get or make a —(1) or —s(1) in. **2** make, cause to make, a —(2) or —s(2). **3** (of the voice) undergo a change (esp of a boy's voice when he is reaching manhood). **4** — **up**, lose strength (eg as the result of old age). adj first-rate: a —polo-player. **'—er** n **1** thin, hard, dry biscuit. **2** firework which makes a sharp noise or series of noises when let off. **3** (pl) instrument for —ing nuts. '—le v & n (make) small —ing sounds.

'cradle n small bed for a newborn baby. v place, hold, in or as in a —: to — a baby in one's arms.

craft n 1 occupation, esp one in which skill in the use of the hands is needed: the — of the potter. 2 cunning; skill in deceiving. 3 boat(s); ship(s); air—. '—sman-(ship) n skilled workman(ship). '—y adj (-ier, -iest) cunning. '—ily adv. '—iness n.

crag n high, sharp rock.

cram v (-mm-) make too full; put, push, too much into.

cramp n painful tightening of the muscles, usu caused by cold (eg while swimming) or overwork (eg while writing). v keep in a narrow space; stop or hinder movement or growth.

crane n 1 large water-bird with a long neck and legs. ⇨ p 26. 2 machine for lifting heavy loads. v stretch out (the neck) to see.

crank¹ n person with fixed (often strange) ideas, esp on one matter.

crank² n L-shaped arm and handle used to turn a machine. v move, cause to move, by turning a crank-handle: to — (up) a car engine.

crape n silk or cotton material with a wrinkled surface.

crash v fall or strike suddenly and noisily (esp of things that break): A stone —ed through the window. n (noise made by a) violent fall, blow, or breaking. 'crash-,helmet, one worn (eg by a motor-cyclist) to protect his head in a —. 'crash-'landing, (esp of an aircraft) landing(2) by —ing.

crate v & n (make a) wooden framework to protect goods being transported.

'crater n mouth of a volcano; hole in the ground made by a bomb.

crave v ask earnestly for; have a strong desire (for). 'craving n strong desire.

crawl v 1 move on hands and knees. 2 go very slowly. 3 be full of (—ing things). n 1 —ing movement or pace. 2 a way of swimming.

'crayon n stick or pencil of coloured chalk or charcoal.

'crazy adj (-ier, -iest) 1 mad. 2 distraught; excited: — with pain; —

about the films. 3 foolish: a — idea. craze v make —(1). n strong enthusiasm, esp for sth which is popular for a short time.

creak v & n (make a) sound like that of a dry or rusty door-hinge or of badly fitting floor-boards when trodden on. '—y adj making such sounds.

cream n 1 fatty or oily part of milk which rises to the surface and can be made into butter. 2 substance like — or containing —; the best part. 3 the colour of —. '—y adj (-ier, -iest).

crease n 1 line made (in cloth, etc) by folding, pressing or crushing. 2 (cricket) chalk line marking certain players' positions by the wicket. v make, get, —s(1) in.

cre'ate v cause (sth) to exist; make (sth new and original). cre'ation n act of creating; sth —d, esp the world or universe as —d by God. 'cre'ative adj of creation; able to —.

cre'ator n 1 (sb who is) full of ideas (esp artistic) for creating. 2 C—, God.

'creature n living being, esp an animal.

cre'dentials n pl letters or papers showing that a person is what he claims to be.

'credible adj that can be believed.

'credit n 1 belief; trust. 2 reputation. 3 honour coming to a person because of what he is or does. 4 person, thing, act, etc, that adds to the good name or reputation of the person(s), etc, responsible: Be a — to your school! 5 belief of others that a person can pay his debts or will keep a promise to pay. letter of —, letter from one bank to another authorizing a stated payment to the holder. 6 money shown as owned by a person in his bank account. 7 (book-keeping) record of money possessed by or due to (sb, etc) (opp debit). v 1 put trust in; believe. 2 enter on the —(7) side of an account. —able adj bringing —(2),(3). —or n person to whom one owes money.

'credulous adj (too) ready to believe things. cre'dulity n.

creed n (system of) beliefs or opinions.

creek n narrow inlet of water on

the seashore or a river bank; small river.

creep v (pt & pp crept) **1** move along with the body close to the ground or floor. **2** move slowly, quietly, or secretly. **3** (of plants) grow along a surface (eg a wall). **'—y** adj (-ier, -iest) causing a feeling as of being touched by a —ing thing.

cre'mate v burn (a dead body) to ashes. **cre'mation** n. **,crema-'torium** n place for cremating..

'crescent n curve of the moon as seen in the first or last quarter. ⇨ p 176. adj (of the moon) growing larger.

crest n **1** top of a slope or hill; white top edge of a wave. **2** tuft of feathers on top of a bird's head. ⇨ p 26. **3** design forming part of a coat of arms. v **1** get to the —(1) of. **2** have, decorate with, a —(2). **'crest-,fallen** adj looking disappointed (at failure, etc).

crew¹ n all the persons working a ship or aircraft.

crew² ⇨ crow.

'cricket¹ n small, brown, jumping insect that makes a shrill noise. ⇨ p 144.

'cricket² n ball game played on a grass field with a ball, bats and wickets by two teams of eleven players.

cried, crier ⇨ cry.

crime n **1** offence(s) for which there is severe punishment by law. **2** foolish or wrong act. **'criminal** adj of —; guilty of —. n criminal person.

'crimson adj & n deep red.

cringe v move (the body) back or down in fear; cower.

'cripple n person unable to walk properly through injury or disease in his backbone or legs. vt make a — of.

'crisis n (pl **'crises**) turning-point (in illness, life, etc); time of danger, of anxiety about the future.

crisp adj (-er, -est) **1** (esp of food) hard, dry, and easily broken. **2** (of the weather) dry and frosty. **3** (of style, manners) quick and decided. n thin fried slice of potato. **'—ly** adv. **'—ness** n.

cri'terion n (pl **cri'teria**) n standard of judgement or value.

'critic n **1** sb who judges and writes about literature, art, music, etc. **2** person who finds fault. **'criticism** n. **'criticize** v.

'critical adj **1** of or at a crisis. **2** of the work of a critic(1). **3** faultfinding. **—ly** adv.

croak n hoarse sound (as) made by frogs and ravens. v make this sound.

crock n pot or jar for containing liquids. **'—ery** n pots, plates, etc.

'crocodile n river reptile. ⇨ p 233.

crook n **1** stick with a rounded hook, esp as used by shepherds. **2** person who makes a living by dishonest means. v bend into the shape of a —. **'—ed** adj not straight or level; dishonest.

crop¹ n yearly (or season's) produce of grain, grass, fruit, etc; (pl) agricultural plants in the fields.

crop² v (-pp-) **1** (of animals) bite off the tops of (grass, plants, etc). **2** cut short (hair, a horse's tail or ears). **3 — up**, (eg of difficulties) appear or arise. **— up (out)**, (of rock, minerals) show above the earth's surface. n very short haircut; bag-like part of a bird's throat.

cross n **1** mark (+, ×, †, etc) made by drawing a line across

crosses

a crown

another. **2** offspring of two animals or plants of different sorts. **3** the C—, on which Jesus was crucified. adj **1** bad-tempered. **2** passing or lying across; (of winds) contrary. **at — purposes**, (of persons) talking of different things, having different purposes, without realizing it. v **1** pass from one side to the other of. **2 — a cheque**, draw two lines across it so that payment can be made only into a bank account. **— one's mind**, (of an idea) come into the mind. **3** obstruct (sb, his plans, wishes). **'cross-ex'amine** v question closely. **'cross-'question** v interrogate. **'cross-'reference** n reference from one part of a book to sth in another book or to another part of the same book. **'crossroads** *n sing* place where two roads —. **'—word (puzzle)** *n* square with spaces in which letters forming words are to be written across and downwards from numbered clues.

crouch *v* stoop with the limbs together, in fear, or to hide, or (of an animal) get ready to jump.

crow[1] *n* large black bird with a harsh cry. ⇨ p 26.

crow[2] *v* (*pt* crowed *or* crew, *pp* crowed) **1** (of a cock) cry; (of persons) express triumph (*over* sb). **2** (of a baby) make sounds showing happiness.

'crowbar *n* long iron bar or rod, useful in moving heavy objects.

crowd *n* large number of people together without order. *v* come together in a —; (cause to) fill a space: — *into a room.*

crown *n* **1** head-dress of gold, jewels, etc, worn on special occasions by a king or queen. **2** sign of royal power or of victory. **the C—**, royal authority. *v* put a —(1) on; reward with a —(2). ⇨ p 67.

'crucial *adj* critical(1).

'crucible *n* pot in which metals are melted.

'crucifix *n* small model of the Cross with the figure of Jesus on it. **'crucify** *v* put to death by nailing to a cross. **,cruci'fixion** *n* crucifying. **the Crucifixion,** that of Jesus.

crude *adj* (-r, -st) **1** (of materials) not refined or manufactured. **2** (of persons, their behaviour) rough; not polite. **3** of unskilled workmanship. **'—ly** *adv.* **'—ness** *n.* **'crudity** *n.*

'cruel *adj* causing pain; enjoying the suffering of others. **'—ly** *adv.* **'—ty** *n.*

'cruet *n* (stand with) container(s) for vinegar, salt, pepper, etc, for use at table.

cruise *v* sail about, either for pleasure or, in war, looking for enemy ships. *n* cruising voyage.

crumb *n* tiny broken-off bit of, eg, bread or cake. **—le** *v* break or rub into —s.

'crumple *v* press or crush into, become full of, folds or creases.

crunch *v* crush noisily.

cru'sade *n* **1** any one of the wars made by the Christian rulers and people of Europe during the Middle Ages to get the Holy Land back from the Muslims. **2** any struggle or movement in support of sth good or against sth bad. *v* take part in a —.

crush *v* press, be pressed, so that there is breaking or harming. **'—ing** *adj* overwhelming.

crust *n* hard outer part of bread; piece of this; hard surface or covering. **'—y** *adj* (-ier, iest) (of bread) having much — or a hard —.

crutch *n* support put under the arm to help a lame person to walk.

crux *n* part of a problem that is most difficult to solve.

cry *n* (*pl* cries) sound expressing a feeling of pain, fear, sadness, etc; loud or excited shout. *v* **1** make the sound of a cry. **2** shed tears (with or without sounds). **3** (often **cry out**) call out loudly in words. **in full cry,** (of dogs) barking together as they hunt an animal. **'crier** *n* (town crier) official making public announcements.

crypt *n* underground room of a church.

'cryptic *adj* with a hidden meaning.

'crystal *n* **1** clear, natural substance like quartz; piece of this cut as an ornament. **2** best quality glass-ware. **3** (science) one of the fragments, regularly and clearly defined in shape, into which certain minerals separate naturally: *salt —s.* **—line** *adj* of or like —. **—lize** *v* form into —s; (fig, of ideas, etc) (cause to) become clear.

cub *n* young lion, bear, fox, tiger.

cube *n* solid body having six equal sides. ⇨ p 68. **'cubic** *adj* of a —; *cubic foot,* volume of a — whose edge is 12 inches long.

'cubicle *n* small division of a larger room, esp for sleeping in.

'cuckoo *n* bird whose call sounds like its name.

'cucumber *n* (plant with) long, green-skinned, fleshy fruit. ⇨ p 306.

cud *n* food which oxen bring back from their first stomach and chew again.

'cuddle *v* hold close and lovingly in one's arms.

'cudgel *v & n* (-ll-) (beat with a) short thick stick.

cue *n* sth (eg the last sentence in an actor's speech) which shows when sb else is to do or say sth.

cuff[1] *n* bottom part of a sleeve.

cuff[2] *v & n* (give sb a) light blow with the hand.

'culminate *v* — **in**, (of efforts, career, etc) reach the highest point. **culmi'nation** *n*.

'culprit *n* person who has done wrong; offender.

cult *n* system of religious belief and worship.

'cultivate *v* 1 prepare (land) for crops by ploughing, etc; encourage the growth of (crops). 2 give care, thought, time, etc, in order to develop sth. —**d** *adj* (of a person) having good manners and éducation. **,culti'vation** *n*.
'cultivator *n* (esp) machine for breaking up ground.

'culture *n* 1 advanced development of the human powers; development of body, mind, and spirit by training and experience. 2 evidence of intellectual development in a particular nation. —**d** *adj* having — of the mind.

'culvert *n* channel(3) built to carry water across and under a road, etc.

'cumbersome, 'cumbrous *adj* heavy or awkward to move.

'cunning *n & adj* (quality of being) clever at deceiving.

cup *n* 1 small (usu china) bowl with a handle on the side for containing drinks. 2 (usu gold or silver) vessel given as a prize. **'cupful** *n* as much as a cup(1) will hold.

'cupboard *n* piece of furniture with doors and shelves, used for storing clothes, crockery, etc.

cur *n* bad-tempered or worthless dog.

'curate *n* clergyman who helps a rector or vicar. **'curacy** *n* —'s office and work.

cu'rator *n* official in charge, esp of a museum.

curb[1] *n* chain or strap under a horse's lower jaw, used to control it; sth that restrains. *v* control.

curb[2] ⇨ **kerb**.

curd *n* thick, soft substance formed when milk turns sour, used to make cheese. **'—le** *v* form —s.

cure *v* 1 bring back to health; make well again. 2 get rid of sth wrong or evil. 3 treat (meat, skins, etc) in order to keep in good condition. *n* curing or being —d; substance or treatment which —s. **'curable** *adj*.

'curfew *n* (old use) ringing of a bell as a signal for fires to be covered, lights put out; (modern use) time or signal for people to remain indoors (eg under martial law).

'curio *n* strange or unusual work of art valued because it is curious(3).

'curious *adj* 1 eager to learn and know. 2 having too much interest in the affairs of others. 3 strange; unusual. **—ly** *adv*. **,curi'osity** *n* 1 being —. 2 —(3) thing.

curl *n* sth shaped like the thread of a screw. *v* make into —s; be or grow in —s. **'—y** (-ier, -iest) *adj*: —**y** hair.

'currant *n* 1 small, sweet, dried grape. 2 (bush with) small juicy fruit growing in clusters.

'currency *n* being current(1); money in present use.

'current[1] *adj* 1 in common or general use. 2 of the present time: — events.

'current[2] *n* 1 stream of water, air, or gas, esp one flowing through slower-moving or still water, etc. 2 flow of electricity through sth or along a wire, etc. 3 course or movement (of events, thought, life).

cur'riculum *n* course of study in a school, college, etc.

'curry *n* dish of food (meat, eggs, etc) cooked with a hot-tasting spice (called curry-powder). *v* cook (food) with curry-powder.

curse *n* 1 words calling for the punishment, injury, or destruction of sb or sth; word(s) used in violent language. 2 cause of misfortune or ruin. *v* use a — against; use violent language. **be —d with**, suffer because of.

curt *adj* (of a speaker or what he says) hardly polite. **—ly** *adv*.

cur'tail *v* make shorter than was at first planned. **—ment** *n*.

'curtain *n* 1 piece of cloth or lace hung in front of a window or door. 2 sheet of heavy material to draw across the front of a stage before and after each act of a play.

'curtsey, 'curtsy *n* (*pl* **'curtseys, 'curtsies**) movement of respect (bending the knees) as made by women and girls presented to the queen. v make a —.

curve n line of which no part is straight, thus: ⌒. v have, cause to have, the form of a —.

'**cushion** n small bag filled with feathers, etc (to make a seat more comfortable).

'**custard** n soft mixture of eggs and milk (or cornflour, milk, etc) sweetened and flavoured, baked or boiled.

'**custody** n (duty of) keeping safe, caring for.

'**custom** n 1 generally accepted behaviour among members of a social group. 2 regular support given to a tradesman by those who buy his goods. 3 (pl) tax due to the government on certain goods imported into a country; import duties; department of government collecting such taxes. —ary adj according to — (1). —er n person buying things from a shopkeeper.

cut v (-tt-) (pt & pp cut) 1 divide or separate, make an opening (using a knife, scissors, etc). 2 cut sth down, make smaller in size or amount. cut sth or sb off, stop, separate, interrupt. cut sth out, remove by cutting, make or shape by cutting. be cut out for (work etc), be suited to; have the necessary qualities for. cut sth up, cut into pieces; destroy. 3 pass (a person) and pretend not to know (him): to cut sb in the street 4 stay away from (a class or lecture at school, etc). 5 cut a loss, accept it and make a fresh start. cut and dried, (of opinions, etc) all decided and ready. n 1 act of cutting. 2 sth obtained by cutting. 3 style in which clothes are made by cutting the cloth. 4 sharp, quick stroke. '**cutter** n 1 person or thing that cuts: wire-cutters. 2 warship's boat for rowing or sailing to and from a ship. '**cutting** n 1 way dug (for a canal, road, etc). 2 sth cut from a newspaper, etc. adj (of words, etc) hurting the feelings.

cute adj (-r, -st) sharp-witted; quick-thinking; (colloq) attractive.

'**cutlass** n sailor's short sword.

'**cutlery** n cutting instruments (eg knives and scissors); implements used at table.

'**cutlet** n thick slice of meat or

fish (to be) cooked for one person.

'**cycle** n 1 series of events taking place in a regularly repeated order; complete series. 2 (short for) bicycle. v ride a bicycle. '**cyclist** n person who —s.

'**cyclone** n violent wind moving round a calm central area.

'**cylinder** n 1 solid or hollow body shaped. ⇨ p 253. 2 cylinder-shaped chamber (in an engine) in which gas or steam works a piston. **cy'lindrical** adj.

'**cymbal** n one of a pair of round brass plates struck together to make loud ringing sounds.

'**cynic** n person who finds pleasure in sneering at human weaknesses. —al adj of or like a —. '**cynicism** n.

'**cypher** n = cipher.

D

dab v (-bb-) touch, put on, lightly and gently. n small quantity (of paint, powder, etc) dabbed on sth.

'**dabble** v splash (the hands, etc) in water. — in (art, etc), take some (not very serious) interest in.

'**dad(dy)** n (child's word for) father.

daft adj (colloq) stupid.

'**dagger** n short, pointed, two-edged knife used as a weapon.

'**daily** adj & adv occurring, appearing each day. n newspaper published each weekday.

'**dainty** adj (-ier, -iest) 1 delicate in appearance or to taste: — cups and saucers; — cakes. 2 (of a person) having delicate tastes; difficult to please. n choice and delicate food. '**daintily** adv.

'**dairy** n 1 building, part of a building, where milk is kept and butter made. 2 shop selling milk, eggs, butter, etc. '**dairy-maid** n girl or woman working in a farm —.

'**dais** n low platform for speakers.

'**daisy** n common wild flower.

dale n valley.

dally v 1 waste time. 2 — with, trifle with; think idly about.

dam[1] n wall built to keep back water. v make a — across; hold back with a —.

dam² *n* mother (of an animal).

'damage *n* 1 harm, injury, causing loss of value. 2 (*pl*) (law) money asked from or paid by a person causing loss or injury. *v* cause — to.

dame *n* 1 (old use) woman, esp a married woman. 2 (title of a) woman who has received an honour corresponding to that of knighthood.

damn *v* 1 (of God) condemn to everlasting punishment. 2 say that sth is worthless. *int* word used to express annoyance. **'—able** *adj* deserving to be —ed. **'—ably** *adv*. **dam'nation** *n* ruin; being —ed.

damp *adj* (-er, -est) not thoroughly dry; having some moisture in or on. *n* state of being —. *v* make —: — *down a fire*, cause it to burn slowly. **'—er** *n* (in a stove or furnace) metal plate which regulates the flow of air into the fire. **'—ness** *n*.

dance *v* & *n* (make a) particular pattern of movement to music. **'—r** *n*.

dancing

'dandy *n* person who pays great attention to his clothes and personal appearance.

'danger *n* risk of suffering, injury, death, anxiety, etc; sb or sth that may cause —. **—ous(ly)** *adj* & *adv*.

'dangle *v* hang or swing loosely; hang or carry (sth) so that it swings loosely.

dank *adj* (-er, -est) unpleasantly damp.

'dappled (*pp*) marked with patches of different colours or shades, esp of an animal, sunlight and shadow.

dare *v* 1 be brave or bold enough to: *I — say*, I agree, think it likely. 2 face the risks of. 3 challenge (sb to do sth). **'dare-,devil** *adj* & *n* foolishly bold (person). **'daring** *n* & *adj* (quality of being) bold and adventurous.

dark *adj* (-er, -est) & *n* (having) very little or no light. **keep sb in the —**, keep things secret from him. **be in the — about**, have no news or knowledge of. **'—en** *v* make or become —. **'—ly** *adv*. **'—ness** *n*.

'darling *n* & *adj* much loved person; (before a noun) delightful.

darn *v* mend (esp a hole in sth knitted, eg a sock) by passing thread in and out and across in two directions. *n* place mended by —ing.

dart *v* (cause to) move forward suddenly and quickly. *n* 1 quick, sudden movement. 2 small, sharp-pointed object, esp one thrown at a —board in the indoor game called —s.

dash *v* 1 send or throw violently; move, be moved, quickly and violently; (fig) destroy (hopes, etc). 2 splash (with water, mud, etc). *n* 1 sudden and violent forward movement. 2 sound made when water strikes or is struck (eg by oars). 3 small amount of sth added or mixed. 4 long mark — in writing or printing. ⇨ Morse.

'data *n pl* known facts (from which to draw conclusions): *computer —*.

date¹ *n* 1 statement of the day, month, and year. **out of —**, no longer used. **up to —**, using, having, the latest information, etc. 2 (colloq) arranged outing with a friend. *v* have, put, a — on; give a — to. **— from (back to)**, have existed since.

date² *n* small, sweet, brown fruit of the date-palm.

daub *v* 1 put (clay, plaster, etc) roughly on a surface. 2 make dirty marks on. 3 paint (pictures) without skill. *n* 1 material used for —ing(1) (eg clay). 2 badly painted picture.

'daughter *n* female child. **'daughter-in-law**, son's wife.

daunt *v* discourage. **'—less** *adj* persevering; not —ed.

'dawdle *v* be slow; waste time.

dawn *n* first light of day; (fig) beginning. *v* begin to grow light; (fig) begin to appear. **— on sb**, suddenly grow clear to his mind.

day *n* 1 period of 24 hours from midnight; time between sunrise and sunset. **pass the time of day**, chat, exchange greetings. **one day**, on a certain day (past or future). **some day,** some day in the future. **2** event; contest: *to win the day*. **'daybreak** *n* dawn. **'daydream** *v & n* (have) idle, pleasant thoughts.

daze *v* make (sb) feel stupid or unable to think clearly. *n* **in a —,** in a **—d** state.

'dazzle *v* make (sb) unable to see clearly or act naturally because of too much light, splendour, brilliance, etc.

'deacon *n* minister or officer with various duties in certain Christian churches. **—ess** *n*.

dead *adj* **1** no longer living; never having had life; not existing any longer; not responding. **2** without movement or activity. **3** thorough; complete: *in — earnest; to come to a — stop*. **4** used; not usable: *a — match; the telephone is —*. **5** exact. **— heat,** race, etc, in which two or more horses, etc, reach the winning-post together. **6 —letter,** (a) rule, law, etc, to which attention is no longer paid; (b) letter kept by the post office because the person to whom it is addressed cannot be found. **7 '—line,** fixed limit of time (eg before which sth must be done). *adv* completely: **— beat,** exhausted; **— level.** *n* **the — of night,** the darkest and quietest part. **'—en** *v* take away the force or feeling of. **'—ly** *adj* as of death. *adv* in a death-like manner.

'deadlock *n* complete failure to reach agreement.

deaf *adj* (-er, -est) unable to hear; unwilling to listen. **'—en** *v* make hearing difficult or impossible. **'—ness** *n*.

deal¹ *n* (board of) fir or pine wood.

deal² *n* **a good (great) —** (*of*), very much.

deal³ *v* (*pt & pp* dealt) **1** give out to a number of persons. **2** to do business; trade: *to — with a grocer* (*at a shop; in all sorts of goods*). **3 — with,** (a) be about; (b) manage; attend to: *to — with a problem*. *n* **1** the act of **—ing** playing-cards. **a square —,** fair treatment. **2** business agreement; (colloq) bargain. **'—er** *n* **1** trade. **2** person who **—s** playing-cards. **'—ings** *n pl* business relations.

dealt ⇨ **deal³.**

dean *n* **1** church officer in charge of a cathedral and its services. **2** head of a university department.

dear *adj* (-er, -est) **1** expensive. **2** much loved, lovable; polite form of address: *D— Sir (Miss Smith)*. *n*—(2) person. **'—ly** *adv* **1** at great cost. **2** very much. **'—ness** *n*.

dearth *n* scarcity (esp of food).

death *n* act or moment of dying; ending of life. **put to —,** kill. **'—less** *adj* never dying. **'—ly** *adj* like **—. 'death-rate** *n* average number of **—s** each year among every 1,000 persons.

de'bar *v* (-rr-) shut out (*from*); prevent by a regulation (*from* doing or having sth).

de'base *v* make lower in value, poorer in quality, etc. **—ment** *n*.

de'bate *n* discussion (esp at a public meeting, in Parliament, etc). *v* have, take part in, a **—** (*about*). **-r** *n*. **de'batable** *adj* that can be **—d;** open to question.

de'bauch *v* cause to lose virtue, to act immorally. **—ery** *n* evil living.

de'benture *n* certificate given by a business corporation as a receipt for money lent at a fixed rate of interest until the loan is repaid.

'debit *n* entry (in an account) of a sum owing; left-hand column of an account. *v* put on the **—** side of an account.

'débris *n* scattered broken pieces.

debt *n* payment that must be, but has not yet been, paid to sb. **in (out of) —,** owing (not owing) money. **'—or** *n* person in **—** to another.

'decade *n* period of ten years.

'decadent *adj* (of a person, nation, art, literature) becoming less worthy, moral, etc. **'decadence** *n*.

de'cay *v* go bad; lose health or power, etc. **—ing.**

de'ceased *adj* dead.

de'ceive *v* cause (sb) to believe sth false; play a trick on (sb) in order to mislead. **-r** *n*. **de'ceit** *n* instance of deceiving. **de'ceitful** *adj* intended to **—;** in the habit of deceiving. **de'ception** *n* deceiving or being **—d;** trick intended to **—. de'ceptive** *adj* deceiving; causing a person to be **—d.**

De'cember *n* last month of the year.

'decent *adj* **1** right and suitable: — *clothes*. **2** unlikely to cause other people to feel shame: — *behaviour*. **3** (colloq) satisfactory. **—ly** *adv.* **'decency** *n.*

de'ception, de'ceptive ⇨ **deceive.**

'deci- *prefix* one-tenth: *decimetre.*

de'cide *v* **1** think about and come to a conclusion(2). **2** give judgement, settle (a question, doubt, etc). **—d** *adj* definite; (of a person) having definite opinions, etc. **—dly** *adv.*

de'ciduous *adj* (of trees) losing their leaves regularly; not evergreen.

'decimal *adj* of tens or one-tenths: *the — system* (for money, weights, and measures); *the — point* (eg the point in 15·62).

de'cipher *v* find the meaning of (sth in cipher, in bad handwriting).

de'cision *n* **1** deciding; making up one's mind; what is decided. **2** ability to decide and act on what is decided.

de'cisive *adj* **1** resulting in a decision. **2** showing decision(2).

deck¹ *n* floor of a ship, usu of wood planks. **clear the —s,** make ready for a fight or (fig) any kind of activity.

deck² *v* = decorate.

de'claim *v* speak with strong feeling (*against*); speak as though addressing an audience. **,decla-'mation** *n.*

de'clare *v* **1** make known publicly and clearly; say solemnly, without doubt or hesitation. **2** make a statement (to customs officers) of dutiable goods brought into a country. **,decla'ration** *n.*

de'cline *v* **1** say 'no' to; refuse (sth offered, to do sth). **2** (of the sun) go down. **3** continue to become smaller, weaker, lower. *n* declining; gradual, continued, loss of strength.

,de'clutch *v* disconnect the engine (of a motor-car, etc) from the gears that drive the car-wheels.

,de'code *v* put in plain language (sth written in code).

,decom'pose *v* **1** separate (a substance) into its parts. **2** (cause to) become bad or rotten. **,decompo'sition** *n.*

'decorate *v* **1** put ornaments on; make more beautiful or gay: *streets —d with flags*. **2** paint (a building); put new paper, colouring material, etc, on (walls of rooms, etc). **3** give (sb) a mark of honour (eg a title or a medal). **,deco'ration** *n.* **'decorator** *n* (esp) workman who —s(2).

de'corum *n* right and proper behaviour, as required by good manners.

de'coy *n* (real or imitation) bird or animal used to attract others so that they may be caught; sb or sth used to attract others into a position of danger. *v* use a —.

de'crease *v* (cause to) become shorter, smaller, less. **'decrease** *n* decreasing; amount by which sth —s.

de'cree *n* order which has the force of a law. *v* make a —.

de'crepit *adj* made weak by old age. **—ude** *n.*

'dedicate *v* **1** give up (one's strength, life, etc *to* a special purpose). **2** devote with solemn ceremonies (*to* a sacred use). **3** (of an author) put sb's name at the beginning of a book (to show gratitude or friendship). **,dedi'cation** *n.*

de'duct *v* take away (an amount or part): *to — 5 per cent of his wages for insurance.* **—ion** *n.*

deed *n* **1** sth done; act. **2** (law) written and signed agreement, esp about ownership or rights.

deem *v* consider; believe.

deep *adj* (-er, -est) **1** going far down. **2** going far in from front to back: *a — shelf.* **3** (of colour) dark; strong. **4** (of sounds) low. **5** (of thoughts, etc) serious, concentrated. *n* **the —,** (poetry) the sea. **'—en** *v* make or become —(er). **—ly** *adv.*

deer *n* graceful, quick-running animal, the male of which has horns, called antlers. ⇨ p 317.

de'face *v* spoil the appearance of (by marking the surface); make (engraved lettering) unreadable.

de'fame *v* hurt the reputation of by saying evil things about.

de'fault *v* fail to perform a duty or to appear when required to do so, or to pay a debt. *n* act of —ing. **by —,** because the other person did not appear or act. **in — of,** in the absence of; if (sth) cannot be obtained. —er n (esp) soldier who fails to perform a duty.

de'feat v 1 overcome; win a victory over. 2 bring to nothing; make useless. n —ing or being —ed.

'defect n fault; imperfection; sth needed for completeness. de'fective adj having a — or —s.

de'fence n 1 defending from, fighting against, attack. 2 sth which defends. 3 (law) argument(s) used in favour of an accused person; lawyer(s) defending an accused person. —less adj without —.

de'fend v keep off attack (from); protect (against, from). —er n. —ant n person against whom a legal action is brought. de'fensible adj able to be —ed. de'fensive adj used for —ing. n on the defensive, ready to —; resisting, expecting, attack.

de'fer¹ v (-rr-) put off to a later time: —red telegram, one sent later at a cheaper rate. —ment n.

de'fer² v (-rr-) —to, yield, give way (to another's opinions, etc, often as a sign of respect). 'deference n —ring; respect. ,defe'rential adj showing great respect.

de'fiance, de'fiant ⇨ defy.

de'ficient adj wanting (in); not having enough of. de'ficiency n.

de'file v make unclean or impure. —ment n.

de'fine v 1 explain the meaning of (eg a word). 2 state or show clearly. 3 decide the shape, outlines or limits of. 'definite adj clear; not doubtful. ,defi'nition n 1 defining; statement that —s. 2 clearness of outline.

de'flate v opposite of inflate.

de'flect v (cause to) turn aside or change course (from).

de'form v spoil the shape or appearance of. —ed adj badly or unnaturally shaped. —ity n badly or wrongly shaped part of the body.

de'fraud v trick (sb) out of what is rightly his.

de'fray v supply money needed for sth; pay (expenses, costs).

'de'frost v remove frost (from a refrigerator, etc).

deft adj (-er, -est) quick and clever (esp in the use of the hands); (of work) showing such skill.

de'fy v 1 say that one is ready to oppose or fight. 2 refuse to obey or show respect to. 3 — sb to do sth, call on sb to do sth which one believes he cannot and will not do. de'fiance n —ing. de'fiant adj showing defiance.

de'generate v become less good than before. adj having —d. de,gene'ration n.

de'grade v 1 move (eg a soldier) down to a lower rank or position, usu as a punishment. 2 cause (sb) to be less moral or less deserving of respect. ,degra'dation n.

de'gree n 1 unit of measurement for angles, temperature, etc. 2 step or stage in a scale or process showing extent, quantity, or progress: a high — of excellence. by —s, step by step; gradually. 3 position in society: people of low —. 4 rank or grade given by a university: the — of M.A.

'de-ice v remove ice from (a windscreen, etc).

deign v be kind and gracious enough (to do sth).

'deity n 1 god(dess). the D—, God. 2 quality or nature of a god or God.

de'jected adj in low spirits; hopeless. de'jection n.

de'lay v 1 make or be slow or late. 2 put off until later. n —ing or being —ed.

'delegate v appoint and send as a representative to a meeting; entrust (duties, etc) (to sb). n person who is —d or to whom sth is —d. ,dele'gation n group of —s.

de'lete v strike or take out (sth written or printed). de'letion n.

de'liberate v think or talk about carefully. adj 1 done on purpose. 2 slow and cautious (in action, speech). —ly adv. de,libe'ration n.

'delicate adj 1 of fine or thin material; soft; easily injured; needing careful handling or treatment: — cups (plants); a delicate-looking child; a — surgical operation. 2 (of colours) soft; not strong. 3 (of the senses) able to appreciate very small differences; (of instruments) able to show or measure such differences. 4 (of food) not coarse in flavour; appealing to a —(3) sense of taste. 5 taking or showing care not to be immodest or to hurt the feelings of others. **'delicacy** n (esp) choice kind of food.

de'licious adj giving delight (esp to the senses of taste and smell and to the sense of humour).

de'light v give great pleasure to; find great pleasure (in). n (sth giving) great pleasure. **—ed** adj filled with, showing, —. **—ful** adj causing —; charming.

de'lirium n wild dreams and talking, esp during feverish illness. **de'lirious** adj suffering from —; wildly excited.

de'liver v 1 take (letters, goods, etc) to houses, to the person(s) to whom they are addressed. 2 save; set free (from danger, temptation, etc). 3 give or recite (a speech, sermon, etc). 4 be —ed of (a child), give birth to. **—y** n —ing or being —ed.

'delta n land at the mouth of a river which has two or more branches: the Nile Delta.

de'lude v deceive; mislead (on purpose). **de'lusion** n false idea or belief, esp as a form of madness.

'deluge n great flood; heavy rainfall. v send down on (sth or sb) like a —.

de'mand v 1 ask for (sth) as if ordering or with authority. 2 need. n 1 act of —ing(1); sth —ed(1). 2 desire (by people ready to pay) (for goods, services): goods in great —.

de'mean v — oneself, lower oneself in dignity.

de'meanour n behaviour; manner.

de'mented adj mad; wild with worry.

'demi- prefix half.

de'mist v wipe condensation from (a windscreen, etc).

de'mobilize v release after military service. **de,mobili'zation** n.

de'mocracy n (state¹(3) having) government freely elected by adult citizens.

'democrat n 1 sb supporting democracy. 2 D—, member of one of the main political parties in the USA. **,demo'cratic** adj of democracy, paying no attention to class divisions based on birth or wealth.

de'molish v pull down; destroy. **,demo'lition** n.

'demon n evil, wicked supernatural being or spirit.

'demonstrate v 1 show (by giving proofs, examples, etc). 2 make known (one's feelings, etc). **,demon'stration** n.

de'moralize v 1 hurt or weaken the morals of. 2 weaken the confidence, discipline or courage of (eg an army). **de,morali'zation** n.

de'mur v (-rr-) raise an objection to, protest or hesitate about, sth. n hesitation: without —.

de'mure adj quiet and serious; shy.

den n 1 animal's hiding-place (eg a cave). 2 secret place for ill-doers. 3 private room for study, etc.

de'nial n ⇨ deny.

de,nomi'nation n 1 name of a particular class or kind, esp a religious body. 2 class of units for measuring (length, weight, money).

de'note v 1 be the sign of. 2 stand as, be a name for.

de'nounce v 1 speak publicly against; betray. 2 give notice that one intends to end (a treaty, etc).

dense adj (-r, -st) 1 (of liquids, vapour) thick; not easily seen through: a — fog. 2 (of things and people) packed close together: a — forest (crowd). 3 (of a person) stupid. **'—ly** adv. **'density** n being —; (physics) relation of weight to volume.

dent n hollow in a hard surface made by a blow or pressure. v make a — in.

'dental adj of or for the teeth.

'dentist n sb responsible for the care of the teeth. **—ry** n work of a —.

de'nude v make bare; uncover; take away coverings, possessions: hillsides —d of trees.

de,nunci'ation n denouncing.

de'ny v say that (sth) is not true; say 'no' to a request; refuse to give. **de'nial** n —ing; refusal.

de'odorant n substance that removes (esp) bad smells from sb or sth.

de'part v leave; go or turn away (from). **—ure** n —ing.

de'partment n one of a number of branches or divisions of a government, business, university, large shopping centre, etc.

de'pend v — (up)on 1 need, rely

on (the support, etc, of), in order to exist, to be true, to succeed: *to — upon one's own earnings*; *Good health —s on good food, sleep, and exercise.* *that —s, it all —s.* *it —s on sth else*; other things have to be considered. **—able** *adj* that can be —ed(2) (up)on. **—ant,** *n* person who —s(1) upon another for a home, food, etc. **—ence** *n* the state of —ing(1), (2) on sb or sth. **—ency** *n* country governed by another country. *adj* —ing(1), (2). **—ent** *adj* —ing(1), (2). *n = —ant.*

de'pict *v* draw or paint; describe in words.

de'plete *v* use up, empty out, until little or nothing remains. **de'pletion** *n*.

de'plore *v* regret. **de'plorable** *adj* that is or should be —d.

de'populate *v* lessen the number of people living in (a country). **de'popu'lation** *n*.

de'port[1] *v* send (an unwanted person) out of the country. **,depor'tation** *n* —ing or being —ed.

de'port[2] *v* — oneself, behave. **—ment** *n* behaviour.

de'pose *v* remove (sb, esp a king) from his position of authority; dethrone.

de'posit *v* 1 put (money, valuables, etc) in sb's charge(5), in a bank, etc, for safe-keeping. 2 (esp of a liquid, a river) leave a layer of (sand, soil, etc). 3 make part payment of money in advance. *n* sth —ed.

'depot *n* storehouse; warehouse.

de'praved *adj* morally bad; (of tastes, habits) evil; corrupt. **de'pravity** *n* — state.

de'preciate *v* make or become less in value. **de,preci'ation** *n*.

de'press *v* 1 press, push, or pull down: *to — a lever.* 2 make sad. 3 make less active; cause (prices) to be lower. **—ion** *n* 1 being —ed(2). 2 hollow place in the surface of the ground. 3 time when trade is —ed(3).

de'prive *v* — (sb) of (sth), take away from; prevent from using or enjoying.

depth *n* 1 being deep. 2 measure from top to bottom or from front to back. **out of one's —,** in water deeper than one's own height;

(fig) considering sth beyond one's understanding.

de'pute *v* give (one's work, authority, etc) to a substitute; give (sb) authority (to do sth) as one's representative. **'deputy** *n* person to whom authority, etc, is —d. **,depu'tation** *n* party of representatives. **'deputize** *v* act as deputy (for).

de'rail *v* cause (a train, etc) to go off the rails. **—ment** *n*.

de'range *v* put into disorder: *mentally —d,* mad.

'derelict *adj* 1 (esp of a ship at sea) deserted (usu because dangerous). 2 made squalid by industrial activity, neglect, etc: *— areas, buildings.*

de'ride *v* laugh scornfully at; mock. **de'rision** *n*. **de'risive** *adj*.

de'rive *v* 1 get. 2 have as a starting-point or origin. **,deri'vation** *n* (esp) original form and meaning of a word. **de'rivative** *adj & n* (thing, word, etc) —d from another.

de'rogatory *adj* tending to hurt one's credit or reputation.

'derrick *n* machine like a crane(2) for lifting or moving heavy things, esp a ship's cargo.

des'cend *v* 1 come or go down. 2 (of property, etc) pass (from father to son) by inheritance. 3 — **upon,** attack suddenly. **—ant** *n* person —ed from the person(s) named. **des'cent** *n* 1 —ing. 2 downward slope. 3 ancestry.

des'cribe *v* say what sth or sb is like. **des'cription** *n* picture in words: *of any description,* of any kind; at all. **des'criptive** *adj*.

'desecrate *v* use (a sacred place or thing) in an unworthy or wicked way. **,dese'cration** *n*.

de'sert[1] *v* 1 leave without help or support, esp in a wrong, cruel way. 2 leave (esp service in the army, etc) without authority or permission. 3 (of courage, confidence, etc) fail. **—er** *n* person (esp a member of the forces) who —s(2). **—ion** *n* —ing or being —ed.

'desert[2] *n* large area of dry, waste land, esp sand-covered. *adj* barren; uninhabited.

de'sert[3] *n* (usu *pl*) what sb deserves, esp sth bad.

de'serve *v* be worthy of (reward,

etc) because of one's behaviour, qualities, etc. **de'serving** *adj* worthy (*of* help, etc). **—dly** *adv* justly; as —d.

de'sign *n* 1 drawing from which sth may be made. 2 general arrangement or plan (of a picture, machine, etc). 3 pattern: *—s on a bowl (carpet)*. 4 purpose; intention. *v* 1 make —s(1) for. 2 intend (for a purpose). **—er** *n* person who —s(1). **—ing** *adj* (esp) cunning.

'designate *v* 1 point out or mark (eg boundaries). 2 name or choose for a position or office. **,desig-'nation** *n*.

de'sire *n* strong wish (*for*); request; sth —d. *v* have a — for; request. **de'sirable** *adj* to be —d; causing —. **de,sira'bility** *n*. **de'sirous** *adj* feeling —.

desk *n* table at which one reads, writes or does business: *reception-desk*.

'desolate *adj* 1 (of a place) un-lived in or unfit to be lived in. 2 (of a person) lonely; neglected; wretched. *v* make —. **,deso'la-tion** *n* making or being —.

des'pair *v & n* (be in) the state of having lost all hope. **—ing** *adj* feeling or showing —.

des'patch ⇨ dispatch.

'desperate *adj* 1 (of a person) filled with despair; lawless; violent. 2 (of illness, etc) extremely serious. **,despe'ration** *n*.

des'pise *v* feel contempt for. **'despicable** *adj* deserving to be —d.

des'pite *n* in spite of.

des'pondent *adj* having or show-ing loss of hope. **des'pondency** *n* low spirits.

'despot *n* ruler using unlimited powers cruelly, wrongly. **des-'potic** *adj*. **—ism** *n* (State with a) despotic government.

des'sert *n* course of fresh fruit, etc, at the end of dinner.

,desti'nation *n* place to which sb or sth is going or being sent.

'destined *pp* intended, designed (by God, fate, or a person) to be or do sth, or *for* sth. **'destiny** *n* power believed to control events; that which happens to sb, thought of as determined in advance.

'destitute *adj* 1 without food, clothes, and other things necessary

for life. 2 — *of*, lacking; without: *— of sympathy*. **,desti'tution** *n*.

des'troy *v* break to pieces; put an end to. **—er** *n* (esp) small fast war-ship. **des'truction** *n*. **des'truc-tive** *adj* causing destruction; fond of, in the habit of, —ing.

de'tach *v* 1 unfasten and take away (*from*). 2 send (a party of men be-longing to the armed forces) away from the main body. **—ed** *adj* (of the mind, etc) not influenced by others; (of a house) not joined to another on either side. **—able** *adj*. **—ment** *n* —ing or being —ed; —ed group of armed forces.

'detail *n* small point or item. **in —**, with all —s. **go into —s**, give or ex-amine all the —s. **de'tail** *v* 1 give —s of; describe fully. 2 give orders to (eg soldiers) to do certain work.

de'tain *v* keep waiting; prevent from leaving. **de'tention** *n*.

de'tect *v* discover (the presence or existence of sb or sth, the identity of sb guilty of wrongdoing). **—ion** *n*. **—ive** *n* person whose business is to — criminals.

de'ter *v* (-rr-) discourage, hinder (sb *from* doing sth). **de'terrent** *n & adj* (sth) tending to — or dis-courage.

de'tergent *n* substance used for loosening dirt when washing clothes.

de'teriorate *v* make or become worse, of less value. **de,terio-'ration** *n*.

de'termine *v* 1 be the fact that decides (sth). 2 decide (sb's future); make up one's mind. 3 cause to decide. 4 find out exactly. **—d** *adj* of fixed purpose; strong-willed. **de,termi'nation** *n* sth —d; firmness of purpose.

de'test *v* hate. **—able** *adj* deserv-ing to be hated.

de'throne *v* remove (a king) from the throne. **—ment** *n*.

'detonate *v* (cause to) explode.

de'tour *n* roundabout way; turn-ing aside.

de'tract *v* take away (credit or value) (*from*). **—ion** *n*. **—or** *n*.

'detriment *n* harm (to health).

'devastate *v* ruin; make desolate. **,devas'tation** *n*.

de'velop *v* 1 (cause to) grow larger, fuller, or complete; (cause to) un-fold. 2 (cause to) appear, become clearly defined, take a more definite shape. **3** make a picture appear on a photographic film. **—ment** *n* **—ing** or being **—ed**; growth; sth which shows itself as the result of earlier conditions, etc: *the latest —ments in foreign affairs.*

'**deviate** *v* turn away (*from* what is right or usual). ,**devi'ation** *n*.

de'**vice** *n* **1** plan; scheme; trick. **leave sb to his own —s**, leave him without help or advice. **2** sth invented for a special purpose.

'**devil** *n* the spirit of evil; cruel or wicked person or spirit.

'**devious** *adj* roundabout; not straightforward.

de'**vise** *v* invent; plan; design.

de'**void** *adj* **— of**, empty of; without; lacking.

de'**volve** *v* **— upon**, (of work, duties) be passed on to (sb else).

de'**vote** *v* give up (one's time, energy, etc) (*to* sb or sth). **—d** *adj* loving; loyal. de'**votion** *n* strong, deep love or loyalty; (*pl*) prayers.

de'**vour** *v* eat (fig, look at, hear) hungrily and anxiously. **be —ed by**, have the whole of one's attention taken up with (curiosity, anxiety, etc).

de'**vout** *adj* paying serious attention to religious duties; (of prayers, wishes, etc) deep-felt; earnest.

dew *n* tiny drops of water formed overnight on cool surfaces (eg leaves, petals, etc).

dex'**terity** *n* neatness and cleverness, esp in the use of the hands. '**dexterous** *adj* having, showing, such skill.

dhow *n* single-masted ship, as used by Arab sailors.

dia'**bolic(al)** *adj* very wicked.

'**diagnose** *v* determine(4) the nature of (esp disease). ,**diag-'nosis** *n* (*pl* ,diag'noses) diagnosing; statement about this.

di'**agonal** *n & adj* (straight line) across a straight-sided figure (eg an oblong) from corner to corner. **—ly** *adv* across and from corner to corner; at a slant.

'**diagram** *n* drawing, design, or plan to explain or illustrate sth.

'**dial** *n* **1** face (of a clock); marked face or flat plate with a pointer for measuring (weight, pressure, etc). **2** part of an automatic telephone used when calling a number. *v* (-ll-) call by means of a telephone **—**.

'**dialect** *n* form of spoken language, way of speaking, used in a part of a country or by a class of people: *a Scottish* **—**.

'**dialogue** *n* conversation between two persons.

di'**ameter** *n* (length of a) straight line passing from side to side and through the centre of a geometrical figure, esp a circle; width or thickness.

'**diamond** *n* **1** brilliant precious stone or jewel, the hardest substance known. **2** figure with four equal sides and angles which are not right angles; this figure printed in red on some playing-cards: ♦.

,**diar'rhoea** *n* too frequent emptying of the bowels.

'**diary** *n* daily record of events, thoughts; book for this.

dice *n pl* small cubes of wood, bone, etc, marked with spots (1 to 6), used in games of chance. *v* **1** play with **—**. **2** cut into small cubes (esp vegetables).

dic'**tate** *v* **1** say (words, etc) for another person to write down. **2** give authoritative orders to: *to* **—** *(terms) to a defeated enemy.* dic'**tation** *n* dictating(1); sth **—d**(1). dic'**tator** *n* ruler with absolute power, esp when power has been obtained by force or in an irregular way. ,**dicta'torial** *adj* in the manner of a dictator.

'**diction** *n* choice and use of words; style or manner of speaking.

'**dictionary** *n* book dealing with the words of a language or with parts of a special subject (eg the Bible) and arranged in ABC order.

did ⇨ **do**.

die[1] *v* come to the end of life; cease to exist. **be dying** (*for* sth, *to do* sth), have a strong wish.

die[2] *n* metal block for shaping coins, medals, etc, or for stamping (words, designs, etc) on paper, etc:

'**diesel 'engine** *n* one burning heavy oil (not petrol).

a diagonal

diamonds

'diet n sort of food a person usually eats or to which he is limited (eg by a doctor). v be on, put sb on, a —.

'differ v 1 be unlike. 2 disagree with. —**ent** (*from, to*) adj unlike; various. —**ence** n 1 that which makes sb or sth unlike. 2 quarrel.

'difficult adj 1 (of problems) requiring much thought, skill, etc. 2 (of people) unco-operative; hard to please. —**y** n 1 hard problem; sth that is —(1). 2 obstacle to getting sth done, solved, etc.

'diffident adj not having, not showing, much belief in one's abilities, judgement, etc. **'diffidence** n.

dif'fuse v spread in every direction. adj spread about; using too many words. **dif'fusion** n.

dig v (-gg-) (*pt & pp* dug) 1 make a hole in; excavate. 2 use a spade to break up earth. **digs, diggings** n pl (colloq) lodgings.

di'gest v 1 (of food) change, be changed, in the stomach and bowels so that it can be used in the body. 2 (fig) take into the mind. **'digest** n short, condensed account (of news, etc). —**ible** adj that can be —ed. —**ion** n person's power to — food. —**ive** adj of —ion.

'digit n any one of the figures o to 9; finger or toe.

'dignify v give dignity to.

'dignity n 1 true worth; quality that wins or deserves respect. 2 calm and serious behaviour: *to lose one's* —. 3 high rank or position. **'dignitary** n person holding a high position (eg a bishop).

di'gress v (in speaking or writing) turn aside from the main subject. —**ion** n.

dike, dyke n ditch for carrying away water from land; wall (of earth keeping back water).

di'lapidated adj in an unrepaired state. **di,lapi'dation** n.

di'late v 1 (cause to) become further open: *—d eyes (nostrils)*. 2 —**upon**, speak or write at great length about.

'dilatory adj slow; causing delay.

di'lemma n situation in which one has to choose between two things, courses of action, etc, both undesirable.

'diligent adj hard-working; showing care and effort. **'diligence** n.

'dilly-dally v waste time by not making up one's mind.

di'lute v make (a liquid or colour) weaker or thinner (by adding water or other liquid). **di'lution** n.

dim adj ('dimmer, 'dimmest) not bright; not clearly seen; (of the eyes) unable to see clearly. v(-mm-) make or become dim. **'dimly** adj. **'dimness** n.

di'mension n measurement (of length, area, etc); (*pl*) size.

di'minish v make or become less.

'dimple n small hollow in the chin or cheek (eg one which appears when sb smiles).

din n long, confused noise. v (-nn-) make a din. **din sth into sb**, get it into his head by loud repetition.

dine v have dinner. **'dining-room** n room in which meals are eaten.

'dinghy n small open boat.

'dingy adj (-ier, -iest) dirty-looking.

'dinner n main meal of the day.

dint n **by — of**, by force of; by means of.

'diocese n district under the care of a bishop.

dip v (-pp-) 1 put, lower, sth *into* a liquid and take it out again: *to dip a pen into the ink*. 2 put (one's hand, a bucket, etc, *into* sth) and take out (liquid, grain, etc); get (liquid, etc) in this way. 3 go below a surface or level; (of land) slope downwards. 4 (cause to) go down and then up again. 5 **dip into** (*a book*, etc), look into; study, but not thoroughly. n dipping or being dipped; liquid in which sheep are dipped; downward slope (eg in a road).

'diphthong n union of two vowel sounds in one compound sound, eg as in *pipe*.

di'ploma n educational certificate.

di'plomacy n (skill in) management of international relations; skill in dealing with people so that business is done smoothly. **'diplomat** n person engaged in — for his government; person clever in dealing with people. **,diplo'matic** adj of —; tactful.

di'rect adj & adv 1 (going) straight; not turned aside; not curved or crooked. 2 straightforward; going straight to the point. 3 in an unbroken line. 4 — **action**, use (by workers) of strike action to get their demands. — **current**, electric current flowing continuously ($\triangleright$ alternating). — **speech**, the actual words of a speaker. *v* 1 tell or show (sb) how to do sth, get somewhere. 2 manage; control. 3 address (a letter, etc); speak or write (remarks, etc, *to* sb). 4 guide, turn (the eyes, one's attention) straight to sb or sth. —**ion** *n* 1 course taken by a moving person or thing; point towards which a person looks, moves, etc. 2 (often *pl*) information about what to do, where to go, how to do sth; command. 3 (usu *pl*) address (on a letter, parcel, etc). 4 act of —ing or managing. —**ly** *adv* 1 in a — manner. 2 at once; now. 3 (colloq, as *conj*) as soon as. —**ness** *n*. —**or** *n* person who —s(2), esp one of a group —ing the affairs of a business company. —**ory** *n* list of names (and usu addresses) in ABC order: *a telephone —ory*.

dirt *n* unclean matter (eg *dust*, *mud*) esp where it is not wanted. '—**y** *adj* (-ier, -iest) 1 covered with —. 2 (of weather) rainy, stormy. 3 unclean in thought or speech. '—**ily** *adv*.

dis- *prefix* indicating the opposite of. ,disad'vantage, ,disap'prove, ,disbe'lieve ,discon'tent, ,discon'tinue, disem'bark, dis'honest, dis'like, dis'loyal, ,diso'bey, dis'please, dis'prove, dis'satisfy, dis-'similar, dis'trust(ful).

di'sable *v* make unable to do sth, esp take away the power of using the limbs: —*d soldiers*. ,disa'bility *n* lack of ability; sth that —s or disqualifies.

,disa'buse *v* free from false ideas.

,disaf'fected *adj* discontented; disloyal; unfriendly.

,disa'gree *v* 1 take a different view; not agree (*with*). 2 — with, (of food, climate, etc) be unsuited to; have bad effects on. —**able** *adj* unpleasant; bad-tempered.

,disap'pear *v* go out of sight; be seen no more. —**ance** *n*.

,disap'point *v* fail to do or be equal to what is hoped or expected. —**ed** *adj* sad at not getting what was hoped for, etc. —**ment** *n* being —ed; person or thing that —s.

dis'arm *v* 1 take away weapons, etc, from. 2 (of a country) reduce, give up the use of, armed forces. 3 make it difficult for sb to feel anger, etc. —**ament** *n* —ing(2) or being —ed(2).

di'saster *n* great misfortune. **di'sastrous** *adj* causing —.

dis'band *v* (of a force of soldiers, etc) break up (as an organized body).

disc (= **disk**) *n* thin, flat round plate (eg gramophone record, coin); an apparently round, flat surface. '**disc-,jockey** *n* sb who plays popular music (on the radio or TV).

dis'card *v* throw or put out or away (sth unwanted).

dis'cern *v* see with an effort (of the eyes or mind). —**ment** *n*.

dis'charge *v* 1 unload (cargo). 2 fire (a gun); shoot (an arrow, etc). 3 give or send out (a liquid, gas, current). 4 send away (from prison, employment, etc). 5 pay (a debt); perform (a duty). *n* discharging or being —d; sth which is —d.

dis'ciple *n* follower of a leader of religious thought, art, learning, etc; one of the twelve personal followers of Jesus Christ.

'**discipline** *n* 1 training of mind and character. 2 self-control; orderly behaviour. *v* apply — to.

dis'close *v* allow to be seen or known. **dis'closure** *n* disclosing; sth —d.

dis'colour *v* spoil the colour of; become spoilt in colour.

dis'comfort *n* absence of comfort; hardship.

,**discon'cert** *v* upset (sb's plans, etc); upset the calmness of.

dis'consolate *adj* unhappy; without hope.

'**discord** *n* disagreement; sound that jars¹(2). **dis'cordant** *adj* not in agreement; unpleasing to the ear.

'**discount** *n* amount which may be taken off the full price of sth to be paid for.

dis'courage *v* lessen the courage or confidence of; try to persuade (sb not to do sth).

'**discourse** *n* speech, sermon, etc.

dis'course v write or speak at length (*on*).

dis'cover v find out, bring to view (sth already existing but not known). **—er** n. **—y** n sth —ed.

dis'credit v cause the value or credit of sb or sth to seem doubtful. n loss of credit; person or thing causing such loss. **—able** adj bringing —.

dis'creet adj careful, tactful, in what one says or does; prudent. **dis'cretion** n 1 being —. 2 freedom to use one's own judgement in doing things.

dis'crepancy n (of statements, accounts) failure to agree; difference.

dis'criminate v see, make, a difference between; make distinctions; treat differently. **dis,crimi'na-tion** n.

'discus n disc, thicker in the centre than at the edge, thrown as a sport.

dis'cuss v examine and talk about (a problem, etc). **—ion** n.

dis'dain v & n (look at with) scorn. **—ful(ly)** adj & adv.

di'sease n illness of the body or mind, of a plant, etc.

dis'figure v spoil the appearance or shape of. **—ment** n.

dis'grace n 1 loss of respect or favour; fall from high position; public shame. 2 person or thing causing —. v bring — upon; be a — to; remove (sb) from his position with —. **—ful** adj.

dis'guise v change the appearance of, in order to deceive. n disguising; being —d; that which is used in order to —.

dis'gust n strong feeling of distaste. v cause — in.

dish n plate, bowl, etc, from which food is served at table; food served from a —: *a tasty dish.*

dis'honour n 1 disgrace; loss or absence of honour. 2 person or thing bringing —. v cause — to, bring — on. **—able** adj.

disil'lusion v set free from mistaken beliefs. **—(ment)** n.

disin'clined pp unready, unwilling (to do sth). **,disincli'nation** n.

disin'fect v make free from infection by disease germs. **—ant** adj & n —ing (substance).

disin'herit v take away (sb's) right to inherit. **—ance** n.

dis'integrate v (cause to) break up. **dis,inte'gration** n.

dis'interested adj not influenced by personal feelings or interests.

dis'jointed adj not connected.

disk ⊳ disc.

'dislocate v put (eg a bone) out of position; put (eg traffic) out of order. **,dislo'cation** n.

dis'lodge v force out of place.

'dismal adj gloomy; miserable.

dis'mantle v take away fittings, etc, from (eg a warship); take to pieces (eg machines).

dis'may n feeling of fear and discouragement. v fill with —.

dis'miss v send away (esp from one's employment); put away (from the mind). **—al** n.

dis'mount v (esp) get down from a horse.

dis'order n 1 absence of order; confusion. 2 political trouble marked by angry outbursts. 3 disease; disturbance of the body's normal working. v put into —. **—ly** adj in —; lawless.

dis'organize v upset the order or system of. **dis,organi'zation** n.

dis'own v say that one does not know, does not wish to have any connection with, (sb or sth).

dis'parage v suggest that (sb or sth) is of small value or importance. **—ment** n.

dis'patch, des- v 1 send off (to a destination, on a journey, for a special purpose). 2 finish (business, a meal, etc) quickly. n 1 —ing or being —ed. 2 sth —ed, esp a message or report. 3 speed; promptness.

dis'pel v (-ll-) drive away; scatter (*clouds, doubts, fears*).

dis'pense v 1 — with, do without. 2 distribute; administer. 3 mix, prepare, and give out (medicine). **—r** n person who —s(3). **dis-'pensary** n place where medicine is —d(3). **,dispen'sation** n 1 sth looked upon as ordered by God. 2 permission to disregard a rule or requirement.

dis'perse v (cause to) go in different directions. **dis'persal** n.

dis'place v put out of the right or usual place; take, put sb or sth, in the place of. **—ment** n (esp) amount of water —d by a solid body in it, or floating in it.

dis'play v show; allow to be seen. n —ing; sth —ed.

dis'pose v 1 — of, deal with; finish with; get (sth or sb) out of the way. 2 arrange (persons, objects) in good order. 3 be (feel) —d, be willing or ready (*for* sth, *to do* sth); **well-disposed**(*towards*) friendly; favourable. **dis'posal** n the act of disposing(1), (2). **at one's disposal**, to be used as one wishes. **,dispo'sition** n 1 arrangement. 2 natural qualities of mind and character: *a dog with a nasty disposition.*

,dispos'sess v — sb of sth, take away property (esp land) from; compel to give up a house, etc.

dis'pute v 1 argue, quarrel (*with* sb, *about* or *on* sth); question the truth or justice of sth. 2 oppose. n disputing. **beyond —**, undoubted(ly).

dis'qualify v make unfit or unable (*to do* sth, pass a test, etc).

dis'quiet v make troubled in mind. n troubled condition of mind.

disre'gard v pay no attention to. n indifference; inattention.

disre'pair n state of needing repair.

dis'reputable adj having a bad reputation; not respectable.

dis'rupt v break up; separate by force (a state, communications, etc). **—ion** n. **—ive** adj.

dis'sect v cut up (parts of an animal, plant, etc) in order to study its structure. **—ion** n.

dis'semble v hide one's real feelings, thoughts, etc, or give a wrong idea of them.

dis'sent v — from, refuse to agree with or to assent to. **dis'sension** n quarrelling; disagreement.

'dissipate v 1 drive away (fear, ignorance, clouds); disperse. 2 waste (time, energy). **—d** adj given to foolish and often harmful pleasures. **,dissi'pation** n.

,disso'lution n ending (of a marriage, partnership, and esp of Parliament before a general election).

dis'solve v 1 (of liquid) soak into a solid so that the solid itself becomes liquid: *water —s salt.* 2 (of a solid) become liquid as the result of being taken into a liquid: *salt —s in water.* 3 cause (a solid) to —. 4 end (a marriage; Parliamentary session, etc).

dis'suade v (try to) turn (sb) away (*from* sth, *from* doing sth).

'distance n 1 measure of space between two objects, places, etc. **in the —**, a long way off. 2 period of time: *at this — of time.* **'distant** adj far away.

dis'taste n dislike. **—ful** adj causing —; disagreeable.

dis'temper n colouring matter (to be) mixed with water and brushed on ceilings and walls. v colour with —.

dis'tend v (cause to) swell out.

dis'til v (**-ll-**) turn (a liquid) to vapour by heating, cool the vapour and collect the drops that condense; purify (a liquid) thus; get the essence (of a liquid or substance) thus; make whisky, etc, thus. **—lery** n place where —ing (esp of whisky, gin, etc) is carried on. **,distil'lation** n —ling or being —led.

dis'tinct adj 1 easily heard, seen, understood; clearly marked. 2 different in kind; separate. **—ly** adv. **—ive** adj serving to mark a difference.

dis'tinction n 1 being, keeping things, different or distinct; distinguishing; being distinguished as different. 2 that which makes one thing different from another. 3 quality of being unusual, superior. 4 mark of honour or reward.

dis'tinguish v 1 see, hear, understand well, the difference (*between*). 2 be a mark of difference, of identity or character. 3 make (oneself) well known; bring distinction(3) on (oneself). **—ed** adj showing, having won, distinction(3).

dis'tort v pull, twist, out of the usual shape; give a wrong idea of (facts, etc). **—ion** n.

dis'tract v draw away (a person's thoughts, attention, etc, *from* sth). **—ed** adj with the attention drawn in different directions; confused. **—ion** n —ing or being —ed; sth that —s.

dis'traught adj distracted; violently upset in mind.

dis'tress n 1 (cause of) great pain, sorrow, discomfort, danger; (suffering caused by) want of money or other necessary things. 2 serious danger or difficulty. v cause — to.

dis'tribute v 1 give or send out (to or among, persons or places). 2 spread out (over a large area). ,distri'bution n. dis'tributive adj.

'district n part of a country or town, esp one marked out for a special purpose.

dis'trust v & n (have) doubt or suspicion (about).

dis'turb v break the quiet or order of; put out of the right or usual position. —ance n (esp) social or political disorder.

dis'use n state of being no longer used. —d adj no longer used.

ditch n narrow channel dug in or between fields to hold or carry off water.

'ditto, (abbr do.) n the same.

di'van n long, low, soft backless seat, also used as a bed.

dive v 1 go head first into water. 'diving-board, platform for diving from. 2 go quickly to a lower level. n act of diving. '—r n (esp) person who works under water in a special dress (a diving-suit).

di'verge v (of lines, paths, opinions, etc) get farther apart from each other or from a point as they progress; turn aside (from). —nt adj.

di'verse adj of different quality, character, etc. di'versify v make —; give variety to. di'versity n variety; difference.

di'vert v turn in another direction; amuse. di'version n turning aside from a route, duty, etc; (esp) sth giving rest or amusement. —ing adj amusing.

di'vest v — sb of (sth), take off or away from. — oneself of, give up; get rid of.

di'vide v 1 separate into parts; take sides in a debate. 2 find out how many times one number is contained in another: $4 \div 2 = 2$.

di'visible adj that can be —d.

di'vision n 1 act of dividing; line that —s. division-sign, the sign $\div$ in arithmetic. 2 (army) unit of two or more brigades. 3 (after a debate, esp in Parliament) vote.

'dividend n 1 number to be divided by another. 2 periodical payment of interest (5) to shareholders.

di'vine¹ adj 1 of, from, or like God. D— Service, public worship of God. 2 (colloq) excellent; beautiful. n priest trained in theology.

di'vinity n 1 quality of being —. 2 (study of) theology.

di'vine² v guess: to — a person's thoughts. ,divi'nation n.

di'visible, di'vision ▷ divide.

di'vorce n 1 legal ending of a marriage. 2 ending of a connection or relationship. v put an end to a marriage by law; separate (non-physical things).

di'vulge v make known (sth secret).

'dizzy adj (-ier, -est) (of a person) feeling as if everything were turning round; giddy; (of a place, etc) causing such a feeling. 'dizzily adv. 'dizziness n.

do¹ v (do, does), pt did, pp done) 1 (used to make neg & interr): (I want) I do not want. Do I want? (Go!) Do not go! or Don't go! 2 perform, carry out an action: He does his homework regularly. 3 be suitable or satisfactory (for); serve (for). 4 have dealings (with): have nothing to do with him. 5 deal with, solve (a problem, etc). 6 cook: meat that is well done (underdone). 7 (colloq) cheat; get the better of. do sb out of sth, get it from him by trickery. 8 (colloq) ruin; spoil. done for, ruined; made worthless. 9 done up, tired out. do sth up, (a) clean; make like new. (b) tie up into a parcel. (c) fasten up (clothing, etc). can (could) do with, (a) be ready for; welcome. (b) need. do without, manage without. do away with, put an end to. do for (sb), (a) be housekeeper to. (b) (colloq) kill or injure.

do.² ▷ ditto.

'docile adj easily trained or controlled. do'cility n.

dock¹ n 1 place in a harbour where ships are (un)loaded or repaired. dry —, one from which water may be pumped out. 2 (pl; also '—yard), row of —s with wharves, sheds, etc. v (of ships) come, go, bring into a —. '—er n.

dock² n place for the prisoner in a criminal court.

'doctor n 1 person trained in medical science. 2 person who has received the highest university degree. v 1 (colloq) give medical treatment. 2 make (esp food and drink) inferior by adding sth.

'doctrine n beliefs and teachings (of a church, political party, etc).

'document n sth written or printed, to be used as a record or in evidence. **,docu'mentary** adj.

dodge v move quickly to one side, change position or direction, in order to escape or avoid sth. n act of dodging.

does (doesn't = does not) ⇨ do¹.

dog n domestic animal that barks. ⇨ below. **lead a dog's life**, have many misfortunes. v (-gg-) keep close behind; follow in the footsteps of.

'dogged adj obstinate.

'dogma n belief(s) put forward by an authority (esp the Church) to be accepted without question. **dog'matic** adj (of a person) putting forward his own opinions as if they were.—s.

dole v — **out**, give out (food, money, etc) in small amounts (eg to poor people). n sth —d out.

'doleful adj sad. **'—ly** adv.

doll n model of a baby or a child, usu for a child to play with.

dollar n ($) unit of decimal currency in some countries (USA, Australia, etc).

'dolphin n sea animal like a porpoise. ⇨ p 247

do'main n **1** lands ruled by a king, etc. **2** province (of thought, knowledge, etc).

dome n rounded roof with a circular base.

do'mestic adj **1** of the home, family, household. **2** of one's own country. **3** (of animals) kept by, living with, man (cf wild). **do'mesticate** v (of animals) tame.

some domestic animals

'dominate v have control or authority over; (of a place) overlook. 'dominant adj dominating; commanding. ,domi'nation n dominating or being —d. ,domi-'neer v act, speak, in a dominating manner.

do'minion n 1 authority to rule. 2 (often pl) territory of a sovereign government; used formerly to describe certain self-governing territories of the British Commonwealth of Nations.

don n university teacher.

do'nate v give (to charity, etc). do'nation n giving; sth given.

done ⇨ do¹.

'donkey n animal like a small horse with coarse(2) hair. ⇨ p. 84. 'donkey-work, most physically tiring part of a job.

'donor n sb who gives sth: a blood —.

don't = do not. ⇨ do¹.

doom n ruin; death; sth evil that is to come. '—ed pp condemned (to sth); facing certain death.

door n that which closes the entrance to a room, building, etc. next —, the next house. out of —s, outside. '—way n opening in a wall that a — fits into. '—step n step in front of an outside —.

'dormant adj inactive and awaiting development or activity, like certain plants in winter: a — volcano.

'dormitory n sleeping-room with several or many beds (eg in a boarding school).

dose n amount (of medicine) to be taken at one time.

dot n small, round pen-mark (as over the letter i). ⇨ Morse. v (-tt-) mark with a —; make of —s: a —ted line. dotted about, scattered here and there. 'dotty adj (-ier, -iest) (colloq) silly.

dote v — on (sb or sth), show much, or too much, fondness for.

'double adj 1 twice as much (large, wide, etc): a — share; — width. 2 being, having, two like things or parts: — doors; a knife with a — edge. 3 intended for two persons or things: a — bed (room). 4 (of flowers) having more than one set or circle of petals. adv 1 twice (as much): to pay —. 2 in twos. n 1 — quantity. 2 person or thing exactly like another. 3 at the —, at a slow run. 4 sharp turn or

twist back. v 1 make or become —. 2 bend or fold in two. — back, turn back quickly. — up, fold up; (of a person) bend the body in pain. 'double-'bass n ⇨ bass¹. 'double-cross v deceive. 'double-'dealer n person who deceives (esp in business).

doubt n (feeling of) uncertainty, in —, uncertain. without (a) —, certainly. no —, very probably. v feel — about. '—ful adj feeling, full of, causing, —. '—fully adv. '—less adv.

dough n mixture of flour, water, etc, in a paste (for making bread).

dove n kind of pigeon; symbol of peace. '—tail v join pieces of wood together with the joint shaped like a —'s tail.

down¹ adv 1 (indicating motion) from a high(er) to a low(er) level. 2 (indicating motion) from a vertical to a horizontal position: Go and lie —. 3 (indicating a reduction to a smaller volume, quantity, etc): My savings are —. The water-level is —. 4 (used with reference to writing): Write it —. 5 (indicating a lowering of spirits): He's feeling —. prep 1 from a high(er) to a low(er) level: Tears ran — her face. 2 at a lower part: Oxford is farther — the river. 3 along: walk — the street. v — tools, refuse to work. — an enemy, knock him —. '—cast adj sad; (of eyes) looking —wards. '—fall n heavy fall (of rain); sudden fall from power or fortune. '—pour n heavy fall (of rain). '—right adj straightforward in manner.   adv thoroughly. '—'stairs adv to, at, on, of, a lower floor. '—'trodden adj kept — and ill-treated. '—ward adj moving, pointing, etc, to what is lower. '—wards adv towards what is lower.

down² n (usu pl) stretch of bare, open highland.

down³ n soft hair or feathers, esp the underfeathers of young birds. '—y adj covered with, soft like, —.

'dowry n property, money, etc, given to or with a daughter when she marries.

doz. ⇨ dozen.

doze v sleep lightly; be half asleep. n short, light sleep.

'dozen n (abbr doz.) (set of) twelve

drab *adj & n* dull muddy brown; (fig) uninteresting; monotonous.

draft *n* 1 outline (in the form of notes or a sketch) of sth to be done or made (eg a speech, letter, drawing, plan). 2 written order for payment of money by a bank. 3 group of men (esp soldiers) chosen from a larger group for a special purpose. *v* make a —(1) of. '—sman *n* man who makes —s(1) (esp in engineering).

drag *v* (-gg-) 1 pull along (esp with effort or difficulty). 2 (allow to) move slowly and with effort: *with —ging feet.* 3 (of time, etc) pass, go on, slowly in a dull manner. *n* sth which is —ged (eg a '—net); sth which slows down progress.

'dragon *n* (in old stories) winged fire-breathing creature.

drain *n* 1 pipe, channel, etc, for carrying away waste liquids. 2 sth that continually uses up force, wealth, time, etc. *v* 1 lead off (liquid) by means of —s(1); (of liquid) flow away. 2 cause (sb) to lose (strength, wealth, etc) by degrees. 3 drink; empty (a cup, etc). '—age *n* —ing or being —ed; system of —s(1).

dram *n* $\frac{1}{16}$ ounce (avoirdupois); $\frac{1}{8}$ ounce for medical substances.

'drama *n* 1 play for the theatre; art of writing and performing plays. 2 series of exciting events. **dra'matic** *adj* of —; exciting, like events in a —(1). **—tist** *n* writer of —s. **—tize** *v* make (a story, etc) into a —(1).

drank ⇨ drink.

drape *v* hang (cloth, clothes) in folds, round or over sth.

'draper *n* shopkeeper selling cloth and articles of clothing. **—y** *n* 1 goods sold by a —. 2 shawls, curtains, etc.

'drastic *adj* having a violent effect. **—ally** *adv.*

draught *n* 1 current of air in a room, chimney, or other shut-in place. 2 depth of water needed to float a ship. 3 — beer, beer on —, beer drawn from a barrel. 4 (amount drunk during) one continuous act of swallowing: *a — of cold water.* 5 — animal, one used for pulling (a cart, etc). 6 (*pl*) table game for two players. '—sman *n*

= draftsman. '—y *adj* (-ier, -iest) with —s(1) blowing through.

draw *v* (*pt* drew, *pp* drawn) 1 move by pulling; take out by pulling. 2 obtain from a source: *to — money from the bank.* 3 take (a breath) into the body; (of a chimney) allow air to flow through. 4 make longer by pulling. 5 attract. 6 cause (sb) to show his feelings, tell what he knows, etc: *to — sb out; to — tears; to — information from sb.* 7 move or come (towards, forward, near, away from, level with, to an end). 8 (of two players, teams, etc) end (a game, etc) without either winning or losing. 9 (of a ship) need (a certain depth of water) in order to float. 10 make (with a pen, pencil, chalk, etc): *— a line (bird, sketch);* use a pencil, etc, to make pictures, etc: *She —s very well.* 11 write out (a cheque); (also — up) put into writing (an agreement, etc). 12 (of days) — in (out), become shorter (longer). 13 — oneself up, stand up straight. 14 — up (at), (of a car, etc) stop (at). *n* (esp) 1 sb or sth that attracts attention or large audiences. 2 a game in which neither side wins. 3 lottery. '—back *n* that which lessens one's satisfaction. '—er *n* box-like container which slides in and out of a piece of furniture. '—ers *n pl* two-legged undergarment fastened at the waist. '—ing *n* art of —ing(10); sth —n(10). '—ing-room *n* room in which guests are received.

drawl *v* speak so that the sounds of the vowels are longer than usual.

dread *v & n* (feel) great fear and anxiety. '—ful *adj* causing —; (colloq) unpleasant. '—fully *adv* (colloq) extremely: *I'm —fully sorry.*

dream *n* 1 sth which one seems to see or experience during sleep. 2 mental picture(s) of the future: *—s of wealth.* *v* (*pt & pp* dreamed or dreamt) have —s; imagine. '—y *adj* (of a person) with thoughts far away; (of things) unreal. '—ily *adv.*

'dreary *adj* (-ier, -iest) dull; gloomy.

dredge *n* apparatus for bringing up mud, etc, from the bed of the sea, rivers, etc. *v* make (a channel,

etc) with a —; bring up with a —.
'—r *n* boat carrying a —.

dregs *n pl* bits of worthless matter which sink to the bottom of a glass, bottle, barrel, etc; of liquid.

drench *v* wet all over, right through.

dress *v* **1** one-piece garment with a skirt as worn by women and girls. **2** clothing. full —, for special occasions. evening —, for formal social occasions. *v* **1** put on clothes. be —ed in, be wearing. **2** make ready for use: *to — leather*; *to — a salad* (with oil, etc). **3** clean and bandage (a wound, etc). **4** comb and brush (one's hair). **5** decorate (a ship with flags, a shop-window with goods). '—er *n* (esp) **1** person employed to help a doctor to — wounds. **2** piece of furniture with shelves for dishes. '—ing *n* (esp) **1** covering used in —ing wounds. **2** oil, etc, for salads. '—ing-gown *n* loose gown worn over night-clothes.

drew ⇨ draw.

drier, driest ⇨ dry.

drift *v* (cause to) be carried along by, or as by, a current of air or water; (of persons) go through life without aim or purpose. *n* —ing movement; pile, etc, made by —ing: —*s of snow*.

drill[1] *n* pointed instrument for making holes. *v* make (a hole) with a —; use a —.

drill[2] *n* physical training (in groups); army training in the handling of weapons, marching, etc; training by practical exercises. *v* train, be trained, by means of —s.

drill[3] *n* long channel cut where seeds are to be sown in the ground; row of seeds sown in this way; machine for making —s and sowing seeds.

drink *v* (*pt* drank, *pp* drunk) **1** take in liquid through the mouth. **2** take in too much alcoholic drink. *n* liquid for —ing. ⇨ drunk. '—able *adj* fit for —ing.

drip *v* (-pp-) (of a liquid) fall, allow to fall, in drops. *n* the drop-by-drop fall of a liquid.

drive *v* (*pt* drove, *pp* 'driven) **1** cause (an engine, tram, car, etc) to work or move as required; cause (cattle, persons, dust, etc) to move in a certain direction. **2** (usu passive) be the power to operate: *—n*

by steam. **3** go, take, be taken, in a carriage, motor-car, etc. **4** force: *—n to steal by hunger*. **5** (of clouds, rain) be carried along violently by the wind: *driving rain*. **6** force (a nail, screw, post, etc) (*into* sth); strike hard (eg a golf-ball). *n* **1** driving or being —n in a car, etc: *to go for a —*. **2** private road to a house. **3** (force behind a) stroke given to a ball; (fig) energy. '—r *n* person who —s (a vehicle, animals, etc); tool for driving(6) (eg '**screw-driver** ⇨ p 293).

'**drizzle** *v & n* rain (in fine drops).

'**dromedary** *n* fast, one-humped, riding-camel. ⇨ p 317.

drone *n* **1** male bee. **2** low humming sound made by bees.

droop *v* bend or hang down (through tiredness or weakness).

drop *n* **1** tiny ball of liquid: '*rain-drops*; sth like a — in size and shape. **2** movement from higher to lower level. *v* (-pp-) **1** (allow to) fall. **2** (allow to) become weaker or lower. **3** — behind, fail to keep up (with). — in (on sb), pay an informal visit (to).

dross *n* waste material rising to the surface of metals when liquid.

drought *n* continuous dry weather causing distress.

drove[1] ⇨ drive.

drove[2] *n* large number of animals moving together.

drown *v* (cause sb to) die in water through being unable to breathe.

'**drowsy** *adj* (-ier, -iest) feeling sleepy; making one feel sleepy.

drudge *n & v* (person who must) work hard and long at unpleasant tasks. '**drudgery** *n*.

drug *n* substance used for medical purpose, either alone or in a mixture, esp one having an effect upon the senses. *v* (-gg-) **1** add harmful —s to (food or drink). **2** give —s to. '—gist *n* tradesman who sells —s, etc.

drum *n* **1** musical instrument with a skin pulled tightly over a hollow cylinder or hemisphere, beaten with the hands or sticks. ⇨ p 180. **2** drum-shaped container (for oil, etc). *v* (-mm-) play the —; tap with the fingers.

drunk *adj* in a helpless state through drinking alcoholic drinks. '—en *adj* caused by, showing the effects of, drinking too much alcoholic liquor. '—ard *n* person who is often —.

dry *adj* ('drier, 'driest) **1** containing no moisture; not wet. **2** (of books, lectures, etc) uninteresting. **3** (of people) without humour; (of weather) not rainy. *v* remove the moisture from. **dryer, drier,** machine for drying: *clothes-(hair-)drier.* '**drily** *adv.* '**dryness** *n.*

'**dual** *adj* of two: *— control,* for or by two persons. '**dual 'carriageway,** road divided along the centre so that the two streams of traffic are separated.

'**dubious** *adj* doubtful.

'**duchess** *n* wife or widow of a duke.

duck[1]*n* common water-bird ⇨ p 211; its flesh as food.

duck[2] *v* move quickly down or to one side (so as not to be seen or hit); go, push sb, quickly under water. *n* **1** act of —ing. **2** (in cricket) score of no runs.

due *adj* **1** owing; to be paid. **2** suitable; right. **3** (to be) expected. **4** — **to,** caused by, *adv* — **north,** etc, exactly north, etc. *n* **1** that which sb deserves. **2** (*pl*) sums of money to be paid (eg for club membership, use of a harbour).

'**duel** *n* unlawful fight with swords or pistols, arranged between two persons who have quarrelled; any two-sided contest. *v* (-ll-) fight a —.

du'et *n* piece of music for two voices or instruments.

dug ⇨ dig.

duke *n* nobleman of high rank.

dull *adj* (-er, -est) opposite of clear or bright; not sharp; (of trade) inactive. *v* make or become —. '**-y** *adv.* '**-ness** *n.*

'**duly** *adv* in a right or suitable manner; at the right time.

dumb *adj* unable to speak; silent. —'**found** *v* make — with surprise.

'**dummy** *n & adj* (object) made to look like and serve the purpose of the real person or thing: *a baby's —,* artificial teat.

dump *n* place for unloading and leaving rubbish or for military stores. *v* put on a —; put or throw down carelessly.

dunce *n* slow learner.

dung *n* solid food waste dropped by domestic animals, used on fields as manure.

'**dungeon** *n* dark underground room formerly used as a prison.

'**duplicate** *v & n* (make an) exact copy (of a letter, etc); (make a) thing exactly like another. *adj* exactly like. '**duplicator** *n* machine that —s sth written or typed.

du'plicity *n* deceit.

'**durable** *adj* likely to last for a long time. ,**dura'bility** *n.*

du'ration *n* time during which sth lasts or exists.

'**during** *prep* in the time (of): *— the afternoon.*

dusk *n* time just before it gets quite dark.

dust *n* finely powdered dirt; any powdered mineral: *chalk-dust.* *v* remove — from. '**-er** *n* cloth for taking — off furniture, etc. '**-bin** *n* rigid container for rubbish(1). '**-y** *adj* (-ier, -iest) covered with —; like —.

'**duty** *n* **1** what one is obliged to do (by conscience, law, morality, etc). **2** inner force urging one to behave in a certain way. **3** payment demanded by the government on goods exported, imported, or manufactured, or when property is transferred to a new owner by sale ('**stamp —**) or death ('**death duties**). '**duty-'free** *adj* (of goods) allowed to enter without payment of customs —. '**dutiable** *adj* on which customs — must be paid. '**dutiful** *adj* doing one's —(1); showing respect and obedience.

dwarf *n* (*pl* dwarfs) *& adj* (person, animal, plant) much below the usual size. *v* prevent from growing to normal size; cause to appear small by comparison.

dwell *v* (*pt & pp* dwelt) **1** live (*in, at*). **2** — **upon,** think, speak or write at length about. '**—ing** *n* house, etc, to live in.

'**dwindle** *v* become less or smaller by degrees.

dye *v* **1** colour, usu by dipping in a liquid. **2** take colour from dye. *n* substance used for dyeing cloth.

dyke ⇨ dike.

dy'namic *adj* (of physical power and force) producing motion; (of a person) having energy and force of character.

'dynamite n powerful explosive.

'dynamo n machine for changing steam-power, water-power, etc, into electrical energy.

'dynasty n succession of rulers belonging to one family.

E

each adj every individual one of a group. pron — thing, person, group, etc. We see — other, — of us see the other.

'eager adj full of, showing, strong desire (for, to do, sth). —ly adv.

'eagle n large bird of prey.

ear¹ n 1 organ(1) of hearing. ⇨ p 30. 2 have a good ear for music, be able to distinguish musical sounds. 'ear-drum n hollow part of the middle ear. 'ear-mark v put (money, etc) on one side (for a purpose). 'earshot n out of earshot, too far away to be heard.

ear² n part of a grain plant on which the seeds appear.

earl n title of a British nobleman of high rank.

'early adj (-ier, -iest) & adv near to the beginning of a period of time, sooner than usual or than others. earlier on, at an earlier stage.

earn v get as a reward for work or for one's qualities. '—ings n pl money —ed.

'earnest adj serious; determined. in —, in a determined, not a joking, way. —ly adv.

earth n 1 this world. 2 dry land. 3 soil. '—enware n dishes, etc, made of baked clay. '—ly adj of this world, not of heaven. '—quake n violent shaking of the —'s surface.

ease n freedom from work, discomfort, or anxiety. stand at —, with the legs apart in a restful position. ill at —, feeling troubled. with —, easily. v 1 give — to (the body or mind). 2 make less tight; lessen (speed, efforts).

'easel n wooden frame to support a blackboard, picture, etc.

east n, adj, & adv part of the sky or point of the horizon where the sun rises. the Far E—, Eastern Asia. the Middle E—, Iran, Turkey, Jordan, etc. '—ern adj lying towards the —; of, from, or in the —. '—wards adv.

'Easter n anniversary of the Resurrection of Jesus Christ.

'easy adj (-ier, -iest) 1 not difficult; simple. 2 free from pain or anxiety. 3 comfortable in, or for, body and mind: — chair, soft, restful one. 'easy-,going adj not causing or taking trouble. go —, take things —, not work too hard. 'easily adv.

eat v (pt ate, pp 'eaten) 1 take food in through the mouth. eat one's words, humbly take back one's own statement. 2 eat away, eat into, destroy as if by eating. 'eat-able adj fit to be eaten.

eaves n pl parts of a roof that overhang the walls of a house. '—drop v (-pp-) listen secretly to a private conversation.

ebb v (of the tide) flow back from the land. n flowing out of the tide.

'ebony n hard, dark wood.

ec'centric adj (of a person, his behaviour) peculiar; strange; not normal. ,eccen'tricity n.

ec,clesi'astical adj of the Christian Church; of clergymen.

'echo n sound sent back from a wall, hill-side, etc. v send back an —; be sent back as an —; be an — of; repeat (the words, etc of).

e'clipse n total or partial cutting off of the light of the sun (when the moon is between it and the earth) or of the reflected light of the moon (when the earth's shadow falls on it). v cause an —; cut off the light from; (fig) make (sth or sb) appear dull by comparison.

e'conomy n 1 avoidance of waste of money, strength, etc. 2 control and management of the money, goods, and other resources of a society or household. ,eco'nomic adj 1 of economics ⇨ below. 2 designed to give a profit. ,eco-'nomics n science of the production and distribution of money and goods. ,eco'nomical adj careful in the use of money, time, goods, etc. e'conomist n 1 expert in economics. 2 person who is economical. **e'conomize** v use or spend less than before.

'ecstasy n feeling of great joy and spiritual uplift. **ec'static** adj of, having, causing, —.

'eddy n (pl **'eddies**) circular or spiral movement (of wind, dust, etc). v move in eddies.

edge n 1 sharp, cutting part of a knife, sword, or tool. 2 (line marking the) outer limit of a flat surface: the — of a table (lake). v (cause to) move slowly forward or along: to — one's way through a crowd. '—ways, '—wise adv with the — forwards or outwards.

'edible adj fit to be eaten.

'edict n order sent out by authority (esp by the Pope).

'edifice n large building.

'edit v prepare (another person's writing) for publication, eg in a newspaper, etc. **e'dition** n. the whole number of copies printed from the same type. **'editor** n. **edi'torial** adj of or by an editor.

'educate v give teaching, training, etc to. **,edu'cation** n.

eel n long, snake-like fish. ⇨ p 247.

ef'face v rub or wipe out.

ef'fect n 1 result; outcome: of no —. take —, have a result, come into use. bring into —, cause to become active or to have an —. 2 impression made on the mind; general appearance. to this —, to the — that, with the general meaning of. 3 (pl) goods; property. v cause to happen. **—ive** adj having an —; making a strong impression. **—ual** adj bringing about the result required.

ef'feminate adj womanish.

,effer'vesce v give off gas bubbles. **—nce** n. **—nt** adj.

,effi'cacious adj (of things) producing the desired result.

ef'ficient adj (of a person) capable; able to do things well. **ef'ficiency** n.

'effigy n person's portrait or image (in wood, stone, etc).

'effort n use of the powers of the body or mind; trying hard.

ef'frontery n impudence.

ef'fusion n pouring out. **ef'fusive** adj (of feelings) pouring out, shown, too freely.

egg n oval, shelled object containing an embryo, laid by birds and reptiles. **egg 'on** v urge persistently.

'egoism n continual selfishness. **'egoist** n selfish person. **'egotism** n practice of talking about oneself. **'egotist** n person who talks too much about himself.

'eiderdown n bed covering filled with soft feathers.

eight n & adj 8. **'—een** n & adj 18. **'eighth** n & adj 8th; ⅛. **'eighty** n & adj 80. **—ieth** n & adj 8oth; ¹⁄₈₀.

'either adj, pron, conj, & adv one or the other of two.

e'jaculate v say suddenly.

e'ject v expel (sb from a place); send out (liquid, etc).

eke v eke out, make (small supplies of money, food, etc) enough for a purpose or one's needs by adding small amounts.

e'laborate adj worked out in great detail. v work out, describe, in detail. **e,labo'ration** n.

e'lapse v (of time) pass.

e'lastic adj having the tendency to go back to the normal size or shape after being pulled or pressed. n cord or material made — by weaving rubber into it.

e'late v be —d, be in high spirits. **e'lation** n.

'elbow n 1 (outer part of) the joint half way down the arm. ⇨ p 29. 2 sharp bend or angle in a pipe, etc. v push (one's way through, forward, etc), using the —s.

'elder adj (of two persons) older. n (usu pl) person deserving respect, having authority, because of age. **—ly** adj rather old. **'eldest** adj (of persons) oldest; first-born.

e'lect v 1 choose (sb) by vote. 2 choose (sth, to do sth). adj chosen: the bishop —. **—ion** n choosing, esp by vote, for Parliament. **—or** n person having the right to — (esp by voting).

,elec'tricity n property or condition, developed in and around substances, by rubbing, by chemical change, etc, which can be used to produce heat, light, and sound and to drive machines; science of this. **e'lectric** adj of, producing, worked by, —. **e'lectrical** adj of —: electrical engineering. **,elec'trician** n expert in setting up and managing electrical apparatus.

e'lectrify v 1 fill (sth) with —; adapt (eg a railway) for working by —. 2 excite, shock, sb as by —. e'lectrifi'cation n. e'electrocute v put to death, kill accidentally, by electric current.

e'lectron n negative electric charge. ,elec'tronic adj.

,elec'tronics n study and application of facts about electrons (as in transistors, computers, etc).

'elegant adj graceful; showing, having, good taste. 'elegance n.

'elegy n poem or song of sorrow.

'element n 1 substance which has not so far been separated into simpler substances. 2 one of the parts of which sth is composed. 3 the —s, the weather; storms. in (out of) one's —, in (not in) natural or pleasing surroundings. ,ele'mental adj of the forces of nature; uncontrolled. ,ele'mentary adj of or in the beginning stages; not developed; simple.

'elephant n largest mammal with a long hanging nose (trunk) and two long round, curved teeth (tusks). ⇨ p 317. 'white-'elephant useless possession.

'elevate v lift up; make (the mind, etc) higher and better. ,ele'vation n 1 elevating or being —d. 2 height (esp above sea-level); hill or high place. 3 flat drawing of one side of a building. 'elevator n 1 = lift. 2 machine for lifting hay, etc.

e'leven n & adj 11. —th n & adj 11th; 1/11.

elf n (pl elves) small fairy.

e'licit v 1 draw out (from sb) (a quality or power of which he is unaware). 2 get (an answer, the truth, applause, etc, from sb).

'eligible adj fit, suitable, to be chosen (for). ,eligi'bility n.

e'liminate v put or take away, remove (because not wanted).

el'lipse n regular oval. ⇨ p 253.

elo'cution n art or style of speaking well, esp in public.

'elongate v make longer.

e'lope v run away from one's family in order to marry secretly.

'eloquence n skilful use of language to persuade or to appeal to the feelings; fluent speaking. 'eloquent adj.

'else adv 1 besides; in addition. 2 or —, otherwise; if not.

'—'where adv in, at or to some other place.

e'lucidate v explain; make clear.

e'lude v escape from (by means of a trick); avoid. e'lusive adj not easy to find.

elves ⇨ elf.

e'maciated adj (of a person's body, appearance) wasted away; lean.

e'mancipate v set free (from restraint, etc). e,manci'pation n.

em'bankment n wall of earth, stone, etc, to hold back water or support a raised road or railway.

em'bargo n (pl em'bargoes) order forbidding (trade, movement of ships, etc).

em'bark v 1 go, put, or take on board a ship. 2 — (up)on, start; take part in.

em'barrass v 1 cause worry, perplexity, or uneasiness to. 2 hinder the movement of. —ment n.

'embassy n duty, mission, residence, of an ambassador.

em'bed v (-dd-) fix firmly (in a surrounding mass).

em'bellish v make beautiful; add ornaments to. —ment n.

'ember n (usu pl) small piece(s) of burning coal or wood in a dying fire.

em'bezzle v use (money placed in one's care) in a wrong way for one's own benefit. —ment n.

em'bitter v arouse bitter feelings in.

'emblem n design representing sth or sb. ,emble'matic adj serving as an —.

em'body v give form to (ideas, feelings); include.

em'brace v 1 put one's arms round (lovingly). 2 accept (an offer, etc). 3 (of things) include. n act of embracing (1).

,embro'cation n liquid rubbed into an aching part of the body.

em'broider v ornament (cloth) with needlework. —y n.

'embryo n offspring of an animal before birth, or of bird, etc, before coming out of the egg.

e'mend v take out errors from.

'emerald n bright green jewel.

e'merge v 1 come into view; (esp) come out (from water, etc). 2 (of facts, ideas) become known. —ncy n sudden happening which makes quick action necessary.

'emigrate v go away *from* one's country *to* another to settle there. **'emigrant** n person who does this. **,emi'gration** n.

'eminent adj (of a person) distinguished; (of qualities) remarkable in degree. —**ly** adv. **'eminence** n 1 being —. 2 high or rising ground.

e'mir n Arab prince or governor.

e'mit v (-tt-) give or send out (light, liquid, sound, etc). **e'mission** n.

e'motion n deep feeling; excited state of the mind or the feelings. —**al** adj of the —s; having —s easily aroused.

'emperor n ruler of an empire.

'emphasis n force or stress laid on word(s) in order to show significance or importance; the placing of special value or importance on sth. **'emphasize** v give — to. **em'phatic** adj having, showing, using, —. **em'phatically** adv.

'empire n group of countries under one ruler, called an emperor.

em'placement n prepared position for artillery.

em'ploy v 1 give work to, usu for payment. 2 make use of. —**ment** n being —ed; one's regular work. **,employ'ee** n person —ed for wages.

em'power v give authority (to do sth).

'empress n wife of an emperor; woman ruling an empire.

'empty adj (-ier, -iest) not containing anything. **make an — promise**, have no intention of fulfilling one's promise. v make or become —.

'emulate v try to do as well as or better than. **,emu'lation** n.

e'nable v make able, give authority or means (to do sth).

e'nact v 1 make a (law); make a law (*that*). 2 play (a scene or part in a play or in real life). —**ment** n law that is —ed.

e'namel n 1 glasslike coating, often coloured, on metal surfaces. — paint, paint which hardens to form such a coating. 2 hard outer covering of teeth. v (-ll-) cover, decorate, with —.

en'chant v charm; delight. —**er**, —**ress** n man, woman, who —s. —**ment** n being —ed; thing which —s; charm; delight.

en'circle v surround.

en'close v 1 put a wall, fence, etc, round; shut in on all sides. 2 put (sth) in (an envelope, parcel, etc), esp with a letter. **en'closure** n sth —d (esp with a letter) in an envelope, etc; enclosing.

en'core int Again! More! v & n (call for a) repetition (of a song, etc) or further performance by the same person(s).

en'counter v & n (have a) sudden or unexpected meeting (with sb, with danger, etc).

en'courage v give hope, courage, or confidence to. —**ment** n encouraging; sth that —s.

en'croach v — (up)on, go beyond what is right or natural. —**ment** n.

en'cumber v get in the way of; be a burden to. **en'cumbrance** n.

en,cyclo'paedia n book, set of books, giving information about every branch of knowledge, or on one subject, with articles in ABC order.

end n 1 farthest or last point. (*get hold of*) **the wrong end of the stick**, (believe sth that is) the opposite of the truth. **on end**, (of a barrel, etc) upright. **for weeks on end**, without an interval; continuously. **make both ends meet**, (fig) manage to earn as much as one needs to spend. **put an end to**, **make an end of**, abolish, stop, destroy. 2 purpose; aim: *gain one's end.* v (cause to) come to an end; reach an end. **end up** (*with*), reach an end (with). **'ending** n end of a story; end of a word. **'endless(ly)** adj & adv. **'endways**, **'endwise** adv with the end forward or up.

en'danger v put in danger.

en'dear v make dear. —**ment** n (act, word, expression of) affection.

en'deavour n & v try.

en'dorse v 1 write one's name on the back of (a cheque, etc). 2 support (a statement, etc). —**ment** n.

en'dow v 1 give (money, etc) to provide an income for (a college, etc). 2 **be —ed with**, possess naturally or be born with. —**ment** n.

en'dure v 1 suffer (pain, hardship, etc). 2 bear; put up with. 3 continue in existence. **en'durance** n ability to —; act, instance of, enduring.

enemy *n* person or group (eg military forces) threatening harm or injury.

'energy *n* force; (person's) power (that may be) used in working. **ener'getic** *adj* full of, done with, —. **,ener'getically** *adv*.

en'fold *v* put one's arms round; cover or wrap up.

en'force *v* **1** compel obedience to (a law, etc). **2** get (sb) by force (to do sth). —**ment** *n*.

en'franchise *v* **1** give political rights to. **2** set free (slaves).

en'gage *v* **1** get the right to occupy (a seat, a taxi, etc) or to employ (a workman, guide, etc). **2** promise. **3** be —**d** in, be busy with. **4** begin fighting (*with*). —**d** *adj* (esp) having given a promise of marriage. —**ment** *n* **1** promise, esp (a) to marry or (b) to go or be somewhere, to meet sb, at a fixed time. **2** battle.

en'gender *v* be the cause of.

'engine *n* machine producing power or motion. **'engine-,driver** *n* man who drives a railway —. **,engi'neer** *n* **1** person who designs machines, bridges, railways, ships, docks, etc. **2** person in control of a ship's —**s**. *v* construct as an engineer; contrive.

en'grave *v* cut (lines, words, etc) into stone, metal plates, or other hard material. **en'graving** *n* picture, etc, printed from an —**d** plate.

en'gross *v* fully occupy (time, attention): —*ed in one's work.*

en'hance *v* add to (the attraction, power, value, etc of).

e'nigma *n* thing, person, circumstance, that is puzzling. **,enig'matic** *adj.*

en'join *v* order.

en'joy *v* **1** take pleasure in. **2** have the use of. —**able** *adj.* —**ment** *n.*

en'large *v* make or become larger. —**(up)on**, say or write more about. —**ment** *n* sth —**d** (esp a photograph); sth added to.

en'lighten *v* give more knowledge to; free from ignorance. —**ment** *n.*

en'list *v* **1** obtain (sb's help, etc). **2** enter, take into, the armed forces.

en'liven *v* make lively.

'enmity *n* hatred.

e'normity *n* great wickedness.

e'normous *adj* very great. —**ly** *adv.*

e'nough *adj, n, & adv* as much or as many as is necessary.

en'quire *v* ⇨ inquire.

en'rage *v* fill with rage; make angry.

en'rapture *v* fill with great delight.

en'rich *v* make rich; improve.

en'rol(l) *v* put (sb's name) on a list or register.

'ensign *n* flag (esp as flown on a ship).

en'sue *v* take place as a result; follow.

en'sure *v* make certain or sure.

en'tail *v* make necessary.

en'tangle *v* catch in a net or among obstacles; (fig) cause (sb) to be in difficulty. —**ment** *n.*

'enter *v* **1** come or go into; become a member of. **2** put (notes, names, records, etc) down in writing. **3** — **into**, take part in; begin to deal with or talk about.

'enterprise *n* **1** undertaking, esp one that needs courage, or offers difficulty. **2** courage, eagerness, to start new —**s**. **'enterprising** *adj* having, showing, —(2).

,enter'tain *v* **1** receive (people) as guests; give food or drink to. **2** amuse; interest. **3** be ready to consider; have in the mind. —**ing** *adj* amusing. —**ment** *n.*

en'thral(l) *v* (-**ll**-) please greatly; take the whole attention of.

en'throne *v* place on a throne.

en'thusiasm *n* strong feeling of interest in, admiration (*for*). **en-'thusiast** *n* person filled with —. **en,thusi'astic** *adj* having, showing, —.

en'tice *v* tempt or persuade (sb) (*away from* sth, *to do* sth). —**ment** *n.*

en'tire *adj* whole; complete; unbroken. —**ly** *adv.* —**ty** *n.*

en'title *v* give a title to (a book, etc); (of conditions, qualities, etc) give (sb) a right (*to*).

'entrails *n pl* bowels.

'entrance[1] *n* way in; act or right of entering.

en'trance[2] *v* be —**d**, be overcome, be carried away as in a dream, with joy.

'entrant *n* person entering (a profession, for a competition, etc).

en'treat v beg earnestly. —y n earnest request.

en'trust v give (sth to sb, as a duty or responsibility); trust (sb with sth).

'entry n 1 entering; (place of) entrance; list, number, of persons, etc, entering for a competition. 2 word with information about it as listed in a dictionary.

e'numerate v count; go through (a list of articles), naming them. e,nume'ration n.

e'nunciate v 1 say, pronounce (words). 2 express (a theory, etc) clearly. e,nunci'ation n.

en'velop v wrap up, cover, on all sides.

'envelope n wrapper or covering, esp one made of paper for a letter.

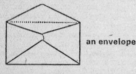

an envelope

'enviable, 'envious ⇨ envy.

en'vironment n (person's) surroundings, influences, etc.

'envoy n messenger, esp one sent on a special mission.

'envy v (pt & pp 'envied) & n (be filled with) feeling of disappointment or ill will at another person's better fortune. 'enviable adj causing —; likely to be envied. 'envious adj having, feeling, or showing —.

'epic n & adj (poetic account) of the deeds of one or more great heroes or of a nation's past history.

'epicure n person who understands the pleasures to be had from delicate(4) food and drink.

,epi'demic n & adj (disease) widespread among many people in the same place for a time.

'epigram n short saying expressing an idea in a clever and amusing way.

e'piscopal adj of, governed by, bishops. e,pisco'palian n & adj (member) of an — church.

'episode n (description of) one event in a chain of events.

e'pistle n (old word for) letter(2). the E—s, (Bible) those written by the Apostles to churches and persons.

'epitaph n words (eg on a tombstone) briefly describing a dead person.

'epoch n (beginning of) a period of time (in history, life, etc) marked by special characteristics, etc.

'equable adj regular; not changing.

'equal adj 1 the same in size, amount, number, quality, etc. 2 — to, having the strength, ability, etc. for. v (-ll-) be — to. —ly adv. e'quality n the state of being —. —ize v make —.

,equa'nimity n calmness of mind.

e'quate v consider, treat, one thing as being equal to (with) another. e'quation n making or being equal; mathematical expression of equality between two quantities by the sign =.

e'quator n imaginary line round the earth, line drawn on maps, to represent points at an equal distance from the north and south poles. ,equa'torial adj.

,equi'distant adj separated by equal distance(s).

,equi'lateral adj having all sides equal.

,equi'librium n state of being balanced.

'equinox n time of the year when day and night are equally long.

e'quip v (-pp-) supply (with what is necessary for a purpose). —ment n things needed for a purpose.

'equity n fairness; right judgement. 'equitable adj just; reasonable.

e'quivalent adj equal in value, amount, meaning, etc (to).

'era n period in history, starting from a particular time or event: the Christian —.

e'radicate v pull up by the roots; put an end to; destroy.

e'rase v rub out.

e'rect adj upright. v 1 set upright. 2 build; establish. —ion n.

'ermine n small animal with (in winter) white fur; (garment made of) its fur.

e'rode v (of rain, currents, acids, etc) wear away; eat into. e'rosion n eroding; being —d.

err v do or be wrong.

'errand n short journey to take or get sth; object or purpose of such a journey.

er'ratic *adj* irregular in behaviour, opinion, etc.

er'ratum *n* (*pl* er'rata) mistake in printing or writing.

er'roneous *adj* incorrect; mistaken.

'error *n* 1 mistake. 2 condition of being wrong in belief or conduct.

erudite *adj* having, showing, great learning.

e'rupt *v* (eg of a volcano) burst out. —ion *n* outbreak.

escalator *n* moving stairs carrying people up or down.

an escalator

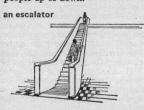

es'cape *v* 1 get free; get away from; avoid. 2 (of gas) flow out. 3 be forgotten or unnoticed by. *n* escaping; means of escaping.

escort *n* person(s), ship(s), going with another or others to give protection or as a sign of honour. es'cort *v* go with as an —.

es'pecial *adj* particular; exceptional. —ly *adv*.

es'quire *n* title of address (written as Esq) used *after* a man's name, instead of using Mr *before* it.

essay *n* piece of writing (not poetry), usu short, on a given subject. —ist *n*.

essence *n* 1 that which makes a thing what it is; the inner nature or most important quality of a thing. 2 extract (usu a liquid) (obtained from a substance, eg by boiling away everything except the most valuable part): meat —.

es'sential *adj* 1 necessary; indispensable. 2 of an essence(2). —ly *adv*.

es'tablish *v* 1 set up on a firm foundation. 2 settle, place (a person, oneself) in a position, place, etc. 3 cause people to accept (a belief, custom, etc). 4 make (a church) national by law. —ment *n* doing or being —ed; that which is —ed.

es'tate *n* 1 piece of property in the form of land, esp in the country. — agent, (esp) person who buys and sells buildings and land for others. 2 all a person's property.

es'teem *v* 1 have a high opinion of. 2 consider. *n* high regard.

'estimate *v* form a judgement about; calculate (the cost, value, etc) of sth. *n* judgement; calculation (eg of cost).

,esti'mation *n* judgement; regard.

es'trange *v* cause (sb) no longer to feel friendly. —ment *n*.

'estuary *n* river mouth into which the tide flows.

et 'cetera (Latin, usu shortened to etc) and other things.

etch *v* (use acid and) engrave (a picture, etc) on a metal plate from which copies may be printed. '—ing *n*. '—er *n*.

e'ternal *adj* without a beginning or an end. e'ternity *n* time without end; the future life.

'ether¹ *n* colourless liquid made from alcohol, used as an anaesthetic.

'ether² *n* the —, substance present throughout all space providing a means for waves of light, etc, to pass across. e'thereal *adj* of unearthly delicacy; spiritual.

'ethics *n* science of morals; rules of conduct. 'ethical *adj* of morals or moral questions; moral.

'etiquette *n* customary rules of behaviour.

'eulogy *n* (speech or writing full of) high praise.

'euphemism *n* (example of the) use of other, usu more pleasing or less exact, words in place of words required by truth or accuracy.

e'vacuate *v* 1 (esp of soldiers) withdraw from; leave empty. 2 require people to leave a place or district. e,vacu'ation *n*.

e'vade *v* 1 get, keep, out of the way of: *to — a blow*. 2 find a way of not doing: *to — paying one's debts*. e'vasion *n* evading; statement or excuse made to — sth. e'vasive *adj* trying to, intended to, —: *an evasive answer*.

e'valuate *v* decide the value of.

,evan'gelic(al) *adj* of, according to, the teachings of the Gospel.

e'vangelist *n* 1 one of the writers (Matthew, Mark, Luke or John) of the Gospel. 2 preacher of the Gospel, esp one who travels.

e'vaporate v 1 (cause to) change into vapour. 2 remove liquid from (a substance, eg by heating). e,vapo'ration n.

evasion, evasive ⇨ evade.

eve n 1 day or evening before a special day: New Year's Eve (31 Dec). 2 on the eve of (great events, etc), at the time just before.

'even¹ adv 1 more than might be expected: It is warm here, — in winter. E— a child can understand it. 2 — if (though), although: I'll go — if you won't. 3 still(2): I can run — faster than you.

'even² adj 1 level; smooth. 2 regular. 3 having the same quality throughout: — writing. 4 (of amounts, distances, values) equal. be (get) — with sb, have revenge on. 5 (opposite of odd) that can be divided by two with no remainder: 2, 4, 6, and 8 are — numbers. v make — or equal. —ly adv.

'even³ n (poet) evening. —song n Evening Prayer in the Church of England. —tide n (poet) evening.

'evening n part of the day between afternoon and nightfall.

e'vent n 1 happening, usu an important one. at all —s, whatever happens. in that —, if that happens. 2 one of the races, etc, in a sports programme. —ful adj full of important —s. —ual adj likely to happen in certain circumstances; coming at last (as a result). —ually adv in the end. e,ventu-'ality n possible event.

'ever adv 1 — (since), at all times; always (since). 2 at any time: Have you — been there? —green n & adj (tree) having green leaves throughout the year. ,—'lasting adj going on for —. the E—lasting, God. ,—'more adv for —.

'every adj 1 all or each one of a group. 2 — other one, each alternate one. — now and then, occasionally. '—body, —one pron each person or all people. —thing pron (all) each thing(s). —day adj happening or used daily; common. —where adv at, in, to — place.

e'vict v turn (sb) out from, dispossess (sb) of, house or land, by authority of the law. —ion n.

'evidence n anything that gives a reason for believing sth; facts, statements, etc, giving support for or proof of a belief. to bear — of, to show signs of. in —, clearly or easily seen. 'evident adj plain and clear (to the eyes or the mind). 'evidently adv.

'evil adj wicked; sinful. the E-One, Satan. n wickedness; sin; — thing; disaster. adv in an — manner.

e'vince v show that one has (a feeling or quality).

e'voke v call up; bring out (memories, feelings).

,evo'lution n 1 process of opening out and developing. 2 Theory of E—, theory that living things have been developed from earlier simpler forms and are not each the result of special creation. 3 movement according to plan (of dancers, soldiers, warships, etc).

e'volve v (cause to) unfold; develop, be developed, naturally and gradually.

ewe n female sheep.

ex- prefix former(ly): the ex-king.

ex'act¹ adj correct in every detail; free from error. —ly adv. —ness n.

ex'act² v demand and get by force; insist upon. —ing adj making great demands; severe.

ex'aggerate v make sth seem larger, better, worse, etc, than it really is. ex,agge'ration n.

ex'alt v make high(er) in rank, great(er) in power, etc; praise highly. —ed adj. ,exal'tation n.

ex'amine v 1 work at carefully in order to learn about or from. 2 put questions to in order to test knowledge or get information. ex,ami-'nation n.

ex'ample n 1 fact, thing, etc, that illustrates a general rule. 2 specimen showing the quality of others in the same group or of the same kind. 3 person's conduct to be imitated. 4 warning: make an — of sb.

ex'asperate v make angry; make (ill-feeling, etc) worse. ex,aspe'ration n.

'excavate v make, uncover, by digging. 'excavator n (esp) machine for doing this.

ex'ceed v be greater than; go beyond what is necessary or allowed. —ingly adv extremely.

ex'cel v (-ll-) do better than; be very good (at sth).

excellent adj very good. **—ly** adv. **'excellence** n. **Your (His) Excellency**, title used when speaking to (of) an ambassador or governor.

ex'cept prep not including; but not. v set apart (as not to be included). **—ion** n sth or sb **—ed**; sth not covered by a general rule. **—ional(ly)** adj & adv unusual(ly).

excerpt n extract(2) from a book, etc (printed separately).

ex'cess n 1 fact of being, amount by which sth is, more than sth else or more than is expected or proper: **—** *postage*, charged when a letter, etc, is understamped. 2 (pl) personal acts which go beyond the limits of good behaviour, morality, or humanity. **—ive** adj too much; too great.

ex'change v give (one thing) and receive (another for it). **— blows, fight.** n 1 act of exchanging. 2 the giving and receiving of the money of one country for that of another; relation in value between kinds of money used in different countries. 3 place where financiers or merchants meet for business: *the Stock E—; the Corn E—.* 4 **telephone —**, central office where telephone lines are connected.

ex'chequer n 1 **the E—**, government department in charge of public money. 2 person's supply of money (public or private).

ex'cise n government tax on certain goods manufactured, sold, or used within a country.

ex'cite v stir up the feelings of; cause (sb) to feel strongly; cause (a feeling, the nerves) to be active. **ex'citable** adj easily **—d. ex,cita-'bility** n. **ex'citement** n.

ex'claim v say suddenly or loudly. **,excla'mation** n sudden short cry, expressing surprise, pain, etc.

ex'clude v 1 prevent (sb *from* getting in somewhere). 2 prevent (the chance of doubt, etc, arising). **ex'clusion** n excluding or being **—d:** *to the exclusion of,* so as to **—.** **ex'clusive** adj 1 (of a person) not willing to mix with others; (of a group) not readily admitting new members. 2 (of goods in a shop, etc) not of the sort to be found

elsewhere; uncommon. 3 reserved to the person(s) concerned: *exclusive privileges.* 4 **exclusive of,** not including.

,excom'municate v exclude (as a punishment) from the privileges of a member of the Church (eg Christian burial). **'excom,muni-'cation** n.

'excrement n solid waste matter discharged from the body.

ex'cruciating adj (of pain) very severe.

ex'cursion n short journey, esp one made by a party for pleasure.

ex'cuse v 1 give reasons showing, or intended to show, that a person or his action is not to be blamed; overlook (a fault, etc). 2 say that sb need not do sth which he ought to do, or that he need not be punished. 3 **— oneself** (*from* a duty, etc), ask to be set free from it. n reason (true or invented) given to explain or defend one's conduct. **ex'cusable** adj that may be **—d.**

'execute v 1 do (what one is asked or told to do). 2 give effect to (eg a will). 3 make legally binding. 4 carry out punishment by death on (sb). 5 perform (by singing, dancing, etc). **,exe'cution** n. **,exe'cutioner** n public official who **—s(4)** criminals. **ex'ecutive** adj having authority to manage affairs, carry out decisions, etc. **ex'ecutor** n person who is chosen to carry out the terms of a will.

ex'empt v & adj (set) free (*from* taxes, work, etc). **—ion** n.

'exercise n 1 use, practice (of mental or physical powers, rights). 2 training (of mind or body); activity, drill, etc, designed for this purpose. v 1 take **—;** give **— to.** 2 trouble (the mind).

ex'ert v put forward, bring into use (one's strength, influence, etc). **— oneself,** make an effort. **—ion** n.

ex'hale v breathe out; give off (gas, vapour).

ex'haust v 1 use up completely; make empty. 2 tire out. 3 say, find out, all there is to say about (a subject). n (outlet in an engine, etc, for) steam, vapour, etc, which has done its work. **ex'haustion** n.

ex'hibit v show publicly; give clear

evidence of (a quality). *n* sth —ed.

¡exhi'bition *n* 1 collection of things publicly —ed. 2 display of goods, etc, for commercial advertisement; act of —ing (a quality, etc).

ex'hilarate *v* make glad; fill with gladness or high spirits. ex,hila-'ration *n*.

ex'hort *v* advise earnestly (to do good, give up bad ways, etc).

'exile *v* send (sb) away from his country as a punishment. *n* (condition of) being —d; person who is —d.

ex'ist *v* be; live. —ence *n* —ing; everything that —s; way of living.

'exit *n* (passage, etc, for) going out. *v* go out (of a theatre, etc).

'exodus *n* a going out or away of many people.

ex'onerate *v* free (sb *from* blame or responsibility).

ex'orbitant *adj* (of a price asked, of a charge made) much too high or great.

ex'otic *adj* foreign; attractive and pleasing because foreign: — *fruit*.

ex'pand *v* make or become larger or wider; spread out. ex'panse *n* wide area. ex'pansion *n* —ing or being —ed. ex'pansive *adj* able to —; covering a large area.

ex'pect *v* regard as likely; feel confident about sth. ,expec'tation *n* —ing; what one —s to receive.

ex'pedient *n & adj* (plan, action) likely to be helpful or useful for a purpose. ex'pediency *n*.

,expe'dition *n* (men, ships, etc, making a) journey or voyage with a definite purpose.

ex'pel *v* (-ll-) send away as a punishment; drive or send out by force. ex'pulsion *n*.

ex'pend *v* spend. —iture *n* —ing; money —ed.

ex'pense *n* spending (of money, time, etc); (usu *pl*) money used or needed for sth. ex'pensive *adj* causing —; high priced.

ex'perience *n* 1 the gaining of knowledge or skill by doing and seeing things; knowledge or skill so gained. 2 event, activity, which has given sb —(1). *v* have — of; find by —.

ex'periment *n* careful test or trial made in order to study what happens and gain new knowledge.

v make —s. ex,peri'mental(ly) *adj & adv*.

'expert *n* person with special skill or knowledge. *adj* skilful.

ex'pire *v* 1 (of a period of time) end. 2 breathe out; (liter) die.

ex'plain *v* 1 tell the meaning of; make sth understood. 2 account for: *Can you — your absence yesterday?* —oneself, make one's meaning clear; defend one's conduct. ¡expla'nation *n*.

ex'plicit *adj* clearly expressed.

ex'plode *v* (cause to) burst with a loud noise. ex'plosion *n*. ex'plosive *n & adj* (substance) tending to —.

ex'ploit¹ *v* 1 use, work, or develop (mines, water-power, other natural resources). 2 use for one's own profit. ,exploi'tation *n*.

'exploit² *n* adventurous act.

ex'plore *v* 1 travel into or through (a country, etc) for the purpose of discovery. 2 examine (problems, etc) thoroughly. —r *n*, ,explo-'ration *n*.

ex'plosion; ex'plosive ⇨ explode.

ex'port *v* send (goods) to another country. 'export *n* —ing; the business of —ing; sth —ed.

ex'pose *v* 1 uncover; leave unprotected. 2 display; show the true character of. 3 allow light to reach (a camera film, etc). ex'posure *n*.

ex'pound *v* explain by giving details.

ex'press *v* 1 make (one's thoughts, etc) known (by words, looks, actions). 2 send (a letter, etc) fast by special delivery. *adj* 1 clearly indicated. 2 going, sent, quickly. *n* —(2) train. —ion *n* 1 process of making known (one's meanings, feelings, etc). 2 word or phrase. 3 sth (esp a look) showing the feelings. —ive *adj* serving to —(1) the feelings.

ex'pulsion ⇨ expel.

'exquisite *adj* 1 of great excellence; 2 (of power to feel) keen; delicate(3).

ex'tant *adj* still in existence.

ex'tend *v* 1 make longer (in space or time). 2 stretch or reach out; offer: *to* — one's hand (*an invitation*) *to sb*. 3 lay out (legs, arms) to full length. 4 (of space, land) reach or stretch. ex'tension *n*

—ing or being —ed; sth —ed; sth added. **ex'tensive** adj far-reaching. **ex'tent** n 1 length; area; range. 2 degree.

ex'tenuate v make (wrongdoing) seem less serious by finding an excuse. **ex,tenu'ation** n.

ex'terior adj & n outer; outside.

ex'terminate v make an end of; destroy. **ex,termi'nation** n.

ex'ternal adj outside; for the outside.

ex'tinct adj no longer burning or active; no longer in existence.

ex'tinguish v 1 put out (a light, fire). 2 put an end to (hope, etc).

ex'tol v (-ll-) praise highly.

ex'tort v obtain (money, promises, etc) by threats or violence. **—ion** n. **—ionate** adj (of a demand, price, etc) too high.

'extra adj & n more than usual.

ex'tract v 1 take, pull, or get out (usu with effort); get (information, money, etc) from sb unwilling to give it. 2 obtain (juices, etc) by crushing, boiling, etc. 3 select and copy out examples, passages, etc (from a book). **'extract** n 1 liquid —ed(2). 2 passage —ed(3) from a book, etc.

ex'traordinary adj unusual; remarkable.

ex'travagant adj 1 wasteful; (in the habit of) wasting money. 2 (of ideas, behaviour, etc) going beyond what is reasonable. **ex'travagance** n. **—ly** adv.

ex'treme adj 1 farthest possible. 2 (of qualities, etc) reaching the highest degree. 3 (of persons, their ideas, etc) far from moderate. n 1 — part or degree. 2 (pl) qualities, etc, which are as wide apart as possible. **go to —s, take —(3)** measures. **ex'tremity** n 1 — point, end, or limit; (pl) hands and feet. 2 — degree (of misfortune, etc). 3 (pl) — measures (eg for punishing wrongdoers).

'extricate v set free, get (sb, oneself) free (from difficulties, etc).

ex'uberant adj full of life and vigour. **ex'uberance** n.

ex'ult v rejoice greatly (at, in). **—ant** adj. **,exul'tation** n.

eye n 1 organ(1) of sight. ⇨ p 30. **have an eye (a good eye) for,** be a good judge of. **see eye to eye,** agree. **with an eye to,** hoping for. **'eyebrow** ⇨ brow. **'eyelid** n upper and lower movable fleshy covering over the eye. 2 thing like an eye, eg the hole in a needle. **'eyesight** n ability to see. **'eyesore** n ugly thing. **'eye,witness** n person who can describe an event because he himself saw it. v look at.

F

'fable n short tale (esp about animals that talk) with a moral (1-). *Aesop's —s.* **'fabulous** adj 1 of or in —s; such as exists only in tales; incredible. 2 (colloq) very good.

'fabric n 1 material, esp woven. 2 framework. **—ate** v make up (sth false).

face n 1 front part of the head. ⇨ p 30. **— to —,** looking directly at one another. **make (pull) a —at,** pull the face out of shape to show disgust, etc. 2 front part of anything: *— of a clock.* **— value,** value marked on a coin, banknote, etc. 3 **on the — of it,** from what it appears to be. v 1 have or turn the — towards; be opposite to. **— the music,** be prepared to suffer the consequences. 2 cover (wall, etc) with a layer of different material.

fa'cetious adj (intended to be) funny; fun-making.

'facile adj 1 easily done. 2 (of a person) able to do things easily. 3 (of speech, writing) produced effortlessly but without enough care. **fa'cilitate** v make easy. **fa'cility** n (esp pl) things that are helpful (in work, travel, etc).

fac'simile n exact copy (of a picture, sth written, etc).

fact n sth known to be true or accepted as true; sth that has been done or that has happened. **as a matter of —, in —,** really; in truth.

'factor n 1 whole number (except 1) by which a larger number can be divided exactly. 2 fact, circumstance, that helps to bring about a result.

'factory n building(s) where goods are made (esp by machinery).

'**faculty** *n* **1** power of mind; power of doing things; sense (eg hearing or sight). **2** branch of learning, esp as studied in a university.

fad *n* fanciful preference, fashion, unlikely to last.

fade *v* (cause to) lose colour and freshness; go slowly out of view or memory.

fag *v* (-gg-) do very tiring work; (of work) make very tired. *n* (colloq) hard work.

'**Fahrenheit** *n* name of a thermometer scale with freezing-point at 32° and boiling-point at 212°. ⇨ p 336.

fail *v* **1** be unsuccessful (in doing sth one tries to do). **2** be too little or not enough; come to an end while still needed. **3** (of health, eyesight, etc) become weak. **4** neglect (to do sth). **5** (of a business, etc) become bankrupt; (of examiners) decide that a candidate has —ed. *n* (only in) **without** —, certainly. '**—ing** *n* weakness or fault (of character). '**—ure** *n* act of —ing; person or thing that has —ed.

faint *adj* (-er, -est) **1** weak; not distinct. **2** feel (look) —, as if about to lose consciousness. *v* become unconscious (because of loss of blood or from hunger, etc). *n* act, state, of —ing. '**—ly** *adv*. **—ness** *n*. '**faint-'hearted** *adj* having, showing, little courage.

fair *adj* (-er, -est) **1** just and honourable; agreeing with justice or the rules of a game. **2** average; quite good; (of the weather) dry and fine; (of winds) favourable. **3** (of the skin and hair) pale; light. **4** (old use) beautiful. **5** — **copy**, new and clean copy. *adv* in a —(1) manner: *to play* —. '**—ly** *adv* **1** justly. **2** moderately. '**—ness** *n*.

fair² *n* **1** sale or exhibition of goods, cattle, often with entertainments, held regularly in a particular place, **2** large-scale exhibition (2).

'**fairy** *n* small imaginary being (usu female) with magic powers. '**fairy-tale** *n* **1** tale about fairies. **2** untrue story.

faith *n* **1** trust, strong belief, or confidence. **2** religion. **3** promise: *to keep (break)* — *with sb.* **4 in good (bad)** —, with (without) sincerity. '**—ful** *adj.* **1** keeping —(3); loyal and true (*to*). **2** exact;

true to the facts. '**—fully** *adv.* '**—less** *adj* false; disloyal.

fake *v & n* (make up) sth that looks genuine but is not.

fall *v* (*pt* **fell**, *pp* **fallen**) **1** come or go downwards or to the ground by force or weight, loss of balance or support, etc; become lower or less: *the temperature is falling (fell, has fallen).* **2** (of a fort, town, etc) be captured in war. **3** give way to temptation. **4** drop down, wounded or killed (in war, etc). **5** become; occur: *Christmas Day —s on a Saturday this year.* — **in love** (*with*), become filled with love (of). — **asleep**, begin to sleep. **6** (with *adv & prep*) — **back**, move or turn back. — **back (up)on**, make use of (when sth else has failed). — **behind**, fail to keep level with. — **in**, (of soldiers, etc) get into line. — **in with**, agree to (sb's plans, etc). — **off**, (esp) become fewer, less. — **on**, make an attack on. — **on one's feet**, be lucky. — **out (with)**, quarrel (with). **it fell out that**, it happened that. — **through**, come to nothing. — **to**, begin. *n* **1** moment or act of —ing. **2** (USA) autumn. **3** (often *pl*) place where a river —s suddenly to a lower level. **4** amount (of rain, etc) that —s.

'**fallacy** *n* mistaken belief or argument. **fal'lacious** *adj.*

'**fallible** *adj* liable to error.

'**fallow** *n & adj* (land) ploughed but not sown or planted.

false *adj* (-r, -st) not true or genuine. *adv* **play sb** —, act —ly towards sb. '**—ly** *adv.* '**—hood** *n* untrue statement. '**falsify** *v* **1** make (records, etc) —. **2** tell, describe, sth —ly.

'**falter** *v* move, act, speak, in an uncertain or hesitating way.

fame *n* condition of being widely known or talked about.

fa'miliar *adj* **1** — **with**, having a good knowledge of. **2** common; often seen, met, heard, etc. **3** close; knowing and known well: —*friends.* **4** claiming more friendship than there is. **fa,mili'arity** *n* being —.

'**family** *n* **1** parents and children. **2** all descendants of a man and wife. **3** all persons related by blood. **4** group of living things (plants, animals, etc) or of languages having a common source.

'famine *n* extreme scarcity of food in a region.

'famish *v* **be —ed**, be suffering from extreme hunger.

'famous *adj* known widely (*for*, *as*).

fan¹ *n* object (waved in the hand) or apparatus (operated by electricity) for making a current of air. *v* (-nn-) send a current of air on to.

fan² *n* enthusiastic supporter or admirer.

fa'natic *n & adj* (person) having excessive enthusiasm for sth.

'fancy *n* **1** (power of creating a) mental picture; sth imagined. **2** idea, belief, without foundation. **3** fondness (*for*). *adj* **1** (esp of small things) decorated; made to please the eye. **2 — dress**, dress of an odd or unusual kind, as worn at some parties. *v* **1** picture in the mind. **2** have a desire for (sth). **3** have a —(2) (that sth is happening, etc). **4 Just —!** How surprising! **5 —** oneself, have a high opinion of oneself. **'fanciful** *adj* full of fancies(2); unreal.

fang *n* long, sharp tooth; snake's poison-tooth.

fan'tastic *adj* **1** wild and strange. **2** (of ideas, plans, etc) absurd; impossible. **—ally** *adv*.

'fantasy *n* **1** fancy(1). **2** sth highly imaginative and dreamlike.

far *adv* ('further or, less· usu, 'farther, 'furthest or, less usu, 'farthest). **1** at or to a great distance. **Far East**, countries in East Asia. **far flung**, spread widely. **2 far and away** (better, etc), very much. *adj* a long way off; distant. **'far-away** *adj* distant; (of sb's look) as if fixed on sth far away in space or time. **'far-'fetched** *adj* (of a comparison, etc) forced; unnatural. **'far-off** *adj* distant. **'far-'seeing, 'far-'sighted** *adj* (fig) wise; having good judgement of future needs, etc.

farce *n* **1** (style of) play for the theatre full of ridiculous situations. **2** series of events like a —. **'farcical** *adj* ridiculous.

fare *n* **1** money charged for a journey (by ship, bus, etc). **2** food and drink. *v* travel; progress.

'fare'well *int* good-bye.

farm *n* **1** land for growing crops, raising animals, etc. **2** (also **'farm-**

house) house on a —. *v* **1** use (land) for growing crops, etc. **2 — out** (*work*), send out to be done by others. **'—er** *n* man who manages a —. **'farmyard** *n* space enclosed by — buildings.

'farther, 'farthest ⇨ far.

'farthing *n* former British coin worth one quarter of an old penny.

'fascinate *v* **1** charm or attract greatly. **2** take away the power of movement by a fixed look, as a snake does. **,fasci'nation** *n* (esp) thing that —s.

'fashion *n* **1** (of clothes, behaviour, thought, etc) that which is considered best and· is imitated by most people in a place at a time: *the Paris —s; in —; out of —*. **2** manner of doing or making sth. **after a —**, somehow or other but not well. *v* form or shape. **—able** *adj* following the —(1); used by, visited by, many people, esp of the upper classes. **—ably** *adv*.

fast¹ *adj* **1** firmly fixed: **— in the ground; — colours**. **2** close and loyal: **— friends**. *adv* firmly; strongly. **— asleep**, in a deep sleep.

fast² *adj* (-er, -est) **1** quick. **2** (of a watch) going too quickly (eg at 2 o'clock the watch indicates 2.10). **3** (of a person, his way of living) too fond of worldly pleasures. *adv* quickly.

fast³ *v* go without (certain kinds of) food, esp as a religious duty. *n* act of, period of, —ing.

'fasten *v* **1** make fast; fix firmly. **2** become —ed; join together. **3 — (up)on**, take firm hold of. **—er** *n*, **—ing** *n* sth that —s things.

fas'tidious *adj* not easily pleased.

fat *n* **1** oily substance in animal bodies; this substance purified for cooking purposes. **2** oily substance obtained from certain seeds. *adj* (-ter, -test) **1** having much fat(1): *fat meat*. **2** thick; well-filled. *v* (-tt-) (also **'fatten**) make or become fat(1).

'fatal *adj* causing, ending in, death or disaster. **—ly** *adv*. **—ism** *n* belief that events are determined by fate. **—ist** *n* person who holds this belief. **fa'tality** *n* a death in an accident, in war, etc.

fate *n* 1 power looked upon as

controlling all events. **2** the future fixed by — for sb or sth. **3** death; destruction. **'—d** adj fixed by —. **'—ful** adj deciding the future.

'father n **1** male parent. **2** founder or first leader. **3** priest (esp in the Roman Catholic Church). v become the — of. **— sth on sb,** cause him to seem responsible for it. **'father-in-law** n — of one's wife or husband. **'—ly** adj of or like a —.

'fathom n measure (six feet) of depth of water. v (fig) understand; get to the bottom of.

fa'tigue n **1** condition of being very tired. **2** (army) task such as cleaning, cooking, etc. v cause — to; make tired.

'fatten ⇨ fat.

fault n **1** sth making a person or thing imperfect; error. **find — with,** point out —s in. **at —,** in the wrong. **2** responsibility for being wrong. **'—less** adj. **'—lessly** adv. **'—y** adj imperfect. **'—ily** adv.

'fauna n all the animals of an area or a stated period of time.

'favour n **1** friendly feeling; willingness to help. **in — of,** (a) in sympathy; willing to help; (b) on behalf of. **out of — (with),** not popular or liked by. **2** sth done from kindness. v **1** show — to. **2** show — to (one person) more than to others. **—able** adj giving or showing approval; helpful. **—ably** adv. **—ite** n & adj (person or thing) specially —ed. **—itism** n practice of —ing persons unequally.

fawn¹ n **1** young deer. **2** light yellowish-brown.

fawn² v **1** (of dogs) show pleasure by jumping up, tail-wagging, etc. **2** (fig) try to win favour by flattery.

fear n **1** painful feeling caused by the possibility of harm or injury. **2** risk; likelihood. **3** reverence and awe: _the — of God._ v have —; feel — of; be anxious. **'—ful** adj causing —. **'—less** adj without —.

'feasible adj that can be done.

feast n **1** day kept(2) in memory of some great event. **2** meal (esp in public) with many good things to eat and drink. v give a —(2) to; take part in a —(2).

feat n difficult action, deed well done.

'feather n one of the light growths from a bird's skin. **birds of a —,** persons of the same sort. v **— one's nest,** save money to spend on oneself. **—ed** adj covered or filled with —s.

feathers

'feature n **1** one of the named parts of the face; (pl) the whole face. **2** characteristic; striking part or point. v be a —(2) of; make (sb or sth) a —(2) of. **—less** adj without —s(2).

'February n second month of the year. ⇨ leap.

fed ⇨ feed. **fed up,** (colloq) discontented (_with_).

'federal adj of, based on, federation. **—ism** n — union. **'federate** v (of states, societies) organize, combine, as a — group. **,fede-'ration** n **1** political system (eg in Australia) in which federated States govern themselves but leave foreign affairs, defence, etc, to a central (F—) government. **2** such a union of States; (also) similar union of societies, trade unions, etc.

fee n charge, payment, for professional advice or services.

'feeble adj (-r, -st) weak. **'feebly** adv.

feed v (pt & pp fed) **1** give food to; provide (one's family, etc) with food. **2** (of animals) eat. **3** — (up)on, take as food. n food for animals.

feel v (pt & pp felt) **1** touch with the hand; be aware of by touch; learn about by touching. **2** be aware through the senses; know that one is (happy, cold, etc). **— like** (_doing sth_), have a wish (to do it). **3** seem (smooth, rough, etc) to the senses. **4** have a vague idea (_that_). **5** be moved by (eg sorrow); be sensitive to (eg the heat). n by the —, by —ing. **'—er** n part of some insects with which they feel. **'—ing** n **1** sth felt in the mind: _a_

—ing *of joy.* **2** physical awareness: *a —ing of pain.* **3** (*pl*) rouse the —ings of, make excited. hurt sb's —ings, offend him; make him sad. **4** sympathy; considerateness: *to show —ing for others. adj* having, showing, sympathy.

feet ⇨ **foot.**

feign *v* pretend.

'feline *adj* of or like a cat.

fell¹ ⇨ **fall.**

fell² *v* cause to fall; knock (sb) down; cut (a tree) down.

'fellow *n* **1** (colloq) man. **2** (*pl*) those sharing experiences: *one's —s,* other men; *— travellers.* **3** member of a learned society or of the governing body of some university colleges. **'fellow-'feeling** *n* sympathy. —**ship** *n* **1** friendly association. **2** (membership of) a group or society.

'felon *n* person who has committed a serious crime. **'felony** *n* serious crime.

felt¹ ⇨ **feel.**

felt² *n* material (1) made of wool, hair, etc, pressed and rolled flat.

'female *adj* **1** of the sex able to give birth to young or lay eggs. **2** of women. *n* — animal or person.

'feminine *adj* **1** of, like, suitable for, women; womanly. **2** of female gender (cf masculine).

fence¹ *v & n* (surround, divide, with a) barrier of wooden boards, posts, wire, etc.

fence² *v* **1** practise the art of fighting with swords. **2** (fig) avoid giving a direct answer.

fend *v* **1** — **off** (*a blow,* etc), defend oneself from. **2** — **for** (*oneself,* etc), provide (food) for; care for.

'fender *n* **1** metal frame bordering an open fireplace to keep burning coals from rolling on to the floor. **2** (on machines, on ships' sides, motor-cars, etc) part or appliance that keeps things off or lessens damage in a collision.

fer'ment *v* **1** (cause to) undergo chemical change, through the action of substances such as yeast. **2** (fig) (cause to) become excited. **'ferment** *n* substance (eg yeast) causing others to —(1). in a —, (fig) in an excited condition. **,fermen'tation** *n* process of —ing.

fern *n* sorts of green-leaved flowerless plant.

fe'rocious *adj* fierce; cruel; violent. **fe'rocity** *n.*

'ferro-'concrete *n* concrete strengthened with an iron or steel framework.

'ferry *n* (place where there is a) boat or aircraft that carries people and goods across a river, channel, etc. *v* take, go, across in a —.

'fertile *adj* **1** (of land, plants, etc) producing much; (of a person, his mind, etc) full of ideas, plans, etc. **2** (opposite of *sterile*) able to produce fruit, young; capable of developing: *— eggs.* **fer'tility** *n* being —. **'fertilize** *v* make (land) —. **,fertili'zation** *n.* **'fertilizer** *n* substance for making land —.

'fervent *adj* hot; (fig) passionate. **'fervour** *n* deep feeling.

'fester *v* **1** (of a wound) become poisoned. **2** (of injustice, etc) act like poison on the mind.

'festival *n* (day or season for) public celebrations or merry-making. **'festive** *adj* of a —. **fes'tivity** *n* **1** (often *pl*) joyful celebration.

fes'toon *n* chain of flowers, leaves, etc, hanging between two points. *v* make into, decorate with, —s.

fetch *v* **1** go for and bring back (sb or sth). **2** cause (blood, tears, etc) to come out; (of goods) be sold for (a price).

fête *n* (usu outdoor) festival.

'fetish, 'fetich *n* object worshipped by pagan people because they believe a spirit lives in it; anything to which too much respect is foolishly given.

'fetter *n* chain for the ankle of a prisoner or the leg of a horse. *v* put —s on; (fig) hinder.

feud *n* bitter quarrel between two persons, families, or groups over a long period of time.

'feudal *adj* of the method of holding land (by giving service to the owner) during the Middle Ages in Europe. —**ism** *n* the — system.

'fever *n* **1** condition of the human body with a temperature higher than normal, esp as a sign of illness. **2** disease in which there is a high —(1). **3** (fig) excited state: —**ish** *adj* of, caused by, having, —.

few *adj* (-er, -est) not many: *few books. n* small number of: *for a few days.*

fez *n* red felt head-dress worn by some Muslim men.

fi'ancé(e) *n* man (woman) to whom one is going to be married.

fi'asco *n* complete failure.

fibre *n* **1** one of the slender threads of which many animal and vegetable growths are formed (eg cotton, nerves). **2** substance formed of a mass of —. **'fibrous** *adj*.

'fickle *adj* (of moods, the weather, etc) often changing.

'fiction *n* **1** sth invented or imagined (contrasted with the truth). **2** (branch of literature concerned with) stories, novels, romances. **fic'titious** *adj* not real; invented.

'fiddle *n* violin. **as fit as a —**, in perfect health. *v* **1** play the —. **2** play aimlessly (with sth in one's fingers).

fi'delity *n* loyalty; faithfulness (*to*).

'fidget *v* move (part of) the body about restlessly; make (sb) nervous.

field *n* **1** area of open land (usu fenced or with boundaries) for farming, playing games, etc: *football* —. **2** (usu in compound words) land from which minerals, etc, are obtained: *oil-field*. **3** expanse; open space: *ice-field*. **4** branch of study; range of activity or use; (esp) place where fighting occurs: *take the* —, *begin a war*. **'field-hospital**, one that can be moved from place to place (in war). **'field-glasses** *n* *pl* long-distance glasses for outdoor use with both eyes. **'—marshal** *n* army officer of highest rank.

fiend *n* devil; very wicked person.

'fierce *adj* (-r, -st) **1** violent; cruel. **2** (of heat, desire, winds, etc) very great or strong.

'fiery *adj* **1** flaming; looking like, hot as, fire. **2** (of a person) quickly or easily made angry.

fif'teen *n* & *adj* 15. **fifth** *n* & *adj* 5th; ⅕. **'fifty** *n* & *adj* 50. (British decimal currency) fifty new pence (50p) coin. ⇨ p 334.

fig *n* (tree having) soft, sweet fruit full of small seeds. ⇨ p.115.

fight *v* (*pt* & *pp* fought) attack with the hands, weapons, etc; struggle against sb or sth. **— it out**, decide by —*ing*. **— shy of**, keep away from. *n* act of —*ing*.

'figment *n* sth invented or imagined: *a — of the imagination*.

'figurative *adj* (of words) applied in an imaginative way, not literally, as when an angry man is described as 'fiery'. **—ly** *adv*.

'figure *n* **1** sign for a number, esp 0 to 9. **2** price: *at a high* —. **3** human form, esp the appearance and what it suggests: *a — of distress*. **4** person, esp one who is famous or important. **5** person's —(3) drawn or painted, cut in stone, etc; diagram or illustration in a book, etc. **6 — of speech**, word(s) used figuratively. *v* **1** have or take a part (*as* sb, *in* history, etc). **2 —** sth out, get a result (esp by using numbers). **3** (esp in *pp*) mark with designs. **'figure-head** *n* person with position but no power; one who is head only in name.

'filament *n* slender thread (esp of wire).

file¹ *n* holder for keeping papers, etc, together and in order; papers, etc, kept in such a holder. *v* put in or on a —.

file² *n* metal tool with a rough face for cutting or smoothing. *v* use a — on. **'filings** *n* *pl* bits —of.

file³ *n* **in (single) —**, in one line one behind the other. *v* **— in (out)**, go in (out) in —(s).

'filial *adj* of a son or daughter.

fill *v* **1** make or become full. **2 — in (out)**, (esp) write what is needed to complete (a form(5), etc); **— out**, (esp) become or make rounder, larger, etc. **— one's —**, eat as much as one can.

'fillet *n* thick slice of fish or meat without bones.

film *n* **1** thin coating or covering (eg of dust, mist). **2** sheet or roll of gelatine prepared for photography. **3** cinema picture: — *actors*. *v* **1** cover, become covered, with a —(1). **2** make a —(3) of. **'—y** *adj* like a —(1).

'filter *n* apparatus (containing, eg, sand) for holding back solid substances in impure liquid poured through it. *v* pass through a —.

filth *n* disgusting dirt. **'—y** *adj* (-ier, -iest).

fin *n* one of those parts of a fish with which it swims. ⇨ p 247.

'final *adj* **1** at the end. **2** putting

an end to doubt or argument: — *judgements*. *n* (also *pl*) — set of university degree examinations, races, etc. **fi'nale** *n* end of a play, musical piece, etc. '—ly *adv* lastly.

fi'nance *n* 1 (science of) the management of (esp public) money. 2 (*pl*) money (esp of a government or business company). *v* provide money for (a scheme, etc). **fi'nancial** *adj*. **fi'nancier** *n* person skilled in —.

find *v* (*pt & pp* found) 1 come across; discover; look for and get back (sth or sb lost, etc). 2 — one's **feet**, discover one's powers and begin to do well. 3 learn by experience. 4 (often — out) learn by inquiry; discover. — sb out, discover that he has done wrong, is at fault, etc. 5 — favour with, win the favour of. 6 (legal) — *a prisoner (guilty)*, decide that he is (guilty). *n* sth found, esp sth valuable or pleasing. '—ing *n* (often *pl*) sth decided or discovered after inquiries.

fine¹ *adj* (-r, -st) 1 (of weather) bright; not raining. 2 enjoyable; splendid. 3 (of workmanship, etc) delicate. 4 consisting of very small particles: — *dust*. 5 very thin: — *thread*; sharp: *a — point*. 6 (of metals) refined; pure. '—ry *n* elegant, well-made clothes, ornaments, etc.

fine² *adv* cut (run) it —, leave oneself hardly enough time.

fine³ *n* sum of money (to be) paid as a punishment for breaking a law or rule. *v* make (sb) pay a —.

fi'nesse *n* delicate or artful way of dealing with a situation.

'finger *n* ⇨ p 29. *v* touch with the —s. **'finger-print** *n* mark made by the finger-tip(s), eg as used to detect criminals.

'finish *v* 1 bring or come to an end. 2 make complete and perfect. *n* 1 the last point. 2 polish: *That table has a good —*.

'finite *adj* having limits.

fir *n* (wood of an) evergreen tree with needle-like leaves.

fire *n* 1 condition of burning: *a forest —*. 2 burning wood, coal, etc, for heating and cooking. **catch (take)** —, start burning. 3 shooting (from guns). **under** —, being shot at. 4 angry or excited feeling. *v* 1 cause to begin burning. 2 harden (eg bricks) in an oven. 3 supply (a furnace, etc) with fuel. 4 shoot(4) with, pull the trigger of, discharge(2) (rifle, etc); send (a bullet, etc) from a gun; (of a gun) go off. 5 excite (the imagination). **'fire-alarm** *n* bell, etc, sounded as an alarm when — breaks out. **'fire-arm** *n* rifle or revolver. **'fire-brigade** *n* company of men who put out —s. **'fire-engine** *n* motor pump manned by —men. **'fire-escape** *n* kind of ladder or outside stairs for escaping from a burning building. '—man *n* member of a fire-brigade. '—place *n* place where a — may be made in a room. **'fire-proof** *adj* that does not burn; that does not break if heated. **'—work** *n* device containing gunpowder, etc, used for display or signals.

firm¹ *adj* (-er, -est) 1 solid; not easily shaken or moved. 2 not easily influenced or changed. *adv* (= —ly): *to stand —*. '—ly *adv*. '—ness *n*.

firm² *n* (two or more) persons carrying on a business.

'firmament *n* sky.

first *adj*, *n*, *& adv* earliest; at the beginning; number one. **'first-'aid** *n* temporary medical assistance (usu in an emergency). **'first-'hand** *adj & adv* obtained through practice, observation of facts, etc, not from books, etc. **'first-'class**, **'first-'rate** *adj* excellent; of the best quality. '—ly *adv* in the — place.

'fiscal *adj* of public money.

fish *v & n* (try to catch an) animal that lives underwater with fins and a tail for swimming. ⇨ p 247. — sth up (out of), find, pull up (eg from one's pocket). '—ing-rod (—ing line), for catching —. '—erman *n* man who catches —, esp for a living. '—monger *n* person who sells —. '—y *adj* (colloq) causing a feeling of doubt: *a very —y excuse*.

'fissure *n* deep crack (in rocks, etc).

fist *n* hand when tightly closed.

fit¹ *adj* ('fitter, 'fittest) 1 suitable or right (*for*); good enough (*for sth, to be* sth). 2 think (see) fit to, decide or choose to. 3 in good health or condition. *v* (-tt-) 1 be the right size and shape for (sb or sth); put on (esp clothing) to see that it is the right size, etc. 2 make (sb) fit(1) (*for, to do, to be*). 3 put into place: *to fit new doors*. 4 fit in, be in harmony (*with*). fit sth or sb in, find the right or a suitable place or time for. fit out (up), equip. *n* the way sth fits; the result of fitting: *a good (bad, exact) fit.* 'fitter *n* (esp) mechanic who fits parts of machinery, apparatus, etc, together. 'fitting *adj* suitable; right (for the purpose). *n* 1 trial of wearing clothes to see if they fit(1). 2 (usu *pl*) things fixed in a building: *electric light fittings.*

fit² *n* 1 sudden attack of illness, esp one with violent movements or unconsciousness. 2 sudden outburst (of anger, laughter, etc). by fits and starts, in efforts that start and stop irregularly. 'fitful *adj* irregular.

five *n* & *adj* 5; (British decimal currency)—new pence (5p) coin = former shilling.

fix *v* 1 make (sth) fast so that it cannot be moved. 2 determine or decide; establish definitely: *to fix a date, fix the position of a ship.* 3 direct (one's eyes, attention) steadily (*on*). 4 treat (photographic films, colours, etc) so that light does not affect them. 5 fix sb up (*with* sth), arrange (sth) for him. *n* in a fix, in a difficult or awkward position. 'fixed *adj* unchanging; fast(1). 'fixedly *adv.* look fixedly at, look at with a fixed stare. 'fixture *n* 1 (esp *pl*) built-in cupboards, fireplaces, etc, bought with a building. 2 (day fixed for a) sporting event.

fizz *v* & *n* (make a) hissing sound (as of gas escaping from a liquid). '—le *v.* —le out, end feebly or in failure. '—y *adj* (-ier, -iest) gassy.

'flabby *adj* (-ier, -iest) (of the muscles, etc) not hard and firm.

flag¹ *n* (usu square or oblong piece of) cloth with a special design to represent a country, activity, group of people, etc. 'flag-staff *n* pole from which a — is flown.

flag² *n* (also 'flag-stone) flat square or oblong piece of stone for floors, etc.

flag³ *v* (-gg-) (of plants) droop; (fig) become tired or weak.

'flagon *n* large rounded bottle in which wine is sold.

'flagrant *adj* (of wrongdoing) openly and obviously wicked.

flair *n* instinctive ability (to do sth well): *have a — for learning languages.*

flake *n* small, light, leaf-like piece: *snow-flakes; —s of rust.* *v* (cause to) fall (*off*) in —s.

flame *n* 1 burning gas. 2 blaze of colour. *v* 1 send out —s; be like —s. 2 (fig) blaze with anger.

flank *n* 1 side of a human being or animal, between ribs and hip. 2 side of a mountain or (esp) an army or fleet. *v* 1 be at or on the — of. 2 go round the — of (the enemy).

'flannel *n* 1 soft, smooth woollen material; ('face-),—, small square of this for washing oneself. 2 (*pl*) — clothes, eg for informal wear in summer. ,flanne'lette *n* cotton material made to look like —.

flap *v* (-pp-) 1 (of wings, sails, etc) move up and down or from side to side. 2 hit lightly, with sth soft and wide. *n* 1 (sound of a) —ping movement or blow. 2 bit, piece, of material that hangs down or covers an opening: *the — of an envelope (a pocket).* 3 (colloq) nervous excitement.

flare *v* burn with a bright, unsteady flame; burst into bright flames. *n* flaring flame.

flash *n* sudden burst of flame or light. in a —, in an instant. *v* 1 send, give, out a — or —es. 2 come suddenly (into view, into the mind). 3 send (news, etc) instantly (eg by radio). 'flash-light *n* small electric torch; brilliant light used for taking photographs. '—y *adj* (of persons, their clothes, etc) smart and bright, but not in good taste.

flask *n* 1 narrow-necked bottle, eg as used in laboratories. 2 (also 'vacuum flask) bottle made to keep liquids very hot or very cold. 3 small bottle for carrying drink in the pocket.

flat *adj* (-ter, -test) 1 smooth; with a broad, level surface. 2 dull; uninteresting. 3 (of beer, etc) tasteless, lifeless, because the gas has gone. 4 (music) below the true pitch. 5 (colloq) absolute; downright: *a* — denial. *adv* in a —(5) manner. *n* 1 — part of sth (eg a sword). 2 stretch of — land, esp near water. 3 set of living-rooms, kitchen, etc on one floor.

'flatter *v* 1 praise too much; praise insincerely (in order to please). 2 (of a picture, artist, etc) show (sb) as better looking than he is. 3 — oneself (that), be pleased with one's belief that. —er *n*. —y *n*.

flaunt *v* display proudly and shamelessly, esp to attract attention.

'flavour *n* quality giving taste and smell to food. *v* give a — to.

flaw *n* crack; sth that lessens the value, beauty or perfection of a thing. '—less *adj* perfect.

flax *n* plant cultivated for the fibres obtained from its stems; — fibres (for making linen). '—en *adj* (of hair) pale yellow.

flay *v* take the skin off; whip.

flea *n* small jumping insect that feeds on blood. ⇨ p 144.

fleck *n* 1 small spot or patch (eg of colour). 2 particle (eg of dust).

fled ⇨ flee.

fledged *adj* (of birds) with fully grown wing feathers; able to fly. 'fledg(e)ling *n* young bird just able to fly; (fig) inexperienced person.

flee *v* (*pt & pp* fled) run away.

fleece *n* sheep's woolly coat; any similar covering. *v* rob (sb) of money, property, etc, by trickery. 'fleecy *adj* (of clouds, the sky) looking like —.

fleet[1] *n* 1 number of warships under one commander; all the warships of a country. 2 number of ships, aircraft, buses, etc, moving or working under one command or ownership.

fleet[2] *adj* quick-moving.

'fleeting *adj* (of thoughts, etc) passing quickly.

flesh *n* soft substance, esp muscle, between the skin and bones of animal bodies. one's own — and blood, one's near relations. '—y *adj*: of —; fat.

flew ⇨ fly.

flex *n* (length of) flexible insulated wire for electric current.

'flexible *adj* easily bent without breaking; (fig) easily changed to

suit new conditions. ,flexi-'bility *n*.

flick *v & n* (give a) quick, light blow (eg with a whip, the tip of a finger, etc).

'flicker *v* shine or burn unsteadily; flash and die away by turns. *n* —ing light.

flight[1] *n* 1 flying. 2 journey made by flying. 3 number of birds or objects in —: *a — of arrows*. 4 set of stairs between two landings(1).

flight[2] *n* 1 act of running away (from danger, etc). put (*the enemy*) to —, cause (them) to flee. take to —, flee. 2 group of aircraft.

'flimsy *adj* (-ier, -iest) (of materials) light and thin; (of objects, etc) easily injured or destroyed.

flinch *v* move back or away (*from*).

fling *v* (*pt & pp* flung) 1 throw violently. 2 put (*out*) or move (oneself, one's hands, etc, *about*) violently. *n* act of —ing; a —ing movement. have one's —, have a time of unrestricted pleasure.

flint *n* very hard stone, esp a piece of this struck against steel to produce sparks.

'flippant *adj* not respectful.

flirt *v* 1 make love without serious intentions: — *with* (sb). 2 consider (a scheme, etc), but not seriously. *n* person who —s(1).

flit *v* (-tt-) fly or move lightly and quickly (from place to place).

float *v* 1 be held up in air, gas, or (esp) on the surface of a liquid. 2 cause to —; keep —ing. *n* piece of cork, etc, used to keep a fishing-line, fishing-net, etc, from sinking.

flock *n* 1 number of birds or certain animals (eg sheep) of one kind either kept together or feeding and travelling together. 2 a Christian congregation. *v* gather, come together, in great numbers.

flog *v* (-gg-) beat with a rod or whip.

flood *n* 1 (coming of a) great quantity of water in a place usually dry. in —, (of a river) overflowing its banks. 2 outburst (of rain, tears, words, anger, etc). *v* 1 cover over or fill with water. 2 come, send, in large numbers or amounts. 'flood-tide *n* incoming tide.

floor *n* surface of a room on which one walks. (Not in USA) ground —, level with the street, etc; first

—, that above the ground —. **have the** —, have the right to speak. **—ed** adj (colloq) defeated.

flop v (-pp-) move, fall, put, or throw down, clumsily or helplessly. **'—py** adj hanging down loosely.

'flora n all the plants of a particular region or period.

'floral adj of flowers.

'florid adj 1 (of the face) naturally red. 2 too rich in ornament or colour.

'florin n former British coin worth two shillings.

'florist n shopkeeper selling (and sometimes growing) flowers.

flo'tilla n fleet of small warships.

'flounder v 1 make violent and usu unsuccessful efforts (as when one is in deep water and unable to swim). 2 (fig) hesitate, make mistakes, when trying to do sth (eg talking).

flour n fine powder made from grain, used for making bread, etc.

'flourish v 1 grow in a healthy way; be well and active; prosper. 2 wave about and show (eg a sword). n —ing movement.

flow v 1 move along or over as a river does; move smoothly. 2 (of hair, articles of dress, etc) hang down loosely. 3 (of the tide) come in; rise. n a —ing(1) movement; quantity that —s(1).

'flower n (usu colourful) part of a flower that produces seeds.

flown ⇨ fly.

flu n ⇨ influenza.

'fluctuate v (of levels, prices, etc) move up and down; be irregular. **,fluctu'ation** n.

flue n pipe in chimney, etc, for carrying away smoke; passage for taking hot air through a boiler, etc.

'fluent adj (of a person) able to speak smoothly and readily. **—ly** adv. **'fluency** n.

fluff n soft feather-like stuff that comes from blankets or other woolly material; soft, woolly fur, feathers, hair, etc. **'—y** adj.

'fluid n & adj (substance) able to flow (as gases and liquids do); (of ideas, etc) not fixed; changing.

fluke n (sth resulting from a) fortunate accident: to win by a —.

flung ⇨ fling.

'flurry n 1 short, sudden rush of wind or fall of rain or snow. 2 nervous hurry. v cause (sb) to be in a —(2).

flush v 1 (of a person, his face) become red through a rush of blood to the skin. 2 (of heat, health, feelings, etc) cause the face to become red in this way: —ed with success (wine). 3 clean or wash (eg drains) with a flood of water; (of liquid) rush out in a flood. n 1 rush of water. 2 a —ing(1) of the face. 3 rush of strong feeling.

'fluster v make nervous or confused. n —ed condition.

flute n musical instrument in the form of a wooden pipe. ⇨ p 180.

'flutter v 1 (of birds) move the wings hurriedly but without flying, or in short flights only. 2 (cause to) move in a quick, irregular way. n —ing movement; nervous condition; excitement: to cause a —.

fly[1] v (pt flew, pp flown) 1 move through the air as a bird or an aircraft does. 2 (of flags) wave in the air; cause to do this; put up. 3 go or run quickly; move quickly. **a flying visit**, a brief visit. **let fly at**, shoot or hit at. **fly into a rage**, lose one's temper. **'flier, 'flyer** n airman. **'fly-wheel** n heavy wheel in a machine, to keep its speed regular.

fly[2] n (the common **'house-fly**) two-winged insect. ⇨ p 144.

foal n young horse or ass.

foam n white mass of small bubbles formed in or on sth (esp liquids, eg beer). v form —; break into —; send out —. **'—y** adj.

'focus n meeting-point of rays of light (heat, etc); point, distance, at which the sharpest outline is given (to the eyes, through a telescope, on a camera plate, etc): in (out of) —. v (cause to) come together at a —; adjust (an instrument, etc) so that it is in —.

'fodder n dried food, hay, etc, for cattle and horses.

foe n enemy.

fog n thick mist (on land or sea surface) which is difficult to see through. **'foggy** adj (**'foggier, 'foggiest**).

'foible n a certain slight peculiarity of character.

foil[1] n 1 metal rolled or hammered

thin like paper. 2 person or thing that contrasts with, and thus shows up, the qualities of another.

foil² v make (sb's schemes, a plot, etc) ineffective; prevent (a person) from carrying out a plan, etc.

foist v — sth (off) on (sb), trick (sb) into accepting a useless or valueless article.

fold¹ v 1 bend one part of a thing over on itself; become —ed; be able to be —ed. 2 — one's arms, cross them over the chest. — (a child) in one's arms, hold it to one's breast. n part that is —ed; line made by —ing. '—er n —ing card; holder for loose papers.

fold² n enclosure for sheep.

'foliage n leaves (on trees, etc).

folk n pl 1 people in general. 2 one's —, (colloq) one's relatives. **'folk-dance (-song)** n old-time dance (song) handed down, esp among country —. '—lore n (study of) old beliefs, tales, customs, etc, of a people.

'follow v 1 come, go, have a place, after (sb or sth). 2 go along, keep to (a road, etc); understand (sth said, studied, etc). 3 engage in (as a profession, trade, etc): to — the plough, to work on the land. 4 take or accept (as a guide, example, etc): to — the fashion. 5 be necessarily true: That does not — at all. It —s, from what you say, that. . . . 6 — sth up, pursue, work at, further. as —s, as now to be given. —er n supporter. —ing n body of supporters.

'folly n foolishness; foolish act.

fo'ment v 1 put warm water or cloths, lotions, etc, to (a part of the body, to lessen pain). 2 excite (disorder, discontent, etc). ,fomen'tation n —ing; sth used (eg hot cloths) for —ing.

fond adj (-er, -est) 1 be —of, like very much; take pleasure in. 2 loving and kind. 3 (of hopes and ambitions) held but unlikely to be realized.

font n basin to hold water for baptism, in a church.

food n anything eaten by living things to keep them alive and make them grow. — for thought, sth that needs to be thought about. '—stuffs n pl materials used as food.

fool n 1 stupid or rash person. April F—'s Day, April 1st. make a — of, cause (sb) to seem a —. —'s errand, one that in the end is seen to be useless. 2 jester. play the —, make silly jokes, play silly tricks. v 1 behave like a —. 2 trick (sb) so that he looks —ish. '—hardy adj —ishly bold. '—ish adj silly; senseless. '—proof adj so simple that even a —cannot make a mistake.

'foolscap n size of a sheet of paper, (usu 17 inches × 13¾ inches).

foot n (pl feet) 1 lowest part of the leg below the ankle on which one stands. on —, walking. set sth on —, set it going. put one's — in it, blunder. 2 bottom (eg of a mountain, page). 3 measure of length, 12 inches: ten feet long; a three-foot rod. 4 infantry. v — the bill, agree to pay the bill. '—ball n (ball(1) used in a) game with eleven players on each side(2) in which the ball(1) is kicked. '—fall n sound of a —step. '—hills n pl low hills at the — of a mountain range. '—hold n safe place for the — (when rock-climbing, etc). '—ing n 1 foothold. 2 relationship (with people); position (in society, etc). 3 foundation. '—lights n pl lights along the front of the stage in a theatre. '—man n man-servant who admits visitors, waits at table, etc. 'footnote n note at the — of a printed page. '—path n narrow path, esp across fields or open country, or at the side of a country road. '—print n mark left by a — on the ground. '—step n tread; —print.

for prep 1 as far as; as long as: for a mile (minute). 2 in favour of. 3 in order to obtain: He paid £10 for it. conj because.

'forage n food for horses and cattle. v search (for food).

for'bear v (pt for'bore, pp for'borne) keep oneself back (from doing sth one wants to do). —ance n patience.

for'bid v (pt for'bade, pp for-'bidden) order (sb) not to do sth; order that sth must not be done: to — a girl to marry; to — a marriage. —ding adj stern; threatening.

force n 1 strength; power of body or mind: the — of a blow (*argument, explosion*); the —s of nature (eg storms). **2** sth tending to cause change (eg in society). **3** influence or pressure exerted at a point, tending to cause movement: *the — of gravity.* **4** body of armed men: *to join the Forces* (ie the *Navy, Army, Air Force*). **in —**, in great numbers. **5** (law) **come into —**, become binding; begin to operate. **put** (*a law*) **into —**, make it binding. *v* use —(1) to get or do sth, to make sb do sth; **break** *open* **by using —.** – **a person's hand**, make him do sth earlier than he wishes to do it. **a —ed march**, rapid one made by soldiers for a special purpose. **'—ful** *adj* (of a person, his character, of arguments, etc) full of —. **'forcible** *adj* done by the use of —; showing —. **'forcibly** *adv.*

ford *n* shallow place in a river where it is possible to walk across. *v* cross (a river) at a —.

fore *n* front part. **come to the —**, become active or prominent. *adj & adv* in front.

fore- *prefix* **1** before (in place). **'—foot** *n.* **'—leg** *n.* **2** before (in time). **—'tell** *v.* **—'warn** *v.*

'forearm *n* arm from elbow to wrist.

fore'bode *v* be a sign or warning that, have a feeling that, trouble is coming. **fore'boding** *n* feeling that trouble is coming.

fore'cast *v* say in advance what is likely to happen. **'forecast** *n* the weather —.

'forefathers *n pl* ancestors.

'forefinger *n* first finger, next to the thumb.

'forefront *n* most forward part.

fore'going *adj* which goes before (in time, space, or order).

fore'gone *adj* **— conclusion**, ending that can be or could have been seen from the start.

'foreground *n* part of a view nearest the person looking.

'forehead *n* part of the face above the eyes; brow.

'foreign *adj* **1** of or from another, not one's own, country. **2 — to**, not natural to; unconnected with. **3** coming from outside. **—er** *n* person from a — country.

'foreman *n* workman in authority over others; chief member (of a jury).

'foremost *adj & adv* first(ly); most important.

'forename *n* given name.

fore'see *v* (*pt* fore'saw, *pp* fore-'seen) see, know in advance.

fore'shadow *v* be a sign or warning of.

'foreshore *n* beach.

'foresight *n* ability to see future needs; care in preparing for these.

'forest *n* large area of tree-covered land. **—ry** *n* (science of) planting and caring for —s.

fore'stall *v* do sth before sb else and so prevent him from doing it.

fore'tell *v* forecast.

'forethought *n* careful thought or planning for the future.

for'ever *adv* for always; at all times.

'foreword *n* introductory comments printed in front of the text of a book, esp by sb other than the author (cf *preface*).

'forfeit *v* (have to) suffer the loss of sth as a punishment or consequence, or because of rules. *n* sth (to be) —ed. **—ure** *n* —ing.

for'gave ⇨ forgive.

forge¹ *v* **— ahead**, go forward, get in front, by making efforts.

forge² *n* workshop with fire and anvil where metal is heated and shaped. *v* shape (metal) by heating, hammering, etc.

forge³ *v* make a copy of sth (eg a signature, banknote) in order to deceive. **'—r** *n* person who does this. **'—ry** *n* forging; sth —d.

for'get *v* (*pt* for'got, *pp* for'gotten) fail to keep in the memory; put out of one's mind; fail to do sth: *He always —s his hat.* **— oneself**, behave thoughtlessly in a way not suited to the circumstances. **—ful** *adj* in the habit of —ting.

for'give *v* (*pt* for'gave, *pp* for-'given) release from punishment, blame; show mercy; give up one's anger towards sb else; excuse from payment of a debt. **—ness** *n* forgiving; willingness to —; being —n.

for'go *v* (*pt* for'went, *pp* for'gone) do without.

fork *n* **1** handle with two or more points (*prongs*) used for lifting food. **2** farm tool for breaking up ground, lifting hay, etc. **3** place where a road, tree trunk, etc.

divides into branches. v 1 lift, move, carry, with a —(2). 2 (of a road, etc) divide into branches.

for'lorn adj unhappy; forsaken.

form n 1 shape or outward appearance. 2 general arrangement or structure; sort; variety. 3 (grammar) shape taken by a word (in sound or spelling) to show its use, etc: past tense —s. 4 fixed order; manner of behaving or speaking required by custom, etc. 5 printed paper with spaces to be filled in: telegraph —s. 6 physical condition (esp of horses, athletes): in good —; out of —. 7 long wooden bench, usu without a back, for several persons to sit on. 8 class in a secondary school. v 1 give — or shape to; make. 2 (of ideas, etc) give shape to; take shape. 3 be, become; come into existence. '—al adj 1 in accordance with rules and customs. 2 of the outward shape (not the reality or substance). 3 regular or geometric in design: —al gardens. 4 (of behaviour) stiff or ceremonious. for'mality n —al behaviour; observance required by custom or rules. for'mation n —ing; sth —ed; (esp) arrangement or structure. '—less adj without —(1).

'former adj 1 of an earlier period. 2 (also as n) the first-named of two. —ly adv in — times.

'formidable adj 1 causing fear. 2 needing great effort to deal with.

'formula n 1 form of words (eg 'How d'you do?'). 2 statement of a rule, etc, esp one in signs or numbers. 3 set of directions (usu in symbols) for a medical preparation. —te v express clearly.

for'sake v (pt for'sook, pp for'saken) go away from; give up; desert.

fort n building(s) specially erected or strengthened for military defence.

forth adv 1 out. 2 onwards; forwards: from this day —. —'coming adj about to come out: —coming books. '—right adj straightforward; outspoken.

forth'with adv at once.

'fortify v strengthen (a place) against attack; strengthen (oneself, one's courage, etc). ,fortifi'cation n = fort.

'fortitude n calm courage, self-control, in the face of pain, danger, difficulty.

'fortnight n period of two weeks. —ly adj & adv (occurring) once every —.

'fortress n fortified town; fort.

'fortune n 1 chance; chance looked upon as a power deciding or influencing the future of sb or sth; fate; (bad or good) luck that comes to a person or enterprise. 2 prosperity; success; great sum of money. 'fortune-'teller n person who claims to be able to tell one's future. 'fortunate adj having, bringing, brought by, good —(1).

'forty n & adj 40. 'fortieth n & adj 40th; ¹⁄₄₀.

'forward adj 1 to or in the front. 2 well advanced or early. 3 ready and willing (to help, etc). 4 too eager. n front-line player (in football, etc). v help or send —; send (letters, etc) after a person to a new address. adv (also '—s) in a — direction. look — to, think, usu with pleasure, about sth coming in the future.

'fossil n recognizable (part of or impression(3) of a) prehistoric animal or plant once buried in the earth, now changed to rock. adj of or like a —.

'foster v care for; help the growth or development of. 'foster-,parent n one who acts as a parent in place of a real parent. 'foster-,brother (-,sister) n boy (girl) cared for by one's parent(s) and brought up as a member of the family.

fought ⇨ fight.

foul adj (-er, -est) 1 causing disgust; filthy. 2 wicked; (of language) full of oaths; (of weather) stormy. 3 — play, (a) (in sport) sth contrary to the rules; (b) violent crime, esp murder. adv fall (run) — of, (of ships) collide with; (fig) get into trouble with. v make or become dirty.

found¹ ⇨ find.

found² v 1 begin the building of; lay the base of. 2 get sth started (eg by providing money for a new school). foun'dation n 1 —ing; sth —ed, esp an institution such as a school or hospital; fund of money to be used for such an institution. **2** (often *pl*) strong base of a building, usu below ground level, on which it is built up. '—er *n* person who —s a school, etc, by providing money.

'**founder** *v* (of a ship) (cause to) fill with water and sink.

'**foundling** *n* deserted infant of unknown parents.

'**foundry** *n* place where metal or glass is melted or moulded.

'**fountain** *n* spring of water; water forced through holes (in pipes, etc) for ornamental purposes, etc. '**fountain-pen** *n* pen with a nib and with ink in the holder.

four *n & adj* 4. **on all —s**, on the hands and knees. '—**teen** *n & adj* 14. '—**th** *adj & n* 4th.

fowl *n* **1** domestic cock or hen. **2** (old use) any bird.

fox *n* wild animal like a dog with red fur and a bushy tail.

'**fraction** *n* **1** small part of a whole. **2** number that is not a whole number (eg $\frac{1}{3}$, $\frac{2}{3}$, 0·76).

'**fracture** *n* (esp of a bone) breaking; breakage. *v* break; crack.

'**fragile** *adj* easily injured or broken.

'**fragment** *n* part broken off; incomplete part (of a book, etc).

'**fragrant** *adj* sweet-smelling. '**fragrance** *n*.

frail *adj* (-er, -est) physically or morally weak; fragile.

frame *n* **1** main structure (eg steel girders, brick walls, wooden struts) of a ship, building, aircraft, etc, which gives it its shape. **2** human or animal body. **3** border of wood, etc, round a picture, door, or window; part of spectacles (3) that holds the lenses. **4** — **of mind**, state or condition of mind. *v* **1** put together; build up. **2** put a —(3) on or round. **3** take shape. '—**work** *n* part of a structure giving shape and support.

franc *n* (F) unit of decimal currency in some countries (France, Belgium, Cameroon, etc).

'**franchise** *n* full rights of citizenship given by a country or town, esp the right to vote at elections.

frank *adj* (-er, -est) showing one's true thoughts, feelings, etc. '—**ly** *adv*.

'**frantic** *adj* wildly excited (*with* pain, anxiety, etc). —**ally** *adv*.

fra'ternal *adj* brotherly. **fra'ter-**

nity *n* (esp) society of men (eg monks) who treat each other as brothers; men sharing the same interests. '**fraternize** *v* make friends (*with*).

fraud *n* **1** criminal (act of) deception. **2** person or thing that deceives. '—**ulent** *adj*.

fraught *adj* — **with**, involving, attended with (usu unpleasant consequences); filled with (meaning).

fray *v* (of cloth, rope, etc) become worn, make worn, by rubbing, so that there are loose threads.

freak *n* **1** absurd or most unusual idea, act, or occurrence; person full of absurd ideas. **2** person, animal, or plant that is abnormal in form. '—**ish** *adj* abnormal.

'**freckle** *n* one of the small light-brown patches sometimes caused by the sun on a fair skin.

free *adj* (-r, -st) **1** (of a country) self-governing; having a system of government which allows private rights. **2** (of a person) not a slave; not in prison; not prevented from doing what one wants to do. **3** (of things) not fixed, controlled, or held back. **have (give sb) a — hand**, authority to do what seems best without consulting others. **the F— Churches**, the nonconformists. **4** without payment. **— trade**, the admission of goods into a country without duty. **5** (of place or time) not occupied or engaged; (of a person) having — time. **6** (of a translation) giving the general meaning but not word for word. **7 be — with** (*one's money*), etc), give readily. **be — from** (*error*, etc), be without. *v* **make —**. '—**dom** *n* condition of being —. '**free-hand** *adj* (of drawing) done without the help of ruler, compasses, etc. '**free-handed** *adj* generous (with money). '—**hold** *adj* absolute ownership of land. '—**ly** *adv* in a — manner; readily.

freeze *v* (*pt* froze, *pp* 'frozen) **1** be freezing, be so cold that water becomes ice. **2** (of water) become ice; (of other substances) become hard or stiff from cold; (of a person) feel very cold. **3** make cold; make hard: *frozen meat* (*roads*). '**freezing-point** *n* temperature at which a liquid (esp water) —s.

freight *n* (money charged for) the

carriage of goods from place to place; the goods carried. *v* load (a ship) with cargo. **'—er** *n* cargo ship.

french *adj* — **window,** one that serves as both a door and a window. **take — leave,** go away, do sth, without asking permission.

'frenzy *n* violent excitement. **'frenzied** *adj* filled with, showing, —.

'frequent *adj* often happening; numerous; common. **fre'quent** *v* go —ly to. **'frequency** *n* being —; rate of occurrence. **—ly** *adv* often.

fresh *adj* (**-er, -est**) **1** newly made, produced, gathered, grown, arrived, etc. **2** new or different. **3** (of food) not salted or tinned; (of water) not salt; (of a person's complexion) healthy-looking; (of weather, the wind) cool. **— air,** clean out-of-doors air. **'—ly** *adv.*

fret *v* (**-tt-**) **1** worry; (cause to) be discontented. **2** wear away by rubbing or biting at. **'—ful** *adj* irritable.

'friar *n* man who is a member of one of certain religious orders, esp one who has vowed to live a life of poverty.

'friction *n* **1** the rubbing of one thing against another, esp when this wastes energy. **2** difference of opinion leading to argument, etc.

'Friday *n* sixth day of the week; Muslims' day of prayer (cf Sabbath). **Good F—,** the F— before Easter.

fridge *n* (colloq) refrigerator.

friend *n* **1** sb, not a relative, whom one likes and whose company one enjoys. **make —s with,** become the —(s) of. **2 F—,** member of the Society of Friends (Quakers). **'—ly** *adj* (**-ier, -iest**) behaving like a —. **'—liness** *n* —ly feeling or behaviour. **'—ship** *n.*

fright *n* great and sudden fear. **'—en** *v* fill with —; give a — to. **'—ful** *adj* (colloq) unpleasant. **'—fully** *adv* (colloq) very.

'frigid *adj* **1** cold(2). **2** unfriendly.

frill *n* (ornamental) wavy border sewn on to the edge of a sleeve, collar, etc. **'—ed** *adj* having —s.

fringe *n* **1** ornamental border of loose threads (eg on a shawl or rug). **2** edge (of a crowd, forest, etc). **3** part of the (usu woman's) hair allowed to cover the forehead. *v* put a — on; serve as a — to.

frisk *v* jump and run about playfully. **'—y** *adj* ready to —; lively.

'frivolous *adj* not serious; unimportant; (of persons) lacking in seriousness. **fri'volity** *n.*

fro *adv* **to and —,** backwards and forwards.

frock *n* woman's dress or gown; child's dress.

frog *n* small, cold-blooded, tailless jumping animal living in water and on land. **'—man** *n* sb wearing special clothes and equipment so that he can stay under water for a long time.

'frolic *v* play about in a lively way. *n* happy, lively play. **—some** *adj.*

from *prep* (indicating) **1** a starting-point in space: *travelling — London to Hong Kong.* **2** the beginning of a period: *— the first of May.* **— time to time,** occasionally. **3** place concerned with distance, absence, etc: *ten miles — the coast; be away — home.* **4** giver, sender: *a letter — my brother.* **5** source, origin: *a quotation — Shakespeare. Wine is made — grapes.* **6** escape, separation, release: *free — suspicion.* **7** motive, cause: *collapse — weakness.* **8** distinction, difference: *This is different — that.*

front *n* **1** the forward part; most important side. **2** (war) place where fighting is taking place. **3 put on (show) a bold —,** show no fear. *v* be opposite; have the — facing towards.

'frontier *n* part of a country bordering on another country; boundary.

'frontispiece *n* picture coming before the text of a book.

frost *n* **1** weather condition with temperature below the freezing-point of water. **2** white, powder-like coating of frozen vapour on the ground, roofs, plants, etc. *v* cover with —(2); damage (plants, etc) by —(1). **'frost-bite** *n* injury to a part of the body from —(1). **'frost-bitten** *adj* having frost-bite. **'—y** *adj* (**-ier, -iest**) freezing; covered with —(2).

froth *n* creamy mass of small bubbles; foam. *v* give off —. **'—y** *adj* of, like, covered with, —.

frown *v* (showing displeasure,

puzzlement, etc) draw the eyebrows together causing lines on the forehead. **— on,** show disapproval. of. n **—ing** look.

froze, 'frozen ⇨ freeze.

'**frugal** adj **1** economical (esp of food). **2** costing little. **—ly** adv. **fru'gality** n.

fruit n **1** part of a plant containing the seed(s); (esp) sweet — that can be used as food. ⇨ p 115. **2** (fig) profit, result (of industry, labour, study, etc). v (of trees and plants) bear —. '**—erer** dealer in —. '**—ful** adj producing —. **fru'ition** n realization of hopes; outcome hoped for. '**—less** adj without — or (fig) success. '**—y** adj of or like — (eg in taste or smell).

frus'trate v prevent (sb) from doing sth; prevent (sb's plans) from being carried out. **frus'tration** n.

fry v cook, be cooked, in boiling fat.

'**fuddle** v make stupid, esp with drink.

'**fuel** n material for burning (eg coal, oil, petrol). v (-ll-) supply with —; take in —.

'**fugitive** n & adj (person) running away (from justice, danger, etc).

ful'fil v (-ll-) perform (a task, duty, etc); do what is required (by conditions, etc); complete (an undertaking). **—ment** n.

full adj (-er, -est) **1** holding as much or as many as possible, all there is space for. **2** complete. **in —,** with all details. **to the —,** to the limit. **— face,** not a side view. **— moon,** seen as a complete disc. **at — speed,** at the highest speed. adv completely: full-grown. '**—y** adv.

'**fumble** v feel about uncertainly or awkwardly with the hands.

fume n (usu pl) strong-smelling smoke, gas, or vapour. v give off —s; (fig) show signs of discontent or anger. '**fumigate** v disinfect by means of —s.

fun n amusement, enjoyment. **in fun,** not seriously. **make fun of, poke fun at,** tease; cause others to laugh at. '**funny** adj ⇨ funny.

'**function** n **1** special activity or purpose (of sb or sth). **2** public ceremony or event. v **1** fulfil a —(1). **2** —as, do the job or duty of.

fund n **1** store or supply (of non-material things): a — of common

sense. **2** (also pl) sum of money available for a purpose: a relief —.

,**funda'mental** adj of or forming a foundation; of great importance. n (usu pl) — rule or principle.

'**funeral** n burying or burning of a dead person with the usual ceremonies.

'**fungus** n (pl '**fungi**) plant, without green leaves, which usu grows on other plants or decaying matter such as old wood.

'**funnel** n **1** pipe or tube, wide at the top and narrowing at the bottom, for pouring liquids or powder into small openings. **2** outlet for smoke from a steamer, railway engine, etc.

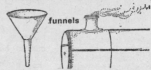

.funnels

'**funny** adj (-ier, -iest) **1** causing fun or amusement. **2** strange; surprising. '**funnily** adv.

fur n **1** soft thick hair covering certain animals (eg cats). **2** animal skin with the fur on it, used as clothing: a fur coat; dressed in furs. **3** rough coating on a person's tongue when he is ill, or on the inside of a kettle or boiler when the water is chalky. v coat (the tongue, inside of a boiler, etc) with fur(3). '**furry** adj (-ier, -iest).

'**furious** adj full of fury; violent.

furl v (of sails, flags, umbrellas) roll up.

'**furlong** n measurement of 220 yards or 201·2 metres.

furlough n (permission for) absence from duty (esp persons employed abroad) for a holiday at home.

'**furnace** n **1** shut-in fire-place for heating water. **2** enclosed space for heating metals, making glass, etc.

'**furnish** v supply or provide (with); put furniture in. '**furniture** n such things as tables, chairs, beds, etc, needed for a room.

'**furrow** n **1** long, deep cut made in the ground by a plough. **2** line on the forehead. v make —s in.

'**further** adv **1** at a greater distance

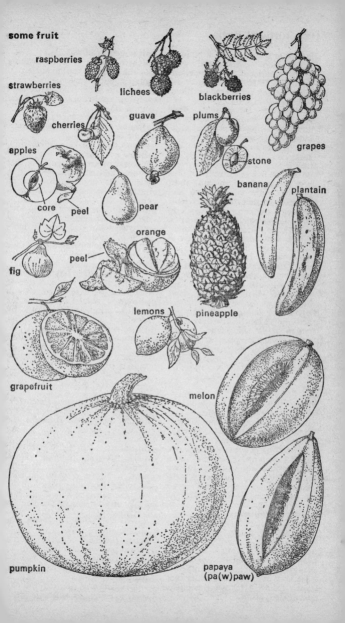

some fruit

raspberries

strawberries

lichees

blackberries

cherries

guava

plums

grapes

apples

stone

core   peel

pear

banana

plantain

fig

peel

orange

pineapple

grapefruit

lemons

melon

pumpkin

papaya
(pa(w)paw)

in time or space. ⇨ far. **2** besides; in addition. *adj* beyond what exists; additional. *v* help forward (plans, etc). '**furthest** *adv & adj* most distant (in space or time). —**more** *adv* in addition.

'**furtive** *adj* (of actions) done secretly or without wishing to attract attention; (of persons) wishing to escape notice.

'**fury** *n* violent excitement, esp anger; outburst of wild feeling.

fuse *v* melt with great heat; join or become one as the result of this. *n* **1** (in an electric circuit) short piece of wire which melts and breaks the circuit if a fault develops. **2** device for carrying a spark to explode powder, etc. '**fusion** *n* mixing or blending of different things into one: (fig) *a fusion of races.*

'**fuselage** *n* body of an aircraft.

fuss *n* unnecessary excitement, esp about unimportant things. *v* get into a —; cause to be in a —. '**—y** *adj* (-ier, -iest) worrying about little things.

'**futile** *adj* useless; unlikely to accomplish much. **fu'tility** *n*.

'**future** *n & adj* (time, events) coming after the present.

G

'**gabble** *v* talk quickly and not very clearly. *n* such talking.

'**gable** *n* three-cornered part of an outside wall between sloping roofs.

gag *n* **1** sth put in a person's mouth to keep it open, or over it to stop him talking. **2** actor's own addition to his part; stage joke. *v* (-gg-) **1** put a gag(1) in or over the mouth of. **2** use gags(2).

'**gaiety**, '**gaily** ⇨ gay.

gain *v* **1** obtain (sth wanted or needed). **2** make progress; be improved: *to —in strength.* **—time**, improve one's chances by delaying or postponing sth. **— upon**, (a) get closer to (persons being pursued, eg in a race); (b) get farther away from (sb following behind). *n* sth —ed; profit.

gait *n* manner of walking.

'**gaiter** *n* leather or cloth covering for the leg from knee to ankle.

'**gala** *n* public merry-making.

'**galaxy** *n* irregular band of stars not seen separately but as a bright band across the sky.

gale *n* very strong wind; storm.

'**gallant** *adj* **1** brave. **2** fine; stately. **—ry** *n* bravery.

'**galleon** *n* old Spanish sailing-ship.

'**gallery** *n* **1** room(s) for the display of works of art. **2** (people in the) highest and cheapest seats in a theatre. **3** floor or platform extending from the inner wall of a hall, church, etc.

'**galley** *n* **1** (in ancient times) low, flat ship with one deck, rowed by many slaves or criminals. **2** ship's kitchen.

'**gallon** *n* liquid measurement of four quarts or 4·5 litres.

'**gallop** *n* (of a horse) fastest pace, with all four feet off the ground together at each stride; a ride at this pace. *v* (cause to) go at a —.

'**gallows** *n* wooden framework for putting criminals to death by hanging.

ga'lore *adv* in plenty.

'**galvanism** *n* (science of, medical use of) electricity produced by chemical action. '**galvanize** *v* coat (sheet iron, etc) with metal (eg zinc) by galvanism; (fig) shock or rouse (a person *into* doing sth).

'**gambit** *n* opening move (in chess).

'**gamble** *v* play games of chance for money; take great risks for the chance of winning sth. *n* risky undertaking. **—r** *n*.

'**gambol** *v* (-ll-) *& n* (usu *pl*) (make) quick, playful, jumping movements.

game¹ *n* **1** form of play, esp with rules (eg football). **play the —**, keep the rules; be honest and fair. **2** (*pl*) athletic contests. **3** plan or undertaking; trick. **having a — with**, playing a trick on. **the — is up**, the attempt has failed. **4** (collective) (flesh of) animals and birds hunted for sport and food. **big —**, lions, elephants, etc. '**game,keeper** *n* man employed to breed and protect —(4).

game² *adj* having, showing, willingness or energy (*for* sth, *to do* sth).

'gander n male goose.

gang n number of labourers, slaves, prisoners, criminals, etc, working together. **'—ster** n member of a — of criminals.

'gangway n 1 opening in a ship's side; movable bridge from this to the land. 2 passage between rows of seats or persons.

gaol n (= jail) public prison. v put in —. **'—er** n person in charge of prisoners in —.

gap n 1 break or opening (in a wall, hedge, etc). 2 unfilled space; wide separation; interval.

gape v yawn; open the mouth widely; stare open-mouthed (at).

'garage n building, shed where motor-cars are stored, repaired, etc.

garb n (style of) dress (esp as worn by persons of a particular profession or trade).

'garbage n waste food put out as worthless, or for pigs, etc.

'garble v make an unfair selection from (facts, statements, etc) in order to give a wrong idea.

'garden n 1 (piece of) ground used for growing flowers, fruit, vegetables, etc. 2 (often pl) public park. **—er** n person who works in a —.

'gargle v wash the throat with liquid kept in motion by a stream of breath. n liquid used for this.

'garish adj too bright; overdecorated.

'garland n circle of flowers or leaves as an ornament or decoration.

'garlic n onion-like plant with a strong taste and smell.

'garment n article of clothing.

'garnish v decorate (esp a dish of food).

'garret n room on the top floor of a house, esp one in the roof.

'garrison n military force stationed in a town or fort. v supply with a —.

'garrulous adj talkative. **gar'rulity** n.

'garter n elastic band worn to keep a stocking in place.

gas n (pl 'gases) 1 any air-like substance (air is a mixture of gases). 2 (esp) the gas, natural or manufactured from coal, used for heating, etc. 3 (USA, colloq) gasolene (= petrol). v (-ss-) poison or overcome by gas. **'gaseous** adj.

gash n long deep cut or wound. v make a — in.

'gasolene n (USA) petrol.

gasp v take short quick breaths as a fish does out of water. n painful catching of the breath. **at one's last —**, exhausted.

'gastric adj of the stomach.

gate n opening in a wall, fence, field, etc, with a movable barrier across it. **'—way** n way in or out closed by —(s).

'gather v 1 get, come, or bring together. 2 pick (flowers, etc). collect (one's papers, etc). 3 understand; conclude: What did you — from his remarks? 4 draw (cloth, the brows) together into small folds. 5 (of an abscess) fester. **—ing** n a coming together of people.

'gaudy adj (-ier, -iest) too bright and showy. **'gaudily** adv.

gauge n 1 standard measure; size or extent. 2 distance between rails or a pair of wheels; thickness of wire, sheet-metal; diameter of a bullet, etc. 3 instrument for measuring rainfall, strength of wind, size of tools, thickness of wire, etc. v measure accurately; (fig) form an opinion or estimate of.

gaunt adj lean; thin.

'gauntlet¹ n strong glove covering the wrist.

'gauntlet² n run the —, run between rows of men who strike the runner with sticks, etc, as a punishment.

gauze n thin, transparent, net-like material of silk, cotton, etc, or of fine wire (for screening windows, etc).

gave ⇨ give.

gay adj ('gayer, 'gayest) cheerful; happy and full of fun. **'gaily** adv. **'gaiety** n cheerfulness; (pl) merrymaking.

gaze v & n (take a) long and steady look (at sb or sth).

ga'zelle n (kinds of) small antelope.

ga'zette n government periodical with news of appointments, promotions, etc, of officers and officials.

gear n 1 equipment or apparatus for a special purpose: an aircraft's landing-gear. 2 set of toothed wheels working together in a machine, esp such a set to connect a motor-car engine with the wheels on the road. **in (out of)** —, with the wheels connected with (disconnected from) the engine. **high (low)** —, that which causes a high (low) speed: *the low — is used when starting or going up hill.* v put in —: — *up (down)*, put into high (low) —.

geese ⇨ **goose.**

gem n 1 precious stone or jewel. 2 sth valued because of its great beauty.

'gender n any of the three classes *masculine, feminine,* and *neuter* used of nouns and pronouns.

,gene'alogy n descent of persons from ancestors; diagram or table illustrating this.

'genera ⇨ **genus.**

'general adj 1 of, affecting, all or nearly all; not special or particular. **a — election,** one for parliamentary representatives over the whole country. **as a — rule, in —,** usually. 2 not in detail: *a — outline of a plan.* 3 (after an official title) chief: *inspector-general.* n army officer with the highest rank below field-marshal. **,gene'rality** n —(1) rule or statement. **'generalize** v 1 draw a —(1) conclusion (*from*); make a —(1) statement (eg '*All boys are lazy.*'). 2 bring into —(1) use. **—ly** adv usually; widely; in a —(1) sense.

'generate v cause to exist or occur; produce (eg heat, electricity). **,gene'ration** n 1 generating. 2 single stage in family descent: *three generations* (children, parents, grandparents). 3 all persons born about the same period. 4 average period (regarded as thirty years) in which children grow up, marry, and have children. **'generator** n machine, apparatus, etc, for generating steam, electric current, etc.

'generous adj 1 ready to give, giving, freely; given freely; noble-minded. 2 plentiful. **,gene'rosity** n.

'genesis n beginning; starting-point.

'genial adj 1 kindly; sympathetic. 2 (of climate, etc) favourable to growth; warm. **—ly** adv. **,geni'ality** n quality of being —.

'genie n (*pl* 'genii) (in Arabian stories) spirit with strange powers

'genitive n & adj (grammar) possessive. **— case,** showing source or possession.

'genius n (*pl* 'geniuses) (person with) unusually great powers of mind or imagination.

gen'teel adj 1 polite and well-bred. 2 (modern use) imitating the ways of living, speaking, etc, of the upper classes. **gen'tility** n.

'Gentile adj & n (person) not of the Jewish race.

'gentle adj (-r, -st) 1 kind; friendly; not rough or violent. 2 (of a slope) not steep. 3 (of a family) with a good social position. **—man** n man of honourable and kindly behaviour. **—manly** adj well-behaved. **'gently** adv in a —(1), (2) manner.

'genuine adj really what it is said to be; true. **—ly** adv.

'genus n (*pl* 'genera) 1 (science) division of animals or plants within a family. 2 sort; class.

ge'ography n science of the world, its structure and its people. **geo'graphic(al)** adj.

ge'ology n science of rocks and soils. **ge'ologist** n expert in —. **,geo'logical** adj.

ge'ometry n science of the properties and relations of lines, angles, surfaces, and solids. **,geo'metric(al)** adj.

germ n 1 part of a living organism capable of becoming a new organism; (fig) starting-point (of an idea, etc). 2 microbe or bacillus, esp one causing disease. **'germinate** v (of seeds) (cause to) begin growth.

ges'ticulate v make movements of the hands, arms, or head instead of, or while, speaking. **ges,ticu'lation** n.

'gesture v & n (use a) movement of the hand or head to indicate or illustrate an idea, feeling, etc.

get v (-tt-) (*pt & pp* got) 1 obtain; buy; earn; win; fetch; be given; receive; understand or see (a meaning, etc). 2 (cause to) become; (cause to) arrive, come or go somewhere: *to get there.* 3 catch; suffer; experience: *to get influenza.* 4 cause sth to be done; have: *to get your hair cut.* 5 engage, persuade, (sb to do sth): *to get the doctor to call.* 6 (with *adv & prep*) **get about,** (of news, etc) spread; (of people) travel. **get sth across**, cause people to understand or accept (eg a new idea, a joke). **get along**, make progress; manage; live sociably (*with* sb). **get at**, reach; find out. **get by heart**, learn. **get in**, arrive; be elected. **get sth in**, collect (eg crops, debts). **get off**, start; escape (punishment). **get on**, (*with*); approach: *it's getting on for tea-time.* **get on with sb**, be friendly together. **get out of**, escape (doing sth); give up (a habit). **get over**, overcome (difficulties); recover from (an illness); finish (a task). **get round** (a rule, etc), evade it. **get round sb**, persuade him to do what is desired. **get through**, pass (an examination); reach the end of (work, money, etc). **get to** (*work, business*, etc), start. **get to know** (*like*, etc) reach the stage of knowing (liking, etc). **get up**, stand; get out of bed; (of wind) become strong. **get up to**, reach; overtake. **get up to mischief**, become naughty, etc. **get sth up**, prepare (clothes, goods, etc) for use or display; organize (an entertainment); produce. **7** (in the perfect tenses) *have got* = have; *have got to* = must; *have not got to* = need not. **get-'at-able** *adj* able to be reached. **'get-up** *n* style in which sth appears.

geyser *n* **1** natural spring sending up at intervals a column of hot water or steam. **2** apparatus for heating water (eg by gas) in a bathroom, etc.

ghastly *adj* **1** death-like; pale. **2** causing horror or fear.

ghost *n* **1** spirit of a dead person appearing to sb living. **give up the —**, die. **'—ly** *adj* like a —.

giant *n* **1** (in fairy-tales) man of very great height and size. **2** man, animal, or plant, larger than normal.

gibe *v* mock (*at*). *n* mocking look or word(s).

giddy *adj* (-ier, -iest) **1** causing, having, the feeling that everything is turning round. **2** too fond of pleasure. **'giddily** *adv*. **'giddiness** *n*.

gift *n* **1** sth given or received without payment. **2** natural ability or

talent. **'—ed** *adj* having great natural ability.

gi'gantic *adj* of immense size.

'giggle *v & n* (give a) silly (often nervous) laugh.

gild *v* cover with gold-leaf or gold-coloured paint. **gilt** *adj* **—ed**; gold-coloured. *n* material for **—ing**. ⇨ guild.

gill[1] *n* (usu *pl*) parts of the body with which a fish breathes in water.

gill[2] *n* one quarter of a pint.

gilt ⇨ gild.

gimlet *n* tool for making a small hole in wood.

'gimmick *n* ingenious method of attracting attention.

gin *n* colourless alcoholic drink made from grain.

'ginger *n* **1** plant with a hot-tasting root used in cooking and as a flavouring. **2** light reddish-yellow.

'gingerly *adj & adv* cautious(ly).

'gipsy, gypsy *n* member of a wandering race (in Europe) making a living by horse-dealing, fortune-telling, etc.

gi'raffe *n* animal with dark spots on yellow skin, and a long neck and legs. ⇨ p 317.

'girder *n* wood, iron, or steel beam used to support the joists of a floor, bridge, etc.

'girdle *n* **1** cord or belt fastened round the waist. **2** sth that encircles. *v* encircle.

girl *n* female child; (colloq) young woman. **'—ish** *adj* of, for, like, a —.

girth *n* measurement round sth: *a tree* 30 *feet in —.*

gist *n* the **—** of (sb's remarks, etc), the substance or general sense.

give *v* (*pt* gave, *pp* 'given) **1** hand sth over (without payment); hand sth over in exchange for sth else. **2** (with *adv & prep*, special senses only) **—** sth away, allow (a secret) to become known. **— sb away**, betray, be false to. **— the bride away** (at a wedding ceremony), give her to the bridegroom. **— in**, stop trying to do or get sth. **— out**, (of supplies) come to an end, be used up. **— sth out**, distribute; announce. **— over**, stop (doing sth). **— up**, stop (doing sth); discontinue (a habit); surrender. **3** (with nouns) **—** *a laugh* (*a push*, etc, = laugh (push, etc). **—** a hand, help. — **evidence of,** show that one has. — **ground,** (of an army) retire. — **rise to,** cause, produce. — **way,** (of ice, a rope, structure) break; (of an army) be forced back; (of one's feelings, etc), surrender oneself (*to* despair, etc), — **place** (*to*). **4** — *sb* **to understand that,** assure him, lead him to believe, that. **5** yield; be able to be forced or pressed out of the natural or usual shape. be elastic: *The foundations are giving. The floor of a dance-hall should — a little.* **6** — (**up**)**on,** (of windows, etc) overlook; open on to. *n* quality of being elastic, of yielding to pressure. — **and take,** willingness to compromise(1). **'given** (*pp*) (special senses) **1** agreed upon: *at a given time.* **2** **given to,** addicted to (eg boasting). **3** **given name,** name given to a child in addition to the family name.

'glacial *adj* of ice.

'glacier *n* mass of ice, formed by snow on mountains, moving slowly along a valley.

glad *adj* (-der, -dest) pleased; joyful. **'—ly** *adv.* **'—ness** *n.* **'—den** *v* make —.

'glamour *n* charm; enchantment; the power of beauty or of romance to move the feelings. **'glamorous** *adj.*

glance *v* **1** take a quick look (*at, over,* etc). **2** (of bright objects, light) flash. **3** (of a weapon or a blow) slip or slide (*off*). *n* quick look.

gland *n* one of certain organs that separate from the blood substances that are needed or not needed for the body's use: *sweat —s; a snake's poison —s.* **'—ular** *adj* of the —s.

glare *v & n* (shine with a) strong, bright light; (give an) angry or fierce look (*at*). **'glaring** *adj* (of errors) easily seen.

glass *n* **1** hard, clear substance that one can see through. **2** — drinking-vessel. **3** looking-glass; — mirror.

glasses

4 telescope; (*pl*) binoculars. **5** barometer. **6** (*pl*) eye-glasses; spectacles. **7** (collective) vessels made of — (eg bowls and dishes): — **and china.** **'glass-,blower** *n* workman who blows molten — to shape it into bottles, etc. **'glasshouse** *n* building with — sides and roof (for growing plants, etc). **'—y** *adj* like —; (of the eyes, a look) dull; fixed.

glaze *v* **1** fit (windows, etc) with glass. **2** cover (pots, etc) with a glass-like coating. **3** (of the eyes) become lifeless in appearance. *n* substance used for, surface obtained by giving a) thin glass coating on pottery, etc. **'glazier** *n* workman who —s window-frames, etc.

gleam *v & n* (give or send out a) ray of soft light (esp one that comes and goes); (fig) brief show (of hope, etc).

glean *v* pick up grain left in a field by the harvesters; (fig) gather (news, etc) in small quantities.

glee *n* delight given by success. **'—ful** *adj.* **'—fully** *adv.*

glib *adj* (of a person, what he says) ready and smooth but not sincere: *a — speaker* (*excuse*).

glide *v* move along smoothly and continuously. *n* such a movement. **'—r** *n* aircraft without any driving-power. **'gliding** *n* sport of flying in —rs.

'glimmer *v & n* (send out a) weak, uncertain light. **not a —** of hope, (fig) no hope at all.

glimpse *v & n* (catch a) short and not very clear view (of sb or sth).

'glisten *v* (esp of wet or polished surfaces, eyes) shine.

'glitter *v & n* (shine brightly with) flashes of light.

gloat *v* — **over,** look on, think about (one's possessions, successes, another person's misfortunes), with selfish delight.

globe *n* object shaped like a ball, esp one with a map of the earth on it.

gloom *n* **1** semi-darkness; deep shade; obscurity. **2** feeling of sadness and hopelessness. **'—y** *adj.* (-ier, -iest). **'—ily** *adj.*

'glorify ⋄ glory.

'glory *n* **1** high fame and honour won by great deeds. **2** adoration and thanksgiving offered to God. **3** reason for pride; sth deserving fame and respect. **4** quality of being beautiful or magnificent. *v* — **in**, rejoice in, take great pride in. **'glorify** *v* give —(2) to; worship. **'glorious** *adj* having or causing —; (*colloq*) enjoyable.

gloss¹ *n* smooth shiny surface. **'—y** *adj* (-ier, -iest) smooth and shiny.

gloss² *n* explanation (in a footnote or list at the end of a book) of difficult word(s) or phrase(s). *v* add —(es) to; write —(es). **'—ary** *n* collection of —es.

glove *n* covering of leather, wool, etc, for the hand, usu with the fingers separate.

glow *v & n* **1** (send out) brightness and warmth without a flame. **2** (have a) warm or flushed look or feeling (as after exercise or when excited). **'glow-worm** *n* insect of which the female gives out a green light at its tail.

glower *v* look in a threatening or angry way (*at*).

glue *n* sticky substance used for joining (esp wooden) things. *v* stick, make fast, with —.

glum *adj* (-mer, -mest) gloomy; sad.

glut *v* over-supply; over-eat. *n* supply greatly in excess of demand. **'—ton** *n* person who eats too much. **'—tonous** *adj* very greedy for food (fig, for work, etc). **'—tony** *n*.

gnarled *adj* (of tree trunks) rough and twisted; covered with knobs.

gnash *v* **1** (of teeth) strike together (in rage, etc). **2** (of a person) make the teeth do this.

gnat *n* small blood-sucking fly. ⇨ p 144.

gnaw *v* continue biting (*at sth*) hard; (fig, of anxiety, etc) torment.

gnome *n* (in tales) imp living underground.

go *v* (3rd person, present tense, **goes**; *pt* **went**, *pp* **gone**) **1** start; move or pass; leave; travel; proceed. **2** extend. **3** become: *to go bad* (eg food). *to go to sleep*, to fall asleep. **4** (of machines, etc) work; operate: *This clock goes by electricity*. **5** be or live (esp as a habit): *to go armed (naked)*. **6** be usually or normally placed or kept. **7** give way; break: *The masts went in the storm*. **8** (of money) be spent on: *Half his wages goes on rent and clothes*. **9** (with *adv & prep*) **go about sth**, set to work at it (in a certain way). **go ahead**, start, make progress. **go after**, try to obtain or overtake. **go away**, leave home, move to a distance. **go back (up)on**, withdraw from (a promise, etc). **go by**, pass; be guided by: *a good rule to go by*. **go by the name of**, be called. **go down**, (of a ship) sink; (of the sea, wind, etc) become calm. **go for**, attack; be sold for (eg ten pence); be expended: *All his work went for nothing*. **go in for**, take part in (eg an examination or competition); take up as a hobby, pursuit, etc: *to go in for golf*. **go into**, enter: *to go into business*; examine: *to go into the evidence*; occupy oneself with: *to go into details*. **go off**, (of a gun, explosives, etc) be fired with a loud noise; (of food, etc) lose quality: *The milk has gone off* (ie become bad). **go off well (badly)**, (of an entertainment, plan, etc) have (fail to have) the result hoped for. **go on**, continue; happen. **be going on for**, be getting near to (eg midnight). **go out**, (of a fire or light) stop burning. **go over (through) sth**, examine or study it carefully. **go round**, (of supplies) be enough for everyone. **go through**, suffer, undergo (hardships, etc. **go through with**, complete (an undertaking, etc). **go together**, be satisfactory when together. **go with**, (of colours, etc) be in harmony with. **go without**, endure the lack of. **10 go to sea**, become a sailor. **go halves**, divide equally. **go shares**, share equally. **go to law**, start legal action against (sb). **go to pieces**, break up (physically or mentally). **go to seed**, (fig) become less active intellectually. *n* (*pl* **goes**) **1** energy; enthusiasm: *full of go*. **2 have a go** (*at sth*), attempt. **3 on the go**, busy; active. **all the go**, fashionable. **'go-between** *n* person making arrangements for others who have not yet met. **'goings-'on** *n pl* (colloq) (usu strange or surprising) behaviour or happenings.

goad *n* pointed stick for urging

animals on; sth urging a person to activity. *v* urge to do sth.

goal *n* **1** point marking the end of a race; (football, etc) posts between which the ball is to be kicked or hit; point made by doing this. **2** (fig) object of efforts: *one's — in life.* **'goal-keeper** *n* player whose duty is to keep the ball out of the —.

goat *n* small, horned animal kept for its milk and hair. ⇨ p 84

'goblet *n* drinking-glass with a stem.

'goblin *n* naughty ugly demon.

god *n* **1** any being regarded as, worshipped as, having power over nature and control over human affairs (eg *Jupiter*); image in wood, stone, etc, to represent such a being. **2** **God**, creator and ruler of the universe. **'god-child** *n* person for whom a god-parent acts as sponsor at baptism. **'god-parent** *n* person who undertakes, when a child is baptized, to see that it is trained as a Christian. **'goddess** *n* female god. **'god-forsaken** *adj* (of places) wretched. **'godless** *adj* wicked; not having belief in God. **'godly** *adj* (-lier, -liest) loving and obeying God; deeply religious. **'godsend** *n* sth welcomed because it is a great help; unexpected good fortune.

goes ⇨ go.

'goggle *v* roll the eyes about; (of the eyes) open widely (in surprise, etc). *n* (*pl*) large glasses worn to protect the eyes from wind and dust.

gold *n* yellow metal of extremely high value; coins from this metal; colour of this metal. **'gold-'leaf** *n* sheet of — beaten very thin for use in gilding, etc. **'—smith** *n* person who makes articles of —. **'gold-standard** *n* market value of — used to compare the wealth of different countries. **'—en** *adj* of — or like — in value or colour.

golf *n* ball game played with golf-clubs over a golf-course.

gone ⇨ go.

gong *n* round metal plate struck with a stick as a signal (esp for meals).

good *adj* (better, best) **1** having the right or desired qualities; giving satisfaction; of a high social posi-

tion: *from a — family.* **2** thorough: *to give sb a — beating.* **3** rather more than: *it's a — five miles; a — half of the cake.* **4** considerable in number or quantity: *a — many people; a — way.* **5** **as — as**, (esp) what is almost the same thing as: *He is as — as dead.* **6** **be in — time** (*for sth*), be early enough. **all in — time**, when the right time comes. **7** fit to be eaten: *Is this meat —?* **8** **make** (**sth**) **—**, pay (expense); carry out (a promise); accomplish (a purpose); pay sb back (for a loss, etc). **9** **— for**, having a — effect upon: *— for the health.* **10** **be — for** (*a twelve-mile walk*, etc), be fit to undertake. **— for** (£20), able to pay (£20). *n* **1** that which is —. **2** advantage; benefit. **3** use: *It's no — trying.* **4** **for — (and all)**, for ever. **5** profit or gain: *£5 to the —.* **6** (*pl*) property; things to be bought and sold; things carried by road and rail: *a —s train.* **'good-for-,nothing** *n & adj* (person who is) useless. **good-'looking** *adj* handsome. **good-'natured** *adj* having, showing, kindness. **'—ness** *n* quality of being —. *int* My **—ness!** How surprising! **'—will** *n* friendly feeling.

goose *n* (*pl* **geese**) water-bird larger than a duck. ⇨ p 211.

gorge *n* **1** contents of the stomach. **make one's — rise**, cause a feeling of disgust. **2** narrow opening between hills or mountains. *v* eat greedily; fill oneself (*with*).

'gorgeous *adj* richly coloured; magnificent.

go'rilla *n* man-sized, tree-climbing ape. ⇨ p 317.

'gospel *n* (the life and teaching of Jesus Christ as recorded in) the first four books of the New Testament; any one of these four books.

'gossip *n* (person fond of) idle talk about the affairs of other people. *v* talk —.

got ⇨ get.

gouge *n* tool with sharp, semi-circular edge for cutting grooves in wood. *v* force out with, or as with, a —. ⇨ p 293.

gourd *n* (hard-skinned fleshy fruit of) kinds of climbing or trailing plant; container or bowl made from this fruit.

'govern *v* **1** rule (a country, city,

etc). 2 control (eg one's temper). 3 influence; determine. —**ment** n (system of) —ing; body of people who —; body of Ministers of State. —**or** n 1 person who —s. 2 regulator in a machine.

'**governess** n woman paid to teach children in their own home.

gown n 1 woman's dress. 2 loose, flowing robe worn by members of a university, judges, etc.

grab v (-bb-) take roughly or selfishly; snatch (at).

grace n 1 quality of being pleasing or beautiful, esp in structure or movement. 2 (usu pl) pleasing accomplishment. 3 favour; goodwill. **be in sb's good —s**, enjoy his favour and approval. 4 **with a (bad) good —**, (un)willingly. 5 short prayer of thanks before or after a meal: to say (a) —. 6 God's mercy and favour towards mankind; influence and result of this. v add — to; confer honour or dignity on. '—**ful** adj having or showing — of looks or movement. '—**fully** adv. '—**less** adj without shame; without a sense of what is right and proper.

'**gracious** adj 1 kind; agreeable. 2 (of God) merciful. 3 (in exclamations) How surprising! —**ly** adv.

grade n step or stage (in rank, quality, value, etc); number or class of things of the same —. **on the up (down) —**, rising (falling). v 1 arrange in order of —s. 2 make land (esp for roads) more nearly level.

gradient n degree or rate of slope: a — of one in twenty.

gradual adj taking place by degrees; (of a slope) not steep. —**ly** adv.

graduate v 1 mark with degrees for measuring: a ruler —d in inches. 2 = grade(1). 3 take a university degree. n person who holds a university degree.

graft[1] n piece of living animal or plant taken out and attached elsewhere to grow there; place where a — is (to be) attached. v put a — in or on.

graft[2] n the getting of business advantages, etc, by using dishonest methods (esp political influence).

grain n 1 seed of food-plants such as wheat and rice. 2 tiny hard bit (of sand, gold, etc). 3 smallest British unit of weight, 1/7000 of one pound (avoirdupois). 4 natural arrangement of lines of fibre in wood, etc. **against the —**, (fig) contrary to one's inclination.

'**grammar** n study or science of, rules of, the words and structure of a language. '**grammar-school** n one that prepares its pupils for entrance to college, university, etc. **gram'marian** n expert in —. **gram'matical** adj of, conforming to the rules of, —.

gram(me) n metric unit of weight; weight of one cubic centimetre of water.

'**gramophone** n machine for reproducing music and speech recorded on discs. ⇨ **record-player**, now the usu word.

'**granary** n storehouse for grain.

grand adj (-er, -est) 1 chief; most important. 2 complete: the — total. 3 splendid. 4 self-important. 5 — **piano**, large one with horizontal strings. ⇨ p 180. '—**stand** n roofed rows of seats in a stadium, etc. '—**eur** n greatness.

grand-prefix '—**child** n child of one's own son or daughter. '—**parent** n parent of one's own father or mother. '—**father('s) clock** n clock in a tall wooden case.

'**granite** n hard, usu grey, stone used for building.

'**granny, 'grannie** n grandmother.

grant v 1 consent to give or allow (what is asked for). 2 agree (that sth is true). **take (sth) for —ed**, regard it as true or certain. n sth —ed, esp money or land by a government.

'**granulated** adj in the form of grains: — sugar.

grape n green or purple berry growing in clusters on vines, used for making wine. ⇨ p 115.

'**grapefruit** n yellow citrus fruit, like a large orange. ⇨ p 115.

graph n diagram on squared paper in the form of a line showing the relation between two quantities (eg the temperature at each hour).

'**graphic** adj 1 of writing, drawing, and painting. 2 (of descriptions) causing one to have a clear picture in the mind. —**ally** adv.

'**grapple** v seize firmly; struggle (with) at close quarters; (fig) try to deal (with a problem).

grasp v 1 seize firmly with the hand(s) or in the arm(s); understand with the mind. 2 — at, try to seize; accept eagerly. n (power of) —ing. '—ing adj greedy (for money, etc).

grass n common low-growing plant of which the green leaves are eaten by cattle, sheep, etc; lawn. '—y adj.

'grasshopper n insect with long hindlegs that makes a shrill noise. ⇨ p 144.

grate¹ v 1 rub small bits off; rub into small bits, usu against a rough surface; make a harsh noise by rubbing. 2 have an irritating effect on (a person, his nerves): a grating noise. '—r n device with a rough surface for grating food.

grate² n (metal frame for holding fuel in a) fireplace.

'grateful adj feeling or showing thanks (for help, kindness, etc). —ly adv.

'gratify v give pleasure or satisfaction to. ,gratifi'cation n.

'grating n framework of bars placed across an opening.

'gratis adv & adj free of charge.

'gratitude n being grateful; thanks.

gra'tuitous adj, 1 given, obtained, or done, without payment. 2 unjustifiable.

gra'tuity n 1 gift (of money) etc, for services. 2 money given to a soldier at the end of his period of service.

grave¹ n resting-place of a dead person in the ground. '—stone n stone over a —, usu with an inscription. '—yard n burial ground.

grave² adj (-r, -st) serious; needing careful consideration. '—ly adv.

'gravel n small stones with coarse sand, as used for roads and paths.

'gravitate v move or be attracted (to or towards). ,gravi'tation n.

'gravity n 1 degree of attraction between any two objects, esp that force which attracts objects towards the centre of the earth. 2 seriousness; serious or solemn appearance. 3 weight. specific —, relative weight of any kind of matter and the same volume of water or air.

'gravy n juice which comes from meat while cooking; sauce made from this.

gray adj = grey.

graze¹ v 1 (of animals) eat growing grass. 2 put (cattle, etc) in fields to —.

graze² v touch or scrape lightly in passing; scrape the skin from.

grease n 1 animal fat, melted soft. 2 any thick semi-solid oily substance. v put or rub — on or in (the parts of a machine). 'greasy adj (-ier, -iest) covered with —; slippery.

great adj (-er, -est) 1 above the average in size, quantity, or degree. 2 noted; important. 3 of great ability. '—ly adv much. '—ness n.

great- prefix **'great-'grandfather**, one father's or mother's grandfather. **'great-'grandson**, grandson of one's son or daughter.

greed n strong desire for more (food, wealth, etc), esp for more than is right. '—y adj (-ier, -iest). '—ily adv. '—iness n.

green adj (-er, -est) 1 of the colour of growing grass. 2 (of fruit) not yet ripe; (of wood) not yet dry enough for use; (of persons) inexperienced. n 1— colour. 2 (pl) — vegetables. 3 area of grass-land, esp one for public use in a village. '—grocer n shopkeeper selling vegetables and fruit. '—house n glass-house for plants that need protection from the weather.

greet v 1 say words of welcome to; express one's feelings on receiving (news, etc); write (in a letter) words expressing politeness (Dear Sir) or friendship, etc (Dear Tom). 2 (of sights and sounds) meet the eyes (ears). '—ing n first words used on meeting sb or in writing to sb.

gre'nade n small bomb.

grew ⇨ grow.

grey adj & n (have the) colour between black and white like clouds on a dull day, or ashes.

grid n 1 system of overhead cables for sending out electric current. 2 system of squares on maps, numbered for reference.

grief n 1 deep or violent sorrow; sth causing this. 2 come (bring to) —, (cause to) be injured or ruined. **grieve** v cause — to; feel —. **'grievance** n real or imagined cause for complaint.

grill n 1 grating. 2 part of a cooker where food (esp meat) can be cooked under the heat; (dish of) meat, etc, cooked in this way; meat, etc, cooked over a fire. v cook, be cooked, over or under a fire or other direct heat.

grim adj (-mer, -mest) stern; severe; cruel.

gri'mace n ugly, twisted expression (on the face), expressing pain, disgust, etc, or to cause laughter. v make —s.

grime n dirt, esp a thick coating on the surface of sth. **'grimy** adj.

grin v (-nn-) & n (give a) broad smile.

grind v (pt & pp ground) 1 crush to grains or powder; produce (eg flour) by doing this. 2 polish or sharpen by rubbing: to — knives. 3 rub together: to — one's teeth. 4 — away (at sth), work hard at. '—stone n wheel-shaped stone, used for sharpening tools, etc. **keep one's nose to the —stone**, work very hard.

grip v (-pp-) take and keep a firm hold of. n (power, manner, act of) —ping. **come to —s with** (a problem), work at it in earnest.

gristle n part of an animal's flesh, usu too hard to eat.

grit n 1 grains of stone, sand, etc. 2 quality of courage and endurance. v — one's teeth, press one's teeth together as when in pain or under stress. '—ty adj (-er, -iest) like, containing, —(1).

groan v & n 1 (make) deep sound(s) forced out by pain, despair, etc. 2 be weighted down (with).

grocer n person who sells tea, sugar, tinned foods, etc. '—ies n pl things sold by a —.

groggy adj weak and unsteady.

groom n 1 servant in charge of horses. 2 bride—.

groove n 1 long, hollow cut in the surface of wood, esp one made to guide the motion of sth that slides into it. 2 way of living that has become a habit. v make —s in.

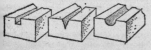

grooves

grope v feel about (for or after sth) as one does in the dark.

gross adj 1 vulgar. 2 (of errors, etc) obviously bad. 3 (of the senses) dull; heavy; (of a person) too heavy; (of food) coarse. 4 total; whole (opposite of net). n (pl unchanged) 12 dozen, 144. '—ly adv obviously.

gro'tesque adj absurd; fantastic; comically extravagant(2).

ground¹ n 1 solid surface of the earth. **hold one's —**, stand firm. **suit sb down to the —**, be completely satisfactory. 2 sea bottom: to touch —. 3 piece of land for a special purpose: a cricket —. 4 (pl) land, gardens, round a building, usu enclosed with walls or fences. 5 (pl) particles of solid matter that settle to the bottom of a liquid: coffee —s. 6 reason(s) for saying, doing, or believing sth: no —s for anxiety. v base (a belief, etc) (on sth); give (sb) training (in sth). '—less adj without reasons. '—nut n (= peanut) tropical plant with seeds that ripen in the soil; seed of this plant (as food). **'ground-rent** n rent paid to an owner of land used for building on. '—work n (fig) elementary studies.

ground² ⇨ grind.

group n number of persons or things gathered or placed together or naturally associated. v form into, gather in, a —.

grove n group of trees:

'grovel v (-ll-) lie down on one's face in front of sb whom one fears, (as if) begging for mercy; show by behaviour, etc, that one has no respect for oneself.

grow v (pt grew, pp grown) 1 increase in size, height, length, etc. — up, become adult. 2 cause or allow to —: to — fruit (a beard). 3 become: to — old. '—er n 1 person who —s things. 2 plant that —s in a certain way: a rapid —er. **'grown-up** adj & n adult (person). **growth** n 1 process of —ing. 2 increase. 3 sth that —s or has —n.

growl v & n (esp of dogs) (make a) low threatening sound.

'grubby adj (-ier, -iest) dirty.

grudge v be unwilling to give or allow. n have a — against sb, **bear (owe) sb a —**, feel ill will against him for causing oneself trouble, etc. 'grudgingly adv unwillingly.

'gruel n liquid food of oatmeal boiled in milk or water.

'gruesome adj frightful; filling one with horror and fear.

gruff · adj (-er, -est) (of sb, his voice, behaviour) rough and unfriendly.

'grumble n bad-tempered complaint; noise like distant thunder. v utter —s; say with —s. —r n.

grunt v & n (eg of pigs) (make a) low rough sound.

,guaran'tee n 1 security against loss on a purchase (given by the seller), or on a loan (given by a friend of the borrower). 2 (also guarantor) person offering such security. v give a — for; (colloq) promise.

guard n 1 state of watchfulness against danger, attack, or surprise: on —; keeping —; off one's —. 2 soldier(s) keeping —. to stand —, to act as sentry. 3 man in charge of a railway train. 4 (esp in compounds) apparatus designed to prevent injury or loss: 'mud-guard (over the wheel of a bicycle, etc). v 1 protect; keep from danger; control (exit). 2 — against, use care to prevent. '—room n room for soldiers on — or for soldiers under arrest.

'guardian n person legally responsible for the care of a young or incapable person and his property. —ship n.

'guava n (tropical tree with) pink fruit in a yellow rind. ⇨ p 115.

guer'(r)illa n. — war, war carried on by fighters not members of a regular army; sb fighting in such a war.

guess v & n (form an) opinion, (give an) answer, (make a) statement, based on supposition, not on definite knowledge or calculation.

guest n 1 person staying at or paying a visit to another's house, or being entertained at a meal. 2 person staying at a hotel or having a meal at a restaurant.

guide n 1 person who shows others the way. 2 sth that directs or influences (conduct, etc). 3 book with information about a place or subject. 4 G—, member of an association for girls like the Scouts Association for boys. v act as — to, for. 'guidance n guiding; being —d.

guild (old spelling, gild) n society of persons for helping one another or for forwarding common interests, eg trade, social welfare.

guile n deceit; cunning.

'guillotine n mechanical chopper for beheading, trimming paper, etc.

guilt n condition of having done wrong; responsibility for wrongdoing. '—y adj (-ier, -iest) having done wrong; showing or feeling —: a —y look (conscience).

'guinea n (formerly) sum of twenty-one shillings.

'guinea-pig n 1 animal a little larger than a rat. ⇨ p 12. 2 sb used in an experiment (esp medical).

gui'tar n six-stringed musical instrument plucked with the fingers. ⇨ p 180.

gulf n 1 part of the sea almost surrounded by land. 2 deep hollow in the ground; (fig) division (between opinions, etc).

'gullet n (food passage in the throat.

'gullible adj easily tricked or cheated.

'gully n narrow channel cut or formed by rain-water, or made for carrying away water from a building.

gulp v swallow (down) food or drink quickly or greedily; work the throat as if swallowing.

gum¹ n firm pink flesh round the teeth. 'gumboil n abscess on the gum.

gum² n sticky substance obtained from some trees. v (-mm-) put gum on; fasten with gum.

gun n firearm that sends shot(3), bullets, shells(3) from a metal tube. 'gunpowder n explosive powder. 'gunshot n range of a gun: within gunshot.

'gurgle v & n (make a) bubbling sound as of water flowing from a narrow-necked bottle.

gush v & n (come out with a) rushing outflow: oil —ing from a new well.

gust n sudden, violent rush of wind; burst of rain; (fig) outburst of (anger, etc).. '—y adj (-ier, -iest).

gut *n* (*pl*) intestines; (fig) courage and determination. *v* (-tt-) take the guts out of (fish, etc); destroy the inside or contents of: *buildings gutted by fire.*

gutter *n* channel fixed under the edge of a roof, channel at the side of a road, to carry off rain-water.

guttural *n & adj* (sound) formed in the throat.

guy *n* (colloq) youth, man.

gym'nasium *n* room with apparatus for physical training.

gym'nastic *adj* of bodily training. **—s** *n pl* forms of exercises for physical training.

gypsy *n* ⇨ gipsy.

gy'rate *v* move in circles.

H

habit *n* 1 person's regular practice, esp sth that cannot easily be given up: *in the — of getting up late.* 2 set of clothes: *riding- —.*

habitable *adj* fit to be lived in.

habitat *n* (of plants, animals) natural home or place of growth.

habi'tation *n* 1 living in: *unfit for —.* 2 place to live in.

ha'bitual *adj* regular; from habit. **—ly** *adv* as a usual practice.

ha'bituate *v* accustom; get (sb, oneself) used to.

hack *v* cut roughly; chop. **'hacksaw** *n* saw for cutting metal.

hackneyed *adj* (esp of sayings) common; too often seen.

had ⇨ have.

haddock *n* sea-fish much used as food, esp when smoked.

hag *n* ugly old woman; witch.

haggard *adj* (of the face) looking tired and lined (from anxiety, etc).

haggle *v* argue (*about* prices, etc).

hail¹ *n* frozen rain-drops; balls of ice falling like rain. *v* 1 (of —) fall: *it —ed.* 2 (fig) come down on like —. **'—stone** *n* small ball of ice.

hail² *v* 1 give a welcoming cry to; cry or call out to (sb, a ship) to attract attention. 2 **— from**, have come from: *She —s from Nairobi.*

hair *n* fine thread-like growth on the skin of animals; (esp) the mass of these on the human head. ⇨ p 29.

not turn a —, give no sign of being troubled; **make one's — stand on end**, fill one with terror. **'—do** *n* style or process of —dressing. **'—dresser** *n* person who dresses (4) and cuts —. **'—pin** *n* one for keeping the — in place. **'hair,splitting** *adj* making, showing, differences too small to be important. **'hairspring** *n* very delicate spring in a watch. **'—y** *adj* (-ier, -iest) of or like —; covered with —.

hale *adj* (usu of old persons) healthy.

half *n & adj* (*pl* halves) one of two equal parts into which sth is divided; ½. **go halves** (*with* sb *in* sth), share equally; **too clever by —**, far too clever; **one's better —**, (colloq) one's wife. *adv* **not — bad**, (colloq) quite good. **'half-breed, 'half-caste** *n* person with parents of different races, esp differently coloured races. **'half-,brother, 'half-,sister** *n* by one parent only. **'—crown** *n* former British coin worth 2s. 6d. **'half-'hearted** *adj* showing, done with, little interest or enthusiasm. **'half-'holiday** *n* day of which the afternoon is free from work or duty. **'halfpenny** *n* (British decimal currency) coin (½p) worth — a new penny. **'half-'witted** *adj* weak-minded.

hall *n* 1 (building with a) large room for meetings, concerts, public business, etc. 2 space into which the main entrance or front door of a building opens. 3 residence for students at a college or university; room in a college for meals: *dine in —.*

hal'lo *int* cry to attract attention; greeting.

hallow *v* make, regard as, holy.

hal,luci'nation *n* seeming to see sth not present; sth so imagined.

halo *n* circle of light round the sun or moon or (in art) shown above the heads of sacred beings.

halt *v. & n* 1 (eg of soldiers) (come to a) stop on a march or journey; (bring to a) stop. 2 act, speak in a hesitating way. **'—ingly** *adv* hesitatingly.

halter *n* rope, leather strap, put round a horse's head; rope used for hanging (2) a person.

halve *v* divide into two equal parts; lessen by one half.

ham n (salted and smoked) upper part of a pig's leg.

'**hamlet** n small village.

'**hammer** n tool for hitting nails, breaking things, etc. ⇨ p 293. **go at it — and tongs**, fight, argue, with great energy and noise. — strike with, or as with, a —. — **away at**, (fig) work hard at.

'**hammock** n hanging bed of canvas or rope network.

'**hamper**[1] v hinder.

'**hamper**[2] n basket with a lid.

hand n 1 part of the arm below the wrist. ⇨ p 29. **at (to)** —, within reach; present. **live from — to mouth**, spend money as soon as it is earned, saving nothing. **in** —, available for use; receiving attention. **out of** —, out of control. **win —s down**, win easily. 2 (pl) care; keeping: *I leave the matter in your* —s. 3 worker in a factory, etc; member of a ship's crew. 4 pointer on a clock or watch. 5 **at first (second)**, directly (indirectly). **second-hand**, not new; bought from or given by a previous owner or user. 6 side; direction: *on all* —s. 7 handwriting; signature. v give; pass: *to* — *on the news*; *to* — *down customs from one generation to the next.* '**—bag** n woman's bag for money, handkerchief, etc. '**—bill** n printed advertisement distributed by —. '**—book** n small book with information on one subject. '**—cart** n one pushed or pulled by —. '**—cuff** n one of a pair of metal rings joined by a chain, place on a prisoner's wrists. '**—ful** n as much as a — holds; a small number. '**—icraft** n art or craft needing skill with the —s. '**—iwork** n sth done or made by —, or by a named person. '**—writing** n person's style of writing by —. '**—ly** adj ⇨ handy.

'**handicap** n sth likely to lessen one's chance of success. v give or be a — to.

'**handkerchief** n square piece of cotton, etc, carried in the pocket or worn for ornament.

'**handle** n part of a tool, cup, door, etc, by which it is held. v touch with, take in, the hands; control (men). '**—bars** n bars for steering a (motor-)bicycle.

'**handsome** adj of fine appearance; (of a gift, etc) generous.

'**handy** adj (-ier, -iest) 1 clever with one's hands. 2 available; useful: *That box will be* —. —**man** n sb who does small repairs in the house.

hang v (pt & pp hung) 1 support, be supported, from above so that the lower end is free. 2 (pt & pp hanged) put (sb) to death by —ing him with a rope round the neck. 3 — **the head**, let it fall forward (eg when ashamed). 4 — **fire**, (fig, of events) be slow in developing. 5 — **about**, be or remain near while waiting. — **back**, hesitate. — **on to**, refuse to give up. **be hung up**, be delayed. n ⊤ the way in which sth (esp a garment) —s. 2 **get the** — **of** sth, learn how to do or use sth. **not care a** —, care not at all. '**—er** (or '**coat-hanger**) bar with a hook on which to — a coat, etc. ,**hanger-'on** n follower, esp one looking for an advantage. '**—ings** n pl curtains. '**—man** n sb who —s (2) criminals.

'**hangar** n shed for aircraft.

hank n coil of yarn or thread.

'**hanker** v — **after**, be continually wishing for.

hap'hazard adv & n (by) mere chance.

'**ha'p'orth** n halfpennyworth.

'**happen** v 1 take place; come about. 2 — **on**, meet or find by chance. —**ing** n event.

'**happy** adj (-ier, -iest) feeling or showing pleasure and contentment; satisfied; lucky. '**happily** adv. '**happiness** n.

ha'rangue v & n (make a) long loud (often scolding) speech (to).

'**harass** v trouble; worry repeatedly.

'**harbour** n place of shelter for ships. v keep safe; hide (eg a criminal); (fig) hold (ill feeling, etc) in the mind.

hard adj (-er, -est) 1 firm, solid; not easily cut or dented. — **cash**, coins and banknotes. 2 difficult. — **of hearing**, rather deaf. — **labour**, imprisonment with — physical labour. — **and fast** (*rules*, etc), that cannot be altered to fit special cases. — **luck (lines)**, worse fortune than is deserved. — **times**, times of money shortage, unemployment, etc. adv with great energy; severely; heavily; with difficulty. — **up**, short of money. **be — pressed**, be in difficult circumstances. — **by**, near. — **upon**, not far behind. '**hard-'headed** *adj* unsympathetic; practical. '**hard-'hearted** *adj* unfeeling; pitiless. '—**ship** *n* severe suffering; painful condition. '—**ware** *n* metal goods such as nails, locks, pans.

'**harden** *v* make or become hard(1).

'**hardly** *adv* **1** with difficulty; severely. **2** scarcely; only just. — **any**, very few, very little.

'**hardy** *adj* (-ier, -iest) able to endure suffering or severe conditions. '**hardily** *adv*.

hare *n* field animal with divided upper lip, like but larger than a rabbit. ⇨ p 12.

hark, 'harken *v* listen.

harm *v & n* (cause) damage or injury (to). '—**ful** *adj* causing —. '—**less** *adj* causing no —.

'**harmony** *n* **1** agreement (of feeling, interests, opinions, etc): **in** — (**with**). **2** (pleasing) combination of musical notes sounded together or of colours seen together. **har-'monious** *adj* in agreement; pleasingly combined or arranged; tuneful. '**harmonize** *v* bring into, be in, — (**with**); add notes (to a tune) to make chords.

'**harness** *n* all the leather-work and metal-work by which a horse is controlled and fastened to whatever it pulls or carries. *v* put a— on (a horse); use (eg a river) to produce (eg electric) power.

harp *n* stringed musical instrument played with the fingers. ⇨ p 180. *v* **1** play the —. **2** — **on**, talk tiringly on (eg one's misfortunes).

har'poon *n* spear attached to a rope, as used for catching whales.

'**harrow** *n* heavy frame with metal teeth for breaking up ground after ploughing. *v* (fig) distress.

harsh *adj* (-er,-est) **1** rough and disagreeable, esp to the senses. **2** stern; cruel. '—**ly** *adv*. '—**ness** *n*.

'**harvest** *n* **1** (season for) cutting or gathering in of grain and other food crops; the quantity obtained. **2** consequence(s) of actions. *v* cut, gather, dig up, a crop. —**er** *n* person or machine that —s.

hash *v* cut up (cooked meat) into small pieces. *n* dish of —ed meat. **make a — of sth**, do it badly.

hasp *n* left-hand part of a metal fastening used with a staple to lock doors, etc.

'**hassock** *n* cushion for kneeling on.

haste *n* quickness of movement; hurry: *make* —, hurry. **in** —, hastily; in a hurry. '—*n v* **1** move or act with speed. **2** cause (sb) to hurry. **3** cause (sth) to be done quickly or earlier. '**hasty** *adj* (-ier, -iest) **1** made, done, or said (too) quickly. **2** quick-tempered. '**hastily** *adv*. '**hastiness** *n*.

hat *n* covering for the head worn out of doors. '**hatter** *n* sb who makes and sells hats.

hatch¹ *n* (movable covering over an) opening in a wall or floor through which goods may be put, esp (—**way**) one in a ship's deck.

hatch² *v* **1** (cause to) break out (of an egg): *to* — *chickens, eggs.* **2** think out and develop (a plot).

'**hatchet** *n* short-handled axe.

hate *v & n* (have a) violent dislike (of). '—**ful** *adj* showing, causing, —. '**hatred** *n* = **hate**.

'**haughty** *adj* (-ier, -iest) too proud; feeling or showing contempt. '**haughtily** *adv*.

haul *v* pull (with effort or force). *n* act of —ing; quantity —ed in or up (esp of fish in a net). '—**age** *n* transport of goods.

haunt *v* visit, be with, habitually or repeatedly. *n* place frequently visited by person(s) named. '—**ed** *adj* frequently visited by ghosts.

have *v* (3rd person, present tense **has**; *pt & pp* **had**) (used to form the perfect tenses) **1** possess, keep. **2** allow: *I won't* — *such behaviour here.* **3** cause (sb) to do sth. **4** experience: *to* — *one's purse stolen.* **5** (indicating necessity, etc) *You* — *to* (= you must) *be home by ten.* **6** (colloq) trick: *He said you were here yesterday but I was had,* deceived. **7** — **to do with**, be concerned with. — **something (nothing) to do with**, be connected (unconnected) with. — (**sth**) **out with sb**, discuss fully in order to settle it (esp a dispute).

'**haven** *n* harbour; (fig) place of safety or rest.

'**haversack** *n* canvas bag for food, as carried by soldiers, hikers, etc.

'havoc n widespread damage.

hawk[1] n strong, swift, keen-sighted bird of prey. ⇨ p 26.

hawk[2] v go from street to street, house to house, with goods for sale. **'—er** n person who **—s**.

hay n grass cut and dried for use as animal food. **make hay while the sun shines**, use one's opportunities before it is too late. **'hay-'fever** n disease causing liquid to run from the nose; (fig) excitement.

'hazard n risk; danger. v take the risk of; expose to danger. **—ous** adj risky.

haze n thin mist. **'hazy** adj (-ier, -iest) misty; (fig) vague; not clear (about).

'hazel n (small tree producing a) light brown edible nut. adj light brown colour: **— eyes**.

he pron referring to a male as the subject(2): *He can see me.* ⇨ him.

head n 1 part of the body above the neck. ⇨ p 29. 2 sth like a — in shape or position. 3 striking part (eg of a hammer, an axe). 4 image of a —, esp on a coin: *H—s or tails?* 5 brain; imagination; power to reason: **lose (keep) one's —**, become over-excited (remain calm). **off one's —**, mad. **take it into one's —** (*that*), have the idea. **go to the —**, (fig, of success, etc) make over-confident. 6 chief person; person or place in the highest position: *at the — of the list (valley); the — of the school* (,**—'master**, **,—'mistress**). **,head-'quarters**, place from which activities are controlled. 7 (for each) person or animal: *five pence a —; fifty — (pl unchanged) of cattle.* 8 main division (in a speech, essay, etc). 9 **'—'** wind, wind that hinders progress. **'head-lamp**, **'head-light**, large lamp at the front of a car, etc. **come to a —**, reach a crisis. v 1 be at the —of. 2 move in the direction indicated: *—ing for home; — sb off.* 3 strike with the —: *to — the ball.* **'head-dress** n (esp ornamental) — covering. **'—ing** n word(s) at the top of a section of printed matter. **'—land** n cape[2]. **'—line** n newspaper heading, usu in large type. **'—long** adj & adv with the — first; (fig) thoughtless(ly) and hurried(ly).

'head-on adj & adv (of collisions or colliding) front striking front. **'—phones** n pl receivers fitting over the head (for radio, etc). **'—strong** adj obstinate. **'—way** n forward movement. **'—word** n word used as a heading, esp the first word, in heavy type, of a dictionary entry.

heal v make or become well.

health n condition of the body or the mind, esp the state of being well and free from illness. **'—y** adj (-ier, -iest) having, likely to produce or maintain, good —.

heap n 1 number of things, mass of material, piled up like a small hill. 2 (pl colloq) plenty: *—s of time.* v 1 put in a —; make into a —. 2 fill, load.

hear v (pt & pp heard) 1 become aware of (sounds) through the ears. **— from sb**, receive a letter, etc, from. **— of**, receive news about. 2 (of a judge) try (a case); judge. int. **H—!** expression of approval. **'—ing** n 1 within (out of) **—ing**, near enough (too far off) to be heard. 2 trial. **'—say** n common talk; rumour.

hearse n carriage for a coffin.

heart n 1 part of the body that pumps blood through the blood vessels ⇨ p 30; shape of this (esp in red on some playing cards): ♥. 2 centre of the affection or emotions. **change of —**, change to make oneself a better person. **—to —**, frank, friendly. **take (lose) —**, take (lose) courage. **take sth to —**, feel much affected by it. **after one's own —**, of the sort one most likes. 3 centre: *be at the — of things.* **—ache** n deep sorrow. **'heart-beat** n one movement of the **—'s** regular motion. **'heart-,breaking** adj causing great sorrow. **'heart-,broken** adj suffering from deep sorrow. **'—en** v give courage to. **'—less** adj unkind; without pity. **'heart-,rending** adj causing deep sorrow. **'—y** adj (-ier, -iest) 1 (of feelings) sincere. 2 strong and healthy. 3 (of meals, appetites) big. **'—ily** adv in a —y manner: *eat —ily.*

hearth n floor of a fireplace.

heat n 1 hotness produced by the sun, electricity, etc. 2 intense feeling. 3 race, etc, winners of which take part in further races. v make or become warm or hot. '—er n apparatus for —ing. 'central-'heating n system that —s a building from one source. '—wave n period of unusually hot weather. '—edly adv angrily.

heath n (sorts of shrub growing on hills or) flat waste-land.

'heathen n & adj (person) of a religion neither Christian, Muslim, Jewish, nor Buddhist; (fig) wild, bad-mannered.

'heather n kind of heath plant with small purple flowers.

heave v (pt & pp heaved or hove) 1 lift, raise up, sth heavy; pull (at, on, εg a rope). 2 (colloq) lift and throw. 3 rise and fall: heaving waves.

'heaven n 1 home of God and the Saints. 2 place, condition, of great happiness. 3 (pl) the sky. Good —s! int expressing surprise. —ly adj of, from, like, —; delightful.

'heavy adj (-ier, -iest) 1 having great weight; difficult to lift or move. 2 of more than the usual size, amount, force, etc: — crops (rain). 3 (of persons, their writing, etc) dull; tedious. 'heavy-weight n boxer weighing 175 lb. or more. 'heavily adv.

'Hebrew n (language, religion of a) Jew, Israelite. adj of the — language or people.

'heckle v ask troublesome questions at a public meeting. '—r n.

'hectic adj 1 unnaturally red: — cheeks (esp as a sign of consumption). 2 full of excitement; without rest: a — life.

hedge n row of bushes, etc, usu trimmed, as a boundary (for a garden, field, etc). v put a — or (fig) barrier round. '—row n —.

heed v & n (pay) attention (to): to — a warning; taking no — of advice.' '—ful adj attentive. '—less adj inattentive; ignoring advice.

heel[1] n back part of the human foot ⇨ p 29; part of a sock, etc, covering this; part of a shoe, etc, supporting it. come to —, become obedient. take to one's —s, run away. v put new —s on (shoes, etc).

heel[2] v (of a ship) (cause to) lean (over).

'heifer n young cow that has not yet had a calf.

height n 1 distance from top to bottom; distance to the top of sth from a level, esp sea level. 2 high place. 3 utmost degree: the storm was at its —. '—en v make higher or greater in degree.

heir n person with the legal right to receive a title, property, etc, when the owner dies. '—ess n female —. '—loom n sth handed down in a family for several generations.

held ⇨ hold.

'helicopter n aircraft with rotating blades on top.

a helicopter

hell n 1 (in some religions) place of punishment after death. 2 place, condition, of great misery or suffering.

hel'lo int = hullo.

helm n handle (also tiller) or wheel for moving the rudder of a boat or ship.

'helmet n protective head-covering worn by firemen, soldiers, motorcyclists, etc.

help v & n 1 (do) part of the work of sb else; make it easier for sb to do sth; do sth for sb in need. 2 avoid(ance); escape: I can't — doing it, ie can't stop myself from doing it; it can't be —ed; there's no — for it, there's no way of avoiding it. 3 serve: — sb to food and drink. '—er n person who —s. '—ful adj giving —; useful. '—ing n portion of food served on a person's plate. '—less adj without —; unable to look after oneself.

hem n border or edge of cloth, esp when turned and sewn down. v (-mm-) 1 make a hem on. 2 hem in, about, surround. 'hemstitch v & n (decorate cloth with) ornamental stitching.

'hemisphere n half a sphere; half the earth: the Southern H—.

hemp n 1 Indian plant; its fibre, used in rope-making. 2 kind of drug.

hen *n* female bird (esp domestic bird that lays eggs that are eaten by us as food). ⇨ p 211. **'hen-pecked** *adj* (of a man) ruled by his wife.

hence *adv* **1** from here; from now. **2** for this reason. **'—'forth, '—'forward** *adv* from this time on.

her *pron* object(2) form of *she*: *I can see her. adj: That is her book.* **hers** *pron*: *That book is hers* (belongs to her). **her'self** *pron*: *She hurt herself when she fell over.*

'herald *n* **1** (historical) person making public announcements for, carrying news from, a ruler, etc. **2** person, thing, foretelling the coming of sb or sth. *v* make known the coming of.

herb *n* low, soft-stemmed plant that dies down after flowering, esp one whose leaves are used in medicine or for flavouring food.

herd *n* number of cattle feeding or going about together. **'—sman** *n* man who looks after —s.

here *adv* in, at or to this place. **— and there,** in various places. **neither — nor there,** not to the point. **'—abouts** *adv* near or about —.

he'reditary *adj* (having a position) passed on from parent to child, from one generation to following generations. **he'redity** *n* tendency of living things to pass their characteristics on to their offspring.

'heresy *n.* (holding of) belief or opinion contrary to what is generally accepted, esp in religion. **'heretic** *n* person supporting a —. **he'retical** *adj* of —.

'heritage *n* that which may be inherited.

'hermit *n* person (esp a man in early Christian times) living alone.

'hero *n* **1** boy or man respected for bravery or noble qualities. **2** chief man in a story, drama, etc. **—ine** *n* woman —. **he'roic** *adj* of, like, fit for, a —. **—ism** *n* great courage.

'heron *n* long-legged water bird. ⇨ p 26.

'herring *n* sea-fish much used as food.

her'self ⇨ her.

'hesitate *v* show signs of uncertainty or unwillingness in speech or action. **'hesitant** *adj* inclined to —. **'hesitantly, 'hesi-** tatingly *adv* in a hesitating manner. **,hesi'tation** *n.*

'heterodox *adj* opposite of orthodox.

hew *v* (*pt* 'hewed, *pp* 'hewed or hewn) cut by striking with sth sharp; shape by chopping.

'hexagon *n* straight-sided figure with six (usu equal) angles. ⇨ p 253.

'heyday *n* time of greatest prosperity.

'hibernate *v* (of some animals) sleep through the winter.

'hiccup, 'hiccough *v & n* (have a) sudden, noisy stopping of the breath.

hide¹ *v* (*pt* hid, *pp* 'hidden) put or keep out of sight; prevent from being seen, found, or known. **'hiding** *n* **1** go into hiding, — oneself. **be in hiding,** be hidden. **2** (colloq) slap.

hide² *n* animal's skin, esp one for use as leather. **'hiding** *n* beating or whipping.

'hideous *adj* very ugly.

high *adj* (-er, -est) **1** extending far upwards; measuring (a given distance) from the bottom to the top. **— road,** important road. **— school,** one giving education more advanced than elementary schools. **2** (of time) far advanced: *— summer. it's — time,* its getting late. **3** (of meat, fish) beginning to go bad. *adv* in or to an important degree. **run —,** (fig, of feelings) be excited. **'high-born** *adj* of a noble family. **'high-brow** *adj* showing a taste for intellectual things, esp music and literature. **,high-'handed** *adj* overbearing. **'—lands** *n pl* mountainous country, esp of NW Scotland. **'high-,pitched** *adj* on a — note. **'—ly** *adv* in or to a — degree. **'—ness** *n* **1** (state of) being — or. at a height. **2** His (Her, Your) H—ness,** title used of (to) a prince (princess). **,highly-'strung** *adj* sensitive; easily excited. **'—way** *n* public (esp main) road.

hike *v & n* (colloq) (go for a) long country walk. **'—r** *n.*

hi'larious *adj* noisily merry; very funny. **hi'larity** *n.*

hill *n* small mountain; slope (on a road, etc). **'—y** *adj* (-ier, -iest) **'—ock** *n* small —.

hilt n handle of a sword or dagger.

him pron object(2) form of **he**: I can see him. **him'self** pron: He hurt himself when he fell over.

hind adj (of things in pairs front and back) at the back: the — legs of a horse. **'—most** adj farthest back.

'Hindu n sb whose religion is Hinduism. **'Hinduism** n religion of N India.

'hinder v get in the way of. **'hindrance** n sth that —s.

hinge n joint on which a door, gate, lid, etc, opens and shuts. v 1 attach with a — or —s. 2 —(up) on, turn or depend upon.

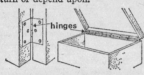
hinges

hint n slight suggestion or indication. v give a —.

hip n large bone on either side of the human body between the ribs and the legs. ⇨ p 29.

,hippo'potamus n large, thick-skinned African river animal. ⇨ p 317.

hire v obtain or allow the use or services of, in return for a fixed payment: to — a horse (a hall). n (money paid for) hiring. **'hire-'purchase** n system by which sth —d becomes the property of the —r after a number of agreed payments have been made. **'—r** n.

his pron & adj: That is his book. That book is his (belongs to him).

hiss v & n (make) the sound of s, the sound made by a snake, esp to show disapproval; the sound of water on a hot surface.

'history n (orderly description of) past events. **his'torian** n writer of —. **his'toric** adj associated with past times; famous in —. **his'torical** adj based on —; really existing in the past (not legendary).

hit v (-tt-) (pt & pp hit) 1 come against (sth) with force; strike (1). **be hard hit (by sth)**, be much troubled, severely affected. **hit upon** (a plan, etc), discover by chance. n blow(1); stroke(1).

hitch v 1 pull (up) with a quick movement. 2 fasten, become fastened, on or to a hook, etc, or with a loop of rope, etc. n 1 sudden pull. 2 kind of knot used by sailors. 3 sth that stops progress: without a —, without difficulty.

'hitch-'hike v travel by begging motorists for free rides.

'hither adv (old use) here. **,—'to** adv up to now.

hive n box (of wood, straw, etc) made for bees to live in.

hoard n carefully saved store of money, food, etc; mass of facts. v save and store (up).

'hoarding n wooden fence round waste land, building work, etc, often covered with advertisements.

hoarse adj (-r, -st) (of the voice) rough and harsh; having a — voice.

hoax n mischievous trick played on sb for a joke. v deceive thus.

'hobble v 1 walk as when lame or with sore feet, etc. 2 tie a horse's legs to prevent it from going away.

'hobby n interesting occupation for one's free time.

'hob-nob v (-bb-) have a friendly talk (with).

'hockey n game played on a field or on ice by two teams of eleven or six players with curved sticks.

hoe n tool for loosening soil and cutting up weeds among growing crops. v work with a —.

hog n castrated male pig. **go the whole hog**, do sth thoroughly.

hoist v & n (lift up with an) apparatus of ropes and pulleys, or kind of elevator (esp on a warship).

hold¹ v (pt & pp held) 1 have and keep in the hand(s) or with a tool. 2 (with adv & prep) — **back**, show unwillingness to do sth. — **sth back**, keep it secret. — **forth**, preach at length. — **(sb) off**, keep at a distance. — **out**, keep one's position or strength; (of supplies, etc) last. — **out** (hopes, etc), offer. — **sth over**, postpone it. **be held up**, be delayed or stopped. —**with**, approve of. 3 (be able to) contain. 4 have or keep in the mind; consider. 5 keep back; restrain. — **one's tongue (peace)**, be silent. 6 be the owner or tenant of; occupy (a place or office). 7 have (a meeting, conversation, examination). 8 remain the same; keep or stay in position, etc. — **good**, be still in force; be still true. n 1 act, manner, or power of —ing. 2 part or place which can be used for —ing. '—all n soft bag of cloth or leather for carrying clothes, etc, when travelling. '—er n person who —s sth; thing for —ing sth. '—ing n sth held(6), esp land or shares.

hold² n part of a ship below decks where cargo is stored.

hole n opening or space in a solid. pick —s in, find fault with. in a —, (colloq) in an awkward situation. v make —s in; put into a —.

'holiday n day(s) of rest from work.

'holiness ⇨ holy.

'hollow adj 1 not solid; with a hole or empty space inside; (of sounds) as if coming from sth —. 2 (fig) unreal; insincere. 3 sunken. n — place; hole; valley. v make a — in.

'holly n evergreen bush with hard, dark-green, sharp-pointed leaves and red berries.

'holster n leather carrying-case for a pistol.

'holy adj (-ier, -iest) 1 of God or religion: the H— Bible; the H— Land (where Jesus lived). 2 devoted to religion. 'holiness n 1 being — or sacred. 2 His (Your) Holiness, title used of (to) the Pope.

'homage n expression of respect: pay — to Shakespeare.

home n 1 place where one lives, esp with one's family. at — (to), expecting and ready to receive (visitors, etc). (feel, make oneself) at —, as if in one's own house. 2 place for the care of old or sick people. 3 (as adj) of the —; of or inside the country in question. adv to, at, in, one's — or country. bring sth — to sb, make him fully conscious of its truth. '—less adj. 'home-like adj. 'home-'made adj. '—sick adj sad because away from —. '—spun n & adj (cloth) made at —. '—ward adj & adv (going) towards —.

'homely adj (-ier, -iest) 1 simple and plain. 2 causing one to think of home or to feel at home.

'homicide n killer or killing of a human being. ,homi'cidal adj.

'homily n moral lecture; sermon.

hone n stone for sharpening tools.

'honest adj speaking the truth; not

stealing or cheating; straightforward. —ly adv. —y n.

'honey n sweet, sticky liquid made by bees. 'honey-comb n structure of six-sided cells made by bees for — and eggs. —moon n holiday taken by a newly married couple.

'honorary adj 1 (of a position) unpaid: the — secretary. 2 (of a university degree, rank, etc) given as an honour, without the usual requirements or duties.

'honour n 1 high public regard; great respect: to do — to the King; a guard of —. 2 good personal character; reputation for good behaviour: on my (word of) —. 3 (as a polite phrase) May I have the — of your company at dinner? 4 Your (His) H—, form of address used to (of) some judges. 5 person or thing bringing credit. 6 the — of knighthood; (pl) marks of respect, distinction, etc. an —s degree, given for work with special distinction at a British university. v 1 feel — for; show — to; confer — on. 2 accept and pay (a cheque) when due. —able adj 1 worthy of, bringing, —(1), (2); upright(2). 2 title, form of respect, used before names of judges and some others. —ably adv.

hood n 1 bag-like covering for the head and neck, often fastened to a cloak. 2 folding roof of a motor-car, etc. 3 hood-shaped or hood-like thing.

hoof n (pl hoofs or hooves) horny outer part of the foot of a horse, camel, etc. ⇨ p 84.

hook n 1 curved or bent piece of metal, etc, for catching hold of sth or for hanging sth on. 2 curved tool for cutting (grain, etc) or for chopping (branches, etc). by — or by crook, by one means or another. v fasten, be fastened with, catch, with a — or —s. '—ed adj made with, having, —s; hook-shaped. '—worm n worm that —s itself to the intestine and causes disease.

'hooligan n one of a disorderly crowd making disturbances in public.

hoop n band of wood or metal put round a barrel; similar band rolled along the ground as a plaything.

hoot n 1 cry of an owl. 2 sound made by a motor-car horn, etc. 3 cry expressing scorn or disapproval. v make a — or —s (at); drive away by —s(3). '—er n steam-whistle (eg in a factory); horn of a motor-car.

hooves ⇨ hoof.

hop[1] n tall climbing plant with flowers growing in clusters; (pl) these flowers, dried and used in making beer.

hop[2] v (-pp-) (of persons) jump with one foot; (of birds) jump forward on both feet. n short jump; stage of a journey by train, etc.

hope n 1 feeling of expectation and desire; feeling of trust. 2 cause for such feeling. v expect and desire. '—ful adj having or giving —. '—fully adv. '—less adj having no —; giving or promising no — —s(1) beer.

horde n wandering tribe; big crowd.

ho'rizon n line at which earth or sea and sky seem to meet. ,hori'zontal adj parallel to the —; flat or level.

horn n 1 one of the hard, pointed, usu curved, outgrowths on the heads of cattle, deer, etc; the substance of these. ⇨ p 84. 2 sorts of musical wind instrument ⇨ p 180; instrument for making warning sounds: fog-horn. '—ed adj having —s(1). '—y adj of, like, —(1).

'hornet n insect with a powerful sting. ⇨ p 144.

'horoscope n diagram or observation of the stars' positions in order to forecast events.

'horror n (sth causing) feeling of extreme fear or dislike. 'horror-struck, 'horror-,stricken adj overcome with —. 'horrible adj, 'horrid adj, causing —; (colloq) disagreeable. 'horrify v fill with horror.

horse n 1 four-legged animal used for riding, pulling carts, etc. ⇨ p 84. 2 soldiers mounted on —s; cavalry. '—man, '—woman n one skilled in riding and managing —s. 'horse-play n rough, noisy fun. 'horse-power n (shortened to HP) unit of power (for engines, etc). '—shoe n U-shaped metal shoe for a —. 'horse-whip v (-pp-)& n (thrash with a) whip for —s.

horticulture n (art of) growing

flowers, fruit, and vegetables. ,horti'cultural adj.

hose[1] n rubber or canvas tube for directing water on to gardens, fires, etc. v water (a garden) with a —; wash (a motor-car, etc) by using a —.

hose[2] n (trade name for) socks and stockings.

'hospitable adj giving hospitality.

'hospital n place where people are treated for, nursed through, their sickness or injury.

,hospi'tality n friendly and generous entertainment of guests, esp in one's own home.

host[1] n 1 person who entertains guests. 2 inn-keeper; hotel-keeper. 'hostess n woman —.

host[2] n great number: a — of friends (difficulties); (old use) army.

Host[3] n bread eaten at Holy Communion.

'hostage n person (less often, thing) given or seized as a pledge that demands will be satisfied.

'hostel n building in which board and lodging are provided (with the support of the authorities concerned) for students and others under training.

'hostess ⇨ host[1].

'hostile adj of an enemy; feeling or showing enmity (to). hos'tility n enmity; (pl) acts of war.

hot adj ('hotter, 'hottest) having great heat; producing a burning sensation in the mouth: a hot curry. get into hot water, get into trouble. 'hot-head n, 'hot-'headed adj hasty (person). 'hot-house n heated building, usu of glass, for delicate plants.

ho'tel n building where meals and rooms are provided for travellers.

hound n kinds of dog used for hunting and racing. v chase, worry with, or as with, —s.

hour n 1 sixty minutes. at the eleventh —, when almost too late. 2 (pl) fixed periods of time, esp for work: office —s. keep late —s, work late, go to bed late. 3 a particular, or the present, point in time: in the — of danger. '—ly adj & adv (done, occurring) every hour.

house n 1 building esp constructed as a home for a family. like a — on fire, very successfully. 2 H—s of Parliament, buildings used by the British Parliament. **3** (audience in a) theatre, etc: *full —* (ie all seats filled). **4** family: *the H— of Windsor* (the present British Royal Family); business firm. *v* **1** provide —s for: *the housing problem.* **2** store in a — or room. **'house-agent** *n* person who sells or lets —s for others. **'house-boat** *n* boat fitted up for living in on a river, etc. **'house-breaker** *n* **1** workman who pulls down old buildings. **2** man who forces his way into a — by day to steal, etc. **'—hold** *n* all persons living in a —. **'—keeper** *n* woman employed to manage —hold affairs. **'—maid,** **'—boy** *n* servant in a —. **'—,master** *n* teacher in charge of school boarding-house. **'—wife** *n* wife who stays at home to look after her family.

hove ⇨ heave.

'hovel *n* small, dirty house.

'hover *v* (of birds) remain in the air over one place; (of persons) wait about. **—craft** *n* craft(3) that can remain still or travel when raised above the surface of land or water by air-pressure.

a hovercraft

how *adv* in what way?: *How did it happen?*; in what state?: *How are you?*; to what extent, amount: *How far (much) is it?*

how'ever *adv* in whatever way or degree. *conj* but yet.

howl *n* long, loud cry (of, eg, a wolf); long cry of sb in pain or of sb expressing scorn, ridicule, etc. *v* utter such cries.

hub *n* central part of a wheel; (fig) centre of activity.

'hubbub *n* confused noise.

'huddle *v* **1** push or crowd together in a confused way. **2 —** (oneself) up, draw the knees up to the body for warmth.

hue[1] *n* (shade of) colour.

hue[2] *n* hue and cry, general outcry of alarm.

hug *v* (-gg-) put the arms round tightly. *n* act of hugging.

huge *adj* very great. **'—ly** *adv.*

hulk *n* old ship no longer used.

hull *n* body or frame of a ship.

hul'lo *int* cry used as a greeting, or to get attention, express surprise, etc.

hum *v* (-mm-) make a continuous sound like that made by bees; sing with closed lips. **make things hum,** make them lively and active. *n* humming sound.

'human *adj* of man or mankind: *a — being,* a person. **—ism** *n* concern for — interests and welfare. **—ly** *adv* (esp) by — means.

hu'mane *adj* tender; kind-hearted.

hu,mani'tarian *adj & n* (of, holding the views of) person working for the welfare of all human beings.

hu'manity *n* **1** the human race. **2** human nature. **3** quality of being humane.

'humble *adj* (-r, -st) **1** having or showing a modest opinion of oneself. **2** poor; mean; low in rank. **'humbly** *adv.*

'humbug *n* dishonest and deceiving act, behaviour, person, etc.

'humdrum *adj* dull; monotonous.

'humid *adj* (esp of air, climate) damp. **hu'midity** *n.*

hu'miliate *v* cause to feel humble or ashamed. **hu,mili'ation** *n.*

hu'mility *n* humble condition or state of mind.

'humour *n* **1** (capacity to cause or feel) amusement. **2** person's state of mind (esp at a particular time): *in a good —; not in the — for work.* *v* give way to, satisfy (a person, his desires). **'humorist** *n* humorous talker or writer. **'humorous** *adj* having or showing a sense of —; causing amusement.

hump *n* fleshy lump (eg on a camel's back). ⇨ p 317. **'—back** *n* = hunchback.

'humus *n* earth formed by the decay of dead leaves, etc.

hunch *n* **1** thick piece or slice. **2** hump. *v* bend (eg the shoulders) to form a —(2). **'—back** *n* person with his back deformed into a —(2).

'hundred *n & adj* 100. **—th** *n & adj* one part of a —; ¹⁄₁₀₀. **—weight** *n* (= cwt) one-twentieth of a ton.

hung ⇨ hang.

'hunger n need, desire, for food; (fig) any strong desire. v feel, suffer from, —; have a desire (for). 'hungry adj (-ier, -iest) feeling, causing, —. 'hungrily adv.

hunt v 1 go after (wild animals) for food or sport. 2 look for; try to find. '—er n. '—sman n.

'hurdle n 1 movable oblong frame of wood, etc, used for temporary fences (eg for sheep). 2 light frame to be jumped over in a hurdle-race. —r n runner in a hurdle-race.

hurl v throw violently.

hur'rah, hur'ray int cry of welcome, joy, or triumph.

'hurricane n violent wind-storm.

'hurry n haste; wish to get sth done quickly; eager haste; (with neg & interr) need for haste. v (cause to) move or do sth quickly. — up, be quick; — away, go off quickly. 'hurried adj done in a —. 'hurriedly adv.

hurt n & v (cause) injury or pain.

'hurtle v (cause to) rush violently.

'husband n man a woman is married to. —ry v farming.

hush v make or become silent; (imperative) Be silent! n silence; quiet.

husk n dry outer covering of (esp grain) seeds. v remove —s from. '—y adj (-ier, -iest) (dry) like —s; (of the voice) hoarse. '—ily adv.

'hustle v push roughly; (make sb) act with speed and energy. n quick, lively activity.

hut n small, roughly-made house or shelter.

hutch n box with a front of wire netting, esp for rabbits.

hy'aena ⇨ hyena.

'hybrid n & adj (animal, plant, etc) from parents of different sorts.

'hydrant n pipe (esp in a street) to which water-hoses can be attached (for putting out fires, etc).

hy'draulic adj of water in motion; worked by water-power.

'hydro- prefix 1 of water. 2 of hydrogen. ,hydro-e'lectric adj of electricity produced by water-power. —gen n gas without colour, taste, or smell that combines with oxygen to form water.

hy'ena n flesh-eating animal like a wolf, with a laugh-like cry.

'hygiene n science of, rules for,

healthy living. hy'gienic adj of —; likely to promote health; free from disease, germs. hy'gienically adv.

hymn n song of praise to God. '—al n book of —s.

'hyphen n the mark -, used for joining words: Afro-American.

'hypnotize v produce in sb a state like deep sleep in which his acts may be controlled by another.

hy'pocrisy n (making a) pretence of virtue. 'hypocrite n person guilty of —. ,hypo'critical adj of — or a hypocrite.

hy'pothesis n (pl hy'potheses) idea put forward as a starting-point for reasoning or explanation. ,hypo-'thetical adj of, based on, a —; not on certain knowledge.

hys'teria n 1 disturbance of the nervous system with (often uncontrollable) outbursts of emotion. 2 foolish excitement. hys'terical adj caused by, suffering from, —. hys'terics n pl attack(s) of —: to go into hysterics.

I

I pron used by a speaker or writer when referring to himself: I can see you. ⇨ me.

ice n frozen water. v make (food, etc) very cold; cover (cake) with sugary mixture. 'iceberg n mass of ice (broken off a glacier) floating

an iceberg

in the sea. 'icecream n frozen cream or custard. 'ice-bound ('ice-free) adj (of harbours, etc) obstructed by (free from) ice. 'icicle n pointed piece of ice formed by the freezing of dripping water. 'icing n sugary coating on a cake; layer of ice (eg on the wing of an aircraft). **'icy** *adj* very cold. **'icily** *adv*.

i'dea *n* **1** thought; picture in the mind. **2** plan; scheme.

i'deal *adj* **1** satisfying one's highest hopes; perfect. **2** existing only as an idea; not likely to be had or reached. *n* idea, example, looked upon as perfect. **—ize** *v* make, think of, as —.

i'dentical *adj* the same: — *with*, like in every way. **i'dentify** *v* **1** say, show, prove, who or what sb or sth is. **2** identify oneself with, give one's support to. **i,dentifi'cation** *n* **i'dentity** *n* who sb is; what sth is.

,ide'ology *n* ideas characteristic of a person or group, esp those of an economic or political system.

'idiom *n* **1** (special form of a) language of a class of people, of a part of a country. **2** word-group (*in order to*) whose meaning must be learnt as a whole. **,idio'matic** *adj* **,idio'matically** *adv*.

'idiot *n* silly person. **,idi'otic** *adj* stupid. **,idi'otically** *adv*.

'idle *adj* (-r, -st) **1** not working; not being used. **2** lazy; not working hard. **3** useless; worthless: — *gossip*. *v* be —. **—r** *n*. **'idly** *adv*. **—ness** *n*.

'idol *n* **1** model (in wood, stone, etc) of a god. **2** sb or sth greatly loved or admired. **i'dolater** *n* idol-worshipper. **i'dolatry** *n* worship of an —. **—ize** *v* love or admire too much.

'idyll *n* short description, usu in verse, of a country scene. **i'dyllic** *adj* simple and pleasant; typical of, suitable for, an —.

if *conj* on condition that; when; although; whether.

'igloo *n* winter hut made of blocks of hard snow (by members of a race living in N Canada, called *Eskimos*).

ig'nite *v* set on fire; take fire.

'ignorant *adj* having, showing, little or no knowledge; not aware (*of* sth). **'ignorance** *n* state of being —.

ig'nore *v* take no notice of.

il- *prefix* not; opposite of: as in *il'legal, il'logical,* etc.

ill *adj* **1** in bad health: *taken ill.* **2** bad: *ill health.* *n* **1** evil. **2** misfortune. *adv* badly; unfavourably.

ill at ease, uncomfortable, embarrassed. **ill-'bred** *adj* badly brought up; badly behaved. **'illness** *n* being ill; disease. **'ill-'treat, ill-'use** *v* treat badly or cruelly.

il'licit *adj* unlawful.

il'literate *n & adj* (person) with little or no education, unable to read or write. **il'literacy** *n*.

il'luminate *v* **1** give light to; throw light on. **2** decorate (streets, etc) with lights (eg as a sign of rejoicing). **il,lumi'nation** *n* lighting; light(s). **il'lumine** *v* give light to or on.

il'lusion *n* (the seeing of) sth that appears to, but does not really, exist; false idea or belief.

'illustrate *v* explain by examples, pictures, etc; provide (a book, etc) with pictures or diagrams. **,illus-'tration** *n* illustrating; sth that —s.

il'lustrious *adj* celebrated.

im- *prefix* opposite of, not: as in *im'moral, im'possible, im'pure,* etc.

'image *n* **1** likeness or copy of the shape of sb or sth, esp one in wood, stone, metal, etc. **2** mental picture. **3** (be) the very — of (*sb*), (be) exactly like. **4** metaphor: *speak in* —s. **— ry** *n* use of —s (4) in writing; —s(1).

i'magine *v* **1** form a picture of in the mind. **2** think of (sth) as probable. **i'maginable** *adj* that can be —d. **i'maginary** *adj* unreal. **i,magi'nation** *n* power of the mind to —; sth —d. **i'maginative** *adj* of, having, using, showing, imagination.

i'mam *n* title of various Muslim leaders.

'imbecile *adj & n* weak-minded (person).

im'bibe *v* drink; take in (ideas).

im'bue *v* —d with, filled with (eg hatred, love of one's country).

'imitate *v* **1** copy the behaviour of. **2** be like; make a likeness of. **,imi'tation** *n* imitating; sth that —s; copy. **'imitator** *n*.

im'maculate *adj* faultless; pure.

im'mediate *adj* **1** without anything coming between. **2** occurring at once. **—ly** *adv* (esp) at once; without delay.

,imme'morial *adj* very old; going back beyond the reach of memory.

im'mense *adj* very large. —ly *adv.* im'mensity *n* great size.

im'merse *v* 1 put under the surface of (a liquid). 2 —d in, deep in (thought, a book, etc). im'mersion *n.*

'immigrate *v* come (*into* a country) to live permanently. 'immigrant *n* sb who does this. ,immi'gration *n.*

'imminent *adj* (esp of danger) likely to come or happen soon. 'imminence *n* nearness (of an event, etc).

im'moral *adj* wicked and evil; contrary(1) to morals. ,immo-'rality *n.*

im'mortal *adj* living for ever; never forgotten. ,immor'tality *n* endless life or fame. —ize *v* make —.

im'mune *adj* free, safe (*from* sth unpleasant or undesirable). im-'munity *n.* 'immunize *v* make — from, esp a disease.

imp *n* child of the devil; (playfully) mischievous child.

im'pact *n* striking (*on, against,* sth) with force; collision.

im'pair *v* weaken; damage.

im'part *v* give, pass on (a share of sth, news, a secret, etc, *to* sb).

im'partial *adj* fair (in giving judgements, etc). —ly *adv.*

im'passive *adj* showing no sign of feeling; unmoved in one's feelings.

im'patient *adj* hasty; not patient. im'patience *n* lack of patience.

im'peach *v* accuse (*of* wrongdoing, esp against the State). —ment *n.*

im'peccable *adj* faultless.

im'pede *v* hinder. im'pediment *n* hindrance, esp a defect in speech.

im'pel *v* (-ll-) drive forward; force.

im'pending *adj* about to happen; imminent.

im'perative *adj* 1 urgent; not to be disregarded or ignored. 2 — mood, form of a verb expressing commands: *Stand up!*

im'perial *adj* of an empire; of an emperor: *an imperial manner.*

im'peril *v* (-ll-) put in, bring into, danger.

im'perious *adj* commanding.

im'personal *adj* 1 not influenced by personal feeling. 2 not referring to a particular person.

im'personate *v* pretend to be (another person); act the part of (in a play).

im'pertinent *adj* impolite; disrespectful. im'pertinence *n.*

,imper'turbable *adj* calm; not easily moved in one's feelings.

im'pervious *adj* 1 (of materials) not allowing (water, etc) to pass through. 2 — to, not moved or influenced by.

im'petuous *adj* acting, done, said, quickly and without much thought. im,petu'osity *n.*

'impetus *n* (*pl* -es) force with which a body moves; driving force.

im'pious *adj* wicked.

'implement *n* tool or instrument.

'implicate *v* show that (sb) has taken part (in a crime, etc). ,impli'cation *n* 1 implicating or being implicated. 2 implying; sth implied.

im'plicit *adj* 1 unquestioning (faith, obedience, etc). 2 implied.

im'plore *v* request earnestly.

im'ply *v* give or make a suggestion (*that*).

im'port *v* 1 bring (goods, etc) into (a country). 2 mean[1]. 'import *n* 1 (usu *pl*) goods —ed. 2 meaning. —er *n* person who —s(1).

.m'portant *adj* of great influence; to be treated seriously. im'portance *n.*

im'portunate *adj* making repeated, inconvenient, requests; urgent. ,impor'tunity *n.*

im'pose *v* 1 place, lay (sth *upon* sb or sth). 2 — upon, take advantage of (sb, his kindness). im'posing *adj* important-looking. ,impo'sition *n* sth —d (eg a tax); unreasonable demand.

im'postor *n* person pretending to be what he is not. im'posture *n* deception.

'impotent *adj* lacking sufficient strength (to do, to resist).

im'poverish *v* cause to become poor.

im'practicable *adj* 1 impossible in practice. 2 (of routes) unusable.

im'pregnable *adj* that cannot be overcome or taken by force.

im'press *v* 1 mark by pressing; have a strong influence on. 2 fix deeply (*on* the mind). —ion *n* 1 effect produced on the mind or feelings. 2 (printing of a) number of copies forming one issue(4) of a book or newspaper. 3 mark, etc, made by pressing. 4 (vague or

uncertain) idea or belief. —**ionable**
adj easily influenced. —**ive** *adj*
—ing the mind or feelings.

im'print *v* print; stamp.

im'prison *v* put, keep, in prison.

im'promptu *adj & adv* without
preparation.

im'prove *v* (cause to) become
better. — **upon**, do (sth) better
than (what is mentioned).
—**ment** *n*.

'improvise *v* 1 compose music
while playing it, verse while
reciting it, etc. 2 provide, make,
or do sth, quickly, in time of need,
using whatever is at hand.

'impudent *adj* shamelessly rude.
—**ly** *adv*. **'impudence** *n*.

'impulse *n* 1 push; impetus. 2 sudden inclination to act. **im'pulsive**
adj acting on, resulting from,
—(2).

im'punity *n* **with** —, with freedom
from punishment or injury.

im'pute *v* — **sth to sb**, consider as
the act, outcome, etc, of. **impu-
'tation** *n* accusation; suggestion.

in *prep* 1 (of place): *in Africa*; *in
the room*; *in bed*; etc. 2 (indicating
motion or activity) into: *He dipped
his pen in the ink. They fell in love.*
3 (of time) during: *in 1066*; *in my
absence*; within a space of: *in a
short time.* 4 (indicating ratio):
One in ten of the boys can't spell.
5 (of dress): *dressed in white*, wearing white clothes. 6 (indicating
physical surroundings): *in the rain
(shade).* 7 (indicating a condition
or state): *in good health.* 8 (indicating the method of expression): *in
ink*; *in English.* 9 (indicating degree
or extent): *in great numbers.* **in 'all**,
as the total: *We were fifteen in all.*
10 (indicating occupation, activity,
etc): *He's in the army.* 11 **in as
far as, in so far as**, in such
measure as; to the extent that.
adv (contrasted with *out*-) 1 (used
with many verbs): *come in*, enter;
give in, surrender; etc. 2 (used
with the verb *be*) (a) at home: *Is
there anyone in?* (b) arrived: *Is the
train in yet?* (c) available: *Oranges
are in now.* (d) fashionable: *Long
skirts are in.* (e) elected; having the
authority: *The Liberal-candidate is
in.* 3 **in for**, likely to experience:
We're in for a storm. **in and out**,
now in and then out: *He's always*

in and out of hospital! 4 (preceding
a noun; contrasted with *out*-): *in-
patient.*

in- *prefix* not; the opposite of:
as in *in'accurate*, *insin'cere*, etc
(cf, im-, il-).

,inas'much *adv* — **as**, because;
since.

i'naugurate *v* introduce at a
special ceremony; open (an exhibition, etc) with formal ceremonies.

inborn, 'in'bred *adj* (of a quality)
possessed from birth.

,inca'pacitate *v* make unfit (*for*).
,inca'pacity *n* inability, unfitness.

in'cendiary *n & adj* 1 (person)
setting fire to property unlawfully.
2 (bomb) causing fire.

in'cense[1] *v* make angry.

'incense[2] *n* (smoke of a) substance
producing a pleasant smell when
burning.

in'centive *n* that which encourages
sb to do sth.

in'cessant *adj* continual. —**ly** *adv*.

inch *n* measure of length, one-
twelfth of a foot or 2·55 cm.

'incident *n* event, esp one of less
importance; event that attracts
general attention. **,inci'dental**
adj small and comparatively unimportant. **,inci'dental to**, likely
to occur in connection with.

in'cision *n* cutting; a cut (esp one
made in a surgical operation).

in'cite *v* stir up, rouse (*to do* sth).

,incli'nation *n* 1 leaning (of the
mind or heart, *to* sth); liking or
desire (*for* sth, *to do* sth), 2 slope
or slant.

in'cline *v* 1 (cause to) slope or
slant. 2 direct the mind in a
certain direction; cause (sb) to
have a wish. **'incline** *n* upward
or downward path.

in'clude *v* bring within, reckon, as
part of the whole. **in'clusion** *n*.
in'clusive *adj* including everything (mentioned, listed, etc).

in'cognito *adv* with one's name
kept secret: *travel* —.

'income *n* money received during a
given period for one's work, from
investments, etc.

in'comparable *adj* that cannot be
compared (*to* or *with*); without
equal.

in'congruous *adj* not in harmony
(*with*); out of place. **,incon-
'gruity** *n*.

,incon'venience n (cause of) discomfort or trouble. v cause — to.

in'corporate v make, become, united in one body, group, or corporation(2). in,corpo'ration n.

in'crease v make or become greater. 'increase n amount by which sth —s.

in'criminate v say, be a sign, that (sb) is guilty of wrongdoing.

'incubate v hatch (eggs), esp by artificial warmth in an apparatus called an 'incubator.

in'cumbent adj. — upon, resting upon (sb) as a duty.

in'cur v (-rr-) bring (debt, sb's anger, etc) upon oneself.

in'cursion n sudden attack or invasion.

in'debted adj in debt, under an obligation (to).

in'decent adj not decent; obscene.

in'deed adv really; truly. int How interesting! (surprising! etc).

in'definite adj vague. — article, (grammar) the words a, an.

in'delible adj that cannot be rubbed or wiped out.

in'delicate adj not refined or modest.

in'demnify v 1 pay back (sb for loss, expenses, etc). 2 make (sb) safe (from, against, harm, loss, etc). in'demnity n (esp) payment to compensate for loss.

in'dented adj (of an edge, esp a coastline) irregular; cut into.

,inde'pendent adj 1 not dependent on or controlled by (other persons or things); self-governing. 2 not needing to work for a living. 3 acting or thinking along one's own lines. —ly adv. ,inde'pendence n being —.

'index n (pl —es, 'indices) 1 sth that points or indicates. 2 list of names, references, etc, in 'ABC order, esp at the end of a book. 'index-finger n finger next to the thumb.

'indicate v point to; point out; make known; be a sign of. ,indi-'cation n that which —s.

'indices ⇨ index.

in'different adj 1 — to, neither for nor against; not interested in. 2 not of good quality or ability. in'difference n.

in'digenous adj native(4) (to).

,indi'gestion n (discomfort from) difficulty in digesting food.

in'dignant adj angry and scornful, esp at injustice, because of undeserved blame, etc. —ly adv. ,indig'nation n.

in'dignity n unworthy treatment causing shame or loss of respect.

'indigo n deep blue (dye).

,indis'cretion n (esp) act, remark, etc, that is not discreet.

,indis'pensable adj that one cannot do without.

,indis'posed adj 1 unwell. 2 not inclined (for sth, to do sth). ,indispo'sition n (esp) slight illness.

,indi'vidual adj 1 (opposite of general) specially for one person or thing. 2 considered or taken by itself: in·an — case. n any one human being (contrasted with society). —ly adv one by one. ,indi,vidu'ality n.

'indolent adj lazy. 'indolence n.

'indoor adj situated, carried on, inside a building. in'doors adv in(to) a house, etc.

in'duce v persuade; bring about. —ment n sth that persuades.

in'dulge v give way to and satisfy (desires, etc). —nce n (esp) sth in which a person —s. —nt adj inclined to —: —nt parents.

'industry n 1 quality of being hardworking; constant employment in useful work. 2 (branch of) trade or manufacture. in'dustrial adj of —(2). in'dustrious adj hardworking; showing —(1).

i'nert adj 1 without power to move or act. 2 (of a person) slow; dull.

i'nestimable adj too great to be estimated or given a value.

i'nevitable adj that cannot be avoided; sure to happen.

,inex'perience n lack or want of experience.

'infamous adj wicked; shameful. 'infamy n — behaviour.

'infant n baby; very young child. 'infancy n 1 state of being an —; period when one is an —. 2 early stage of development. —ile adj childish.

'infantry n part of an army that fights on foot.

in'fatuate v —d with, be foolishly in love with. in,fatu'ation n.

in'fect v give disease germs to;

(fig) give (feelings, ideas, etc) to.
—**ion** n (esp) disease that —s.
—**ious** adj 1 —ing with disease;
(of disease) that can be spread by
germs carried in air or water.
2 (fig) quickly spreading to others:
—*ious laughter.*

in'fer v (-rr-) reach an opinion
(from facts or reasoning). 'infer-
ence n 1 process of —ring. 2 sth
—red.

in'ferior adj low(er) in rank, social
position, importance, quality, etc:
— *to others.* n person who is — (in
rank, etc). in,feri'ority n state
of being —.

in'fernal adj of hell; devilish.

in'fest v (of rats, insects, etc) be
present in large numbers.

'infidel n person with no belief in
the true or accepted religion.

,infi'delity n (act of) unfaithfulness.

in'filtrate v (cause to) pass (*into*
or *through*) gradually. ,infil'tration n.

'infinite adj without limits. the —,
— space. —ly adv. ,infini'tesi-
mal adj too small to be measured.
in'finity n number or quantity
beyond calculation.

in'firm adj weak. —ity n weakness.

in'flame v (cause to) become red,
over-heated, angry. in'flam-
mable adj easily catching fire.
,inflam'mation n —d condition
(esp of part of the body). in-
'flammatory adj (esp of
speeches, etc) likely to rouse angry
feelings and excitement.

in'flate v fill with air or gas; cause
to swell. in'flation n (esp) economic condition when there is more
money than goods for sale and
prices rise.

in'flict v — sth on sb, cause him
to suffer by means of (a blow,
penalty, etc). — **oneself upon** sb,
force one's company on him.

'influence n 1 action of natural
forces (*on, upon*): *the — of climate
upon the growth of crops.* 2 power
to affect character, beliefs, actions;
person or fact that exercises such
power; the exercise of such power
(*on*). v have, use, (an) — upon.
influ'ential adj having —.

,influ'enza n (colloq flu) quickly
spreading disease marked by fever
and catarrh.

'influx n a flowing in (eg of visitors,
wealth, new ideas).

in'form v tell (sb *that, of* sth).
,infor'mation n sth told; news
or knowledge given.

in'formal adj not formal(1), (4).
—ly adv. ,infor'mality n.

in'fringe v break (a law, rule, etc).
— **upon,** trespass upon (sb's rights).

in'furiate v fill with fury.

in'fuse v 1 put, pour (a quality
into). 2 pour liquid on (tea-leaves,
etc) to flavour it. in'fusion n.

in'genious adj having, showing,
skill (at making or inventing
things). ,inge'nuity n.

in'genuous adj frank; innocent;
natural.

in'glorious adj shameful; dishonourable.

'ingot n (usu brick-shaped) lump
of metal (esp a valuable one).

in'grained adj (of stains, habits,
etc) deeply fixed; difficult to get
rid of.

in'gratiate v bring (oneself) into
favour (*with* sb), esp for one's own
advantage.

in'gredient n one of the parts in a
mixture.

in'habit v live in. —ant n person
living in a place.

in'hale v breathe in (air, smoke,
etc).

in'herent adj — in, existing as a
natural and permanent part of.

in'herit v 1 receive (property, a
title) from sb at his death. 2 have
(qualities) from ancestors. —ance
n —ing; sth —ed.

in'human adj unfeeling; cruel.

i'nimical adj unfriendly; harmful
(*to*).

i'nimitable adj too good, clever,
etc, to be imitated.

i'niquitous adj very wicked or
unjust. i'niquity n.

i'nitial adj of or at the beginning.
n — letter, esp (*pl*) first letters of
a person's names. v mark or sign
(sth) with one's —s.

i'nitiate v 1 begin; set (a scheme)
working. 2 admit or introduce (sb
into a secret, a society, etc). n &
adj (person) who has been —d.
i,niti'ation n.

i'nitiative n. take the —; take the
first step(6). on one's own —,
without an order or suggestion
from others. have the —, have the

right or power to take the first step. **show —**, show ability to start new schemes, etc.

in'ject v force (a liquid, etc, *into* sth) (as) with a syringe; fill (sth *with* a liquid) in this way. **—ion** n. **—ing**; instance of this (as with a medical syringe); substance to be **—ed**.

in'junction n order (esp from a law court) demanding that sth shall or shall not be done.

injure v hurt; damage. **'injury** n wrong; damage; **—d** part of the body. **in'jurious** adj causing, likely to cause, injury.

in'justice n 1 unjust act. **do sb an —**, judge him unfairly. 2 lack of justice.

ink n coloured liquid used for writing and printing. v mark, make dirty, with ink. **'inky** adj (-ier, -iest) like, covered with, ink.

'inkling n slight hint or idea (*of*).

inland adj 1 in the interior of a country. 2 carried on, obtained, within the boundaries of a country: **— revenue. in'land** adv away from the coast.

in'lay v set pieces of (designs in) wood, metal, etc, in the surface of another kind of material so that the resulting surface is smooth and even: *ivory inlaid with gold.* **'inlay** n inlaid work.

inlet n strip of water extending into the land from a larger body of water, or between islands.

inmate n one of a number of persons living together (eg in a hospital, prison, etc).

inmost adj farthest from the surface.

inn n public house where lodging, drink, and meals may be had.

in'nate adj (of a quality) in one's nature; possessed from birth.

inner adj inside. **—most** adj = inmost.

innings n (cricket, etc) time during which a player or team is batting; (fig) chance to show one's abilities; period of power.

innocent adj not guilty (*of* wrongdoing); harmless. **'innocence** n.

inno'vation n new practice; change in an old custom.

innu'endo n (*pl* -es) indirect reference, usu sth unfavourable to sb's character or reputation.

in'numerable adj too many to be counted.

i'noculate v protect (usu by injection with a germ to produce a mild form of a disease) against a severe attack. **i,nocu'lation** n.

'in-,patient n person lodged in and receiving treatment at a hospital.

'inquest n official inquiry to learn facts (esp concerning sb's death).

in'quire v ask to be told. **— after**, ask about (sb's health, etc). **— into**, try to learn the facts about. **—r** n person who **—s. in'quiry** n asking; inquiring. **in'quisitive** adj fond of, showing a fondness for, inquiring into, the affairs of other people.

in'satiable adj that cannot be satisfied; very greedy.

in'scribe v write (words, one's name, etc, *in* or *on*); mark (sth *with* words, etc). **in'scription** n sth **—d** (eg the words on a coin).

in'scrutable adj mysterious; that cannot be known.

'insect n sorts of small animal with no backbone and six legs (eg ant, fly). ⇨ p 144. (incorrectly) any small creeping or flying creature. **in'secticide** n substance for killing **—s.**

in'sensible adj 1 unconscious (as the result of illness, a blow, etc). 2 not aware (*of* danger, etc). 3 (of changes) too small or gradual to be observed. **in'sensibly** adv. **in,sensi'bility** n.

in'sert v put (sth *in*, *into*, *between*). **—ion** n **—ing**; sth **—ed.**

'inside n 1 inner side or surface. 2 part of a road, etc nearest to the pavement; part of a pavement farthest from the roadway. 3 (colloq) stomach and bowels. **in'side** adj situated on or in; coming from the inner part or edge. adv on or in the **—. prep** on the inner side.

inside-'out adv with the inner side outside; thoroughly: *know the plans —.*

in'sidious adj doing harm secretly.

'insight n power of seeing with the mind (*into* a problem, etc).

in'sinuate v 1 make a way for (oneself, sth) gently and secretly (*into* sth). 2 suggest unpleasantly and indirectly (*that*). **in,sinu'ation** n.

in'sipid adj tasteless; uninteresting; dull.

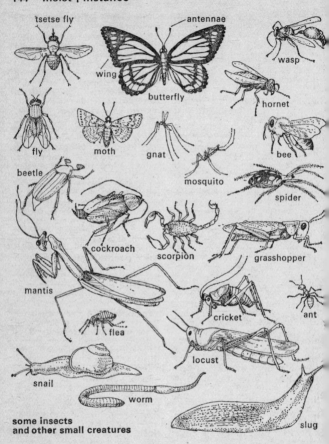

tsetse fly

antennae

wasp

wing

butterfly

hornet

fly

moth

gnat

bee

beetle

mosquito

spider

cockroach

scorpion

grasshopper

mantis

cricket

ant

flea

locust

snail

worm

slug

**some insects
and other small creatures**

in'sist v urge strongly, against dis-
belief or opposition (*on* sth);
declare emphatically. —ent *adj*
compelling attention; urgent.
—ence *n*.

'insolent *adj* insulting; contemptuous. 'insolence *n*.

in'somnia *n* inability to sleep.

in'spect *v* examine carefully; visit
officially to see that rules, etc, are
obeyed. —ion *n*. —or *n*.

in'spire *v* fill with noble aims,

thoughts, feelings, creative power
,inspi'ration *n* 1 inspiring o
being —d; person or thing that —s
2 good idea coming to the min
suddenly.

in'stall *v* put (a telephone, a heating system, etc) into a building
place (sb) in his new post (4).

in'stalment *n* any one of the part
of sth supplied, paid for, etc, a
intervals over a period of time.

'instance *n* example.

'**instant** *adj* coming, happening, or given, at once: — *obedience*. ,—'**coffee,** that which can be made —ly with coffee powder and boiling water or milk. *n* moment. —**ly** *adv* at once. ,**instan'taneous** *adj* happening, done, in an —.

in'stead *adv* in place (of).

'**instep** *n* upper surface of the foot or shoe between toes and ankle.

'**instigate** *v* excite and urge (sb to do sth); cause (eg a strike) in this way.

in'stil *v* (-ll-) introduce (ideas, etc, *into* sb's mind) gradually.

'**instinct** *n* natural tendency to do sth or to behave in a certain way without reasoning. **in'stinctive** *adj* based on —.

'**institute** *n* society or organization for a special (usu social or educational) purpose. *v* get (an inquiry, rules, etc) started. ,**insti'tution** *n* 1 instituting. 2 long-established custom, law, etc. 3 (building occupied by an) organization for social welfare (eg an orphanage).

in'struct *v* 1 teach. 2 give orders to. —**ion** *n* 1 teaching. 2 (*pl*) orders; directions (about how to use sth, etc). —**ive** *adj* giving knowledge.

'**instrument** *n* 1 sth used in the performance of an action, esp in delicate or scientific work. 2 ,**musical** —, violin, piano, etc. ⇨ p 180. ,**instru'mental** *adj*. 1 (of music) for —s, not voices. 2 causing sth to happen.

insu'bordinate *adj* disobedient. '**insu,bordi'nation** *n* disobedience.

'**insular** *adj* of an island; of or like islanders; narrow-minded.

'**insulate** *v* cover or separate with non-conducting materials in order to prevent loss of heat, electricity, etc. ,**insu'lation** *n*.

'**insult** *n* sth said or done intended to hurt a person's feelings or dignity. **in'sult** *v* treat (sb) with —s.

in'superable *adj* (of difficulties, etc) that cannot be overcome.

in'surance *n* 1 safeguard against loss, provision against sickness, death, etc, by means of payment(s) to a company, society, or (eg in Gt Brit) the State. 2 payment made to or by such a company,

etc. **in'sure** *v* make an agreement about the — of: *to insure one's house against fire*.

,**insur'rection** *n* planned rising against the government.

in'tact *adj* untouched; undamaged.

'**intake** *n* 1 place where water, etc, is taken into a pipe, channel, etc. 2 that which enters or is taken in (during a given period).

'**integral** *adj* whole; necessary for completeness.

in'tegrity *n* quality of being honest.

'**intellect** *n* power of the mind to reason. ,**intel'lectual** *adj* having, showing, connected with, the power to reason. *n* —ual person.

in'telligence *n* 1 (power of) understanding. 2 news; information. **in'telligent** *adj* having, showing, —. **in'telligible** *adj* clear to the mind; easily understood. **in,telli-gi'bility** *n*.

in'tend *v* have in mind as a purpose.

in'tense *adj* 1 (of qualities) high in degree. 2 (of feelings, etc) strong. —**ly** *adv*. **in'tensify** *v* make, become, —. **in'tensity** *n* being —; strength (of feeling, etc).

in'tent *adj* 1 (of looks) eager. 2 (of persons) — **on,** closely occupied with. *n* purpose. **to all —s and purposes,** in all essential points.

in'tention *n* purpose; sth intended. —**al** *adj* said or done on purpose. —**ally** *adv* on purpose.

in'ter *v* (-rr-) bury.

inter- *prefix* between; among; one with another.

,**inter'cede** *v* plead. ,**inter'cession** *n*.

,**inter'cept** *v* stop or seize (sb or sth) between the starting-point and the destination.

,**inter'change** *v* 1 make an exchange of (views, etc). 2 put (each of two things) in the other's place. '**inter-change** *n* an interchanging.

'**intercourse** *n* 1 dealings or communications, exchange (of trade, ideas, etc, between persons, societies, nations). 2 sexual communication between a man and a woman.

'**interest** *n* 1 condition of wanting to know about sth. 2 quality that excites curiosity. 3 sth to which one gives time and attention: *your chief —s in life*. 4 (what is to sb's) advantage. **5** money charged or paid for the loan of capital. *v* cause (sb) to give his attention to. **—ed** *adj* having an —(3) in; seeking one's own advantage. **—ing** *adj* holding the attention.

,inter'fere *v* — **in**, break in upon (other person's affairs) without right. — **with**, disturb, put out of place. **—nce** *n* interfering.

'interim *n* **in the** —, meanwhile.

in'terior *adj* of or in the inside; inland. *n* the inside parts of sth; inland areas.

,inter'jection *n* word(s) used as an exclamation: *Oh! Good gracious! Indeed!* etc.

,inter'lock *v* lock or join together.

'interloper *n* person who pushes his way in where he has no right.

'interlude *n* interval (of time).

,inter'mediary *n & adj* (sb or sth) acting between (persons, groups, etc).

,inter'mediate *adj* coming between (in time, space, degree, etc).

in'terminable *adj* endless; far too long.

,inter'mittent *adj* with some intervals; that keeps coming and going.

in'tern *v* compel (esp aliens in war) to live inside certain limits or in a special camp. **—ment** *n*.

in'ternal *adj* **1** of or in the inside; of the domestic affairs of a country. **2** derived from what is shown by the thing itself: — *evidence*. **—ly** *adv*.

,inter'national *adj* existing, carried on, between nations.

in'terpret *v* **1** make clear the meaning of; consider as the meaning of. **2** act as **—er**. **—er** *n* person who gives an immediate translation of words spoken in another language. in,terpre'tation *n*.

in'terrogate *v* question. ,inter'rogative *adj* of or for questions.

,inter'rupt *v* **1** stop, for a time: *traffic —ed by floods.* **2** speak to sb while he is saying sth. **—ion** *n*.

,inter'sect *v* (of lines) cut or cross.

'interval *n* time or space between, esp time between two parts of a play, concert, etc. **at —s, with —s** between.

,inter'vene *v* **1** (of events) come between. **2** (of persons, etc) interfere so as to stop sth or change the result. ,inter'vention *n*.

'interview *v & n* (conduct a) meeting with sb for discussion, esp of a newspaper man and sb whose views are requested for publication.

in'testine *n* lower part of the food canal below the stomach. ⇨ p 30.

'intimate[1] *adj* **1** close and familiar: **on — terms with. 2** private and personal. **—ly** *adv*. 'intimacy *n*.

'intimate[2] *v* make known (eg one's approval of sth, *that* one approves).

in'timidate *v* frighten, esp in order to force sb *into* doing sth.

'into *prep* **1** (indicating movement towards a point within): *go — the room.* **2** (indicating a result from an action): *get — trouble.*

in'tone *v* recite (eg a prayer) in a singing tone; speak with a particular tone. ,into'nation *n* (esp) the rise and fall of the voice in speaking.

in'toxicate *v* make drunk; excite beyond self-control. in,toxi'cation *n*.

in'trepid *adj* fearless.

'intricate *adj* complicated; puzzling.

in'trigue *n* secret plot(ting).

in'trinsic *adj* (of value, beauty) existing within, not coming from outside.

,intro'duce *v* **1** bring in or forward; bring (sth) into use, into operation, or to the attention. **2** make (persons) known to each other in the usual formal way. ,intro'duction *n* introducing; being **—d**; sth **—d** or sth that **—s**, esp an explanatory article at the beginning of a book, etc.

in'trude *v* force (oneself *into* a place, *upon* sb); enter without invitation. **—r** *n*. in'trusion *n*.

,intu'ition *n* (power of) immediate understanding of sth without reasoning.

'inundate *v* flood (*with*). ,inun'dation *n*.

in'vade *v* enter (a country) in order to attack or conquer. **—r** *n*. in'vasion *n*.

'invalid[1] *n & adj* (person who is) weak or disabled through illness or injury; suitable for such persons: *an — chair (diet).*

in'valid[2] *adj* not valid.

in'valuable *adj* having a value too high to be measured.

in'vasion ⇨ invade.

in'vent *v* **1** create or design (sth not existing before). **2** make up (a story, excuse, etc.). **—or** *n*. **—ion** *n*.

'inventory *n* detailed list (of goods, etc.).

in'verse *adj* in **— proportion**, that between two quantities, one of which decreases in the same proportion that the other increases.

in'vert *v* put upside down or in the opposite order, position, or relation. **in'version** *n* —ing or being —ed.

in'vest *v* **1** put (money *in* a business, *in* stocks, etc); (colloq) **— in**, buy (sth considered to be profitable or useful): **—** *in a new hat.* **2** surround (eg a town) with armed forces. **—ment** *n* the —ing of money; sum of money —ed; business in which money is —ed. **—or** *n* person who —s money.

in'vestigate *v* examine; inquire into. **in,vesti'gation** *n*.

in'vidious *adj* likely to cause ill will because of injustice, etc.

in'vigorate *v* make strong or confident.

in'vite *v* ask (sb to accept hospitality, do sth); ask for; attract. **,invi'tation** *n* (esp) request to do sth, come somewhere, etc.

'invoice *v* & *n* (make a) list of goods with the price(s) charged.

in'voke *v* call upon (God, the law) for help; ask earnestly for (help, protection, etc).

in'voluntary *adj* done without intention; done consciously.

in'volve *v* **1** cause (sb or sth) to be in a complicated or difficult situation: **—d** *in debt (crime, mystery).* **2** have as a necessary consequence. **—d** *adj* complicated.

inward *adj* inner; placed in, moving or turned towards, the inside. **—ly** *adv* (esp) in mind or spirit.

'inward(s) *adv* towards the inside.

IOU *n* (= I owe you) signed paper acknowledging that one owes the sum of money stated.

ir- *prefix* not: as in *ir'relevant*, etc.

i'rate *adj* angry. **ire** *n* (liter) anger.

iris *n* coloured part of the eyeball.

'irksome *adj* troublesome; tiring.

'iron *n* **1** commonest metal from which steel is made. **2** too many **—s in the fire**, too many plans, etc, needing attention at once. **strike while the — is hot**, act while circumstances are favourable. **3** (also **'flat-iron**) tool heated and used for smoothing clothes, etc.

ironing

ivy

4 (*pl*) chains for a prisoner. *v* smooth (clothes, etc) with an —(3). **—monger** *n* dealer in metal goods. **—mongery** *n* business of an —monger; his goods. **'iron-mould** *n* discoloration caused by **—** rust or ink.

'irony *n* **1** the expression of one's meaning by saying sth that is the direct opposite, in order to make one's remarks forceful. **2** event, situation, which would normally be desirable but is of no value because of circumstances. **i'ronic(al)** *adj* of, using, showing, irony.

,irre'sistible *adj* that cannot be resisted; very attractive, etc.

,irres'pective *adj*. **— of**, not taking into consideration.

,irres'ponsible *adj* doing things, done, without proper care and thought; not responsible.

'irrigate *v* **1** supply (land, crops) with water (by means of water-channels, etc). **2** construct reservoirs, canals, etc, for distribution of water for crops. **,irri'gation** *n*.

'irritate *v* **1** make angry or annoyed. **2** make (part of the body) inflamed or sore. **'irritable** *adj* easily —d. **,irri'tation** *n*.

is ⇨ be.

'island *n* piece of land surrounded by water. **isle** *n* (liter, except in proper names) —.

'isn't = is not. ⇨ be.

'isolate *v* separate; put or keep away from others. **,iso'lation** *n*.

'issue *v* **1** come, go, flow, out. **2** give or send out; distribute. *n* **1** a flowing out. **2** result or outcome.

3 question arising for discussion. **4** new coins, banknotes, stamps, edition of newspaper, **—d** at one time. **5** offspring: *He died without —*.

'isthmus *n* neck of land joining two larger bodies of land.

it *pron* (*pl* they, them) **1** referring to animals, plants, objects, ideas, etc: *I can see it.* **2** used to refer to a phrase or clause that follows: *It is easy to learn Russian.* **3** used as a subject for the verb *be*, etc: *It's raining.* **its** *adj* (indicating possession) of it: *The dog wagged its tail.* **itself** *pron* The dog hurt *itself when it stepped on a nail.*

i'talic *adj* (of letters) sloping: *This is – type.* **n** *pl* — letters.

itch *v & n* **1** (have a) feeling of irritation in the skin, causing a desire to scratch. **2** (have a) restless longing (*for* sth, *to do* sth).

'item *n* **1** single article in a list, etc. **2** detail or paragraph of news.

its ⇨ it.

it's = it is.

'ivory *n* white, bone-like substance forming the tusks of elephants, walruses, etc. ⇨ pp 247, 317.

'ivy *n* climbing, evergreen plant with dark, shiny leaves. ⇨ p 147.

J

jab *v* (-bb-) force (a pointed weapon, the elbow, etc) suddenly and roughly (*into* sb or sth); aim a blow (*at* sb or sth). **n** blow of this sort.

'jabber *v* talk excitedly, or indistinctly. **n** rapid, confused talk.

jack *n* **1** machine for raising heavy objects off the ground (eg a motorcar in order to remove a wheel). **2** Union J—, flag of the United Kingdom. **3** Jack-of-all-trades, sb with many different skills. *v* — up, raise with a —(1).

'jackal *n* wild, dog-like animal.

'jacket. *n* **1** short coat. **2** outer covering (eg the skin of a potato, loose paper cover for a book).

jade *n* hard, usu green, stone.

'jaded *adj* tired out; worn out.

'jagged *adj* with rough, uneven edges and sharp points: *— rocks.*

jail *n* = gaol.

jam¹ *v* (-mm-) **1** crush, be crushed, between two surfaces or things: *ships jammed in the ice.* **2** (of parts of a machine, etc) (cause to) become fixed so that movement or action is prevented: *to jam on the brakes of a bus.* **3** push together (into a mass, or into sth). **n** number or quantity of things, etc, crowded together so that movement is impossible or difficult: *a traffic jam.*

jam² *n* fruit boiled with sugar and preserved in jars, tins, etc.

jambo'ree *n* merry meeting, rally (2), eg of Scouts.

'jangle *v & n* (give out, cause to give out, a) harsh metallic noise.

'January *n* first month of the year.

jar¹ *v* (-rr-) **1** strike (*on* or *against* sth) with a harsh sound. **2** have an unpleasant effect (*on*). **n** jarring sound; bodily or mental shock.

jar² *n* tall vessel, usu round, with a wide mouth, of glass, stone, earthenware, etc; (such a vessel and) its contents.

'jargon *n* experts' language full of technical or special words.

'jaundice *n* illness causing the skin to become yellow. **—d** *adj* jealous and spiteful.

jaunt *v & n* (take a) short journey for pleasure.

'jaunty *adj* (-ier, -iest) feeling, showing, self-confidence. **'jauntily** *adv.*

'javelin *n* light spear for throwing, usu in sport.

a javelin

a jam-jar

jaw *n* **1** lower (upper) —, one or other of the bone structures containing the teeth. **2** (*pl*) the mouth, its bones and teeth; (fig) entrance (esp to a dangerous place). (colloq) talk a lot; scold.

jazz *n* popular music (often improvised) of USA Negro origin with strong rhythms.

'jealous *adj* **1** feeling or showing

fear or ill will because of possible or actual loss of rights or love. **2** feeling or showing unhappiness because of the better fortune, success, etc, of others. **3** taking watchful care (of one's reputation, etc). **—y** n.

jeans n pl workman's overalls; tough (usu cotton) trousers similar to overalls, worn informally by men, women and children.

jeep n strong motor vehicle that can travel easily across fields and over rough roads.

jeer v mock, laugh rudely (at sb). n **—ing** remark.

'jelly n clear, soft food substance, eg one made by boiling fruit juice with sugar. **'—fish** n jelly-like sea animal. ⇨ p 247.

'jeopardy n **in —**, in danger. **'jeopardize** v put in danger.

jerk v & n (give a) sudden pull or twist: *The bus stopped with a —.* **'—y** adj (-ier, -iest) with sudden stops and starts.

'jersey n close-fitting knitted woollen garment with sleeves.

jest v & n joke. **in —**, not seriously.

jet n strong stream of gas, liquid, steam, or air forced out of a small opening. **jet aircraft**, one driven forward by jets of gas directed backwards from it.

'jettison v throw (goods) overboard in order to lighten a ship (eg during a storm).

'jetty n structure built out into the sea as a breakwater, etc.

Jew n sb of the Hebrew race. **'Jewish** adj of the Jews.

'jewel n precious stone (eg a ruby); ornament with —s in it. v adorn with —s. **—ler** n trader in —s; person who sets —s. **—(le)ry** n —s.

jib v (-bb-) **1** (of a horse) refuse to go forward; (fig) refuse to go on with sth. **2 jib at**, show unwillingness (to do sth).

jig n (music for a) quick lively dance. v (-gg-) dance a jig; move up and down quickly and jerkily.

'jig-saw ,puzzle n picture cut in irregularly shaped pieces which are to be fitted together again.

jilt v give up, send away (sb one has promised to marry).

'jingle v & n (make) light, ringing sound (as of keys striking together).

job n **1** complete(d) piece of work.

make a good job of sth, do it well. **odd jobs**, bits of work not connected with each other. **2** That's a good job, That's fortunate. **3** employment: **out of a job**, unemployed.

'jockey n person (esp a professional) who rides horses in races. ⇨ disc.

jo'cose, 'jocular adj humorous.

jog v (-gg-) & n **1** (give a) slight knock or push; (fig) **jog sb's memory**, cause him to remember sth. **2** (run, move, at a) pace causing a shaking motion. **jog along**, (fig) make slow, uneventful progress.

join v **1** put or come together; unite; connect with a line, rope, bridge, etc. **2** become a member of (a society, the armed forces, etc). **3** come into the company of; associate with (sb in sth). n **join(1)**.

'joiner n skilled workman who makes furniture and the wooden parts of buildings. **—y** n work of a —.

joint n **1** place at which two things are joined. **2** structure by which two things (eg two pipes, two bones) are joined. **3** limb or other

joints

division of a sheep, ox, etc, which a butcher serves to customers. adj held or done by, belonging to, two or more persons together: **— ownership**. v fit together by means of —s.

joist n one of the pieces of timber (from wall to wall) to which floorboards are nailed.

joke n sth said or done to cause amusement; circumstance that causes amusement. v make —s. **'—r** n. **'jokingly** adv.

'jolly adj (-ier, -iest) joyful; gay; merry. adv (colloq) very: — **good**. **'jollity** n — condition.

jolt v & n **1** (give sb or sth a) jerk or sudden shake. **2** (of a cart, etc) move with —s: *an old bus —ing along.*

'jostle v push roughly (*against*).

jot[1] v (-tt-) jot sth down, make a quick written note of it.

jot[2] n not a jot, not a bit, not at all.

'journal n 1 newspaper; other periodical. 2 daily record of news, events, accounts[1], etc. **—ism** n work of writing for, editing, or publishing, newspapers. **—ist** n person employed in —ism.

'journey n (*pl* 'journeys) (distance travelled in) going to a place, esp a distant place: *a three days' —; to go on a — (from . . . to . . .).* v make a —.

'jovial adj full of fun and good humour; merry. **—ly** adv. **,jovi'ality** n.

joy n (sth that gives) great pleasure. **'joyful** adj filled with, showing, causing, joy. **'joyfully** adv. **'joyless** adj sad. **'joylessly** adv. **'joyous** adj full of joy.

'jubilant adj triumphant; showing joy. **,jubi'lation** n.

'jubilee n (celebration of the) fiftieth anniversary of some event.

'Judaism n religion of the Jews.

judge n 1 public officer with authority to hear and decide cases in a law court. 2 person who decides in a contest, competition, dispute, etc. 3 person able to give opinions on merits or values. v 1 act as a —(1), (2). 2 estimate; consider; form an opinion about. **'judg(e)ment** n 1 judging or being **—d**; decision of a — or court. 2 power, ability, to —(2), (3); good sense. 3 misfortune considered as a punishment from God.

ju'dicial adj of or by a judge or law court.

ju'dicious adj having, showing, good sense. **—ly** adv.

'judo n Japanese art of wrestling and self-defence.

jug n deep vessel for liquids, with a rounded handle and lip(2).

'juggle v 1 perform (*with* objects, eg by throwing many balls up into the air and catching them). 2 play tricks with (objects, facts, figures, etc) in order to deceive. **—r** n.

juice n liquid part of fruits, vegetables, and meat; fluid in animal organs: *digestive —s.* **'juicy** (-ier, -iest) adj.

'juke-box n coin-operated record-player.

Ju'ly n seventh month of the year.

'jumble v mix, be mixed, in a confused way. n confused mixture.

'jumble-sale, sale of second-hand clothes, books, etc.

jump v 1 move quickly, rise suddenly (up) lifting both feet off the ground (or from a height): — *down from a wall.* 2 make a sudden movement (eg from fear). 3 — *at (an offer, etc),* accept eagerly. 4 (cause to) pass over by **—ing.** n 1 act of **—ing.** 2 sudden rise (eg in prices). **—y** adj nervous.

'jumper n outer (usu woollen) garment pulled on over the head and coming down to the hips.

'junction n (place of) joining, esp a railway station where lines join.

'juncture n at this —, with affairs as they now are.

June n sixth month of the year.

'jungle n (land covered with) thickly growing trees and undergrowth (esp in the tropics).

'junior n & adj (person) younger, lower in rank, than another: *John Green Junior (Jun, Jr).*

junk[1] n old things of little or no value.

junk[2] n Chinese flat-bottomed sailing vessel.

a junk

,juris'diction n administration of justice; (extent of) legal authority.

'jury n body of (usu twelve) persons who swear to give a true decision (*a verdict*) on a case in a law court. **'juror, —man** n member of a —.

just[1] adv 1 exactly. 2 almost not: *We — caught the train.* 3 — *now,* now; a moment ago.

just[2] adj 1 fair; in accordance with what is right. 2 well deserved. **'—ly** adv. **'—ice** n 1 the quality of being right and fair; *treated with —ice.* do **—ice to,** show that one has a — opinion of or knows the value of. 2 the law and its administration: *brought to —ice; a court of —ice.* 3 judge of the Supreme Court. 4 J**—ice of the Peace,** magistrate.

justify *v* 1 show that (sb, sth) is right and reasonable. 2 be a good reason for (doing sth). '**justifiable** *adj* that can be justified. ,**justifi'cation** *n*.

jut *v* (-tt-) **— out,** stand out from (a mass of sth, an edge, shore, etc).

jute *n* fibre from the outer skin of certain plants, used for making canvas, rope, etc.

juvenile *n* young person. *adj* of, characteristic of, suitable for,**—s.**

K

kanga'roo *n* Australian animal that jumps along. ⇨ p 317.

keel *n* wood or steel structure forming the base of a ship's framework. **on an even —,** (fig) steady.

keen *adj* (-er, -est) 1 (of points and edges) sharp. 2 (of interest, the feelings) strong; deep. 3 (of the mind, the senses) active; sensitive; sharp. 4 (of persons, their characters, etc) eager. '**— on,** interested in, fond of. '**—ly** *adv*. '**—ness** *n*.

keep *v* (*pt & pp* kept) 1 have and not give back or away; not lose. **— hold of,** not let go. **— in mind,** remember. **— one's temper,** remain calm. 2 celebrate (the Sabbath, Christmas, etc); observe (the law); be faithful to (a promise, treaty, etc). 3 provide what is needed for; support: *earn enough to — one's family.* 4 own and look after, esp for profit: *to — a shop; to — poultry and pigs.* 5 **— house,** maintain a household in good order. (cf housekeeper.) 6 make entries in or records of: *to — a diary; to — accounts.* (cf bookkeeping.) 7 conceal; not let others know: *to — a secret.* 8 (cause to) continue in a certain place, direction, relation, condition, etc: *to — quiet; to — the children quiet; to — straight on; kept indoors by illness.* 9 (of food) not go bad. 10 do (sth) repeatedly or fre-

quently: *My shoe-lace —s coming undone.* 11 **— sb or sth from (doing sth),** prevent or hold back: *What kept you from joining me?* 12 (with adv & prep) **— at,** (cause to) work persistently at. **— away,** avoid going, prevent (sb) from going, to or near. **— down,** hold under; make (expenses, etc) low. **— from,** abstain from or prevent or restrain (sb or sth) from (doing sth). **— in,** restrain (one's feelings, etc); see that (a fire) continues burning; detain (a pupil) at school after school hours as a punishment. **— off,** (cause to) stay at a distance; say nothing about (a question, etc). **— on,** continue (to have, do, use, wear, etc): *to — one's coat on; to — on although one is tired; He kept on asking silly questions,* did so repeatedly. **— under,** hold down, control. **— up,** prevent from sinking; observe (old customs); cause (sb) to wait up at night. **— up with,** go on at the same rate as. 13 **— sth to oneself,** refuse to share it. **— early (good) or late (bad) hours,** finish work, go to bed, early (late). **— watch,** be on watch (for sth). **— one's feet (balance),** not fall. *n* 1 (food needed for) support: *to earn one's —.* 2 **for —s,** (colloq) permanently. '**—er** *n* as in: *shopkeeper,* etc, esp *gamekeeper.* ⇨ game[1](4). '**—ing** *n* 1 care: *in safe —ing.* 2 **in (out of) —ing with,** in (not in) harmony or agreement with. '**—sake** *n* sth kept in memory of the giver.

keg *n* small cask or barrel.

'**kennel** *n* hut for a dog.

kept ⇨ keep.

kerb *n* stone edging of a raised path. '**kerb-stone** *n* stone in such an edging.

'**kernel** *n* inner part (seed) of a nut or fruit-stone; (fig) centre of a subject, problem, etc.

'**kerosene** *n* paraffin.

'**kettle** *n* metal vessel with a lid, spout, and handle, for boiling water in.

key *n* 1 metal instrument for moving the bolt of a lock; instrument for winding a clock or watch. 2 (fig) sth that provides an answer to a problem. 3 place which, from its position, gives control of a route or area. 4 **key industries,** those essential to the carrying on of others. **5** operating part of a piano, typewriter, etc, pressed down by the finger; **'keyboard,** row of keys(5). **6** (music) scale of notes definitely related to each other and based on a particular note, called the **'keynote. 'keystone** n middle stone of an arch; (fig) controlling principle.

'khaki n & adj (cloth, military uniform, of a) dull, yellowish-brown.

kick v strike with the foot; make movements as if doing this. **— off,** (football) start. **— up a row,** (colloq) make a disturbance or protest. n act of —ing; blow given by —ing.

kid n **1** young goat. **2** leather made from its skin: *kid gloves.* **3** (colloq) child.

'kidnap v (-pp-) steal (a child); carry (sb) away by force and unlawfully.

'kidney n one of a pair of organs in the abdomen separating waste liquid from the blood. ⇨ p 30. — of sheep, ox, etc, as food.

kill v cause the death of; put to death; destroy. **— time,** do sth to occupy oneself whilst waiting.

kiln n large furnace or oven for burning (*lime-kiln*), baking (*brick-kiln*) or drying (*hop-kiln*).

'kilo- prefix 1,000, esp in —*gram,* —*metre,* —*watt.*

kilt n short skirt worn by men in the Scottish Highlands.

kin n family; relations. **next of kin,** nearest relation(s).

kind[1] n **1** sort, natural group, of animals: *man—.* **2** sort, class, or variety: *What — do you want? Something (nothing) of the —,* something like (not at all like) the thing mentioned. **3 pay in —,** pay in goods instead of in money.

kind[2] adj (-er, -est) having or showing thought, sympathy or love for others. **'—ly** adv *Will you —ly . . .?* will you please . . .? adj (-lier, -liest) sympathetic; behaving with, showing, —ness. **'—ness** n — behaviour; — act.

'kindle v **1** (cause to) catch fire or burst into flame. **2** (fig) rouse, be roused, to a state of strong feeling or interest.

'kindly ⇨ kind[2].

'kindred n **1** members of a family. **2** all one's relations. adj related; similar.

king n male sovereign (usu hereditary) ruler of an independent state. **'—dom** n **1** country ruled by a — or queen. **2** any one of the three divisions of the natural world; *the animal, vegetable, and mineral* —*doms.* **'—ly** adj royal; like, suitable for, a —.

kink n **1** irregular or back twist in wire, thread, cord, etc. **2** mental twist. v form a — (in).

'kinsfolk n pl relations. **'kinship** n relationship.

ki'osk n public telephone call-box; small covered stall in a street, railway station, etc, for the sale of newspapers, tobacco, sweets, etc.

a kite

a kiosk

'kipper n salted and smoked herring.

kiss v & n touch with the lips to show affection.

kit n **1** all the equipment (esp clothing) of a soldier, sailor, or traveller. **2** equipment needed by a workman for his trade. **3** equipment for a special activity.

'kitchen n room used for cooking.

kite n **1** bird of prey of the hawk family. **2** framework of wood, etc covered with paper or cloth, made to fly at the end of a long string or wire.

kith n **— and kin,** friends and relations.

'kitten n young cat.

knack n cleverness in doing sth well, gained through experience.

'knapsack n bag carried on the back by soldiers, travellers, etc.

knave n dishonest man.

knead v make (flour and water, wet clay, etc) into a firm paste by working with the hands; make (bread, pots) in this way.

knee n joint(2) between the upper and lower leg. ⇨ p 29. **'—cap** n flat bone forming front part of the —. ⇨ p 30.

kneel v (pt & pp knelt) go down on one's knee(s); rest on one's knee(s).

knell n slow sounding of a bell, esp for a death.

knew ⇨ know.

'knickerbockers n pl loose, wide breeches gathered in below the knees. **'knickers** n pl woman's or girl's lower undergarment.

'knick-knack n small unimportant ornament, piece of furniture, etc.

knife n (pl 'knives) blade(1) with a handle used to cut or as a weapon.

knight n 1 (in the Middle Ages) man raised to honourable military rank. 2 man whom the Sovereign has honoured with the title *Sir* before his usual names. v make a —(2).

knit v (-tt-) 1 make (an article of clothing, etc) by looping yarn on long needles(2). 2 unite firmly or closely. 3 — the brows, frown.

knob n 1 rounded end of a handle on a door or drawer, of a walking-stick, etc. 2 rounded swelling or rounded part standing out from a surface. 3 small lump (eg of coal). **'—bly** adj (-ier, -iest) covered with —s(3).

knock v 1 hit; strike; get (down, in, etc) by hitting: — the bottom of a box out; — at a door. 2 — off work, (colloq) stop working. — sb up, wake him (by —ing at his door). — sb out, (boxing) send him to the floor with a blow so that he cannot go on fighting. n (short, sharp sound of a) blow. **'—er** n (esp) device for —ing at a door. **'knock-out** n blow that —s sb out.

knoll n small hill.

knot n 1 string, rope, etc, twisted together (and tied). 2 piece of ribbon twisted and tied as an ornament. 3 difficulty; hard problem. **tie oneself (up) in(to)** —s, get badly confused about sth. 4 hard lump in wood where a branch grew out from a bough or trunk. 5 group (of persons). 6 measure of speed for ships; nautical mile (= 6,080 feet). v (-tt-) make —(s) in; tie with —s; form —s. **'—ty** adj (-ier, -iest) (esp) puzzling.

know v (pt knew, pp known) have news or information about; have in one's mind through experience or learning; be acquainted with. — what's what, — one's business, have good judgement, practical experience. **'—ing** adj having, showing that one has, intelligence, sharp wits, etc. **'—ingly** adv consciously; in a —ing manner. **'—ledge** n 1 —ing; understanding. 2 all that is —n; what a person —s.

'knuckle n bone at a finger-joint. v — under, submit; yield.

Ko'ran n holy-book of the Muslim religion (cf Bible).

kraal n (S Africa) fenced-in village of huts; enclosure for animals.

L

'label v & n (-ll-) (put on or tie on a) piece of paper, metal, etc, for describing what sth is, where it is to go, its price, etc.

la'boratory n place for scientific experiments, esp in chemistry.

'labour n 1 work. 2 a piece of work. 3 L—, one of two main British political parties, representing Socialist opinion. L—ite member of the L— party. v 1 work hard, esp with the hands. 2 try hard (for sth, to do sth). 3 move, act, be troubled, suffer (under difficulty or weakness). **—er** n man who does heavy work with his hands. **la'borious** adj hard-working; needing, showing signs of, great effort.

'labyrinth n network of winding paths, roads, etc, through which it is difficult to find one's way without help.

lace n 1 delicate ornamental work made of threads. 2 string or cord for fastening a shoe, etc. v fasten or tighten with —s(2).

lack v 1 be without; have less than enough of. 2 be —ing, be wanting. n need; shortage. **for — of**, because of the absence of.

'lacquer n sorts of varnish giving a hard, bright coating. v put — on.

lad, 'laddie n boy; young man.

'ladder n 1 two poles (ropes) with many short planks (ropes) joining them, used to climb up and down. **2** fault in a stocking, caused by a broken thread.

'**laden** adj. — **with**, weighted or burdened with.

'**lading** n. **bill of —**, list of cargo.

'**ladle** n large deep spoon for serving liquid foods, e g soup.

'**lady** n **1** woman of good manners; polite term for any woman. **2** L—, title used of and to the wives and daughters of some nobles. **3 Our** L—, Mother of Jesus. —**like** adj behaving as a —. **L—ship** n used (Your, Her, L—ship) instead of a titled woman's name.

lag v (-gg-) move too slowly; fall (behind) others). '**laggard** n one who —s.

la'**goon** n salt-water lake separated from the sea by sand bank(s).

laid ⇨ lay.

lain ⇨ lie².

lair n wild animal's den.

lake n large area of water surrounded by land.

lamb n young sheep. ⇨ p 84; its flesh as food.

lame adj (-r, -st) not able to walk easily because of an injury or defect. v make —. !—**ly** adv. '—**ness** n.

la'**ment** v feel or express great sorrow or regret. n (also ,lamen-'**tation**) expression of grief.

lamp n container for oil and wick used to provide light; other device for giving light: gas and electric —s. '—**post** n post for a street —.

lance¹ n long spear used by soldiers on horseback.

lance² v cut into, cut open, with a surgeon's knife.

land n **1** solid part of the earth's surface. **2** ground used for farming. **3** country: my native —. v go, come, put, on — (from a ship, aircraft, etc). '—**ed** adj owning —. '—**ing** n **1** platform at the top of each flight of stairs. **2** act of reaching —. **3** (also '—**ing stage**) platform on which passengers — from a ship. '—,**lady** n woman keeping an inn or a boarding-house, or letting rooms to tenants. '—**lord** n person from whom another rents land or building(s); person keeping an inn, a hotel, a boarding-house. '—**mark** n **1** sth marking the boundary of a piece of —. **2** object, etc, easily seen from a distance and helpful to travellers.

'—**scape** n (picture of) inland scenery. '—**slide** n sliding down of a mass of earth, rock, etc, from the side of a cliff or a mountain.

lane n narrow country road; way made or left between rows of persons; width of one line of traffic along a road: the inside (outside) —.

'**language** n **1** words and their use. **2** form of — used by a nation or race. **3** manner of using words; words; phrases, etc, used by a class; legal —. **4** bad (**strong**) —, — full of vulgar words.

'**languid** adj lacking in energy; slow-moving. '**languish** v become —; lose health and strength; be unhappy because of a desire (for sth). '**languor** n weakness; stillness.

lank adj (of hair) long and lying limp or flat. '—**y** adj (-ier, -iest) (of a person) tall and lean.

'**lantern** n case (usu metal and glass) protecting a light from wind, etc.

lap¹ n legs above the knees when sb is sitting.

lap² v (-pp-) **1** fold (cloth, etc) (round or in). **2** arrange (cloth, etc) so that the edge is folded back or over. n one run round a race-track: on the last lap.

lap³ v (-pp-) **1** drink by taking up (water, etc) with the tongue as a cat does. **2** (of waves, etc) move (against) sth) with a lapping sound.

lapse n **1** slight error in speech or behaviour. **2** slip of the memory. **3** wandering from what is right. **4** (of time) passing away; interval. v fail to keep up one's position; turn aside from good ways into bad ways.

'**larceny** n stealing; theft.

lard n pork fat for use in cooking.

'**larder** n room or cupboard where food is stored.

large adj (-r, -st) of great size; able to contain much. **at —**, free, not in prison. **the world** (**people**) **at —**, people in general. '—**ly** adv to a great extent.

lark n small song-bird.

'**larva** n (pl '**larvae**) insect in the first stage of its life history after coming out of the egg.

lash v **1** beat and strike violently. **2** make violent movements; move up and down. **3** scold angrily; excite to anger. **4** fasten tightly with rope, etc. *n* **1** ('eye-lash), short hair growing on the upper and lower eyelid. **2** part of a whip with which strokes are given; stroke given with a whip.

lass, 'lassie *n* girl.

las'so *n* long rope looped with a slip-knot, used for catching horses and cattle, esp in America.

last[1] *n* that which comes at the end: at —, in the end, after a long delay; the only remaining (one). *adj* coming after all the others in order or time; coming immediately before the present: — *week*. *adv* after all others.

last[2] *v* go on; be enough (for). '—ing *adj* continuing (for a long time).

latch *n* **1** simple fastening for a door or window. **2** small spring lock. *v* fasten with a —.

late *adj* (-r, -st) **1** after the agreed or usual time; far on in the day, month, year, etc. **2** no longer living. **3** who or which was until recently. **4** of —, recently. of — years, in the last few years. *adv* after the usual, expected or proper time. —r on, afterwards. sooner or —r, at some future time. '—ly *adv* a short time ago; recently. '—st *adj* newest (fashions, etc). at (the) —st, before or not —r than the time mentioned.

'latent *adj* present but not active and not seen: — *energy*.

lathe *n* machine for holding and turning wood and metal while being shaped.

'lather *n* soft mass of white froth from soap and water. *v* form —; put — on.

'Latin *n* language of ancient Rome. *adj* of the — language: of peoples speaking languages based on —.

'latitude *n* **1** distance north or south of the equator measured in degrees. **2** (degree of) freedom in action or opinion.

la'trine *n* (in camps, etc) pit or trench to receive waste matter from the human body.

'latter *adj* **1** recent; belonging to the end of a period. **2** the —, the second of two already named.

'lattice *n* framework of crossed strips of wood, metal, etc: *a — window*.

laugh *v & n* (make) vocal sounds indicating amusement or pleasure. **'laughing-stock** *n* person or thing causing general ridicule. '—able *adj* causing people to —. '—ter *n* —ing.

launch[1] *v* **1** set (esp a newly built ship) afloat. **2** send (a blow, etc) (at or against). **3** get (an attack, a scheme) started. **4** — out (into), make a start on (sth new). *n* —ing (of a ship).

launch[2] *n* passenger-carrying boat (for use on rivers, in harbours, etc) driven by steam, petrol, or electricity.

'launder *v* wash (and iron) clothes. **'laundry** *n* clothes-washing place or business; clothes (to be) —ed.

'laurel *n* evergreen shrub; (*pl*) victory; honour (in war, art, etc).

'lava *n* molten material flowing from a volcano; this material when it has cooled and hardened.

'lavatory *n* water-closet. ⇨ water[2].

'lavish *v* give abundantly. *adj* giving, given, generously and abundantly.

law *n* **1** rule made by authority for the proper government of a community or society or for correct conduct in life. **2** the law, system of laws. **3** such rules as a subject of study and as a profession. **4** correct statement of what always happens (in nature, science) in certain circumstances: *Newton's Law*. **'law-abiding** *adj* obeying the law. **'law court** *n* court of justice. **'lawful** *adj* allowed by, according to, the law. **'lawless** *adj* not obeying, contrary to, the law. **'lawsuit** *n* claim made in a law court. **'lawyer** *n* person who has studied law and advises others in matters of law.

lawn *n* area of grass kept closely cut and smooth. **'lawn-,mower** *n* machine for cutting grass on —s.

a lawn-mower

playing leap-frog

lax *adj* inattentive; not strict or severe. **'laxity** *n*.

lay¹ *v* (*pt & pp* laid) **1** put on to a surface; put down in a certain position or place. **2** (of birds, insects, and reptiles) produce (eggs). **3** (with various objects) put down; cause to be down: *lay the dust.* **lay the table (the supper)**, place what is needed on the table. **4** (phrases) **lay sth aside**, put away, save. **lay sth by**, save for future use. **lay down one's life**, sacrifice it. *(can't)* **lay one's hands on sth**, (can't) find where it is. **lay in**, provide a store of. **lay on**, supply (water, gas, etc) through pipes into a building. **lay out**, prepare, make a plan for. **be laid up**, be forced by illness, etc, to stay in bed.

lay² ⇨ **lie²**.

lay³ *adj* **1** of, for, done by, persons who are not priests. **2** of, for, done by, non-professional persons (esp of law and medicine). **'layman** *n* lay person.

¹layer *n* thickness of material (esp one of several) laid or lying or spread over a surface.

'layout *n* arrangement; general design.

'lazy *adj* (-ier, -iest) unwilling to work; doing little work. **laze** *v* be —; do nothing. **'lazily** *adv*. **'laziness** *n*.

lead¹ *n* **1** heavy soft grey metal. **2** lump of this, tied to a line, for measuring the depth of the sea. **3** graphite, as used in — pencils. **'—en** *adj* heavy as —; lead-coloured.

lead² *v* (*pt & pp* led) **1** be or go in front; take, guide, towards some place; be, do sth, first. **2** control, manage, direct, by persuasion or example. **3** (cause to) pass, go through. **4 — to**, (of a road, etc) go to; (of acts, etc) have as a result. *n* **1** action of —ing or guiding; example. **2** —ing position; distance by which one —s: *a — of five yards.* **3** (in card games) right to start the play. **'—er** *n* person who —s. **'—ership** *n*. **'—ing** *adj* chief; most important.

leaf *n* (*pl* leaves) **1** one of the flat (usu green) parts growing from the stem of a plant or branch of a tree. **2** sheet of paper forming two pages of a book. **turn over a new —**, (fig) make a new and better start. **'—let** *n* **1** young —. **2** printed sheet (often folded) with announcements, etc. **'—y** *adj* (-ier, iest) of or like, shaded by, leaves.

league¹ *n* **1** agreement between persons, groups, or nations for their common welfare. **2** group of sports-clubs playing matches among themselves. *v* form into, become, a —.

league² *n* (old) measure of distance (about 3 miles or 4·8 kilometres).

leak *n* hole, crack, etc, through which liquid, gas, etc, may wrongly get in or out. *v* **1** (allow liquid, etc, to) pass in or out through a —. **2** (fig, of news, a secret) — **out**, become known. **'—age** *n* —ing; sth that —s out or in. **'—y** *adj* (-ier, -iest) having a —.

lean¹ *adj* (-er, -est) having less than the usual amount of fat. *n*. meat without fat.

lean² *v* (*pt & pp* leaned or leant) **1** be or put in a sloping position, esp for support. **2** support. **3** have a tendency (*towards*). **4 — upon**, (fig) depend upon (*for* sth). **'—ing** *n* tendency (of mind, *towards* sth). **'lean-to** *n* building whose roof is supported by the wall of another building.

leap *v & n* (*pt & pp* leapt or leaped) jump. **'leap-frog** *n* game. ⇨ p 155. **'leap-year** *n*. ⇨ **year**.

learn *v* (*pt & pp* learnt or learned) **1** gain knowledge of or skill in by study, practice, or being taught. **2** be told or informed. **'—ed** *adj* having or showing much knowledge: *the —ed professions* (eg the law). **'—ing** *n* knowledge from careful study.

lease *n* legal agreement allowing the use of land or a building. *v* give, take, the right to use (land, etc) by —.

least *adj & n* smallest (quantity, degree, etc). **at —**, at any rate; even if more is impossible. *adv* in the — degree.

'leather *n* material (for shoes, etc) made from animal skins.

leave¹ *v* (*pt & pp* left) **1** go away from. **2** neglect or forget to take, bring, or do, sth. **3 — go (of)**, stop holding. **— off**, stop, give up. **— out**, omit, not put in. **4** give (money, etc) by will²(6) to sb at one's death. **5** be left, remain.

leave² n **1** permission (to do sth, esp to be absent from duty in the armed forces or government service): go home on —; period of such absence. **2 by your —**, with your permission. **3 take — of sb**, go away, say good-bye.

'leaven n substance (eg yeast) used to make bread rise before baking.

leaves ⇨ leaf.

'lecture v & n **1** (give a) talk (to an audience or class) for the purpose of teaching. **2** (give a) scolding (to).

led ⇨ lead.

ledge n narrow shelf coming out from a wall, cliff, etc.

'ledger n book for business accounts.

lee n (place giving) protection against wind; side away from the wind. **'leeway** n drift of a ship caused by the wind; make up leeway, (fig) make up for lost time, get back into position.

leek n onion-like vegetable. ⇨ p 306.

leer n unpleasant look suggesting evil desire or ill will. v — **at**, look at in this way.

left¹ ⇨ leave.

left² adj **1** (opposite of right) (of, in, on the) side of the body that is to the west when one faces north. **2** (political) radical; socialist. **'left-'handed** adj using the —(1) hand more easily or more often than the right. **the — n —(2)** group(s).

leg n one of the two limbs used for standing on, walking, etc. **pull sb's leg**, try, for a joke, to make him believe sth that is untrue; one of the supports of a table, chair, etc. **on its last legs**, almost useless or worn out.

'legacy n money, etc (to be) received by a person by the will²(6) of someone at his death.

'legal adj of, connected with, in accordance with, authorized or required by, the law. **'-ly** adv. **le'gality** n being —. **-ize** v make —.

'legate n Pope's ambassador.

le'gation n (house, offices, staff, etc, of a) diplomatic minister below the rank of ambassador, representing his government in another country.

'legend n old story handed down from the past, esp one of doubtful truth. **—ary** adj famous, known only, in —s.

'legible adj (of handwriting, print) that can be read easily. **'legibly** adv.

'legion n division of 3,000 to 6,000 men in the ancient Roman army.

'legislate v make laws. **,legis'lation** n making laws; the laws made. **'legislative** adj law-making. **'legislator** n member of a law-making body. **'legislature** n law-making body.

le'gitimate adj **1** lawful; regular. **2** reasonable; that can be justified. **3** born of married parents.

'leisure n time free from work. **—ly** adj & adv unhurried(ly).

'lemon n (tree with) pale yellow fruit having acid juice used for flavouring. ⇨ p 115. **,lemo'nade** n drink made from —s.

lend v (pt & pp lent) give (sb) the use of (sth) with the understanding that it will be returned. **— a hand**, help. **— oneself to**, give one's support to. **— itself to**, be useful or helpful for a purpose.

length n **1** measurement from end to end (space or time): at —, at last; for (after) a long time. **at full —**, with the body stretched out and flat. **go to all (any) —s**, do anything necessary to get what one wants. **2** piece of cloth, etc, long enough for a purpose. **'-en** v make or become longer. **'-ways**, **'-wise** adv in the direction of the —.

'lenient adj not strict. **—ly** adv. **'leniency** n.

lens n piece of glass, etc, with one or both sides curved, for use in eye-glasses, cameras, telescopes, etc.

lent ⇨ lend.

Lent n (in the Christian Church) period of forty days before Easter.

'lentil n kind of bean plant; its seed as food: — soup.

'leopard n large flesh-eating animal with yellowish coat and dark spots. ⇨ p 317.

'leper n person with leprosy. **'leprosy** n skin disease that gradually eats into the body.

less adj **1** not so much (in amount); small in quantity or degree of.

2 — than not so much as: *I have — money than you.* **n** smaller amount, quantity, shorter time, etc. **adv 1** to a smaller extent; not so much. **2** not so: *Tom is — clever than John.* **prep** minus: *£10 — £3 equals £7.* **'—en** *v* make or become —. **'—er** *adj* not so great as the other.

'lesson *n* **1** sth to be learnt or taught; period of time for learning or teaching. **2** sth experienced, esp sth serving as a warning or example.

lest *conj* for fear that; in order that . . . not; (after *be afraid, fear*) that.

let *v* (-tt-) **1** allow. **2 let sth down,** allow it to go down. **let sb down,** fail to help him in time of need. **let sb into a secret,** share it with him. **let off,** fire or discharge (a gun, etc); allow (sb) to go unpunished or with slight punishment. **3 let (sth or sb) alone,** leave undisturbed, not touch or trouble. **let alone,** (as *prep*) not to mention; still less; still more. **let go (of),** stop holding. **let oneself go,** stop controlling one's feelings. **4** allow the use of a building, etc, in return for rent: *to let a house; houses to let;* (often **let out**) hire. **5** (with first and third persons only) used to make suggestions and give orders: *Let's start at once!* **6** (with third person only) used to challenge: *Let him do his worst!*

'lethal *adj* causing, designed to cause, death: *— weapons.*

'lethargy *n* state of being tired, uninterested; want of energy.

'letter *n* **1** written character or sign representing a sound. **capital —,** *A, B, C,* etc. **small —,** *a, b, c,* etc. **2** written message, etc, sent from one person to another. **3** (*pl*) literature; books; authorship: *a man of —s.*

'lettuce *n* garden plant with green leaves used in salads. ⇨ p 306.

'level *n* **1** surface parallel with the horizon. **sea —,** from which the height of land is measured. **on a — with,** at the same height as. **2** instrument for testing whether a surface is —: *a spirit-level.* **adj 1** having a horizontal surface. **— crossing,** place where a railway and a road cross each other on the same level. **2 do one's — best,**

do all that one can do. **,level-'headed,** steady and well balanced, with good judgement. **3** in line (*with*); on an equality (*with*): *a — race; drawing — with the other runners.* *v* (-ll-) **1** make —; make (social classes) equal. **2** — **up (down),** raise (lower) to a certain —. **3** aim (a gun, an accusation) (*at, against*).

'lever *n* bar or other tool turned on a pivot, to lift sth or force sth open. *v* move (sth *up, into position,* etc) with a —.

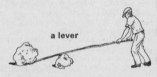

a lever

'levity *n* lack of seriousness.

'levy *v* **1** collect (taxes, etc) by authority or force; raise (an army) by compulsion. **2** — war (**upon, against**), declare and make war on. *n* act of —ing; the amount of money, number of men, so obtained.

'liable *adj* **1** — for, responsible according to law: *— for his wife's debts.* **2** be — to, have a tendency to (make mistakes, etc); be likely to (suffer, experience sth, undesirable); be subject to (tax, punishment, etc). **,lia'bility** *n* **1** being —. **2** (*pl*) debts or other personal responsibilities.

li'aison *n* — officer, one who keeps two military, etc, units (esp of different nationalities) in touch with each other.

'liar *n* person who tells lies.

'libel *n* **1** (publishing of) written or printed statement about sb that damages his reputation. **2** (colloq) anything that brings discredit (*on*). *v* (-ll-) publish a — against; give a poor idea of (sb). **—lous** *adj.*

'liberal *adj* **1** giving or given freely; generous. **2** open-minded; having or showing a broad mind. **3** L—, (member of a) British political party. *n* person favouring equality of opportunity for all and opposing too much government control. **libe'rality** *n* generosity.

'liberate *v* set free. **,libe'ration** *n.*

liberty n **1** state of being free. **2** right or power to decide for oneself what to do, how to live, etc.

library n (building, room, for a) collection of books. **li'brarian** n person in charge of a —.

lice ⇨ louse.

licence n **1** (written or printed statement giving) permission from someone in authority for sb to do sth. **2** wrong use of freedom; disregard of laws, customs, etc.

license v give a licence to: *licensed to sell tobacco.*

lichee n (also **'litchi**) (Chinese tree with) white fleshy fruit in a thin brown shell. ⇨ p 115.

lick v **1** pass the tongue over. **2** (colloq) beat(2). n act of —ing with the tongue.

lid n movable top forming part of a container: *the teapot lid; the lid of a box.* ⇨ eye.

lie¹ v (pp & pt lied) & n (make a) statement that one knows to be untrue.

lie² v (pt lay, pp lain) **1** be, put oneself, flat on a horizontal surface. **2** be resting flat on sth. **3** be kept, remain, in a certain position or state: *ships lying at anchor; towns lying in ruins.* **4** be; exist: *the trouble lies in the engine.* **5** lie in, stay in bed after one's usual time. n the way sth lies: *the lie of the land,* (fig) state of affairs.

lieu n in — of, instead of.

lieu'tenant n army officer below a captain; junior officer in the navy. **2** (in compound words) officer with highest rank under; *lieu,tenant-'colonel.*

life n (pl lives) **1** condition that distinguishes animals and plants from earth, rocks, etc. **2** all living things. **3** state of existence as a human being. **4** period between birth and death; period since one's birth. **5** way of living. **6** written account of sb's —, **7** activity, interest: *put more — into your work.* **'—belt** n inflated ring(2) worn

round the chest to save one from drowning. **'—boat** n one for saving lives at sea or along the coast. **'life-,jacket** n inflated jacket to save one from drowning. **'—less** adj dead. **'—'long** adj lasting throughout —.

lift v **1** raise to a higher level or position. **2** (of clouds, etc) rise. **3** dig up (root-crops). n **1** act of —ing: *give sb a —,* take him (into a car, etc) to help him on a journey. **2** apparatus for taking persons or goods up or down to another floor.

light¹ n **1** (opposite of *darkness*) that which enables things to be seen. **come to —, be brought to —,** become known as the result of inquiry, etc. **2 strike a —,** strike a match. **3** new knowledge helping to explain sth adj (-er, -est) (opposite of *dark*) exposed to —; pale in colour. v (pt & pp lit or **'lighted**) **1** cause to burn or shine. **2** (often + up) make, become, bright. **3** give — to. **'—en** v **1** make or become —(er). **2** send out —ning: *it thundered and —ened.* **'—house** n tower, building (on cliff, rocks, etc) with strong — to guide and warn ships. **'—ning** n flash of bright — produced by natural electricity in the sky, with thunder. **'—ning-rod,** **'—ning-con,ductor** n metal rod fixed on top of high buildings, etc, and connected with earth, to prevent damage by —ning. **'—ship** n moored ship with the same purpose as a —house.

light² adj (-er, -est) **1** of little weight, esp for its size. **2** not made to support anything heavy. **3** gentle; delicate. **4** (of books, plays, etc) for entertainment; (of food) easily digested; (of sleepers) easily waked; (of beer, wines) not strong. adv travel —, with little luggage. **'—en** v make, become, —(er). **'light-'headed** adj dizzy. **'light-'hearted** adj gay; free from care. **'—ly** adv. **'—ness** n.

'lighter n boat for carrying goods to and from ships in a harbour.

like¹ adj similar (to); resembling. **nothing — as** (good, etc), not nearly so (good, etc). *It looks — rain,* rain seems probable. *I don't feel — working,* I have no

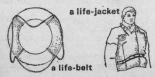

a life-jacket

a life-belt

wish to work. '**—ly** adj **1** probable. **2** that seems right or reasonable: a long – excuse. '**—lihood** n degree to which sth is —ly. '**—n** v point out the — ness of one thing (to another). '**—ness** n quality of being —. '**—wise** adv in the same way. conj also.

like² v **1** be fond of; find agreeable or satisfactory; have a taste (4) for. **2** (in negative sentences with infin) be unwilling: I don't – to get up. **3** (with would, should) expressing a wish. n (pl only) things one —s. **likable** adj pleasing; of a kind that is —d. '**liking** n have a liking for, be fond of. **to one's liking**, as one —s (it); satisfactory.

'**lily** n flowering bulb plant.

limb n leg, arm or wing; bough of a tree.

lime¹ n white substance obtained by burning —stone, used in making cement and mortar. '**—stone** n kinds of stone containing much —.

lime² n round, juicy fruit like, but more acid than, a lemon.

'**limit** n **1** line or point that may not or cannot be passed. **2** greatest or smallest amount, degree, etc, of what is possible, to be allowed, etc. v put a – or – s to; be the – of. **—ed** adj (of quantity) small; (of views, etc) restricted; narrow. **—less** adj without —s. **,limi'tation** n —ing; condition that —s; disability.

limp¹ adj not stiff or firm.

limp² v walk lamely or unevenly as when one leg or foot is hurt or stiff. n a lame walk.

line¹ n **1** mark made by drawing the point (of a pen, etc) along a surface. **2** length of thread, string, wire, etc, for various purposes: fishing (telephone) —s. **3** row of persons or things: boys standing in a —. **4** organized system of transport: an air —. **5** row of written or printed words. **read between the —s**, find more meaning than the words express. **6** short written message. **7** series of connected military defence posts: the front —; behind the —s. **8** direction; way of dealing with a situation: on the right —s. **9** the equator. **10** kind of business or commercial activity: in the drapery —. **11** class of commercial goods. **12** number of

people who succeed each other in time (esp with the same ancestry): a long – of kings. v mark (sth) with —s; form a – or —s. '**linear** adj —ar measure, measure of length. '**—r** n ship, aircraft, of a —(4). '**—sman** n (sport) man who helps the referee by deciding whether the ball has crossed the —.

line² v add a layer of (usu different) material to the inside of (bags, boxes, articles of clothing): coats —d with silk. '**lining** n this layer.

'**linen** n & adj (cloth) made of flax; articles made of —, eg shirts, sheets.

'**linger** v be slow in going away or dying; stay long(er than others).

'**linguist** n person skilled in foreign languages.

'**liniment** n liquid for rubbing on stiff or aching parts of the body.

'**lining** n ⇨ line².

link n **1** one ring or loop of a chain. **2** person or thing that connects two others. v join, be joined.

li'noleum n strong floor-covering of canvas treated with oil.

lint n soft linen or cotton material used for dressing wounds.

'**lintel** n piece of wood or stone forming the top of a door or window-frame.

'**lion** n large, pale-brown, meat-eating cat (2). ⇨ p 317. **the —'s share**, the larger part. '**—ess** n female —.

lip n **1** one of the two edges of the opening of the mouth. **2** edge of a cup, etc; part like a lip. '**lip-,service** n approval, respect, etc given in words but not sincere. '**lipstick** n (stick of) cosmetic material for colouring the lips.

'**liquid** n substance, like water or oil, that flows freely and is neither a solid nor a gas. adj **1** in the form of a —: – food. **2** clear; bright. '**liquefy** v make or become —.

'**liquidate** v **1** pay (a debt). **2** bring (eg an unsuccessful business company) to an end by dividing up it property to pay debts. **,liqui'dation** n.

'**liquor** n **1** alcoholic drink. **2** liquid produced by boiling or fermenting a food substance, eg as used in cooking.

lisp v fail to use the sounds s and z correctly (eg by saying thickth *teen* for *sixteen*). *n* a —ing way of speaking.

list[1] *n* number of names (of persons, things, etc) written or printed. *v* make a — of; put on a —.

list[2] *v* (esp of a ship) lean over to one side. *n* —ing of a ship.

'listen *v* pay attention and hear; try to hear. — in, listen to a radio programme, a conversation, etc. —er *n*.

'listless *adj* too tired to do anything or to show interest.

lit ⇨ light.

'litany *n* form of prayer in the Church of England.

'litchi ⇨ lichee.

'literacy *n* being literate.

'literal *adj* corresponding exactly to the original: *a — translation*. —ly *adv*.

'literary *adj* of literature or authors.

'literate *n & adj* (person) able to read and write.

'literature *n* 1 (the writing or study of) books, etc, valued as works of art. 2 all the writings of a country or a period; the books dealing with a special subject.

lithe *adj* (of a person, body) bending, twisting, turning easily.

'litigate *v* contest (sth) at a lawcourt. liti'gation *n*.

'litre *n* unit of measure (about 1¾ pints) in the metric system.

'litter *n* 1 various articles, scraps of paper, etc, left lying about untidily. 2 straw, etc, used as bedding for animals. 3 newly born young ones of an animal: *her — of puppies*. *v* 1 put, leave, — about. 2 put — down (for animals).

'little *adj* 1 small; young; not tall; unimportant. 2 of the smaller or smallest size. 3 (*less*, *least*) not much. a —, a small quantity (of). *n* after (for) a —, after (for) a short time. *adv* not much; hardly at all. a —, rather: *a — better*. — by —, gradually.

live *v* have existence as an animal or plant, breathe; be alive; make one's home (in, at, etc). — and let —, be tolerant. — on, have as food or diet; get what one needs for support from. *adj* (used only *before* nouns) having life; full of energy, activity, interest; — wires, charged with electric current. '—lihood *n* means of living. '—ly *adj* full of

life and gaiety; quick-moving. '—liness *n*. '—long *adj*. the —long day, the whole length of the day. '—n *v* —n up, become or make —ly. '—stock *n* animals kept for use or profit. 'living *adj* 1 alive. 2 (of a picture, etc) true to life. *n* 1 = —lihood: *to earn one's living*. 2 manner of living. living-room, room for general use. living wage, one that is enough to — on.

'liver *n* reddish-brown organ in the body, purifying the blood. ⇨ p 30; animal's — eaten as a food.

'livery *n* special dress worn by men servants in a royal palace, etc.

'livid *adj* of the colour of lead: — *with cold* (*anger*), very cold (angry).

'lizard *n* small, long-tailed, four-legged reptile. ⇨ p 233.

load *n* 1 that which is (to be) carried or supported. 2 amount which a cart, etc, can take. *v* 1 put a —(1) on or in; put goods into or on. 2 put (a cartridge, shell, etc) into a(gun).

loaf[1] *n* (*pl* loaves) mass of bread cooked as a separate quantity.

loaf[2] *v* waste time; wait about idly.

loan *n* 1 sth lent, esp a sum of money. 2 lending or being lent: *books on —; have the — of*. *v* lend.

loath, loth *adj* unwilling.

loathe *v* dislike greatly; feel disgust for. 'loathing *n* disgust.

loaves ⇨ loaf.

'lobby *n* entrance hall.

lobe *n* lower rounded end of ear.

'lobster *n* shellfish; its flesh as food. ⇨ p 247.

'local *adj* 1 of a place or district: — *news*. 2 of a part, not of the whole. —ly *adv*. lo'cality *n* thing's position; place; district.

lo'cate *v* 1 discover, show, the position of. 2 be —d, be situated. 3 establish in a place. lo'cation *n* place; (in S Africa) suburb for Non-Europeans.

loch *n* (Scotland) 1 long narrow inlet of the sea. 2 lake.

lock *n* 1 mechanism, turned by a key, for fastening a door, gate, etc. 2 mechanism by which a gun is

a canal lock

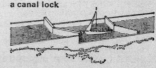

fired. **3** section of a canal, closed
at each end by gates, in which boats
are raised or lowered to another
water-level. *v* **1** fasten by using
a —(1). — **(sb) in (out)**, keep in
(out) by —ing the door, gate, etc.
— **sth up**, put in a —ed place; — **the
doors**, etc, of a building. **2** become,
cause to be, fixed and unable to move:
jaws tightly —ed. '—**er** *n* small cupboard with a —. '**lockout** *n* refusal of employers to allow workers
to enter their place of work until they
accept certain conditions. '—**smith**
n maker and repairer of —s(1).

'**locket** *n* small case for a portrait,
lock of hair, etc, worn hung from
the neck.

ˌloco'**motion** *n* (power of) going
from one place to another. ˌloco-
'**motive** *n* railway engine.

'**locust** *n* winged insect that flies in
great numbers and destroys plant
life. ⇨ p 144.

lodge *n* house for a servant at the
entrance to a large private estate.
v **1** supply (sb) with room(s) for
living in. **2** live (*in, at, with*) as a
lodger. **3** (cause to) enter and
become fixed (*in*). **4** put (money,
etc) for safety (*with sb, in a place*).
'—**r** *n* person paying for room(s),
etc, in sb's house. '**lodging** *n*
(usu *pl*) place where one —s(2);
room(s) occupied by a —r.
'**lodging-house** *n.*

loft *n* room in the highest part of a
house under a roof gable.

'**lofty** *adj* (-ier, -iest) **1** very high.
2 (of thoughts, aims, feelings)
noble.

log[1] *n* rough length of a tree trunk
that has been cut down; short
piece of this for a fire.

log[2] *n* **1** apparatus for measuring
a ship's speed. **2** (also '**logbook**)
daily record of a ship's progress,
events of a voyage, etc.

'**logarithm** *n* one of a series of
numbers set out in tables to make
it possible to work out multiplication and division sums by adding
and subtracting.

'**loggerhead** *n* at —s (*with*), on bad
terms; in disagreement (with).

'**logic** *n* science, method, of reasoning. —**al** *adj* in accordance with
the laws of —; able to reason
rightly. —**ally** *adv.*

loin *n* **1** (*pl*) the lower part of the

back between the hip-bones and
the ribs. **2** joint of meat from this
part of an animal.

'**loiter** *v* go slowly with frequent
stops on the way; stand about;
pass time (*away*) thus. '—**er** *n.*

loll *v* **1** rest, sit, or stand (*about*) in
a lazy way. **2** (of the tongue) hang
(*out*).

'**lonely** *adj* (-ier, -iest) **1** without
companions: *feeling —*, sad because
alone. **2** (of places) without many
people; far from inhabited places
or towns. '**loneliness** *n.*

long[1] *adj* (-er, -est) measuring much
from end to end in space or time.
in the — run, in the end. **the —
and the short of it**, the general
effect or outcome. *adv* as (so) —
as, for as — a time as; on condition
that. '—**hand** *n* ordinary writing
(not shorthand). '—**ways**, '—**wise**
adv lengthways.

long[2] *v* desire earnestly. '—**ing** *n*
strong desire. '—**ingly** *adv.*

'**longitude** *n* distance east or
west, measured in degrees, from
a meridian, esp that of Greenwich,
in London.

look *v* **1** try to see; turn one's eyes
in the direction of. — **after** (sb or
sth), take care of; watch over. —
down on, scorn. — **for**, try to
find; be on the watch for. —
forward to, expect, wait for (with
pleasure). — **in on** (sb), visit while
passing. — **out**, be on one's guard;
watch (*for* sth). — **sth over**, inspect it. — **sth through**, glance at,
read, it. — **to**, attend to; take care
about. — **sth up**, find (eg a word
in a dictionary). — **up to**, respect.
— **upon**, regard (2)(as). **2** — **like**,
seem to be; seem likely: *it —s
like rain*, rain seems likely. *n* **1** act
of —ing. **2** appearance; what sth
suggests when seen. **3** (*pl*) person's
appearance: *good —s*, beauty.
'—**er-on** (*pl* —ers-on) spectator.
'—**ing-glass** *n* mirror. '**look-out**
n **1** place for keeping watch; person
keeping watch. **2** prospect; future.
3 *That's his (your) look-out*, (a risk,
etc) for him (you) and no one else
to watch for.

loom[1] *n* machine for weaving cloth.

loom[2] *v* appear indistinctly (esp a
storm, danger or other threatening
thing).

loop *n* (shape produced by a) curve

crossing itself; part of a length of string, wire, ribbon, etc, in such a shape. *v* 1 form or bend into a — or —s. 2 — sth up (back), keep or fasten up (back) in the form of, or with, a —. **'loop-hole** *n* narrow opening in a wall; (fig) way of escape from control, esp one provided by inexact wording of a rule.

loose *adj* (-r, -st) 1 free; not held together, tied up, fastened, packed, or contained in sth. 2 not tight or close-fitting. 3 moving more freely than is right: *a — screw.* 4 (of talk, behaviour, etc) not sufficiently controlled. 5 not tightly packed. *v* make —. **'—ly** *adv.* **'—n** *v* set or become —; make less tight.

loot *v* take (goods, esp private property) unlawfully and by force, eg in time of war. *n* property so taken.

lop *v* (-pp-) cut (branches, etc) off (a tree, etc); cut off or away.

,lop-'sided *adj* with one side lower than the other.

lord *n* 1 supreme ruler. 2 **L—**, God. **the L—s Day**, Sunday. 3 peer; nobleman. **the House of L—s**, the upper division of the British Parliament. 4 (person with) official position of authority. *v* — **it over** (*sb*), rule over like a —. **'L—ship** *n* **His** (*Your*) **Lordship**, used when speaking of (to) a —.

'lorry *n* strong wagon (usu long, low, open) usu driven by petrol. (USA = *truck.*)

lose *v* (*pt & pp* lost) 1 have taken away from one by accident, carelessness, death, etc. 2 — **one's way, — oneself, be lost,** not know where one is; be unable to find the right road, etc. 3 fail to be in time for; fail to see, hear, etc; fail to keep: — *one's train* (*the post, one's temper*). — **one's head,** become too excited. 4 (of a watch or clock) go too slowly. **loss** *n* losing; sth lost; waste. **at a loss,** uncertain what to do or say.

lost ⇨ lose.

lot¹ *n* (colloq) **the (whole) lot,** all; everything. **a lot (of), lots (of),** a great number or amount (of). **a lot,** (*better,* etc), much (better).

lot² *n* 1 draw (cast) lots, decide sth by lot, select, decide, by methods depending on chance. 2 that which comes to a person by luck or destiny. 3 object or number of objects offered together for sale at an auction.

loth *adj* unwilling.

'lotion *n* medicinal liquid for use on the skin.

'lottery *n* arrangement for giving money prizes to holders of numbered tickets previously bought by them and drawn by lot(2).

loud *adj* (-er, -est) easily heard; noisy. 2 (of a colour, behaviour, etc) of the kind that forces itself on the attention. **'loud-,speaker** *n* part of a radio receiver that changes electric waves into sound waves — enough to be heard without earphones. **'—ly** *adv.*

lounge *v* sit, stand about (leaning against sth) in a lazy way. *n* room (esp in a hotel) with comfortable chairs for lounging.

louse *n* (*pl* lice) sorts of small insect living on the bodies of human beings and animals under dirty conditions; similar insect living on plants.

love *n* warm and tender affection (as between husband and wife, children and parents, close friends, etc). **in — (with),** having — and desire (for). **make.— to,** show that one is in — with. *v* 1 have the feeling of — (towards sb). 2 find pleasure in. **'lovable** *adj* deserving —; having qualities that cause —. **'—less** *adj* not feeling, showing, having, —. **'—r** *n* 1 person who —s sth. 2 man who is in —. 3 (*pl*) man and woman in —. **'loving** *adj* feeling or showing —. **'—sick** *adj* unhappy through being in —; desiring to be —d.

'lovely *adj* (-ier, -iest) 1 beautiful; pleasant; attractive. 2 delightful. **loveliness** *n.*

low *adj* 1 (-er, -est) not reaching far up; not easily heard; deep(4). 2 not highly organized: *low forms of life.* 3 feeble: *feeling low.* **in low spirits,** sad. 4 vulgar; common: *low tastes.* 5 **lower animals,** all except man. *adv* in or to a low position. **be laid low,** be forced to stay in bed by illness, injury, etc. **be running low,** (of supplies, etc) be getting near the end. **'lowbrow** *n & adj* (person) having or showing little taste for intellectual things, esp art, music, and literature.

'lower v 1 let down (a flag, sail, etc). 2 make or become less high.

'lowly adj (-ier -iest) humble.

'loyal adj true, faithful (to). —ly adv. —ist n — subject, esp during a revolt. —ty n.

'lubricate v put oil or grease into (machine parts) to make (them) work smoothly.

'lucid adj clear, easy to understand.

luck n 1 good or bad fortune; sth that comes by chance. in (out of) —, having (not having) good —. 2 good fortune; the help of chance. '—y adj (-ier, -iest) having, bringing, resulting from, —. '—ily adv.

'ludicrous adj ridiculous.

'luggage n bags, trunks, etc, and their contents, taken on a journey.

'lukewarm adj neither hot nor cold; (fig) not eager either in supporting or in opposing.

lull v make or become less active. n interval of quiet or lessened activity. '—aby n song to make a baby fall asleep.

'lumber n 1 roughly prepared timber (eg boards). 2 useless or unwanted articles taking up space. v 1 — along (past), move in a heavy, noisy way. 2 — up, fill space.

'luminous adj bright.

lump n 1 mass without regular shape: —s of clay (coal). 2 swelling or bump. 3 a — sum, one payment covering a number of payments. v 1 form into —s. 2 group together in a mass. '—y adj (-ier, -iest) full of, covered with, —s.

'lunar adj of the moon: a — month, twenty-eight days. ⇨ p 336.

'lunatic n madman. 'lunacy n madness.

lunch n meal taken in the middle of the day. v eat —.

lung n either of the two breathing organs in the chest of man and other animals. ⇨ p 30.

lunge n sudden forward push (eg with a sword) or forward movement of the body (when striking a blow). v make a —.

lurch[1] n leave sb in the —, leave him when he is in difficulties.

lurch[2] n sudden change of weight to one side; sudden roll. v move (along) with a — or —es.

lure n sth that attracts; the attrac-

tion that sth has. v attract, tempt (to do sth, go somewhere).

'lurid adj 1 highly coloured, esp suggesting burning. 2 sensational.

lurk v be, keep, out of view, lying in wait or ready to attack.

'luscious adj rich and sweet in taste or smell.

lust n impure desire. v — after (for), have — for.

'lustre n quality of being bright, esp of a smooth surface; (fig) glory.

lu'xuriant adj strong in growth; abundant: — vegetation. lu'xuriance n — growth.

'luxury n 1 state of life in which one has and uses things that please the senses: living in —. 2 sth pleasing to have but not essential. lu'xurious adj loving, having, —.

'lychee ⇨ lichee.

'lying ⇨ lie.

lynch v put to death without a lawful trial (sb believed guilty of serious crime).

lynx n wild animal of the cat family, noted for its keen sight. ⇨ p 317.

'lyric adj of, composed for, fit for, singing. n — poem; (pl) — verses. —al adj 1 = —. 2 enthusiastic.

M

'ma(mma) n mummy; mother.

'ma'am n short for madam.

macaroni n flour paste made in the form of long tubes, cooked for food.

mace n rod or staff carried as a sign of office or authority.

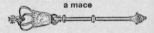

a mace

ma'chine n 1 apparatus or appliance with parts working together to apply power: printing-machine, sewing-machine. 2 persons organized to control a political group. ma'chine-gun n one firing a continuous stream of bullets. —ry n 1 (parts or works of) —s. 2 methods, organization (eg of government).

'mackerel n sea-fish much used as food.

'mackintosh n rainproof coat made of cloth treated with rubber.

mad adj ('madder, 'maddest) **1** having, resulting from, a diseased mind. **2** (colloq) very foolish; much distressed: mad with pain. **'madden** v make mad, esp make angry. **'madly** adv. **'madness** n.

'madam n respectful form of address to a woman.

made ⇔ make.

¡Mademoi'selle n (French) title used before the name of an unmarried girl. (cf Miss)

Ma'donna n (picture or statue of) Mary, Mother of Jesus Christ.

¡maga'zine n **1** store for arms, ammunition, explosives, etc. **2** chamber for holding cartridges in a rifle or gun. **3** paper-covered periodical, issued regularly, with stories, articles, etc, by various writers.

'maggot n larva.

'magic n **1** art of controlling events by the (pretended) use of supernatural forces. **2** witchcraft. **3** art of obtaining mysterious results by clever tricks. adj (also —al) done by, or as by, —; possessing —; used in —. **ma'gician** n person practising —(3), or claiming — power.

'magistrate n civil officer acting as a judge in the lowest courts. **¡magis'terial** adj of a —; having, showing, authority.

mag'nanimous adj having, showing, a generous character. **¡magna'nimity** n.

'magnet n piece of iron, etc able to attract other pieces of metal. **mag'netic** adj of, like, produced by, a —: —ic needle. **'magnetize** v give the properties of a — to; attract as a — does.

mag'nificent adj splendid; important-looking; remarkable. **mag'nificence** n.

'magnify v make (sth) appear larger or more important; give praise to (God).

'magnitude n largeness; (degree of) importance.

'magpie n noisy black-and-white bird, noted for thieving.

ma'hogany n (tropical tree with) dark-brown wood much used for furniture.

maid n **1** (liter) girl. **2** (old use) unmarried woman. **old —**, woman now unlikely to marry. **3** woman employed to do housework.

'maiden n (liter) girl; young unmarried woman. adj **— name**, woman's family name before marriage. **— speech**, sb's first speech made in public or in Parliament. **— voyage**, ship's first voyage.

mail¹ n body armour of metal rings or plates: coat of —.

mail² n **1** letters, parcels, etc., sent or delivered by post. **2** government system of carrying and delivering letters, etc. **— order**, order for goods to be delivered by post. v send (sth) by post.

maim v hurt, wound, so that some part of the body is useless.

main adj chief; most important. n **1** one of the principal pipes for carrying water or gas, or wires for electric current, from the supply centre: connect a house to the —s. **2** in the —, for the most part. **'—land** n country or continent without its islands. **'—ly** adv chiefly. **'main-spring** n driving force. **'—stay** n (fig) chief support. **main'tain** v keep in good order; support; claim (a statement as true).

maize n grain plant with a large, yellow head of seeds (called a cob).

'majesty n kingly or queenly appearance, conduct, etc; stateliness; royal power. **His, Her (Your) M —**, form used when speaking of (to) a king or queen. **ma'jestic** adj having, showing, —.

'major adj greater or more important of two (parts, etc). n army officer between a captain and a lieutenant-colonel. **'major-'general** n army officer next above a brigadier. **ma'jority** n **1** greater number or part (of); esp number by which votes for one side exceed those for the other side. **2** legal age of reaching manhood or womanhood.

make v (pt & pp made) **1** create; bring into existence; construct; prepare; produce. **— fun (sport) of** (sb), laugh at, ridicule. **— light of** (sth), treat as not serious or difficult. **— the most of sth**, use to the greatest advantage. **2** compel, force, persuade. **3** cause to become, do, sth: — sb happy; — the *fire burn.* **4** reach; accomplish: *we made the journey in two days.* **5** consider to be; reckon. **6** — for, go towards; rush at. — off, go or run away. — out, write out (eg a cheque); succeed in seeing, reading, understanding; give the idea (*that*). — up, invent (a story); supply (what is needed for completion); prepare (medicine, etc); put (things) together (in parcels, etc); settle (a quarrel); prepare (an actor for the stage); put cosmetics on the face. — up one's mind (*to*), determine (to). — believe, pretend. *n* way a thing is made; structure. **'make-believe** *n* pretending. **'M—r** *n* God. **'make-shift** *n* sth used until sth better is obtained. **'make-up** *n* **1** arrangement; composition. **2** powder, paint, etc, used by an actor, or by a woman on her face. **'making be the making of,** bring about the well-being of. **have the makings of,** have the necessary qualities for becoming.

mal- *prefix* **1** bad(ly): *maltreat*; *malformation.* **2** not: *malcontent.*

'malady *n* illness; disease.

ma'laria *n* fever due to the bite of certain kinds of mosquito.

male *adj* of the sex that does not give birth to offspring. *n* — person, animal, etc.

ma'levolent *adj* spiteful. **ma'levolence** *n*.

,malfor'mation *n* the state of being badly formed; badly formed part.

'malice *n* active desire to harm sb: *bear sb (no)* —. **ma'licious** *adj* feeling, showing, —.

ma'lign *v* speak ill of (sb); tell lies about. *adj* injurious. **ma'lignant** *adj* **1** filled with, showing, desire to hurt. **2** (of diseases) very harmful to life.

'malleable *adj* **1** (of metals) that can be hammered or pressed into new shapes. **2** (fig, esp of character) easily trained.

'mallet *n* wooden-headed hammer. ⇨ p 293.

,malnu'trition *n* condition caused by not getting enough food or not enough of the right sort of food.

malt *n* grain (usu barley) prepared for use in beer-making.

mal'treat *v* treat roughly or cruelly. —ment *n*.

'mammal *n* any of the class of animals that feed their young with milk from the breast.

'mammoth *n* large kind of hairy elephant, now extinct. *adj* immense.

man *n* (*pl* **men**) **1** human being; male human being. **the man in the street,** person considered as representing the tastes or opinions of ordinary people. **a man of the world,** man with a wide experience of business, society, etc. **2** the human race; all mankind. *v* supply (ships, etc) with the men needed. **'manful** *adj* fearless; determined. **'manhood** *n* the state of being a man; manly qualities. **man'kind** *n* the human race. **'manlike** *adj* having the qualities, good or bad, of a man. **'manly** *adj* (-ier, -iest) having the strong qualities expected of a man. **'manslaughter** *n* act of killing a human being unlawfully but not wilfully.

'manacle *n* (usu *pl*) chain for a prisoner's hands or feet. *v* put —s on.

'manage *v* **1** control (a business, etc). **2** be able (to do sth). —able *adj* easily controlled. —ment *n* managing or being —d; the persons who — a business. —r, ,—'ress *n* man, woman, who controls a business.

'mandate *n* **1** order from a superior; command given with authority; the authority so given. **2** control over certain territories authorized by the League of Nations after the First World War. **'man'dated** *adj* under a —(2): *—d territories.*

mane *n* long hair on the neck of some animals (eg a lion). ⇨ p 317.

mange *n* skin disease, esp of dogs. **'mangy** *adj* (-ier, -iest) having —; dirty or neglected.

'manger *n* long open box or trough for horses and cattle to feed from.

'mangle¹ *v & n* (put through a) laundry machine with rollers for pressing out water from and smoothing clothes, etc.

'mangle² *v* cut up, tear, damage badly.

'mango *n* (*pl* **'mangoes**) tropical fleshy fruit with yellow pulp.

mangrove *n* tropical tree growing in salt-water swamps and sending down new roots from its branches.

a mangrove swamp

manhood, man'kind ⇨ man.

mania *n* **1** violent madness. **2** great enthusiasm (*for* sth). **—c** *n* violent madman; (fig) enthusiast.

manicure *n* care of the hands and fingernails. *v* give a — to.

manifest *adj* clear and obvious. *v* **1** show clearly; give signs of. **2** come to light, appear: *Malaria did not — itself during the voyage.* *n* list of a ship's cargo. **,manifes'tation** *n*.

manifold *adj* having or providing for many uses, copies, etc.

ma'nipulate *v* operate, handle, use with skill (instruments, etc); manage (sb or sth) cleverly. **ma,nipu'lation** *n*.

mannequin *n* woman (also called a **model**) employed to display new clothes by wearing them.

manner *n* **1** way a thing is done or happens. **2** person's way of behaving towards others. **3** (*pl*) habits and customs. **4** (*pl*) social behaviour: *good —s*, polite behaviour. **5** sort: *all — of*, every kind of. **ill- (well-)mannered** *adj* having bad (good) —s(4). **—ism** *n* habitual peculiarity of behaviour.

ma'nœuvre *n* planned movement (of military forces); movement or plan, made to deceive or to escape from sb, to win or do sth. *v* (cause to) perform —s; force (sb or sth *into* doing sth, *into* or *out of* a position) by clever handling.

manor *n* piece of land (in England) with a house over which the owner has certain rights. **ma'norial** *adj*.

mansion *n* grand house.

mantelpiece *n* shelf above a fire-place.

mantis *n* long-legged insect. ⇨ p 144.

mantle *n* loose sleeveless cloak.

manual *adj* of, done with, the hands: **—** *labour*. *n* **1** text-book; handbook. **2** organ keyboard. **—ly** *adv*.

,manu'facture *v* make, produce (goods, etc), esp on a large scale by machinery. *n* the making of goods; (*pl*) **—d** goods and articles. **—r** *n* person who **—s**.

ma'nure *n* animal waste or other material, natural or artificial, used for making soil fertile. *v* put — on (land).

manuscript *n* book, etc, as first written out by hand or typed and ready for printing.

many *adj* (⇨(few, more, most) large number; a lot of. **be one too —** for, be cleverer than. **'many-,sided** *adj* (fig) having — capabilities, aspects, etc.

map *n* flat drawing representing an area of land, a country, the world, etc. *v* (-pp-) make a map of. **map sth out**, plan, arrange.

a map

mar *v* (-rr-) injure; spoil.

'marathon ('race) *n* long-distance race on foot; test of endurance.

'marble *n* **1** sorts of hard lime-stone used, when cut and polished, for building and works of art. **2** small ball of stone or glass used in children's games.

march *v* walk as soldiers do, with regular and measured steps; cause to do this: *The soldiers —ed (the prisoners) away.* *n* **1** the act of —ing: *soldiers on the —; distance —ed; music for —ing to.* **a dead —**, piece of music in slow time for a funeral. **2** (fig) progress; onward movement.

March *n* third month of the year.

mare *n* female horse. **—'s nest**, discovery which turns out to be worthless.

,marga'rine *n* butter substitute made from vegetable or animal (e g whale) fat.

'margin *n* **1** blank space round the printed or written matter on a page. **2** edge or border (eg of a lake). **3** amount (of time, money, etc) above what is calculated as necessary. **—al** *adj* of or in a —(1): *—al notes*.

ma'rine *adj* **1** of, by, found in, produced by, the sea. **2** of ships. *n* **1** merchant —, all the merchant ships of a country. **2** soldier serving on a warship. **'mariner** *n* (*liter*) sailor.

,mario'nette *n* doll or puppet moved by strings on a small stage.

'maritime *adj* of, near, the sea.

mark *n* **1** line, cut, stain, etc, that spoils the appearance of sth. **2** noticeable spot on the body. **3** natural sign or indication (of quality, character, intelligence). **4** figure, design, line, etc, made as a sign: *price-marks*; *trade-marks*. **5** unit for measuring quality or result (eg for school work); *95 —s out of 100*. **6** sth aimed at. **7** normal level. **up to (below) the —**, as good as (not so good as) the normal. **8 make one's —**, become famous. *v* **1** put or be a —(4) on or against. **2** give —s(5) to: *—ing examination papers*. **3** pay attention to. **4 — time**, move the feet in turn up and down without going forward; (*fig*) wait and do nothing. **5 — sth off**, separate by a limit. **— sth out**, make lines to show the limits of (eg a tennis-court). **'—ed** *adj* clear; readily seen: *a —ed difference*. **'—sman** *n* person skilled in shooting.

'market *n* **1** public place (open space or building) where people meet to buy and sell goods. **2** trade in a certain class of goods. **black —**, (place of the) illegal sale of rationed or controlled goods, etc. **3** buying and selling: *come into the —*, be offered for sale. **4** area, country, in which goods may be sold. *v* take or send to —; buy or sell in a —. **'market-,garden** *n* one where vegetables, etc, are grown for a —.

'marmalade *n* jam made from oranges.

ma'roon *v* put (sb) on a desert island, uninhabited coast, etc, and leave him there.

mar'quee *n* large tent.

'marrow *n* **1** soft fatty substance in the hollow parts of the bones. **2** (often **vegetable —**) vegetable like a very large, fat cucumber.

'marry *v* take as a husband or wife;

join as husband and wife; give (eg one's daughter) in marriage. **'marriage** *n* state of being married; wedding ceremony. **'marriageable** *adj* (of age) fit for marriage.

marsh *n* area of low-lying wet land.

'marshal *n* officer of the highest rank: *Field-M—* (army); *Air M—* (Air Force). *v* (-ll-) arrange (military forces, facts, etc) in order.

'martial *adj* of, associated with, soldiers or warfare: *— music. — law*, military government replacing the operation of ordinary law for a time.

'martyr *n* **1** person put to death or caused to suffer for his religious beliefs or for a noble cause. **2 be a — to**, suffer severely from (eg rheumatism). *v* put to death, cause to suffer, as a —. **—dom** *n* —'s suffering or death.

'marvel *n* **1** sth causing great surprise, pleased astonishment. **2** sb or sth showing a good quality in a surprising way: *a — of patience (ingenuity)*. *v* (-ll-) be much surprised (*at*). **—lous** *adj* wonderful; causing pleased surprise.

ma'scara *n* cosmetic for dyeing the eyelashes.

'mascot *n* person, animal or object considered likely to bring good fortune.

'masculine *adj* of, like, the male sex.

mash *v & n* (beat or crush into a soft damp mass.

mask *n* **1** covering for (part of) the face or head. **2** covering for the head worn as a protection against gas or smoke. *v* wear, cover with a —; keep (sth) from view.

'mason *n* stone-cutter; worker who builds with stone. **—ry** *n* stone work.

,masque'rade *n* dance at which masks and other disguises are worn. *v* be, appear, in disguise.

mass *n* **1** quantity, lump, without regular shape; large number, quantity, or heap. **the —es**, the general public. **a — meeting**, large meeting, esp of people wanting to express their views. **— production**, manufacture of large numbers of identical articles. **2** (*science*) quantity of matter in body. *v* form or collect into a —.

Mass *n* Holy Communion, esp in the Roman Catholic Church.

'massacre n cruel killing of a large number of (esp defenceless) people. v make a — of.

'massage n rubbing and pressing of the body to lessen pain, stiffness, etc. v apply — to.

'massive adj heavy and solid; heavy-looking.

mast n upright support (wood or metal) for a ship's sail, a flag, etc; tall steel structure for the aerials of a radio or television transmitter.

'master n 1 man who has others working for or under him; male owner of a dog, horse, etc; captain of a merchant ship; male head of a household; male teacher. 2 M — of Arts (Science, etc), one who has received the second university degree. 3 great painter: the old —s, esp those of 1200-1700, and the pictures they painted. 4 person who has control (of): make oneself — of a subject. 5 (with a boy's name): Master Tom Smith (abbr Mr). v become the — of; overcome. —ful adj fond of controlling others. —ly adj skilful; expert. —piece n sth made or done with great skill. —y n complete control or knowledge (of).

'masticate v grind up (food) with the teeth.

mat n 1 piece of material used for a floor-covering or ('doormat) to wipe dirty shoes on; piece of material placed on a table, etc, to prevent damage (eg from hot dishes). 'matted adj (of hair, etc) tangled; knotted.

match¹ n small stick of wood with a head(2) that lights easily.

match² n 1 contest; game: a football —. 2 person able to meet another as his equal in strength, skill, etc: to meet one's —. 3 marriage. 4 person or thing exactly like, corresponding to, or combining well with another: colours that are a good —. v 1 put in competition (with or against). 2 be equal to or correspond (with) (in quality, colour, etc): a brown dress with a hat to —. 3 be, obtain, a —(2) for: a well-matched pair. '—less adj unequalled.

mate n 1 fellow workman. 2 merchant ship's officer below the captain: first (second, etc) —. 3 one of a pair of birds or animals living

together: the lioness and her —. v unite, cause to unite to produce young: the mating season.

ma'terial n cloth; that of which sth is or can be made or with which sth is done: writing —s, pen, paper, etc. adj 1 made of, connected with, matter or substance (contrasted with spiritual). 2 of the body; of physical needs. 3 important; essential. ma'terialist n person who ignores religion, art, etc.

ma'ternal adj of or like a mother: — aunt, aunt on the mother's side of the family. ma'ternity n being a mother.

mathe'matics n science of space and number, including arithmetic, algebra, geometry. mathe'matical adj of —. mathema'tician n expert in —.

'matinée n afternoon performance at a theatre.

'matins n pl morning prayer (Church of England); prayers at daybreak (Roman Catholic Church).

ma'triculate v (allow to) enter a university as a student, usu after passing an examination. ma'triculation n matriculating; examination for this.

'matrimony n state of being married. matri'monial adj.

'matron n 1 woman housekeeper in a school or other institution. 2 woman controlling the nursing staff in a hospital.

'matter n 1 physical substance (contrasted with mind and spirit). 2 printed —, anything printed. 3 subject; sth to which thought and attention is given: money —s; —s I know nothing about. a — of course, sth naturally to be expected. as a — of fact, in reality, although you might not think so. 4 pus. 5 be the — (with), be wrong (with). no — when (where, who, how), it is unimportant when, etc. v be important (to sb). 'matter-of-'fact adj keeping to facts; unimaginative.

'matting n woven material for floor coverings, for packing goods, etc.

'mattock n tool. ⟹ p 293.

'mattress n long, flat thick pad of springs, straw, etc, on which to sleep.

ma'ture v come or bring to full

development or to a state ready for use. *adj* ripe; fully grown or developed; carefully thought out; ready for use. **ma'turity** *n.*

maul *v* injure by rough or brutal handling.

mauve *adj & n* pale purple (colour).

'maxim *n* widely accepted truth or rule of behaviour briefly expressed.

'maximum *n* greatest possible or recorded degree, quantity, etc; opposite of *minimum*.

May *n* fifth month of the year.

may *v* (*pt* might) **1** (used to show possibility, likelihood, or permission): *That may or may not be true. May I come in?* (cf *can*). **2** (used for a wish): *May you always be happy!* **'maybe** *adv* perhaps. **as soon as maybe**, as soon as possible.

mayor *n* head of a town corporation. **—'ess** *n* woman —; **—'s** wife.

maze *n* network of paths, lines, etc; number of confusing facts. **in a —**, puzzled; bewildered.

me *pron* used by a speaker or writer in referring to himself: *You can see me.* ⇨ **I**.

'meadow *n* piece of grassland, esp one used for hay.

'meagre *adj* thin; not enough.

meal *n* occasion of eating: *three —s a day*; food for (eaten at) a —.

mean¹ *v* (*pt & pp* meant) **1** (intend to) convey the sense(1) of sth that can be understood: *The word 'many' —s 'a large number'*. **2** design(2). **3** have as a purpose or plan. **— mischief**, have an evil plan in mind. **— business**, be ready to act, not merely to talk. **4** be a sign of. **5 — much (little) to,** be of much (little) importance to. **'—ing** *n* **1** that which is meant. **2** purpose. **'—ingless** *adj.* **'—ingly** *adv.*

mean² *adj* **1** poor in appearance: *a — house in a — street.* **2** selfish; ungenerous. **3** (of a person, his behaviour) small-minded; unworthy. **4** low in quality. **'—ness** *n.*

mean³ *n & adj* (condition, quality, number) equally distant from two opposites or extremes: *the — annual temperature.* **'—time** *adv & n* (in) the time between. **'—'while** *adv & n* = —time.

mean⁴ *n* **1** (usu *pl*; often *a —s*) method, process, way by which a result may be obtained. **by —s of,**

through, with the help of. **by all —s**, certainly, at all costs. **by no —s**, not at all. **2** (*pl*) money, property: *live within one's —s*, not spend more than one's income.

'measles *n* infectious disease causing fever and red spots on the body.

'measure *n* **1** size, quantity, degree. **give full (short) —**, give the full (less than the full) amount. **made to —**, (clothes) specially made for sb after taking his —ments. **2** unit, standard, or system used in stating size, quantity, or degree: *an inch is a — of length.* **3** sth with which to test size, quantity, etc: *a tape-measure; a pint —.* **4** extent, esp: *in some —; beyond —,* great(ly). **5** (proposed) law. **6** proceeding; step; *take —s against wrongdoers.* *v* **1** find the size, amount, etc, of. **2 — out,** give a —d quantity of, mark out. **3** be (a certain length, etc). **—ment** *n* (*esp pl*) detailed figures about length, breadth, height, etc.

meat *n* flesh of animals used as food.

me'chanic *n* skilled workman, esp one who makes or works machines. **—s** *n* science of motion and force; science of machinery. **—al** *adj* of, connected with, produced by, machines. **'mechanism** *n* working parts of a machine; way in which sth works. **'mechanize** *v* use machines in or for.

'medal *n* flat piece of metal, usu shaped like a coin, with words and a design stamped on it, given as an award or to commemorate an event.

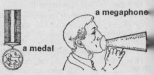

a megaphone

a medal

'meddle *v* busy oneself without being invited, interfere (*with* others' things, *in* sb else's affairs). **—some** *adj* in the habit of meddling.

'mediate *v* act as peace-maker (*between*). **,medi'ation** *n.* **'mediator** *n.*

'medical *adj* of the art of medicine: *— students.* **'medicine** *n* **1** the art and science of the prevention and cure of disease. **2** substance (esp one taken through the mouth) used in medicine. **'medicine-,man** n witch-doctor.

,medi'(a)eval adj of the Middle Ages (from A.D. 1000–1400).

'mediocre adj not very good; second-rate. **,medi'ocrity** n (esp) — person.

'meditate v think about; consider; give oneself up to thought (upon). **,medi'tation** n serious thought.

'medium n **1** that by which and through which sth is done: newspapers are a — for advertising. **2** middle quality or degree: the happy —. adj coming half-way between: of — height; — waves (in radio).

'medley n mixture of different articles, sounds, colours, etc.

meek adj (-er, -est) humble; unprotesting. **'—ly** adv. **'—ness** n.

meet v (pt & pp met) **1** come together from different directions or places. **2** — with, experience (eg bad weather); have (eg an accident). **3** go to a place and wait for the arrival of sb or sth. **4** make the acquaintance of: M— Miss Jones. **5** satisfy; come into agreement with (sb, his wishes). **'—ing** n a coming together of persons for some purpose, esp discussion.

'megaphone n horn for speaking through, carrying the voice to a distance. ⇨ p 170.

melancholy n & adj (being) sad.

mellow adj (-er, -est) **1** soft and sweet in taste; soft, pure, and rich in colour or sound. **2** made sympathetic and wise by experience. v make or become —.

melodrama n exciting and emotional drama, usu with a happy ending. **,melodra'matic** adj sensational.

melody n **1** tunefulness. **2** song or tune. **me'lodious** adj musical.

melon n large juicy round fruit growing on a plant that trails along the ground. ⇨ p 115.

melt v **1** (cause to) become liquid through heating. **2** soften, be softened. **3** fade, go slowly (away). **'molten** (old pp now used only of metals, lava.) **—ed**: molten steel.

member n person belonging to a group, society, etc. **—ship** n

being a —; the number of —s (in a society, etc).

'membrane n soft, thin, skin-like substance covering or connecting inside parts of an animal or plant.

me'mento n sth that serves to remind one of a person or event.

'memo n ⇨ memorandum.

'memoir n **1** short life-history of someone. **2** (pl) sb's own written account of his life and experiences.

,memo'randum n (abbr memo) **1** note or record for future use. **2** informal business communication.

'memory n **1** power of remembering. **2** period over which one's — can go back. **3** in — of, to keep (sb or sth) in the —. **4** sth that is remembered; sth from the past stored in the —. **'memorable** adj deserving to be remembered. **me'morial** n & adj (sth) made or done to remind people of an event or person. **'memorize** v learn by heart; commit to —.

men ⇨ man.

'menace n threat; danger. v threaten.

me'nagerie n collection of wild animals in cages, etc, esp for a travelling show.

mend v **1** remake, repair, set right (sth broken, worn out, torn, etc); restore to working order. **2** = amend. n —ed place. **on the —,** improving (in health).

'menial adj & n (suitable for, to be done by, a) household servant.

'mental adj of or in the mind. **—ly** adv. **men'tality** n general character of a person's mind.

'mention v speak or write sth about; say the name of. n —ing.

'menu n list of food dishes at a meal (in a restaurant, etc).

'mercantile adj of trade and merchants. **,— ma'rine** n country's merchant ships, seamen.

'mercenary adj working only for the sake of money or reward; based on love of money: — motives.

'merchandise n goods bought and sold.

'merchant n (usu wholesale) trader, esp one doing business with foreign countries. **— service,** ships and seamen engaged in carrying goods and passengers. **—man** n — ship.

'mercury n heavy silver-coloured

metal, usu liquid (as in ther-mometers).

'mercy n 1 (capacity for) holding oneself back from punishing, causing suffering to, sb whom one has the right or power to punish or hurt. (be) at the — of, in the power of. 2 piece of good fortune; sth to be thankful for. 'merciful adj having, showing, —. 'merciless adj without —; cruel.

mere adj nothing more than; only: a — (the —st) trifle. '—ly adv only.

merge v 1 (cause to) become part of sth greater, esp (of two companies) become, cause to become, one. 2 — into, be absorbed in (sth else).

me'ridian n (half-)circle round the globe, passing through a given place and the north and south poles.

'merit n 1 quality deserving praise. 2 (pl) what is deserved (whether reward or punishment). v deserve; be worthy of.

'mermaid n (in stories) woman with a fish's tail in place of legs.

'merry adj (-ier, -iest) happy; cheerful. make —, hold, join in, a — party. 'merrily adv. 'merriment n. 'merry-,making n.

mesh n one of the spaces in netting; (pl) net, (fig) snares.

mess¹ n dirty or untidy state: make a — of sth. v make a — of. — sth up, spoil it. — about, waste time, work or play without doing very much. '—y adj (-ier, -iest).

mess² n group of persons taking meals together (esp in the armed forces); room in which the meals are taken.

'message n piece of news sent to sb. 'messenger n sb who carries a —.

Mes'siah n person expected by the Jews to come and free them; Jesus Christ.

'Messrs title used before names of business partners, a plural of Mr.

met ⇨ meet.

'metal n 1 any one of a class of simple substances such as tin, iron, gold. 2 'road-metal, broken stone for making roads. me'tallic adj of or like —.

'metaphor n (an example of) the use of words to indicate sth different from the literal meaning:

She has a heart of stone. ,meta-'phorical adj.

'meteor n small body rushing from outer space into the earth's atmosphere and becoming bright as it burns up.

,meteo'rology n science of the weather.

'meter n apparatus that measures, esp one that records the amount, strength, etc, of whatever passes through it (eg electric current).

'method n 1 way of doing sth. 2 system; orderliness. me'thodical adj.

'methylated 'spirit n form of alcohol used for lighting and heating.

'metre n 1 unit of length (= 39·37 inches) in the metric system. 2 rhythm in poetry. 'metric adj. the metric system, system of measuring by tens and tenths based on the —. ⇨ p 335. 'metrical adj of rhythm in verse.

me'tropolis n chief city of a country. ,metro'politan adj of a —.

'mettle n on one's —, in a position that moves one to do one's best.

mice ⇨ mouse.

'microbe n tiny living creature, esp a kind of bacteria causing diseases.

'microphone n instrument for changing sound waves into electrical waves, as used in telephones and radio.

a microphone

a microscope

'microscope n instrument for making very small near objects appear larger.

mid adj in the middle of; middle in mid Atlantic; in mid air, high above the ground. 'mid'day n noon. the 'Midlands n pl the central counties of England. 'midnight n 12 o'clock at night. 'mid'summer n middle of the summer. 'mid'way adj & adv half-way.

mid- prefix in the middle of.

middle n & adj (position that is) at an equal distance from two or more points; between the beginning and the end. **— age,** period of life midway between youth and old age. **the M — Ages,** time (in European history) from A.D. 1000 to 1400. **the — class(es),** those between the highest and lowest classes of society. **the — watch,** (on ships) period from midnight to 4 a.m. **—man** n any trader through whose hands goods pass between producer and consumer. **'middling** adj & adv of — or medium size, etc; moderately (well or good).

midget adj & n extremely small (person or thing).

midst n **in the — of,** in the middle of, while occupied with. **in our —,** among us. prep (liter) among.

midwife n (pl **'midwives**) woman trained to help women in childbirth.

might¹ ⇨ **may.**

might² n great power or size. **'—y** adj (-ier, -iest) of great power or size.

mi'grate v **1** move from one place to another (to live there). **2** (of birds) come and go regularly with the seasons. **'migrant** n (esp) bird that **—s. mi'gration** n.

mild adj (-er, -est) **1** soft; gentle; not severe: **— weather (punishment).** **2** (of food, drink, tobacco) not sharp or strong in taste. **'—ly** adv.

mildew n (usu destructive) growth of tiny fungi on plants, leather, food, etc, in damp places.

mile n measure of distance, 1,760 yards or 1·6 kilometres. **'—age** n distance travelled measured in —s. **'—stone** n roadside stone marking distances in —s; (fig) important event.

militant adj prepared to use force; actively engaged in war. n sb using or prepared to use force (esp for political gain).

military adj of or for soldiers, an army; of war, esp on land.

mi'litia n force of civilians trained as soldiers but not part of the regular army.

milk n white liquid produced by female mammals as food for their young; cow's **—.** v draw the — from (a cow, etc). **'—maid** n woman who **—s** cows and makes butter, etc. **'—man** n man who

delivers — to customers' houses. **'—tooth** n early temporary tooth in young mammals.

mill n **1** (building with) machinery for grinding grain into flour. **2** building, factory, workshop for industry: **paper- (cotton-, steel-, saw-) mills. 3** small machine for grinding: **coffee-mill.** v grind, produce by grinding, in a **—. '—stone** n either of the two round stones between which grain is ground; (fig) burden. **'—er** n man who works a flour-mill.

mil'lennium n **1** 1,000 years. **2** future time of complete happiness for everyone.

'millet n grain plant with tiny seeds.

'milli- prefix one thousandth part of: **—gram; —metre.**

'milliner n person who makes or sells women's hats. **—y** n (things needed for making) women's hats.

'million n 1,000,000. **,millio'naire** n extremely rich person.

mime v & n (tell a) story using actions and no words.

'mimic adj imitated or pretended: **— battles.** n person who copies the speech, gestures, etc, of others. v (pt & pp **'mimicked**) **1** imitate (others), esp to cause amusement. **2** be very like: **insects that — leaves.**

'minaret n tall, slender spire of a mosque. ⇨ p. 177.

mince v cut up (meat, etc) into very small pieces. n minced meat.

'mincemeat n mixture of currants, sugar, suet, etc for pastries.

mind¹ n **1** memory. **keep (bear) sth in —, come to —,** remember. **put sb in — of,** remind him of. **2** way of thinking, feeling, wishing; opinion; purpose. **make up one's —,** come to a decision. **change one's —,** change one's purpose or intention. **be in two —s about sth,** feel doubtful, hesitate. **be of one —,** (of two or more persons) be in agreement. **speak one's —,** say plainly what one thinks. **have a good — to,** be almost decided or ready to. **take one's — off** (sth), turn one's attention from. **3** power to reason. **out of one's right —,** mad. **presence of —,** ability to decide or act quickly when there is danger. **'—ful** adj **—ful of,** giving thought to. **'—less** adj **—less of,** paying no attention to.

mind² v 1 take care of: — *the baby*; attend to: — *the step*, take care not to stumble over it. M — (out) ! Be careful! 2 be troubled by; feel objection to: *Do you — my smoking? Would you — closing* (= please close) *the window?*

mine¹ *pron* of me; belonging to me: *That book is —.* ⇨ my.

mine² n 1 hole made in the earth to get coal, ores, etc. 2 (underground tunnel for) charge of high explosive; metal case filled with high explosive for use in war: *ships sunk by —s.* v 1 get (coal, etc) from a —(1). 2 put —s(2) in (the sea) or under (a fort); destroy, sink, or damage with a —(2). 3 (also undermine) make holes or tunnels under. 'mine-field n (esp) area of land or sea where —s(2) have been laid. 'mine-layer (-,sweeper) n ship laying (sweeping up or destroying) —s(2). '—r n (esp) man working in a —(1).

'mineral n substance (eg coal) not vegetable or animal, got from the earth by mining, etc. 'mineral-,water n water containing gas (and often a flavouring), such as *soda-water.*

'mingle v mix (*with*).

'miniature n small-scale copy or model of sth.

'minimum n & adj least possible or recorded amount, degree, etc (of); opposite of *maximum.*

'minister n 1 person at the head of a Department of State: *M— of Health.* 2 person representing his Government in a foreign country. 3 Christian priest or clergyman. v give help or service (*to*). 'ministry n 1 Department of State: *the Air Ministry.* 2 Cabinet (2). 3 enter the ministry, become a —(3).

'minor adj 1 smaller; less important. 2 younger of two brothers: *Jones —.* n (legal) person under the age of 18 (in Gt Brit). mi'nority n 1 the state of being a —. 2 the smaller number or part, esp of a total of votes.

'minster n church, esp one that once belonged to a monastery.

mint¹ n place where coins are made, usu under State authority. v make (coins) by stamping metal.

mint² n plant used for flavouring, sweet with this flavour.

'minus prep less; with the deduction of: *7 minus 3 equals 4* (7 − 3 = 4). a — quantity, one less than o eg — 15. minus-sign, sign — i arithmetic.

'minute¹ n 1 sixtieth part of an hour 2 one-sixtieth of a degree in an angle. 3 official record (with comments, advice, etc) of an interview, etc. 4 (pl) records o what is said and decided at a meeting.

mi'nute² adj (-r, -st) very small giving small details: *a — description.*

'miracle n 1 act or event which doe not follow the known laws o nature; remarkable or surprising event. 2 remarkable example (o a quality). mi'raculous adj.

'mirage n false picture or vision a seen, eg, in the air over a desert.

mire n soft deep mud; wet ground

'mirror n polished (formerly meta now glass) surface in which on can see oneself; looking-glass. give back a picture or reflection o

mirth n laughter; being merry.

mis- prefix badl(y); wrong(ly), a in *misbehave, miscount, misspell.*

'misanthrope n person who hate mankind. ,misan'thropic adj.

,misbe'have v behave improperl be naughty. ,misbe'haviour n.

mis'carriage n 1 — of justice mistake in judging or punishmen 2 failure, esp the delivery of child before it is able to live.

mis'carry v (of plans) fail; hav a result different from what wa hoped; have a miscarriage(2).

,miscel'laneous adj of mixed sort having various qualities an characteristics.

'mischief n 1 injury or damage don on purpose. 2 foolish or though less behaviour likely to caus trouble. 'mischievous adj caus ing, engaged in, fond of, —.

,miscon'ception n mistaken idea

mis'conduct n wrong or bad b haviour. miscon'duct v mana (sth) badly; behave (onese badly.

,miscon'strue v form a wron idea of.

mis'deed n wicked act; crime.

'miser n person who loves mon

for its own sake and spends as little as possible. —ly adj.

'miserable adj 1 wretched; causing wretchedness. 2 poor in quality. 'miserably adv. 'misery n state of being —; suffering; poverty.

'mis'fire v (of a gun) fail to go off; (of a motor-car engine) fail to start. n such a failure.

'misfit n article of clothing which does not fit well; (fig) person not well suited to his position.

mis'fortune n (happening caused by or marked by) bad luck.

mis'giving n doubt; distrust.

mis'guided adj wrong because of bad guidance or influences.

'mishap n unfortunate accident (usu not serious).

mis'lay v (pt & pp mis'laid) put (sth) by accident where it cannot easily be found.

mis'lead v (pt & pp mis'led) cause to be or do wrong; give a wrong idea to.

mis'place v 1 put in a wrong place. 2 give (love, affections) wrongly.

mis'rule n bad government.

miss v 1 fail to hit, hold, catch, read, see, be at, what it is desired to hit, etc: fire at sth and — it; — one's train. 2 realize or feel regret at the absence of sth: They all —ed their brother when he went away. 3 — (sth) out, fail to put it in or say it. n failure (to hit, etc). '—ing adj not to be found; not in the place where it ought to be.

Miss n form of address for an unmarried girl or woman without a title: Miss Smith.

'mis-'shapen adj wrongly shaped.

'missile n object thrown or sent through the air to hurt or damage; object or weapon fired at high speed from a rocket.

'mission n 1 (the sending out of a) number of persons entrusted with special work, usu abroad: a trade —. 2 work done by such persons, their building(s), organization, etc. 3 special work which a person feels he must do. —ary n person sent (usu abroad) to preach his religion.

mist n water vapour in the air, less dense than fog: hills hidden in —. '—y adj (-ier, -iest) 1 with —. 2 not clear.

mis'take n wrong opinion or idea

or act; error. v (pt mis'took, pp mis'taken) 1 be wrong, have a wrong idea about. 2 — (sb or sth) for, wrongly suppose that (sb or sth) is (sb or sth else).

mis'took ⇨ mistake.

'mistress n 1 housewife in charge of a household. 2 woman school teacher.

mis'trust v & n (feel) doubt or suspicion (about). —ful adj suspicious.

'misunder'stand v take a wrong meaning from (sth said or written); form a wrong opinion of (sb or sth). —ing n failure to understand rightly.

mis'use n & v use (using) wrongly or for a wrong purpose; treat unkindly.

'mitigate v make less severe or painful. ,miti'gation n.

mix v (of different substances, people, etc) put, bring, or come together so that the different substances, etc, are no longer separate; make or prepare (sth) by doing this: mix flour and sugar; Oil and water do not mix. feel mixed up, be puzzled and confused. 'mixed adj of different sorts. 'mixture n mixing; being mixed; sth that is mixed or made by mixing.

moan v & n (utter, give a) low sound of pain, regret, or suffering.

moat n deep wide ditch with water, round a castle, etc, as a protection.

mob n 1 disorderly crowd. 2 the common people; the masses. v (-bb-) crowd round in a disorderly manner.

'mobile adj moving, able to move, easily: — artillery. mo'bility n.

'mobilize v collect together (forces, materials, etc) and prepare for service and use, esp in war. ,mobili'zation n.

mock v make fun of; ridicule (esp by mimicking). adj not real: — battles. '—ingly adv. '—ery n 1 —ing. 2 sb or sth that is —ed. 3 bad or contemptible example.

mode n style or fashion (of dress, etc).

'model n 1 small-scale copy of sth; design to be copied. 2 person or thing to be copied. 3 mannequin. v (-ll-) 1 shape (in some soft substance): —ling in clay. 2 make from a —; take as a copy or example: M— *your behaviour upon his.*

'moderate *adj* not extreme; midway (eg in opinions, habits). *v* make, become, less violent or extreme. **—ly** *adv* to a — extent; fairly. **,mode'ration** *n.*

'modern *adj* **1** of the present or recent times: — *history.* **2** new and up to date: — *methods.* **—ize** *v* bring up to date; make suitable for present-day needs.

'modest *adj* **1** taking, showing, care not to do or say anything impure or improper. **2** having, showing, a not too high opinion of oneself. **3** not very large, fine, etc. **—ly** *adv.* **—y** *n.*

'modify *v* make changes in; make less severe, violent, etc. **,modifi'cation** *n.*

'module *n* (esp a) self-contained part of a spacecraft that can perform a specific task when separated from it: *a lunar* —, one that can land on the moon.

moist *adj* (-er, -est) slightly wet. **'—en** *v* make, become, —. **'—ure** *n* slight wetness.

'molar *n & adj* (one) of the teeth used for grinding food.

mole *n* small dark-grey fur-covered animal living in tunnels which it makes under the ground. ⇨ p 12. **'mole-hill** *n* heap of earth thrown up by a —.

'molecule *n* smallest unit into which a substance can be divided without a change in its chemical nature.

mo'lest *v* trouble or annoy on purpose.

'molten ⇨ melt.

'moment *n* **1** point of time. **in a —,** very soon, at once. **the — that,** as soon as. **2** importance. **—ary** *adj* last for, done in, a —. **mo'mentous** *adj* very important.

'monarch *n* supreme ruler, esp king or emperor. **—y** *n* (country with) government by a —.

'monastery *n* building in which monks live. **mo'nastic** *adj* of monasteries and monks.

'Monday *n* second day of the week.

'money *n* metal coins and paper bank-notes used in buying and selling.

'mongrel *n* dog of mixed breed.

'monitor *n* school pupil given authority over other pupils.

monk *n* one of a society of men living together under religious vows.

'monkey *n* small ape-like mammal. ⇨ p 317. *v* — **about with,** (colloq) play mischievously with.

mo'nogamy *n* custom of being married to one wife (husband) at a time.

'monologue *n* scene in a play, etc, in which only one person speaks.

mo'nopoly *n* **1** (possession of the) sole right to supply; the product or service thus controlled. **2** complete possession of trade, talk, etc. **mo'nopolist** *n* person who has a —. **mo'nopolize** *v* get, keep, a — of.

'monosyllable *n* word of one syllable. **,monosyl'labic** *adj.*

'monotone *n* (keeping a) level tone in talking or singing. **mo'notonous** *adj* (uninteresting because) unchanging. **mo'notony** *n* sameness; dullness.

mon'soon *n* wind blowing in the Indian Ocean from SW in summer and from NE in winter.

'monster *n* **1** wrongly-shaped (usu over-sized) animal or plant. **2** (in stories) imaginary creature (eg half animal, half bird). **3** very cruel person. **'monstrous** *adj* of or like a —; of great size; (colloq) absurd.

month *n* twelfth part of a year; period of 28 days. **'—ly** *adj & adv.*

'monument *n* building, column, statue, etc, serving to keep alive the memory of a person or event.

mood *n* state of mind or spirits: *in a cheerful* —. **'—y** *adj* (-ier, -iest) having —s that often change. **—ily** *adv* gloomily.

moon *n* small body (6) that moves round the earth and shines at night. **'moon-flight,** journey to the —. **'moon-struck,** mad.

phases of the moon

moor[1] *n* area of open uncultivated land, esp heather-covered land.

moor[2] *v* make (a boat, ship, etc)

secure (to land or buoys) by means of cables, etc. **'—ings** *n pl* cables, etc, by which a ship is —ed; place at which a ship is —ed.

mop *v* (-pp-) *&* *n* (use a) bundle of coarse strings, cloth, etc, fastened to a handle, for cleaning floors, dishes, etc.

mope *v* pity oneself.

'moral *adj* **1** concerning principles(2). **2** good and virtuous: *living a — life.* *n* **1** that which a story, event, or experience teaches. **2** (*pl*) standards of behaviour; principles of right and wrong. **mo'rality** *n* (standards, principles, of) good behaviour. **'moralize** *v* deal with — questions; point out —s. **—ly** *adv.*

mo'rale *n* confidence under discipline; fighting spirit.

mo'rass *n* area of soft wet land.

'morbid *adj* diseased; unhealthy; having or showing unnatural ideas or feelings. **—ly** *adv.*

more *n, adj, & adv* (the) greater in quantity, quality, size, etc. **— and —**, increasingly. **— or less**, approximately. **—'over** *adv* in addition (to this); besides.

'morning *n* part of the day between dawn and midday.

mo'rose *adj* ill-tempered.

'morphia, 'morphine *n* drug for relieving pain.

'morrow *n* **the —**, the day after (that spoken of).

Morse *n* **— code**, system of dots and dashes representing letters of the alphabet to be signalled by lamp, wireless, etc.

'morsel *n* tiny piece (eg of food).

'mortal *adj* **1** which must die; which cannot live for ever. **2** causing death: *— injuries.* **3** lasting until death. *n* human being. **—ly** *adv.* **mor'tality** *n* **1** being —. **2** number of deaths caused by sth (eg a disease).

'mortar *n* **1** mixture of lime, sand, and water used in building. **2** bowl made of hard material in which substances are crushed to powder with a pestle. ⇨ p 202.

'mortgage *v* give a money-lender a claim on (property) as a security for money borrowed. *n* act of mortgaging; agreement about this.

'mortify *v* **1** cause (sb) to be hurt in his feelings. **2** subdue (bodily

desires). **3** (of flesh, eg a wound) go bad; decay. **,mortifi'cation** *n.*

'mortuary *n* room or building to which dead bodies are taken to await burial.

mo'saic *n & adj* (form or work of art) of designs made by fitting together bits of differently coloured stone, etc.

mosque *n* a building in which Muslims worship God.

a mosque

mos'quito *n* small flying bloodsucking insect. ⇨ p 144.

moss *n* sorts of small green or yellow plant growing in thick masses on wet surfaces. **'—y** *adj.*

most *n & adj* (contrasted with *least* and *fewest*) (the) greatest in quantity, size. *adv: the — beautiful* (*useful*, etc), more beautiful (useful, etc) than anyone (anything) else. **at (the) —**, not more than. **make the — of**, use to the best advantage. **for the — part**, nearly all. **'—ly** *adv* chiefly; generally.

moth *n* winged insect flying chiefly at night, attracted by light. ⇨ p 144.

'mother *n* female parent. **— tongue**, one's own language. *v* watch over as a — does her children. **—hood** *n.* **—ly** *adj* having the qualities of a —. **mother-in-law** *n* — of one's wife or husband.

'motion *n* **1** (manner of) moving. **in —**, moving. **2** particular movement; gesture. **3** proposal to be discussed and voted on at a meeting. *v* direct (sb) by a —(2): *— sb to a seat.* **—less** *adj* not moving.

'motive *n* that which causes sb to act.

'motley *adj* of various colours or sorts: *a — collection of plates.*

'motor *n* **1** machine (esp one worked by petrol or electricity) that supplies power or causes motion, esp one that drives a vehicle or aircraft. **2** (with nouns) **motor-bike** **(-car, -boat,** *etc*), worked or driven by a —. v travel, take (sb), in a motor-car.

'motto n (pl 'mottoes) short saying giving a rule of conduct.

mould[1] n container into which liquid metal or a soft substance is put to take a desired shape; food (eg jelly) shaped in such a container. v give a shape to: — a head in (out of) clay; (fig) — sb's character.

mould[2] n woolly or furry growth of fungi appearing on moist substances. '—y adj covered with —.

moult v (of birds) lose feathers before a new growth.

mound n small hill; heaped up earth.

mount n 1 (in proper names) mountain: Mount (Mt) Kenya. 2 card, etc, on which a picture, etc, is fixed. 3 horse for riding on. v 1 go up (a ladder, hill, etc); get on (a horse, etc). 2 put and fix in position: — a gun (on a gun-carriage). 3 — up, become greater in amount. 4 — guard (over), be on duty as a guard (over).

'mountain n mass of very high land going up to a peak: Everest is the highest — in the world. ,mountai'neer n person living among —s or clever at climbing —s. '—ous adj having many —s; immense: —ous waves.

mourn v feel or show sorrow for a death or loss. '—er n one who —s, esp at a funeral. '—ful adj. '—fully adv. '—ing n 1 grief. 2 (the wearing of) black clothes as a sign of grief: go into —ing (for sb).

mouse n (pl mice) small rodent found in houses and chased by cats. ⇨ p 12.

mous'tache n hair allowed to grow on the upper lip.

mouth n 1 opening in the face through which food is taken. ⇨ p 30. down in the —, sad. 2 opening or outlet (in a bag, bottle, etc, of a tunnel, river, etc). '—ful n. 'mouth-,organ n small musical instrument played by passing it across the lips while blowing. '—piece n part of a pipe, musical instrument, etc, placed to or in the —.

move v 1 (cause to) change position. — house, take one's furniture, etc, to another house. 2 affect the feelings of: —d to tears by the sad story. 3 put forward for discussion and decision (at a meeting). n 1 change of place or position. 2 sth (to be) done to achieve a purpose: the next —. 3 on the —, moving about. '—ment n 1 moving or being —d; activity. 2 moving part of a machine; group of such parts. 3 united action of a group of people for a special purpose. 'movable adj that can be —d.

mow v (pt mowed, pp mowed or mown) cut (grass, etc) with a scythe or machine: new-mown hay; mowing the lawn. 'lawn-mower, —ing machine. ⇨ p 155.

Mr n (Mister) form of address to a man with no title: Mr Smith.

Mrs n form of address to a married woman with no title: Mrs Smith.

much pron, adj, & adv great in quantity.

muck n 1 farmyard manure. 2 dirt. v make dirty. '—y adj (-ier, -iest).

mud n soft wet earth. '—dy (-ier, -iest) adj.

'muddle v bring into confusion; do (sth) badly. n —d state: in a —.

'muffle v 1 cover up for warmth. 2 make the sound of sth (eg a bell) less by wrapping it up in a cloth.

mug n straight-sided drinking vessel, usu of plastic or metal, with a handle, for use without a saucer.

mule n animal which is the offspring of a male ass and a mare. 'mulish adj stubborn.

'multi- prefix having many (of).

'multiply v 1 6 multiplied by 5 is 30 (6 × 5 = 30). 2 produce a great number of. 3 make or become great in number. ,multipli-'cation n act of —ing. multi-plication-sign, the sign × in arithmetic.

'multitude n great number (esp of people gathered together).

'mumble v say sth, speak (one's words) indistinctly. n —d words.

'mummy[1] n dead body preserved from decay by being embalmed, esp as by the ancient Egyptians.

'mum(my)[2] n (child's word for) mother.

mu'nicipal adj of a —ity. ,munici-'pality n town or city with local self-government; governing body of such a town.

mu'nitions n pl military supplies, esp guns, shells, bombs, etc.

'mural *adj* of or on a wall. *n* — painting.

'murder *n* unlawful killing of a human being on purpose. *v* kill (sb) unlawfully and on purpose. —er. —ess *n* male (female) who commits a —. —ous *adj* planning, suggesting, designed for, —.

'murky *adj* (-ier, -iest) dark, gloomy.

'murmur *v & n* 1 (make a) low, continuous, indistinct sound: *the* — (= hum) *of bees.* 2 say (sth), talk, in a low voice: —*ing a prayer.*

'muscle *n* stringy part of flesh which produces movement of the limbs, etc. ⇨ p 30. 'muscular *adj* of the —s; having much —.

muse *v* think dreamily (*upon, over,* sth), paying no attention to what is happening around oneself.

mu'seum *n* building in which objects (esp of art, history, science, etc) are displayed.

'mushroom *v & n* (grow rapidly like a) kind of fungus that can be eaten. ⇨ p 306.

'music *n* (act of producing) pleasing combinations of sounds and rhythms; written or printed signs for these. face the —, meet expected criticism or punishment with courage. —al *adj* fond of, skilled in, —. mu'sician *n* person skilled in —; composer of —.

'Muslim *n* follower of the religion of the Prophet Muhammad.

'muslin *n* thin, fine, soft cotton cloth (for dresses, curtains, etc).

'mussel *n* sorts of shell-fish with a shell in two parts.

must *v* be obliged to: *I — go home soon;* (expressing a feeling of strong probability or certainty): *I think you — have been here before.*

mustard *n* plant; its seeds crushed to a yellow powder, mixed with water to make a hot-tasting sauce.

'muster *n* gathering of persons, esp of soldiers for inspection. *v* collect, call, come, together.

'musty *adj* (-ier, -iest) stale; smelling or tasting of damp earth.

mute *adj* 1 silent; saying nothing. 2 dumb; unable to speak. 3 (of a letter in a word) not sounded (as *b* in *dumb*). *n* person unable to speak.

'mutilate *v* damage by tearing, breaking, or cutting off a part. ,muti'lation *n*.

'mutiny *n* open rising (esp of soldiers and sailors) against authority. *v* rise against authority. ,muti'neer *n*. person guilty of —. 'mutinous *adj* rebellious.

'mutter *v* speak, say sth, in a low voice not meant to be heard.

'mutton *n* flesh of the sheep.

'mutual *adj* 1 given and received by two or more persons, etc, to and from each other. 2 (of feelings, opinions) held in common with others. 3 common to two or more: *our — friend Robin.* —ly *adv.*

'muzzle *n* 1 (covering of wires or straps put over an) animal's nose and mouth. 2 open end or mouth of a gun. *v* put a —(1) on (an animal); prevent (a person, newspaper, etc) from expressing views freely.

my *adj* belonging to me: *That is my book.* ⇨ mine. myself *pron: I hurt myself when I fell over.*

'mystery *n* sth of which the cause or origin is hidden or impossible to understand. mys'terious *adj* full of, suggesting, —.

'mystic *adj* of hidden meaning or spiritual power; causing feelings of awe. *n* person who seeks union with God and, through that, the realization of truths beyond man's understanding. —al *adj* —; unreal. —ism *n.*

'mystify *v* bewilder; puzzle.

myth *n* 1 story, handed down from old times, about the early beliefs of a race. 2 false belief; person, thing, etc, that does not exist or has never existed. '—ical *adj* of —s; unreal. my'thology *n* study of —s(1). ,mytho'logical *adj.* my'thologist *n* student of —ology.

N

'nadir *n* lowest level or state (of one's hopes, ambitions, etc).

nag *v* (-gg-) scold continuously.

nail *n* 1 hard substance covering the end of a finger or toe. fight tooth and —, fight very fiercely. 2 piece of metal with a point at one end and a flattened head at the

nails

some musical instruments

other, for holding things together, etc. **hit the — on the head,** say or do the right thing. *v* make fast with a — or —s.

na'ive *adj* natural and innocent (because young or inexperienced). **—ness** *n.*

'naked *adj* bare; without the usual covering. **—ness** *n.*

name *n* **1** word(s) by which a person, animal, place, etc, is known. **in the — of,** with the authority of (eg the law); for the sake of (eg common sense); **call sb —s,** call him insulting —s (eg liar, coward). **2** reputation: *lose one's good —.* *v* **1** give a — to; say the — of. **— sb after,** give him the same — as. **2** mention; state. **'—ly** *adv* that is to say. **'—sake** *n* person with the same — as another.

'nan(ny) *n* (child's word for) grandmother.

nap¹ *n* short sleep (esp during the day, not in bed). **be caught napping,** be caught by surprise or not ready.

nap² *n* surface (on cloth, etc) of soft, short hairs, smoothed and brushed up.

nape *n* (esp) back of the neck.

'napkin *n* **1** table —, piece of cloth used at meals for protecting clothing, etc. **2** (colloq **'nappy**) towel tied round a baby's buttocks.

nar'cotic *n & adj* (substance) producing sleep or other insensible condition; harmful drug.

nar'rate *v* tell (a story); give an account of. **'narrative** *adj & n* (of, in the form of, a) story.

'narrow *adj* (-er, -est) **1** measuring little across in comparison with length. **2** limited. **3** with a small margin: *a — majority.* **4** strict: *a — search.* **—ly** *adv* **1** with little to spare; only just. **2** strictly; carefully. **'narrow-'minded** *adj* having little sympathy for other persons' beliefs, etc.

'nasal *adj* of the nose.

'nasty *adj* (-ier, -iest) **1** dirty; disgusting. **2** dangerous; threatening.

'natal *adj* of birth.

'nation *n* body of people usu living in the same country(1) under the same government. **—al** *adj* of, common to, a —. *n* person of a certain —. **—alism** *n* (esp) movement for —al self-government.

—alist *n* supporter of —alism. **—alize** *v* (esp) transfer (eg land, railways) from private to State ownership. **,nationali'zation** *n.* **,nation'ality** *n* being a member of a —.

'native *adj* **1** of the place, circumstances, etc, of one's birth: *This is my own, my — land!* **2** (of qualities) belonging to a person by nature, not by education: *The defendant relied on his — wit.* **3** (of plants and animals) belonging by origin (*to*): *plants — to America.* *n* **1** person belonging by birth to a place or country: *a — of Wales.* **2** animal or plant natural to and having its origin in a certain region: *The kangaroo is a — of Australia.*

na'tivity *n* birth. **the N—,** the birth of Jesus Christ: *a N— play.*

'natural *adj* **1** of, concerned with, produced by, nature(1),(2): **— history** (ie botany, zoology, etc); *animals living in their* — (ie wild) *state.* **2** normal; to be expected: *die a — death* (ie not by violence). **3** (of a person, his behaviour, etc) simple; not cultivated or self-conscious: *speak in a — way* (voice); *a — orator.* **—ly** *adv* **1** in a — way. **2** by nature. **3** of course; as might be expected. **—ist** *n* student of, expert in — history.

'naturalize *v* give (sb from another country) rights of citizenship. **,naturali'zation** *n.*

'nature *n* **1** the whole universe and all created things: **— worship** (of trees, oceans, etc); **— study** (of plants, insects, animals, etc). **2** the forces that control life, weather, etc: *mankind's struggle against —.* **3** simple life without the arts and aids of civilization: *living in a state of* — (eg as primitive men did). **4** real or necessary qualities (of sth). **5** character, feeling, etc, with which a person is born: *proud by —.* **good —,** kindness, unselfishness. **6** sort: *things of this —.* **in the —'of,** almost the same as.

naught *n* nothing.

'naughty *adj* (-ier, -iest) (of children, their behaviour, etc) bad; disobedient; causing trouble.

'nausea *n* feeling of sickness in the stomach. **'nauseate** *v* cause — to.

'nautical *adj* of ships or sailors.

'naval *adj* of a navy: **— officers.**

nave *n* central part of a church, where the congregation sits.

'navigate *v* direct the course of (a ship or aircraft). **'navigable** *adj* (of a river, etc) that can be used by ships; (of ships) in good condition for sailing, etc. **,navi'gation** *n* science of navigating.

'navy *n* a country's warships; their officers and men. — **'blue** *adj & n* dark blue (colour).

near *adv & prep* within a short distance in space or time. *adj* (-er, -est) **1** not far away in space or time. **2** close in relationship or friendship. **3** not generous (*with* one's money). **4** on the side of a horse, carriage, etc) —er to the side of the road. (cf off.) *v* come — (to). —'**by** *adv* close at hand. '—**ly** *adv* almost. **not**—**ly** (*enough*), far from (enough). '—**ness** *n*.

neat *adj* (-er, -est) **1** (liking to have everything) tidy, in good order, done carefully: *a* — *worker* (*desk*). **2** simple and pleasant: *a* — *dress*. **3** cleverly said or done: *a* — *answer*. '—**ly** *adv*. '—**ness** *n*.

'nebula *n* (pl **'nebulae**) group of stars, mass of gas, so distant that it is seen only as an indistinct patch of light. **'nebulous** *adj* indistinct; vague.

'necessary *adj* which must be (done); which cannot be done without or escaped from. *n* (usu *pl*) thing(s) — for living. **'necessarily** *adv*. **ne'cessitate** *v* make —. **ne'cessity** *n* **1** urgent need. **2** sth that is —. **3** condition of being poor.

neck *n* **1** part of the body between the head and the shoulders. ⟹ p 29. — **and** —, side by side. **2** anything like a — in shape: *the* — *of a bottle*. '—**lace** *n* string of beads, pearls, etc, worn round the —. '—**tie** *n* band of material worn round a collar and tied in a knot in front.

need *v* **1** want; require: *We — more help*. **2** be obliged: *N— you go so soon?* *n* **1** in — of, wanting; not having enough of. **2** sth wanted or necessary. '—**ful** *adj* necessary. '—**less** *adj* unnecessary. —**s** *adv* (only in) **must**—**s** or —**s must**, be compelled to. '—**y** *adj* (-ier, -iest) poor; not having what is necessary for living.

'needle *n* **1** sharp steel instrument with a hole (called an *eye*) at one end for thread, used in sewing and darning. **2** long, thin needle-like instrument of wood, bone, steel, etc, for knitting. **3** pointer in a compass or on a dial.

'negative *adj* **1** (opp of *positive*) (of words and answers) meaning *no* or *not*. **2** (maths, of a quantity) that has to be subtracted from another quantity or from zero (o). **3** (photography) with the lights and shades reversed. *n* **1** — word or statement. **2** — quantity. **3** (photography) film or plate from which (positive) prints are made.

ne'glect *v* **1** fail to pay attention to or care for (eg one's children). **2** leave undone (what one ought to do). *n* —ing or being —ed: *in a state of —*.

'negligent *adj* taking too little care —**ly** *adv*. **'negligence** *n*. **'negligible** *adj* of little or no importance or size.

ne'gotiate *v* **1** discuss (sth *with sb*) in order to reach an agreement **2** arrange (*for* a sale, etc) by discussion. **3** get past or over (an obstacle). **ne,goti'ation** *n*.

'Negro *n* (pl -es) member (or, outside Africa, descendant) of one of the African races south of the Sahara. **'Negress** *n* woman —.

neigh *v & n* (make the) cry of a horse.

'neighbour *n* person living in a house, street, etc, near oneself person, thing, or country near (nearest) another. —**hood** *n* **1** (people living in a) district; area near the place or thing referred to **2** condition of being near. —**ing** *adj* bordering upon. —**ly** *adj* friendly; helpful.

'neither *adj & pron* not one nor the other (of two). *adv & conj* **1** — . . .

a necklace   a necktie (or tie)

nor, N— *you nor I could have been there.* **2** nor; and not: *If you don't go,* — *shall I.*

'**nephew** *n* son of one's brother or sister.

nerve *n* **1** fibre or bundle of fibres carrying feelings, etc, between the brain and parts of the body. **2** (*pl*) condition of being easily excited or worried: *suffering from* —*s; noises that get on her* —*s.* **3** quality of being bold and confident. **4** **strain every** — (to do sth), make the greatest possible effort. '**nervous** *adj* **1** of the —*s*(1). **2** having or showing —*s*(2): *feeling nervous* (ie worried or frightened).

nest *n* place made or chosen by a bird for its eggs; kind of place in which certain living things (eg wasps, ants) have and keep their young. *v* make and use a —.

'**nestle** *v* settle (*down*) comfortably and warmly; press against closely and lovingly.

net[1] *n* material of knotted string, hair, wire, etc; such material made up for a special purpose: *fishing-nets; mosquito-nets.* *v* (-tt-) catch (fish, etc) in or with a net. '**netting** *n* net material: *wire netting for the windows.* '**network** *n* complex system of lines that cross: *a network of railways (canals).*

net[2] *adj* remaining when nothing more is to be taken away. **net profit,** (when working expenses have been deducted). **net weight,** (of the contents only).

'**nettle** *n* common wild plant with leaves that sting when touched. *v* (fig) make rather angry; annoy.

neu'rotic *n & adj* (person) suffering from nervous disorder; (colloq) (sb who is) very excitable.

'**neuter** *adj* without male or female sex organs; (of words) neither feminine nor masculine.

'**neutral** *adj* **1** helping neither side in a war or quarrel; belonging to a — country. **2** not clearly one thing (eg colour) or another. *n* — person, country, etc. **neu'trality** *n* state of being —. —**ize** *v* make —.

'**never** *adv* not at any time; on no occasion. **N— mind !** Don't bother, it doesn't matter. —'**more** *adv* — again. —**the'less** *conj* in spite of that; yet.

new *adj* ('**newer,** '**newest**) **1** not

existing before; experienced for the first time. **2** rediscovered. **3** beginning again: *a new moon, New Year.* *adv* newly; just; recently: *new-laid eggs.* '**newcomers,** those recently arrived. '**newly** *adv* recently; in a new way.

news (*pl* news) *n* report or account of what has recently happened, of new facts, etc. '—**agent** *n* shopkeeper selling —papers, periodicals, etc. '—**paper** *n* set of printed and folded sheets containing —, etc; these printed sheets as material.

next *adj & n* coming nearest or immediately after; immediately following in time. —**door,** in or to the — house. *adv* after this (that); in the nearest place (to). *prep* — to.

nib *n* pointed metal tip of a pen.

'**nibble** *v* take tiny bites (*at* sth).

nice *adj* (-r, -st) **1** pleasant; agreeable. **2** with particular tastes; delicate; fussy: *too* — *about his food.* —'**ly** *adv.* —'**ty** *n* exactness.

nick *v & n* (make a) small V-shaped cut, esp as a record. **in the** — **of time,** only just in time.

'**nickel** *n* silver-white metal used in alloys; (USA) coin worth five cents.

'**nickname** *n* name given in addition to or altered from or used instead of the real name.

'**nicotine** *n* poisonous substance in tobacco.

niece *n* daughter of one's brother or sister.

night *n* period when there is no light from the sun. '—**dress,** '**nightgown** *n* long loose garment worn by women and children in bed. '**night-fall** *n* end of daylight. '—**mare** *n* dream causing fear. '—**ly** *adj & adv* done, happening, at — or every —. '**night-'watchman** *n* man employed to keep watch (eg in a factory) during the —.

'**nightingale** *n* small bird which sings sweetly.

nil *n* nothing; score of zero.

'**nimble** *adj* (-r, -st) quick-moving; (of the mind) sharp; quick to understand.

nine *n & adj* 9. **a — days' wonder,** sth that excites attention for a few days only. '—'**teen** *n & adj* 19. '—**ty** *n & adj* 90. **ninth** *n & adj* 9th; ⅑. '—**tieth** *n & adj* 90th; 90.

nip *n* **1** small, quick pinch or bite. **2** **a nip in the air,** a feeling of frost. *v* (-pp-) **1** give a nip to; stop or check the growth of. **2** hurry: *nip along (off, in)*. '**nipper** *n* **1** (*pl*) pincers. **2** (colloq) small child. '**nippy** *adj* (-ier, -iest) (of weather) cold.

'**nipple** *n* part of the breast through which milk comes.

'**nitrogen** *n* part of air which is not oxygen.

no *adj & adv* not any; not one. *int* stating disagreement or any negative.

no. =(serial) number: *No. 10*.

'**noble** *adj* (-r, -st) **1** having, showing, high character and qualities. **2** (of families) of high rank or birth. **3** splendid; that excites admiration. *n* person of high birth; peer. **no'bility** *n* **1** quality of being —. **2** the —s as a class. '**nobly** *adv*. —**man** *n* = —.

'**nobody** *n* not any person; no-one.

noc'turnal *adj* of, in, or done, active, or happening in, the night.

nod *v* (-dd-) **1** bow (the head) slightly and quickly to show agreement or as a familiar greeting. **2** let the head fall forward when sleepy. *n* nodding movement of the head.

No'el *n* Christmas.

noise *n* sound, esp loud unpleasant sound. —**less** *adj* silent. '**noisy** *adj* (-ier, -iest) making much —; full of —. '**noisily** *adv*.

'**nomad** *n* member of a tribe wandering from place to place with no fixed home. **no'madic** *adj* of —s.

'**nominal** *adj* **1** existing, etc, in name or word only, not in fact: *the —ruler*. **2** a — rent (sum), a small or inconsiderable one. —**ly** *adv*.

'**nominate** *v* put forward sb's name for election to a position. ,**nomi-'nation** *n* (right of) nominating. **nomi'nee** *n* person —d.

non- *prefix* who (which) is not; who (which) does not, etc: '*non-'smokers*.

'**Noncon'formist** *n* Protestant not conforming to the ritual, etc, of an established (4) Church.

'**nondescript** *adj* not easily classed; not having a definite character.

none *adj & n* not anything; not any person. *adv* (with *too*) not at all: *— too large*; (with comparative) not very much: *— the worse for his experiences*.

no'nentity *n* unimportant person.

'**nonplus** *v* (-ss-) surprise (sb) so that he does not know what to do.

'**nonsense** *n* foolish or meaningless talk, behaviour, etc. **non'sensical** *adj*.

nook *n* corner; sheltered place.

noon *n* 12 o'clock midday.

noose *n* loop of rope (with a knot) that becomes tighter when the rope is pulled.

nor *conj* (after *neither* or *not*) and not; and . . . not. ⇨ neither.

'**normal** *adj* in agreement with what is usual or regular. *n* **above (below)** —, above (below) what is usual or average. —**ly** *adv*.

north *n, adj, & adv* direction to one's left when facing the sunrise and to which a compass needle points. '—**erly** *adj & adv* (of winds) from the —; in or towards the —; '—**ern** *adj* in or of the —. '—**ward(s)** *adv* towards the —.

nose *n* **1** part of the face with which we smell. ⇨ p 30. **pay through the** —, pay a very high price. **2** any prominent feature at the front of an object: *the — of an aircraft*. **3** sense of smell. *v* **1** smell (about, for); discover by smelling: *— sth out*. **2** go forward carefully: *a ship nosing (its way) through the ice*. '**nose-dive** *v & n* (of an aircraft) (make a) quick descent with the — of the plane pointing to the earth. '**nosy** *adj* ('nosier, 'nosiest) (colloq) inquisitive.

nos'talgia *n* homesickness.

'**nostril** *n* either of the two openings into the nose.

not *adv* used to show the opposite or negative: *This is not true. I am not coming*.

'**notable** *adj* deserving to be noticed. '**notably** *adv*. ,**nota'bility** *n* (esp) important person.

'**notary** *n* (often — public) official with authority to write out legal documents and to record that he has witnessed signatures to them.

no'tation *n* system of signs or symbols representing numbers, amounts, musical notes, etc.

notch *v & n* (make a) V-shaped cut.

note *n* **1** short record (of facts, etc) made to help the memory. **2** short letter: *a — of thanks*. —**paper**, for writing letters, —s, etc. **3** short comment on or explanation of sth in a book, etc. **4** written or printed promise to pay money: *a £5 —; bank-notes.* **5** simple sound of a certain pitch or duration; sign (eg ♩, ♪) used to represent such a sound; any one of the keys of a piano or organ moved with the fingers. **6** quality (esp of voice) showing the nature of sth: *a — of triumph in his voice.* **7** distinction; importance. **8** notice; attention: *take — of; worthy of —.* *v* **1** notice; pay attention to. **2 — sth down**, write down. **'—d** *adj* well-known; famous. **'note-,worthy** *adj* deserving attention.

'nothing *n* not anything; o. **come to —**, have no result or success. **make — of**, be unable to understand; fail to use (eg opportunities); treat as if unimportant. **there is — for it but to**, the only possible way to is; we can only.

'notice *n* **1** (written or printed) news of sth about to happen or sth that has happened: *put up a —.* **2** warning given to or by sb about the ending of an agreement, etc: *give a servant a month's —.* **3 at short —**, with little warning. **4** attention. **take no — of**, ignore. **bring sth to the — of** sb, inform sb of sth. *v* take — of; see. **—able** *adj* easily seen or **—d**.

'notify *v* give notice of; report (*to*).

'notion *n* idea; opinion.

no'torious *adj* widely known (esp for sth bad). **,noto'riety** *n*.

,notwith'standing *conj* although. *prep* in spite of.

nought *n* nothing; the figure o.

noun *n* (grammar) word by which a person, thing, quality, etc, is named.

'nourish *v* **1** keep or make strong with food. **2** have or encourage (hope, hatred, etc). **—ment** *n* food; power of **—ing**.

'novel¹ *adj* strange; of a new kind. **—ty** *n* **1** newness; strangeness. **2** previously unknown thing, idea, etc; (*pl*) manufactured articles of various kinds and usu low value.

'novel² *n* made-up story in prose long enough to fill one or more books, about either imaginary or historical people. **—ist** *n* writer of **—s**.

No'vember *n* eleventh month of the year.

'novice *n* person who is still learning and who is without experience.

now *adv* at this time. **now and again, now and then**, sometimes; from time to time. **'nowa-days** *adv* in these days.

'nowhere *adv* not anywhere.

'nozzle *n* metal end of a hose.

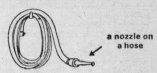

a nozzle on a hose

'nucleus *n* (*pl* **'nuclei**) central part round which other parts group or collect: *— of an atom.* **'nuclear** *adj* of a **—**, esp of an atom: *— physics, — war.*

nude *adj* unclothed. *n* (in art) **—** human figure.

nudge *v* push slightly with the elbow to attract attention. *n* push given in this way.

'nugget *n* lump of metal (esp gold) as found in the earth.

'nuisance *n* thing, person, act, etc, that causes trouble or offence.

null *adj* **— and void**, (legal) no longer binding(4). **'—ify** *v* make **—**.

numb *v* & *adj* (-er, -est) (make) without power to feel or move: *fingers —(ed) with cold.*

'number *n* **1** sign representing counted people, objects, etc: 1, 479, 2½, etc. **2** quantity or amount: *a large — of people.* **3** one issue of a periodical, esp for one day, week, etc. *v* **1** give a **— to**; put a **— on**. **2** add up to. **3 — sb among**, regard him as being among. **—less** *adj* more than can be counted.

'numeral *n* word or sign standing for a number. **nu'merical** *adj* of, in, numbers. **'numerous** *adj* very many; great in number.

nun *n* woman who lives in a society with other women in the service of God. **'nunnery** *n* house of nuns; convent.

'nuptial *adj* of marriage: *— Mass.* **—s** *n pl* wedding.

nurse *n* **1** woman who looks after babies and small children for a living. **2** person trained to carry out treatment of sick or injured people. v 1 act as a —. 2 feed (a baby) at the breast. 3 hold a baby (or child) in the arms. 4 look after carefully; try to cause the growth of (eg a new business). '—ry n 1 room or building for the special use of young children. 2 place where young plants and trees are raised.

nurture n training; care; education (of children). v give — to.

nut n 1 (often eatable) seed with a hard shell: *walnut, groundnut.* 2 small piece of metal for screwing on to the end of a bolt. '**nut-crackers** n pl instrument for cracking nuts. '**nutshell** n (esp) **in a nutshell**, in the smallest possible space, in the fewest possible words.

kernel

nutshell

nut

nuts

'**nutmeg** n hard nut grated for use in flavouring food.

nu'trition n 1 giving or taking nourishment. 2 science of food values. **nu'tritious** adj having a high value as food; nourishing.

'**nuzzle** v press or rub the nose (*against, into*): *The horse* —d (*against*) *my shoulder.*

'**nylon** n 1 man-made substance used for making clothes, ropes, etc. 2 (pl) stockings.

nymph n (Greek and Roman stories) one of the lesser goddesses, living in rivers, trees, etc.

O

O, oh int cry of surprise, fear, etc.

oak n (hard wood of) sorts of a large forest tree.

oar n pole with a flat blade used in rowing. '**oarsman** n rower.

an oarsman rowing

oar

o'asis n (pl o'ases) fertile place, with water and trees, in a desert.

oath n 1 undertaking, with God's help, to do sth; solemn declaration that sth is true: *on one's* —. 2 wrongful use of God's name or of sacred words; swear-word.

oats n pl (seed grains of a) plant grown in cool climates, providing food (esp for horses). '**oatmeal** n ground —, used for porridge, etc.

o'bedient adj doing, willing to do, what one is told to do. —**ly** adv. **o'bedience** n.

o'bese adj (of people) very fat. **o'besity** n fatness.

o'bey v do what one is told to do.

o'bituary n printed notice of sb's death, often with a short account of his life.

'**object¹** n 1 sth that can be seen or touched; material thing. **an object-lesson,** one (to be) taught or learnt from an example before the learner. 2 person or thing to which action or feeling or thought is directed; purpose: *succeed in one's* —; *with no* — in life.

ob'ject² v say that one is opposed (*to*). —**ion** n. —**ionable** adj likely to be —ed to; unpleasant.

ob'jective n object aimed at; purpose; (military use) point to which armed forces are moving in order to capture it. adj impartial.

obli'gation n promise, feeling of duty, condition, etc, that indicates what action ought to be taken. **be under an — to sb,** (feel) obliged to do sth for sb. **o'bligatory** adj required by law, rule, or custom.

o'blige v 1 bind by a promise, require (sb to do sth). 2 do sth for sb as a kind act or in answer to a request. **o'bliging** adj willing to help.

o'blique adj sloping; slanting.

o'bliterate v rub or blot out; remove all signs of. **ob,lite'ra-tion** n.

o'blivion n state of being quite

forgotten. o'blivious *adj* having no memory (*of*); unaware (*of*).

'oblong *n & adj* (figure) having four straight sides at angles of 90°, longer than it is wide. ⇨ p 253.

ob'noxious *adj* nasty; offensive.

'oboe *n* musical instrument similar to a clarinet. ⇨ p 180.

ob'scene *adj* (of words, behaviour) indecent, esp referring to sex; corrupting(2). ob'scenity *n*.

ob'scure *adj* 1 dark; hidden; not clearly seen or understood. 2 not well known. *v* make —. ob'scurity *n*.

ob'sequious *adj* too eager to obey, please, or show respect.

ob'serve *v* 1 see and notice; watch carefully. 2 pay attention to (laws, rules); celebrate. 3 say (*that*). ob'servance *n* observing(2) (of a law, etc). ob'servant *adj* quick to —(1); careful to —(2). ,obser'vation *n* 1 observing or being —d. 2 remark or statement. ob'servatory *n* building from which the stars, etc, may be —d. —r *n* person who —s.

ob'sess *v* (of fears, fixed or false ideas) be continually present in the mind of; distress. —ion *n*.

obsolete *adj* no longer in use. ,obso'lescent *adj* becoming —.

'obstacle *n* sth in the way that stops progress or makes it difficult.

obstinate *adj* 1 hard to persuade; self-willed. 2 not easily overcome. —ly *adv*. 'obstinacy *n*.

ob'struct *v* be, get, put sth in the way of; block up (a road, etc); prevent free movement; make (the development or progress of sth) difficult. —ion *n*.

ob'tain *v* 1 get; become the owner of; secure for oneself. 2 (of customs, rules, etc) be established or in use. —able *adj* that can be —ed.

ob'tuse *adj* 1 stupid. 2 (of an angle) over 90° and under 180°.

obvious *adj* easily seen or understood.

oc'casion *n* 1 time at which a particular event takes place; right time (for sth). rise to the —, show that one is equal to what needs to be done. 2 reason; cause. *v* be the —(2) of. —al *adj* not frequent. —ally *adv* now and then; at intervals.

oc'cult *adj* 1 hidden; secret. 2 mysterious; magical.

'occupy *v* 1 live in, use (a house, farm, etc); take and keep possession of (towns, etc, in war). 2 take up, fill (space, attention, time). ,occu'pation *n* (esp) employment; trade.

oc'cur *v* (-rr-) 1 take place; happen. 2 exist; be found. 3 — to, come into (the mind): *it —red to me that, I had the idea that.* —rence *n* happening.

'ocean *n* (one of the main divisions of the) great body of sea-water surrounding the land: *the Pacific —*.

'octagon *n* shape with eight angles and sides. ⇨ p 253. oc'tagonal *adj*.

Oc'tober *n* tenth month of the year.

'octopus *n* sea-animal with a soft body and eight tentacles. ⇨ p 247.

odd *adj* 1 of numbers other than even numbers (eg 1, 3, 5, 7, 9). 2 of one of a pair: *an odd sock*; of one or more of a set or series when not with the rest: *odd volumes of a set.* 3 with a little added: *20-odd miles.* 4 (-er, -est) strange. 5 odd jobs, various, unconnected pieces of work. at odd times (moments), at various and irregular times. 'oddity *n* (esp) peculiar person, thing, way of behaving. 'oddly *adv* strangely. 'oddments *n pl* various bits and pieces. odds *n pl* 1 the chances in favour of or against sth happening. 2 be at odds (with), be quarrelling (with). 3 odds and ends, small articles of various sorts and usu of small value.

ode *n* poem, usu in irregular metre and expressing noble feelings.

'odious *adj* hateful; repulsive.

'odour *n* smell. —less *adj*.

o'er *adv & prep* (poet) over.

of *prep* 1 belonging to; related to. 2 made with: *a ring of gold*; describing: *a woman of great beauty.* 3 about: *I think of her often.* 4 (cause): *He died of malaria.*

off *prep* 1 at a distance; away from. 2 close by: *an island off the coast.* 3 branching out from: *a street off London Road. adv* 1 at or to a distance. 2 (separation): *Take off your coat*; (disconnection): *Switch off the light.* 3 (completion): *Finish off that job by tomorrow.* 4 (decay): *That meat is off.* off and on, at times; at intervals. *adj* **1 the off side**, the further or far side; (of horses, cars, etc) of the side farther from the side of the road (in Gt Brit the right side). **2 off chance**, very small likelihood. **in one's off time**, in one's spare time. **'off'hand** *adj* (of behaviour) without enough respect. *adv* without thought or preparation.

'offal *n* inner parts of an animal used as food: *liver, heart*, etc.

of'fence *n* **1** crime; sin; the breaking of a rule. **2** the hurting of sb's feelings; condition of being hurt in one's feelings. **3** that which annoys the senses or makes sb angry. **4** attacking: *weapons of —*. **of'fend** *v* **1** do wrong; commit an —(1). **2** give —(2) to. **3** be displeasing to. **of'fender** *n*. **of'fensive** *adj* **1** causing —(2). **2** used for, connected with, attack. *n* **take the offensive**, begin the attack. **of'fensively** *adv*.

'offer *v* **1** hold out, put forward, to be taken or refused; say what one is willing to pay, give, or exchange for sth. **2** present to God: — (*up*) *a prayer*. **3** attempt: *—ing no resistance*. *n* statement —ing to do or give sth; that which is —ed. **—ing** *n* sth —ed or presented.

'office *n* **1** (often *pl*) room(s) used as a place of business for clerical work. **2** (buildings of a) government department, including the staff, their work and duties: *the Foreign O—; a post —*. **3** the work which it is sb's duty to do, esp a public position of authority: *to resign —*. **4** (*pl*) attentions; help. **through the good —s**, because of (sb's) kind help. **'office-boy** *n* boy employed to do the less important duties in an —.

'officer *n* **1** person appointed to command others in the armed forces, in ships and aircraft, the police force, etc. **2** person with a position of authority or trust, esp in the Government service: *customs —s*. **3** (of a society) the secretary, treasurer, etc.

of'ficial *adj* **1** of a position of trust or authority; said, done, etc, with authority. **2** suitable for, characteristic of, persons holding office(3). *n* person holding a senior government position or engaged in

public work. **—ly** *adv* in an — manner; with — authority. **of'ficiate** *v* perform the duties of an office or position. **of'ficious** *adj* too ready to offer help, advice, etc.

'offing *n* **be in the —**, be likely to occur.

'offset *v* compensate for; balance.

'offshoot *n* stem or branch growing out from a main stem, etc.

'offspring *n* (*pl* **'offspring**) child-(ren); young animals.

'often *adv* (-er, -est) many times; in a large proportion of instances.

'ogre *n* (in fairy tales) cruel man-eating giant. **'ogress** *n* female —.

oil *n* (sorts of) (usu easily-burning) liquid which does not mix with water, obtained from animals (e g whale oil), plants (e g coconut oil), or from wells (e g petroleum). *v* put oil on or into. **'oil-colours** *n pl* (also **oils**) paint made by mixing colouring matter in oil. **'oilskin** *n* (coat, etc, of) cloth treated with oil to make it keep out water. **'oily** *adj* (-ier, -iest) of or like oil; covered with oil.

'ointment *n* paste made from oil or fat and used on the skin.

'O'K *int* indicating agreement, satisfaction; all right.

old *adj* ('older, 'oldest) **1** of age: *How old is the baby?* **2** (contrasted with *young*) having lived (existed) for a long time; having been used on many occasions; very familiar: *an old friend*. ⇨ **elder**. **'old fashioned** *adj* out of date; keeping the old ways and customs.

'olive *n* (tree with) small fruit with a stone-like seed. **hold out the — branch**, show that one is ready to discuss peace. *adj* yellowish-green or yellowish-brown.

'omelet(te) *n* eggs beaten together and fried or baked quickly.

'omen *n* sign of good or evil fortune. **'ominous** *adj* of bad —; threatening.

o'mit *v* (-tt-) fail (to do sth); fail to include (sth); leave out: — *the next chapter*. **o'mission** *n* —ting sth —ted.

om'nipotent *adj* having power over all.

om'niscient *adj* knowing all things.

om'nivorous *adj* eating all kind of food.

on *prep & adv* **1** in contact with (from above); covering; near: *a town on the coast.* **2** about: *a book on history.* **3** towards: *hurry on.* **4** connected; available.

once *adv* on one occasion; at some time during the past. **— in a while**, occasionally. **— and for all**, now and for the last time. **— upon a time**, at some time in the past. **at —**, now; immediately. **all at —**, all together; suddenly. *conj* from the moment that.

one *adj & pron* **1** a single; I: *one new penny* (1p). **2** any person: *One does not know who one may meet here.* **one by one**, one after the other, one at a time. **it's all one to me**, it doesn't affect me. **one'self** *pron* referring to the speaker or people in general: *One should not be too proud of oneself.* **'one-'sided** *adj* (esp) concerning with, seeing, only one side of an argument.

onerous *adj* needing effort.

onion *n* vegetable plant with a sharp taste and smell. ⇨ p 306.

onlooker *n* person who looks on while sth is happening.

only *adj* that is the one; single example; single; the one group: *the — men who can go.* *adv* solely; no one more; nothing more: *Only five men went home.* **if —**, ⇨ if. *conj* except that; but it must be added that.

onset *n* attack; vigorous start.

onslaught *n* furious attack.

onus *n* responsibility for, burden of, doing sth.

onward(s) *adj & adv* forward(s).

ooze *n* soft liquid mud (eg at the bottom of a lake). *v* (of thick liquids) pass slowly through small openings.

opal *n* precious stone in which changes of colour are seen.

o'paque *adj* not allowing light to pass through.

open *adj* **1** not closed, so that people and things can go in, out, or through; not covered; spread out or unfolded (maps, charts, etc); (of a book) showing some pages inside. **2** in the **— air**, outdoors. **an — boat**, one with no deck. **— competitions (scholarships,** *etc*), not limited to any special persons. **the — country**, land not built over, not covered with forests, etc. **have an — mind**, be ready to consider new ideas, etc. **an — question**, one not yet settled or decided. **the — sea**, part of it far from land. **3 — to**, willing to listen to (reasons, etc) or to consider (an offer, etc); not protected against (attack). *n* **the —**, the **— air**, the country. *v* **1** cause to be **—**, unfastened, uncovered; cut or make an **—ing in**. **2 — out**, unfold, spread out. **— up**, make **—**; make possible the development of (a country, etc). **3 — fire** (*at*, *on*), start shooting. **—ing** *n* **1 — space**; way in or out; beginning (of a play, game, music, etc). **2** vacant position (in a business firm, etc). **—ly** *adv* without secrecy; frankly. **,open-'handed** *adj* generous. **,open-'hearted** *adj* sincere; kind.

'opera *n* dramatic composition with music in which the words are sung. **,ope'ratic** *adj.*

'operate *v* **1** (cause to) work, be in action, have an effect. **2 — on sb** (*for sth*), perform a surgical operation on. **,ope'ration** *n* **1** working; way in which sth works. **come into operation**, start operating; become effective. **2** sth (to be) done: *start operations.* **3** (*pl*) movements of men, ships, etc, by the armed forces. **4** cutting of the body by a surgeon (to remove diseased parts, etc). **'operative** *adj* operating; effective. *n* worker at a machine (esp in a factory). **'operator** *n* person who works sth (eg a piece of apparatus): *telephone-operator.*

o'pinion *n* belief or judgement not founded on complete knowledge. **in my —**, it seems likely to me. **public —**, what most people think.

'opium *n* substance used to relieve pain and as a harmful drug.

op'ponent *n* person against whom one fights, plays games, argues, etc.

'opportune *adj* **1** (of time) good for a purpose. **2** done, coming, at a favourable time. **,oppor'tunist** *n* person who is more anxious to gain an advantage than to consider whether he is gaining it fairly. **,oppor'tunity** *n* favourable time or chance (*for* sth, *of doing* sth, *to do* sth).

op'pose *v* 1 set oneself against (sb or sth). 2 put (sth) forward as a contrast (*to*). **'opposite** *adj* 1 facing: *the house opposite* (*to*) *mine.* 2 entirely different from; contrary. **,oppo'sition** *n* 1 resistance: *under heavy opposition*; opposing. 2 **the Opposition,** members of the political party or parties opposing the Government.

op'press *v* 1 rule unjustly or cruelly. 2 cause to feel troubled (in mind or spirit) or uncomfortable: *—ed by the heat* (*by the fear of poverty*). **—ion** *n.* **—ive** *adj* unjust; hard to bear. **—ively** *adv.* **—or** *n* unjustly cruel person.

'optical *adj* of the sense of sight; for helping eyesight: *— instrument* (eg a microscope). **op'tician** *n* person who makes or sells — instruments, esp spectacles.

'optimism *n* confidence in success; tendency to look upon the bright side of things. **'optimist** *n* optimistic person. **,opti'mistic** *adj* expecting the best.

'option *n* right or power of choosing; thing that is or may be chosen. **—al** *adj.*

'opulent *adj* rich; plentiful; luxuriant. **'opulence** *n.*

or *conj* expressing a choice between two alternatives: *Is it a boy or a girl?*; if not: *Run, or you will be late*; expressing a similarity between two things, ideas, etc: *a pound or one hundred new pence.*

'oral *adj* using the spoken, not the written, word: *an — examination.*

'orange *n* (evergreen tree with) round, thick-skinned juicy fruit, ⇨ p 115; colour of the peel of some varieties between yellow and red. **—'ade** *n* drink made from — juice.

o,rang-u'tan *n* long-armed ape. ⇨ p 317.

o'ration *n* formal speech made in public. **'orator** *n* person who makes speeches (esp a good speaker). **,ora'torical** *adj* of speech-making. **'oratory** *n* art of speaking in public.

'orbit *n* path followed by a heavenly body round another: *the earth's — round the sun*; path followed by a spacecraft round the earth, moon, etc. *v* make an — round.

'orchard *n* piece of ground (usu enclosed) with fruit-trees.

'orchestra *n* band of persons playing musical (including esp stringed) instruments in a theatre or at a concert; place in a theatre for such a band. **or'chestral** *adj.*

'orchid *n* sorts of plant, many of which have flowers of bright colours and unusual shapes.

or'dain *v* 1 (of God, fate, the law etc) decide; appoint; give orders (*that*). 2 make (sb) a priest, etc.

or'deal *n* 1 (in former times) method of deciding sb's guilt or innocence by requiring him to endure a physical test such as passing through fire unharmed: *trial by —.* 2 any severe test of character or endurance.

'order *n* 1 way in which things are placed in relation to one another: *in — of size.* 2 condition in which everything is carefully arranged; working condition: *out of —.* 3 (condition brought about by) good and firm government, obedience to the laws. 4 rules at a public meeting: *called to — by the Chairman.* 5 command given with authority. 6 request to supply goods. **on —,** asked for but not yet supplied. **made to —,** made according to special or personal requirements. 7 written direction (esp to a post office) to pay money. 8 **in — that,** so that, with the intention that. **in — to** (*do* sth), with the purpose of (doing sth). 9 rank or class in society; group of people belonging to or appointed to a special class (eg a brotherhood of monks). **take holy —s,** become a priest. *v* 1 give an —(5),(6) (sb) or for (sth). 2 put sth in —(2); arrange. **—ly** *adj* 1 well arranged; in good —(2). 2 peaceful; well-behaved. *n* army officer messenger; army hospital attendant.

'ordinal *n & adj* (number) showing order or position in a series, as *first, second, third*, etc.

'ordinance *n* order given by an authority: *—s of the City Council.*

'ordinary *adj* normal; usual; average. *n* **out of the —,** unusual. **,ordi'nation** *n* ceremony of ordaining(2).

'ordnance *n* artillery.

ore n rock, earth, etc, from which metal can be extracted.

organ n 1 any part .of an animal body or plant serving an essential purpose (eg the nose or heart; stamens in flowers). ⇨ p 30. 2 means for making known what people think (—s of public opinion) or for getting sth done (—s of government). 3 musical instrument from which sounds are produced by air forced through pipes. **organic** adj 1 of the bodily —s. 2 having —s(1). 3 an —ic whole, an organized whole. an —ic part, a structural part. —ism n living being with parts that work together. —ist n person who plays the —(3).

organize v put into working order; arrange in a system; make preparations for. **organization** n (esp) —d body of persons; —d system. —r n person who —s.

orgy n occasion of wild merry-making.

orient n the O—, (poetical name for) countries of Asia east of the Mediterranean. **oriental** adj of the O—. n —al person.

origin n starting-point; (person's) parentage.

original adj 1 first or earliest. 2 newly formed or created; not copied or imitated: —ideas. 3 able to produce new ideas, etc. n 1 that from which sth is copied. 2 the language in which sth was first written. —ly adv. o,rigi'nality n quality of being —; ability to create. **originate** v 1 come into being (from or in a place, with sb). 2 be the inventor of; start; give origin to.

ornament n 1 sth designed or used to add beauty to sth else. 2 person, act, quality, etc, adding beauty, charm, etc (to). v be an — to; make beautiful. **orna'mental** adj.

or'nate adj richly decorated.

orphan n child who has lost one or both of its parents by death. —age n charitable home for —s.

orthodox adj (having opinions, beliefs, etc, that are) generally accepted or approved. —y n being —.

oscillate v (cause to) swing or move to and fro between two points as a pendulum does.

os'tensible adj (of reasons, etc) put forward in an attempt to hide the real reason. **os'tensibly** adv.

osten'tation n display (of wealth, learning, etc) to obtain admiration, envy, etc. **osten'tatious** adj fond of, showing, —.

ostracize v shut out from society; refuse to meet, talk to, etc. **ostracism** n.

ostrich n large, fast-running bird, unable to fly. ⇨ p 26.

other pron & adj not the same as that already referred: You go this way and I'll go the — way. adv in a different way: I could not treat him — than fairly. the — day, a few days ago. — than, different from. —wise adv differently; in different conditions; in — respects. conj if not; or else.

otter .n fur-covered, fish-eating water animal ⇨ p 12; its fur.

ought v 1 indicating obligation: I — to go home soon. 2 indicating probability: He — to be here soon.

ounce n unit of weight, $\frac{1}{16}$ of a pound¹(1) or 28·3 grams.

our adj of or belonging to us: That is our book. **ours** pron & adj belonging to us: That book is ours. **ourselves** pron: We hurt ourselves when we fell over.

oust v drive or push (sb) out (from his position, etc).

out adv away from, not in or at a place; not in the usual condition. **out and out**, thorough(ly). **out of date**, old-fashioned. **out of breadth**, breathing fast. **out of doors**, in the open air. **out-of-the-way**, remote; unusual. **outer** adj of or for the outside; further from the middle or inside. **outermost** adj furthest from the middle or the inside.

out'bid v (⇨ bid) bid higher than (sb else) at a sale, etc.

outbreak n a breaking out (of war, disease, etc).

outburst n a bursting out (of anger, etc).

outcast n & adj (person or animal) driven out from home or society.

out'class v be much better than.

outcome n effect or result of an event, of circumstances.

outcrop n layer or mass (of rock, etc) not covered with soil.

outcry n loud shout (of fear, etc); public protest (against sth).

out'distance v travel faster than; leave (others) far behind.

out'do v do more or better than.

'out'door adj for, done in, the open air: — games. —s adv.

'outer ⇨ out.

'outfit n all the clothing or articles needed for a purpose: a camping —. —ter n shopkeeper selling equipment, esp clothing.

out'grow v grow too large or too tall for (eg one's clothes); grow faster or taller than (sb else); leave behind, as one grows older (childish ways, bad habits, etc).

'outgrowth n 1 natural development or product. 2 offshoot.

'outing n short pleasure trip.

out'landish adj looking or sounding strange or foreign.

out'last v last or live longer than.

'outlaw n (olden times) person punished by being placed outside the protection of the law; criminal. v make (sb) an —.

'outlay n spending; money spent (for materials, work, etc).

'outlet n 1 way out for water, steam, etc. 2 means or occasion for releasing (one's feelings, energies, etc).

'outline n 1 line(s) showing shape or boundary. 2 statement of the chief facts, points, etc: an — of British history. v draw in —(1); give an —(2) of.

out'live v live longer than; live until (sth) is forgotten.

'outlook n 1 view on which one looks out. 2 what seems likely to happen in future. 3 person's way of looking at a problem.

'outlying adj remote; far-off.

out'number v be greater in number than.

'out-of-'date adj ⇨ date¹.

'out-,patient n person visiting a hospital for treatment but not lodged there. (cf in-patient.)

'outpost n (soldiers in an) observation post¹(1) at a distance from the main body of troops.

'output n quantity of goods, etc, produced or work done.

'outrage n (act of) extreme violence or cruelty; act that shocks public opinion, the feelings. v be guilty of —; do sth that shocks people. **out'rageous** adj shocking; cruel; immoral.

,out'right adv 1 openly, with nothing held back. 2 completely, at one time. adj positive, thorough.

'outset n start.

'out'side n, adj, & adv (of, on, nearer the) outer side, surface, or part. **have an — chance**, be very unlikely to. **—r** n 1 sb who is not, or who is considered unfit to be, a member of a group, society, etc. 2 sb with an — chance of winning a game, passing an examination, etc. **at the (very) —**, at the most.

'outskirts n pl borders or outlying parts (esp of a town).

out'spoken adj frank.

out'standing adj 1 easily noticed or visible. 2 (of work, payments, etc) still to be attended to.

out'strip v (-pp-) do better than; pass (sb) in a race, etc.

'outward adj 1 of or on the outside. 2 going out: the — voyage. **—(s)** adv towards the outside. **—ly** adv on the surface; as far as can be seen.

out'weigh v be greater in weight, value, or importance than.

out'wit v (-tt-) get the better of by being cleverer or more cunning.

'oval adj & n (having the) shape of an egg. ⇨ p 253.

o'vation n enthusiastic expression of welcome or approval.

'oven n enclosed box-like space that is heated for baking food.

'over adv 1 indicating loss of balance, change from one side to another: fall —; cross —; change —; etc. 2 from beginning to end: Think (Read) it —. Go — it again. 3 remaining: money left —; ended: the meeting is —. prep partly or completely covering a surface; at or to a higher level than and not touching; from one side to the other: — a bridge; more than: — £5. **— and above**, in addition (to).

,over- prefix too (much): ,overpo'lite; ,—'tired; ,—'heated; ,—'charge.

'overall(s) n loose-fitting garment worn over ordinary clothes to keep them clean.

,over'balance v (cause to) lose balance; fall over.

,over'bearing adj masterful; forcing others to do one's will.

'overboard adv over the side of a ship into the water: fall —.

overcast adj (of the sky) covered with dark clouds; (fig) gloomy.

overcoat n long coat worn out of doors over ordinary clothes.

overcome v (pt ,over'came, pp ,over'come) 1 get the better of; be too strong for. 2 make weak: — by emotion.

overdo v (pt ,over'did, pp ,over'done) do too much; exaggerate.

overdraw v (pt ,over'drew, pp ,over'drawn) draw a cheque for a greater sum than one has in the bank. **'overdraft** n amount of money by which a bank account is overdrawn.

overdue adj beyond the time fixed (for delivery, payment, etc).

overgrown adj 1 having grown too fast. 2 covered (with sth that has grown over): flower-beds — with weeds.

overhang v (pt & pp ,over'hung) be or hang over like a shelf.

overhaul v examine thoroughly in order to learn about the condition of; put into good condition. **'overhaul** n -ing.

overhead adj 1 raised above the ground: — cables. 2 —s, (business) charges, expenses, etc, needed for carrying on a business (eg for rent, salaries, advertising), not manufacturing costs. adv above.

overhear v (pt & pp ,over'heard) hear without the knowledge of the speaker(s); hear what one is not intended to hear.

overjoyed adj greatly delighted (at).

overlap v (-pp-) cover partly and extend beyond one edge: —ping tiles.

overlook v 1 have a view of from above. 2 fail to see or notice; pay no attention to.

overnight adv 1 on the night before. 2 for the night. **'overnight** adj during the night: an — journey.

overpower v overcome; be too strong for. **-ing** adj too strong.

overreach v get the better of (by trickery). — oneself, fail in one's object, damage one's own interests, by being too ambitious.

override v (pt ,over-rode, pp ,over-'ridden) decide against (sb's decisions, claims, etc) (esp by using one's higher authority).

overrule = override.

overrun v (pt ,over'ran, pp ,over-'run) 1 spread over and occupy. 2 go beyond (a limit).

oversea(s) adj & adv (at, to, from, for, places) across the sea.

oversee v (pt ,over'saw, pp ,over-'seen) look after, control (work, workmen). **'overseer** n foreman.

oversight n failure to notice sth or do sth: through an unfortunate —.

oversleep v (pt & pp ,over'slept) sleep too long; continue sleeping after the (agreed) time for waking.

overstep v (-pp-) go beyond: He —ped his authority.

overt adj done openly and publicly, not secretly. **—ly** adv.

overtake v (pt ,over'took, pp ,over'taken) 1 come or catch up with; outstrip. 2 (of storms, troubles) come upon suddenly, by surprise.

overthrow v (pt ,over'threw, pp ,over'thrown) defeat; put an end to. **'overthrow** n defeat; fall.

overtime n & adv (time spent at work) after the usual hours.

overture n 1 (often pl, make —s to) approach made to sb with the aim of starting discussions: peace —s. 2 musical composition played as an introduction to an opera.

overwhelm v (weigh down; crush; cover over; overcome completely: —ed by the enemy's forces; —ed by grief.

overwrought adj tired out by too much work or excitement.

owe v 1 be in debt to (sb, for sth). 2 be under an obligation to give: owe loyalty to the king. **'owing** adj still to be paid. **'owing to** prep because of.

owl n night-flying bird that lives on mice and small birds. ⇨ p 26.

own adj emphasizing the ownership or special characteristic of sth: This is my (very) own pen. hold one's own, keep one's position against attack; not lose strength. on one's own, independent(ly); without a companion. v 1 possess. 2 agree; confess; recognize: own (up) to a fault, confess to it. **'owner** n person who owns(1) sth.

ox n (pl 'oxen) 1 general name (esp in pl) for domestic cattle kept for supplying milk and meat. 2 (esp) fully-grown castrated bullock used to pull a wagon, etc.

'oxygen *n* gas without smell, colour, or taste, necessary for life.

'oyster *n* kind of shellfish, usu eaten uncooked, whose shell sometimes contains a pearl. ⇨ p 247.

oz. written short form of *ounce*.

P

p *n* abbr for penny or pence in British decimal currency.

pa *n* (child's name for) father.

pace *n* 1 (distance covered by the foot in a) single step in walking or running. 2 rate or speed. **keep — with**, go at the same speed as. 3 **put sb through his —s**, test his abilities. *v* 1 walk with slow or regular steps. 2 measure by taking —s: *— out (off) a distance of* 3 *yards*.

pa'cific *adj* peaceful; making or loving peace. **'pacifism** *n* principle that war should and could be abolished. **'pacifist** *n* believer in pacifism. **'pacify** *v* calm and quieten.

pack *n* 1 bundle of things tied or wrapped together. 2 number of dogs (*hounds*) kept for hunting, or of wild animals (eg wolves) that go about together. 3 number of (bad) persons or things: *a — of thieves*. 4 complete set of playing-cards. *v* 1 put (things) into a box, bundle, bag, etc; fill (a box, etc) with things. 2 crush or crowd (into a place). 3 put soft material into or round (to keep sth safe or to prevent loss or leakage). 4 — **sb off**, **send sb —ing**, send him away quickly. **'—age** *n* parcel; bundle. **'—et** *n* small bundle, esp of letters or papers. **'—ing** *n* act of —ing; material used in —ing goods.

pact *n* a solemn agreement.

pad *n* 1 kind of cushion used to prevent damage, give comfort, improve the shape of sth, etc. 2 number of sheets of writing-paper fastened together along one edge. *v* (-dd-) put a pad(1) or pads(1) on or in.

'paddle *n* short oar with a broad blade at one or both ends. *v* 1 send

(a canoe) through the water by using —(s). 2 walk with bare feet in water; move the hands about in water.

'paddock *n* small grass field.

'paddy *n* rice in the husk.

'padlock *v & n* (fasten with a) lock with a movable part that can be passed through a staple[1].

'pagan *n & adj* (person who is) not a believer in one of the chief religions of the world.

page[1] *n* one side of a leaf of paper in a book, newspaper, etc.

page[2] *n* boy servant (in a club or hotel).

'pageant *n* 1 public entertainment, often outdoors, in which historical events are acted. 2 procession of finely dressed people (eg at a coronation). **—ry** *n* splendid display.

paid ⇨ pay.

pail *n* metal bucket.

pain *n* 1 suffering of the body or mind. 2 (*pl*) trouble(2). **take —s**, work carefully. 3 **penalty**. *v* cause —to. **'—ful(ly)** *adj & adv*. **'—lessly** *adj & adv*. **'—staking** *adj* taking great trouble.

paint *n* colouring matter (to be mixed with oil or other liquid). *v* 1 coat with —. 2 make a picture (of), with —. **'—er** *n* 1 workman who —s (buildings), etc). 2 artist who —s (pictures). **'—ing** *n* art, act of —ing; painted picture.

pair *n* 1 two things of the same kind used together: *a — of shoes*. 2 single article with two parts always joined: *a — of trousers (scissors)*. *v* join in —s. **— off**, form into —s; arrange in —s.

pal *n* (colloq) comrade; friend.

'palace *n* house of a ruler (eg king) or bishop; large, splendid house.

'palate *n* 1 roof of the mouth. 2 sense of taste. **'palatable** *adj* agreeable to the taste or (fig) to the mind.

pale[1] *adj* (-r, -st) 1 (of a person's face) having little colour; looking ill. 2 (of colours) faint. *v* become —.

pale[2] *n* 1 long pointed piece of wood used for fences. 2 limits of what is considered good social behaviour: *outside the —*. **'paling(s)** *n* fence of —s(1).

'palette *n* board on which an artist mixes his colours.

pall¹ *v* become uninteresting.

pall² *n* heavy cloth spread over a coffin; (fig) any dark heavy covering: *a — of smoke.*

'palliate *v* lessen the severity of (pain, disease); excuse the seriousness of (a crime, etc).

'pallid *adj* pale(1); ill-looking.

'pallor *n* paleness (of face).

palm¹ *n* inner part of the hand between the wrist and fingers. *v —* sth off on sb, persuade him, by trickery, to take sth of little value. **'—ist** *n* person who claims to tell a person's future by examining the lines on his —.

palm² *n* 1 (sorts of) tree with no branches and a mass of large wide leaves at the top: *coconut —.* 2 palm-leaf as a symbol of victory or success.

'palpitate *v* (of the heart) beat rapidly; (of a person) tremble (eg with terror). **'palpi'tation** *n*.

'paltry *adj* (-ier, -iest) worthless; contemptible.

'pamper *v* indulge too much.

'pamphlet *n* small paper-covered book, esp on a topical question.

pan *n* flat dish, often shallow and without a cover, used for cooking. **pan-** *prefix* of or for all: *pan-Asian.*

'pande'monium *n* (scene of) wild and noisy disorder.

'pander *v* give help or encouragement (*to* sb, *to* sb's evil acts and desires).

pane *n* single sheet of glass in (a division of) a window.

'panel *n* 1 separate part of the surface of a door, wall, etc, usu raised above or sunk below the surrounding area. 2 list of names of persons summoned to serve on a jury, etc. *v* (-ll-) put —s on or in. **—ling** *n* —led work.

pang *n* sudden feeling of pain or remorse.

'panic *n* unreasoning, uncontrolled, quickly spreading fear. **—ky** *adj*.

'pannier *n* one of a pair of baskets placed across the back of a horse, a motor-bike, etc, for carrying things.

'pano'rama *n* wide, uninterrupted view; constantly changing scene.

pant *v* 1 take short, quick breaths. 2 have a strong wish (*for* sth, *to do* sth). 3 — out, say while —ing(1).

'panther *n* kind of leopard.

'pantomime *n* 1 Christmas drama for children, usu based on a fairy-tale. 2 mime.

'pantry *n* 1 room (in a hotel, ship, mansion) in which glass, table-linen, etc, are kept. 2 (in a house) larder.

pants *n pl* 1 two-legged under-garment for men hanging from the waist. 2 (colloq) trousers.

'pa(pa) *n* (child's name for) father.

'papacy *n* position of, authority of, the Pope. **'papal** *adj* of the —.

pa'paya, pa(w)paw *n* tropical tree; its fruit, like melon, green outside and yellow inside. ⇨ p 115.

'paper *n* 1 (substance usu made from wood-pulp and produced as) thin sheet(s) for writing, printing, drawing, etc. 2 newspaper. 3 (*pl*) documents showing who sb is, what authority he has, etc. 4 set of examination questions on a given subject. *v* paste — on (walls, etc).

par *n* 1 average or normal amount or degree. **above (below) par,** (of shares) above (below) the original price. 2 **on a par with,** equal to.

'parable *n* story designed to teach a moral lesson.

'parachute *n* apparatus used when jumping from an aircraft or for dropping supplies.

pa'rade *v* 1 (of troops) gather together for drilling, etc; march in procession. 2 make a display of. *n* 1 a parading of troops: *on —.* **parade-ground,** place used for this. 2 wide, often ornamental, pathway, esp on a sea front.

'paradise *n* 1 the Garden of Eden. 2 Heaven. 3 place of perfect happiness.

'paradox *n* statement which seems to say sth opposite to the truth: *'The child is father of the man'.*

'paraffin — oil, oil obtained from coal, petroleum, used for heating.

'paragon *n* (apparently) perfect example of a person or thing.

'paragraph *n* division of a piece of writing, usu dealing with one main idea, started on a new line.

'parallel *adj* 1 (of lines) continuing at the same distance from one another. 2 exactly corresponding (*to*). *n* **1** — **of latitude**, line marking degree of latitude. **2** comparison: *draw a* — *between*. *v* be — *to*. ,**paral'lelogram** *n* four-sided figure whose opposite sides are —. ⇨ p 253.

pa'ralysis *n* loss of feeling or power to move in any or every part of the body. '**paralyse** *v* affect with —; make helpless.

'**paramount** *adj* of the greatest importance; having supreme authority.

'**parapet** *n* low wall (eg at the side of a bridge or enclosing a flat roof).

,**parapher'nalia** *n pl* various things used for carrying, sending or for sb's work.

'**paraphrase** *v & n* (give a) restatement of the meaning of (a piece of writing) in other words.

'**parasite** *n* animal or plant living on or in another and getting its food from it: *A flea is a* —.

,**para'sol** *n* umbrella for the sun.

'**paratrooper** *n* soldier trained to use a parachute.

'**parcel** *n* thing(s) wrapped and tied up for carrying, sending by post, etc. *v* (-ll-) — **out**, divide; distribute.

parch *v* **1** (of the sun, thirst, etc) make hot or dry. **2** make dry by heating.

'**parchment** *n* writing material prepared from sheepskin; parchment-like paper.

pardon *v* forgive; excuse. *n* forgiveness. —**able** *adj* that can be —ed.

pare *v* cut away the outer part, edge, or skin of. — **sth down**, reduce. '**paring** *n* sth —d off.

'**parent** *n* father or mother; (*pl*) father and mother. —**age** *n*: *of unknown* —*age*, of unknown —s. **pa'rental** *adj* of a —.

pa'renthesis *n* (*pl* pa'rentheses) sentence within another, enclosed by brackets or commas; (*pl*) a pair of brackets ( ), [ ], etc.

'**pariah** *n* outcast.

'**parish** *n* division of a county for local government (in England and Wales), centred on a church: — *church* (*council*).

'**parity** *n* being equal or at par.

park *n* **1** public garden or recreation ground in a town. **2** area of grassland and trees round a large country house. **3** '**carpark**, place

a parking-meter

a parked car

where cars, etc, may be left for a time. *v* put or leave a motor-car in a —(3). '—**ing**-,**meter** *n* coin-operated machine for charging and timing parking spaces for cars.

'**parley** *n* conference, esp between leaders of two opposed armies.

'**parliament** *n* (esp in Gt Brit and other countries with representative government) supreme law-making council or assembly. ,**parlia'mentary** *adj*.

'**parlour** *n* sitting-room.

pa'rochial *adj* **1** of a parish. **2** (fig) limited; narrow: *a* — *outlook* (*mind*).

'**parody** *n* (piece of) writing imitating the style used by sb else. *v* make a — of.

pa'role *n* prisoner's promise, on being given certain privileges, that he will not try to escape.

'**paroxysm** *n* sudden attack (of pain, etc) or outburst (of anger, grief, etc).

'**parrot** *n* sorts of bird with a hooked bill, some of which can be taught to say words. ⇨ p 26.

'**parry** *v* turn aside (a blow, etc).

,**parsi'monious** *adj* too economical.

'**parsnip** *v* vegetable. ⇨ p 306.

'**parson** *n* (colloq) parish priest; any clergyman. —**age** *n* —'s house.

part *n* **1** some but not all of a thing or a number of things. **2** (*pl*) **these** (**those**) —**s**, this (that) district. **3** any one of a number of equal divisions. **4** person's share in some activity; his duty: *play a* — *in a play* (*in a conference*); *take* — *in an event*. **for my** —, as far as I am concerned. **5** what an actor says or does in a play, etc: *learning his* —**s**. **6 take sb's** —, give him support or approval. **take sth in good** —, not be offended. *v* **1** (cause to) separate or divide. — **company** (*with*), end a relationship (with). **2** — **with**, give up, give away. '—**ing** *n* (esp) line from which the hair is combed in opposite ways.

'—ly *adv* in —, not completely.
'— time *adj & adv* for only —
of the working week: — *time
teaching.*

par'take *v* (*pt* par'took, *pp*
par'taken) 1 have or take a share
(*in* sth). 2 have some (*of* the food,
drink, etc, provided): — *of a meal.*
3 have some of the characteristics
(*of* sth).

'partial *adj* 1 forming only a part;
not complete. 2 — to, having a
liking or taste for. 3 showing too
much favour to one person or side.
—ly *adv.* ,parti'ality *n* being
—(3) in treatment, judgement, etc.

par'ticipate *v* have a share, take
part (*in* a common act, feeling,
etc). par,tici'pation *n.*

'participle *n* verb form (eg *writing*
and *written*, the present and past
—s of *write*). ,parti'cipial *adj.*

'particle *n* very small bit: —*s of
dust; atomic —s.*

par'ticular *adj* 1 relating to one
as distinct from others: *in this —
case.* 2 especial. 3 hard to satisfy:
very — about what he eats. n
detail: *go into —s.* —ly *adv*
especially.

,parti'san *n* person devoted to a
political party, group, or cause.

par'tition *n* 1 division into parts.
2 that which divides, eg a thin
wall. 3 part formed by dividing.
v divide.

'partner *n* 1 person who takes part
with another or others in the work
and proceeds of some activity:
business —s; my tennis —. 2 husband
or wife. *v* be a — to.

par'took ⇨ partake.

'partridge *n* sorts of bird like the
pheasant; its flesh as food.

party *n* 1 body of persons united
in opinion or in support of a cause,
etc, esp in politics. 2 group of
persons travelling or working together. 3 meeting, by invitation,
of a group of persons, usu at a
private house, for pleasure.

pass *v* 1 go past; move towards
and beyond (a person, place, etc).
2 give by handing; give information: — *sth on* to others. 3 — a
remark, speak (about). — the
time of day (*with*), exchange a
greeting, etc, with. 4 change (*from*
one state of things to another).
5 come to an end. — away, die.

6 examine and accept; be examined
and accepted. 7 take place, be
done and said (*between* persons).
8 (of time) spend; be spent. 9 give
(an opinion, judgement, etc, *upon*
sb or sth). 10 — (sb or sth) by,
pay no attention to. — for, be
accepted as. — off, (of events) take
place (quietly, etc). — sb over,
disregard him. *n* 1 success in an
examination (without distinction
or honours). 2 (paper, ticket, etc,
giving) permission to travel, enter
or leave a building, etc. 3 come to
—, happen. bring to —, cause to
happen. 4 narrow way over or
between mountains. '—able *adj*
1 that can be —ed(1) over. 2 that
can be accepted as fairly good.
'—book *n* book with a customer's
bank account record. '—key *n* key
opening a number of different
locks. '—word *n* secret word
that enables sb to be known as a
friend by sentries, etc.

'passage *n* 1 act of going past,
through, or across; journey by sea.
2 way through; corridor. 3 enact-
ment of a bill²(3). 4 short extract
from a piece of writing.

'passenger *n* person travelling by
bus, tram, train, ship, etc.

'passion *n* strong feeling, esp of
love, hate, anger. —ate *adj* filled
with, showing, —; quickly or easily
moved by —.

'passive *adj* acted upon but not
acting; not offering active resistance: — *obedience* (*resistance*). —ly
adv.

'Passover *n* Jewish feast.

'passport *n* government document
to be carried by a traveller abroad,
giving personal particulars.

past *adj* of the time before the
present. *n* 1 — time; — events.
2 person's — life or experiences.
prep 1 after (in time). 2 up to and
further than. 3 beyond. *adv*
beyond in space; up to and further
than: *walk — the gate.*

paste *n* 1 soft mixture of flour,
fat, etc, for making pastry. 2 paste-
like mixture made from meat, fish,
etc. 3 mixture of flour and water
for sticking things together, esp
paper on walls or boards. *v* stick
(things *down, together, on,* etc)
with —(3). '—board *n* cardboard.

'pasteurize v rid bacteria from by heating and cooling it: —d milk.

'pastime n sth done to pass time pleasantly; a game.

'pastor n Christian minister (esp in a Nonconformist church).

'pastoral adj of shepherds and country life: — poetry.

'pastry n (pl -ies) paste(1) baked in an oven, with fruit, meat, etc.

'pasture, 'pasturage n grassland for cattle; grass on such land.

'pasty adj like paste¹(1): a — complexion, white and unhealthy.

pat v (-tt-) hit gently with the open hand or with sth flat: pat sb on the back (to show approval). n 1 a touch of this kind. 2 small mass of sth, eg butter, shaped by patting it.

patch n 1 small piece of material put on or over a hole or damaged place. 2 differently coloured part of a surface, etc. 3 small area of ground, esp for gardening. 4 not a — on, not nearly· so good as. v 1 put a — or —es on. 2 —sth up, mend roughly. — up a quarrel, settle it. '— y adj (-ier, -iest) (fig of work) of uneven quality.

'patent adj 1 — medicine, medicine made and sold by one company only. 2 — leather, leather made with a hard, smooth, shiny surface. n invention, process, etc, given protection by the law against imitation. v obtain protection for (an invention, etc).

pa'ternal adj of or like a father. pa'ternity n being a father; person's origin on the father's side.

path n 1 way made (across fields, through woods, etc) by people walking. 2 (also 'foot-) · pavement. 3 line along which sb or sth moves: the — of a comet, a rocket, etc.

pa'thetic adj sad; pitiful.

pa'thology n science of diseases. ,patho'logical adj of —; of the nature of disease. pa'thologist n expert in —.

'pathos n quality that arouses feelings of pity.

'patience n 1 (power of) enduring trouble or suffering without complaining; ability to wait for results, for other people, etc, or to work calmly and without haste. lose (one's) —, become angry. out of — (with), no longer able to endure.

2 kind of card game (usu for one person). 'patient adj having or showing —. n person receiving medical treatment.

'patriarch n old man who is highly respected.

'patriot n person who loves and is ready to defend his country. —ism n qualities and feelings of a —. ,patri'otic adj.

pat'rol v (-ll-) go round (a camp, town, the streets, etc) to see that all is well, keep a look-out (for wrongdoers, the enemy, etc). n 1 the act of —ling: soldiers on —. 2 person(s), ship(s), or aircraft on — duties.

'patron n 1 person who supports with money, etc, the artistic, etc, work of a person or society. 2 regular customer (at a shop, restaurant, etc). 3 — saint, saint looked upon as protecting (a church, town, etc). —age n support given by a —(1),(2). 2 —izing manner. —ize v 1 be a —(1),(2) to. 2 treat (sb) as if he were inferior.

'patter n sound of quick light taps or footsteps: the — of rain on a roof. v make this sound.

'pattern n 1 sth serving as a model, esp shape of a garment, cut out in paper, used in dressmaking, etc. 2 sample, esp a small piece of cloth. 3 ornamental design (on a carpet, wallpaper, etc).

'paucity n smallness of number or quantity.

'pauper n person with no income, esp one supported by charity.

pause n short interval or stop: a — in the conversation. v make a —.

pave v lay flat stones, bricks, etc on (a road, etc). — the way for, (fig) make conditions easy or ready for. '—ment n —d path at the side of a road for people on foot (cf USA sidewalk.)

pa'vilion n 1 ornamental building for concerts, dancing, etc. 2 building on a sports ground for the use of players, spectators, etc. 3 big tent.

paw n animal's foot that has claws. v feel, scratch, with the paws.

pawn¹ n least valuable piece in the game of chess; person made use of by others for their own advantage.

pawn² v leave (clothing, jewellery,

etc) as a pledge for money borrowed. *n* in —, —ed. '—broker *n* person licensed to lend money on the security of goods left with him. '—shop *n*. ..

pay *v* (*pt & pp* paid) **1** give (sb) money *for* goods, services, etc. **pay sb off**, pay him his wages and discharge him. **2** suffer pain or punishment (*for* sth done). **3** give (attention *to* sth); make (a call, a visit, *on* sb); offer (a compliment *to* sb). **4 pay out** (*rope*), let (it) pass out through the hands. *n* money paid for regular work or services, eg in the armed forces. **'payable** *adj* which must or may be paid. **'payment** *n* paying or being paid; sum of money paid; reward or punishment. .

pea *n* plant with seeds in pods, used as food; a seed. ⇨ p 306.

peace *n* **1** state of freedom from war and disorder. **2** rest; quiet; calm. **'—able** *adj* —ful; not quarrelsome. **'—ful** *adj* **1** loving —. **2** calm; quiet.

peach *n* (tree with) juicy round fruit with yellowish-red skin and a rough stone-like seed.

'peacock *n* large male bird. ⇨ p 26.

peak *n* **1** pointed top, esp of a mountain. **2** pointed front part of a cap (1) to give shade.

peal *n* **1** loud ringing of a bell, or of a number of bells with different notes. **2** loud echoing noise: —s of thunder (*laughter*). *v* (cause to) ring or sound loudly.

'peanut = groundnut. ⇨ ground.

pear *n* (tree with) sweet juicy fruit. ⇨ p 115.

pearl *n* silvery-white gem which forms in some oyster-shells, valued for its beauty.

'peasant *n* person working on the land, either for wages or on a very small farm which he rents or owns. —ry *n* the —s of a country; —s as a class.

peat *n* plant material partly decomposed by the action of water; piece of this cut out to be burnt as fuel.

'pebble *n* small smooth stone found in the sea, on a beach or in a river.

peck¹ *n* measure for dry goods (eg beans) equal to two gallons.

peck² *v* **1** strike (at) with the beak; get by doing this: *hens —ing corn*;

make (a hole) by —ing. **2** (colloq) — at one's food, eat little because one has no appetite. *n* stroke made by a bird with its beak.

pe'culiar *adj* **1** strange; unusual. **2** special. **3** — to, used, adopted, practised only, by: *a style of dress — to this region.* —ly *adv.* **pe,culi'arity** *n* sth strange or characteristic.

pe'cuniary *adj* of money.

'pedal *n* part of a machine or instrument (eg bicycle, sewing-machine, piano) worked by the foot or feet. *v* (-ll-) use —s.

'pedant *n* person who values book-learning, rules, etc, too highly. **pe'dantic** *adj.* —ry *n* tiresome or unnecessary display of learning.

'peddle *v* go from house to house selling small articles.

'pedestal *n* base of a column; base for a statue or other work of art.

pe'destrian *n* person walking in the street.

pedigree *n* line of family descent.

'pedlar *n* person who peddles goods.

peek *v* peep (*at* sth).

peel *v* **1** take the skin off (fruit, etc). **2** (of the skin of the body, wallpaper, etc) come off in bits or strips. *n* skin of fruit, potatoes, etc. ⇨ p 115. '—ings *n pl* pieces —ed off: *potato —ings.*

peep *v & n* (take a) short, quick look (usu without wanting to be seen).

peer¹ *v* look (*at, into,* sth) closely, as if or when unable to see well.

peer² *n* **1** person's equal in rank, merit, etc. **2** (in Gt Brit) nobleman; person with the right to sit in the House of Lords. **'—age** *n* the —s(2); the rank of a —(2). **'—ess** *n* wife of a —(2); woman —. **'—less** *adj* without an equal.

peg *n* wooden or metal pin or bolt used to fasten parts of woodwork together, to hang things on (eg *hat pegs*), to fasten things to a clothes-line, to stop up the hole in a barrel, etc. **a square peg in**

pegs

a round hole, a person unfitted for his position. v (-gg-) **1** fasten with pegs. **2** fix (prices, etc) by regulations. **3** mark (out) by putting pegs in the ground.

'pelican n large water-bird with a long beak under which is a pouch for storing food.

'pellet n small ball of sth soft (eg wet paper.

'pell-'mell adv in hurried disorder.

pelt¹ n animal's skin with the hair or fur on it.

pelt² v **1** attack (with stones, sticks, etc). **2** (of rain, etc) beat down; fall heavily. n at full —, at full speed.

'pelvis n cavity of the hip bones and lower backbone. ⇨ p 30.

pen¹ n instrument for writing with ink. v (-nn-) write (a letter, etc). 'pen-knife n small pocket-knife.

pen² n small closed-in space for sheep, cattle, etc. v (-nn-).

'penal adj connected with punishment: a — offence, one for which there is legal punishment; — servitude, imprisonment with hard labour for three years or more. —ize v **1** make (an act) punishable by law. **2** give a penalty(2) to (a player, etc). —ty n **1** punishment for wrongdoing, for failure to obey rules or keep an agreement, etc; suffering which wrongdoing brings. **2** (sport, etc) loss of points for breaking the rules.

penance n self-punishment undertaken to show repentance.

pence ⇨ penny.

'pencil n instrument for writing with a rod of lead(3) or coloured wax. v (-ll-) write or draw with a —.

'pending adj waiting to be settled. prep while waiting for.

'pendulum n weighted rod hung from a fixed point so that it swings freely, esp one regulating the movement of a clock.

'penetrate v make a way into or through; (fig) see into or through. 'penetrating adj (of a person, his mind) able to see and understand quickly and clearly; (of cries, voices) loud and clear; piercing. ,pene'tration n.

'penguin n flightless sea-bird of the Antarctic. ⇨ p 26.

pe'ninsula n area of land (eg Italy) almost surrounded by water.

'penitence n sorrow and regret for wrongdoing. 'penitent n & adj. (person) feeling regret; showing —.

'pennant, 'pennon n long, narrow triangular or swallow-tailed flag.

'penny n (pl 'pennies for a number of coins; pence, for value or cost). (p) British coin worth one hundredth of a pound¹(1). —worth, 'penn'orth n as much as a — will buy. 'penniless adj without money or property.

'pension n regular payment made by a government or former employer to a person no longer employed.

'pensive adj deep in thought.

pent · adj shut (up) in: pent-up feelings.

'pentagon n straight-sided figure with five (usu equal) angles. ⇨ p 253.

'penury n poverty.

'people n **1** men and women in general. **2** all those persons forming a nation or race. **3** (with pl form —s) race; nation: the —s of Asia. v fill with —; put — in.

'pepper n **1** hot-tasting powder made from dried berries. **2** red, yellow or green seed-pods of certain plants, used as vegetables. v **1** put —(1) on. **2** — sb with, pelt with. —y adj (fig) hot-tempered.

per prep for each, in each: per pound; per annum (year). per 'cent for (in) each hundred (abbr %) per'centage n rate or number per cent.

pe'rambulator n (colloq and more commonly pram) small four-wheeled carriage for a baby.

per'ceive v become aware of, esp through the eyes or the mind. per'ceptible adj that can be —d. per'ception n act or power of perceiving.

perch n bird's resting-place; rod or bar provided for this purpose. v come to rest (on); take up a position (on).

'percolate v (of liquid) pass slowly (through). —d adj: —d coffee.

per'dition n complete ruin.

pe'remptory adj (of persons, their

orders, etc) not to be questioned or disobeyed.

'perfect *adj* **1** complete, with everything needed. **2** without fault. **3** — **tense**, one using *have*, *has*, *had* and a past participle. **per'fect** *v* make —. **—ly** *adv*. **per'fection** *n* —ing or being —ed; — quality, person, etc.

'perforate *v* make a hole or holes through, esp a line of holes in paper (as round a postage stamp).

per'form *v* **1** do (a piece of work, esp one requiring skill). **2** act (a play); play (music), sing, do tricks, etc, before an audience. **—ance** *n* **1** —ing; (esp) sth done or acted. **2** the —ing of a play; a concert. **—er** *n* one who —s, esp in a play or at a concert.

'perfume *n* (liquid with a) sweet smell, esp that of flowers. *v* give a — to; put — on.

per'functory *adj* done, doing things, with little care or interest.

per'haps *adv* possibly; it may be.

'peril *n* danger. **—ous** *adj*.

pe'rimeter *n* (length of the) outer boundary of a drawn shape, enclosed area of land, etc.

'period *n* **1** any portion of time, esp one between events that occur regularly. **2** portion of time in the life of a person, nation, etc. **,peri'odic** *adj* occurring or appearing at regular intervals. **,peri'odical** *n* newspaper, magazine, etc, published every week, month, etc.

'periscope *n* tube with mirrors by which a view from a level above that of the viewer's eyes can be obtained, esp the kind used in submarines for seeing what is on the sea's surface.

'perish *v* **1** (cause to) be destroyed, come to an end, die. **2** —ed with cold, feeling very cold. **—able** *adj* quickly or easily going bad (eg food).

'perjure *v* — **oneself**, knowingly make a false statement after taking an oath to tell the truth. **'perjury** *n* act of perjuring oneself.

perk *v* **1** — **up**, become lively and active. **2** — **up the head (tail)**, (of an animal) show liveliness. **'—y** *adj* (-ier, -iest) lively. **'—ily** *adv*.

'permanent *adj* going on for a long time; intended to last. **—ly** *adv*. **'permanence** *n*.

'permeate *v* — **through**, spread, pass, into every part of.

per'mit *v* (-tt-) **1** allow. **2** — **of**, admit(3). **'permit** *n* written authority to do sth, go somewhere. **per'missible** *adj* which is —ted. **per'mission** *n* consent; statement that —s.

per'nicious *adj* harmful; injurious.

,perpen'dicular *adj* **1** at an angle of 90° to (another line or surface). **2** upright. *n* — line.

'perpetrate *v* commit (a crime, an error); do (sth wrong).

per'petual *adj* **1** never-ending; going on for a long time or without stopping. **2** often repeated. **—ly** *adv*. **per'petuate** *v* preserve from being forgotten. **,perpe'tuity** *n* **in perpetuity**, for ever.

per'plex *v* puzzle; bewilder. **—ity** *n* —ed condition; —ing thing.

'perquisite *n* profit, allowance, etc, in addition to regular wages, etc.

'persecute *v* **1** punish, treat cruelly, esp because of religious beliefs. **2** worry (*with* questions, etc). **,perse'cution** *n*.

,perse'vere *v* keep on, continue (*at*, *in*, *with*, sth). **,perse'verance** *n*.

per'sist *v* — **in**, go on (doing sth, believing, etc) in spite of failure, opposition, etc. **—ence** *n* —ent adj —ing. **—ently** *adv*.

'person *n* **1** man, woman, or child. **2 be present in —**, be present oneself (not represented by sb else). **—al** *adj* **1** private; individual. **2** done, made, etc, by a — himself; for, concerning oneself: *a —al call*. **3** of a —'s looks, qualities, etc. **4** of, about, or against a —. **—ally** *adv* **1** in —. **2** as a —. **3** speaking for oneself. **,person'ality** *n* qualities that make up a —'s character. **per'sonify** *v* represent (sth, eg a quality) as a —. **,person'nel** *n* staff; —s employed in any work, esp public undertakings and the armed forces.

per'spective *n* art of drawing solid objects on a flat surface so that their depth, size, and distance are suggested.

per'spire *v* give out liquid through the skin as when hot. **,perspi'ration** *n* sweat.

per'suade *v* cause (sb) by reasoning (*to do* sth) or to be certain (*of*, *that*). **per'suasion** *n* persuading or being —d; conviction or belief.

per'suasive *adj* able to —; convincing.

pert *adj* saucy; disrespectful.

'pertinent *adj* referring directly (*to*).

per'turb *v* trouble; make anxious.

pe'ruse *v* read. pe'rusal *n*.

per'vade *v* get into every part of; spread through. per'vasive *adj*.

per'verse *adj* 1 wilfully continuing in wrongdoing. 2 contrary to reason.

per'vert *v* 1 turn (sth) to a wrong use. 2 cause (a person, his mind) to turn away from right behaviour, beliefs, etc. 'pervert *n* —ed person. per'version *n* —ing or being —ed.

'pessimism *n* tendency to expect the worst thing to happen. 'pessimist *n* person inclined to —. ‚pessi'mistic *adj*.

pest *n* troublesome or destructive thing (esp animals, insects, attacking crops). 'pestilence *n* fatal, infectious, quickly-spreading disease.

'pester *v* trouble; annoy.

'pestle *n* instrument used for crushing substances in a mortar.

pestles and mortars

pet *n* 1 animal, etc, kept as a companion: *pet dog*. 2 person treated as a favourite; sb especially loved. pet name, name used affectionately instead of the real name. *v* (-tt-) treat with affection; touch lovingly.

'petal *n* one of the leaf-like divisions of a flower.

‚peter 'out *v* come to an end gradually.

pe'tition *n* earnest request; prayer. *v* make a — to (sb *for* sth).

'petrify *v* (cause to) change into stone; take away the power to think, act, etc (through fear, etc). ‚petri'faction *n*.

'petrol *n* refined oil used to drive engines (in motor-cars, etc).

pe'troleum *n* mineral oil from which —, paraffin, etc, are obtained.

'petticoat *n* woman's loose underskirt; slip(4).

'petty *adj* (-ier, -iest) 1 unimportant. 2 having or showing a narrow mind: — *spite*. 3 — cash, (business) money for or from small payments. 4 — officer, naval officer below commissioned rank.

'petulant *adj* unreasonably impatient or irritable. 'petulance *n*.

pew *n* long bench with a back, usu fixed to the floor, in a church.

'pewter *n* grey alloy of tin and lead; vessels made of —.

'phantom *n* ghost; sth unreal, as seen in a dream.

'pharmacy *n* chemist's shop.

phase *n* 1 stage of development. 2 (of the moon) area of bright surface visible from the earth (*new moon, full moon*, etc).

'pheasant *n* long-tailed game[1] bird.

phe'nomenon *n* (*pl* phe'nomena) 1 thing that appears to the senses or can be observed. 2 remarkable person or thing. phe'nomenal *adj* extraordinary.

phi'lanthropy *n* love of mankind; practice of helping people who are in need. phi'lanthropist *n* person who helps those who are in need. ‚philan'thropic *adj*.

phi'losophy *n* 1 the search for knowledge, esp concerning nature and the meaning of existence. 2 calm acceptance of events; self-control in the face of suffering or danger. phi'losopher *n*. ‚philo-'sophical *adj* devoted to, guided by, —; resigned.

phlegm (pronounced *flem*) *n* thick semi-fluid substance forming on the skin of the throat and in the nose, brought up by coughing.

phone *n & v* (colloq) telephone.

pho'netic *adj* of, corresponding to, the sounds of speech: — *spelling* (eg *flem* for *phlegm*). —s *n* science of speech sounds.

'phoney *adj* not genuine.

'phosphorus *n* yellowish substance which catches fire easily and gives out a faint light in the dark. phospho'rescent *adj*. ‚phospho'rescence *n*.

'photograph *n* picture taken with a camera. *v* take a — of. pho-

'tographer n. pho'tography n art or process of taking —s. ,photo-'graphic adj.

phrase n small group of words forming part of a sentence (eg *in order to*). v express in words.

'**physical** adj 1 of material (contrasted with moral and spiritual) things: *the — world*. 2 of the body: *— strength*. —ly adv.

phy'sician n doctor of medicine and surgery, esp one who does not practise surgery.

'physics n group of sciences dealing with matter and energy (eg heat, light, sound).

,physi'ognomy n (person's) face or features; general features of a country.

,physi'ology n science of the normal functions of living things.

,physio'therapy n medical treatment by means of massage, exercise, and heat and light.

phy'sique n structure of the body: *a man of strong —*.

pi'ano n musical key-board instrument. ⇨ p 180. '**pianist** n person who plays the —. ⇨ grand.

pick[1] n 1 (also '**pick-axe**) heavy tool, used for breaking up roads, brickwork, etc. ⇨ p 293. 2 small sharp-pointed instrument: *a tooth-pick*.

pick[2] v 1 take or gather (flowers, fruit) from plants, trees; get the meat off (a bone); tear or separate with the fingers. — **choose**. — **sth out**, choose it, distinguish it, from among others. 3 — **up**, take hold of and lift up (eg sth on the floor); learn by chance (bits of news, etc); take (passengers) on to or into (a train, bus, etc); recover (one's health, spirits). — **oneself up**, get to one's feet after a fall. 4 — **sb's pocket**, steal sth from his pocket. — **a lock**, open it without a key, by using sth else. — **a quarrel** (*with sb*), start one on purpose. n that which is —ed or chosen.

'**picket** n 1 pointed stake set upright in the ground. 2 small group of men on police duty; worker(s) on guard during a strike, to try to stop others from going to work. v 1 put —(s)(1) round; fasten a horse to a —(1). 2 place a —(2) in or round; act as a —(2).

'**pickle** n 1 salt water, vinegar, etc, for keeping meat, vegetables,

etc, in good condition. 2 (usu *pl*) vegetables kept in —. v preserve in —(1).

'**picnic** n pleasure trip during which food is eaten in the open air: v take part in a —.

pic'torial adj of, having pictures.

'**picture** n 1 painting, drawing, etc, of sth or sb, esp as a work of art. 2 be the — of (*health*, etc), appear to be very (healthy, etc). 3 the —s, (colloq) the cinema. v make a — of; describe in words; imagine. ,**pictu'resque** adj 1 (of scenes, places) striking and charming in appearance. 2 (of a person, his language, behaviour, etc) striking; original.

'**pidgin** n kind of imperfect English used in some parts of the world (esp in trade).

pie n meat or fruit covered with paste and baked in a dish.

piece n 1 part or. bit of a solid substance. in —s, broken. take to —s, break up; undo; take apart. 2 separate instance or example: *a — of news* (*bad luck*). 3 unit or definite quantity in which goods are prepared for distribution: *sold only by the —*. 4 single composition (art, music, etc): *a — of poetry*. 5 single thing out of a set: *a tea-service of* 30 —s; one of the wooden, metal, etc, objects moved on a board in such games as chess. 6 coin: *a ten pence —*. v put (parts, etc, *together*); make by joining or adding —s. '—**meal** adv (done) bit by bit. '—**work** n work paid for according to the amount done, not the time taken.

pier n 1 long structure of wood, iron, etc, built out into the sea as a landing-stage or for walking on for pleasure. 2 pillar supporting a span of a bridge, etc.

pierce v 1 (of sharp-pointed tools) go into or through; make (a hole) by doing this. 2 (fig, of cold, pain, sounds, etc) force a way into or through; affect deeply.

'**piety** n being pious.

pig n (farm) animal. ⇨ p 84; its flesh as meat. ⇨ bacon, pork. **pig-'headed** adj obstinate. '**pigsty** n building for pigs. '**pigtail** n plait of hair hanging down over the back of the neck.

'**pigeon** n bird, wild or tame, of the

dove family. ⇨ p 26. —**hole** n one of a number of small open boxes for keeping papers, letters, etc, in.

'**pigment** n colouring matter.

'**pigmy** ⇨ pygmy.

pile[1] n heavy piece of timber driven into the ground, esp under water, as a foundation for a building, etc.

pile[2] n 1 number of things lying one upon the other. 2 large amount. **make a —**, (colloq) earn and save a large amount of money. v put in a —; make a — of: —things up.

pile[3] n soft, thick, hair-like surface of velvet, some kinds of carpet, etc.

'**pilfer** v steal (small things or things of small value).

'**pilgrim** n person who travels to a sacred place (eg Mecca). —**age** n journey of a —.

pill n ball of medicine for swallowing whole.

'**pillage** n & v plunder.

'**pillar** n column(1). '**pillar-box** n box in a street in which letters are posted.

'**pillion** n seat for a second person behind the rider of a horse or the driver of a motor-bike.

'**pillow** n soft cushion for one's head, esp in bed.

'**pilot** n 1 person trained to take ships into or out of a harbour, up a river, etc. 2 person trained to fly aircraft. 3 guide. v act as a — to.

'**pimple** n small, hard, inflamed spot on the skin.

pin n 1 piece of thin, stiff, pointed wire, used to fasten things together. '**safety-pin**, one with a shielded end. 2 short thin length of wood or metal for holding things together. v (-nn-) 1 fasten (things together, up, to sth, etc) with a pin or pins. 2 prevent from moving: pinned (down) by a fallen branch. '**pin-point** n sth very small. v find (the target, cause of a disease, etc) accurately. '**pin-prick** n (fig) trifling cause of annoyance.

'**pinafore** n (colloq 'pinny) article of clothing worn (usu by children) over other clothes to protect them.

'**pincers** n pl instrument for gripping things, pulling out nails, etc. ⇨ p 293.

pinch v 1 take or have in a tight grip between the thumb and finger, or between two hard things which are pressed together: — one's finger in a doorway. 2 be too tight; hurt by being too tight. n 1 painful squeeze; act of —ing(1). 2 amount that can be taken up with the thumb and finger: a — of salt. 3 at a —, if necessary and if no other way is possible.

pine[1] n kinds of evergreen tree with needle-shaped leaves and cones; the wood of this tree.

pine[2] v 1 waste away through sorrow or illness. 2 wish strongly (for sth, to do sth).

'**pine,apple** n (tropical plant with) sweet juicy fruit. ⇨ p 115.

'**pinion**[1] v hold or bind fast (sb's arms) to his sides. n bird's wing.

'**pinion**[2] n small cog-wheel.

pink adj & n pale red (colour).

'**pinnacle** n 1 tall, pointed ornament built on to a roof. 2 (fig) highest point: at the — of his fame

pint n unit of measure for liquids and dry goods (eg peas); eighth of a gallon or 0·57 of a litre.

,**pio'neer** n person who goes first into a country to develop it; explorer. v act as a —.

'**pious** adj having or showing deep love for religion. —**ly** adv.

pip[1] n 1 small seed, esp of lemon, orange, apple, pear. 2 note of time-signal on the telephone or radio. 3 star on a military uniform indicating rank.

pip[2] v (-pp-) fail or cause to fail; be defeated. **pipped at the post** only just[1](2) defeated.

pipe n 1 tube through which liquid or gases may flow. 2 kinds of musical wind instrument. 3 tube with a bowl, used for smoking tobacco. v convey (water, etc through —s(1). '**piping** adj shrill adv: piping hot, very hot. n length of —s(1): ten feet of lead piping.

'**piquant** adj pleasantly sharp to the taste.

pique v 1 hurt the pride or self-respect of. 2 stir the curiosity of.

'**pirate** n sea-robber. '**piracy** n.

'**pistol** n small fire-arm held in one hand.

'**piston** n short cylinder or thick round plate fitting closely inside another cylinder or tube, pushed backwards and forwards (by gas or steam in an engine, a pump, etc) on the end of a rod.

pit n **1** deep hole in the earth, with steep sides, esp one from which material is dug out: *a gravel-pit; a coal-pit* (= a coal-mine). **2** (people in) seats in the back part of the ground floor of a theatre. **3** small mark left in the skin (esp by smallpox). v (-tt-) **1** mark with pits(3). **2** match(1) (a person, one's strength, etc *against*). **'pitfall** n pit with a covered opening to trap wild animals; (fig) unsuspected danger.

pitch[1] v **1** put up (*a tent*, etc). **2** throw (*a ball*, etc). **3** (cause to) fall forwards or outwards: *He (was) —ed from the lorry.* **4** (of a ship) move up and down from end to end as the bows rise and fall. (cf roll.) **5** (music) set in a certain key: — *a tune too high.* **6** — **in**, set to work with energy. **— into**, attack violently. n **1** place where sb (esp a street trader) usually does his business. **2** (cricket) part of the field between the wickets. **3** amount of slope (esp of a roof). **4** (music and speech) degree of highness or lowness. **5** degree (of a quality). **6** (of a ship) process of —ing(4). **'—fork** n long-handled two-pointed fork for lifting hay, etc.

pitch[2] n black sticky substance made from coal-tar, used to fill spaces between boards, etc. v put — on. **'pitch-'black, 'pitch-'dark** adj quite black or dark.

pitcher n large jug.

piteous adj arousing pity.

pith n soft substance filling the stems of some plants; (fig) most important or necessary part (*of*). **'—y** adj (-ier, -iest) (esp) full of forceful meaning; concise.

pittance n low payment or allowance (for work, etc).

pity n **1** feeling of sorrow for the troubles, sufferings, etc, of another: *have (take) — on sb.* **2** (event which gives) cause for regret or sorrow. v feel — for. **'pitiable** adj exciting —; (esp) deserving only contemptuous —. **'pitiful** adj feeling or causing —. **'pitiless** adj feeling or showing no —.

pivot n central pin or point on

which sth turns. v place on, supply with, a —; turn (*on* sth) as on a —.

'placard n written or printed announcement, displayed publicly.

pla'cate v soothe; pacify.

place n **1** particular portion of space occupied by sth or sb. **out of —**, not in the correct order or position. **— of worship**, church, etc. **—s of amusement**, theatres, etc. **2 take —**, (of an event) be held, happen. **in — of**, instead of. **3** passage or part of a book, etc, reached in reading: *find (lose) one's —.* **4** work; job. **lose one's —**, (esp) become unemployed. **5 keep sb in his —**, not allow him to become too familiar. v **1** put (sth) in a certain —; find a — for. **2** put (confidence *in* sb, etc). **3** give: *— an order (for* goods, *with* sb).

'placid adj calm; untroubled; (of a person) not easily irritated. **—ly** adv. **pla'cidity** n.

plague n **1** = pestilence. **2** cause of trouble or disaster: *a — of locusts.* v annoy (e g with repeated requests).

plaice n kind of flat sea-fish.

plain[1] adj (-er, -est) **1** easy to see, hear, or understand. **2** simple; ordinary; without luxury or ornament: *— food; a — blue dress;* in *— clothes,* (esp) in ordinary clothes, not in uniform. **3** (of thoughts, actions, etc) straightforward; frank. **4** (of a person's appearance) not pretty or handsome. adv clearly. **'—ly** adv. **'—ness** n.

plain[2] n area of level country.

'plaintiff n person who starts an action in a law-court.

'plaintive adj sounding sad.

plait v weave or twist (three or more lengths of hair, straw, etc) under and over one another into one rope-like length. n sth made in this way: *wearing her hair in a —.*

plan n **1** outline drawing (of or for a building) showing the relative size, positions, etc, of the parts, esp one showing the various floors. **2** diagram (of the parts of a machine). **3** diagram showing how a garden, park, or other small area of land has been or is to be laid out. **4** the arranging of sth to be done in the future: *my —s for the holidays.* v (-nn-) make a — of or for; make —s (*to do* sth).

plane n **1** flat or level surface. **2** tool with a flat end for smoothing wood, etc. **3** (wing, or supporting part, of an) aircraft. v make smooth with a —(3). adj perfectly flat: a — figure.

'planet n one of the heavenly bodies (eg Mars, Earth) moving round the sun. **—ary** adj.

plank n board; long, flat piece of wood. v cover with —s.

plant n **1** any living thing that is not an animal and (usu) grows out of the ground (with a stem and leaves), esp one smaller than a tree or bush. **2** machinery, tools, etc, used in an industrial process: a farm with its own lighting — (eg generator for electric light). v **1** put —s in (a garden, etc). **2** put (seeds, plants, trees, etc) in the ground to grow. **3** place firmly in position. **— oneself** (in the doorway), stand there.

plan'tation n **1** area of land —ed with trees. **2** large estate producing tea, tobacco, cotton, etc. **'—er** person growing crops on a —ation.

'plantain n (tropical tree producing) kinds of large banana. ⇨ p 115.

'plaster n **1** paste of lime, sand, and water used for coating walls and ceilings. **2** medical preparation spread on a piece of cloth, etc, for protecting wounds. v **1** put —(1) on (walls, etc). **2** put a —(2) on (the body). **3** cover thickly with —.

'plastic adj **1** (of materials) easily shaped. **2** (fig) easily bent or changed. n substance derived from a — material. **—s** n science of — substances.

plate n **1** flat dish, usu made of china, from which food is eaten. **2** flat, thin sheet of metal, glass, etc. **3** gold or silver articles (eg spoons, dishes) for use at meals. **4 dental** —, frame with artificial teeth, fitting the upper or lower jaw. **5** helping (of food) served on a —(1). v **1** cover (a ship, etc) with metal —s(2). **2** coat (one metal) with another.

'plateau n expanse of land with a flat surface high above sea level.

'platform n **1** flat surface built at a higher level than railway lines in a railway station, used by travellers. **2** flat structure raised above floor level for speakers in a hall, etc. **3** programme of a political party.

'platinum n white heavy metal of great value.

'platitude n statement obviously true, esp one often heard before.

'plausible adj **1** (of excuses, arguments, etc) seeming right or reasonable. **2** (of persons) clever at producing — arguments, etc.

play v **1** amuse oneself alone or with others: — football; perform on a musical instrument: — the piano. **2** act; take a part in a stage drama. **— the fool**, act foolishly. **3 — a joke (trick) on sb**, carry out a joke, etc, against him. **— upon** (sb's fears, etc), make use of them for one's own advantage. **be —ed out**, have no strength or money left. **4** (of light, water) move about in a lively way. **5** send; be sent; direct (light, water, on or over sth). n **1** sth done for amusement, recreation, etc. in —, not seriously. **2** a drama. **3** gambling **4 — on words**, pun. **5** (space for) free and easy movement. **6 come into —**, begin to operate. **bring into —**, begin to use. **'—er** n. **'—mate** n child who —s with another. **'—ful** adj full of fun; ready for —; not serious. **'—goer** n person who often goes to the theatre. **'—thing** n toy. **'—wright** n person who writes —s(2).

plea n **1** request (for sth); excuse offered for wrongdoing. **2** (law) statement made by or for defendant in a law court.

plead v **1** speak in defence of sb or of oneself in a law court. **— guilty**, admit that one is guilty. **2** ask earnestly (for sth, etc). **3** offer as an excuse: Don't — ignorance.

'pleasant adj (-er, -est) giving pleasure; agreeable; friendly. **—ly** adv. **—ness** n.

please v give pleasure. int (polite if it —s (you): May I come in, — . **'pleasing** adj agreeable; giving pleasure.

'pleasure n **1** feeling of being happy or satisfied. **take — in**, enjoy. **with —**, willingly. **2** thing that gives happiness. **'pleasurable** adj giving —.

pleat n fold made by doubling cloth on itself. v make —s in.

plebiscite n (decision made upon a political question by) the votes of all qualified citizens.

pledge n 1 sth left with sb to be kept by him until the giver has done sth which he is under an obligation to do; article left with a pawnbroker. 2 sth given as a sign of love, approval, etc: a — of my friendship. 3 under — of secrecy, after having promised secrecy. v give (sth) as a —; give (sb) a promise.

plenty n more than enough (of). **'plentiful** adj in large quantities of numbers. **'plenteous** adj (liter) plentiful.

pliable adj easily bent or twisted; (of the mind) easily influenced. **'pliant** adj = pliable.

pliers n small scissors-like tool for holding, turning, or twisting things.

plight¹ n condition, esp a sad or serious one.

plight² v — one's word, promise.

plod v (-dd-) continue walking, working, etc, slowly but without resting.

plot n 1 small piece of land. 2 plan or outline of the events in a story (esp a novel or a drama). 3 secret plan. v (-tt-) 1 make secret plans(4). 2 mark the position of (sth) on a chart or graph.

plough n instrument for cutting and turning up the soil. v 1 break up (land) with a —; use a —. 2 force (a way through). **'—share** n blade of a —.

a plough

pluck v 1 pull the feathers off (a hen, etc). 2 pick (flowers; fruit); pull (weeds, etc) up or out. 3 snatch (at sth); take hold of and pull (at). 4 — up courage, overcome one's fears. n courage. **'—y** adj (-ier, -lest) brave. **'—ily** adv.

plug n 1 piece of rubber, metal, etc, used to stop up a hole (eg in a bath). 2 device for making a connection with a supply of electric current. 3 **'sparking-plug.** v (-gg-) 1 stop

plugs

up (a hole) with a —(1). 2 — in, make a connection with a —(2).

plum n (tree having a) soft, round, smooth-skinned fruit with a stone-like seed. ⇨ p 115. **'plum-cake**, **'plum-'pudding** n one made with currants and raisins.

plumage n bird's feathers.

plumb n out of —, not perpendicular. **'plumb-line** n cord with a piece of lead for finding the depth of water or for testing whether a wall, etc, is perpendicular.

'plumber n workman who fits pipes (for water, etc) into buildings and repairs them. **'plumbing** n the pipes, water-tanks, etc, in a building.

plume n feather; sth suggesting a feather by its shape. v (of a bird): — itself (its feathers), smooth the feathers.

plump¹ adj (-er, -est) (of an animal, a person) rounded; pleasantly fat. v (— up, out) make or become —.

plump² v (cause to, allow to) fall or drop, suddenly and heavily. adv suddenly; abruptly.

'plunder v take goods from (places) by force; rob (people), esp during war or civil disorder. n —ing; goods taken.

plunge v 1 put (sth), go, suddenly and with force (into): — into a lake. 2 (of a horse, ship, etc) move forward or downward violently. n act of plunging (eg from a diving-board).

'plural n & adj (form of a word) used with reference to more than one.

plus prep with the addition of. **'plus-sign**, sign + in arithmetic.

plush n kind of silk or cotton cloth with a soft nap(2).

plu'tocracy n (government by a) rich and powerful class. **'plutocrat** n person who is powerful because of his wealth. **'pluto'cratic** adj.

ply¹ n layer of wood, etc; one strand of wool yarn, rope, etc: three-ply wood (wool).

ply² *v* **1** use, work with (a tool, etc): *plying her needle*. **2** (of ships, buses, etc) go regularly (*between*; *from . . . to*). **3** ply a trade, work at it. **4** ply sb with, keep him constantly supplied with (food and drink, questions, etc).

pneu'matic *adj* worked or driven by, filled with, compressed air: — *drills* (*tyres*).

pneu'monia *n* serious illness with inflammation of the lung(s).

poach¹ *v* cook (an egg) by boiling it without the shell.

poach² *v* (go on sb else's property and) take without right (pheasants, salmon, etc). **'—er** *n* sb who —es.

'pocket *n* **1** small bag in an article of clothing for putting things in. **2** hole in earth or rock filled with ore. *v* **1** put in one's —. **2** hide, keep under (one's feelings): — *one's pride*. **'pocket-book** *n* leather case for paper money; (USA) small handbag. **'pocket-,money** *n* money (esp that given to children) for occasional needs.

pod *n* long narrow case for seeds: *pea-pod, bean-pod*. ⇨ p 306.

'poem *n* piece of writing in verse form. **'poet** *n* writer of —s. **po'etic(al)** *adj* of poets or poetry; in the form of verse. **'poetry** *n* —s; art of a poet; quality that produces a poetic feeling.

'poignant *adj* sharp in taste or smell; intense to the feelings; keen.

point *n* **1** sharp end (of a pin, pencil, cape(2), etc). **2** dot made by or as by the — of a pencil, etc. a decimal —, as in 3·13. **3** mark, position, real or imagined, in space or time. **be on the — of doing sth**, be ready to do it. **when it comes to the —**, when the time for action or decision comes. **4** mark on a scale; degree: *the boiling-point of water*. **5** —s of the compass, one of the thirty-two marks (eg NNE). **6** chief idea, purpose, etc, of sth said, done, planned, etc: *come to the —* (of an explanation, etc). **see the —**, understand a joke or story. **7** detail, step, esp one marking stages in the development of an argument, etc. **8** unit for measuring scores in some games and sports. **9** (*pl*) tapering movable rails for moving trains, etc, from one track to another. *v* **1** — to (at), direct attention to, show the position or direction of. **2** — (sth) out, show, call attention to. **3** make a —(1) on (eg a pencil). **'point-'blank** *adj* aimed, fired, at very close range; (fig, of sth said) in a way that leaves no room for doubt. *adv* in a point-blank manner. **'—ed** *adj* **1** (fig) directed definitely against sb or his behaviour. **2** (of wit) sharp. **'—er** *n* stick used to — to things; indicator on a dial. **—less** *adj* with little or no sense, aim, or purpose.

poise *v* be or keep balanced. *n* balance; (fig) appearance of quiet self-confidence.

'poison *n* substance causing death or injury if absorbed by a living thing. *v* give — to; put — on; kill with —. **—er** *n*. **—ous** *adj*.

poke *v* **1** push (with a stick, one's finger, etc). — the fire, stir or break the coal with a —r. **2** make (a hole) by pushing sth in or through; get (a stick, one's head, etc) into or through by pushing. **3** — fun at, make fun of. *n* act of poking. **'—r** *n* metal rod or bar for poking coal in a fire. **'poky** *adj* (-ier, -iest) (of a room) small.

pole¹ *n* **1** North P—, South P—, the two ends of the earth's axis; the two points in the sky about which the stars seem to turn. **'pole-star** *n* star seen near the North P— of the sky. **2** either of the terminal points of an electric battery: *the negative* (*positive*) —. **'polar** *adj* of or near the P—s: *polar bear*.

pole² *n* **1** long thick rod of wood or metal as used for supporting telegraph wires, tents, etc, or for flying a flag. **2** unit for measuring of distance, 5½ yards.

po'lice *n* department of government, body of men, concerned with the keeping of public order. *v* keep order in (a place) with — or as with —. **'—man** *n* member of the — force. **po'lice-,station** *n* office of the — in a district.

'policy¹ *n* plan of action, esp one made by a government.

'policy² *n* written statement of the terms of a contract of insurance.

'polish *v* **1** make or become smooth and shiny by rubbing. **2** (esp ?

pp) improve in behaviour, intellectual interests, etc. *n* 1 (surface, etc, obtained by) —ing. 2 substance used for —ing: *shoe-polish*.

po'lite *adj* (-r, -st) 1 having, showing the possession of, good manners and consideration for other people. 2 refined. —ly *adv.* —ness *n.*

'politic *adj* prudent; well judged.

po'litical *adj* of the State; of government; of public affairs.

'politics *n pl* the science or art of government; political views, questions, etc. ,poli'tician *n* person taking part in — or much interested in —.

poll *n* voting at an election; list of voters; counting of votes; place where voting takes place. *v* vote at an election; receive (a certain number of) votes. 'poll-tax *n* tax to be paid equally by every person.

'pollen *n* fine powder formed on flowers and carried (by the wind, insects, etc) to other flowers to fertilize them.

pol'lute *v* make dirty. pol'lution *n.*

poly- *prefix* many. po'lygamy *n* (custom of) having more than one wife at the same time. ,poly'technic *n* school where many subjects, esp trades, are taught.

'pommel ⇨ pummel.

pomp *n* splendid display, esp at a public event.

'pompous *adj* full of, showing, self-importance. pom'posity *n.*

pond *n* small area of still water, eg one made as a drinking place for cattle.

'ponder *v* consider; be deep in thought.

'ponderous *adj* not moved or moving easily; (fig) dull; tedious.

'pontiff *n* the Pope.

pon'toon *n* flat-bottomed boat.

'pony *n* horse of small breed.

pooh *int* expression of contempt.

pool¹ *n* 1 small area of still water, esp one naturally formed. 2 puddle.

pool² *v* put (money, etc) together for the common advantage: *— our resources. n* sum of money made up of payments from many persons (eg in business or gambling).

poor *adj* (-er, -est) 1 having little or no money and nothing of value.

2 deserving or needing help or sympathy. 3 small in quantity: *a — supply.* 4 low in quality: *— soil.* 'poor-'spirited *adj* lacking in courage. '—ly *adv* badly. *adj* (-ier, -iest) (colloq) ill; in — health.

pop *v* (-pp-) 1 (cause to) make a sharp quick sound (as when a cork comes out of a bottle). 2 (cause to) go or come (*in, out,* etc) quickly. *n* 1 popping(1) sound. 2 sorts of popular music and song.

Pope *n* Bishop of Rome, head of the Roman Catholic Church.

'poplin *n* cloth for shirts, etc.

'populace *n* the common people.

'popular *adj* 1 of or for the people. 2 suited to the tastes, educational level, etc, of the general public. 3 liked and admired by the public: *— songs (singers).* ,popu'larity *n* condition of being —(3). —ize *v* make —.

'populate *v* people. ,popu'lation *n* (total number of) people living in a place, country, etc. 'populous *adj* thickly —d.

'porcelain *n* fine china (plates, cups, etc) with a coating of glaze.

porch *n* roofed doorway or entrance.

pore¹ *n* tiny opening in the skin.

pore² *v* — over, study, examine (a book, etc) with close attention.

pork *n* meat of a pig, esp unsalted.

'porous *adj* allowing liquid to pass through (as sandy soil does).

'porpoise *n* sea animal. ⇨ p 247.

'porridge *n* soft food made by boiling oatmeal in water or milk.

port¹ *n* (town with a) harbour.

port² *n* doorway in a ship's side. '—hole *n* small round glass window in a ship's side.

port³ *n* left side of a ship or aircraft.

port⁴ *n* (kinds of) sweet red wine.

'portable *adj* that can be carried about: *a — radio, typewriter,* etc.

por'tend *v* be a sign or warning of. 'portent *n* thing, esp sth marvellous or mysterious, which —s some coming event.

'porter *n* 1 person whose work is to carry luggage, etc, at railway stations, hotels, etc. 2 doorkeeper or gate-keeper.

port'folio *n* 1 holder (usu leather) for loose papers, etc. 2 position and duties of a Minister of State.

'portion *n* 1 part, esp a share,

(to be) given when sth is divided up. 2 some (of). v divide into —s.

'portly adj (-ier, -iest) (of elderly persons) stout; dignified looking.

'portrait n painted picture, drawing, photograph (of a person or animal). por'tray v make a — of; describe vividly in words.

pose v 1 put (sb) in a position before making a picture of him; take up an attitude. 2 behave in an affected way hoping to impress others. 3 — as, pretend to be. 4 put forward (a difficult question or problem). n 1 attitude taken when posing(1) for a picture, etc. 2 behaviour intended to impress people. '—r n awkward or difficult question, etc.

posh adj (slang) smart²(1).

po'sition n 1 place where sth or sb is or stands, esp in relation to others. 2 right place for sth or sb: in (out of) —. 3 way in which the body is placed: in a comfortable —. 4 person's place or rank, in relation to others, in employment or in society. 5 condition or circumstances: not in a — to help. v place (sth or sb) in a —; find the — of.

'positive adj 1 definite; leaving no room for doubt; certain. 2 constructive: a —suggestion. 3 (maths) greater than 0. 4 (of electricity) that which is produced by rubbing glass with silk. 5 (grammar) of the simple form (of an adj or adv), not the comparative or superlative degree. n photograph printed from (negative) film. —ly adv definitely.

pos'sess v 1 own; have. 2 keep control over. 3 — oneself of, become the owner of. be —ed of, have. be —ed, be mad. —ion n 1 —ing. in —ion (of), owning; in the —ion of, owned by. 2 sth —ed; property. —ive adj of or showing —ion: —ive adjective; eager to — or retain.

'possible adj 1 that can be done; that can exist or happen. 2 that is reasonable or satisfactory for a purpose. 'possibly adv 1 by any possibility. 2 perhaps. ,possi'bility n 1 (degree of) being likely or possible. 2 sth that is —.

post¹ n 1 place where a soldier is on watch; place of duty; place occupied by soldiers. 2 last —,

military bugle call sounded at bedtime and at funerals. 3 trading station. 4 position or appointment. v put at a —(1): — a sentry at the gate, send to a —(1).

post² n government transport and delivery of letters and parcels; one collection or distribution of letters, etc; letters, etc, delivered at one time; — office or pillar-box. v 1 send (letters, etc) by —. 2 (old use) travel by stage-coach; make a quick journey. 3 — (up), (business) write items in a ledger. 4 keep sb —ed, keep him supplied with news. 'postage n payment for the carrying of letters, etc. '—al adj of the — or — office. —al order, official receipt for a small sum paid in by the sender, to be cashed by the receiver at another — office instead of sending cash by —. '—card n card carried by — instead of a letter. 'post'haste adv in great haste. '—mark n official mark, showing place and date of —ing, stamped on letters, etc. '— office n government department in charge of —al services; office, building, in which —al work is carried on.

post³ n upright piece of wood, metal, etc, supporting or marking sth: 'gate-posts; the 'winning-post. v 1 — sth up, display publicly on a —, on a notice-board, etc. 2 make known by means of a —ed notice. '—er n public advertisement (to be) —ed up; large decorative picture on paper (to be) —ed up.

post- prefix after; later than. 'post-'date v put (on a letter, cheque etc) a date later than the date of writing. '—'graduate n & adj, (student doing a course of studies after taking a degree. '—script n sth added to a letter after the signature.

pos'terity n 1 person's descendants. 2 future generations.

'posthumous adj coming or happening after death.

post'pone v put off until later —ment n.

'postulate v demand, take for granted, as a necessary fact. —sth.—d.

'posture n 1 position of the body in a sitting —. 2 attitude of the body or mind. v take up a —.

posy n small bunch of flowers.

pot n round vessel of earthenware, metal, etc, for keeping things in, for cooking, etc: a *flower-pot*; a *coffee-pot*. v (-tt-) 1 put (meat or fish paste, etc) into a pot to preserve it. 2 plant in a flower-pot. **pot-hole** n hole made by rain and traffic in a road. **potter** n maker of pottery. **pottery** n pots; earthenware.

potato n (pl potatoes) plant with rounded tubers eaten as a vegetable. ⇨ p 306.

potent adj powerful; effective: — *forces (reasons)*. **potency** n.

potential adj that can or may come into existence or action.

potter[1], **pottery** n ⇨ pot.

potter[2] v work (at sth) with little energy; move (about) from one little job to another.

pouch n small bag (eg for pipe tobacco); bag of skin on some animals (eg kangaroos) in which they carry their young.

poultice n soft hot mass put on the skin to lessen pain. v put a — on.

poultry pl n hens, ducks, geese, turkeys, etc.

poultry

goose

duck

chicken (hen)

turkey

chicks

pounce v & n (make a) sudden attack or downward swoop (on).

pound[1] n 1 unit of weight, 16 ounces avoirdupois, 12 ounces troy. 2 (£) decimal unit of money in Britain (formerly worth 20 shillings) worth 100 new pence; unit of money worth 20 shillings in some other countries.

pound[2] v 1 strike heavily and repeatedly (at, on). 2 crush to powder; break to pieces.

pour v 1 (of liquids, of substances that flow like liquids) flow, cause to flow, in a continuous stream. 2 (of people) come (in, out, etc) in large numbers: —ing into the station. 3 (of rain) come (down) heavily.

pout v push out (the lips), esp when bad-tempered, or discontented.

poverty n state of being poor. **poverty-stricken** adj very poor; shabby-looking.

powder n 1 substance that has been crushed, rubbed, or worn to dust; special kind of —, eg for use on the skin. 2 ⇨ gun —. v put —on (the face, etc); make into —.

power n 1 ability to do or act. 2 strength or force. 3 energy or force that can be used to do work: *water-power*; *an engine of sixty horse-power*. 4 control; authority: *the — of the law*. 5 person or organization or State having great influence in (inter)national affairs. 6 capacity to magnify: *the — of a lens*. **power-house**, **power-station** n place where —(3) (esp electrical) is produced or distributed. **-ful** adj having or producing great —. **-less** adj without —; unable (to do sth).

practice n 1 performance; the doing of sth: *put a plan into —*. 2 way of doing sth that is common or habitual; sth done regularly. 3 frequent or regular repetition in order to become or remain skilful: *piano —*. in —, skilful through —. out of —, not having practised recently. 4 work of a doctor or lawyer; all persons who consult a certain doctor or lawyer: *a doctor with a large —*. **practicable** adj that can be put into —; that can be done or used. **practical** adj 1 concerned with —(1): *practical difficulties*. 2 (of persons) clever at doing and making things; fond of action. 3 useful; doing well what it is intended to do. **practically** adv 1 in a practical manner. 2 really. 3 almost.

practise v 1 do sth repeatedly or regularly in order to become or remain skilful. 2 make a custom of. — what you preach, do what you advise others to do. 3 — the law (medicine), work as a lawyer (doctor).

prairie n wide area of level land

with grass but no trees, eg in N America.

praise v 1 speak with approval of; say that one admires. 2 give honour and glory (to God). n act of praising; expressions of approval. '—,worthy adj deserving —.

pram n ⇨ perambulator.

prance v (of a horse) jump on the hind legs; (of a person) move or jump about gaily and happily.

prank n playful or mischievous trick: play a — on sb.

'prattle v go on talking as a child does, about unimportant things. n such talk.

pray v 1 offer thanks, make requests (to God, for sth or for the good of sb). 2 ask (sb) (for, to do, sth) as a favour. '—er n —ing to God; thing —ed for; form of worship or of words used in —ing.

pre- prefix before: pre-'war.

preach v deliver(3) (a sermon); give a talk, esp in church, about morals; give moral advice (to). '—er n.

pre'carious adj uncertain; depending upon chance.

pre'caution n sth done in advance (against a possible danger or risk).

pre'cede v come or go before (in time, place, order). **'precedence** n (right to a) higher or earlier position. **'precedent** n earlier happening, decision, etc, taken as an example or rule.

'precept n guide for behaviour.

'precious adj 1 of great value. 2 highly valued; dear (to).

'precipice n perpendicular or very steep face of a rock or cliff.

pre'cipitate v 1 throw down or send violently from a height. 2 cause (an event) to happen suddenly or earlier than necessary. 3 condense (vapour) into drops which fall as rain or dew. adj (done, doing things) without enough thought.

pre'cipitous adj like a precipice.

'précis n chief ideas, points, etc, of a speech or a piece of writing restated in a shortened form.

pre'cise adj 1 exact; correctly stated; free from error. 2 taking care to be exact. —ly adv exactly. int quite so. **pre'cision** n.

pre'cocious adj (of a person) having developed earlier than is

usual; (of actions, knowledge) marked by such development.

,precon'ceive v form (ideas, etc) in advance (before getting knowledge, etc).

'predecessor n person who held a position before (the person mentioned).

pre'dicament n awkward or unpleasant situation from which escape seems difficult.

'predicate n (grammar) the part of a statement that says sth about the subject. **pre'dicative** adj: predicative adjective, one used only in a — (eg asleep).

pre'dict v say, tell, in advance (that sth will happen): — (that it will) rain. **—ion** n —ing; sth —ed.

,predis'pose v cause (sb) to be liable or inclined (to sth, to do sth) before the occasion comes. **,predis-po'sition** n.

pre'dominant adj having most power or influence; most noticeable. **pre'dominate** v be —.

pre-'eminent adj best of all.

'preface n author's explanatory remarks at the beginning of a book. v begin (a talk, etc, with sth).

'prefect n 1 school pupil given responsibility for keeping order.

pre'fer v (-rr-) 1 like better. 2 put forward (a complaint, request, etc). 3 appoint (sb) to a higher position. **'preferable** adj superior (to); to be —red. **'preference** n 1 —ring; sth —red. 2 the favouring of one person, country, etc, more than another.

'prefix n 1 word or syllable (eg co-) placed in front of a word to add to or change its meaning. 2 word (eg Mr, Dr) used before a person's name. v add a — to or in front of; add (a note, etc, to sth) at the beginning.

'pregnant adj (of a woman or a female animal) carrying offspring in the body in the process of development before birth. **'pregnancy** n.

,prehis'toric adj of the time before recorded history.

'prejudice n 1 opinion, like, or dislike, formed before one has adequate knowledge or experience a — against modern poetry. 2 to the — of, so as to injure (sb' interests, etc). ˌpreju'dicial adj causing — or injury (to).

'prelate n bishop or other church-man of equal or higher rank.

pre'liminary adj coming first and preparing for what follows. n — step, etc.

'prelude n introductory action, event, piece of poetry or music.

'premature adj done, happening, doing sth, before the right or usual time.

pre'meditate v consider, plan, in advance: a —d crime.

'premier adj first in position, importance, etc. n prime minister.

'premises n pl house or other building with its land.

'premium n 1 amount or instalment paid to a society, etc, for an insurance policy. 2 reward; bonus. 3 at a —, (of stocks and shares) at more than the par value.

ˌpremo'nition n feeling of uneasiness considered as a warning (of approaching danger, etc).

pre'occupy v take all the attention of (sb, his mind) so that it is not given to other matters.

pre'pare v 1 get or make ready. 2 be —d to, be able and willing to. ˌprepa'ration n preparing or being —d; food, medicine, etc, specially —d. pre'paratory adj introductory; needed or used for preparing.

pre'pay v (pt & pp 'pre'paid) pay in advance.

pre'ponderate v be greater in number, strength, influence, etc. pre'ponderant adj.

prepo'sition n word used with a noun or pronoun to show its relation with another word: walk to school; born in 1960; good at football, etc. —al adj. —al phrase, (eg in front of).

pre'posterous adj foolish; unreasonable; unnatural.

pre'rogative n (ruler's) special right or privilege(s).

pres'cribe v direct (that); order (medicine) to be taken (for an illness); require (books) to be studied (for an examination). pres'cription n sth —d, esp (written directions for preparing) medicine.

present[1] adj 1 at the place referred to. — company, those who are here. 2 existing now. 3 not past or

future: at the — time. n the — time. at —, now. for the —, for now, until later. 'presence n 1 being — in a place. 2 presence of mind, ability to act quickly and sensibly in time of danger, etc. —ly adv soon.

pre'sent[2] v 1 give, offer, put forward: — a cheque at the bank (for payment); — a petition to the Governor. 2 introduce (sb, esp to a person of high rank). 3 — oneself, appear, attend (for examination, trial, etc). 4 hold (a rifle, etc) in a certain way as a salute, etc: Present arms! 'present n sth given: birthday —s. pre'sentable adj fit to appear, be shown or seen, in public. ˌpresen'tation n —ing or being —ed; sth —ed (esp at a public ceremony).

pre'sentiment n premonition.

pre'serve v 1 keep safe; keep from loss, risk of going bad, etc: — eggs (one's eyesight). 2 care for or protect land and rivers, with the animals, birds, and fish. n 1 woods, streams, etc, where animals, birds, and fish are —d(2). 2 (usu pl) jam. ˌpreser'vation n 1 act of preserving. 2 condition of sth —d: in a good state of preservation, well —d. pre'servative n & adj (substance) for preserving.

pre'side v have or take the position of authority (over a business, at a meeting). 'president n 1 head of a government, esp in a republic. 2 head of certain government departments, of some business companies, colleges, societies, etc. ˌpresi'dential adj of a president or his duties.

press v 1 push against: — the trigger of a gun. 2 use force or weight to make sth flat, to get sth into a smaller space, to get juice out of fruit, etc. 3 keep close to and attack: — the enemy. 4 — for, make repeated requests for. 5 be —ed for (time, money, etc), have hardly enough, be in need of more. 6 demand attention: —ing affairs. 7 Time —es, there is need for speed, immediate action, etc. 8 — sb's hand, grasp it to show affection or sympathy. — sth into sb's hands, give sth to sb. 9 — sth on sb, urge him again and again to take (food, money, etc). n 1 act of —ing. 2 machine,

apparatus, for —ing: *a* '*wine-press.*
3 printing-machine. in the —,
being printed. 4 business for printing (and sometimes publishing)
books or newspapers. 5 the —,
newspapers, periodicals, journal-
ists. 6 cupboard for clothes, books,
etc. '—ing *adj* (of business) needing immediate attention; (of persons, their requests) insistent.

'pressure *n* 1 pressing; (the
amount of) force exerted continuously on or against sth by sth
else that touches it. — gauge,
apparatus for measuring the —
of a liquid or gas at a given point.
'pressure-,cooker, pot for cooking under high —. atmospheric
—, weight of the atmosphere as
measured by a barometer. 2 bring
— to bear (*on sb*), put — on (*sb*),
do sth that forces him (to do what
is required). work under —,
work hard owing to oppression,
having a great many things to get
done, etc. 'pressurized *adj* (of
an aircraft cabin) with air-pressure,
etc, adjustable for comfortable flying at great heights.

pres'tige *n* respect resulting from
the good reputation (of a person,
nation, etc); power or influence
caused by such respect.

pre'sume *v* 1 take for granted
(that); suppose to be true. 2 venture, dare: *May I — to . . .?* 3 —
upon, make a wrong use of, take
an unfair advantage of. pre-
'sumption *n* 1 sth —d(1). 2 behaviour that takes unfair advantage.
pre'sumptuous *adj* (of behaviour,
etc) too bold and self-confident.

,presup'pose *v* 1 presume before-
hand (*that*). 2 imply the existence
of. ,presuppo'sition *n.*

pre'tend *v* 1 make oneself appear
(to be sth, to be doing sth) either
in play or to deceive others. 2 claim,
say falsely: — *to like sb.* 3 — to,
put forward a false claim to. pre-
'tence *n* —ing; make-believe.
pre'tension *n* (statement of a)
claim. pre'tentious *adj* suggesting a claim to great merit or
importance.

'pretext *n* false reason for an action:
under the — of (that).

'pretty *adj* (-ier, -iest) pleasing and
attractive. *adv* (colloq) quite.
'prettily *adv.*

pre'vail *v* 1 gain the victory (*over*);
get control (*over*); fight successfully (*against*). 2 be generally
seen, done, etc. 3 — upon (sb to
do sth), persuade. 'prevalent *adj*
common; seen or done' everywhere.

pre'varicate *v* make untrue or
partly untrue statements. pre-
,vari'cation *n.*

pre'vent *v* 1 stop (sth) from
happening: — *an accident.* 2 keep
(sb *from* doing sth). —able *adj*
that can be —ed. —ion *n* —ing.
—ive *adj* serving or intended to —.

'previous *adj* coming earlier in time
or order: — *to,* before. —ly *adv.*

prey *n* 1 animal, bird, etc, killed
and eaten by another: *bird of* —,
kind that kills and eats other birds
and animals. 2 be a — to (*fears,*
etc), be greatly troubled by. *v* —
upon, take, hunt, (other animals,
etc) as —(1); (of fears, losses, etc)
trouble greatly.

price *n* money for which sth is (to
be) sold or bought; that which
must be done, given, or experienced to obtain or keep sth: *the —
of liberty. v* fix, ask about, the
— of sth; mark (goods) with a —.
'—less *adj* too valuable to be —d.

prick *v* 1 make a hole or mark in
(sth) with a sharp point; make
(a hole or mark) in this way. 2 hurt
with a sharp point: — *one's finger
with a needle.* 3 (of things) cause
sharp pain; (of parts of the body)
feel sharp pain. 4 — up the ears,
(esp of dogs, horses) raise the ears.
n small mark or hole, pain, caused
by the act of —ing. '—le *n* pointed
growth on the stem of a plant or
on the skin of some animals. *v* give
or have a —ing feeling. '—ly *adj*
having —les; —ling.

pride *n* 1 feeling of satisfaction
arising from what one does or
from persons, things, etc, one is
concerned with: *take — in one's
work.* 2 object of such feeling.
3 self-respect. 4 too high an
opinion of oneself, one's position,
etc. *v* — oneself (up)on, take —
in, be pleased and satisfied about.

priest *n* 1 clergyman of the
Roman Catholic and Anglican
Churches. 2 (of non-Christian
religions) person trained to perform special acts of religion.

prig *n* self-satisfied, self-righteous person. '**—gish** *adj*.

prim *adj* (**-mer, -mest**) neat; disliking, showing a dislike of, anything improper.

'**primary** *adj* **1** leading in time, order or development: *of* — (chief) *importance*. **— school,** first or earliest school. **2 — colours,** those from which other colours can be obtained: *red, yellow, blue*.

prime *adj* **1** chief; most important: **— minister** (in the Cabinet). **2** of best quality: **— beef.** *n* finest part. *v* get ready for use or action: *a — pump* (by putting water in it).

'**primitive** *adj* of the earliest times; of or at an early stage of social development: *— weapons, man,* etc.

primrose *n* pale yellow (flower).

prince *n* **1** ruler, esp of a small State. **2** son of a ruler, esp of a king or emperor. '**princess** *n* wife of a —; daughter, granddaughter, of a king or emperor. '**—ly** *adj* of or for a —; magnificent; very generous.

principal *adj* highest in order of importance. *n* **1** head of certain organizations, esp colleges. **2** person for whom another acts as business agent. **3** money lent, put into a business, etc, on which interest is payable. **—ly** *adj* chiefly.

principle *n* **1** basic truth; general law of cause and effect. **2** guiding rule for behaviour: *a man of high —s,* one who is honest and upright. **on —,** because of, obeying, —s, not because of self-interest.

print *v* **1** make marks on (paper, etc) by pressing it with inked type, etc; make (books, pictures, etc) in this way. **2** make (a photograph) on paper from a negative film or plate. **3** shape (one's letters, etc) like those used in —. *n* **1** mark(s), letters, etc, made by —ing(1) on paper, etc. **in —,** (of a book) —ed and on sale. **out of —,** (of a book) no more —ed copies available from the publisher. **2** (in compounds) mark made on a surface by sth pressed on it: '*finger-prints*. **3** (any special kind of) —ed lettering: *in small —*. **4** picture, design, made by —ing; photograph —ed from a negative. **5** cotton cloth with coloured designs, etc, —ed on it. '**—er** *n*.

'**—ing-press** *n* machine for —ing books, etc.

'**prior**[1] *adj* earlier in time or order. *adv* **— to,** before. **pri'ority** *n* being —; right to have or do sth before others.

'**prior**[2] *n* head of a religious order or house. '**—ess** *n* woman —. '**—y** *n* house governed by a —(ess).

prise ⇨ *prize*[2].

'**prism** *n* solid figure esp a glass — that separates sunlight into colours. ⇨ p 253.

'**prison** *n* building in which wrongdoers serve their sentences(2). **—er** *n* person held in —; person captured in war: *take a soldier —er*.

'**private** *adj* **1** (opp of *public*) of, for the use of, concerning, one person or a group of persons, not people in general: *a — letter*. **2** secret; kept secret: *— information*. **3** having no official position: *retiring to — life*. **4 a — soldier,** ordinary soldier (of the lowest rank). *n* **1** — soldier. **2 in —,** not in the presence of others. **—ly** *adv* in —; alone. '**privacy** *n*.

pri'vation *n* **1** lack of the necessaries of life: *suffering many —s*. **2** state of being deprived of sth.

'**privilege** *n* right or advantage held only by a person, class(1), etc. **—d** *adj* having, granted, a — or —s.

prize[1] *n* **1** sth (to be) awarded to one who succeeds in a competition, etc. **2** sth worth working for. **3** sth (esp a ship, its cargo) captured from the enemy in war. **4** (as *adj*) given as a —; awarded a —: *— cattle*. *v* value highly. '**prize-fight** *n* boxing match for which a money — is offered.

prize[2], **prise** *v* use force (to get a box, a lid *open, up, off*), eg with a lever.

pro- *prefix* supporting; favouring: *pro-British*. **pros and cons** *n pl* arguments for and against.

'**probable** *adj* likely to happen or to prove true or correct. '**probably** *adv*. ,**proba'bility** *n* being —; sth which is —.

pro'bation *n* **1** testing of a person's conduct, abilities, etc, before he is finally accepted for a position or admitted into a society, etc: *on —*. **2** (law) the **— system,** that by which (esp young) offenders are allowed to go unpunished for their first offence as long as they continue to live an honest life.

probe n slender instrument with a blunt end, used by doctors. v examine (as) with a —.

'problem n question to be solved or decided, esp sth difficult. ,prob-le'matic(al) adj (esp of a result) doubtful.

pro'cedure n regular order of doing things, esp legal and political affairs.

pro'ceed v 1 go forward (to a place); continue, go on (to do sth, with one's work, etc). 2 come, arise (from a cause). **—ing** n sth done or being done. **'proceeds** n pl results, profits, of an undertaking.

'process n 1 connected series of actions, changes, etc: the — of digestion. 2 method, esp industrial. 3 forward movement. **in — of** (completion), being (completed). v put (materials) through a —(2); treat in order to preserve: **—ed** leather (cheese).

pro'cession n number of persons, vehicles, etc, moving forward and following each other in an orderly way: a funeral —; marching in —.

pro'claim v make known publicly and officially. ,procla'mation n.

pro'crastinate v delay taking action. pro,crasti'nation n.

pro'cure v obtain, esp with care or effort. **pro'curable** adj.

prod v (-dd-) push or poke (at) with sth pointed. n poke or thrust.

'prodigal adj wasteful (of sth).

pro'digious adj surprisingly great.

'prodigy n sth surprising because it seems contrary to the laws of nature; person who has unusual or remarkable abilities.

pro'duce v 1 put or bring forward to be looked at or examined. 2 manufacture; create (works of art, etc). 3 yield (crops, etc); give birth to (young). 4 bring about; cause. 5 get (a play) ready for public performance in a theatre. **'produce** n that which is —d, esp by farming. **— r** n person who —s goods or plays. **'product** n 1 sth —d (by nature or man). 2 quantity obtained by multiplying numbers. **pro'duction** n process of producing; sth —d; quantity —d. **pro'ductive** adj 1 able to —;

fertile. 2 **productive of,** producing. ,produc'tivity n (esp) rate at which goods are produced per man per hour.

pro'fane adj 1 worldly (contrasted with holy, sacred). 2 having or showing contempt for God or sacred things: — language. v treat (sacred places, things) with contempt, without proper reverence. **pro'fanity** n (esp) — language.

pro'fess v 1 declare that one has (beliefs, likes, ignorance, etc). 2 have as one's profession. 3 represent oneself (to be, to do sth): I don't — to be an expert. **—ion** n 1 occupation requiring higher education and special training: the law, teaching, medicine, etc. 2 declaration of belief, feeling, etc: a —ion of loyalty.

pro'fessional adj 1 of a profession(1): — skill. 2 (opp of amateur) connected with, engaged in, the doing of sth for payment: — football; — musicians. n person who teaches or engages in some kind of sport for money; person who does sth for payment that others do for pleasure.

pro'fessor n university teacher of the highest rank.

'proffer v & n offer.

pro'ficient adj skilled, expert (in, at, sth). **pro'ficiency** n.

'profile n 1 side view, eg of the face. 2 edge or outline of sth.

'profit n 1 advantage or good obtained from sth. 2 money gained in business. v 1 get — (from); bring — to. 2 — by, be helped by. **—able** adj bringing —.

pro'found adj (-er, -est) 1 deep 2 needing, showing, having, great knowledge. 3 needing much thought and study to understand. **—ly** adv deeply; sincerely. **pro'fundity** n.

pro'fuse adj 1 plentiful; abundant. 2 — in (of), giving, using, producing, very (or too) generously. **—ly** adv. **pro'fusion** n great quantity.

'program(me) n 1 list of items, events, etc. (eg for a concert). 2 plan of what is to be done.

'progress n 1 forward movement: making good —. 2 development. **in —,** being carried on. 3 improvement. **pro'gress** v make —. pro-

'gressive *adj* 1 making continuous forward movement. 2 increasing by regular degrees. 3 getting better; supporting or favouring —.

pro'hibit *v* forbid (by law, etc) (sb *from* doing sth) say that sth must not be done, that sb must not do sth: *smoking* —ed. —ive *adj* (esp of prices) high enough to prevent use, purchase, etc: —*ive rents*. ,prohi'bition *n* —ing; order that —s sth, esp law —ing the sale of alcoholic drinks.

'project *n* (plan for a) scheme or undertaking. pro'ject *v* 1 make a plan for. 2 cause (a shadow, an outline, a picture from a film or slide) to fall on a surface (eg a wall, a screen). 3 stand out from the surrounding surface: —*ing eyebrows*. pro'jectile *n* sth (to be) shot forward, esp from a gun. pro'jection *n* —ing; sth —ed. pro'jector *n* apparatus for —ing pictures on a screen.

,prole'tariat *n* wage-earners (unskilled and semi-skilled workers, etc) contrasted with managers, professional people, landowners, etc.

pro'lific *adj* producing much or many.

'prologue *n* introductory part of a poem or play; (fig) first of a series of events.

pro'long *v* make longer. —ed *adj* continuing for a long time.

,prome'nade *n* (place suitable for, or specially made for, a) walk or ride taken for pleasure in public. *v* have, take sb for, a —.

'prominent *adj* 1 standing out; easily seen. 2 important; distinguished. 'prominence *n*.

'promise *n* 1 written or spoken undertaking to do, or not to do, sth, give sth, etc. 2 (sth that gives) hope of success or good results. *v* 1 make a —(1) to: —(sb) *help*; — *to do sth*; — *that* . . . 2 give cause or hope for expecting.

pro'mote *v* 1 give (sb) higher rank or position. 2 help forward; support: — *peace*. 3 help to organize and start (new business companies, etc). pro'motion *n*.

prompt¹ *adj* (-er, -est) acting, done, sent, given, without delay. '—ly *adv*. '—ness, '—itude *n*.

prompt² *v* 1 be the reason causing sb (*to* do sth). 2 follow the text

of a play and remind actors, when necessary, of their lines(5).

prone *adj* 1 (stretched out, lying) face downwards. 2 — *to*, inclined to.

prong *n* any one of the pointed parts of a fork.

'pronoun *n* word used in place of a noun: *he, she*, etc). pro'nominal *adj*.

pro'nounce *v* 1 say, make, the sound of (a word, etc). 2 declare, announce (esp sth official): —*judgement*. 3 give one's opinion. —d *adj* definite; strongly marked. pro,nunci'ation *n* way of pronouncing a word; way in which sb usually —s his words.

proof *n* 1 fact(s), method(s), reasoning, etc, showing that sth is true, that it is a fact. 2 act of testing whether sth is true, a fact, etc: *put sth to the* —. 3 trial copy of a book, picture, etc, for approval before other copies are printed. *adj* (esp in compounds) giving safety or protection against sth: *a fire-proof nightdress*.

prop *n* 1 support used to keep sth up: 'pit-props (supporting the roof of a coal-mine, etc). 2 person who supports sth or sb. 3 (also property) article used for a set in a play or film other than scenery, costumes, or furniture. *v* (-pp-) (often — up) support; keep in position.

,propa'ganda *n* (measures for the) spreading of information, ideas, etc, to advance a cause(3); 'propagate *v* 1 increase the number of (plants, animals, etc) by natural reproduction. 2 spread (news, etc) more widely. ,propa'gation *n*.

pro'pel *v* (-ll-) drive forward. —ler *n* shaft with blades for —ling a ship or aircraft.

'proper *adj* 1 right, fitting. 2 as required or expected by society: — *behaviour*. 3 — *noun*, noun used for one particular(1) person, place, etc: *Adam; Paris; Monday*. —ly *adv*.

'property *n* 1 sth which a person owns; possession(s); (esp) land, or land and building(s). 2 special quality belonging to sth: *a substance with the* — *of dissolving grease*. 3 ⇨ prop(3).

'prophecy *n* power of telling, statement of, what will happen in the future. **'prophesy** v say what will happen in the future. **'prophet** n 1 person who teaches religion and claims that his teaching comes to him direct from God: *the — Isaiah*; *Muhammad, the P— of Islam*. 2 person who tells what is to happen in the future. **'prophetess** n woman prophet. **pro'phetic** adj of — or a prophet.

pro'pitiate v lessen the anger of; win the favour of.

pro'pitious adj likely to bring success; favourable.

pro'portion n 1 relationship of one thing to another in quantity, size, etc; relation of a part to the whole. 2 (often pl) the correct relation of parts or of the sizes of the several parts. 3 (pl) size, measurements: *a building of magnificent —s*. 4 part; share. v put into — or right relationship. **—al** adj in proper —.

pro'pose v 1 offer or put forward. for consideration, as a suggestion, plan, or purpose. 2 offer marriage (to sb). 3 put forward (sb's name) for an office. **pro'posal** n 1 sth —d. 2 offer (esp of marriage). **,propo'sition** n 1 statement, esp for consideration or proof. 2 question or problem.

pro'pound v put forward (a theory, riddle, etc) for consideration or solution.

pro'prietor n person owning (esp landed) property; owner (esp of a hotel, shop). **pro'prietress** n woman —.

pro'priety n 1 state of being proper(2). 2 correctness; suitability.

pro'pulsion n propelling force.

pro'saic adj dull; commonplace.

prose n language not in verse form.

'prosecute v 1 continue with (one's trade, studies). 2 start legal proceedings against. **,prose'cution** n prosecuting or being —d; person, and his advisers, who —(2): *the case for the prosecution*.

'prospect n 1 wide view over land or sea or (fig) before the mind, in the imagination. 2 sth expected or hoped for. **pros'pect** v search underground (*for* gold, etc). **pros'pective** adj of the future.

pros'pector n person who prospects.

pros'pectus n. printed account giving details of and advertising sth (eg a school, a new business undertaking).

'prosper v succeed; do well. **pros'perity** n good fortune; state of being successful. **—ous** adj **—ing**.

'prostrate adj 1 lying stretched out on the ground, usu face downward (eg to show deep respect). 2 overcome (with grief, etc). **pros'trate** v 1 make (oneself) —. 2 be —d, be overcome (with grief, etc); be made helpless. **pros'tration** n being —d; complete exhaustion.

pro'tect v 1 keep safe (*from* harm, etc). 2 help (home industry) by taxing imports. **—ion** n **—ing** or being **—ed**; sth that **—s**. **—ive** adj giving **—ion**. **—orate** n country under the **—ion** of one of the great powers.

pro'test v 1 declare, against opposition (*that*). 2 raise an objection, say sth (*against*). 3 say that one is displeased (*about*). **'protest** n statement **—ing**. **do sth under —**, do it unwillingly, with the feeling that it is not right. **,protes'tation** n solemn declaration.

'Protestant n & adj (member) of any branch of the Christian Church except the Roman Catholic and Greek Orthodox Churches.

pro'tract v prolong: *a —ed visit*.

pro'trude v (cause to) stick out or project: *— the tongue*.

proud adj (-er, -est) 1 having, showing, pride: *— of one's success*. 2 causing pride. 3 (of things) looking splendid or important. **'—ly** adv.

prove v 1 supply proof of. 2 make certain of, by experiment or test: *— sb's worth*. 3 be seen or found in the end (*to* be).

'proverb n short saying, with words of advice or warning, in general use. **pro'verbial** adj widely known and talked about; admitted by all.

pro'vide v 1 give, supply (what is needed, esp what a person needs in order to live): *— for one's family*; *— one's family with food and clothing*. 2 make ready, do what is necessary (*for*); take steps to guard (*against*). 2 conj on condition (*that*). **pro'viding** conj on the condition or understanding (*that*).

'Providence n God; God's care: trust in —. **¡provi'dential** adj of, coming (as) from, P—: a providential escape.

'provident adj (careful about) providing for future needs.

'province n **1** large administrative division of a country. **2** branch of learning. **pro'vincial** adj **1** of a —. **2** of the speech, manners, ideas, etc, of a person living away from the capital. n person from the —.

pro'vision n **1** providing or preparation (esp for future needs). **2** (pl) food. **make — for**, provide for. **—al** adj for the present time only, and to be changed or replaced later. **—ally** adv.

pro'viso n limiting clause; condition(1).

pro'voke v **1** make angry; vex. **2** cause, arouse (discussion, laughter, etc). **3** drive (sb to do sth, into doing sth, etc). **pro'voking** adj annoying. **¡provo'cation** n provoking or being —d; sth that —s. **pro'vocative** adj likely to cause anger, argument, discussion, etc.

prow n pointed front of a ship.

'prowess n bravery; skill in fighting.

prowl v go about cautiously looking for a chance to get food (as wild animals do), to steal, etc. n on the —, **—ing**.

prox'imity n nearness.

'proxy n (document giving sb the) authority to represent or act for another, esp at an election; person given a —.

prude n person who is too modest or delicate in behaviour. **—ry** n.

'prudent adj careful; acting only after careful thought or planning. **—ly** adv. **'prudence** n.

prune¹ n dried plum.

prune² v cut away parts of trees, bushes, etc, to control growth or shape.

pry¹ v **pry into**, inquire too curiously into (other people's affairs, conduct).

pry² v lift up, get open, by force, esp with a lever.

psalm n sacred song or hymn, esp one of those in the Bible.

pseudo-prefix seeming to be but not really; false: **¡pseudo-intel'lectual**.

'pseudonym n name taken by a writer, etc, instead of his real name.

psy'chiatry n treatment of mental illness. **psy'chiatrist** n expert in —.

'psychic adj of the soul or the mind. **psy'chology** n science, study, of the mind and its processes. **¡psycho'logical** adj.

pub n short for public house.

'public adj (opp of private) of, for, owned by, done by or for, known to, people in general: a — library. **— house**, house (not a hotel, club, etc) whose chief business is to sell beer, spirits, etc, to be drunk there. **— spirit**, readiness to work for the good of all. n the —, people in general. **in —**, openly, not in secret or in private. **—ly** adv in —. **pub'licity** n **1** state of being known to, seen by, everyone: trying to avoid —ity. **2** advertising.

¡publi'cation n **1** (act of) publishing. **2** sth published; a book, periodical, etc.

'publish v **1** make known to the public. **2** announce (a book, etc) as on sale and sell it. **—er** n (person engaged in the) business of magazines, etc; —ing of books.

'pucker v draw together into small folds or wrinkles. n small fold or wrinkle.

'pudding n dish of food, usu a sweet soft mixture, served as part of a meal, usually after the meat course.

'puddle n small dirty pool of rainwater, eg on a road.

puff n (sound of a) short, quick sending out of breath or wind; steam, smoke, etc, sent out at one time. v **1** send out —s; move along with —s; breathe quickly (as after running). **2** cause to swell out with air: —ing out his chest with pride. **'—y** adj (-ier, -iest).

pug'nacious adj fond of, in the habit of, fighting. **pug'nacity** n.

pull v **1** (opp of push) take hold of (sth, sb) and bring (it, him) nearer; move (it, him) along from in front: — a cart; remove sth from where it is fixed: — a tooth out. **2** (with adv) — through, come safely through illness, trouble, etc. — oneself together, get oneself, one's feelings, etc, under control.

— up, stop. — sb or sth up, cause to stop. 3 (with *nouns*) — a face, show dislike, disgust, disappointment, etc. — sb's leg, try to deceive him in order to have a joke. — one's weight, do one's fair share of work with others. *n* act of —ing; force used in —ing.

'pull,over *n* knitted garment —ed on over the head.

'pulley *n* wheel with rope or chain, used for lifting things.

pulp *n* 1 soft fleshy part of fruit. 2 soft mass of other material, esp of wood fibre as used for making paper. *v* make into — or like —; become (like) —.

'pulpit *n* raised and enclosed structure in a church, used by the priest or clergyman for sermons, etc.

pulse *n* the regular beat of the arteries (eg as felt at the wrist) as blood is pumped through them by the heart. pul'sate *v* throb.

'pulverize *v* become, grind to, powder.

'pummel *v* (-ll-) beat repeatedly with the fist(s).

pump *n* machine for forcing liquid, gas, or air into or out of sth. *v* use a —; force (water, etc) (*out, up,* etc); make (a tyre, etc) full of air.

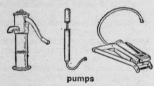

pumps

'pumpkin *n* (creeping plant with) large round yellow fruit with many seeds in it. ⇨ p 115.

pun *n* humorous use of words which sound the same but have different meanings: *The current cost of electricity is rising.* *v* (-nn-) make puns; make a pun (*on, upon,* a word).

punch[1] *v* strike hard with the fist. *n* blow given with the fist.

punch[2] *n* tool, machine, for making holes (eg in leather, in tickets). *v* use a — to make a hole in sth.

'punctual *adj* neither early nor late; coming, doing sth, at the right time. —ly *adv.* ,punctu'ality *n.*

'punctuate *v* put marks (eg , ; : ! ?) into a piece of writing. ,punctu'ation *n.*

'puncture *n* small hole (esp in a bicycle or car tyre) made by sth pointed. *v* make (get) a — in.

'pungent *adj* sharp; stinging.

'punish *v* cause (sb) to suffer pain or discomfort for wrongdoing. —ment *n* (method of) —ing or being —ed. 'punitive *adj* (intended for) —ing.

'puny *adj* (-ier, -iest) small and weak.

pup *n* short for *puppy.*

'pupil[1] *n* person who is being taught in school or by a private teacher.

'pupil[2] *n* circular opening in the centre of the eye, regulating the passage of light.

'puppet *n* doll, etc, with jointed limbs moved by wires, etc.

'puppy *n* (*pl* -ies) young dog.

'purchase *v* buy. *n* 1 buying. 2 sth bought. 3 firm hold or grip.

'purdah *n* (esp in Muslim communities) curtain or veil for, convention of, keeping women out of the sight of men: *in* —.

pure *adj* (-r, -st) 1 unmixed with any other substance. 2 clean; without evil or sin: — *in body and mind.* 3 (of sounds) clear and distinct. 4 complete: — *nonsense.* '—ly *adv* (esp) entirely; completely. '—ness *n.* 'purity *n.* 'purify *v* make —. ,purifi'cation *n.*

purge *v* make clean or free (*of, from,* impure matter). *n* purging; medicine for purging the bowels.

'puritan *n* person who is strict in morals and the Christian religion.

'purple *n & adj* (colour of) red and blue mixed together.

'purpose *n* 1 what one means to do, get, be, etc; intention. 2 what sth is designed for. 3 power of forming plans and keeping to them. 4 on —, by intention, not by chance. to no —, without result. *v* have as a —(1). —ly *adv* on —.

purr *v & n* (make the) cat's low throbbing sound of contentment.

purse *n* small bag, of leather, plastic, etc, for money. *v* draw (the lips) together in tiny folds or wrinkles.

'purser *n* officer responsible for a ship's accounts, stores, etc.

pur'sue v 1 go after in order to catch up with, capture or kill. 2 go on with (eg one's studies). **pur'suit** n pursuing; sth occupying one's time: *literary pursuits*.

pur'vey v supply (esp food *to*).

pus n thick yellowish-white liquid formed in and coming out from a poisoned place in the body.

push v 1 (opp of *pull*) use force directly on (sth, sb) and send (it, him) further away; move (it, him) from behind; exert pressure against. 2 — on (along, forward), go on with one's journey, work, etc. **be —ed for** (*time*, etc), have hardly enough for one's needs. 3 (fig) urge, force (sb, oneself, *to do* sth). n 1 act of —ing. 2 determination to make one's way, attract attention, etc. 3 **at a —**, if compelled.

puss n cat. **'pussy** n (*pl* -ies) (child's name for a) cat.

put v (*pt & pp* put) 1 cause to be in a certain place or position or in a certain relation or condition. 2 (with *adv*) **put sth away**, put into the proper place. **put by**, save for future use. **put down**, write down; suppress. **put sb down as**, consider him to be. **put in**, advance (a claim); submit (a document). **put in for**, be a candidate for (a position). **put off**, make the time (of an event, for doing sth) later; make excuses in order not to have to do sth one has promised to do or that one ought to do. **put on**, give oneself (a certain appearance, etc); arrange for, make available (eg extra trains); increase (speed, weight). **put out**, cause (sth) to stop burning; cause (sb) to be troubled or annoyed. **put up**, raise; offer (a prayer); offer (goods for sale); provide, obtain, food and lodging. **put up with**, bear patiently, without protest. 3 (in phrases) **put an end to**, cause to end. **be hard put to it**, be in difficulties. **put to death**, kill. **put sb in mind of**, cause him to recall. **put sth in hand**, make a start in doing sth. 4 express in words an idea for consideration: *I put it to you that. . . .*

putrefy v (cause to) become rotten. **putre'faction** n. **'putrid** adj rotten; decomposed: *putrid fish*.

'puttee n long band of cloth wound round the leg from ankle to knee.

'putty n soft paste of powder and oil for fixing glass in window frames. v fix with —.

'puzzle n 1 question or problem difficult to understand or answer. 2 problem (eg *crossword* —) or toy designed to test a person's skill or knowledge. v 1 cause (sb) to be perplexed. 2 — sth out, (try to) find the answer by hard thought.

'pygmy, pigmy n member of a race of very short persons in Africa.

py'jamas n *pl* loose-fitting jacket and trousers for sleeping in.

'pylon n tall steel framework for supporting power cables.

'pyramid n solid figure with a triangular or square base and sloping sides meeting at a point ⇨ p 253; structure of this shape, esp one of those built in ancient Egypt.

pyre n large pile of wood for burning a dead body.

'python n large snake that kills its prey by twisting itself round it and crushing it.

Q

quack[1] v & n (make the) cry of a duck.

quack[2] n 1 person dishonestly claiming to have knowledge and skill (esp of medicine).

'quadrangle n 1 plane four-sided figure, esp a square or rectangle. 2 space enclosed by buildings on three or four sides, esp in a college.

'quadrant n 1 a fourth part of a circle or its circumference. 2 instrument for measuring angles (of altitude) in astronomy and navigation.

,quadri'lateral adj & n (four-sided) plane figure, eg a square.

'quadruped n four-footed animal.

quad('ruplet n one of four people born together of the same mother.

quaff v (liter) drink deeply.

'quagmire n bog; marsh.

quail v feel or show fear.

quaint adj attractive or pleasing

because unfamiliar or old-fashioned.

quake v shake; tremble.

'qualify v 1 make or become trained or entitled (*to do sth, for doing sth, for a post, as a teacher*). 2 limit; make less inclusive or less general. **,qualifi'cation** n 1 training, test, etc, that qualifies(1) a person: *a doctor's qualifications.* 2 sth that qualifies(2) or limits.

'quality n 1 (degree, esp high degree, of) goodness or worth: *material of the best —; a poor — of cloth.* 2 sth that is special in sth or sb; sth that distinguishes a person or thing: *One — of honey is sweetness.*

qualm n 1 feeling of doubt, esp about sth one is doing or has just done. 2 feeling of faintness or sickness that lasts for only a few moments.

'quandary n state of perplexity.

'quantity n (*pl* -ies) 1 the property(2) of things that can be measured (eg size, weight, amount, number). 2 a certain amount or number: *buy things in* — (*in large quantities*).

'quarantine n (period of) separation from others until there is no danger of spreading disease: *in — for a week.* v put or keep in —.

'quarrel n 1 angry argument or disagreement. 2 cause for being angry; reason for complaint. v (-ll-) have, take part in, a —; find fault (*with*). **—some** adj in the habit of —ling; fond of —ling.

'quarry[1] n place where stone, slate, etc, is got out of the ground. v get (stone, etc) from a —.

'quarry[2] n animal, bird, etc, that is hunted.

quart n two pints or 1·14 litres.

'quarter n 1 one part of sth divided into four equal parts; ¼. 2 period of three months ending on a *quarter-day.* 3 part; direction: *travel in every — of the globe.* 4 (USA) (coin worth) 25 cents. 5 district (esp of a town): *the business —.* 6 one-fourth of a lunar month; the moon's phase at the end of the first or third week. 7 eight bushels. 8 unit of weight, 28 pounds. 9 mercy to a defeated enemy: *give (ask for)* —. 10 (*pl*)

lodgings, esp the place where soldiers are lodged. 11 at close **—s**, close together. v 1 divide into —s(1). 2 find —s(10) for; place (soldiers) in —s(10). **'quarter-day** n one of the four days in the year on which three three-monthly accounts are due. **—ly** adv & adj (happening) once every three months.

quar'tet(te) n (piece of music for) four players or singers.

quartz n sorts of hard mineral including some that contain gold.

'quaver v 1 (of the voice or a sound) shake; tremble. 2 say or sing in a shaking voice. n —ing sound.

quay n (usu stone) landing-place built for ships in a harbour, on a river bank, etc.

queen n 1 wife of a king. 2 woman ruler. 3 (— *bee*, etc) egg-producing (bee, etc). **'—ly** adj of, suitable for, a —.

queer adj 1 strange; unusual. 2 causing doubt or suspicion. 3 (colloq) ill or faint. **'—ly** adv. **'—ness** n.

quell v subdue (a rebellion).

quench v put out (flames); satisfy (thirst); put an end to (hopes).

'query n question, esp one raising a doubt about the truth of sth. v ask (*if, whether*).

quest n in — of, in search of.

'question n 1 sentence asking for information, permission, etc. **question-mark**, sign ? used at the end of a printed or written —. 2 problem, etc, needing to be discussed and decided. **out of the —**, impossible. (*the man*, etc) **in —**, being talked about. **beyond —**, without doubt. v 1 ask —(s) of 2 express doubt (about); feel doubt (*whether*). **—able** adj which may be —ed(2); doubtful.

queue n line of people waiting for their turn (eg to enter a cinema). v (often — up) get into, be in, a —.

quick adj (-er, -est) 1 moving fast done in a short time; able to move fast and do things in a short time 2 lively; bright; active. n sensitiv part of flesh (esp under the nails). **cut to the —**, (*fig*) hurt in one' feelings. **'—ly** adv. **—en** v 1 mak or become —er. 2 (cause to become (more) lively and active **'—sand** n (area of) loose, wet deep sand which sucks down men, animals, etc, that try to walk on it. **'—silver** n mercury.

'quiet adj (-er, -est) **1** with little or no movement or sound. **2** free from excitement, trouble, anxiety. **3** gentle. **4** (of colours) not bright. v (also **—en**) make or become **—(1),(2)**. **—ly** adv. **—ness** n.

quill n large wing or tail feather, esp one used (formerly) for writing with.

quilt n bed-cover placed over a blanket.

qui'nine n bitter liquid used as a medicine for fevers.

quin('tuplet) n one of five people born together of the same mother.

quit v (-tt-) **1** go away from. **2** stop (doing sth). adj be **—** of, be no longer burdened or troubled with. **—s** adj be **—s**, be on even terms (with sb) by paying a debt.

quite adv **1** completely. **2** rather. **3** (in an answer) **—** (so), expressing understanding or agreement.

'quiver v (cause to) tremble slightly.

quix'otic adj generous; unselfish; acting in disregard of one's own welfare.

quiz v (-zz-) ask questions of, as a test of knowledge. n such a test. **'—zical** adj **1** teasing. **2** comical.

'quota n agreed share, amount, or number, esp the quantity of goods (number of immigrants) allowed to enter a country.

quote v **1** repeat, write (words used by another); repeat or write words (from a book, etc). **2** give (a reference, etc) to support a statement. **3** name, mention (a price). **quo'tation** n sth **'—d(1),(3)**. **quotation marks**, the marks (' ' or " ") placed before and after the word(s) **—d**.

R

'Rabbi n (title of a) Jewish priest.

'rabbit n small animal living in a burrow. ⇨ p 12.

'rabble n disorderly crowd.

'rabid adj **1** suffering from rabies. **2** furious.

'rabies n fatal disease spread by dogs, cats, etc.

race¹ n **1** competition in speed (eg in running). **2** strong, fast current of water in a river, the sea, etc. v **1** run a **—** (with, against). **2** cause (a horse, etc) to **—**. **3** (cause to) move at great speed. **'race-course** n ground prepared for horse-races.

race² n **1** tribe or nation (group of tribes or nations) having, or thought to have, the same original ancestors. **2** main division of living things: the human **—**. **'racial** adj of a **—**; concerning differences between **—s** of men: racial·harmony.

rack¹ n **1** wooden or metal framework for holding food (esp hay) for animals. **2** framework for holding things, hanging things on,

a luggage rack

etc. **3** instrument used in olden days for torturing a victim by stretching. v **1** torture; (fig) cause severe pain to. **2** **—** one's brains (for an answer, etc), make great mental efforts.

rack² n go to **—** and ruin, fall into a ruined state.

'racket¹ n uproar; loud noise.

'racket², **'racquet** n stringed bat used in tennis, etc.

'radar n radio apparatus that indicates solid objects which come within its range, used by pilots, eg in fog or darkness.

'radiate v **1** send out rays of (light or heat); come or go out in rays. **2** give out, show (joy, etc). **3** spread out like radii from a centre. **'radiant** adj **1** radiating. **2** (of sb's face, looks) bright; happy. **'radiator** n **1** apparatus for radiating heat, esp heat from steam or hot water supplied in pipes. **2** device for cooling a motor-car's engine.

,radi'ation n the sending out of heat, energy, etc, in rays; sth radiated.

'radical adj **1** (fig) thorough and complete: **—** changes. **2** favouring **—** changes in political systems, etc. n person with **—(2)** opinions.

'radio n **1** wireless telegraphy;

broadcasting. **2** apparatus for receiving broadcasts. *v* send by —.

'**radio-** *prefix* of rays, esp X-rays. —**graph** *n* X-ray photograph.

'**radium** *n* metal that gives out radiation that is able to pass through solid substances.

'**radius** (*pl* '**radii**) *n* **1** straight line from the centre of a circle or a sphere to any point on the circumference or surface of it. **2** circular area measured by its —: *within a* — *of ten miles.*

'**raffia** *n* fibres from dried leafstalks of a palm, for making baskets, bats, etc.

'**raffle** *n* sale of an article by lottery. *v* sell (sth) by this method.

raft *n* number of logs or boards fastened together in order to float on a river or to serve as a boat.

'**rafter** *n* one of the sloping beams supporting a roof.

rag[1] *n* **1** odd bit of cloth. **2** (*pl*) old or torn clothes: *dressed in rags.* '**ragged** *adj* **1** (with clothes) badly torn or in rags. **2** rough; irregular.

rag[2] *v* (-**gg**-) play rough practical jokes (on).

rage *n* (outburst of) furious anger; violence. *v* be violent.

raid *v & n* (make a) sudden attack on, surprise visit to. '—**er** *n* person, ship, aircraft, etc, making a —.

rail[1] *n* **1** wooden or metal bar or rod, or number of such bars or rods placed end to end, as a fence or barrier, to hang things on, etc. **2** steel bar forming a railway or tramcar track. **by** —, by train. *v* put —s(1) round; shut (*in* or *off*) by means of —s(1). '—**ing** *n* (often *pl*) fence of —s(1). '—**road** *n* (USA) —**way**. '—**way** *n* (system of) track(s) on which trains run.

rail[2] *v* complain angrily.

rain *n* **1** water falling in drops from clouds. **2** thick, fast, fall like —: *a —of bullets.* **3** the —**s**, the rainy season in some tropical countries. *v* **1** send down —. **2** come, fall, send, (*down, upon*) like —. '—**bow** *n* many-coloured arch seen in the sky when the sun shines on falling —drops. '—**fall** *n* amount of —falling on a place in a certain period. '—**proof** *adj* able to keep — out. '—**y** *adj* (-**ier**, -**iest**) having much —: *a —y day.*

raise *v* **1** lift up (eg a weight, one's hat, voice, etc); make (prices, the temperature, sb's hopes, etc) higher; put up, build (eg a monument). **2** cause to rise or appear: *— the dust* (*trouble*). **3** bring up for attention or discussion: *— a protest* (*a new point*). **4** grow or produce (crops); breed (cattle, etc); bring up (a family). **5** get or bring together; manage to get: *— an army* (*a loan*). **6** *—a siege* (*blockade*), end it.

'**raisin** *n* dried grape.

'**rajah** *n* Indian prince; Malay chief.

rake *n* long-handled tool, used for smoothing soil, gathering together dead leaves, etc. ⇨ p 293. *v* use a — on (soil, etc); get (sth *together*, *out*, etc) with a —.

'**rally**[1] *v* **1** (cause to) come together, esp after defeat or confusion, to make a new stand and new efforts. **2** (cause to) recover (health, strength). *n* **1** —**ing**. **2** public meeting, esp to support a cause. **3** gathering of cars or motorbikes, etc.

'**rally**[2] *v* tease in a good-humoured way; make fun of.

ram *n* **1** male sheep. **2** instrument for —**ming** or battering. *v* (-**mm**-) strike and push heavily.

'**ramble** *v* walk for pleasure with no special destination in the countryside; (fig) wander in one's talk, not keeping to the subject. *n* rambling walk. '**rambling** *adj* (esp) (of buildings, streets) extending in various directions irregularly, as if built without planning.

'**ramify** *v* form or produce branches; make or become complicated.

ramp *n* rising bank of earth; sloping way joining two levels.

'**rampant** *adj* (esp of diseases, social evils) unchecked; beyond control.

'**rampart** *n* earthen bank, broad wall, etc, for defence.

'**ramshackle** *adj* almost collapsing.

ran ⇨ run.

ranch *n* (esp USA) large farm.

'**rancid** *adj* (esp of fat, butter) stale, ill-smelling.

'**rancour** *n* deep, long-lasting hate or ill will. '**rancorous** *adj*.

'**random** *n* **at** —, without aim or system. *adj* done or made at —.

rang ⇨ ring.

range n **1** line or series of things, esp mountains. **2** area of land with targets for firing at. **3** distance to which a gun will shoot or to which a shell, etc, can be fired: *in (out of) —.* **4** distance between limits: *a wide — of colours.* **5** cooking-stove with an oven. v **1** arrange in order, in a row or rows. **2** go, move (*over, through,* etc). **3** extend in a line. **4** vary between limits: *prices ranging between 5p and 10p.* **'range-,finder** n instrument for measuring the distance of sth to be fired at.

rank¹ n **1** line of persons or things, esp (army) a row of soldiers standing side by side: *the —s, the — and file.* **other —s,** private(4) soldiers and corporals. **2** position in a scale, esp·in the armed forces: *promoted to the — of captain.* v **1** arrange in a —(1) or —s(1). **2** have, put in, a certain —(2), compared with others. **rank²** adj (-er, -est) **1** (of plants, land, etc) overgrown. **2** offensive; having a bad smell or taste. **3** unpardonable.

'rankle v (of thoughts, insults, etc) continue to be bitter in the mind.

'ransack v **1** search (sth) thoroughly (*for*). **2** rob; plunder.

'ransom n freeing of a prisoner upon payment to his captor(s); the money paid. v set (make) free on payment of —.

rant v speak noisily, without restraint.

rap v & n (-pp-) (give a) quick, light blow (with the knuckles, a stick, etc).

ra'pacious adj greedy (esp for money). **ra'pacity** n greed.

'rapid adj very quick. n (usu pl) part of a river where a steep slope causes the water to·flow fast. **-ly** adv. **ra'pidity** n.

rapt adj so deep in thought or moved by joy that one is unaware of other things: *— in a book.* **'rapture** n state of deep pleasure: *go in (go into) raptures about sth.*

rare adj (-r, -st) **1** not often seen or happening. **2** unusually good. **3** (of substances) thin, not dense. **'—ly** adv seldom. **'rarefied** adj = —(3). **'rarity** n scarcity; sth —(1).

'rascal n **1** dishonest person.

2 (playfully) mischievous person (esp a child).

rash¹ n (breaking out of) many tiny red spots on the skin.

rash² adj too hasty; done, doing things, without enough thought of the consequences. **'—ly** adv.

'rasher n slice of bacon or ham.

rasp n metal tool with surfaces covered with sharp points, used for scraping. v **1** scrape with a —. **2** make a harsh grating sound; (fig) irritate (the feelings).

'raspberry n (bush with) small, sweet, (red) berry. ⇨ p 115.

rat n animal like, but larger than, a mouse. ⇨ p 12.

rate¹ n **1** standard of reckoning, by bringing two numbers or amounts into relationship: *travelling at the — of thirty miles an hour.* **the annual birth —,** the number of births in relation to a number (eg 1,000) of people during one year. **2** at this (that) —, if this (that) is true, if this (that) state of affairs continues. **at any —,** in any case, whatever happens. **3** —s, charges payable by householders to local authorities for education, water-supply, etc. **4** first (second, third) —, excellent (fairly good, rather poor). v judge or estimate the value or worth of; consider: *— sb's abilities high.*

rate² v scold.

'rather adv **1** more willingly; by preference: *I would — visit you tomorrow.* **2** more precisely: *He arrived late last night, or —, early this morning.* **3** somewhat: *Look at that — tall boy over there.*

'ratify v confirm (an agreement) by signature or other formality. **,ratifi'cation** n.

'rating n **1** class or grade, esp of ships (according to tonnage). **2** (in a ship) person's rank. **3** (Navy) sailor who is not an officer.

'ratio n relation between two amounts expressed by dividing one by the other: *The —s of 20 to 100 and 1 to 5 are the same.*

'ration n fixed quantity, esp of food, allowed to one person. v limit (people, goods) to —s.

'rational adj of reason(ing); able to reason; sensible; that can be tested by reason.

'rattle v **1** (cause to) make short,

sharp sounds quickly one after the other: *windows that — in the wind.* 2 talk, say sth, in a fast, lively way. 3 move, fall (*down, past*, etc) with a rattling ·noise. *n* (baby's toy making a) rattling noise.

'**rattlesnake** *n* poisonous American snake that makes a rattling noise with its tail.

'**raucous** *adj* (of sounds) harsh; rough.

'**ravage** *v* 1 destroy; damage badly. 2 rob with violence. *n* (usu *pl*) destruction; destructive effects (*of*).

rave *v* talk wildly or angrily; talk with foolish enthusiasm (*of*, *about*). '**ravings** *n pl* such talk.

'**raven** *n* large, black bird like a crow. *adj* (esp of hair) black.

'**ravenous** *adj* very hungry.

'**ravishing** *adj* giving great pleasure.

raw *adj* 1 uncooked. 2 in the natural state; not manufactured or prepared for use. 3 (of persons) untrained, inexperienced. 4 (of the weather) damp and cold. 5 (of a place on the flesh) with the skin rubbed off.

ray *n* 1 line, beam, of light, heat, energy: *the rays of the sun.* 2 any one of a number of lines coming out from a centre.

'**rayon** *n* silk-like material.

raze *v* destroy (towns, buildings) completely, esp by knocking them down to the ground.

'**razor** *n* instrument for shaving.

re- *prefix* 1 again: *reappear.* 2 again and in a different way: *regroup.*

reach *v* 1 stretch (the hand *for*, or out, *out for*, sth); stretch out the hand for and take sth: — (*out one's hand*) *for a book.* 2 get to, go as far as; amount to. *n* (extent or. distance of) —ing: *within easy — of London.* **out of —,** too far away to be —ed. **within —,** near enough to get at (to).

re'act *v* 1 have an effect *on* the person or thing acting. 2 — **to,** behave differently, be changed, as the result of being acted upon, —**ion** *n* action resulting from, in answer to, sth, esp a return to an earlier condition after a period of the opposite condition. —**ionary** *n & adj* (person supporting) political —ion; opponent of progress.

read *v* (*pt & pp* read) 1 look at and

(be able to) understand printed or written words; say what is written or printed. 2 study (a subject, esp at a university): —*ing physics.* *n* period of time given to —ing: *have a quiet —.* '—**able** *adj* that can be read; that is easy or pleasant to —. '—**er** *n* 1 sb in the act of —ing(1). 2 school —ing-book. 3 university teacher junior to a professor. '—**ing** *n* (esp) 1 knowledge, esp of books: *a man of wide —ing.* 2 figure of measurement, etc, as shown on a scale, etc, at a particular time: *the —ing on a thermometer.*

'**ready** *adj* 1 in the condition needed for use; in the condition for doing sth; willing (to do sth). 2 quick, prompt: *a — answer.* 3 — **money,** money (esp coins and notes) available for cash payments. **ready-made,** (esp of clothes) made in standard sizes, not made specially to the wearer's measurements. '**readily** *adv* willingly; without difficulty. '**readiness** *n*: *in readiness for,* —(1) for.

real *adj* 1 existing in fact; not imagined or supposed; not made up or artificial. 2 (law) — **estate,** land and buildings. **re'ality** *n* 1 quality of being —. **in —ity,** in actual fact. 2 sth actually seen, experienced, etc. '**really** *adv* truly.

'**realize** *v* 1 be fully aware of; understand: — *that one is wrong.* 2 change or convert (a hope, plan, etc) into a fact: — *an ambition.* 3 exchange (property, etc) for money; (of property) be sold at (a certain price or profit). ,**reali'zation** *n.*

realm *n* kingdom.

ream *n* measurement of 480 sheets of paper.

reap *v* cut (grain, etc); gather in grain from (a field, etc). —**er** *n* person or machine that —s.

rear¹ *n* 1 back part (eg of a building). 2 last part of an army, fleet, etc. **bring up the —,** come or be last. 3 (as *adj*) at the back: *the — entrance.*

rear² *v* 1 cause or help to grow; bring up: — *poultry* (*a family*). 2 (esp of a horse) rise on the hind legs. 3 raise (the head).

'**reason** *n* 1 (fact put forward or

serving as the) cause of or justification for sth. **by —** of, because of. **2** power of the mind to understand, form opinions, etc: *It stands to —*, It is clear (that). *v* **1** make use of one's — (2) (*about* sth). **2** argue, use —s(1) (*with* sb); put forward as a — (1): *he —ed that....* **—able** *adj* **1** able to —; willing to listen to —. **2** acting, done, in accordance with —. **3** moderate; that can be agreed to. **—ably** *adv*.

reas'sure *v* dispel the fears or doubts of (sb).

re'bel *v* (-ll-) **1** rise (against authority); take up arms to fight (*against* the government). **2** show resistance (to authority, etc). **'rebel** *n* person who —s. **re'bellion** *n* —ling, esp an armed rising. **re'bellious** *adj*.

re'bound *v* spring back after striking sth. **'rebound** *n* on the —, while springing back.

re'buff *n* unkind refusal of (an offer of or request for sth). *v* give a — to.

re'buke *v* reprove. *n* reproof.

re'call *v* **1** summon back (eg an ambassador). **2** bring back (an event, etc) to the mind. *n* —ing.

re'cant *v* give up, take back, (a belief, statement) as being false.

reca'pitulate *v* repeat the chief points of (an argument, etc). **'reca,pitu'lation** *n*.

re'cede *v* **1** (appear to) go backwards from the observer or from an earlier position. **2** slope away from the front or from the observer.

re'ceipt *n* **1** receiving or being received. **2** (*pl*) money received (in a business, etc). **3** written statement that sth (esp money) has been received. **4** recipe. *v* write out and sign a — (3).

re'ceive *v* **1** take (sth offered, sent, etc). **2** experience: *— a warm welcome.* **3** allow to enter; be ready to see, welcome, or entertain. **—d** *adj* widely accepted as correct. **—r** *n* **1** radio **—r**, for receiving broadcasts. **2** part of a telephone apparatus that is held to the ear.

'recent *adj* (having existed, been made, happened) not long before; begun not long ago. **—ly** *adv*.

re'ceptacle *n* bag, box, or other container.

re'ception *n* **1** act or manner (1) of receiving sth or sb. **2** formal party: *a wedding —.* **re'ceptive** *adj* ready to receive' (eg suggestions).

re'cess *n* **1** period of time when work is stopped (eg when the law courts, Parliament, are not in session). **2** part of a room where the wall is set back from the main part. **3** dark or secret inner place or part.

'recipe *n* directions for preparing food or for getting a result.

re'cipient *n* person who receives sth.

re'ciprocal *adj* given and received in return: *— affection.* **re'ciprocate** *v* (of two persons) give and receive, each to each; (of one person) give in return.

re'cite *v* **1** say (esp poems) aloud from memory. **2** give a list of, tell, (names, facts, etc) one by one. **re'cital** *n* **1** telling of facts; account (eg of one's adventures). **2** musical performance by one person or of the works of one composer. **reci'tation** *n* **1** reciting. **2** sth (to be) —d.

'reckless *adj* rash; not thinking (*of*): *— of the consequences.*

'reckon *v* **1** find out (the quantity, number, cost, etc) by working with numbers. **— up**, add up. **— in**, include when —ing. **2 — with**, take into account; settle accounts with. **3** look upon (*as*); be of the opinion (*that*). **4 — (up)on**, base one's hopes or plans on. **—ing** *n* (esp) list of charges (*for* sth): *out in one's —ing*, mistaken in one's calculations.

re'claim *v* **1** bring back (waste land, etc) to a useful condition. **2** reform (eg a criminal). **,reclam'ation** *n*.

re'cline *v* be, place oneself, in a position of rest; put (one's arms, etc) in a resting position.

re'cluse *n* person who lives by himself and avoids other people.

'recognize *v* **1** know again, identify, (sb or sth) that one has seen, heard, etc, before. **2** be willing to accept (sb or sth) as what (he or it) is said to be. **3** be aware (*that*); be ready to admit; acknowledge. **,recog-'nition** *n* recognizing or being —d.

re'coil *v* & *n* **1** jump back (*from*, eg in fear). **2** (of a gun) kick back (on being fired).

,recol'lect *v* call back to the mind.

—ion n **1** time over which the memory goes back. **2** sth **—ed**. **3** act or power of **—ing**.

,recom'mend v **1** say that one thinks sth is good (for) or that sb is fitted (for a post, etc). **2** advise; suggest as being suitable or suitable. **3** (of a quality, etc) cause to be or appear pleasing or satisfactory. ,recommen'dation n (esp) statement that —s(1) sb or sth.

're'compense v reward or punish; pay (sb) (for loss or injury). n reward; payment.

'reconcile v **1** cause (persons) to become friends after they have quarrelled. **2** settle (quarrels, differences of opinion); bring into harmony. **3** — oneself (to sth), overcome one's dislike of it. ,reconcili'ation n.

,recon'dition v put into good condition again.

,recon'noitre v go to or go near (the enemy's position, etc) to learn about his strength, position, etc. re'connaissance n.

re'cord v **1** set down in writing for reference. **2** preserve for use, etc, by writing or in other ways (eg by means of photographs, records(2), etc). **3** (of an instrument) mark on a scale, etc. 'record n **1** written account of facts, events, etc; **—ed** facts about sb or sth, esp past history: school —s. **2** disc, etc, on which music, speech, etc, has been **—ed**. 'record-player, ⇨ gramophone. **3** score, point, attainment, mark, etc (high or low), not reached before; (esp in sport) the best yet done: break (beat) the —, do better (worse) than ever before. **4** (as adj) that is a —(3). **—er** n **1** sb who keeps **—s**(1). **2** wooden musical instrument played by blowing.

re'count v give an account of; tell.

re'coup v compensate (sb, oneself, for loss, etc).

re'course n have — to, seek help from; turn to for help.

re'cover v **1** get back (sth lost, etc); get back the use of (one's sight, etc). **2** become well, happy, etc, again. **—y** n.

,recre'ation n (form of) play or amusement; sth that pleasantly occupies one's time after work is done.

re'cruit n new member of a society, group, etc, esp a soldier in the early days of his training. v get **—s** for; get (sb) as a **—**.

'rectangle n oblong ⇨ p 253. rec'tangular adj.

'rectify v put right; take out mistakes from. ,rectifi'cation n.

'rectitude n honesty; honest behaviour.

'rector n **1** (Church of England) priest in charge of a parish. **2** head of certain universities and colleges. **—y** n **—'s** house.

re'cumbent adj (esp of a person) lying down; reclining.

re'cuperate v make or become strong after illness; recover.

re'cur v (-rr-) **1** come, happen, again. **2** go back (to sth) in words or thought. **—rence** n **—ring**; repetition.

red adj & n (having the) colour of fresh blood. see red, lose control of oneself because angry. red tape, (fig) too much attention to rules, esp in public affairs. 'redden v make or become red. 'red-'handed adj catch sb red-handed, in the act of doing wrong. 'red-letter 'day n day on which some happy event occurs.

re'deem v **1** get (sth) back by paying for it or by doing sth. **2** perform (an obligation). **3** set free by payment; rescue (a slave, a prisoner). **4** compensate: his **—ing** feature, that which compensates for his faults, etc. the R**—er** n Jesus Christ. re'demption n deliverance or rescue (esp from evil ways).

re'double v make or become greater or stronger.

re'dress v set (a wrong) right; do sth that makes up for (a wrong).

re'duce v **1** make less in number; make smaller in size, appearance, price, etc. **2** — to, bring or get to a certain condition, way of behaving, etc; change to: **—d** to poverty. **— pounds to pence. re'duction** n **1** reducing or being **—d**: sell goods at a reduction of 10 per cent. **2** copy, on a smaller scale, of a picture, map, etc.

re'dundant adj **1** beyond what is needed. **2** (of workers) dismissed or unemployed because of the lack of work. **re'dundance, re'dun-dancy** n.

reed n 1 (tall firm stem or stalk of) kinds of water-plant. 2 (in wind instruments) part that vibrates to produce sound.

reef¹ n that part of a sail which can be rolled up or folded so as to reduce its area. v reduce the area of (a sail) by rolling up or folding part of it. **'reef-knot** n ordinary double knot.

reef² n ridge of rock, etc, just below or above the surface of the sea.

reek v smell strongly and unpleasantly (of sth).

reel n roller or similar device on which cotton thread, wire, photographic film, etc, is wound. v 1 roll or wind on to, or with the help of, a —. **— off** (a story), tell quickly and easily. 2 walk unsteadily, moving from side to side. 3 be dizzy; (of things) seem to be going round.

re'fectory n dining-hall (in a convent, college, etc).

re'fer v (-rr-) 1 send, take, hand over, to sb or sth to be dealt with, decided, etc. 2 turn to, go to, for information, etc. 3 **— to,** (of a speaker) speak about or of; (of sth said) apply to, be connected with. **,refe'ree** n 1 person to whom questions are —red for decision. 2 (football, boxing, etc) official who judges and controls the match. v act as —ee. **'reference** n 1 —ring: reference book, eg a dictionary. 2 (person willing to make a) statement about a person's character and abilities. 3 **in (with) —ence to,** concerning. **,refe-'rendum** n the —ring of a political question to a direct vote of all citizens.

re'fine v 1 free (eg gold, sugar) from other substances; make or become pure. 2 cause to be more cultured, polished in manners, etc: —d tastes (speech). **—ment** n 1 refining or being —d. 2 purity of feeling, taste, language, etc; delicacy of manners. 3 delicate or ingenious development of sth. **—ry** n place, building, where sth is. **—d(1):** a sugar —ry; an oil —ry.

re'fit v (-tt-) make (a ship) ready for use again by renewing or repairing; (of a ship) be made fit for further voyages. n —ting.

re'flect v 1 (of a surface) throw back (light, heat, sound); (of a mirror) show an image of 2 express; show the nature of. 3 (of actions, results) bring (credit or discredit upon). 4 consider, think (upon, that, how, etc). **—ion** n 1 —ing or being —ed(1); sth —ed, esp in a mirror, water, etc. 2 thought. 3 expression of a thought in speech or writing. **—ive** adj thoughtful.

'reflex adj **— action,** one that is involuntary (eg a sneeze).

re'form v make or become better by removing or putting right what is bad or wrong: — the world (a sinner, one's character). n —ing; improvement; change made in order to improve sth. **,refor'ma-tion** n 1 change for the better in morals, habits, etc, or in society, the Church. 2 **the R—ation,** start of the Protestant churches in the sixteenth century. **—er** n.

re'frain¹ v hold oneself back (from).

re'frain² n lines of a song that are repeated at the end of each verse.

re'fresh v give new strength to, make fresh (by resting, etc). **—ing** adj pleasant and welcome: a —ing sleep (breeze). **—ment** n that which —es, esp (often pl) food or drink (between meals).

re'frigerator n (colloq fridge) box in which food is kept cold.

'refuge n (place giving) shelter or protection from trouble, danger, or pursuit. **,refu'gee** n person taking — (eg from floods, war).

re'fund v pay back (money to sb). **'refund** n —ing; money —ed.

re'fuse¹ v say 'no' to; show unwillingness to accept sth, or to do sth that one is asked to do. **re'fusal** n act of refusing.

'refuse² n waste material.

re'fute v prove (statements, etc) to be wrong or mistaken; prove (sb) wrong in his opinions, etc.

re'gain v get possession of again; get back to (a place).

'regal adj of, for, by, fit for, a king or queen. **—ly** adv.

re'gale v give pleasure to (sb, oneself, with food, drink, etc).

re'gard v 1 look closely at. 2 consider. 3 pay attention to; respect:

— sb's wishes. **4** as —s, —ing, concerning; in the matter of. *n* **1** long or steady look. **2** attention; concern. **3** respect; approval; kindly feelings; (*pl*, esp at the end of a letter) kindly thoughts and wishes. **—less** *adj* **—less of**, paying no attention to.

re'gatta *n* meeting for boat-races.

re'generate *v* **1** reform spiritually; raise morally. **2** give new strength or life to. ,regene'ration *n*.

'regent *n & adj* (person) performing the duties of a ruler who is too young, old, ill, etc, or who is absent: *The Prince R—*. 'regency *n* office, authority, of a —.

ré'gime *n* system of government or of living.

'regiment *n* **1** (army) permanent unit made up of battalions or batteries, commanded by a colonel. **2** large number (*of*). *v* organize; subject to discipline.

'region *n* area or division with, or without, definite boundaries or characteristics. **in the — of**, near, surrounding. **—al** *adj* of a —.

'register *n* **1** (book containing) record or list (of births, marriages, etc). **2** mechanical device for keeping records: *a cash —*. *v* **1** make a written record of, in a list. **2** put or get sb's name, one's own name, on a —. **3** (of instruments, eg a thermometer) indicate; record; (of sb's face) show (a feeling). **4** send (a letter, parcel) by special post, paying a fee for insurance. ,regis'tration *n*. 'registry *n* place where —s are kept.

re'gret *n* feeling of sadness at the loss of sth or of disappointment because sth has or has not been done, etc. *v* (-tt-) have — for; be sorry (*that*). **—ful** *adj* sad; sorry. **—fully** *adv*. **—table** *adj* that should be —ted.

'regular *adj* **1** evenly arranged: *teeth*. **2** coming or happening repeatedly at even intervals: — *breathing*. **3** normal; orderly: — *habits*. **4** properly trained; full-time or professional: *the — army*. **5** in accordance with standards of correctness. *n* soldier of the — army. ,regu'larity *n*. **—ize** *v* make lawful or correct. **—ly** *adv* in a — manner; at — intervals or times.

'regulate *v* **1** control by means of a system or rule(s). **2** adjust (a mechanism, eg a clock) to obtain a desired result. ,regu'lation *n* **1** regulating or being —d; rule; order. **2** (as *adj*) as required by rules. 'regulator *n* (esp) part of a mechanism that —s(2).

re'hearse *v* **1** practise (a play, etc) for public performance. **2** say over again; give an account of. re'hearsal *n*.

reign *n* (period of) rule. *v* rule (*over*).

,reim'burse *v* pay sb what he has already paid on one's behalf.

rein *n* (often *pl*) long narrow strap fastened to a bridle, for controlling a horse. *v* control with, or as with, —s.

,rein'force *v* make stronger by adding or supplying more material, men, etc. **—ment** (esp in *pl*) men, ships, etc, sent to —.

,rein'state *v* put back in a former position or condition. **—ment** *n*.

re'iterate *v* say or do again several times. ,reite'ration *n*.

re'ject *v* put aside, throw away, as not good enough to be kept; refuse to accept. 'reject *n* —ed article. re'jection *n*.

re'joice *v* be or make glad; show signs of great happiness.

re'juvenate *v* make or become young again in nature or appearance. re,juve'nation *n*.

re'lapse *v* fall back into bad ways; become ill again, after improving. *n* relapsing.

re'late *v* **1** tell (a story); give an account of (facts, etc). **2** connect (*to, with,* sth else) in thought or meaning. **3** be —d (*to*), belong to the same family (as). **4** — to, have reference to.

re'lation *n* **1** relating(1) (of facts, etc); sth related (a story, etc). **2** connection; what there is between one thing, person, idea, etc and another: *the — of the weather to the crops*. **out of all — to,** not in proportion to. **in — to,** concerning. **3** (often *pl*) dealings; what one person, group, country, etc has to do with another: *friendly — between countries*. **4** relative. **—ship** *n* —(2).

'relative *adj* **1** — to, having connection with. **2** comparative

3 related to each other. *n* person to whom one is related(3) (*an uncle, aunt, nephew, etc*). —**ly** *adv* comparatively; in proportion (*to*).

re'**lax** *v* **1** (cause to) become less tight or stiff. **2** (allow to) become less severe or strict; weaken. ,relax'**ation** *n* recreation.

're**lay** *n* — race, one between two teams, each member of the team running one section of the total distance. 're**lay** *v* send on further (eg a broadcast programme received from another station).

re'**lease** *v* **1** allow to go; set free; unfasten. **2** allow (news) to be published, (a film) to be exhibited. *n* releasing or being —d.

re'**lent** *v* become less harsh; begin to show mercy. —**less** *adj* pitiless.

're**levant** *adj* connected with what is being discussed.

re'**liable** *adj* that can be relied on. re'**liably** *adv*.

re'**liance** *n* trust. re'**liant** *adj* having trust; trusting.

're**lic** *n* sth that has survived from the past and that serves to keep memories alive.

re'**lied** ⇨ rely.

re'**lief** *n* **1** the lessening or ending or removal of pain, anxiety, etc. **2** that which brings —(1); food, clothes, etc, (to be) sent to people in trouble: *a — fund*, money for such goods. **3** sth that adds interest to what would, without it, be monotonous. **4** freedom from duty; the person(s) replacing other person(s) on duty. **5** method of carving or moulding in which a design or figure stands out from the surface. **6** degree of clearness or outline. **in sharp —**, clearly visible in outline. **— map**, one shaded or coloured to show the height of land. re'**lieve** *v* **1** be, give, or bring, — to. **2** relieve sb of sth, take it from him.

re'**ligion** *n* **1** belief in God as the creator and controller of the universe. **2** system of faith and worship based on such a belief. re'**ligious** *adj* **1** of —. **2** (of a person) devout.

re'**linquish** *v* give up (eg hope); let go (eg one's hold of sth).

're**lish** *n* (sth that gives) special taste, flavour, or quality. *v* enjoy; have a taste, give a suggestion (of).

re'**luctant** *adj* (slow to do sth because) unwilling. re'**luctance** *n*.

re'**ly** *v* (*pt & pp* re'lied) — (up)on, depend upon; look to (sb) for help.

re'**main** *v* **1** be still present after a part has gone or has been taken away. **2** continue to be. —**der** *n* that which —s; those who —. —**s** *n pl* **1** what is left: *the —s of a meal* (*of ancient Rome*). **2** dead body.

re'**mand** *v* send (an accused person) back to prison (from a court of law) until more evidence is obtained. *n* —ing.

re'**mark** *v* **1** see; notice. **2** say (*that*). *n* **1** notice; looking at. **2** comment; sth said. —**able** *adj* deserving notice; out of the ordinary. —**ably** *adv*.

're**medy** *n* cure; method of (or sth used for) putting right sth that is wrong or ending a disease. *v* provide a — for; cure.

re'**member** *v* **1** keep in the memory; call back to the mind. **2** — sb (*to* sb else), give or carry greetings to. re'**membrance** *n* **1** —ing or being —ed: *in remembrance of*. **2** sth given or kept in memory of sb or sth.

re'**mind** *v* cause (sb) to remember; cause (sb) to think (*of* sth or sb). —**er** *n* sth (eg a letter) that —s.

,remi'**niscence** *n* **1** the recalling of past experiences. **2** (*pl*) account of what sb remembers. ,remi'**niscent** *adj* reminding one (*of*); suggestive (*of*); remembering the past.

re'**miss** *adj* careless; not doing one's duties properly.

re'**mission** *n* **1** pardon or forgiveness (of sins, by God). **2** freeing (from debt; punishment).

re'**mit** *v* (-tt-) **1** excuse (sb's) payment (of a debt, etc). **2** send (money, etc) by post. **3** make or become less: — *one's efforts*. —**tance** *n* the sending of money, a sum of money sent, to sb at a distance.

're**mnant** *n* **1** small part that remains. **2** (esp) left-over piece of cloth offered at a reduced price.

re'**monstrate** *v* make a protest (*against* sth); argue in protest (*with* sb, *that*). re'**monstrance** *n*.

re'**morse** *n* deep, bitter regret for

wrongdoing. **—ful** *adj* feeling —.
—less *adj* without —.

re'mote *adj* (**-r, -st**) **1** far away in space or time; widely separated (*from*). **2** slight: *not the —st idea*.

re'move *v* **1** take off, away, or to another place. **2** change one's dwelling-place; go to live in another place. **re'moval** *n*.

re'munerate *v* pay (sb) for work or services. **re,mune'ration** *n* payment or reward.

'render *v* **1** give in return or exchange or as sth due: — *thanks to God.* **2** offer; send in (an account for payment). **3** cause to be (in some condition): *—ed helpless by an accident.*

'rendezvous *n* (place decided upon for) meeting at an agreed time.

re'new *v* **1** make new; make as good as new. **2** replace (sth) with a new thing of the same sort. **3** begin again. **4** get, make, say, or give again. **—al** *n*.

re'nounce *v* **1** say that one will no longer have anything to do with (sb or sth having a claim to one's care, affection, etc). **2** give up; surrender (a claim, etc). **re,nunci'ation** *n*.

'renovate *v* restore (eg old buildings) to good or strong condition. **,reno'vation** *n*.

re'nown *n* fame. **—ed** *adj* famous.

rent *n* regular payment for the use of land, a building, a room, machinery, etc. *v* **1** pay — for. **2** allow (sb) to occupy or use in return for —.

re,nunci'ation *n* ⇨ renounce.

re'pair *v* **1** mend; put into good condition. **2** put right; make up for. **n** under —, being —ed. **2** (often *pl*) work or process of —ing. **,repa'ration** *n* payment compensating for loss or damage.

,repar'tee *n* witty, clever answer(s).

re'past *n* (formal) meal.

re'patriate *v* send or bring (sb) back to his own country.

re'pay *v* (*pt & pp* re'paid) pay back (money, etc); give (sth) in return for. **—ment** *n*.

re'peal *v* cancel (a law). **n** —ing.

re'peat *v* **1** say or do again. **2** say (what sb else has said or what one has learnt by heart). **—edly** *adv*

again and again. **,repe'tition** *n* —ing or being —ed; sth —ed.

re'pel *v* (**-ll-**) **1** drive back or away. **2** cause a feeling of dislike in. **—lent** *adj* tending to —.

re'pent *v* wish one had not done sth; be or feel sorry (esp about wrongdoing). **—ance** *n*. **—ant** *adj*.

,reper'cussion *n* **1** springing back (after striking sth with force). **2** (usu *pl*) far-reaching and indirect effect of an event.

'repertoire, 'repertory *n* plays, songs, etc, which a company, actor, musician, etc, is prepared to perform.

repe'tition *n* ⇨ repeat.

re'place *v* put back in its place; take the place of (sb or sth).

re'plenish *v* fill up (sth) again (*with*): — *one's wardrobe.*

re'plete *adj* filled, well provided (*with*). **re'pletion** *n* being —.

'replica *n* exact copy.

re'ply *v* (*pt & pp* re'plied) *& n* answer.

re'port *v* **1** give an account of (sth seen, heard, done, etc). **2** go to sb, go somewhere, and say that one has come, that one is ready for work, etc. **3** make a complaint about (to sb in authority). **n** **1** account of, statement about, sth done, seen, heard, etc. **2** common or general talk; (a) rumour. **3** noise of an explosion. **—er** *n* person who **—s**(1) for a newspaper.

re'pose *v* **1** rest; give rest or support to. **2** place (belief, confidence, etc, *in*). *n* rest; quietness; restful behaviour or appearance.

,repre'sent *v* **1** be, give, make a picture, sign, symbol, or example of. **2** describe (*as*); put forward (eg grievances, matters for attention, etc) *to* (sb). **3** act or speak for; be an agent for; be a member of Parliament for. **,represen'tation** *n* —ing; sth —ed. **—ative** *adj* **1** serving as an example of a class or group. **2** —ative **government**, government by persons who are elected by the public to —(3) them. **n 1** typical specimen (of a group, etc). **2** person who —s(3) others.

re'press *v* keep or put down or under; prevent from finding an outlet. **—ion** *n*. **—ive** *adj*.

re'prieve *v* cancel the execution of

(sb condemned to death); give relief for a time from (trouble, etc). *n* reprieving or being —d.

'**reprimand** *v* reprove severely. *n* severe reproof.

re'prisal *n* action taken to pay back injury with injury.

re'proach *v* blame regretfully; scold. *n* **1** (words used for) —ing. **2** cause of shame or discredit. —**ful** *adj* full of, expressing, —.

,**repro'duce** *v* **1** copy; cause to be seen, heard, etc, again. **2** produce offspring; bring about a natural increase. ,**repro'duction** *n* process of reproducing; sth —d(1).

re'proof *n* (words of) blame or disapproval. **re'proval** *n* reproving. **re'prove** *v* find fault with; speak severely to (sb *for* doing wrong).

'**reptile** *n* (member of a) class(1) of animals including snakes, crocodiles, lizards, tortoises, etc.

re'public *n* (country with a) system of government in which elected representatives of the people are supreme and the head of the government (the President) is elected. —**an** *adj* **1** of a —. **2 R**—**an**, member of a main political party in the USA.

re'pudiate *v* refuse to accept (eg sb's authority), to pay (a debt), to acknowledge (a friend).

re'pugnant *adj* distasteful. **re'pugnance** *n* strong dislike (*to* sth); unwillingness to do sth.

re'pulse *v* **1** drive back (the enemy); resist (an attack) successfully. **2** refuse to accept. *n*

repulsing or being —d. **re'pulsion** *n* feeling of dislike. **re'pulsive** *adj* causing strong dislike.

,**repu'tation** *n* the general opinion about the character of sb or sth: *a man of high* —. **re'pute** *n* (usu good) —. **re'puted** *adj* generally considered (*to be*).

re'quest *n* act of asking; thing asked for. **in** —, being —ed by people. *v* make a — (*for* sth, *that*).

re'quire *v* **1** need. **2** order (sb to do sth). **3** demand. —**ment** *n*.

'**rescue** *v* deliver from danger; set free (from enemies). *n* rescuing or being —d.

re'search *n* study undertaken in order to discover new facts.

re'semble *v* be like. **re'semblance** *n* (point of) likeness.

re'sent *v* feel indignant or angry at. —**ful** *adj* —ing.

re'serve *v* **1** store for later use. **2** set apart (seats in a theatre, etc) for a particular person or purpose only. *n* **1** sth that is being or has been stored for use later. **in** —, stored for the future. **2** (*pl*) military forces kept back for later use. **3** area of land kept and used for a special purpose: *a game* — (for wild animals). **4** lowest acceptable price or condition of sale. **5** unwillingness to talk about one's thoughts and feelings. ,**reser'vation** *n* reserving; being —d. **without reservation**, without any limiting condition (eg fear). —**d** *adj* (esp) having or showing —(5) of manner.

'**reservoir** *n* place (often an artificial lake) where water is stored.

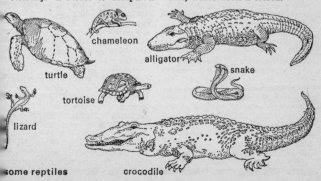

chameleon

alligator

turtle

snake

tortoise

lizard

some reptiles

crocodile

re'side v have one's home (in, at, etc). 'residence n place in which one —s. 'resident n person who —s in a place (contrasted with a visitor). ,resi'dential adj of private houses: the residential district of a town.

'residue n that which remains after part is taken or used.

re'sign v 1 give up (a position, claim, etc). 2 — oneself to, be ready to endure without complaint. —ed adj having or showing patient acceptance of sth. ,resig'nation n 1 —ing a position; letter to an employer, etc, proposing this. 2 being —ed(2) (to conditions).

re'silience n quality of being elastic. re'silient adj.

re'sist v 1 use force against in order to prevent the advance of. 2 be undamaged or unaffected by. 3 (usu neg) keep oneself back from. —ance n 1 (power of) —ing. 2 opposing force.

'resolute adj fixed in determination or purpose; firm. —ly adv. ,reso'lution n 1 quality of being resolute. 2 sth that is resolved(1).

re'solve v 1 decide or determine. 2 put an end to (doubts, etc) by providing an answer. n sth —d(1).

'resonant adj 1 (of sounds) resounding. 2 tending to make sounds echo.

re'sort v — to, 1 make use of, for help or to gain one's purpose. 2 go often to (a place). n 1 —ing(1). in the last —, as the final attempt, when all else has failed. 2 thing or person —ed(1) to. 3 place visited frequently or by large numbers of people: health —s.

re'sound v 1 echo and re-echo; fill (a place) with sound. 2 be filled . with sound; echo back sound.

re'source n 1 (pl) wealth, goods, etc, which a country or person has or can use. natural —s, minerals, water-power, etc. 2 (skill in finding) sth that helps in time of trouble or need. —ful adj quick or good at finding ways of doing things.

res'pect n 1 high opinion or regard. 2 consideration; care. with — to, in — of, concerning. 3 (pl) greetings. 4 detail; particular: in some (many) —s. v 1 have —(1),(2) for. 2 refrain from interfering

with, hurting, breaking, etc: — the law (sb's wishes or feelings). —able adj 1 deserving —. 2 (of a person, his behaviour, clothes, etc) of the sort considered right or good enough. 3 fairly high in degree or amount. —ably adv. —ful adj showing — (to). —ing prep with reference to. —ive adj belonging to, of, for, each of those in question. —ively adv separately or in turn, and in the order given.

'respite n 1 time of relief or rest (from sth unpleasant). 2 reprieve for a time.

re'splendent adj very bright.

res'pond v answer; act in answer to. res'ponse n answer; reaction. res'ponsive adj answering; —ing easily or quickly.

res'ponsible adj 1 (of persons) be — (for), have in one's charge and have to account for (loss, failure, etc). be — (to), have to give an account of what one does (to sb). 2 deserving credit or blame (for). 3 trustworthy. 4 (of work, a position, etc) needing a —(3) person. res,ponsi'bility n 1 being —. 2 sth for which a person is —.

rest¹ n 1 condition of being free from activity, disturbance; (period of) quiet or sleep: (be) at —. 2 support, for keeping sth in position. v 1 be still or quiet. 2 give a — to. 3 (cause to) be supported (on or against sth). '—ful adj giving — or a feeling of —. '—ive adj (of horses) refusing to stand still; (of persons) impatient of control or discipline. '—less adj never still or quiet; unable to —.

rest² v 1 remain in some condition or position: — assured that. 2 depend: Success —s on effort. 3 It — with you to decide, it is you who must decide. n the —, what is left over; the others.

'restaurant n place where meals can be bought and eaten.

,resti'tution n restoring (of sth lost, stolen, etc) to its owner.

re'store v 1 give back (sth stolen, etc). 2 bring back into use (e an old custom); put (sb) back into a former position. 3 repair; re construct. 4 make well or norm again. ,resto'ration n restoring or being —d.

res'train v hold back; keep under control; prevent (from). **—t** n —ing or being —ed; sth that —s.

res'trict v limit; keep within limits. **—ion** n.

re'sult n that which is produced by an activity or other cause. v be a —; have the kind of — indicated: — in failure.

re'sume v 1 go on after stopping for a time. 2 take again: — one's seat. **re'sumption** n.

,resur'rect v 1 take up (a dead body) from the grave. 2 bring back into use or the memory. **—ion** n (esp) **the R—ion**, the rising of Jesus from the tomb.

re'suscitate v bring back (eg sb nearly drowned) to consciousness.

'retail n (cf **wholesale**) selling of goods to the general public: — prices. **re'tail** v 1 sell by —. 2 (of goods) be sold by —. **—er** n tradesman who sells by —.

re'tain v keep; keep in place; continue to have or hold.

re'taliate v return the same sort of ill-treatment, etc, that one has received. **re,tali'ation** n.

re'tard v check; hinder.

'reticent adj (in the habit of) saying little; reserved. **'reticence** n.

'retinue n number of persons (servants, officers, etc) travelling with a person of high rank.

re'tire v 1 withdraw (from or to). 2 give up one's work or position. 3 go to bed. **—d** adj 1 having —d(2). 2 quiet; secluded. **—ment** n condition of being —d, esp (2). **re'tiring** adj avoiding society.

re'tort v answer back sharply (esp to an accusation). n such an answer.

re'touch v make small changes in (a photograph, painting, etc).

re'trace v go back over or along: — one's steps.

re'tract v 1 take back, withdraw (a statement, offer, etc). 2 draw (sth, eg the under-carriage of an aircraft) in or back. **—able** adj that can be —ed.

re'treat v (esp of an army) go back; withdraw. n 1 act of —ing. 2 signal for —ing.

re'trench v reduce (expenses, etc); economize. **—ment** n.

re'trieve v 1 get possession of again. 2 set right (an error). 3 restore (one's fortunes).

'retrospect n view of past events. **seen in —**, looked back upon. **,retro'spective** adj (eg of laws, etc) applying to the past.

re'turn v 1 come or go back. 2 give (put, send, pay) back. 3 say in reply. n 1 —ing or being —ed. **in — (for)**, in exchange (for). **a — ticket**, one for a journey to a place and back again. 2 (often pl) profit (on an investment, etc). **—able** adj that can be, or is to be, —ed.

re'union n (esp) meeting of old friends after long separation.

re'veal v allow or cause to be seen; make known (a secret, etc). **,reve'lation** n —ing; sth —ed, esp a piece of surprising knowledge.

'revel v (-ll-) 1 make merry. 2 — in, take great pleasure in. n (usu pl) joyful merry-making. **—ry** n —s.

re'venge v 1 do sth to a wrongdoer to get satisfaction for (wrong): — an insult; — one's friend. 2 be **—d** (on sb for sth), — oneself. n act of revenging; desire to —. **—ful** adj feeling or showing a desire for —.

'revenue n income, esp the total annual income of the State.

re'verberate v (esp of sound) send, be sent back.

re'vere v have deep respect for (esp sacred things). **'reverence** n deep respect. v treat with —nce. **'reverent** adj feeling or showing —nce. **the 'Reverend (Rev)**, title for a clergyman: the Rev T Wells.

'reverie n (state of enjoying) dreamy, pleasant thoughts.

re'verse adj 1 opposite or contrary: in the — direction. 2 back or backward; under: the — side of a coin, medal, etc. n 1 the opposite or contrary. 2 the back or the under side (of a coin, medal, etc). 3 a change to bad fortune; defeat. v 1 put in a — position. 2 (cause to) go backwards or in the opposite direction. 3 do the opposite of (sth done earlier). 4 cancel (a decision, etc).

re'vert v go back (to a former state, an earlier question, etc).

re'view v 1 consider or examine again; go over again in the mind. 2 inspect formally (troops, etc). 3 write an account of (new books,

etc) for periodicals. n **1** act of —ing.
2 periodical with articles on current events, —s of new books, etc.

re'vile v swear at; call bad names.

re'vise v **1** (read through carefully, esp in order to) correct and improve. **2** review(1) in preparation for an examination. **re'vision** n revising; —d version.

re'vive v **1** come or bring back to consciousness, strength, health, or an earlier state: *Our hopes —d.* **2** come or bring into use again: *— old customs.* **re'vival** n **1** reviving or being —d. **2** (esp) (meetings to bring about an) increase of interest in religion.

re'voke v repeal; cancel; withdraw (a decree, etc).

re'volt v **1** rise in rebellion. **2** be filled with disgust or horror (*at* or *against* sth). **3** cause a feeling of disgust. n rebellion.

ˌrevo'lution n **1** journeying round: *the — of the earth round the sun.* **2** one complete turn (of a wheel, etc). **3** complete change (in conditions, ways of doing things, government, etc). —**ary** n sb supporting a —(3). *adj* of a —(3); bringing, causing, favouring, great (and often violent) changes. —**ize** v make a complete change in.

re'volve v **1** (cause to) go round in a circle (as the rim of a wheel does). **2** turn over in the mind; think about all sides of (a problem).

re'volver n pistol that can be fired a number of times without reloading.

re'vulsion n sudden and complete change of feeling.

reward n sth offered, given, or obtained in return for work, services or for the return of lost or stolen property or for the capture of a criminal, etc. v give a — to; be a — to.

'rhapsody n enthusiastic expression of delight (in words, music, etc).

'rhetoric n **1** (art of) using words impressively. **2** language with too much display. **rhe'torical** *adj* (esp) **rhetorical question,** one asked for the sake of effect(2), no answer being expected.

'rheumatism n disease causing pain and swollen joints. **rheuˈmatic** *adj* of, causing, caused by, suffering from, —.

rhi'noceros n large mammal of Africa and Asia. ⇨ p 317.

rhyme n **1** sameness of sound between the last parts of words or of lines of verse (eg *rhyme, time*). **2** verse(s) with —. **nursery —s,** poems or songs for small children. **3** word which —s with another. v **1** (of words) be in —. **2** write verse(s) with —.

'rhythm n regular succession of weak and strong stresses, sounds, or movements (in speech, music, dancing, etc). —**ic(al)** *adj*.

rib n **1** any one of the curved bones extending from the backbone round the chest. ⇨ p 30. **2** sth like a rib, eg a thick vein in a leaf.

'ribbon n **1** (length or piece of) silk or other material woven in a narrow band, used for ornamenting or tying things. **2** sth like a —: *a typewriter —.*

rice n (plant with) white grain used as food, esp in the East.

rich *adj* (-er, -est) **1** having much money or property. **2** (of clothes, etc) costly; splendid. **3** (of land, etc) producing much; abundant (*in*). **4** (of food) containing much fat, many eggs, etc. **5** (of colours, sounds) deep; strong. **'—es** n *pl* wealth. **'—ly** *adv* **1** in a —(2) manner. **2** fully (esp —*ly deserve*). **'—ness** n quality of being —.

rick n pile of hay, straw, etc.

'rickety *adj* weak, esp in the joints; likely to collapse: *— furniture.*

'rickshaw n two-wheeled carriage pulled by a man.

rid v (*pt & pp* rid) make free (*of*). **get rid of,** get free of, dispose of (sth unwanted). **'riddance** n clearing away or out; being free from.

'ridden (*pp* of ride) (in compounds) oppressed or dominated by *di'sease-ridden.*

'riddle¹ n puzzling question, thing situation, etc.

'riddle² v make many holes in (sth) *The corpse was —d with bullets.*

ride v (*pt* rode, *pp* 'ridden) **1** si on (a horse, bicycle, etc) and b carried along. **2** be carried along (*in* a bus, etc). **3** be supported by float on. **— at anchor,** (of a ship be anchored. n journey on horse back, on a bike, as a passenger in a bus, etc. **'—r** n person who —s.

ridge n **1** upper edge of two sur

faces that slope together. **2** long, narrow stretch of high land; range of hills or mountains. **3** raised narrow strip (esp between furrows). *v* make into, cover with, —s.

ridicule *v* cause (sb or sth) to appear foolish; make fun of. *n* words, acts, used to show humorous contempt. **ri'diculous** adj deserving —; unreasonable.

rife *adj* **1** widespread. **2** — with, full of (eg superstition).

'rifle[1] *v* search thoroughly in order to steal from.

'rifle[2] *n* gun with a long barrel(2).

rift *n* split or crack.

rig *v* (-gg-) **1** supply (a ship) with masts, rigging, sails, etc. **2 rig sb out**, provide him with needed clothes, equipment, etc. **rig sth up**, put together quickly with any materials available: *rig up a shelter*. *n* design of mast(s) and sails. **'rigging** *n* ropes, etc, which support a ship's masts and sails.

right[1] *adj, n, & adv* (opp of *left*) (of, in, on the) side of the body that is to the east when one faces north; (of politics) moderate, conservative. **right-hand 'man**, valuable or chief helper.

right[2] *adj* **1** (opp of *wrong*) (of conduct) just; moral; according to the law; (of statements of fact or opinion) true; correct. **All '—** (**Al'right** is incorrect) used to indicate agreement. **2 the — side** (of cloth, etc), the side intended to be seen or used. **3 — angle**, one of 90°. *adv* **1** directly. **— away**, immediately. **2** completely; quite: *turn — round.* **3** exactly: *— in the middle.* **4** straight: *go — on.* **n 1** that which is —. **be in the —**, have justice or truth on one's side. **2** sth to which one has a just claim; sth one may do or have by law. **by —(s)**, justly, correctly. **by — of**, on account of, because of. *v* put, bring, or come back, into the — or an upright condition; make sth — again. **right-a,bout** *adj* a **right-about turn**, a turn continued until one is facing in the opposite direction. **'—ful** *adj* **1** according to law or justice: *the —ful owner.* **2** (of actions) justifiable. **'—ly** *adv* justly; correctly or truly.

righteous *adj* obeying the law; just. **—ly** *adv.* **—ness** *n.*

'rigid *adj* **1** stiff; unbending; that cannot be bent. **2** strict; not to be changed. **—ly** *adv.* **ri'gidity** *n.*

'rigmarole *n* long, wandering story or statement.

'rigour *n* **1** strictness. **2** (often *pl*) severe conditions (eg of climate). **'rigorous** *adj* **1** strict. **2** harsh.

rim *n* **1** raised or thickened edge, esp of sth round (eg a bowl). **2** outer ring of a wheel (to which a tyre is fitted). *v* (-mm-) make or be a rim for; provide with a rim.

rind *n* hard outside skin (of some fruits, of bacon and cheese).

ring[1] *n* **1** circle. **2** circular band, eg as worn on the finger: *a wedding —.* **3** enclosed space for a circus, etc. **4** square platform for boxers. *v* (*pt & pp* 'ringed*) **1** surround. **2** put a — in the nose of (eg a bull). **'—,leader** *n* person who leads others (against authority).

ring[2] *v* (*pt* rang, *pp* rung) **1** give out a clear musical sound as when metal is struck. **2** cause sth (esp a bell) to —: — *the church bells;* — *for the servant.* **— sb up**, get into communication by telephone. **— off**, end a telephone conversation. **3** — with, (of a place) echo with. *n* —ing sound.

rink *n* stretch of ice for skating; floor prepared for roller-skating.

rinse *v* (often — out) wash with clean water in order to remove unwanted substances: — *the soap out of the clothes;* — *one's hair;* — *out the teapot.* *n* act of rinsing.

'riot *n* **1** violent uprising of people in a district. **2** outburst of uncontrolled behaviour. **run —**, be out of control. *v* take part in a —. **—er** *n* person who —s.

rip *v* (-pp-) **1** pull, tear, or cut (sth) sharply or with force (to divide it, get it off, out, or open): *rip the cover off*; *rip a piece of cloth in two.* **2** (of material) be ripped. *n* torn place; long cut.

ripe *adj* (-r, -st) **1** (of fruit, grain) ready to be gathered and used. **2** fully developed. **3 — for**, ready for. **'—n** *v* (cause to) become —.

'ripple *n* (sound of) small waves (esp moving along the surface); gentle rise and fall. *v* (cause to) move in —s; make —s in.

rise *v* (*pt* rose, *pp* 'risen) **1** go or come up or higher. **2** stand up;

get out of bed. **3** come to the surface of a liquid. **4** have a starting-point (*in, at, from*). **5** rebel (*against*). **6** (of Parliament, etc) adjourn. *n* **1** small hill; upward slope. **2** increase (*in* cost, etc). **3** give — to, cause. **'rising** *adj*. **the rising generation**, the young people of the time referred to. *n* (esp) rebellion.

risk *n* possibility or chance of meeting danger, suffering loss or injury, etc. *v* put or be in danger; take the chance of: — *failure*. **'—y** *adj* (-ier, -iest).

rite *n* religious act or ceremony: *burial —s*. **'ritual** *n* system of —s. *adj* of —s: *ritual dances*.

'rival *n* **1** person who competes with another. **2** (as *adj*) competing: — *shops*. *v* (-ll-) be a — of; claim to be (almost) as good as. **—ry** *n* being —s; competition.

'river *n* natural flow of water to the sea, a lake, or another —: *the — Nile*; liquid flowing in this way: *a — of blood*.

'rivet *n* metal pin or bolt for fastening together metal plates, etc. *v* **1** fasten with —s. **2** fix (the eyes, one's attention *upon* sth).

rivets

road *n* **1** specially constructed route for motor-vehicles, bicycles, etc; such a route with pavements, shops, houses, etc, on either side (⇨ street). **on the —**, travelling. **2** way of getting (*to*): *the — to success* (ruin).

roam *v* wander.

roar *n* loud deep sound as of a lion or of thunder. *v* make such sounds; say (sth) with a —.

roast *v* **1** cook, be cooked, over or in front of a fire or (of meat, potatoes) in an oven.

rob *v* (-bb-) deprive (sb) *of* his property; take property from (a place) unlawfully (and often by force). **'robber** *n*. **'robbery** *n* act of robbing.

robe *n* long, loose (esp official) outer garment. *v* put a — on.

ro'bust *adj* vigorous; healthy.

rock¹ *n* **1** the solid stony part of

the earth's surface. **2** mass of — standing out from the surface or sea floor: *The ship was on the —s*. **3** separate lump of —. **'—y** *adj* (-ier, -iest) full of —s; hard like —.

rock² *v* **1** roll about backwards and forwards or from side to side: — *a baby to sleep*; —*ing with laughter*. **2** shake: *The town was —ed by an earthquake*.

'rocket *n* tube-shaped case filled with fast-burning material, which launches itself into the air as a firework or as a signal of distress, etc, or which is used to launch a space-capsule, missile, etc.

rod *n* **1** thin, straight piece of wood or metal (eg as used for fishing, or hanging curtains on). **2** measure of length, 5½ yards.

rode ⇨ ride.

rodent *n* animal that gnaws things: *rat, rabbit, squirrel*, etc.

roe *n* mass of eggs in a fish.

rogue *n* rascal. **'roguish** *adj* (esp) playful or mischievous.

role *n* (esp) actor's part in a play.

roll *v* **1** move along on wheels; move along by turning over and over: — *a barrel*; *a —ing stone*. **2** turn or fold over and over into the shape of a ball or cylinder: — *string into a ball*; — *up a map* (carpet); — *oneself up in a blanket*. **3** make flat or smooth by pressing with a —ing cylinder of wood, metal, etc: — *the grass*; — *out pastry*. **4** rock or sway from side to side: *a ship —ing in bad weather*. **5** (of surfaces) have long slopes that rise and fall: *miles of —ing country*. **6** make, say sth with, long deep sounds as of thunder: *drums —ing in the distance*. **7** — **in** (along), come in large numbers. — **up**, (fig) increase in number. **8** —**ed gold**, thin coating of gold on another metal. *n* **1** sth made into the shape of a cylinder by being —ed(2): *a — of cloth*; *a bread-roll*. **2** a —ing(6) movement (eg of drums, thunder). **3** official list, esp of names: *call the —*. **'—er** *n* cylinder-shaped object, often part of a machine, for pressing, crushing, smoothing, printing, etc: *a* **'steam-roller** (for road-making). **'roller-skates** (with wheels for use on a smooth surface, not ice).

'Roman *adj*: — *numerals*, I, II, IV, X, etc. ⇨ p 334.

ro'mance *n* **1** story or novel of adventure; love-story. **2** real experience considered to be worth description because like a —(1). **ro'mantic** *adj* having ideas, feelings, etc, suited to —; suggesting —: *romantic tales (adventures).*

romp *v & n* (esp of children) (take part in) active, noisy play.

roof *n* top covering of a building, tent, bus, etc. *v* put a — on; be a — for.

rook *n* large black bird like a crow. ⇨ p 26.

room *n* **1** one of the separate divisions of a building enclosed by its floor, ceiling and walls; (*pl*) set of these occupied by one person or family (cf flat(4)). **2** space that is or might be occupied or that is enough for a purpose. **.'—ful** *n*. **'—y** *adj* (-ier, -iest) having much — (2) in it.

roost *n* branch, pole, etc, on which a bird rests. *v* sleep on a —. **'—er** *n* (USA) cock.

root *n* **1** that part of a plant, tree, etc, which is normally in the soil. **take** —, send down a —, begin to grow. **2** (also **root-crop**) plant with a — used as food: *carrot, yam*, etc. **3** part of a hair, tooth, tongue, which corresponds to a —; (part of a) word on which other forms of that word are based. *v* **1** (of plants, cuttings) (cause to) send out —s. **2** — (sth) up (out), pull up with the —s; get rid of completely. **square-root** ⇨ square.

rope *n* (piece or length of) thick, strong cord or wire made by twisting fines cords or wires together. *v* tie (*up, together*) with —; enclose or mark *off* with —.

'rosary *n* string of beads used in counting prayers.

rose¹ ⇨ rise.

rose² *n* **1** sweet-smelling flower growing on a bush with thorny stems. **2** pinkish-red colour. **'rosy** *adj* (-ier, -iest) rose-coloured; (fig) bright.

rot *v* (-tt-) **1** go bad; spoil: *rotting fruit.* **2** (fig) waste away, decay. *n* **1** decay. **2** (colloq) nonsense. **'rotten** *adj* **1** having rotted. **2** (colloq) bad.

'rota *n* list of persons to do things, of duties to be done, in turn.

ro'tate *v* (cause to) move round a central point; (cause to) take turns, come in succession **ro'tation** *n* (esp) *in rotation*, in turn.

rote *n* by —, by heart, from memory.

ro'tund *adj* (of a person, his face) round and fat. **—ity** *n.*

'rouble *n* unit of money in Russia.

rouge *n* red colouring matter for the face.

rough *adj* (-er, -est) **1** not level, smooth, polished; of irregular surface. **2** (opp of *calm, gentle*) moving or acting violently: — *children (behaviour)*; stormy: *a — sea.* **3** made or done without attention to detail, esp as a first attempt: *a — sketch.* **4** (of sounds) harsh. **5** without comforts or conveniences: *leading a — life in the jungle. n·* — state. **take the — with the smooth**, take pleasant and unpleasant things alike. **in the —**, in an unfinished state. *v* **1** make —. **2 — it**, do without the usual comforts of life. **'—en** *v* make or become —. **'—ly** *adv* (esp) approximately.

round *adj* (-er, -est) shaped like a circle or a ball. **a — trip**, journey that starts and ends at the same place. **in — numbers**, roughly, given in 10s, 100s, 1,000s, etc. *n* **1** a — slice. **2** regular succession or distribution (of duties, pleasures, drinks, etc): *the postman's —; go the —s.* **3** (ammunition for firing a) single shot: *only five —s left.* **4** step or stage in a competition: *a boxing-match of ten —s.* **5** action, etc, performed by a number of people: — *after — of cheers; a — of applause.* *adv* **1** in a circle or half-circle. **all the year —**, throughout the year. **2** on all sides. **3** from one to another of a group in turn: *pass sth —.* **not enough to go —**, not enough for everyone. **4** by a longer route. **5 come —, bring sb —**, back to consciousness (after fainting). *prep* **1** on all sides of; in a circle —. **2** so as to be or go —. *v* **1** make or become —. **2 go —. 3 — sth off**, make it complete, add a suitable finish. **— up** (eg *animals*), get them together. **'round-a,bout** *adj* not by the shortest way. *n* **1** revolving platform with wooden horses, etc, to carry children for amusement. 2 road junction at which traffic must go — a central enclosure.

rouse v 1 wake (up). 2 cause (sb) to be more active, interested, etc: — sb to action; rousing cheers.

rout v & n (cause) complete defeat and disorderly flight.

route n way taken or planned from one place to another.

rou'tine n fixed and regular way of doing things.

rove v roam; wander.

row[1] n line of persons or things, esp a line of seats: in the front row.

row[2] v move (a boat) by using oars; carry or take (sb or sth) in a boat with oars. n journey or outing in a rowing boat: go for a row.

row[3] n 1 violent argument or quarrel. 2 trouble; scolding.

'rowdy adj (-ier, -iest) & n rough and noisy (person).

'royal adj of, like, belonging to the family of, suitable for, a king or queen. —ly adv. —ist n supporter of (government by) a king. —ty n 1 — persons. 2 position, dignity, etc, of a — person. 3 payment to an author on the sales of his books, to an inventor for the use of his patent, etc.

rub v (-bb-) 1 move (one thing) backwards and forwards on the surface of (another): rub oil on the skin; rub the skin with oil. **rub sth out (off)**, remove (esp marks) by rubbing. 2 clean, dry, polish, etc, by rubbing. n act of rubbing.

'rubber n 1 elastic substance made from the juice of certain trees and used for making tyres, balls, etc. 2 piece of similar material used to rub out pencil marks, etc.

'rubbish n 1 waste material; things thrown away or destroyed as worthless. 2 nonsense.

'rubble n bits of broken stone or bricks.

'ruby n red jewel; deep red colour.

'rucksack n canvas bag worn strapped on the back.

'rudder n flat, broad piece of wood or metal hinged on the stern of a boat or ship for steering.

'ruddy adj (-ier, -iest) (of the face) healthily red.

rude adj (-r, -st) 1 impolite.

2 rough or violent: a — shock. 3 primitive; without refinement. '—ly adv. '—ness n.

'rudiments n pl first steps or stages (of knowledge, an art or science). ,rudi'mentary adj elementary; undeveloped.

'ruffian n violent cruel man; (colloq) troublesome youth.

'ruffle v disturb the peace, calm, or smoothness of.

rug n 1 floor mat of thick material. 2 thick, usu woollen, covering.

'Rugby (football) n (colloq 'rugger) football played by two teams of fifteen men using an oval-shaped ball that may be kicked or handled.

'rugged adj 1 rough; rocky: a — coast (hillside). 2 (of a person's face) wrinkled. 3 rough but kindly and honest: — manners.

'ruin n 1 (cause of) overthrow or destruction: Gambling was his —. 2 sth, esp a building, that has fallen to pieces: The church was in —s. v cause the — of. —ous adj causing —; in —s.

rule n 1 law or custom which guides or controls behaviour or action; decision about what must or must not be done: obey the —s of the game. **make it a** — to do sth, make a habit of it. **as a** —, usually. 2 government; authority: under British —. v 1 govern. 2 give a decision (that). 3 — a line, make a line on paper with a —r(2). '—r n 1 person who governs. 2 straight strip of wood, etc, for drawing straight lines and measuring. **'ruling** n (esp) decision made by sb in authority.

rum[1] n alcoholic drink made from sugar-cane.

rum[2] adj (colloq) queer; odd.

'rumble v & n (make, move with, a) deep, heavy, continuous noise.

'ruminate v meditate.

'rumour n hearsay; story, statement, open to doubt. v tell as a —.

run v (pt ran, pp run; -nn-) 1 move with quick steps, faster than walking. 2 (of buses, etc) go along; make a journey. 3 (of machines, etc) keep going: leave the engine running. 4 (cause to) flow: leave the water (the tap) running. 5 get; become: run into debt; supplies *running low*. **6** (cause to) pass or move quickly or lightly (*over*, *through*, etc): *Run your eye over this page*. **7** (of roads, lines, etc) go; extend. **8** (of colours in a material) spread when wet. **9** force; cause (sth) to go (*into*, *through*). **10** control, manage (*a business*, etc). **11** (USA) be a candidate (*for*). **12** (of plays, films, etc) continue to be performed or shown. **13** (with *adv & prep*) **run across** (sb or sth), meet or find by chance. **run after** (sb), try to catch. **run away (with)**, (try to) escape (with). **(be) run down**, (of persons) (be) exhausted, ill; (of clocks) need rewinding. **run sb down**, say unkind things about him. **run into**, collide with; meet unexpectedly. **run out (of)**, become exhausted, have no more. **run up** (*a bill*, etc), let the bill, etc, grow larger. *n* **1** act of running. **2** (usu enclosed) space for domestic birds or animals: *a chicken run*. **3** unit of score in cricket. **4** period; succession: *a run of ill luck*. **in the long run**, in the end. **'runaway** *n & adj* (horse, person) running away. **'runner** *n* **1** person, animal, etc, that runs, esp in a race. **2** part (of a sledge, etc) that slides on sth. **'runner-'up** *n* person taking the second place in a competition. **'running** *adj* continuous: *five times running*, five times in succession. *n* **in (out of) the running**, having (not having) a chance of success in a race, etc. **'runway** *n* track on an airfield, etc, for aircraft.

rung¹ ⇨ ring.

rung² *n* crosspiece forming a step in a ladder.

ru'pee *n* unit of money in India and Pakistan.

'rupture *n* act of breaking apart or bursting; ending of friendly relations. *v* break; end.

'rural *adj* in, of, characteristic of, the country. (cf. urban).

ruse *n* trick.

rush *v* **1** (cause to) go or come with great speed or violence. **2** get through or over by —ing: — *the gates*. *n* —ing: *the — hours*, period when everyone is —ing to or from work.

'russet *n & adj* reddish-brown.

rust *n* reddish-brown coating

formed on iron by the action of water and air. *v* (cause to) become covered with —; (*fig*) become poor in quality because not used. **'—y** *adj* (-ier, -iest) covered with —; (of skill) imperfect through lack of practice.

'rustic *adj* rural; in rough country style: — *dress* (*speech*).

'rustle *n* gentle light sound (as of leaves moved by a breeze). *v* make, move with, such a sound.

rut *n* line or track made by wheels in soft ground. **get into a rut**, get into a fixed way of living which cannot easily be changed.

'ruthless *adj* pitiless; merciless.

rye *n* (plant with) grain used for making flour, as animal food, etc.

S

'Sabbath *n* weekly day of rest and prayer, Saturday for Jews, Sunday for Christians.

'sable *n* (valuable fur of a) small, dark-coated animal. *adj* black.

'sabotage *n* damage done on purpose to machinery, equipment, etc.

'sabre *n* sword with a curved blade.

sack¹ *n* large bag (for heavy goods, eg coal, flour).

sack² *v* (colloq) dismiss (sb) from employment. *n* **get the —**, be dismissed. **give sb the —**, dismiss him.

'sacrament *n* solemn religious ceremony in the Christian Church: *Baptism*, *Holy Communion*, etc.

'sacred *adj* of God; connected with religion. **—ly** *adv*.

'sacrifice *n* **1** offering to God of sth precious; the thing offered. **2** the giving up of sth of value to oneself for a special purpose or to benefit sb else. **3** sth given up in this way. **4** sell sth at a —, sell it below its true value. *v* make a — of; give up as a —: *he —d his life to save the child*.

'sacrilege *n* disrespectful treatment of, damage to what should be sacred. **,sacri'legious** *adj*.

sad *adj* (-der, -dest) unhappy; causing unhappiness. **'sadly** *adv*. **'sadness** *n*. **'sadden** *v* make or become sad.

'**saddle** *n* leather seat for a rider on a horse or bicycle. *v* put a — on (a horse); (fig) burden (sb) (*with* debt, a heavy responsibility, etc).

sa'fari *n* overland journey (esp in East Africa to see wild animals).

safe *adj* (-r, -st) 1 free from, protected from, danger. 2 unhurt. 3 not causing or likely to cause harm or danger. *n* 1 metal box with a strong lock for keeping valuables in. 2 airy cupboard for food. '—**guard** *v & n* protect(ion). '**safe-'keeping** *n* care; keeping —. '—**ly** *adv*. '—**ty** *n* being —. '—**ty-pin** *n* one with a guard for the point.

sag *v* (-gg-) sink or curve down in the middle; hang unevenly.

sa'gacious *adj* showing or having common sense or intelligence.

sage *adj & n* wise (man). '—**ly** *adv*.

said ⇨ say.

sail *n* 1 sheet of canvas spread to catch the wind and move a boat. **under** —, with —s spread. **set** —, begin a voyage. 2 **go for a** —, go for a short trip on water for pleasure. *v* 1 go forward by means of a — or —s. 2 begin a voyage. '—**or** *n* 1 seaman. 2 **a good** —**or**, a person not usually seasick in rough weather.

saint *n* 1 holy person. 2 one who by his holy living on earth is declared by the Church · to have won a high place in heaven. '—**ly** *adj* (-lier, -liest) very good or holy; like a —. '—**liness** *n*.

sake *n* **for the** — **of, for my** (*the country's*, etc) —, for the good or interest of, because of a desire for.

'**salable** ⇨ sale.

'**salad** *n* uncooked vegetables (eg *lettuce, onions*) prepared as food.

'**salary** *n* (usu monthly) payment for regular employment on a yearly basis: *a* — *of £900 a year*.

sale *n* 1 exchange of goods for money; act of selling sth: *on* (*for*) —, to be sold; quantity sold: *a large* —. 2 the offering of goods at low prices for a period. 3 auction. '**salable** *adj* suitable for selling; likely to sell. '—**sman,** '—**swoman** *n* person selling goods in a shop, or (for wholesalers) to shopkeepers. '—**smanship** *n* skill in selling goods.

'**salient** *adj* outstanding; easily noticed: —*points of a speech*.

'**sallow** *adj* (-er, -est) (of the skin) of an unhealthy yellow colour.

'**salmon** *n* large fish valued for food; the colour of its flesh, orange-pink.

sa'loon *n* 1 room for social use in a ship, public house, etc. 2 — **car**, car with a wholly enclosed seating space for the passengers.

salt *n* 1 white substance obtained from mines, present in sea-water, used to flavour and preserve food. **not worth one's** —, not deserving one's pay. 2 (chemistry) compound of a metal and an acid. '—**y** *adj* (-ier, -iest) containing —; tasting of —.

'**salutary** *adj* having a good effect (on body or mind): — *advice*.

sa'lute *n* sth done to welcome sb or to show respect: *military* —, the raising of the hand to the forehead, the firing of guns, etc. *v* 1 make a — to (sb). 2 greet (with a bow, by raising the hat, etc).

a salute

a sandal

'**salvage** *n* 1 the saving of property from loss (by fire or other disaster). 2 (payment due for saving) such property. *v* save from loss in a fire, wreck, etc.

sal'vation *n* 1 the act of saving, the state of having been saved from the power of sin. 2 that which saves sb from loss, etc.

same *adj & pron* unchanged; identical. **be all** (just) **the** — **to,** make no difference to. **all the** —, although that is the case. **at the** — **time,** however, yet.

'**sampan** *n* small flat-bottomed boat used in China.

'**sample** *n* one of a number, part of a whole, taken to show what the rest is like. *v* take a — of.

'**sanctify** *v* make, set aside as, holy.

'**sanction** *n* 1 right or permission given by authority to do sth. 2 approval (of behaviour, etc) by general custom. 3 penalty intended to restore respect for law or authority. *v* give —(1),(2) to.

'sanctity *n* holiness; sacredness.

'sanctuary *n* **1** holy or sacred place (esp a church). **2** place of refuge.

sand *n* **1** tiny grains of worn rock as seen on the seashore. **2** the —s, area of — exposed at low tide. **'—paper** *n* paper with — glued to it, used for rubbing rough surfaces smooth. **'—stone** *n* rock formed chiefly of —. **'—y** *adj* (-ier, -iest) **1** containing, covered with, —. **2** (esp of hair) yellowish-red.

'sandal *n* open shoe with straps to hold it on the foot. ⇨ p 242.

'sandwich *n* slices of bread with meat, etc, between. *v* put (one thing, a person) tightly between others.

sane *adj* (-r, -st) **1** healthy in mind; not mad. **2** sensible. **'—ly** *adv*.

sang ⇨ sing.

'sanguine *adj* **1** hopeful. **2** red-faced.

'sanitary *adj* **1** free from dirt that might cause disease. **2** of, concerned with, the protection of health. **,sani'tation** *n* arrangements to give — conditions.

'sanity *n* being sane.

sank ⇨ sink[1].

sap[1] *n* liquid in a plant, carrying necessary food to all parts.

sap[2] *v* (-pp-) weaken (a wall or other defence) by digging under it; (fig) destroy (sb's faith, confidence, etc).

'sarcasm *n* (use of) bitter remarks intended to wound the feelings. **sar'castic** *adj* of, using, —.

sar'dine *n* small fish tinned in oil.

sash *n* strip of silk, etc, worn over clothing round the waist or across one shoulder.

sat ⇨ sit.

'Satan *n* the Evil One; the Devil.

'satchel *n* leather or canvas bag, used for carrying schoolbooks.

'satellite *n* **1** planet moving round another; man-made object put into orbit (round the Earth), esp one in a fixed position that transmits radio and TV signals. **2** (fig) person, state, depending upon and following the lead of another.

'satiate *v* satisfy (too) fully.

'satin *n* silk material, smooth and shiny on one side.

'satire *n* (piece of) writing that ridicules a person, a society, etc. **sa'tirical(ly)** *adj & adv*. **'satirize** *v* attack with —(s).

'satisfy *v* **1** give (sb) what he wants or needs; make contented. **2** be enough for (one's needs); be equal to (what one hopes or wants). **3** convince (sb, oneself). **,satis'faction** *n* —ing or being satisfied; sth that satisfies; feeling of pleasure. **,satis'factory** *adj* giving pleasure; —ing a need or desire; good enough.

'saturate *v* make thoroughly wet.

'Saturday *n* seventh day of the week; Jewish Sabbath.

'satyr *n* (in Greek and Roman stories) god, half man and half animal.

sauce *n* liquid added to food to give it extra flavour.

'saucepan *n* deep, round, metal cooking-pot with a handle and usu with a lid.

'saucer *n* curved round dish on which a cup is placed.

'saucy *adj* (-ier, -iest) impolite; impudent.

'saunter *n* slow walk. *v* walk slowly.

'sausage *n* chopped-up meat, etc, flavoured and put into a tube of thin skin; one section of this.

'savage *adj* **1** in a primitive or uncivilized state. **2** fierce; cruel. *n* — person.

save *v* **1** make or keep safe (*from* loss, injury, etc). **2** keep or store for future use. **— up**, store money. **3** avoid; make payment of (sth) unnecessary: — *bus fares by walking*. **4** keep (sb) from the necessity to use (money, time, etc). **5** (Christian teaching) set free from the power of, eternal punishment for, sin. **'saving** *n* (esp *pl*) money —d up.

'saviour *n* person who rescues or saves sb from danger. **The S—,** Jesus Christ.

'savour *n* taste, flavour, suggestion (*of* sth). *v* — **of**, suggest.

saw[1] ⇨ see.

saw[2] *n* cutting tool with tooth-edged steel blade. *v* (*pt* 'sawed, *pp* sawn) cut with a saw; use a saw; cut (*up*) into pieces with a saw. **'sawdust** *n* tiny bits of wood falling off when wood is sawn. **'sawmill** *n* workshop where wood is sawn by machine.

'saxophone n brass musical instrument, played by blowing. ⇨ p 180.

say v (pt & pp said) go without saying, be obvious. that is to say, in other words. n have (say) one's say, state one's opinions. have a right to say in the matter, (have a right to) share in a discussion, etc. 'saying n common remark; sth often said.

scab n dry crust formed over a wound or sore. —by adj.

'scabbard n case for the blade of a sword, dagger, or bayonet.

'scaffold n 1 structure put up for workmen to stand on while building or repairing walls, etc. 2 platform on which criminals are (or were) executed. —ing n materials (eg poles and planks) for a —.

scald v 1 hurt with hot liquid or steam. 2 clean (dishes, etc) with boiling water or steam. n injury from hot liquid, etc.

scale¹ n 1 (tool or instrument with a) series of marks for the purpose of measuring (as on a ruler or thermometer). 2 system of units (eg the decimal —) for measuring. 3 arrangement in steps or degrees: a — of wages. 4 proportion between the size of sth and of the map, diagram, etc, which represents it: the — of a map (eg one inch to the mile). 5 relative size. 6 (music) series of notes starting from a keynote. v 1 climb (with a ladder, etc). 2 — up (down), increase (decrease) by a certain proportion.

scale² n 1 one of the two pans of a balance. 2 (often pl) a pair of —s, instrument for measuring weight. turn the —s, decide the result of sth which is in doubt.

scale³ n 1 one of the thin flat plates of hard material covering the skin of some fishes and reptiles. 2 layer of chalky material forming on the inside surface of boilers, waterpipes, or on teeth. v 1 take —s from. 2 come (off) in flakes: paint scaling off a door.

scalp n the skin and hair of the top of the head. v cut the — off.

'scalpel n surgeon's knife.

scamp n worthless person. v do (work) carelessly or too quickly.

'scamper v run along quickly like small animals or children.

scan v (-nn-) look at attentively; run the eyes over every part of: — the horizon.

'scandal n 1 (behaviour causing a) general feeling of indignation; disgraceful action. 2 harmful gossip. —ize v fill with indignation. —ous adj 1 shocking. 2 (of reports, etc) containing —(2).

scant adj (having) hardly enough: — of breath; pay — attention. '—y adj (-ier, -iest) small in size or amount. —ily adv in a — manner.

'scapegoat n person blamed or punished for the mistake(s) or wrongdoing(s) of others.

scar n mark remaining on the surface (of skin, furniture, etc) as the result of injury, etc. v (-rr-) mark with a — or —s.

scarce adj (-r, -st) 1 rare; not available in sufficient quantity. 2 not often seen or found. —ly adv not quite; almost not. 'scarcity n.

scare v frighten. n fright; feeling of alarm among the general public. '—crow n figure made of sticks and old clothes, put in a field to frighten birds away.

scarf n long strip or square of material worn over the shoulders, round the neck, or over the hair.

'scarlet n & adj bright red.

'scathing adj harsh (criticism, etc).

'scatter v 1 send or go in different directions. 2 throw or put here and there: — seed. —ed adj not situated together: —ed villages.

sce'nario n outline of events, etc, for a play, a film, etc.

scene n 1 place of an actual or imagined event. 2 view; sth seen. 3 one of the parts, shorter than an act, into which a play is divided. 4 painted background, canvas, etc, on the stage of a theatre: behind the —s, at the back of the stage, hidden from the audience. 5 angry outburst, display of feelings, etc, in the presence of other people. 'scenery n 1 stage —s(4). 2 country —s(2).

scent n 1 smell, esp sth pleasant. 2 (usu liquid) preparation made from flowers; perfume. 3 smell left by an animal by which dogs can follow its track: throw sb off the —, (fig) deceive him by wrong suggestions, etc. 4 sense of smell (in dogs): *hunt by* —. *v* **1** learn the existence of; suspect: — *a plot.* **2** put —(2) on. **3** give a —(1) to.

'sceptic *n* person who doubts the truth of what he is told, esp of religious teachings. **—al** *adj.* **—ism** *n.*

'sceptre *n* rod or staff of a king, as a sign of power or authority.

'schedule *n* list of details, esp of times for doing things.

scheme *n* **1** arrangement; ordered system. **2** plan for work or activity. **3** secret or dishonest plan. *v* make a — (esp a dishonest one) (*for* sth, *to do* sth).

'scholar *n* **1** (old use) boy or girl at school. **2** student who has won a —ship(2). **3** person with much knowledge. **—ly** *adj* having or showing much learning; of or fit for a —. **—ship** *n* **1** learning or knowledge coming from study. **2** money awarded to a clever student towards his school or college fees (usu after a competition). **scho'lastic** *adj* of —s or education.

school¹ *n* building(s) where pupils or adults are taught; all the pupils in a —. a — of thought, group of people sharing an idea. *v* train; discipline. **'—,fellow, '—mate** *n* person educated or being educated at the same — as another.

school² *n* large number (of fish) swimming together.

'science *n* **1** knowledge arranged in a system, esp knowledge obtained by observation and the testing of facts. **2** a branch of such knowledge (eg *chemistry, biology*). **3** skill, expertness (eg in sport). **,scien'tific** *adj* of, for, used in, guided by the rules of, —. **'scientist** *n* person expert in a — such as physics or biology.

'scissors *n pl* (often *a pair of* —) two-bladed instrument for cutting paper, cloth, etc.

scoff *v* mock (*at*). **'—er** *n.*

scold *v* blame (sb) angrily.

scoop *n* deep shovel-like tool (of many kinds and sizes) for taking up and moving quantities of flour, sand, earth, etc; part of a machine with that purpose. *v* get or take (*up* or *out*) with, or as with, a —; make (a hole or hollow *in* sth) as with a —.

'scooter *n* **1** (child's toy) L-shaped platform with small wheels moved by pushing one foot against the ground whilst standing on it. **2** kind of motor-bike with small wheels.

scope *n* range of observation or activity; extent of opportunity: *seek — for one's energies.*

scorch *v* burn or discolour the surface of (sth) with dry heat.

score¹ *n* **1** (record of) points, goals, runs, etc, made by a player or team in sport. **2** (record of) accounts, esp of money owing. **pay off** (**settle**) **old** —**s,** (fig) take revenge. **3 on that** —, on that point. *v* **1** make or keep a —(1); make as points in a game: — *a goal* (20 *runs*). **2** make a cut, scratch, or line on a surface. **3** — **off** *sb,* get the better of him.

score² *n* (set of) twenty.

scorn *v* feel or behave towards sb as not deserving respect, fear, etc. **2** refuse (*to do* sth) because it is wrong or unworthy. *n* contempt; person, action, etc, that is —ed. **'—ful** *adj* feeling or showing —. **'—fully** *adv.*

'scorpion *n* small animal of the spider family with a poisonous sting in its long tail. ⇨ p 144.

'scot-'free *adv* unharmed; unpunished.

'scoundrel *n* wicked person.

scour *v* **1** rub (a dirty surface) bright or clean. **2** get (rust, etc, *off, out*) by rubbing. *n* —ing.

scourge *n* **1** whip for punishment. **2** (fig) cause of suffering. *v* **1** whip. **2** bring pain or suffering to.

scout¹ *n* **1** member of an organization for boys for training in out-door skills and developing character(1). **2** soldier, ship, etc, sent out to get information (eg about the enemy). *v* go out as a —.

Scouts

scout² *v* consider (an idea, suggestion) worthless or ridiculous.

scowl *v & n* (have a) bad-tempered look on the face.

'scramble v 1 climb or crawl (up, etc). 2 struggle with others (for sth).

scrap[1] n 1 small (usu unwanted) piece. 2 waste or unwanted articles or material: — iron, iron and steel articles to be melted down. v (-pp-) throw away as useless or worn out.

scrap[2] n & v (-pp-) (colloq) fight.

scrape v 1 make clean, smooth, or level by drawing or pushing the hard edge of a tool, or sth rough, along the surface; remove (paint, etc) by doing this. 2 injure by scraping. 3 go, get, past or through sth, touching or almost touching it. — through (an examination), (fig) only just pass. 4 collect together with difficulty. 5 rub with a harsh sound. 6 make (eg a hole) by scraping. n 1 act or sound of scraping. 2 —d place. 3 awkward situation resulting from foolish behaviour. '—r n tool for scraping.

scratch v 1 make lines on or in a surface with sth sharp or pointed: — sth out (by using a knife or drawing a line through it); make (a hole, etc) by —ing. 2 scrape (2) (the skin) with the finger-nails, etc. 3 withdraw from a contest. n 1 mark, cut, sound, etc, made by —ing. 2 act of —ing. 3 starting-line for a race. adj formed or done with whatever is available: a — team. —y adj (-ier, -iest).

scrawl v write or draw quickly and carelessly. n sth —ed.

scream v 1 give a loud, sharp cry of, or as of, fear or pain; say (sth) in a loud, high voice. 2 (of machines, etc) make a loud, shrill noise. n loud, piercing cry or noise.

screech v scream in anger, pain, or excitement; make a harsh, piercing noise. n —ing cry or noise.

screen n 1 upright framework, used to protect from draughts, heat, etc, or to hide sb or sth from view; anything serving this purpose. 2 frame with fine wire netting (screen-door, etc) to keep out flies, mosquitoes, etc. 3 sieve. 4 surface on which films, TV pictures, etc, are shown. v 1 hide, shelter, etc, with a —(1). 2 provide (a house, etc) with —s(2). 3 separate (coal, etc) into

different sizes by putting through a —(3).

screw n 1 metal peg driven into wood or metal by twisting, for fastening and holding things together. 2 propeller of a ship or (air-screw) of an aircraft. v 1 fasten or tighten with a — or —s: — the lid down. 2 twist round: — the lid of a glass jar on (off). 3 — up (one's eyes, face), draw the skin into tight folds to show disgust, to see at long distance, etc. '—driver n tool for turning —s. ⇨ p 293.

'scribble v write quickly or care-lessly; draw meaningless marks.

scribe n professional letter-writer.

script n 1 handwriting; type(3) that imitates this. 2 (short for) manuscript or typescript.

'scripture n the Holy S—s, the Bible.

scroll n roll of paper for writing on; ancient book written on a —.

scrub[1] v (-bb-) clean by rubbing hard, esp with a stiff brush, soap, and water. n —bing. —bing-brush n brush with short, hard bristles for —bing floors, etc.

scrub[2] n (land covered with) trees and bushes of poor quality.

'scruple n (hesitation caused by) fear that some action proposed is morally wrong. 'scrupulous adj strictly honest.

'scrutiny n thorough examination. 'scrutinize v make a — of.

'scuffle v & n (take part in a) rough confused fight or struggle.

scull n oar. v move a boat forward with a — or —s.

'sculpture n 1 art of making forms or ornamenting surfaces by carving stone or wood, by modelling in clay, etc. 2 (a piece of) such work. 'sculptor n.

scum n 1 dirty substance, froth, which comes to the surface of a boiling liquid, a pond, etc. 2 (fig) worst or seemingly worthless part (of the population, etc).

'scurry v run, esp with short, quick steps. n act or sound of —ing.

'scurvy n disease caused by lack of fresh fruit and vegetables.

'scuttle[1] n (also coal—) container for a supply of coal at the fire-side.

'scuttle[2] v make a hole in (one's

ship) in order to sink it (eg to prevent capture by an enemy).

'scuttle³ v scurry (*off, away*).

scythe n tool with a long, curved
blade and a long handle for cutting
grain, etc.

sea n (any part of the) expanse of
salty water surrounding the con-
tinents; one of certain large areas
of inland water: *the Black Sea; the
Dead Sea, etc.* **all at sea,** puzzled.
go to sea, become a sailor. **'sea-
faring** adj of work on the sea;
occupied in sea voyages. **'sea-gull**
n common sea bird with long wings.
'sea level n level of the sea's surface used in reckoning the height of
land and depth of the sea. **'seaman**
n sailor, esp one who is not an
officer. **'seasick** adj sick from the
motion of a ship or boat. **'sea'side**

n & adj (place, town) by the sea.
'seaweed n plant(s) growing in
the sea.

seal¹ n **1** piece of wax, lead, etc,
stamped with a design and attached
to a document, etc, to show that it
is genuine, or to a letter, door, etc,
to guard against its being opened
by persons not having authority to
do so. **2** piece of metal, etc, on
which is the design to be stamped
on the hot wax, etc. v **1** put a
— (1) on; stamp a — (1). **2** close
tightly: — *a jar of fruit* (to make it
airtight). **3** — a bargain, settle it.
his fate is —ed, is decided.
'—ing-wax n kind of wax
melted to — letters.

seal² n fish-eating sea-animal
valued for its fur. ⇨ below.

seam n **1** line where two edges,

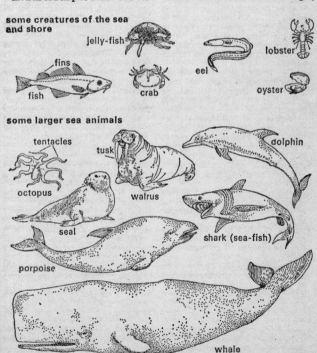

some creatures of the sea
and shore

jelly-fish

fins

fish

crab

eel

lobster

oyster

some larger sea animals

tentacles

tusk

dolphin

octopus

walrus

seal

shark (sea-fish)

porpoise

whale

esp of cloth or leather, are turned back and sewn together. **2** layer of coal, etc, between layers of other materials (eg *rock*). **3** line or mark like a —(1). *v* sew a —(1).

search *v* **1** examine, look carefully at, through or into (*for* sth or sb, *in order to*). **2** go deeply into; go into every part of. *n* act of —ing: *go in — of sb.* '—light *n* powerful electric lamp for —ing the sky, sea, etc.

'**season** *n* **1** period of the year having a particular climate: *winter, spring, the rainy (dry)* —, etc. **2** period suitable or normal for sth: *the football* —. **3** period (in a town) when most of the social events take place. *v* make or become suitable for use. '—**able** *adj* (of the weather) normal for the —. '—**al** *adj* dependent on or changing with the —s. '**season-'ticket** *n* one giving the owner the right to travel between two places, or to go to a place of amusement, as often as he wishes during a certain period.

seat *n* **1** sth made or used for sitting on (eg *a chair, box, rug*). **2** part of a chair, stool, etc, on which one sits. **3** place where sth is or is carried on: *—s of learning,* universities. *v* **1** — oneself, sit down. **Be —ed,** (formal) Sit. **2** have —s for: *The hall —s 500 people.*

se'cede *v* withdraw from membership (of a group of States, etc).

se'cluded *adj* (of a place) quiet, solitary. **se'clusion** *n* — place; solitary condition.

'**second** *n* **1** 60th part of a minute of time or a degree(1): *the — hand of a watch.* **2** (colloq) moment; short time.

'**second** *adj* next after the first in position, time, order, etc. — **lieutenant,** lowest commissioned rank in the army. — **nature,** habit. *n* **1** that which is —. **2** person who supports or helps another in a duel or a boxing match. *v* **1** support. **2** (at a meeting) speak in support of a proposal (so that it may be discussed). '**second-'best** *adj* next after the best. '**second-'class** *adj* of the class after the first. '—'**hand** *adj* **1** already used by sb else: *second-hand books (clothes).* **2** (of news, information) obtained

from others, not based on personal observation, etc. '**second-'rate** *adj* not of the best quality.

'**secondary** *adj* following, less important than, what is first or chief: — *roads.* — **school (education),** between the primary school and university, college, etc.

'**secret** *adj* (to be) kept from the knowledge or view of others; of which others have no knowledge. *n* **1** sth —. **keep a** —, not tell anyone else. **2** way of doing or getting sth not widely known: *What's the — of his success?* **3** in —, —ly. —**ly** *adv* in a — manner. '**secrecy** *n* keeping things —; state of being (kept) —. '**secretive** *adj* having the habit of secrecy.

'**secretary** *n* **1** person employed to send letters, keep papers and records, etc, for another or for an organization. **2** S— **of State,** minister in charge of a government department or a branch of a department. ,**secre'tarial** *adj* of a — or a —'s work.

sect *n* group of people united by (usu religious) beliefs that differ from those more generally held.

'**section** *n* **1** part cut off; slice. **2** one of a number of parts which can be fitted together (eg to make a structure). **3** division: *the factory — of the town.* —**al** *adj* supplied in —s(2) for fitting together by the buyer: —*al buildings.*

'**sector** *n* **1** section of a circle lying between two lines drawn from the centre to the edge. **2** division of a battle area for control purposes.

'**secular** *adj* worldly or material (opp of *spiritual, religious*).

se'cure *adj* **1** safe (*from* or *against* risk, etc). **2** firmly or tightly fixed; not likely to slip or break. *v* **1** make —; lock; tie (up). **2** obtain: — *tickets for a concert.* **se'curity** *n* **1** (sth that provides) safely. **2** pledge for repayment of a loan, etc. **3** certificate showing ownership of stocks, shares, etc.

se'date *adj* (of a person) calm, serious, quiet.

'**sediment** *n* matter (eg sand, mud) that settles to the bottom of a liquid. ,**sedi'mentary** *adj.*

se'dition *n* words, actions, intended to make people rebel · against authority. **se'ditious** *adj.*

see¹ v (pt saw, pp seen) **1** have (the use of) the power of sight;. understand. **2** (with adv & prep). **see about**, take steps to do (sth), get (sth). **see after**, look after, attend to. **see sb off**, go to a railway station, ship, etc, to see sb start a journey. **see through (sb or sth)**, not be deceived by. **see (sb or sth) through**, support as long as necessary. **see to**, attend to. **see to it that**, make certain that. **3 see the last of**, finish with. **see red**, become very angry.

see² n district under a bishop.

seed n (pl seed or seeds) **1** flowering plant's element of life, from which another plant can grow. **2** cause or origin. **'—ling** n plant newly grown from a —.

seek v (pt & pp sought) **1** look for; try to find. **2 — to do**, try to do.

seem v have or give the impression or appearance of being or doing; appear to be.

'seemly adj (-ier, -iest) proper or correct (for the occasion, etc).

seen ⇨ see.

seep v ooze. **'—age** n.

'seesaw n (game played by children seated on a) board that moves up and down; up-and-down or to-and-fro motion. v move or play in this way.

seethe v (of liquids) boil; bubble; (fig) be excited (with anger, etc).

'segment n **1** part cut off or marked off by a line. **2** section (of a sphere).

'segregate v separate, put or keep apart, from others. **,segre'gation** n.

seize v **1** take possession of (property, etc) by law. **2** take hold of, suddenly and violently. **'seizure** n **1** seizing. **2** sudden heart attack.

'seldom n rarely; not often.

se'lect v choose. adj carefully chosen. **—ion** n **1** —ing. **2** group of —ed articles; number of things from which to —.

self n (pl selves) **1** person's nature or special qualities. **2** one's interests considered from one's own point of view. **3 one's better —**, the better side of one's nature.

self- prefix short for itself, myself, himself, etc, as in self-taught, taught by oneself. **'self-'conscious** adj uneasy, esp because unable to forget oneself in the company of others. **'self-'willed** adj determined to go one's own way; refusing advice or guidance.

'selfish adj chiefly thinking of, interested in, one's own needs; without care for others. **—ly** adv. **—ness** n.

sell v (pt & pp sold) **1** give or offer in exchange for money. **2 — off, —** (stocks of goods) cheaply. **— out, —** all of one's stock (of goods, etc). **'—er** n.

'selvage, 'selvedge n edge of cloth woven so that the threads do not become loose.

selves ⇨ self.

'semblance n likeness; appearance.

'semi- prefix **1** half: a —circle. **2** partly: semi-civilized. **3** occurring twice: semi-annual. **—'colon** n the sign; (used in writing and printing). **'semi-de'tached** adj (of a house) joined to another on one side only. **,semi-'final** n the last round but one in a competition.

'senate n **1** Upper House of the two parts of Parliament, esp in France and USA. **2** governing body of some universities, colleges, etc. **3** highest council of state in ancient Rome. **'senator** n member of a —.

send v (pt & pp sent) **1** cause (sb or sth) to go, come or be carried; get (sb or sth) taken. **—away**, send (sb or sth) to a distance. **— for**, ask for sb to come, sth to be brought. **— in**, enter (one's name, work, etc, for a competition, etc). **— off**, dispatch (letters, goods, etc). **— out**, give forth (light, heat); distribute (circulars, etc). **2** cause to become: **— sb mad**. **'send-off** n meeting (eg at a railway station) of a traveller's friends to wish him a good journey, etc.

'senile adj showing signs of, caused by, old age. **se'nility** n.

'senior adj **1** older in years; higher in authority or rank. **2** (after a person's name) indicating the elder with the same name: Tom Brown Senior (abbr Sen or Sr). **n —** person.

sen'sation n **1** feeling: a — of warmth. **2** (sth that causes) deep, strong interest or excitement.

—al *adj* causing deep interest and excitement.

sense *n* **1** any one of the special powers of the body by which one sees, hears, smells, tastes, or feels. **2** awareness (*of* sth) through one or more of these powers. **3** power of judging; practical wisdom. **4** understanding of the value (*of* sth): *the moral —; his — of duty.* **5** (*pl*) normal state of mind. **out of his —s**, mad. **come to one's —s**, stop behaving foolishly. **6** meaning: *It doesn't make —*, it has no meaning. **'—less** *adj* **1** foolish. **2** unconscious.

,sensi'bility *n* power to feel, esp to be responsive to art, music, etc.

'sensible *adj* **1** having or showing good sense(3). **2** aware (*of*).

'sensitive *adj* **1** quick to receive impressions through the senses(1): *a — skin.* **2** easily offended or hurt in spirit: *— to blame.* **3** (of instruments) able to record small changes.

'sensual *adj* of, given up to, the pleasures of the senses(1). **'sensuous** *adj* affecting, appealing to, the senses(1).

sent ⊳ send.

'sentence *n* **1** words, esp with a subject(2) and predicate, that form a statement, question, etc, making complete sense. (cf clause, phrase). **2** (statement by a judge, etc, of) punishment. *v* declare that (sb) is to have a certain punishment: *— sb to five years' imprisonment.*

'sentiment *n* **1** feeling in the mind (eg of pity, loyalty). **2** (tendency to be moved by) tender feeling; (display of) tender feeling. **3** opinion; expression of feeling.

,senti'mental *adj* easily moved by, full of, tender feelings; affecting the feelings: *— novels.* **,senti-men'tality** *n*.

'sentinel *n*. **'sentry** *n* soldier keeping watch or guard.

'separate *adj* apart; not joined; distinct. *v* **1** make, keep or become *—.* **2** (of a number of people) go in different ways. **'separable** *adj* that can be *—d.* **,sepa'ration** *n* (period of) being *—d*; act of separating.

Sep'tember *n* ninth month of the year.

'septic *adj* infected; causing, caused by, infection (with bacteria).

'sepulchre *n* tomb. **the Holy S—**, that of Jesus Christ. **se'pulchral** *adj* of a —; of burial.

'sequel *n* that which follows or arises out of (an earlier happening); further story about the same persons.

'sequence *n* **1** sth that follows as a result. **2** connected line of events, ideas, etc.

'seraph *n* angel. **se'raphic** *adj*.

,sere'nade *n* music (intended to be) played or sung outdoors at night. *v* sing or play a — to (sb).

se'rene *adj* clear and peaceful; calm. **—ly** *adv*. **se'renity** *n*.

serf *n* (in olden times) person not allowed to leave the land on which he worked. **'—dom** *n* social system in which land was cultivated by —s.

serge *n* hard-wearing woollen cloth.

'sergeant *n* **1** non-commissioned army officer above a corporal and below a sergeant-major. **2** police officer with rank below that of inspector.

'serial *adj* **1** (of a story, etc) appearing in (weekly, monthly, etc) parts. **2** of, in, or forming, a series. *n* —(1) story. **—ly** *adv*.

'series *n* (*pl* 'series) **1** number of things, events, etc, each of which is related in some way to the others. **2** succession (*of* numbers, etc).

'serious *adj* **1** solemn; thoughtful; not given to pleasure-seeking. **2** important because of possible danger: *a — illness.* **3** in earnest, not playful. **—ly** *adv*. **—ness** *n*.

'sermon *n* spoken or written address on a religious or moral subject, esp one given in church.

'serpent *n* snake.

'servant *n* person working for another or others for payment, esp in a household.

serve *v* **1** be a servant to (sb): *— as a cook.* **2** perform duties (for): *— one's country* (eg as a statesman). **3** attend to (customers in a shop); supply (*with* goods or services); place (food, etc) on a table for a meal; give (food, etc) to sb at a meal. **4** be satisfactory for a need or purpose. **5** act towards (sb) in a certain way: *— sb shamefully.* **6 It —s him right**, He deserves the loss, punishment, etc, that he has received.

'service n **1** being a servant: go into —, become a domestic servant. **2** department or branch of public work, government employment, etc. **the fighting —s**, the Navy, Army, Air Force. **on active —**, engaged on military duties in time of war. **3** sth done to help or benefit another: get the —s of a lawyer. **4 at your —**, ready to help, ready to be used, etc. **5** system or arrangement that supplies public needs: a bus —; the telephone —. **6** form of worship and prayer to God; religious ceremony for a special purpose: the marriage —. **7** complete set of articles (plates, etc) for use at table: a dinner — of fifty pieces. **0** work done by domestic servants, waiters, etc: add ten per cent to the bill for — (ie as a tip). **—able** adj **1** willing, able, to help. **2** strong and lasting.

servi'ette n table-napkin.

servile adj of or like slaves; suggesting the behaviour, etc, of a slave: — flatiery. **ser'vility** n.

session n meeting of a law court, of Parliament, etc; series of such meetings. **in —**, meeting for business, discussion, etc.

set v (pt & pp set; -tt-) **1** (of the sun, etc) go down below the horizon. **2** put or place (sth in a certain position, condition, or relation): set a stake in the ground. (with certain objects): **set (a broken bone)**, bring the parts together so that they may unite. **set (the hands of) a clock**, move them to show a certain time. **set (sb) an example**, show him, by one's own behaviour, how he ought to behave. **set fire to sth**, cause it to begin burning. **set sail**, begin a voyage. **set a trap**, arrange it so that it is ready. **set type**, arrange it in order, ready for printing. **3** (with objects, followed by adj or adv) cause (sb or sth) to be in a certain state, relation, etc: set sth in order; set sb free; set sb's doubts at rest. **4** (with adv & prep) **set about**, begin. **set forth (out)**, start a journey; state clearly (eg one's opinions). **set off**, start a journey; explode (a mine(2), a firework);

start (a chain of events). **set a dog on (to) sb**, make it attack him. **set up** (a shop, a government, etc), get one started or established. **set up as** (a carpenter, etc), begin business as. **5** cause (sb) to do sth; give as a task to be done: set sb a question; set the men to chop wood. **6 at a set time (date)**, at one fixed in advance. **set books**, books to be studied for an examination. n **1** number of persons or things, of a similar kind, that go together: a set of golf-clubs; a tea-set (= service(1)). **2** apparatus: a TV set. **'set-back** n (cause of) check to progress. **'setting** n (esp) place, scene, etc, considered as the background of a story, event, etc. **'set-to** n quarrel.

set'tee n kind of sofa.

'settle v **1** (cause to) come to rest: — (oneself) (down) in an armchair. **2** make or become calm, untroubled: a period of —d weather. **3** (cause to) become used to a new life or occupation: — (down) to a new job. **4** make one's home (at, in). **5** reach an agreement about; decide. **6** pay (a debt, etc). **7** (of dust, etc, in the air, particles in a liquid) (cause to) come to rest: The rain —d the dust; The dust —d on everything. **8** (of the ground, foundations, etc) sink gradually to a lower level. **—ment** n **1** the act of settling (an argument, etc). **2** (group of persons who —(4) in a) new colony. **—r** n colonist; person who —s(4).

'seven n & adj 7. **—'teen** n & adj 17. **—th** n & adj. **—ty** n & adj 70. **—tieth** n & adj 70th; 1/70.

'sever v **1** cut (eg a rope) in two. **2** break off (relations, friendship).

'several adj three or four; some. pron a few; some.

se'vere adj (-r, -st) **1** stern; strict. **2** (of the weather, a disease) violent. **3** (of style, etc) simple; without ornament. **—ly** adv. **se'verity** n.

sew v (pt sewed, pp sewed or sewn) work with a needle and thread; fasten with stitches; make (sth) by stitching. **'sewing** n clothes, etc, being sewn. **'sewing-machine** n.

'sewer n large underground drain that carries away water, etc, from buildings and roadways.

sex n the state of being male or female; males or females collectively. '—ual adj of —; of the —es.

'**shabby** adj (-ier, -iest) **1** in bad condition because much used, worn, etc. **2** wearing — clothes. **3** (of behaviour) mean; unworthy.

'**shackle** n one of a pair of iron rings joined by a chain for fastening a prisoner's wrists or ankles. v put —s on; (fig) hinder.

shade n **1** partly dark area sheltered from direct rays of light, esp sunlight. **2** darker part(s) of a picture, etc. **3** degree or depth of colour: various —s of blue. **4** sth (eg for a lamp) that shuts out light or lessens its brightness. v **1** keep direct rays of light from: He —d his eyes with his hand. **2** darken (parts of a drawing, etc) to give an appearance of solidity. **3** change by degrees (into . . ., from . . ., to). '**shady** adj (-ier, -iest) **1** giving — from sunlight: the shady side of the street. **2** dishonest: shady dealings.

'**shadow** n **1** dark patch or area on the ground, on a wall, etc, made by sb or sth cutting off direct rays of light. **2** least sign or appearance: without a — of doubt. v **1** darken. **2** secretly follow all the movements of (eg a suspected criminal). —y adj of or like a —.

shaft n **1** (the long, slender stem of an) arrow or spear; long handle of an axe, etc. **2** one of the two wooden poles between which a horse is harnessed to a cart. **3** steel rod which turns car-wheels or a ship's propeller. **4** beam of light. **5** vertical passage in a building or leading to a mine, for ventilation or for a lift (elevator) to travel in.

shake v (pt shook, pp 'shaken) **1** move, be moved, quickly and violently up and down, forwards and backwards. — off (a cold, etc), get rid of. **2** (of sb's voice) become weak and uncertain. '**shaky** adj (-ier, -iest) unsteady.

shall v (pt should) **1** used in expressing the future tense: I (We) — come tomorrow. (cf will.) **2** used in expressing determination: He (She, You, They) — do as I say. (cf will.) **3** used in reported speech: (He said, 'You will fail.') He told me that I should fail. **4** indicating what is advisable or right:

You should come tomorrow. You should have come yesterday. (cf ought.) **5** S— I?, Do you want me to?; You shouldn't, You ought not to.

'**shallow** adj (-er, -est) not deep: a — stream; (fig) not earnest or serious.

sham v (-mm-) pretend: —ming illness. n person who —s; sth intended to deceive. adj false or pretended: a — battle.

shame n **1** distressed feeling; loss of self-respect. **2** dishonour: bring — on one's family. **3** sth that causes —(1): What a — to deceive the old man! v **1**. cause —(2) to; cause (sb) to feel —(1). **2** force or frighten (sb into or out of doing sth) by causing him —(1). '**shame-'faced** adj showing —(1). '—**ful** adj causing or bringing —. '—**less** adj feeling no —(1); done without —(1).

'**sham'poo** v & n (use a) special liquid or powder for washing the hair.

shan't = shall not. ⇨ shall.

shape n outward form, appearance, outline. in any — or form, of any kind, in any way. in good (bad) —, (of things) in a good (bad) condition; (of persons) (un)healthy. v take —; develop; cause to have a certain —. '—**less** adj without a clear or good —; without order. '—**ly** adj (-ier, -iest) having a pleasing —.

share[1] n **1** part (of sth) that one has, gets, or gives, in common with others. **2** part taken by sb in an activity, etc. **3** one of the equal parts into which the capital of a business company is divided. v **1** give a — of to others. **2** have or use (with). **3** have a — (in sth).

share[2] n blade of a plough.

shark n large sea-fish that eats other fish ⇨ p 247; (fig) swindler.

sharp adj (-er, -est) **1** having good cutting edge: a — knife; with a fine point: a — needle. **2** distinct: — outlines. **3** (of curves, slopes, bends) changing direction quickly or abruptly. **4** (of sounds) shrill; piercing. **5** quickly aware of things: — eyes. **6** (of feeling, taste) keen: à — pain. **7** quick in mind: a — child. **8** quick; brisk: a — walk. **9** harsh; severe: a — rebuke.

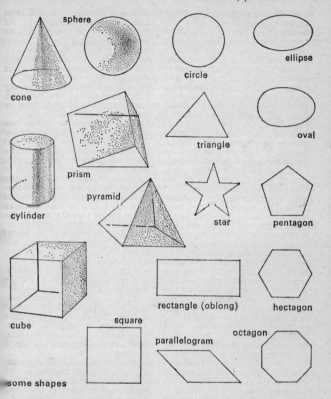

cone

sphere

circle

ellipse

prism

triangle

oval

cylinder

pyramid

star

pentagon

cube

square

rectangle (oblong)

hectagon

parallelogram

octagon

some shapes

10 (music) above the normal pitch. *n* (music) the symbol #. *adv* 1 punctually: *Come at five o'clock —.* 2 abruptly: (*Turn — to the left.* '**—en** *v* make —(1). '**—ly** *adv.*

shatter *v* 1 break violently into small pieces. 2 (fig) end (sb's hopes); shock (sb's nerves).

shave *v* 1 cut (hair) off the chin, etc, with a razor. 2 cut off (a thin slice, etc). 3 pass very close to, almost touching. *n* 1 shaving (of the face). 2 a close (narrow) —, a fortunate escape from injury, etc. '**shavings** *n pl* thin slices **—d** off wood.

shawl *n* large (usu square) piece

of material worn about the shoulders or head by women or wrapped round a baby.

she *pron* referring to a female as the subject(2): *She can see me.* ⇨ her.

sheaf *n* (*pl* sheaves) bundle of corn, barley, etc, tied together after reaping; bundle of papers.

shear *v* (*pp* shorn) cut the wool off (a sheep) with shears. '**—s** *n pl* large scissors for —ing sheep, cutting cloth, grass, etc.

sheath *n* 1 case for the blade of a sword, dagger, etc. 2 long, folded covering, esp as part of a plant.

sheathe *v* 1 put (a sword, etc) into a sheath. 2 protect with casing.

shed[1] n building for storing things, protecting animals, etc.

shed[2] v (pt & pp shed; -dd-) **1** let fall: — tears, leaves, etc. **2** cause (blood) to flow. **3** give forth: a fire —s warmth. — **light on**, help to make clear; provide information about.

sheep n (pl sheep) grass-eating animal kept for its flesh (mutton) and its wool. ⇨ p 84. '—ish adj timid and stupid like a —; lacking self-will.

sheer adj **1** thorough; complete: a — waste of time. **2** straight up or down.

sheet n **1** large piece of linen or cotton cloth, esp for a bed. **2** broad, thin, flat piece (of paper, glass, etc).

sheik(h) n Arab chieftain.

shelf n (pl shelves) **1** board fastened at right-angles to a wall, or in a bookcase, cupboard, etc, to stand things on. **2** shelf-like piece of rock on a cliff, etc. **shelve** v put (sth) on a —; (fig) postpone dealing with (problems, etc).

shell n **1** hard outer covering of birds' eggs, nuts, some seeds, and some water animals (called '—**fish**). **2** outer structure, walls, of an unfinished or ruined building. **3** metal case, filled with explosive, to be fired from a gun. v **1** fire —s(3) at. **2** remove the —(1) from.

'shelter n **1** condition of being protected or safe (eg from rain). **2** sth that gives such protection or safety. v **1** give — to; protect. **2** take — (in, under, etc).

shelve ⇨ shelf.

'shepherd n man who takes care of sheep. v guide or direct.

'sheriff n chief law officer in a county.

shield n **1** (representation of a) piece of armour carried on the arm to protect against arrows, stones, etc. **2** sth (eg in a machine) designed to keep out dust, wind, etc, to protect from danger or damage. v protect; keep safe.

shift v move, be moved, from one place to another. n group of workmen who start work as another group finishes; period of time for which such a group works: on the day (night) —. '—y adj (-ier, -iest) untrustworthy.

'shilling n (formerly) British coin worth twelve old pence.

'shimmer v & n (shine with a) wavering soft light.

shin n front of the leg between the knee and the ankle. ⇨ p 29.

shine v (pt & pp shone) give out or reflect light; be or make bright. n brightness; polish. '**shiny** adj (-ier, -iest).

shingle n small smooth pebbles on (or from) the seashore.

ship n large vessel that travels out to sea: sailing- (steam-)ship. v (-pp-) put, take, send (goods, etc) in a —. '—**mate** n fellow sailor in a —. '—**ment** n putting of goods on a —; amount of goods —ped at one time. '—**per** n person who arranges for goods to be —ped. '—**shape** adj in good order. '—**wreck** n loss or destruction of a — at sea by storm, etc. v (cause to) suffer —wreck. '—**wright** n —builder. '—**yard** n place where —s are built.

ships

shire n county (esp in compounds as York—).

shirk v try to escape (doing sth); avoid (a duty, sth unpleasant).

shirt n loose-fitting garment of cotton, etc, as worn by men. in '**shirt-sleeves**, not wearing a jacket.

'shiver v tremble, esp from cold or fear. n —ing.

shoal n great number of fish swimming together.

shock n **1** (condition of the human body or mind resulting from a violent blow or shaking caused by a collision or explosion. **2** violent effect of the passage of electric current through the body. **3** disturbance of the nervous system. v (of bad news, etc) give a —(3) to; fill with surprised disgust or horror. '—**ing** adj.

shod ⇨ shoe.

'shoddy adj (-ier, -iest) (of work

material) of worse quality than it seems to be.

shoe n outer covering for the foot. **'shoe-lace (string)**, string used to tie up a —. v (pt & pp **shod**) **1** make and fit —(s) on (a horse). **2** (esp **shod**) **well (poorly) shod** wearing strong (poor) —s.

shone ⇨ shine.

shook ⇨ shake.

shoot v (pt & pp **shot**) **1** move, come, go, send, suddenly or quickly (out, in, up, etc). **2** (of plants) send out (new leaves, etc) from a stem. **3** (of pain) go again and again along (a part of the body) suddenly and swiftly. **4** (with rifle, etc) fire(4) a bullet from it; loose (an arrow from a bow); hit with a bullet, shell, arrow, etc; wound or kill by doing this. n new young growth on a plant, etc. **'—ing star** n meteor.

shop n **1** building or room where goods are shown and sold to the public. **2** (also **'work—**) place where goods (esp machines) are manufactured or repaired. v (-pp-) **go —ping**, go to the —s to buy things. **'—keeper** n owner or manager of a retail —. **'shop-lifter** n sb who steals from a —. **'shop-'steward** n member of a local branch committee of a trade union.

shore n land bordering the sea, a lake, etc. **on —**, on land.

shorn ⇨ shear.

short adj (-er, -est) **1** (opp of long) measuring little from beginning to end; (opp of tall) not reaching far up. **2** less than the usual, stated or required (amount, distance, weight, etc): working — time, fewer days per week, etc, than usual. **a — cut**, a way of getting somewhere, doing sth, more quickly than usual. **3 — of**, not having enough of. **in —**, in a few words. **4** (of cake, pastry) easily breaking or crumbling. adv **1** suddenly; abruptly: stop —. **2 come (fall) — of**, fail to reach (what is required, etc). **'—age** n condition of not having enough. **'—'coming** n fault; failure to be as good as is required, etc. **'—en** v make or become —er. **'—hand** n system of rapid writing using special signs. **'short-'handed** adj having not enough workmen. **'—ly** adv **1** soon. **2 —ly after**

(before), a — time after (before). **3** briefly. **'short-'sighted** adj **1** unable to see distant things well. **2** (fig) not thinking sufficiently of future needs, etc. **'short-'tempered** adj easily made angry.

shorts n garment like trousers but with short legs.

shot n **1** (sound of the) firing of a gun, etc. **2** attempt to hit sth, do sth, etc. **have a —**, try. **3** that which is fired from a gun, esp (pl shot) quantity of tiny balls of lead contained in the cartridge of a sporting gun (or **'—gun**). v ⇨ shoot.

should v ⇨ shall.

'shoulder n **1** part of the body where an arm (or foreleg of an animal) is joined to the trunk(2) ⇨ p 29. **2** shoulder-like part of sth. n take on one's —(s); push with the —. **'—-blade** n flat bone of the —, behind and below the neck. ⇨ p 30.

shout n loud call or cry. v give a —; speak, say sth, in a loud voice.

shove v & n (colloq) push.

'shovel n spade-like tool, used for moving coal, sand, snow, etc. ⇨ p 293. v (-ll-) take (up), move with a —; make (a path, etc) with a —.

show v (pt **showed**, pp **shown**) **1** allow to be seen; bring before the light. **2** (with adv) **— off**, make a display of one's abilities, etc. **— sth off**, help to make its beauty, etc, more noticeable. n **1 —ing. 2** collection of things publicly displayed, esp for competition: a flower —. **3** display intended to impress people. **4** (colloq) public entertainment (eg at a theatre). **'—y** adj (-ier, -iest) too much decorated or ornamented.

'shower n **1** short fall of rain, etc. **2** (spray of water coming from an) overhead tap for washing oneself. **3** large number of (small) things together: a — of sparks. v **1** fall, send, give, in a —(3). **2** take a bath by standing under a —(2).

shrank ⇨ shrink.

shred n strip or piece cut, torn, or broken off sth; fragment: torn to —s. v (-dd-) make into —s.

shrewd adj (-er, -est) **1** having, showing, sound judgement and common sense. **2** (of a guess) near the truth.

shriek v & n scream.

shrill adj (-er, -est) (of sounds) sharp; high-pitched.

shrimp n small shell-fish used for food.

shrine n tomb or casket containing holy relics.

shrink v (pt shrank, pp shrunk) 1 make or become smaller (esp of cloth through wetting). 2 move back, show unwillingness to do sth (from fear, shame, etc).

'shrivel v (-ll-) (cause to) become dried or curled up (through heat, frost, dryness, etc).

shroud n sheet (to be) wrapped round a corpse. v wrap or cover in, or as in, a —: —ed in mist.

shrub n plant with a woody stem, lower than a tree and (usu) with several separate stems from the root.

shrug v (-gg-) lift the shoulders slightly (to show doubt, etc). n such a movement.

shrunk ⇨ shrink.

'shudder v shake; tremble with fear or disgust. n a —ing.

'shuffle v 1 walk (along) without raising the feet properly. 2 mix (playing-cards) before dealing; put (papers, etc) into disorder.

shun v (-nn-) keep away from; avoid.

shunt v send (a railway wagon, etc) from one track to another.

shut v (pt & pp shut; -tt-) 1 move a door, gate, lid, one's lips, etc, so as to close an opening; keep sb or sth out (in) by doing this. 2 (with adv) — down, (of a factory, etc) stop work; stop broadcasting. be — in, (of a person, etc) be locked inside. — off, stop the supply of (gas, water, etc); turn off (a radio, TV, etc). — up, fasten doors, windows, etc, in a building (for safety); (colloq) stop talking.

'shutter n 1 movable cover for a window (to keep out light or burglars). 2 part of a camera that opens and admits light to the film.

'shuttle n part of a weaving-machine or sewing-machine that carries the lower thread.

shy adj (-er, -est) 1 (of persons) self-conscious when in the presence of others. 2 showing such self-consciousness: a shy smile. 3 (of animals) easily frightened. 4 fight

shy of, be inclined to avoid. v (pt & pp shied) (of a horse) turn aside, jump up, in alarm (at sth). **'shyly** adv. **'shyness** n.

sick adj (-er, -est) 1 be —, throw up food from the stomach. 2 unwell; ill. 3 (colloq) — of, tired of. — at (about), feeling annoyance about. **'—en** v 1 be —ening for, be in the first stages of (an illness). 2 make or become tired (of), disgusted. **'—ly** adj (-ier, -iest) 1 causing a — feeling. 2 weak; often in bad health. **'—ness** n ill health.

'sickle n curved blade with a short handle, used for cutting grass, etc.

side n 1 one of the (fairly) flat surfaces of an object that is not the top or the bottom; either of the two surfaces of paper, cloth, etc; one of the two surfaces of the body or a house that is not the back or front of it. **on every —**, everywhere. **— by —**, close together or touching. **by the — of**, (fig) compared with. **put sth on one —** put it away, save it. 2 team or players. **take —s (with)**, take sb's —, support, in a dispute v **— with**, support (in a dispute) **—board** n table, usu with drawer and cupboards, in a dining-room **'—car** n one-wheeled carriag fastened to the — of a motor bike **'siding** n short length of railwa track at the — of the main line **'—line** n occupation which is no one's main work. **'—track** branch road. v (fig) avoid. **'—wa** n (USA) pavement. **'—ways** ad to, towards, from, the —; with th — or — edge first.

'sidle v walk (up to, away from, pas sb) shyly or nervously.

siege n (period of) operations armed forces to capture a fortifie place. **lay — to**, besiege.

sieve n utensil with wire networ etc, to separate finer grains fro coarser, etc, or solids fro liquids.

sift v 1 separate by putting throug a sieve: — ashes from cinder 2 shake through a sieve: — flour.

sigh v 1 take a deep breath th can be heard (showing tirednes relief, etc). 2 — for, feel a lon ing for. n act or sound of —ing.

sight n 1 (power of) seeing los one's —, become blind. (know *only*) **by —**, by appearance, not as an acquaintance. **2** sth seen or to be seen, esp sth remarkable; (*pl*) noteworthy buildings, places, etc: *the —s of London*. **3** device to guide the eye (when using a rifle, etc). *v* **1** see (by coming near to): *— land*. **2** adjust the —s(3) (of a gun, etc). **'—,seer** *n* person visiting the —s(2) of a town, etc.

sign *n* **1** mark or object used to represent sth: *mathematical —s* (eg $+$, $-$, $\times$, $\div$). **2** name(s), design, etc, on a board or plate to give information to the public: *traffic —s*. **3** indication: *—s of rain*. **4** movement of the head, hand, etc, used instead of words. *v* **1** write one's name on (a letter, etc) to show that one is the writer or that one agrees with the contents. **2** make known (*to sb*) an order or request by using —s(4). **'—board, '—post** *n* = —(2).

'signal *n* **1** (making of) sign(s) or movement(s), to give warning, instructions, news, etc. **2 railway —**, post, etc, for —s to train-drivers. *v* (-ll-) **1** make a — or —s (*to*). **2** use —s. **3** send (news) by —. **'signal-box** *n* building on a railway with apparatus for —ling.

'signature *n* person's name signed by himself.

'signify *v* **1** make known, show by a sign: *— one's approval*. **2** mean; be a sign of. **sig'nificance** *n* meaning; importance. **sig'nificant** *adj*.

'silence *n* condition of being quiet or silent. *v* make (sb or sth) silent; cause to be quiet. **'silent** *adj* **1** making no or little sound; still. **2** saying little or nothing; giving no answer or news.

silhou'ette *n* picture in solid black on white, showing only the shape; dark shape of sb or sth seen against a light background. *v* show or make a — of.

silk *n* thin soft thread from the cocoons of certain insects; material made from this. **'—y** *adj* (-ier, -iest) (as) of —.

sill *n* flat shelf or block of wood or stone below a window.

silly *adj* (-ier, -iest) foolish; weak-minded; (colloq) careless.

silt *n* sand, mud, etc, left by moving water (at the mouth of a river, etc).

v (of a harbour, etc) cause to become stopped *up* with —.

'silver *n* **1** (spoons, forks, coins, etc, made of a) shining white precious metal. **2** (as *adj*) silver-coloured; (of sounds) soft and clear. **—y** *adj* like —; clear-toned.

'similar *adj* of the same sort. **— to**, almost the same as. **—ly** *adv*. **,simi'larity** *n* likeness.

'simile *n* (use of a) comparison of one thing to another: *He is as brave as a lion*.

'simmer *v* **1** keep (a pot, food) almost at boiling-point. **2 — with rage (excitement)**, be filled with rage, etc, which is only just kept under control.

'simple *adj* (-r, -st) **1** unmixed; not divided into parts; having only a few parts: *a — substance*; *a — machine*. **2** plain: *a — meal*. **3** not highly developed: *— forms of plant life*. **4** easily done or understood: *— language*. **5** foolish; inexperienced: *He's not — enough to believe that*. **6** sincere; straightforward: *behave in a — and pleasant way*. **—ton** *n* foolish, easily deceived person. **sim'plicity** *n* the state of being —. **'simplify** *v* made —r(4). **'simply** *adv* **1** in a — manner. **2** quite. **3** only.

,simul'taneous *adj* happening or done at the same time.

sin *n* breaking of, act that breaks, God's laws. *v* (-nn-) commit sin; do wrong. **'sinful** *adj* wicked. **'sinless** *adj* free from sin. **'sinner** *n* person who sins.

since *adv* after a date in the past; before the present time. *prep* during a period of time after: *We haven't met — her marriage*. *conj* from the time past when: *Where have you been — I last saw you?* because: *S— we are poor, we can't buy anything*.

sin'cere *adj* (-r, -st) **1** (of feelings, behaviour) genuine; not pretended. **2** (of a person) in the habit of showing only — feelings. **—ly** *adv*. **sin'cerity** *n*.

'sinew *n* **1** tendon (strong cord) joining a muscle to a bone. **2** (*pl*) energy; physical strength.

sing *v* (*pt* sang, *pp* sung) make continuous musical sounds with the voice; utter words to a tune. **— out**, call loudly (*for*). **— up**, —

louder. **'sing-song** n 1 wearisome rising-and-falling tone of speech. 2 meeting of friends to — songs together.

singe v blacken the surface of (cloth, etc) by burning; burn the tips of (hair, etc).

'single adj 1 one only. — **ticket**, for a journey to a place but not back again. 2 for the use of, used by, done by, one person. 3 unmarried. v — **out**, select from others (for special attention, etc). **,single-handed** adj & adv without help from others. **'singly** adv one by one; alone.

'singlet n undershirt; vest.

'singular adj 1 uncommon; strange. 2 (grammar) of the form used in speaking of one person or thing. n — form (of a word). —**ly** adv.

'sinister adj suggesting misfortune; showing ill will: a — smile.

sink v (pt sank, pp sunk) 1 go down, esp below the horizon or the surface of water, etc; cause or allow a ship to —. 2 slope downwards; become lower or weaker. 3 make by digging: — a well. 4 (of liquids, and fig) go deep into: The warning sank into his mind. n fixed basin (of stone, porcelain, etc) with a drain for taking off water, used for washing dishes, etc.

'sinuous adj winding; curving.

sip v (-pp-) drink a very small quantity at each swallow. n (quantity taken in) one act of sipping.

'siphon n 1 bent tube so arranged that water in a vessel will be drawn up and then down through it. 2 bottle from which soda-water, etc, can be forced out by the pressure of gas through a —.

sir n 1 respectful form of address to a man: Dear Sir, Good morning, sir. (cf madam). 2 Sir, prefix to the name of a knight or baronet.

'siren n device for producing a loud shrill noise (as a warning).

'sisal n plant with strong fibre used for making string, rope, etc.

'sister n 1 daughter of the same parents as sb else. 2 senior hospital nurse. 3 nun. 4 (as adj) of the same design, type, etc: — ships. **'sister-in-law** n — of one's wife or husband; wife of one's brother.

sit v (pt & pp sat) 1 rest the body on the buttocks. 2 (with adv & prep) **sit for**, take (an examination). **sit on** (a committee), be a member of one. **sit up**, (esp) not go to bed (until later than the usual time). 3 (of a law court, etc) hold meetings. **'sitting** n (esp) time when a law court, etc, sits (3).

'sitar n large stringed musical instrument played with the fingers.

site n place where sth was, is, or is to be: the — of a battle, a new house.

'situated adj (of a town, building, etc) placed; (of a person) placed in (certain) conditions. **,situ'ation** n 1 position (of a building, etc). 2 state of affairs (esp at a certain time).

six n & adj 6. **'sixpence** n (formerly) British coin, value six old pennies. **six'teen** n & adj 16. **sixth** n & adj 6th; $\frac{1}{6}$. **'sixty** n & adj 60. **sixtieth** n & adj 60th; $\frac{1}{60}$.

size n 1 degree of largeness or smallness. 2 one of the standard and (usu) numbered —s in which clothes, etc, are made: — ten shoes. v arrange in —s.

skate n one of a pair of sharp-edged steel blades fastened to a boot for moving smoothly over ice. (cf roller —s.) v go on —s.

'skeleton n 1 bony framework of an animal body. ⇨ p 30. 2 framework of a building, organization, plan, etc. 3 — **key**, one made to open a number of different locks.

sketch n rough, quickly made drawing, account, or description. v 1 make a — of. 2 — **sth out**, give a rough plan of.

'skewer n pointed stick or metal rod for holding meat together while cooking. v fasten with, or as with, a —.

ski n (pl **skis** or **ski**) one of a pair of long strips of wood strapped to the boots for moving over snow. v move over snow on —s.

skies ⇨ sky.

skid n 1 piece of metal fixed under a cart wheel to prevent its turning. 2 slipping movement of the wheels of a car, etc, on a wet or icy road. v (-dd-) (of a car, etc) move or slip sideways.

skill n ability to do sth well and properly. '—**ed** adj trained, experienced: —ed workmen; need ing —: —ed work. **'skilful** ad

having or showing —. '**skilfully**
adv.

skim *v* (-mm-) **1** remove (the scum, cream, etc) from the surface of a liquid: — (*the cream off*) *the milk.* **2** move lightly over (a surface). **3** read through (sth) quickly, noting only the chief points.

skin *n* **1** substance forming the outer covering of the body of a person or animal. **2** animal — with or without the hair or fur; hide. **3** outer covering of a fruit. *v* (-nn-) take the — off. '**skin-'deep** *adj* of or on the surface only. '**—ny** *adj* (-ier, -iest) having little flesh.

skip *v* (-pp-) **1** jump lightly and quickly. **2** jump over a turning rope. **3** go from one place to another; (esp) go from one part of a book to another, without reading what is between: — *the next chapter.* *n* —ping movement.

'**skipper** *n* captain (esp of a small merchant ship).

'**skirmish** *n* minor fight between small sections of armies or fleets.

skirt *n* **1** woman's garment that hangs from the waist. **2** part of a dress that hangs from the waist. **3** (*pl*) = outskirts. *v* be on, pass along, the —s(3) of.

skittles *n* (game in which) bottle-shaped pieces of wood, plastic, etc (are knocked down by a ball rolled at them).

skull *n* bony framework of the head. ⇨ p 30.

sky *n* (*pl* skies) space in which we see the clouds, sun, moon, stars, etc. '**skylight** *n* window in a roof. '**skyline** *n* outline of things, e g on the horizon, seen against the sky. '**skyscraper** *n* very tall building.

slab *n* thick flat piece of stone or other solid substance.

slack *adj* (-er, -est) **1** giving little care or attention to one's work; having or showing little energy. **2** with not much business or work needing to be done. **3** loose; not tight: *a — rope.* *n* the —, part of a rope, etc, that hangs loosely. *v* be lazy or careless in one's work. '**—en** *v* make or become slower, looser, or less active. '**—ly** *adv.*

slain ⇨ slay.

slake *v* satisfy (thirst).

slam *v* (-mm-) thrust *down* or shut (sth) violently. *n* noise of a door, window, etc, being —med.

'**slander** *v & n* (make a) false statement that damages sb's reputation. **—ous** *adj* making or containing such statements.

slang *n* words, meanings, and phrases commonly used in very informal talk.

slant *v & n* slope.

slap *n* (sound of a) quick blow with the open hand or with sth flat. *v* (-pp-) **1** hit with a —. **2** put (sth) *down* with a —ping noise.

slash *v* make long cuts in (or *at* sth) with a sweeping stroke; strike with a whip. *n* act of —ing; long cut.

slat *n* long, thin, narrow piece of wood or metal.

slate *n* **1** kind of blue-grey stone that splits easily; square or oblong piece of this used for roofs. **2** sheet of — for writing on.

'**slaughter** *v* kill (an animal) for food; kill (people) in great numbers. *n* such killing. '**slaughterhouse** *n* place where animals are killed for food.

slave *n* person who is the property of another and obliged to work for him. '**—ry** *n* condition of being a —; custom of having —s. '**slavish** *adj* **1** in the manner of —s; submissive. **2** without originality: *a slavish imitation.*

slay *v* (*pt* slew, *pp* slain) kill; murder.

sled, sledge *n* vehicle with runners (long strips of wood or metal) instead of wheels, used on snow.

'**sledge**(₌hammer) *n* heavy hammer used by blacksmiths.

sleek *adj* (-er, -est) **1** (of hair, fur) soft and smooth. **2** (of sb, his behaviour) over-anxious to please.

sleep *n* the condition of —ing. *v* (*pt & pp* slept) **1** be in a completely restful and inactive condition during which one is unconscious and dreams. **2** (of a hotel, etc) have enough beds for. '**—er** *n* (esp) bed or berth in a railway carriage. '**sleeping-draught** (-pill) *n* medicine to cause —. '**—less** *adj* without —; unable to —. '**—y** *adj* (-ier, -iest) **1** needing, ready for, —. **2** quiet; inactive: *a —y village.* '**—ily** *adv.*

sleet n falling snow or hail mixed with rain.

sleeve n part of a garment covering the arm. **laugh up one's —**, be secretly amused.

sleigh n = sled(ge).

slender adj (-er, -est) 1 small in width or circumference compared with height or length: a — girl. 2 small and poor: a — chance.

slept ⇨ sleep.

slew ⇨ slay.

slice n thin, wide, flat piece cut off sth, esp bread or meat. v cut into —s; cut (such a piece off).

slide v (pt & pp slid) 1 (cause to) move smoothly along a polished surface: children sliding on the ice. 2 (of things) move easily and smoothly: drawers that — in and out. 3 let things —, pay no attention to them. n 1 act of sliding(1). 2 smooth stretch of ice, hard snow, on which to —(1). 3 smooth slope down which persons or things can —(1). 4 picture on photographic film to be slid into a projector and shown on a screen. 5 glass plate on which is put sth to be examined under a microscope.

slight¹ adj (-er, -est) 1 slim; slender. 2 not serious or bad: a — headache. '—ly adv (esp) a little: —ly better.

slight² v treat (sb) without proper respect or courtesy. n act of disrespect or discourtesy.

slim adj (-mer, -mest) slender; small. v (-mm-) exercise and eat certain food to make oneself —.

slime n soft, nasty, thick mud or other greasy liquid. **'slimy** adj (-ier, -iest) like, covered with, —.

sling n band of material, rope, chain, etc, put round an object (eg a barrel, a broken arm) to support or lift it. v (pt & pp slung) 1 throw with force. 2 support (sth) so that it can swing or be lifted.

slink v (pt & pp slunk) go (about, away, off, out, past) in a secret, guilty, or ashamed manner.

slip v (-pp-) 1 fall or almost fall by losing one's footing (as on ice). 2 go or move quietly or quickly. 3 move, escape, get away, by being hard to hold or by not being held or fastened firmly: The fish —ped out of my hands. 4 put, push, or pull with a quick movement: —

into (out of) a dress. 5 make a —(2). 6 escape from: it —ped my memory. n 1 act of —ping. 2 small mistake: — of the tongue (pen), mistake in speaking (writing). 3 narrow strip of paper. 4 petticoat. **'slip-knot** n one that slides along. '—**per** n loose-fitting light shoe worn indoors. '—**pery** adj smooth, wet, polished, etc, so that it is difficult to hold, stand on, move on, etc: a —pery road. '—**shod** adj slovenly.

slit n long, narrow cut, tear, or opening. v (pt & pp slit; -tt-) make a —in; cut or tear into narrow pieces.

slither v slip(1).

slogan n striking and easily remembered phrase used to attract public attention.

slop v (-pp-) 1 (of liquids) spill over the edge. 2 cause (liquids) to do this. n (always pl) 1 dirty, waste water from the kitchen, etc. 2 liquid food (eg soup), esp for ill people. '—**py** adj (-ier, -iest) wet and dirty; too sentimental; careless and untidy.

slope n 1 position or direction that is between horizontal and upright: the — of a roof. 2 a piece of rising or falling ground. v have a —; cause to —.

slot n narrow opening through which to insert sth (eg a coin). v (-tt-) make a — or —s in. **'slot-machine** n one from which sth may be obtained by putting a coin through a —.

sloth n idleness; laziness.

slouch v stand, sit, move, in a lazy, tired way.

slovenly adj (-ier, -iest) careless, untidy, or dirty (in dress, habits, etc).

slow adj (-er, -est) 1 taking a long time; not quick; dull; unintelligent; not lively enough. 2 (of a clock) showing a time that is earlier than the correct time. v (cause to) go at a —er speed than before: The train —ed down (up). '—**ly** adv. '—**ness** n.

sludge n thick mud; thick dirty oil or grease.

slug n slow-moving creature like a snail but without a shell. ⇨ p 144. '—**gish** adj inactive; slow-moving.

sluice n 1 apparatus ('sluice-gate 'sluice-valve) for controlling a flow of water (in a canal, etc); channel carrying off surplus water; current of water through a —. **2** thorough washing with a stream of water. *v* wash with a stream of water.

slum *n* street with poor, dirty crowded houses; (*pl*) district of such streets.

'slumber *v* sleep.

slump *v* **1** drop or fall heavily. **2** (of prices, trade activity) fall steeply or suddenly. *n* general drop in prices, trade activity, etc.

slung ⇨ sling.

slunk ⇨ slink.

slur *v* (-rr-) **1** join words, syllables, musical notes, etc, so that they are not distinct. **2** — **over**, deal quickly with (hoping to conceal) (sb's faults, etc). *n* **1** sth that damages one's reputation. **2** act of —ring sounds.

slush *n* soft melting snow.

sly *adj* (-er, -est) **1** deceitful. **2** appearing to have, suggesting, secret knowledge. **on the —**, secretly. **—ly** *adv*.

smack *n* (sound of a) blow given with the open hand. *v* **1** strike with the open hand. **2** — **the lips**, make a —ing sound to show pleasure (at food, etc).

small *adj* (-er, -est) (opp of *large*) not (as) big in size or degree. **— change**, coins of — value. **the — hours**, about 1 a.m. to 4 a.m. **look (feel) —**, foolish, humbled. **on the — side**, a little (too) —. **'small-'arms** *n pl* weapons light enough to be carried in the hand.

smallpox *n* serious disease which leaves marks on the skin.

smart[1] *v & n* (feel or cause) sharp pain (of body or mind).

smart[2] *adj* (-er, -est) **1** bright; new-looking; well-dressed. **2** clever. **3** fashionable. **4** (of a walk) quick. **'—en** *v* **—en up**, make or become —(1). **'—ly** *adv*.

smash *v* **1** break, be broken, into pieces. **2** rush, force a way, violently (*into*, etc). *n* (sound of) —ing; collision.

smattering *n* a — **of**, a slight knowledge of (a subject).

smear *v* mark with sth oily or sticky; (fig) slander or libel. *n* mark made by —ing.

smell *n* that which is noticed by

means of the nose; (usu) bad or unpleasant quality that affects the nose. *v* (*pt & pp* smelt) **1** be aware of by means of the —; act of —ing. **— of**, have the — of; suggest. **— out**, discover by —ing or (fig) careful inquiry. **2** give out a —: *His breath —ed of beer.*

smelt *v* melt (ore); separate (metal) from ore by doing this.

smile *v & n* (have a) pleased, happy expression on the face.

smith *n* worker in iron or other metals. **'—y** *n* blacksmith's shop.

smoke *n* black, grey vapour from sth burning. *v* **1** breathe in and out the — of burning tobacco. **2** give out —. **3** dry and preserve (*meat, fish*, etc) with —. **4** drive *out* with —. **'—r** *n* person who —s tobacco. **'smoky** *adj* (-ier, -iest) giving out much —; full of —. **'smoke-stack** *n* tall factory chimney; outlet for — from a steamship or railway engine.

smooth *adj* (-er, -est) **1** having a surface like that of glass. **2** (of movement) free from shaking or bumping. **3** (of a paste, etc) free from lumps; well mixed. **4** (of sounds, speech) flowing easily. **5** (of a person, his manner) pleasant but perhaps insincere. *v* **1** make —. **2** — **over**, explain away difficulties deceptively. **'—ly** *adv*.

'smother *v* **1** cause the death of, by stopping the breath of. **2** cover completely or thickly: *—ed in dust.* **3** put out (a fire) by covering it with ashes, sand, etc.

'smoulder *v* burn slowly without a flame. *n* —ing fire.

smudge *n* dirty mark (eg where wet ink has been rubbed).

smug *adj* (-ger, -gest) self-satisfied.

'smuggle *v* **1** get (goods) secretly and unlawfully (*into, out of,* a country). **2** take (sth) secretly (*into*). **'—r** *n* sb who —s.

snack *n* light, quickly eaten, meal.

snag *n* hidden danger; (fig) unexpected hindrance or difficulty.

snail *n* small, soft animal with a shell on its back. ⇨ p 144.

snake *n* long, legless, crawling reptile, often poisonous. ⇨ p 233.

snap *v* (-pp-) **1** make a sudden, often noisy, bite (*at*). **2** open or close with a sudden cracking noise;

break with a sharp noise. *n* **1** act or sound of —ping. **2 a cold** —, a sudden short period of cold weather. **'—shot** *n* photograph taken (quickly) with a hand camera.

snare *n* trap, esp one with a slip-knot, for catching birds and small animals. *v* catch in a —.

snarl *v* (of dogs) show the teeth and growl.

snatch *v* **1** put out the hand suddenly and take: — *sth up* (*off, etc*). **2** get quickly or when one has the chance: — *an hour's sleep*.

sneak *v* go quietly and secretly (*away, out*, etc). *n* cowardly and treacherous person.

sneer *v & n* (show contempt by a) disrespectful smile or words.

sneeze *n* sudden uncontrollable outburst of air through the nose and mouth. *v* make a —.

sniff *v* **1** draw air, etc, noisily through the nose. **2** — *at*, smell.

snip *v* (-pp-) cut with scissors.

snipe *v* shoot (*at* sb) from a hiding-place or in darkness; kill or wound by shooting in this way. **'—r** *n* soldier who —s.

snob *n* person with too much respect for social position, wealth, etc. **'—bery** *n*. **'—bish** *adj*.

snooze *v* (colloq) take a short sleep.

snore *v* breathe roughly and noisily while sleeping. *n* this noise.

snort *v* deliberately force air violently out through the nose: —*ing with indignation*. *n* act or sound of —ing.

snout *n* animal's nose (and mouth). ⇨ p 84.

snow *n* frozen vapour falling in flakes; mass of such flakes on the ground, etc. *v* **1** (of —) come down from the sky. **2 be** —**ed up** (**in**), be prevented by — from going out. **'—y** *adj* of or like —; covered with —.

snub *v* (-bb-) treat with contempt. (esp a younger or less senior person); behave coldly towards (sb, an offer). *n* —bing words or behaviour.

snuff[1] *n* powdered tobacco to be taken up into the nose.

snuff[2] *v* cut off the end of the wick of a candle; put *out* (a candle flame).

snug *adj* (-ger, -gest) **1** warm and comfortable; sheltered. **2** well and conveniently arranged. **'—gle** *v* lie

or get (*close to* sb, *up, down*) so as to be warm or comfortable.

so *adv* **1** to such an extent: *Why are you so late?* **2** in this (that) way: *As you treat me, so shall I treat you.* **3** *I told you so!*, That is what I told you! **4** also: *You are coming and so are they.* *conj* therefore; for this is why: *She told me to come, so I came.* *int* (exclamatory) *So there you are!* **'so-and-so** *pron* used for sb or sth not named. **so-'called** *adj* so described (esp without good reason). **'so-so** *adj* not bad, not good.

soak *v* **1** become wet through by being in and absorbing liquid. **2** cause (sth) to absorb as much liquid as possible. **3** (of rain) make very wet; pass (*through, into*). **4** (of substances) absorb, take *up* or *in* (a liquid).

soap *n* fatty substance used with water to remove dirt by washing, soaking, etc. *v* rub — on; wash with —. **'—suds** *n pl* mass of foam from — and water. **'—y** *adj* (-ier, -iest) of or like —.

soar *v* go high in the air; rise beyond what is ordinary: —*ing prices*.

sob *v* (-bb-) draw in the breath sharply and irregularly from pain or sorrow, esp while crying. *n* act or sound of —bing.

'sober *adj* **1** self-controlled; serious in thought; calm. **2** avoiding drunkenness; not drunk. **3** (of colours) not bright. *v* make or become —. **so'briety** *n* being —.

'soccer *n* game in which a ball is kicked between two teams of eleven players each.

'sociable *adj* fond of the company of others; friendly.

'social *adj* **1** living in groups, not separately. **2** of people living in communities: — *customs* (*welfare*). **3** of or in society. *n* friendly meeting, usu for talk and entertainment, esp one arranged by a club. **—ism** *n* theory of a classless society where land, transport, chief industries, etc, should be owned by the State in the interests of the community as a whole. **—ist** *n* supporter of —ism.

so'ciety *n* **1** social community; persons living together as a group or nation; the organization, customs etc, of such a group. **2** the persons of distinction or the upper classes in a place, district, etc. **3** company: *spend an evening in the — of one's friends.* **4** club or association: *the Dramatic S—.*

soci'ology *n* study of the nature and growth of society.

sock *n* **1** short stocking not reaching the knee. **2** loose sole put inside a shoe.

'socket *n* hollow into which sth fits or in which sth turns.

sod *n* turf; lump of this.

'soda *n* common chemical substance used in making soap, glass, etc. **'soda-,water,** water with gas in it to make it bubble.

'sodden *adj* wet through: *— with rain.*

'sofa *n* long, cushioned seat with a back and arms.

soft *adj* (-er, -est) **1** (opp of *hard*) not firm; easily dented, cut, squeezed, or altered in shape. **2** (of cloth, hair, etc) smooth; delicate. **3** (of light, colours) restful to the eyes; not bright. **4** (of sounds) subdued, not loud. **5** (of words, answers, etc) mild; intended to please. **'soft-'hearted,** gentle; forgiving. '**—en** *v* make or become —. '**—ly** *adv*. '**—y** *n* mild person.

'soggy *adj* (-ier, -iest) (esp of ground) heavy with water.

soil[1] *n* ground; earth, esp the earth in which plants grow.

soil[2] *v* make or become dirty.

'sojourn *v & n* (make a) stay with sb for a time.

'solace *n* (that which gives) comfort or relief (when one is in trouble or pain). *v* give — to.

'solar *adj* of the sun: *the — system.*

sold ⇨ sell.

'solder *n* easily melted metal used to join the surfaces of harder metals. *v* join with —.

'soldier *n* member of an army.

sole[1] *n* the under part of the foot or of a sock, shoe, etc. *v* put a new — on (a shoe, etc).

sole[2] *n* flat sea-fish used as food.

sole[3] *adj* **1** one and only; single. **2** restricted to one person: *have the — rights.* '**—ly** *adv* alone; only.

'solemn *adj* **1** performed with religious or other ceremony; causing deep thought or respect. **2** serious-looking; important. **—ly** *adv*.

so'lemnity *n* (esp) — ceremony. **'solemnize** *v* perform (eg a marriage) with the usual rites.

so'licit *v* ask (*for*) earnestly or repeatedly: *— sb for his vote; — votes.*

so'licitor *n* lawyer who prepares legal documents (eg *wills*) and advises on legal matters.

'solid *adj* **1** not in the form of a liquid or gas; keeping its shape when pressed. **2** without holes or spaces. **3** of strong material or construction. **4** having length, breadth, and thickness. ⇨ p 253. **5** that can be depended on: *— arguments.* **6** of the same substance throughout: *— gold.* *n* body or substance that is —, not a liquid or a gas. **—ly** *adv*. **,soli'darity** *n* unity resulting from common interests or feelings: *national —arity.* **so'lidify** *v* make or become —. **so'lidity** *n* quality of being —.

so'liloquy *n* the act of saying one's thoughts aloud.

'solitary *adj* **1** (living) alone; without companions. **2** one only. **3** (of places) seldom visited. **'solitude** *n* being —; — place.

'solo *n* piece of music or a song (to be) performed by one person. *adv* alone. **—ist** *n* person who sings or plays a —.

'soluble *adj* that can be dissolved (in a liquid).

so'lution *n* **1** answer (to a question, problem, etc). **2** process of dissolving a solid or gas in a liquid; the liquid that results.

solve *v* find the answer to (*a problem*, etc).

'sombre *adj* dark-coloured; gloomy.

some *adj* **1** amount or quantity of sth, unknown or not specified: *— sugar, milk, etc.* **2** (pl of *one, a, an*) *— children.* **3** *— more: Do have — more tea.* **4** *It is — place or other.* ⇨ somewhere. **5** *— time,* a considerable time. *pron* — of, a few (little) of; part of. '**—body,** '**—one** *pron* — (indefinite) person; a person of importance. '**—thing** *pron* (indefinite) object, animal, idea, etc. '**—times** *adv* from time to time; now and then. '**—what** *adv* in — degree. '**—where** *adv* (in an) unknown place.

'somersault *n & v* jump and turn

heels over head before landing on one's feet.

'somnolent adj sleepy.

son n male child. **'son-in-law** n daughter's husband.

song n music for, or produced by, the voice.

'sonic adj relating to sound or the speed of sound. ⇨ **supersonic**.

'sonnet n kind of poem containing fourteen lines and a formal pattern of rhymes.

soon adv (-er, -est) **1** in a short time; not long after the present time; early. **as — as**, at the moment (when); no later than. **2 would as — (would —er)**, would with equal (more) pleasure or willingness.

soot n black powder in smoke, or left by smoke on surfaces. **'—y** adj.

soothe v **1** make (a person, his nerves) quiet or calm. **2** make (pains, aches) less sharp or severe.

sop n sth offered to prevent trouble or to satisfy for a time.

so'phisticated adj no longer simple and childlike; behaving artificially.

'sopping adj & adv wet through.

so'prano n & adj (person having the) highest singing voice of women or boys.

'sorcerer n person who practises magic with the help of evil. **'sorcery** n witchcraft.

'sordid adj **1** wretched; shabby. **2** (of behaviour) contemptible.

sore adj (-r, -st) **1** (of a part of the body) tender and painful. **2** filled with sorrow. **3** causing sorrow and annoyance: a — subject. n bruised or inflamed place on the body. **'—ly** adv greatly: —ly tempted.

'sorrow n (a cause of) sadness; regret. v feel —. **—ful** adj.

'sorry adj (-ier, -iest) **1** feeling sadness or regret. **2** pitiful: in a — state. int Please excuse me!

sort n **1** group or class of persons or things alike in some ways. **2 out of —s**, (colloq) feeling unwell; rather ill. v (often — **out**) arrange in groups (according to size, destination, etc): —ing letters. **'—er** n (esp) post-office worker who —s letters.

'S O 'S n message for help (sent by radio, etc) from a ship, aircraft, etc, in danger.

sought ⇨ **seek**.

soul n **1** non-material or spiritual part of a human being. **2** person's real self, the centre of his feelings, thoughts, etc. **3** human being: not a — to be seen. **4** person looked upon as a fine example of a virtue or quality: She is the — of patience.

sound¹ n that which is heard: within — of (the guns), near enough to hear (them). v **1** make or produce (a). — **2** give a certain impression to the ear or mind. **3** test or examine by listening: The doctor —ed my chest. **'sound-proof** adj that —s cannot enter or leave: a sound-proof room.

sound² n narrow strip of water joining two larger areas of water.

sound³ adj (-er, -est) **1** healthy: — teeth. **2** based on reason; prudent: a — policy. **3** thorough; complete: a — sleep. adv (only in) — **asleep**, in a deep sleep. **'—ly** adv **1** with good judgement. **2** thoroughly. **'—ness** n.

soup n liquid food made by boiling meat, vegetables, etc, in water.

sour adj (-er, -est) **1** having a sharp acid taste (like unripe fruit). **2** (of milk) having spoiled. **3** bad-tempered. v make or become —. **'—ly** adv.

source n **1** starting-point, esp of a river. **2** origin; place where sth (eg information) can be, was, obtained.

south n, adj, & adv direction to one's right when facing the sunrise. **'—ern** adj in or/of the —. **'—ward(s)** adv towards the —.

'souvenir n sth taken, bought, or received as a gift, and kept as a reminder of a person, place, or event.

'sovereign adj **1** (of power) highest. **2** (of a state or ruler) having — power. **3** (of a remedy, etc) of proved value. n **1** ruler, esp a king or emperor. **2** former British gold coin. **—ty** n — power.

'soviet n **1** one of the councils of workers, etc, in Russia; one of the higher groups to which these councils give authority. **2** (as an adj) of Russia.

sow¹ v (pt sowed, pp sowed or sown) put (seed) in the ground; plant (land) with seed.

sow² n female pig.

space *n* **1** that in which sth exists or moves or can be placed: *The universe exists in —. Our earth moves through —.* **spacecraft** (-ship), craft (3) for space travel. **space-flight**, journey into —(1). **'—man** *n* astronaut. **2** amount of —, distance, between two or more objects: *The —s between printed words.* **3** an open —, (esp) land not built on. **4** unoccupied or empty place or area. **5** period of time: *in the — of ten years.* *v* place (esp words, letters) with regular —s(2) between. **'spacious** *adj* having much —; with plenty of room.

spade *n* **1** tool for digging. ⇔ p 293. **2** playing-card with a black design: ♠. *v* dig with a —. **'—work** *n* hard work.

span[1] *n* **1** distance or part between the supports of an arch, esp of a bridge. **2** distance (about 9 inches) between the tips of a man's thumb and little finger when stretched out.. **3** period(2). *v* (-nn-) extend across (from side to side).

span[2] *adj* ⇔ spick.

spank *v* punish (a child) by slapping (him) with the open hand.

'spanner *n* tool for gripping and turning nuts(2), etc. ⇔ p 293.

spar[1] *n* strong pole used to support a ship's sails.

spar[2] *v* (-rr-) make the movement of attack and defence (as in boxing).

spare *v* **1** hold back from hurting, damaging, or destroying; show mercy to: — *sb's life*, not kill him. **2** find (time, money, etc, *for*): — *the time for a rest; Can you — me ten pence until tomorrow?* **3** — no pains (expense), do everything that hard work (money) can do. not — oneself, use all one's powers. **4** use with care, in small quantities: *be sparing with.* **5** enough and to —, more than is needed. *adj* **1** additional to what is needed immediately: — *cash* (*time*); *a — wheel.* **2** (of persons) thin; lean. *n* — part for a machine, etc. **'sparing(ly)** *adj & adv* economical(ly).

spark *n* tiny, glowing bit thrown off from a burning substance or still present in ashes, etc, or produced by striking hard metal and stone together; flash produced by the breaking of an electric current.

'sparkle *v & n* (send out) flashes of light; gleam.

'sparrow *n* small, brownish-grey bird very common in towns.

sparse *adj* (-r, -st) thinly scattered; not dense or thick. **'—ly** *adv*. **!sparsity** *n*.

!spasm *n* sudden fit of pain, outburst of grief, etc. **spas'modic** *adj* taking place, done, at irregular intervals.

spat ⇔ spit.

spate *n* sudden rush (of water, work, etc).

spawn *n* eggs of fish, frogs, etc.

speak *v* (*pt* spoke, *pp* 'spoken) say sth aloud in one's ordinary (not a singing) voice; have a conversation; address an audience; be able to use (a language). **— out (up)**, — clearly or frankly. **— one's mind**, say frankly what one thinks. **nothing to — of**, nothing worth mentioning. **not on —ing terms with**, having quarrelled with. **'—er** *n* (esp) person —ing in public. **the S—**, presiding officer of the House of Commons.

spear *n* weapon with a metal point on a long handle.

'special *adj* **1** of a particular sort; not common, usual or general; of or for a certain person, thing, purpose, etc. **2** (also es'pecial) exceptional. **—ist** *n* person expert in a —(1) branch of work, esp of medicine. **—ize** *v* be or become a —ist (*in* sth).

'species *n* **1** division of a *genus*. **2** kind; sort.

spe'cific *adj* **1** detailed and precise. **2** of one particular thing, not general: *for a — purpose.* **'specify** *v* mention definitely; give the details of. **,specifi'cation** *n*.

'specimen *n* sample; one of a class as an example; part taken to represent the whole.

'specious *adj* seeming true or right but not really so.

speck *n* **1** small spot of dirt or colour. **2** tiny bit (*of dust*, etc). **'—ed** *adj* marked with —s(1). **'—led** *adj* having small marks of distinct colour on the skin, feathers, etc.

'spectacle *n* **1** public display or entertainment, esp one with ceremony. **2** sth seen; sth taking place before the eyes, esp sth noteworthy. **3** (*pl*) pair of glasses for the eyes. **spec'tacular** *adj* making a fine —(1),(2). **spec'tator** *n* onlooker.

'spectre *n* ghost; haunting fear of future trouble: — *of famine.*

'speculate *v* **1** consider, form opinions (without full knowledge). **2** buy and sell goods, shares, etc, with the risk of loss and the hope of profit through changes in their market value. **,specu'lation** *n*.

sped ⇨ speed.

speech *n* **1** power, act, manner, of speaking. **2** talk given in public. **'—less** *adj* unable to speak, esp because of surprise or anger.

speed *n* **1** rate of moving: *at full* —; *the* — *limit.* **2** swiftness. *v* (*pt & pp* sped) (cause to) go quickly. **'—y** *adj* (-ier, -iest) quick; coming, done, without delay. **'—ily** *adv*.

spell¹ *v* (*pt & pp* spelt or spelled) **1** name or write the letters of a word in their proper order. **2** have as a consequence: *Delay may* — *danger.* **'—ing** *n*.

spell² *n* words supposed to have magic power; overpowering attraction: *under a* —. **'—bound** *adj* with the attention held by, or as by, a —.

spell³ *n* period of time, duty, or activity: *a* — *of good weather.*

spend *v* (*pt & pp* spent) **1** pay out (money) for goods, services, etc. **2** use up (energy, time, material, etc).

spew *v* vomit.

sphere *n* **1** ball; globe. **2** person's interests, activities, etc. **'spherical** *adj* shaped like a —. ⇨ p 253.

sphinx *n* stone statue in Egypt with a lion's body and a woman's head; person who keeps his thoughts, plans, etc, secret.

spice *n* **1** flavouring (eg *ginger*, *nutmeg*). **2** (*fig*) flavour, suggestion, or trace (*of*): *a* — *of danger.* *v* flavour with, or as with, —.

spick *adj* (only in) — **and span**, bright, clean, and tidy.

'spider *n* creature with eight legs of which most sorts spin webs in which insects are caught. ⇨ p 144.

spied ⇨ spy.

spike *n* **1** sharp point; pointed piece of metal. **2** ear of grain (eg corn). *v* pierce with a —.

spill *v* (*pt & pp* spilt or spilled) **1** (of liquid or powder) (allow to) flow over the side of the container. **2** (of a horse, carriage, etc) upset; cause (the rider, a passenger) to fall. *n* fall from a horse, a carriage, etc.

spin *v* (*pt* spun, or span, *pp* spun; -nn-) **1** form (thread) by twisting wool, cotton, silk, etc. **2** form by means of threads: *a* — *web.* **3** (often — **round**) (cause to) go round and round as a wheel does. **4** — **sth out**, make it last for a long time. *n* **1** —ning motion. **2** short, quick ride on a bicycle, in a car, etc. **'—dle** *n* bar or pin on which sth turns.

spine *n* **1** backbone. **2** one of the sharp needle-like parts of some plants and animals. **'spinal** *adj* of the —(1). **'spiny** *adj* (-ier, -iest) having —s(2).

'spinster *n* unmarried woman.

'spiral *adj & n* (in the form of a) curve winding round a central point. *v* (-ll-) move in a —.

'spire *n* tall pointed structure on a church or tower.

'spirit *n* **1** the soul. **2** this part of a person thought of as separate from the body. **3** fairy, elf. **4** quality of courage, vigour, liveliness. **5** mood: *in a* — *of mischief.* **6** the — **of the law**, the purpose underlying it. **7** (*pl*) state of mind. **in high** —s, cheerful and happy. **8** (*pl*) strong alcoholic drinks (eg *brandy*). **9** alcohol for burning: *a* — *lamp.* *v* take (sb or sth) *away* or *off* secretly or mysteriously. **—ed** *adj* lively; courageous. **—less** *adj* without energy or courage. **—ual** *adj* **1** of the soul; of religion; not material things. **2** caring much for —ual things.

spit *v* (*pt & pp* spat; -tt-) send (liquid, etc, *out*) from the mouth. *n* **1** act of —ting. **2** liquid of the mouth (usu called *saliva* or **spittle**).

spite *n* ill will; desire to cause sth pain or damage: *do sth from* (*out of*) —. **in** — **of**, not being, not to be, prevented or convinced by. hurt or annoy because of —. **'—ful** *adj* having or showing —. **'—fully** *adv*.

splash *v* **1** cause (a liquid) to fly about in drops; (of a liquid) scatter and fall in drops. **2** make (sb or sth) wet by —ing. **3** move, fall, etc, so that there is —ing: —*ing through the water.* n (mark, sound, etc, made by) —ing. **'splash-down** n & v (the) return (of) a spacecraft to earth by landing in the sea.

'splendid adj magnificent. **'splen-dour** n magnificence; brightness.

splice v join (two ends of rope, etc) by weaving strands together; join (two pieces of wood) by making the ends overlap. n join made by splicing.

splint n strip of wood, etc, bound to an arm, etc, to keep a broken bone in position.

'splinter n sharp-pointed or sharp-edged bit of wood, glass, etc, split, torn, or broken off a larger piece. v break into —s; come off as a —.

split v (pt & pp split; -tt-) **1** break lengthwise: —*ting logs.* **2** divide; break open by bursting. **3** — *one's sides,* (colloq) laugh very heartily. n a —ting; break caused by —ing.

spoil v (pt & pp spoilt or spoiled) **1** make useless or unsatisfactory: *holidays —t by bad weather.* **2** indulge (children) too much. **3** pay great attention to the comfort and happiness of. **4** (of food, etc) become unfit for use.

spoke¹ ⇨ speak.

spoke² n any one of the bars or wires connecting the hub (centre) of a wheel with the rim (edge).

'spokesman n person chosen to speak on behalf of a group.

sponge n simple(3) sea-animal; (its) light structure of soft elastic material, full of holes and able to absorb water easily. v wash, clean, take up (liquid), with a —. **'spongy** adj soft like a —.

a sponge

a spoon

'sponsor n person who makes himself responsible for another; person who puts forward and supports an idea, etc. v act as — for.

spon'taneous adj done, happening, naturally and without apparent cause; not caused or suggested from outside.

spool n small reel (for a camera film, cotton thread, wire, etc).

spoon n utensil for stirring, serving, eating food, etc. —**ful** n.

sport n **1** outdoor recreation. **2** form of this (eg *swimming, football*). **3** (pl) meeting for athletic contests (eg *running, jumping*). **4** fun: *say sth in —,* not seriously. v play about; amuse oneself. **'—ing** adj **1** of —. **2** fond of, interested in, —. **3** willing to take a risk of losing; involving risk of losing: *a —ing offer.* **'—sman** n **1** person who is fond of —. **2** person who plays fairly and is cheerful if he loses. **'—smanlike** adj fair and honourable; ready to obey the rules. **'—smanship** n.

spot n **1** small (esp round) mark different in colour from what it is on. **2** dirty mark. **3** small red place on the skin. **4** particular place: *the — where the accident occurred.* v (-tt-) **1** mark, become marked, with —s(1), (2). **2** pick out, see, (one person or thing) out o, many. **'—less** adj (esp) quite clean. **'—ty** adj (-ier, -iest) marked with, covered with —s.

spout n pipe or lip through or from which liquid pours. v (of liquid) come or send out with force.

sprain v injure (a joint, eg the wrist or ankle) by twisting violently. n injury so caused.

sprang ⇨ spring¹.

sprawl v **1** sit or lie with the arms and legs loosely spread out. **2** (of plants, handwriting, etc) spread out loosely and irregularly.

spray n **1** liquid sent through the air in a shower (by the wind or through an apparatus called a —er). **2** small twig or shoot with its leaves or flowers, esp as a decoration. v scatter liquid, etc, on (sth): — *fruit bushes.*

spread v (pt & pp spread) **1** extend the surface or width of sth by unfolding or unrolling; cover by doing this: — *a cloth on a table;* — *out a map (one's arms).* **2** put (a substance) on a surface and flatten it out: — *butter on bread.* **3** — *the table,* place food, dishes, etc, on it ready for a meal. **4** (cause to) become more widely extended:

water —ing over the floor; diseases that are — by flies. n extent; breadth; extension.

spree n (have) a —, (go out on) a —, (have) a lively, merry time.

spring[1] v (pt sprang, pp sprung) **1** jump suddenly up; move suddenly (up, down, out, etc) from rest or from hiding. **2** (often — up) appear; grow up quickly from the ground or from a stem: weeds —ing up everywhere. **3** arise or come from. **4** bring forward suddenly: — a surprise on sb. n **1** act of —ing(1); —ing(1) movement. **2** (place where there is) water coming up from the ground. **3** length of twisted, bent, or coiled metal or wire that tends to return to its shape when pulled, etc. **4** elastic quality. **5** cause or origin. **6** (as adj) worked by, resting on, containing, a —(3) or —s(3): a — mattress. **7** — tide, very high tide after a new or full moon.

spring[2] n season of the year between winter and summer when vegetation sprouts(1). **'—time** n (liter) period of —.

sprinkle v send a shower of (sand, water, flour, etc) on to (a surface): — a dusty road with water; — water on a dusty road.

sprint v run at full speed.

sprout v **1** start to grow; put out leaves, etc; cause to grow. **2** have, develop, produce (hair, horns, etc). n **1** shoot, newly —ed part, of plant. **2** (Brussels)-sprout, small, round green vegetable. ⇨ p 306.

spruce adj (-r, -st) neat and smart in appearance.

sprung ⇨ spring.

spun ⇨ spin.

spur n **1** sharp-pointed instrument used to make a horse go faster. **2** (fig) sth (eg ambition) that urges a person on to activity. (act) **on the — of the moment**, on a sudden impulse. **3** sharp point at the back of a cock's leg. **4** ridge extending from a hill or mountain. v (-rr-) urge on (as) with —s.

spurn v kick or push away with contempt; treat with contempt.

spurt v **1** (of liquid, flame, etc) (cause to) come (out) in a sudden burst. **2** make a sudden short effort, esp in a contest. n sudden

bursting forth (of water, energy, etc).

'sputnik n spacecraft (as built by Russians).

spy n person who tries to get secret information, esp about the armed forces of another country. v spy upon, spy on, watch secretly.

'squabble v quarrel noisily. n noisy quarrel.

squad n small group of soldiers, policemen, etc, working or being trained together.

'squadron n **1** division of a cavalry regiment (120–200 men). **2** number of warships or military aircraft forming a unit.

'squalid adj wretched and dirty.

squall n sudden wind-storm, often with rain or snow.

'squalor n state of being very dirty and untidy.

'squander v waste (time, money).

square n **1** figure shaped like this: □. ⇨ p 253. **2** space in a town, with buildings round it. **3** result obtained when a number is multiplied by itself: The — of 7 is 49. adj **1** having a — shape. **2** level or parallel with. **3** (of dealings) fair; honest. **4** (of accounts) settled; balanced. **5** — foot (etc), area equal to that of a — with sides one foot in length (etc). **— measure**, expressed in — feet, etc: three feet — (= nine — feet). **— root**, quantity which, when multiplied by itself a certain number of times, produces another quantity: 4 is the —root of 16 (√16 = 4). v **1** make —. **2** make straight or level. **3** (often — up) balance (accounts).

squash v crush; press flat or into a small space.

squat v (-tt-) sit on one's heels. adj (of a person, building, etc) wide in comparison with height. **'—ter** n person who occupies public land, an empty building, etc, without legal right.

squeak n short shrill cry or sound (eg of an unoiled hinge). v make a —ing sound; say in a —ing voice.

squeal v & n (make a) long, shrill cry.

squeeze v press upon from opposite sides or from all sides; change the shape, size, etc, of sth by doing this; get (juice, water, etc) out of sth or force (sth) *into*, etc, by pressing. *n* act of squeezing; condition of being —d; close fit.

squint *v* 1 have one eye turned in a different direction from the other; be cross-eyed. 2 look sideways or with half-closed eyes or through a narrow opening (*at*). *n* —ing position of the eyeballs.

'squire *n* (in Gt Brit, formerly) chief landowner in a country parish.

'squirrel *n* small bushy-tailed animal with red or grey fur, living in trees. ⇨ p 12.

squirt *v* (of liquid) force out, be forced out, in a thin stream or jet. *n* stream of liquid —ing out.

stab *v* (-bb-) pierce with a sharp-pointed weapon or instrument; push (a knife, etc) into. *n* —bing blow.

'stable¹ *n* building in which horses are kept. *v* put or keep in a —.

'stable² *adj* firm; fixed; not likely to change. **sta'bility** *n*. **'stabilize** *v* make —. **,stabili'zation** *n*.

stack *n* 1 large pile of hay, straw, etc, usu covered for storage. 2 neat pile of books, wood, rifles, etc. 3 (also **'chimney-stack**) brick chimney of a house or factory; funnel of a steamship or steam-engine. *v* make into a —; pile up.

staff *n* 1 pole: *a flag* —. 2 group of assistants under (or including) a manager or head. 3 group of senior army officers who organize. *v* provide with, act as, a —(2).

stag *n* male deer.

stage *n* 1 raised platform; (esp) part of a theatre on which the actors appear. 2 profession of acting. **go on the** —, become an actor. 3 point, period, or step in development. 4 journey, distance, between two stopping-places along a road or route. *v* produce (a play) on the ·(1).

'stagger *v* 1 walk or move unsteadily (from weakness, a heavy burden, etc); (of a blow) cause (sb) to do this; (fig, of news) shock deeply. 2 arrange (eg office hours, staff holidays) so that they start and finish at different times.

'stagnant *adj* (of water) without current or tide; still and stale. **stag'nate** *v* be —.

staid *adj* (of persons) steady(3) and serious.

stain *v* 1 (of liquids, etc) change the colour of; make coloured or dirty marks on: *ink-stained fingers*. 2 colour (esp wood) with a substance that penetrates (the wood, etc) to some extent. 3 colour (glass) with transparent colours: —*ed glass* (for church windows, etc). *n* 1 liquid (not paint) for —ing(2) wood, etc. 2 —ed(1) place; dirty mark: *ink* —s. **'—less** *adj* 1 without a —: (fig) *a —less reputation*. 2 —less **steel**, kind that does not become —ed(1).

stair *n* (often *pl*) (any one of a) series of fixed steps leading from one floor of a building to another. **'—case** *n* flight of —s inside or outside the walls of a building.

stake *n* 1 strong pointed stick (to be) driven into the ground as a post, etc. 2 sum of money risked on the unknown result of a future event, eg a horse-race. **at —**, to be won or lost. *v* 1 support (eg a bush) with a —(1). 2 mark (*out* or *off*) with —s(1). 3 risk, place (money, one's hopes, etc) *on*.

stale *adj* (-r, -st) 1 (of food) dry; not fresh. 2 (of news, jokes, etc) uninteresting because heard before.

'stalemate *n* (esp) stage of a dispute at which further action by either side seems to be impossible.

stalk¹ *n* part of a plant supporting a leaf or leaves, flower(s), or (a) fruit.

stalk² *v* 1 move quietly and cautiously towards a wild animal, etc, in order to get near it. 2 walk stiffly or proudly: — *out of the room*.

stall *n* 1 compartment for one animal in a stable or cattle-shed. 2 small, open-fronted shop; table, etc, used by a trader in a market, on a street, etc: *a station book*—. 3 seat in the part of a theatre nearest to the stage. *v* (of a motor-car engine, an aircraft) (cause to) fail through insufficient power or speed to keep going.

'stalwart *adj* 1 solidly built; tall and strong. 2 firm and resolved.

'stamen *n* male part of a flower, bearing pollen.

'stamina *n* energy enabling a person or animal to work for a long time, survive a serious illness, etc.

'stammer *v & n* (speak with a)

tendency to repeat sounds: *G-g-give me that b-b-book.*

stamp v 1 put one's foot down with force (*on*): — *on a spider*; — *out a fire.* 2 print (a design, words, etc) by using a — (2) on paper, cloth, etc. 3 put a postage-stamp (on a letter, etc). *n* 1 act of —ing with the foot. 2 article (as shown here) for —ing(2) or printing designs, words, etc; the design, etc, so printed; (fig) sign. 3 (also **'postage-stamp**) piece of printed paper (to be) stuck on envelopes, etc.

stamps

stam'pede n sudden wild rush of frightened people or animals. v (cause to) take part in a —.

stand v (*pt & pp* **stood**) 1 have, take, keep an upright position. — **up**, rise to one's feet. 2 place (sth) upright. 3 endure: *can't — cold weather.* 4 be in a certain condition or situation: *as affairs now —.* 5 (colloq) provide and pay for: — *sb a good dinner.* 6 — **a good chance of**, be likely to have, get, etc. **It —s to reason** (*that*), all reasonable people must agree. 7 (with *adv & prep*) — **by**, be an onlooker; be ready (for action); be faithful to (eg a friend). — **for**, represent; be a candidate for (Parliament, etc). — **out**, be easily seen above or among others; continue firm (*against* or *for* sth). — **up for**, fight in the cause of. — **up to**, face boldly. *n* 1 **make a —**, fight (*against, for*). **bring (sb or sth) to a —(still)**, cause to stop. 2 small piece of furniture, support, on or in which things may be placed: *a 'music-stand; an 'ink—.* 3 structure (usu sloping) where people may — or sit to watch races, etc. **'—by** n reliable support in time of need. **'—ing** n 1 **of long —ing**, that has existed a long time. 2 **of high —ing**, of high position or reputation. *adj* **—ing order**, (for) sth to be done or delivered regularly. **'—point** n point of

view. **'—still** n stop: *be at a —still,* be stopped.

'standard n 1 flag. 2 (often as *adj*) sth used as a test or measure for weights, lengths, qualities, etc, or for the required degree of excellence: — *weights; a high — of living.* — **authors**, of long-established reputation. 3 — **lamp**, one on a tall upright support. 4 class in a primary school. **—ize** v make —(2) in size, shape, quality, etc: *—ized parts for motor-car engines.* **standardi'zation** n.

stank ⇨ stink.

'staple¹ n U-shaped piece of metal or wire to fasten or support sth.

'staple² n chief sort of article or goods produced or traded in. *adj* forming the —: — *products.*

star n 1 any of the heavenly bodies seen as a source of light at night. 2 five- or six-pointed shape. ⇨ p 253. 3 person famous as a singer, actor, etc. v (-rr-) 1 mark or decorate with a printed — or —s (*** ***). 2 be a —(2) actor, etc (*in a* play or film). **'—ry** *adj* lit by, shining like, —s. **—s, —ry-'eyed**, too enthusiastic and optimistic.

'starboard n right side of a ship as one looks forward. (cf port.)

starch n 1 white, tasteless food substance, plentiful in potatoes, grain, etc. 2 this substance in powder form, used for stiffening cotton clothes. v make (eg shirt collars) stiff with —.

stare v look (*at*) fixedly; (of eyes) be wide open.

stark *adj* 1 stiff, esp in death. 2 complete. *adv* completely.

start v 1 begin a journey; begin an activity. 2 (cause to) come into existence; set going. 3 jump (as) from fear, surprise, etc. *n* 1 act of —ing(1): *make an early —.* 2 sudden jump because of fear, etc. 3 amount of time or distance by which one person —s(1) before (other) competitors. 4 **by fits and —s**, irregularly.

'startle v cause (sb) to move or jump through surprise or fear.

starve v (cause to) suffer or die from hunger: *be starving (for food),* be very hungry. **star'vation** n.

state¹ n 1 way in which sth or sb is (in circumstances, appearance, mind, health, etc); condition: *The* *house was in a dirty —. He's in a poor — of health.* 2 (often as *adj*) dignity; ceremony: *The Queen drove through the streets in — to open Parliament.* **lie in —**, (of a dead person) be placed where the public may pay respect. 3 (often **S—**) self-governing country or self-governing division of a country. '**—ly** *adj* (-ier, -iest) impressive; dignified. '**—room** *n* private bedroom in a ship. '**—sman** *n* person who takes an important part in public affairs.

state² *v* express in words, esp carefully, fully, and clearly. '**—d** *adj* made known: *at —d times.* '**—ment** *n* stating of facts, views, a problem, etc: *make a —ment.*

'**station** *n* 1 position (to be) taken up by sb for some purpose. 2 post of observation or service, esp the local branch or establishment of an organized body, eg army, police, missionary society. 3 stopping-place for railway trains; the buildings, etc, connected with it. 4 social position. *v* put (sb, oneself) at a certain **—(1)**.

'**stationary** *adj* 1 not intended to be moved about. 2 not moving.

'**stationer** *n* dealer in **—y**. **—y** *n* writing materials; notepaper.

sta'tistics *n pl* 1 facts shown in numbers collected and arranged for comparison. 2 the science of **—**. **sta'tistical** *adj*.

'**statue** *n* figure of a person, animal, etc, in wood, stone, bronze, etc.

'**stature** *n* (person's) height.

'**status** *n* person's legal, social, or professional relation to others.

'**statute** *n* law passed by Parliament or other law-making body. '**statutory** *adj* fixed, required, done, by **—**.

staunch *adj* (of a friend, a supporter) trustworthy; firm.

stay *v* 1 be, keep, remain (at a place, in a position or condition): *S—where you are.* **—up late**, not go to bed until late. 2 live for a time (eg as a guest). 3 stop, check (eg the progress of a disease). 4 be able to continue (work, etc). '**—ing-power**, endurance. *n* 1 (period of) **—ing(2)**: *a short — at a friend's house.* 2 rope or wire supporting sth, esp a mast. 3 (*pl*) corset.

'**steadfast** *adj* keeping firm (to); firm and unchanging. '**—ly** *adv*.

'**steady** *adj* (-ier, -iest) 1 standing firm and well balanced; not likely to fall. 2 regular in movement, speed, direction, etc: *a — wind.* 3 regular in behaviour, habits, etc. *v* make or become **—**; keep **—**. '**steadily** *adv*.

steak *n* thick slice of meat or fish for frying, grilling, stewing, etc.

steal *v* (*pt* stole, *pp* 'stolen) 1 take (sb else's) property secretly and unlawfully. 2 move, come, go (*in, out, away,* etc), secretly and quietly. 3 obtain by surprise or by a trick. **—th** *n* do sth by **—th**, do it secretly and quietly. '**—thy** *adj* (-ier, -iest) doing, done, quietly and secretly. '**—thily** *adv*.

steam *n* gas or vapour into which boiling water changes. *v* 1 give out **—**. 2 move, work, etc, (as if) under the power of **—**. 3 cook, soften, etc, with **—** heat. '**steam-engine**, '**—ship**, '**steam-roller** *n* engine, ship, heavy roller, worked or driven by **—** pressure. '**—er** *n* **—ship**. '**—y** *adj* (-ier, -iest) of, like, full of, **—**.

steel *n* hard alloy of iron and carbon or other elements, used for knives, tools, machines, etc. *v* make (oneself, one's will) determined (*to do* sth, etc).

steep¹ *adj* (-er, -est) (of a slope) rising or falling sharply.

steep² *v* soak.

'**steeple** *n* high church tower with a spire. '**—jack** *n* workman who climbs and repairs **—**s, etc.

steer¹ *n* young bullock.

steer² *v* direct the course of (a boat, motor-car, etc). '**—sman** *n* man who **—**s a ship.

'**steerage** *n* part of a ship for passengers paying the lowest fares.

stem¹ *n* 1 part of a plant coming up from the roots. 2 part of a leaf, flower, fruit, etc, that joins it to the stalk, branch, etc. 3 anything that joins like a **—**, eg the **—** of a wine-glass (between the bowl and the base). 4 main part of a word (eg *man*) to which parts may be added (eg un*manly*).

stem² *v* (-mm-) 1 check, stop (a current of water, etc). 2 make progress against (the tide, etc).

stench *n* bad smell.

ste'nographer n (old use) typist who can use shorthand.

step v (-pp-) move the foot, or one foot after the other, forward, or in the direction indicated: — on to (off) a platform (into a boat, etc). n 1 act of —ping once; distance covered by doing this. — by —, gradually. 2 (also foot—) sound made by sb walking. 3 in (out of) —, putting (not putting) the right foot to the ground at the same time as others (walking, marching, dancing). 4 place for the foot when going from one level to another. 5 —s, a pair of —s, 'step-ladder, folding ladder with flat —s, not rungs. 6 one of a series of actions with a view to effecting a purpose: take —s to do sth. What's our next —? 7 rank; rise to a higher grade, etc.

step- prefix '—child, '—son, 'step-,daughter n child of an earlier marriage of one's wife or husband. '—,father (mother) n one's parent's later husband (wife). 'step-,brother, '—,sister n —child of one's father or mother.

'sterile adj 1 not producing, not able to produce, seeds or offspring. 2 (of land) barren. 3 (fig) having no result. 4 free from living germs. ste'rility n. 'sterilize v make —. ,sterili'zation n.

'sterling adj 1 (of gold or silver) of a standard quality fixed by law. 2 genuine; of excellent quality. n British money: payable in —.

stern[1] adj (-er,-est) severe; strict.

stern[2] n back end of a ship or boat.

stew v cook, be cooked, in water or juice, slowly in a closed dish. n dish of —ed meat, etc.

'steward n 1 man who arranges for the supply of food, etc, in a club, college, etc. 2 person who attends to the needs of passengers in a ship or aircraft. 3 man who organizes a public meeting, dance, etc. 4 man who manages another's property (esp a large estate). —ess n woman —(2) (esp in a ship).

stick[1] n 1 thin branch of a tree or bush, cut for some purpose: a walking-stick. 2 rod-shaped piece (of chalk, etc).

stick[2] v (pt & pp stuck) 1 push sth pointed (into, through, etc). 2 (of

a pointed thing) be, remain, in a position by the point: a nail —ing in the tyre. 3 (cause to) be or become joined or fastened with, or as with, paste: — a stamp vn a letter. 4 (colloq) put (in some position), esp quickly or carelessly: He stuck his hands in his pockets. 5 be or become fixed; fail to work properly: The door has stuck. The key stuck in the lock. 6 (with adv & prep) not — at trifles, not hesitate at, be stopped by, trifles. — at one's work, keep on doing it. — out, (cause to) stand or be out: — out your tongue. — out for, insist upon having. — to, be faithful to (one's friends, a promise). — up for, defend, support. '—y adj (-ier, -iest) that —s(3) or tends to —(3) to anything that touches it. '—ily adv. '—iness n.

stiff adj (-er, -est) 1 not easily bent or changed in shape. 2 hard to stir, move, do, etc: a — paste; a — climb. 3 (of a breeze, etc) strong. 4 (of behaviour) formal or cold. '—en v make or become, —(er). '—ly adv. '—ness n.

'stifle v 1 make breathing difficult or impossible. 2 suppress (eg a rebellion). 3 cause a feeling of oppression: stifling heat.

'stigma n (esp) mark of shame or disgrace.

stile n step(s) for climbing over a fence.

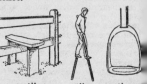

a stile   stilts   a stirrup

still[1] adj & adv without movement or sound: stand —. v make calm. —born adj dead when born.

still[2] adv 1 even up to the present time or the moment mentioned. 2 even; yet; in a greater degree: I like that dress better —.

stilt n one of a pair of poles, with supports for the feet, used as shown above. '—ed adj (of talk, behaviour) too formal.

'stimulant *n* drink (eg coffee), drug, etc, that increases bodily or mental activity.

'stimulate *v* rouse to action; quicken thought or feeling. **'stimulus** *n* sth that —s.

sting *n* **1** sharp, often poisonous, pointed organ(1) of some insects and plants. **2** sharp pain caused by this; (fig) any sharp pain of body or mind. *v* (*pt & pp* stung) **1** prick or wound with a —; be able to —. **2** cause sharp pain to; (of the body) feel such pain.

stink *v & n* (*pt* stank, *pp* stunk) (have a) nasty smell.

stint *v* keep (sb) on a small allowance. **— oneself of sth,** allow oneself little of it.

'stipulate *v* **1** state, put forward, as a necessary condition (*that*). **2 — for,** require (as part of an agreement). **,stipu'lation** *n*.

stir *v* (-rr-) **1** be moving; cause to move: *The wind —red the leaves.* **2** move (a spoon, etc) round and round in (the contents of a bowl, cup, etc). **3** (often — up) excite. *n* **1** —ring. **2 make a —,** excite feeling or a display of interest.

'stirrup *n* foot-rest, hanging from a saddle, for the rider of a horse.

stitch *n* **1** (sewing) the passing of a needle and thread in and out of cloth, etc; (knitting) one complete turn of the wool, etc, over the needle. **2** the thread, etc, seen between two successive holes made in the material: *cut the —es.* *v* sew; put —es in.

stock *n* **1** base, support, or handle of an instrument, tool, etc: *the — of a plough (rifle).* **2** line of ancestry: *a man of Irish —.* **3** store of goods available for sale or use, esp by a trader or shopkeeper: *The book is in (out of) —.* **take —,** examine, and make a list of, goods in —; (as *adj*) usually kept in —: *— sizes in hats.* **4** (also **'live-stock**) farm animals: *a 'stock-farmer, a 'stock-breeder.* **5** money lent to a Government for interest; shares in the capital of a business company. **the S— Exchange,** place where —s and shares are bought and sold. *v* **1** (of a shop, etc) have a —(3) of; keep in —(3). **2** supply or equip (*with*). **'stock-,broker** *n* man whose business is the buying and selling of —(5). **'stock-in-'trade** *n* things needed for trading.

'stocking *n* tight-fitting covering of silk, cotton, wool, etc, for the foot and leg, reaching to or above the knee.

stoke *v* put (coal, etc) on a (fire), on the fire of (an engine, furnace, etc). **'—r** *n* workman who —s.

stole, stolen ⇨ steal.

'stolid *adj* not easily excited; slow to show the feelings.

'stomach *n* **1** bag-like part of the body into which food passes to be digested. ⇨ p 30. **2** belly. *v* endure (3).

stone *n* **1** solid mineral matter other than a metal; piece of this of any shape (usu broken off). **2** jewel: *precious —s.* **3** unit of weight, 14 lb. **4** nutlike seed case in certain tree-fruits, eg plum, cherry. ⇨ p 115. *v* throw —s at. **'stone-'blind (-'deaf)** *adj* completely blind (deaf). **'—mason** *n* man who cuts —, builds with —, etc. **stone's-throw** *n* short distance. **'stony** *adj* (-ier, -iest) **1** having many —s: *stony land.* **2** hard, unsympathetic.

stood ⇨ stand.

stool *n* (usu three-legged) seat without a back, usu for one person.

stoop *v* **1** bend the body forwards and downwards; lower the head forwards so that the neck is bent. **2** (fig) lower oneself morally. *n* —ing position of the body.

stop *v* (-pp-) **1** put an end to (the movement or progress of sb or sth); prevent; discontinue; come to rest. **2** (also — up) fill or close (a hole, an opening, etc). **3** discontinue payment: *— sb's wages.* **— a cheque,** tell the bank not to let it be cashed. **4** stay, remain (*at home, in bed,* etc). *n* **1** —ping or being —ped: *come to a —.* **put a — to,** end. **2** place where buses, etc, — regularly. **3** punctuation mark, esp **full —,** the sign . at the end of a sentence, etc. **4 — press,** latest news added to a newspaper already on the printing machines. **'—gap** *n* thing or person filling the place of another for a time. **'—page** *n* condition of being —ped up; obstruction. **'—per** *n* cork or plug for closing an opening, esp of a bottle.

store n 1 quantity of sth kept for use as needed. **2 in —,** kept ready for use. **in — for sb,** ready for him, coming to him. **3** (pl) goods, etc, of a particular kind or for a special purpose. **4** place where goods are kept; warehouse. **5** (pl) shop selling many varieties of goods; (USA, sing) any kind of shop: a clothing —. **6 set great — by sth,** value it highly. v **1** (often — up) collect, keep, for future use. **2** put (e g furniture) in a warehouse for safe keeping. **3** fill, supply (with): (fig) a mind —d with facts. **'storage** n (space used for, money charged for) the storing of goods.

'storey (pl **'storeys**), **'story** (pl **'stories**) n floor or level in a building: a house of three —s.

stork n large, long-legged, usu white, bird. ⇨ p 26.

storm n **1** violent weather conditions. **2** violent outburst of feeling. **3 take by —,** capture by a sudden and violent attack. v **1** shout angrily (at). **2** force (a way) into (a building, etc); capture by violent attack. **'—y** adj (-ier, -iest). **'—ily** adv.

'story[1] n **1** account of past events. **2** account of imaginary events. **3** (esp by or to children) **tell stories,** make untrue statements.

story[2] ⇨ storey.

stout adj **1** strong, thick, not easily broken or worn out: — shoes. **2** determined and brave. **3** (of a person) rather fat. **'—ly** adv in a —(2) manner.

stove n enclosed apparatus for cooking or for heating rooms by oil, coal, gas, or electricity.

stow v pack, esp carefully and closely: — cargo in a ship's holds. **'—away** n person who hides in a ship or aircraft (until after it leaves) in order to travel without paying.

'straggle v fail to keep up with others on a journey or march.

straight adj (-er, -est) **1** without a curve or bend; continuing in one direction. **2** in line; parallel to (sth else, esp sth level): Put your hat on —. **3** in good order; tidy: Put your desk —. **4** (of a person, his behaviour) honest; truthful; frank. adv **1** by or in the shortest way: come — home. **2 — away (off),** at once. **— on (in, out,** etc**),**

directly on, etc; say sth — out, without hesitation. **'—en** v make or become —. **'—'forward** adj **1** honest. **2** easy to do or understand.

strain v **1** stretch tightly by pulling (at). **2** cause (sb, oneself) to do as much as possible, make the greatest possible use of (powers, muscles, etc); injure or weaken by doing this: — one's eyes (heart, etc). **3** pass (liquids) through a cloth, a network of wire, etc, to separate solid matter. n **1** condition of being stretched; force exerted: The rope broke under the —. **2** sth that tests and —s one's powers, etc: the — of sleepless nights. **3** injury caused by —ing. **4** (pl) music, song, or verse: the —s of an organ. **5** manner of speaking or writing: in a cheerful —. **6** tendency (esp inherited) in sb's character: a — of insanity in the family. **—ed** adj (esp of feelings, behaviour) forced; uneasy. **'—er** n vessel for —ing(3) liquids.

strait n **1** (also pl) channel of water connecting two seas: the S—s of Gibraltar. **2** (pl) trouble; difficulty. **'—en** v in —ened circumstances,** in financial —s(2); poor.

strand[1] v (of a ship) run aground; be **'—ed,** (fig) be left without money or friends or without the means to get to one's destination.

strand[2] n any one of the threads, wires, etc, twisted together in a rope, cable, etc.

strange adj (-r, -st) **1** not seen, heard, known, etc, before; surprising. **2 be — to,** be unaccustomed to. **'—ly** adv. **'—ness** n. **'— r** n person in a place or in company that he does not know.

'strangle v kill by squeezing the throat of; hinder the breathing of. **,strangu'lation** n.

strap n band (usu leather) to fasten things together or to keep sth in place. v (-pp-) fasten or hold in place with a — or —s.

'strategy n act of planning operations, e g in war (the movements of armies and navies into favourable positions for fighting). **stra'tegic** adj of, by, serving the purpose of, —.

straw n cut stalks of dried grain plants (e g wheat); one such stalk.

'strawberry n (plant having) small juicy red fruit covered with tiny yellow seeds. ⇨ p 115.

stray v wander (*from* the right path, etc). *adj* **1** having —ed. **2** seen or happening now and then.

streak n **1** long, thin, usu irregular line or band. **2** trace (2) (of some quality). v mark with —(s). **'—y** *adj* (-ier, -iest) having —s.

stream n **1** river. **2** steady flow or current (of liquid, gas, persons, things, etc). v move as a —; flow freely. **—'lined** *adj* designed so that the shape offers little resistance to the flow of air or water.

street n town or village road with houses, shops, etc: *the high* —, *the principal* —. ⇨ road.

strength n **1** quality of being strong. **2** below —, not having the needed number of men. **in great** —, in great force or numbers. **'—en** v make or become strong(er).

'strenuous *adj* using or needing great effort: — *work(ers).*

stress n **1** pressure; conditions causing hardship, etc: *times of* —, of trouble and danger. **2** weight or force (*on*). **3** (result of) extra force, used in speaking, on a particular word or syllable. v put — on; emphasize.

stretch v **1** make wider, longer, or tighter by pulling; be or become wider, etc, when pulled. **— (out)** one's arms (legs), extend them (eg after sleeping). **2** **— oneself out (on)**, lie at full length (on). **3** **— a point** (in sb's favour), treat him more favourably than is usual. **4** extend (*for* a certain distance or in a certain direction). n **1** —ing or being —ed. **2** unbroken or continuous period of time or extent of country. **—er** n folding bed for carrying sb sick or injured.

strew v (*pt* strewed, *pp* strewn) scatter (sand, flowers, etc) *on* (a surface).

'stricken *adj* overcome: *terror-stricken; — with fever.*

strict *adj* **1** stern; demanding obedience. **2** clearly defined or limited: *the — truth.* **3** requiring exact performance: *in — confidence.*

stride v (*pt* strode) **1** walk with long steps. **2** pass (*over* or *across* sth) with one step. n (distance covered in) one step. **make great —s**, make rapid progress.

strife n quarrelling.

strike v (*pt & pp* struck) **1** hit; aim a blow (*at*). **2** (with *adv*) **— off (out)** (*a word*, etc), cross out by drawing a line through. **— out**, (esp) begin swimming. **— out for oneself**, begin a new business, etc, for oneself. **— up**, begin (playing music, a friendship with sb). **3** (cause to) sound by striking: *The clock struck four.* **4** lower (*a flag, sail*). **5** **— a match**, light it by rubbing. **6** find; arrive at; discover: — *a bargain;* — *oil;* — *the right path.* **7** take (a certain direction): *We struck out across the fields.* **8** — fear (terror, etc) **into**, cause fear, etc, in sb. **be struck dumb** (*blind*, etc), be suddenly made dumb, etc. **9** have (usu a strong) effect upon the mind; attract the attention of: *How does the plan — you?* **10** (of an idea) occur to (suddenly): *It has struck me that . . .* **11** (of workers) stop working, in order to get better conditions, or in protest against sth. n act of striking(11): *The bus-drivers are on* —. **'—r** n (esp) worker on —(11). **'striking** *adj* attracting attention; unusual.

string n **1** (piece or length of) fine cord or ribbon used for tying things. **2** series of things on a —: *a — of beads;* number of things in, or as in, a line: *a — of buses (lies).* **3** tightly stretched length of cord, gut, or wire for producing musical sounds (eg in a violin or piano). v (*pt & pp* usu strung, but —*ed instruments*) **1** put a — or —s on (a violin, a bow, etc). **2** put (beads, etc) on a —. **3** tie or hang on — or on rope: *— lamps across the street.* **4 high(ly) strung**, (of a person) often, or easily becoming, nervous or excited. **'—y** *adj* like —(1).

strip v (-pp-) **1** take off (clothes, covering, etc): — *the bark off a tree.* **2** take away the belongings, contents, rights, etc, of (sb or sth). n long narrow piece of sth (land, cloth, paper, etc).

stripe n **1** long narrow band of different colour or material (eg the —s of a tiger). **2** (usu V-shaped) mark showing the rank (of a soldier, etc).

strive v (pt strove, pp 'striven) struggle.

strode ⇨ stride.

stroke[1] n 1 blow: hammer —s. 2 one of a series of regularly repeated movements, esp as a way of swimming or rowing. 3 single movement of the hand(s), esp in games (eg cricket) or made with a pen or brush. 4 single movement or effort: I haven't done a — of work all day. 5 sound made by a bell striking the hours: on the — of three. 6 sudden attack of illness caused by the bursting of a blood-vessel in the brain, with loss of feeling, etc.

stroke[2] v pass the hand along a surface, usu again and again: — a cat. n act of stroking.

stroll v & n (go for a) quiet walk.

strong adj (-er, -est) 1 (opp of weak) not easily hurt, damaged, broken, etc; having great(er) power of mind or spirit. 2 having much of the substance that gives flavour: — tea; (of a solution) with little water: — acid. 3 **drink**, drink containing alcohol. 4 having a considerable effect on the mind or senses: a — smell of gas. '—ly adv. '—box, '—room n one built for keeping valuables. '—hold n strongly defended or fortified place.

strove ⇨ strive.

struck ⇨ strike.

'structure n 1 way in which sth is put together or organized. 2 building; framework or essential parts. **'structural** adj of a —, esp the framework: structural alterations.

'struggle v fight; make violent efforts (to do sth); try hard (to do sth, for sth). n struggling; great effort.

strum v play a stringed instrument (carelessly): — a guitar.

strung ⇨ string.

strut n piece of wood or metal used as a support, esp in a framework.

stub n short remaining end of sth (eg a pencil, a cigarette). v (-bb-) — one's toe, strike it against sth.

'stubble n 1 ends of grain plants left in the ground after harvest. 2 short stiff growth of beard.

'stubborn adj obstinate.

'stubby adj (-ier, -iest) short and thick: — fingers.

stuck ⇨ stick[2].

stud n button-like device, used to fasten collars, etc. v (-dd-) —ded with, having (jewels, etc) set or scattered in or on the surface.

'studio n 1 well-lit workroom of a painter, photographer, etc. 2 hall, etc, where cinema plays is acted and photographed. 3 room from which cinema and TV programmes are broadcast.

'study v give time and attention to learning or discovering sth: — the map; — medicine. n 1 —ing: begin one's studies. 2 room used by sb for —ing and writing. **'student** n person who is —ing, esp in a university or an art school. **'studious** adj having or showing the habit of —ing; painstaking.

stuff n 1 material or substance. 2 material of which the name is uncertain, unknown, unimportant, or of poor quality. v 1 press (sth) tightly into; fill (sth) tightly with: — feathers into a bag. 2 fill the skin of (a dead bird or animal) with plaster, etc, so that it can be put on show (eg in a museum). '—ing n material for —ing. '—y adj (-ier, -iest) badly ventilated.

'stumble v strike the foot against sth and almost fall. **'stumbling-block** n sth causing difficulty, hesitation, or doubt.

stump n 1 part of a tree remaining when the trunk has fallen or been cut down just above the ground. 2 anything remaining after the main part has been cut or broken off or has worn off. 3 (cricket) one of three wooden sticks forming the wicket. v 1 walk (about, etc) with stiff movements. 2 (colloq) be too hard for; baffle. '—y adj short and thick.

stun v (-nn-) 1 make (sb) unconscious by a blow, esp one on the head. 2 shock: He was —ned by the news.

stung ⇨ sting.

stunk ⇨ stink.

stunt[1] v stop or check the growth of.

stunt[2] n (colloq) sth difficult done to attract attention.

'stupefy v make (sb's mind or senses) dull; make clear thought impossible. ,stupe'faction n.

stu'pendous adj tremendous.

'stupid adj slow-thinking; foolish. —ly adv. stu'pidity n.

'stupor n almost unconscious condition caused by shock, drugs, etc.

'sturdy adj (-ier, -iest) strong; solid; vigorous.

'stutter, v stammer.

sty n pigsty.

style n 1 manner of writing or speaking or doing anything, esp when characteristic of a writer, artist, or of a period of art, etc. 2 quality that marks out anything done or made as superior, fashionable, or distinctive: the latest —s (= fashions) in dress. 3 general form or design: made in three —s. v describe by a certain name or title. 'stylish adj having —(2); fashionable.

sub- prefix 1 (with names of officials and organizations) deputy or junior: sub-lieutenant. 2 not quite; not altogether: sub-tropical. 3 below: sub-normal.

sub'conscious adj of those mental activities of which we are not (wholly) aware.

sub'continent n part of a continent (eg that occupied by India, Pakistan and Bangladesh in Asia).

,subdi'vide v divide again into further divisions.

sub'due v 1 conquer. 2 make quieter or softer: —d light.

'subject n 1 any member of a State except the supreme ruler: British —s. 2 sth (to be) talked or written about or studied; (grammar): They in They came early; book in There is a book on the table. adj 1 governed or protected by another State: — races (nations). 2 — to, likely or liable to experience or to have. 3 — to, conditional upon. sub'ject v 1 bring, get (a country, a person) under control. 2 cause to undergo or experience. sub'jection n 1 —ing(1). 2 being —ed(1).

'sub'let v rent to sb else (a room, etc, of which one is a tenant).

sub'lime adj of the greatest and highest sort, causing wonder and reverence: the — mercy of God.

'submarine n & adj (ship able to travel) under the surface of the sea.

sub'merge v 1 put under water; cover with water. 2 sink out of sight; (of submarines) go down under water.

sub'mit v (-tt-) 1 put (oneself) under the control of another; surrender to. 2 put forward (a plan, etc) for discussion or decision. 3 suggest (that). sub'mission n. sub'missive adj obedient.

su'bordinate adj junior in rank or position (to). n person in a — position. v treat as — or less important; make — (to).

sub'scribe v 1 (agree to) pay (a sum of money), in common with others, to a cause, for sth. 2 — to (a newspaper, etc), place an order for it. 3 — to (opinions, etc), show that one agrees with (them). —r n. sub'scription n (esp) money —d (eg for charity, a newspaper).

'subsequent adj later; following. —ly adv later on.

sub'side v 1 (of flood water) sink to a lower or to the usual level. 2 (of land) sink. 3 (of winds, passions) become quiet again. 'subsidence n.

sub'sidiary adj 1 giving help or support (to). 2 — company, one controlled by a larger one.

'subsidy n financial aid to industry, etc, that is not self-supporting. 'subsidize v give a — to.

sub'sistence n (means of) supporting life.

'substance n 1 material; any particular kind of matter. 2 chief or real meaning of sth (eg of a speech). 3 firmness. sub'stantial adj 1 solidly built or made. 2 having physical existence. 3 large: a substantial meal.

'substitute n person or thing taking the place of or acting for another. v put or use as a — for. ,substi'tution n:

subter'ranean adj underground.

'subtle adj (-r, -st) 1 difficult to perceive or describe because fine or delicate; mysterious: a — charm (flavour). 2 quick and clever at seeing delicate differences: a — critic. 3 elaborate; complex: a — argument. —ty n.

sub'tract v take (a number or quantity) away from. —ion n.

'suburb n outlying district of a town. su'burban adj of or in a —.

'subway n underground passage (esp under a street); (USA) underground railway.

suc'ceed v 1 do what one is trying to do: — in (passing) an examination.

2 do well; have a good result. 3 come next after and take the place of another. 4 — **to**, inherit (a title, property, etc) on the death of the owner. **suc'cess** n 1 —ing(1),(2), 2 person or thing that —s(1),(2). **suc'cessful** adj having success. **suc'cession** n 1 the coming of one thing after another in time or order. **in succession**, one after the other. 2 number of things one after the other. 3 (right of) —ing(3) to a title, property, etc. **suc'cessive** adj coming one after the other. **suc'cessor** n person or thing that —s(3) another.

'**succour** v & n help.

suc'cumb v yield (to a temptation, etc); die.

such adj 1 of the same kind or degree (as): *I've never seen — heavy rain as this!*. 2 suggesting sth is not in good condition, acceptable, etc: *You can borrow my car, — as it is.* 3 so great: *Don't be in a hurry.* **pron** — persons or things.

suck v 1 draw (liquid) into the mouth by using the lip muscles: *— the juice from an orange.* 2 hold (sth) in the mouth and lick, roll about, squeeze, etc, with the tongue. **n** act or process of —ing.

'**suction** n sucking action; force caused by the production of a partial vacuum.

'**sudden** adj happening quickly or unexpectedly. **n all of a —**, **—ly**. **—ly** adv.

suds n pl mass of soap bubbles.

sue v 1 go to law against. 2 beg or ask (for mercy, peace).

suede n kind of soft leather (made from the skin of goats) without a shiny surface: *— shoes.*

'**suet** n solid fat covering the kidneys of sheep and oxen.

'**suffer** v 1 feel or have (pain, loss, etc). 2 allow; tolerate. **—ance** n. **on —ance**, allowed but not welcomed or wanted. **—ing** n pain.

suf'fice v be enough (for). **suf'ficient** adj enough. **suf'ficiency** n sufficient quantity (of).

'**suffix** n letter or syllable(s) added at the end of a word to make another word (as in quick*ly*).

'**suffocate** v choke; kill by stopping the breathing; cause or have difficulty in breathing. ,**suffo-'cation** n.

'**suffrage** n (right to a) parliamentary vote.

'**sugar** n sweet substance obtained from various plants, esp *sugar-cane* and *sugar-beet.* v sweeten or mix with —. **—y** adj tasting of —.

sug'gest v 1 propose; put forward for consideration. 2 bring (an idea, etc) into the mind. **—ion** n idea, plan, etc, that is —ed. **—ive** adj tending to bring ideas, etc, to the mind: *a —ive lecture.*

'**suicide** n self-murder(er). **sui-'cidal** adj very harmful to one's own welfare.

suit n 1 set of articles of outer clothing of the same material. 2 request made to a superior, esp to a ruler. 3 (also **law —**) case in a law court. v 1 satisfy; be convenient or right for. 2 (esp of clothes) look well when worn. 3 make it right or appropriate for: *— the punishment to the crime.* **be —ed** (for), be fitted. '**—able** adj right for the purpose or occasion. '**—ably** adv. ,**suita'bility** n. '**suitcase** n oblong, stiff-sided case for carrying one's clothes, etc, when one is travelling. '**—or** n person bringing a law—; man courting a woman.

suite n 1 personal attendants of an important person, eg a ruler. 2 set of rooms, articles of furniture, etc, to be used together.

sulk v be in a bad temper and show this by refusing to talk. '**—y** (-ier, -iest) —ing; often —ing. '**—ily** adv.

'**sullen** adj 1 silently bad-tempered. 2 (of the sky, etc) dark and gloomy.

'**sully** v stain or discredit.

'**sulphur** n yellow substance that burns with a strong smell.

'**sultan** n Muslim ruler.

'**sultry** adj (-ier, -iest) (of the weather) hot and without a breeze.

sum n 1 total obtained by adding together numbers or amounts. 2 amount of money. 3 problem in arithmetic. v (-mm-) 1 **sum up**, give the total of. 2 **sum up**, express briefly (the chief points of what has been said, etc) '**summary** n brief account of the chief points of sth. '**summarize** v be or make a summary of.

'**summer** n season, usu the warmest between spring and autumn.

'summit n top; highest point.

'summon v 1 command (sb) to come; call (people) together for a meeting, etc. 2 — up, gather together (one's energies, etc). —s n (pl 'summonses) order to appear before a judge, to do sth, etc. v deliver a —s to.

'sumptuous adj costly-looking; magnificent.

sun n 1 heavenly body from which the earth gets warmth and light. 2 the light or warmth of the sun. v (-nn-) put, sit, etc, in the sun's rays. 'sunblind n shade fixed outside a window. 'sunburn n darkening or blistering of the skin caused by the sun. 'sundown n sunset. 'sunlit adj lit by the sun. 'sunny adj (-ier, -iest) lit by the sun; (fig) cheerful; happy. 'sunrise n (time of the) sun's appearance above the horizon. 'sunset n (time of the) sun's disappearance below the horizon. 'sunshade n kind of umbrella used to keep off sunlight. 'sunshine n bright sunny weather. 'sunstroke n illness caused by too much exposure to the sun.

'Sunday n first day of the week; Christian Sabbath.

'sundry adj various. 'sundries n pl various small unnamed items.

sung ⇨ sing.

sunk ⇨ sink.

'super- prefix 1 more or greater than: —human. 2 to an unusually high degree: super-abundant. 3 above; on the top: —structure.

su'perb adj magnificent.

,super'cilious adj showing contemptuous indifference.

,super'ficial adj 1 of or on the surface only. 2 with no depth of knowledge or feeling. —ly adv.

su'perfluous adj more than is needed or wanted. ,super'fluity n.

,superin'tend v manage; watch and direct (work, etc). —ence n. —ent n manager.

su'perior adj 1 better than the average. 2 greater in number. 3 — to, better than; higher in rank than. 4 — to, not giving way to (flattery, etc). n 1 person of higher rank, authority, etc, or who is better, wiser, etc (in sth). 2 S—, head of a monastery or convent. su,peri'ority n.

su'perlative adj 1 of the highest degree or quality. 2 (grammar) the — degree, the form of an adj or adv expressing the highest degree: best, most, lowest, worst, etc.

'supermarket n large self-service store, usu selling food and household goods.

,super'natural adj spiritual; that which is not controlled or explained by physical laws.

,super'sede v (of a person or thing) take the place of; use or put sb or sth in place of.

,super'sonic adj faster than the speed of sound.

,super'stition n 1 unreasoning belief in or fear of what is unknown or mysterious, esp belief in magic. 2 idea, practice, etc, founded on such belief. ,super'stitious adj of, showing, resulting from, —.

'supervise v superintend.

'supper n last meal of the day.

sup'plant v 1 supersede. 2 take the place of (sb), esp after getting him out of his office, etc, by unfair means.

'supple adj easily bent; not stiff: the — limbs of a child.

'supplement n sth added later to improve or complete (eg a dictionary). ,supple'ment v make additions to.

sup'ply v give or provide (sth needed or asked for). n 1 —ing; that which is supplied; amount of sth that is obtainable. 2 (pl) stores necessary for some public need.

sup'port v 1 bear the weight of; hold up or keep in place. 2 help (sb or sth) to go on: — a charity; encourage: — your local football team. 3 provide (a person, one's family) with food, clothes, etc. 4 endure. n —ing or being —ed; sb or sth that —s. —er n.

sup'pose v 1 let it be thought that; take it as a fact that: — the world were flat; — it is true. 2 guess; think. 3 (used to make suggestions): S— we go (= let's go) for a swim. 4 be —d to, be expected to: You're —d to know the rules. sup'posing conj if. —d adj regarded as being so. ,suppo'sition n 1 supposing. 2 sth —d; guess.

sup'press v 1 put an end to the activity or existence of. 2 prevent from being seen or known. —ion n.

su'preme adj highest in rank or authority; of the greatest importance or value: the S— Being, God. —ly adv. **su'premacy** n.

sure adj (-r, -st) 1 of, — that, free from doubt; certain. 2 be — to (come, etc), do not fail to . . . make —, satisfy oneself; do what is necessary in order to feel certain, to get sth, etc. 3 proved or tested; trustworthy. adv — enough, certainly; as expected. '—ly adv 1 certainly. 2 if experience or probability can be trusted.

surf n waves breaking in white foam on the seashore or on reefs.

'surface n 1 the outside of any object, etc; any side of an object; top of a liquid. 2 outward appearance.

'surfeit n too much of anything, esp food and drink.

surge v move forward, roll on, in or like waves. n forward rush of waves.

'surgeon n doctor skilled in operations(4). (cf physician.) **'surgery** n 1 treatment of injuries or diseases by a —. 2 doctor's room where patients come to consult him. **'surgical** adj of or by surgery.

'surly adj (-ier, -iest) bad-tempered and unfriendly. **'surliness** n.

sur'mise v & n guess(ing).

sur'mount v overcome (difficulties, etc); get over (obstacles). be —ed by (with), have on or over the top.

'surname n that part of a person's name common to all members of his family.

sur'pass v do or be better than.

'surplice n wide-sleeved white gown worn by priests and choir in church.

'surplus n amount (esp money) that remains after needs are supplied.

sur'prise n (feeling caused by) sth sudden or unexpected. v 1 give a feeling of — to. 2 catch, find (sb, the enemy) unexpectedly, when they are unprepared. **sur'prising** adj causing —.

sur'render v 1 give up (oneself, a ship, town, etc) (to the enemy, the police, etc); stop fighting. 2 give up possession of (freedom, etc) to sb. 3 — oneself to yield

to (despair, a habit, etc). n act of —ing.

sur'round v be all round; shut in on all sides. —ings n pl everything that —s a place or person.

sur'vey v 1 take a general view of; examine the general condition of. 2 measure and map out the position, size, boundaries, etc, of (land, a coast, etc). **'survey** n 1 general view. 2 (map or record of a) piece of land-surveying. —or n man whose business is —ing(2).

sur'vive v continue to live or exist; live or exist longer than; remain alive after (eg an earthquake). **sur'vival** n 1 surviving. 2 person, custom, etc, that has —d, but is looked upon as belonging to past times. **sur'vivor** n person who has —d (an accident, etc).

sus'ceptible adj 1 easily influenced by feelings. 2 — to, easily affected by (pain, flattery, etc). — of proof, that can be proved.

sus'pect v 1 have an idea or feeling (that . . .). 2 feel doubt about. 3 have a feeling that sb may be guilty of: He is —ed of telling lies. **'suspect** n person —ed of wrongdoing.

sus'pend v 1 hang (sth) up from (a support above). 2 be —ed (in the air, in a liquid), remain in place as if hanging: dust —ed in the still air. 3 delay; stop for a time: — judgement; — payment; become bankrupt. 4 shut out for a time (from membership of a society, from privileges, etc). **sus'pension** n —ing or being —ed. **suspension bridge**, one —ed on or by means of steel cables

a suspension bridge

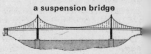

sus'pense n uncertainty. keep sb in —, keep him waiting for news about sth.

sus'picion n 1 feeling of a person who suspects; feeling that sth is wrong. 2 slight taste or suggestion (of). **sus'picious** adj having, showing, or causing —.

sus'tain v 1 (enable to) keep up or last: —ing food (that keeps up one's strength). **2** suffer or experience (a defeat, etc). **—ed** *adj* continued; going on for a long time. **'sustenance** *n* food and drink.

'swagger *v* walk or behave in a self-important manner.

'swallow¹ *v* **1** cause or allow to go down one's throat. **2** take in; use up; absorb. *n* act of —ing.

'swallow² *n* small fast-flying bird with a double-pointed tail. ⇨ p 26.

swam ⇨ swim.

swamp *n* (area of) soft, wet land. *v* **1** flood (eg a boat) with water. **2** (*fig*) overwhelm: *—ed with orders for goods.* **'-y** *adj* (-ier, -iest).

swan *n* large, graceful, long-necked, (usu white) water-bird. ⇨ p 12.

swap, swop *v* (*colloq*) exchange.

swarm *n* **1** large number of insects, birds, etc, moving about together: *a — of ants* (*bees*). **2** (*esp pl*) large numbers (*of* children, etc). *v* **1** (esp of bees when forming a new colony) move or go in large numbers. **2 —with**, be crowded or filled with: *The dog was —ing with fleas.*

'swarthy *adj* of a dark colour.

swat *v* hit at with a flat object: *— a fly.*

swathe *v* wrap tightly round: *His leg was —d in bandages.*

sway *v* **1** move, be moved, unsteadily first to one side and then back again. **2** control or influence. *n* **1** —ing movement. **2** rule or control: *under the — of.*

swear *v* (*pt* swore, *pp* sworn) **1** say solemnly or with emphasis: *— to do sth*; *— that.* **2** (cause to) take an oath: *— sb to secrecy.* **3** use curses and bad words. **'-word** *n* word used in —ing(3).

sweat *n* **1** moisture given off by the body through the skin: *in a —*, very worried. **2** (*colloq*) hard work. *v* **1** give out —. **2** (cause to) work hard. **—ed labour,** workers who are made to work very hard for low wages. **'-er** *n* jersey. **'-y** *adj* (-ier, -iest) wet with, smelling of, —.

sweep *v* (*pt & pp* swept) **1** clear away (dust, dirt, etc) with a brush or broom; clean by doing this. **2** move or pass quickly over or along, esp so as to remove anything in the way: *houses swept away by the floods.* **3** stretch in an unbroken line or curve or expanse. *n* **1** act of —ing(1); —ing(1) movement. **2** long unbroken stretch, esp curved, of a road, coast, etc, or of sloping land. **3** man whose work is —ing soot from chimneys. **'-er** *n* sb (*street-sweeper*) or sth (*carpet-sweeper*) that **—s.** **'-ing** *adj* far-reaching: *—ing changes.* **'-stake(s)** *n* form of gambling, esp on a horse-race.

sweet *adj* (-er, -est) **1** tasting like sugar or honey. **2** fresh and pure: *— milk.* **3** pleasant or attractive: *— scents* (*voices*); *a — temper*; *a little boy.* *n* **1** dish of — food (tart, pudding, etc) as part of a meal. **2** piece of boiled and flavoured sugar, chocolate, etc. **'-en** *v* make or become —.

'sweetheart *n* either of a couple who love each other; beloved child, etc.

swell *v* (*pt & pp* 'swelled or 'swollen) **1** (cause to) become greater in volume, thickness, or force: *Wood often —s when it gets wet.* **2 — up** (**out**), (cause to) have a curved surface. *n* **1** gradual increase of sound. **2** slow rise and fall of the sea's surface. **'-ing** *n* swollen place on the body (eg the result of a blow or of tooth-ache).

'swelter *v* be uncomfortably hot.

swept ⇨ sweep.

swerve *v* (cause to) change direction suddenly. *n* swerving movement.

swift *adj* (-er, -est). **'-ly** *adv* quickly.

swim *v* (*pt* swam, *pp* swum; -mm-) **1** move through the water by using arms, legs, fins, tail, etc. **2** be covered *with*, overflowing *with*, or as if floating *in*: *eyes —ming with tears; rice —ming in water.* **3** seem to be moving round and round; feel dizzy. *n* act of —ming: *go for a —.*

'swindle *v* cheat. *n* piece of swindling; sth sold, etc, that is less valuable than it is described. **'-r** *n* person who —s.

swine *n* (old use) pig.

swing *v* (*pt & pp* swung) **1** (of sth fixed at one end or side) (cause to) move backwards and forwards: *—ing his arms.* **2** (cause to) move along a curve: *The car swung round the corner.* *n* **1** —ing movement. **2 go with a —,** go without trouble, go well. **in full —**, active, in full operation. **3** seat held by ropes or chains for **—ing** on.

swirl v (of liquid, air, dust, etc) (cause to) move or flow at different rates of speed, with twists and turns. n **—ing** movement.

switch n **1** device for making or breaking a connection between railway points (to allow trains to go from one track to another) or in an electric circuit. **2** twig, cane. v **1** turn (electric current) *on* or *off*. **2** move (a train, tram) on to another track. **3** swing or turn suddenly. **'—board** n apparatus with many electric **—es**, esp for making connections by telephone.

'swivel n ring and pivot joining two parts so that one can turn round without turning the other. v (**-ll-**) (cause to) turn on a **—**.

'swollen ▷ swell (esp as *adj*).

swoon v & n faint.

swoop v come (*down*) *on* with a rush. n **—ing** movement.

swop ▷ swap.

sword n long steel blade fixed in a hilt, used as a weapon.

swore, sworn ▷ swear.

swum ▷ swim.

swung ▷ swing.

'syllable n *A-rith-me-tic* is a word of four **—s**. **syl'labic** *adj*.

'syllabus n outline or summary of a course of studies; programme of school studies.

'symbol n sign, mark, object, etc, looked upon as representing or recalling sth: ×, ÷, +, *and — are common mathematical* **—s**. **sym'bolic** *adj* of, using, used as, a **—**. **—ize** v be a **—** of; use a **—** or **—s** for.

sym'metrical *adj* having (usu two) matching parts on either side of a dividing line: *a — design*.

'sympathy n (capacity for) sharing the feelings of others; feeling of pity or tenderness: *feel — for the sick man*; *in — with a proposal*, agreeing with it, approving it. **,sympa'thetic** *adj* having or showing **—**; caused by **—**. **'sympathize** v feel **— (**with**)**.

'symphony n musical composition for an orchestra.

'symptom n **1** change in the body's condition that indicates illness. **2** sign of the existence of sth.

'synagogue n (building used for an) assembly of Jews for religious teaching and worship.

'synchronize v (cause to) happen at the same time; agree in time.

'syndicate n business association esp one that supplies articles, etc, to several newspapers.

'synod n council of ministers, elders, etc, deciding the affairs of a particular Church.

'synonym n word with the same meaning as another in the same language. **sy'nonymous** *adj*.

sy'nopsis n (*pl* **sy'nopses**) summary or outline (of a book, play, etc).

'syntax n (rules for) sentence building.

syn'thetic *adj* (of substances) artificially made: **—** *rubber*.

'syphon n = siphon.

'syringe n device for drawing in liquid and forcing it out again in a fine stream.

'syrup n thick, sweet liquid made from sugar-cane juice or by boiling sugar with water.

'system n **1** group of parts working together in a regular relation: *the nervous* **—**. **2** ordered group of principles, ideas, etc: *a — of government*. **,syste'matic** *adj* methodical; orderly. **,syste'matically** *adv*.

T

tab n small piece or strip of cloth etc, fixed to a garment, etc, as a badge, mark, or holder.

'table n **1** piece of furniture with a flat top and (usu) four legs. **2** people seated at a **—**. **3** list of facts, information, etc: *multiplication* **—s**; *a railway time-table*. **—cloth** n one (to be) spread over a **—**. **—land** n plateau. **—spoon** n large spoon for serving food on to plates at **—**.

'tablet n **1** flat surface with words cut or written on it, eg one fixed to a wall in memory of sb or sth. **2** lump (of soap); pill.

ta'boo n forbidden act or thing. *adj* forbidden.

'tabular *adj* arranged or shown in tables(3). **'tabulate** v arrange (facts, figures, etc) in columns.

'**tacit** *adj* unspoken; understood without being spoken: — *consent*.

'**taciturn** *adj* (in the habit of) saying very little. ,**taci'turnity** *n*.

tack *n* **1** small, flat-headed nail. **2** long, loose stitch used in sewing. **3** sailing-ship's direction as fixed by the direction of the wind and the position of the sails. **on the right (wrong) —**, (fig) following a wise (unwise) course of action. *v* **1** fasten (*down*) with —s(1). **2** stitch loosely with —s(2). **3** (of a sailing-ship) sail a zigzag course.

'**tackle** *n* **1** set of ropes and pulleys for working a ship's sails, or for lifting heavy things. **2** equipment for doing sth: *fishing —*. *v* **1** deal with, attack (a problem, etc). **2** seize, lay hold of (eg a thief, a football player who has the ball).

tact *n* (use of) skill and understanding shown by sb who handles difficult people and situations successfully and without causing offence. '**—ful(ly)** *adj & adv*. '**—less(ly)** *adj & adv*.

'**tactics** *n pl* (often with a *sing v*) art of placing and moving fighting forces for or during battle; (fig) method(s) for carrying out a policy. **tac'tician** *n* expert in —.

'**tadpole** *n* young of a frog or toad before full development.

tag *n* **1** metal point at the end of a string, shoe-lace, etc. **2** label (eg for showing prices, addresses). *v* (-gg-) **1** join (sth, esp a piece of writing) *to* or *on to* sth else. **2** fasten a tag(2) to.

tail *n* **1** movable part of the lower end of the back of an animal, bird, fish, etc. **2** sth like a — in position: *the — of a comet (an aircraft)*. **3** side of a coin without the sovereign's head on it, esp **Heads or —s?** (in spinning a coin to decide sth). *v* — **off**, become smaller in size, fewer in number, etc.

'**tailor** *n* maker of suits and overcoats, esp for men.

taint *n* trace of infection or of some bad quality. *v* make or become infected or spoiled: *—ed meat*.

take *v* (*pt* took, *pp* '**taken**) **1** get hold of with the hand(s), etc, or with an instrument. **2** catch (sb or sth) by surprise or pursuit: — *500 prisoners*; win: — *the first prize in a competition*; become ill with (a disease); get, become: *be —n ill*. (**not much**) **—n with**, (not very) attracted by. **3** carry, go with (sb or sth): — *the box upstairs*; — *a friend home*. **4** have; eat or drink, give, allow, or get, for oneself: — *a bath (a holiday, some medicine, a deep breath)*; — *an interest in sth*; — (hire) *a taxi*; — (rent) *a house*. **5** accept; subscribe to: *I will — £5 for it. What newspaper do you —?* **6** make a record(1): — *notes of a lecture*; — *photographs*. **7** need: *The journey will — two days. It —s two to make a quarrel*. **8** suppose: *I — him to be an honest man*. **9** (with *adv & prep*)—**after** (sb), resemble (a parent or relation) in looks, etc. — **sb down**, lower his pride. — (**sb**) **in**, receive (him) as a guest; get the better of by a trick. — (**sth**) **in**, understand, receive into the mind; see at a glance; receive (eg a newspaper) regularly; reduce the area, width, etc, of (eg a garment). — (**sb or sth**) **for**, consider to be, esp wrongly suppose to be. — **off**, (esp) ridicule by imitation; (of an aircraft) start a flight. — **on**, undertake (work); engage (workers). — **out**, obtain (an insurance policy, a licence, etc). — (**sth**) **over**, succeed to the management or control of; accept the transfer of duties, etc. — **to**, adopt as a habit or practice: — *to drink*; use as a means of escape: *a crew taking to the boats*. — *to one's heels* (run away); form a liking for: — *to a new neighbour*. — **up**, absorb, dissolve; occupy (time, attention); proceed to deal with. **10** (eg of vaccine) have effect; act. '**taking** *adj* attractive. '**takings** *pl n* money —n in business.

tale *n* **1** story: *fairy— —s*. **2** report or account. **tell —s**, tell about sb's wrongdoing.

'**talent** *n* **1** natural power to do sth; ability: *have a — for painting*. **2** local —, local people with —. **—ed** *adj* having —.

'**talisman** *n* charm(2).

talk *v* say things; speak to give information (*to*); discuss matters (*with*); have the power of speech: *Can your parrot —?* — (**sth**) **over**, discuss it. — **sb round**, get his support or agreement by —ing to him. *n* —**ing**; informal lecture.

small-talk, conversation about unimportant topics. **'—ative** adj liking to — a lot.

tall adj (-er, -est) **1** (esp of persons) of more than ordinary height. **2 a — story,** one that is difficult to believe. **a — order,** an unreasonable request.

'tallow n hard (esp animal) fat used for making candles, etc.

'tally v (of stories, amounts, etc) correspond; agree. n reckoning.

'talon n claw of a bird of prey.

tame adj (-r, -st) **1** (of animals) used to living with human beings; not wild or fierce. **2** uninteresting. v make —.

'tamper v interfere (with).

tan n & adj yellowish brown. v (-nn-) **1** make (an animal's skin) into leather. **2** make or become brown with sunburn. **'tanner** n workman who tans skins.

tang n sharp taste or smell.

'tangible adj **1** that can be touched. **2** clear and definite: **—proof.**

'tangle n confused mass (of string, hair, etc). v make or become confused, disordered.

tank n **1** (usu large) container for liquid or gas. **2** (in India) artificial (usu square) pond for water. **3** armoured fighting vehicle. **'—er** n **1** ship with —s. **2** lorry with a large — for transporting oil.

a tank

'tantalize v keep just out of his reach sth that sb desires; raise hopes that are to be disappointed.

'tantamount adj (only in) **— to,** equal in effect to.

tap¹ n device for controlling the flow of a liquid or gas from a pipe, barrel, etc. v (-pp-) **1** let liquid out from (eg a barrel); cut (the bark of a tree) and get (sap, etc). **2** (fig) try to obtain (money, information, etc) from.

tap² n quick, light blow. v (-pp-) give a tap or taps to: tap sb on the shoulder; tap at (on) the door.

tape n **1** long, narrow strip of material (for tying up parcels, etc). **'tape-measure,** one marked in inches, centimetres, etc, for measuring. **2** long, narrow, magnetized strip that can record and reproduce sound. **3** strip (of paper) recording information for a computer. **'tape-recorder** n apparatus for recording and playing **—s(2).**

'taper v make or become gradually narrower towards one end.

'tapestry n cloth with designs, etc, made by weaving coloured threads into it, used for hanging on walls.

tar n black substance, thick and sticky when warmed, obtained from coal. **'tarmac** n mixture of tar and crushed stone for roads, etc; runway.

'tardy adj (-ier, -iest) late; slow. **'tardily** adv.

'target n sth aimed at; thing, plan, etc, against which criticism is directed.

'tariff n **1** list of fixed charges, esp for meals, rooms, etc, at a hotel. **2** list of taxes on goods imported; tax on a particular class of imported goods.

'tarmac ⇨ tar.

'tarnish v (esp of metal surfaces) lose, cause the loss of, brightness.

tar'paulin n (sheet or cover of) waterproof canvas.

'tarry v (liter) wait (for); be slow or late in coming, going, etc; stay.

tart¹ adj acid; sharp. **'—ly** adv.

tart² n fruit pie; piece of pastry with jam, etc, on it.

task n piece of (esp hard) work (to be) done. **take sb to —,** scold him. **'—,master** n person who makes others perform hard —s.

'tassel n bunch of threads, etc, tied together at one end and hanging from sth as an ornament.

taste n **1** sense by which flavour is known: sweet to the —. **2** quality of substances made known by this sense, eg by putting on the tongue: Sugar has a sweet —. **3** small quantity (of sth to eat or drink). **4** liking (for): It's not to my —, I don't like it. **5** ability to enjoy beauty; ability to choose and use what is good (in art, behaviour, etc). **in good (bad) —,** pleasing (displeasing) to people with —(5)

a tap

v **1** be aware of the —(2) of sth. **2** (of food) have a —(2): *It —s good (sour, of onions).* **3** test the —(2) of. **4** experience: *— the joys of freedom.* **'—ful** *adj* in good —(5). **'—fully** *adv.* **'—less** *adj* **1** with little or no —(2). **2** in bad —(5). **'tasty** *adj* (-ier, -iest) pleasing to the —(1).

'tatter *n* (usu *pl*) rag; piece of cloth, paper, etc, torn off or hanging loosely from sth. **—ed** *adj* ragged.

tat'too *v* mark (sb's skin) with permanent designs or patterns.

taught ⇨ teach.

taunt *n* remark intended to hurt sb's feelings. *v* attack (sb) with —s. **'—ingly** *adv.*

taut *adj* (-er, -est) (of ropes, nerves, etc) tense (2).

'tawdry *adj* (-ier, -iest) bright but in bad taste.

tax *n* **1** sum of money (to be) paid by citizens, according to income, value of purchases, etc, to the government for public purposes. **2** a tax on (*one's strength, patience,* etc), sth that is a strain or burden on. *v* **1** put a tax(1) on. **2** be a —(2) on. **3** tax sb with (sth), accuse him of. **'taxable** *adj* that can be taxed(1). **tax'ation** *n* system of raising money by taxes; taxes (to be) paid.

'taxi *n* (*pl* 'taxies) (rarely *taxi-cab*) motor-car with a —meter, which may be hired. *v* **1** go in a —. **2** (of aircraft) move on wheels on the ground. **—meter** *n* device which automatically records the fare to be paid for a journey in a —.

tea *n* **1** (dried leaves of an) evergreen shrub of eastern Asia; drink made by pouring boiling water on these leaves. **2** light meal with tea to drink in the late afternoon. **'tea-cloth** *n* cloth for drying dishes.

teach *v* (*pt & pp* taught) give instruction(s) to sb; cause sb to know or be able to do sth; give lessons (for a living). **'—er** *n.* **'—ing** *n* (esp) that which is taught.

teak *n* hard wood used in making furniture, ship-building, etc.

team *n* **1** two or more horses, oxen, etc, pulling a cart, plough, etc, together. **2** persons playing together and forming one side in some games (eg football, cricket).

tear¹ *v* (*pt* tore, *pp* torn) **1** pull sharply apart or to pieces; make (a hole *in* sth) by pulling sharply: *— a piece of paper to pieces; — a dress on a nail.* **— sth up**, ie into small pieces. **2** cause (sth) to be down, off, out, etc, by pulling sharply. **3** become torn: *Paper —s easily.* **4** go in excitement or at a great speed: *children —ing out of school.* *n* torn place.

tear² *n* drop of salty water coming from the eye. **in —s**, crying. **'—ful** *adj* crying; wet with —s.

tease *v* make fun of, playfully or unkindly. *n* person fond of teasing others. **'teasingly** *adv.*

'technical *adj* of, special to, one of the mechanical or industrial arts (eg printing) or the methods used by experts: *— terms; — skill.* **tech'nician** *n* person expert in the technique of a particular art, etc. **tech'nique** *n* method of doing sth expertly, esp mechanical skill.

'tedious *adj* slow and uninteresting.

teem *v* **— with**, have, be present, in great numbers: *rivers —ing with fish.*

'teenager *n* person in his (her) teens.

teens *n pl* **in their —**, (of people) 13 to 19 years of age.

teeth ⇨ tooth.

teethe *v* (of a baby) be getting its first teeth.

'tele- *prefix* long distance. **'telegram** *n* message sent by —graph. **'telegraph** *n* apparatus for sending messages along wires or by wireless. *v* send (news), etc, by —graph. **tele'graphic** *adj.* **'telephone** *n* means, instrument, for talking to sb at a distance by using electric current or radio. *v* send (news, etc) by —phone; use the —phone. **'telescope** *n* tube-like instrument with lenses for making distant objects appear to the eye to be nearer or larger. **'television** *n* (colloq TV) process of sending pictures to a distant television receiving set and reproducing them.

tell *v* (*pt & pp* told) **1** make known (in spoken or written words); inform about (one's name, etc). **2** (esp with *can, be able to*) recognize the difference between: *Can you*

— *Mary from her twin sister?*
3 There is no —**ing** (*what will happen*, etc.), it is impossible to say.
4 have a marked effect (*upon*).
5 (old use) count: — *one's beads*, say one's prayers with a rosary.
all told, altogether. — **off**, count one by one and give orders (*for a task*, *to do* sth); (colloq) scold.
'—**ing** *adj* effective. **'tell-tale** *n & adj* (person) making known a secret, sb's feelings, etc.

'temper *n* **1** degree of hardness, toughness, elasticity, of a substance, esp steel. **2** state or condition of mind. **in a good** —, calm and pleasant. **keep one's** —, keep one's anger under control. **out of** — (*with*), angry. *v* **1** give the required —(1) to (steel, etc.). **2** soften or modify (sth *with*).

'temperament *n* person's natural tendencies: *a girl with a nervous* —.

'temperance *n* moderation; self-control in speech, behaviour, and (esp) in the use of alcoholic drinks.

'temperate *adj* **1** showing, behaving with, —. **2** (of climate, parts of the world) free from extremes of heat or cold.

'temperature *n* degree of heat or cold. **have a** —, have a fever.

'tempest *n* violent storm.

'temple¹ *n* building used for religious worship.

'temple² *n* flat part of either side of the head between the forehead and ear.

'temporal *adj* **1** of or in time. **2** of this physical world or life only.

'temporary *adj* lasting for, made to be used for, a short time only.

'temporize *v* act so as to gain time; delay decision or action.

tempt *v* **1** (try to) persuade (sb) to do sth wrong or foolish. **2** attract (sb) to have or do sth pleasant and harmless. **temp'tation** *n* —ing or being —ed; sth that —s.

ten *n & adj* 10; (British decimal currency) ten new pence (10p) = former two shillings. —**th** *n & adj* 10th; $\frac{1}{10}$.

te'nacious *adj* holding tightly; refusing to let go (*of*). **te'nacity** *n*.

'tenant *n* person who pays rent for the use of land, a room, building, etc.

tend¹ *v* watch over; take care of.

tend² *v* **1** have a —ency. **2** move

or be directed. **'**—**ency** *n* turning or inclination (*to*, *towards*, *to do* sth): *Your work shows a* —*ency to improve*, shows signs of improvement.

'tender¹ *v* **1** offer (eg one's services, resignation). **2** make an offer (to supply goods, etc). *n* **1** statement of the price at which one offers to supply goods or services. **2** sth offered, esp **legal** —, form of money which must by law be accepted in payment of a debt.

'tender² *adj* (-er, -est) **1** easily hurt or damaged; quickly feeling pain. **2** (of meat) easily chewed; not tough. **3** kind; loving. —**ly** *adv*. —**ness** *n*.

'tendon *n* tough, thick cord that joins a muscle to a bone.

'tendril *n* thread-like part of a climbing plant (eg pea) that twists round any support nearby.

'tenement *n* large dwelling-house for the use of many families.

'tennis *n* game for two or four players who hit a ball backwards and forwards over a net.

'tenor *n* (person with the) highest normal male voice.

tense¹ *n* verb form showing time.

tense² *adj* (-r, -st) **1** tightly stretched. **2** showing or feeling excitement, etc: *faces* — *with anxiety*. **'**—**ly** *adv*. **'**—**ness** *n*.

'tension *n* **1** state of, degree of, being tense. **2** condition when feelings or relations between two persons, groups, States, etc, are strained.

tent *n* shelter made of canvas supported by poles and ropes.

'tentacle *n* long, slender, boneless part of certain animals used for feeling, holding, etc. ⇨ p 247.

'tentative *adj* made or done as a trial, to see the effect: — *suggestions*.

'tenterhooks *n pl* (only in) **on** —, anxiously awaiting news, a decision, etc.

tenth ⇨ ten.

'tenure *n* (period of time, condition of) using land, holding office, etc.

'tepid *adj* lukewarm.

term *n* **1** fixed or limited period of time, esp one during which law courts, schools, etc, are open. **2** conditions offered or agreed to. **come to (make)** —**s with (sb)**, reach an agreement. **3 be on goo**

—s with (sb), be friendly with him. **4** word(s) expressing a definite idea, esp in a branch of study: *scientific —s.* **5** (*pl*) words: *in —s of high praise.* *v* name; give a certain —(4) to.

'**terminal** *adj* **1** of, taking place, each term(1). **2** of, forming, the point or place at the end (eg of a railway). *n* —(2) part or place; either of the free ends for completion of an electric circuit.

'**terminate** *v* come to an end; put an end to. — **in,** have at the end. ,**termi'nation** *n* ending (esp of a word).

'**terminus** *n* station at either end of a railway, a bus route, etc.

'**termite** *n* ant-like insect causing damage to wood, paper, etc, often called a 'white ant'.

'**terrace** *n* **1** level(led) piece of ground on a slope. **2** row of joined houses, esp along the top or side of a slope. —**d** *adj* having —s; cut into —s: *a —d garden.*

'**terrible** *adj* causing great fear, sorrow, or discomfort. '**terribly** *adv* (colloq) very (much).

ter'**rific** *adj* causing fear; (colloq) very large, enjoyable, etc. '**terrify** *v* fill with fear.

'**territory** *n* land, esp land under one ruler or government. ,**terri'torial** *adj* of —. **territorial waters,** the sea near a country's coasts. **2 Territorial Army,** force of part-time soldiers, members being trained in their spare time.

'**terror** *n* (person, thing, etc, causing) great fear. —**ism** *n* use of —, esp for political purposes. —**ist** *n*.

terse *adj* (-r, -st) brief and apt.

test *n* examination or trial (of sth or sb) for quality, value, ability, etc. — **pilot,** one who takes newly built aircraft on — flights. '**test-tube** *n* slender glass tube, closed at one end, used in —ing chemicals. *v* **1** put to the —; examine: — *ore for gold.* **2** be a — of.

'**testament** *n* **1** statement in writing saying how sb wishes his property to be distributed after his death. **2** Old **T**—, New **T**—, the two main divisions of the Bible.

'**testify** *v* **1** give evidence (in a court of law) *against*, on behalf of, *that*. **2** declare *that.* **3** — **to,** be evidence of.

,**testi'monial** *n* **1** written statement testifying to sb's merits, abilities, etc. **2** sth given (usu by a group of persons) to sb to show appreciation of services.

'**testimony** *n* **1** statement, esp in a court of law, testifying that sth is true. **2** open declaration of one's religious beliefs.

'**tetanus** *n* disease marked by the stiffening of some or all of the muscles which are usu under our control.

'**tether** *n* rope or chain by which an animal is fastened while grazing. **at the end of one's —,** at the end of one's self-control, resources, etc. *v* fasten with a —.

text *n* **1** the author's own words, apart from anything else in a book. **2** short quotation (esp from the Bible), as the subject of a sermon or discussion. '—**book** *n* one written to teach a subject.

'**textile** *adj* of the making of cloth. *n* woven material; material for spinning and weaving.

'**texture** *n* **1** arrangement of the threads in a textile fabric: *of fine (close, knitted)* —. **2** structure of a substance, esp when touched or looked at: *skin of coarse* —.

than *conj* **1** (introducing the second part of a comparison): *John is taller — Jane.* **2 no (one) other** —, not any other person but. **nothing else** —, only, entirely: *It was nothing else — bad luck that lost them the game.*

thank *v* express gratitude to sb for sth. —*s* *n* *pl*—**s to,** as the result of, because of. '—**ful** *adj.* '—**fully** *adv.* '—**less** *adj* (esp of actions) for which there are no —s: *a —less task.* '—**s-giving** *n* (form of prayer used in) expressing —s to God (eg for the harvest).

that *adj* & *pron* (*pl* **those**) (contrasted with **this** (**these**)): *Look at — man over there.* **T**— *man is taller than this.* *adv* (colloq) *I couldn't walk — far (as far as —).* *pron* (*pl* unchanged) *I have seen the letters — came yesterday.* *conj* **1 so —:** *Come here so — I can see you.* **2** *I will see — he does it.* **3** *She's so rude that nobody likes her.* **4 on condition —,** providing: *I'll go on condition — you'll be there.*

thatch *n* (roof covering of) dried

straw, reeds, etc. *v* cover (a roof, etc) with —.

thaw *v* **1** It is —ing, the temperature has risen above freezing-point. **2** (cause anything frozen solid to) become liquid or soft again. **3** (of persons, their behaviour) (cause to) become less formal, more friendly. *n* weather causing snow, etc, to —.

the (*definite article*) a particular one. (cf a, an.) *adv* by so much; by that amount: *The more he has, the more he wants.*

'theatre *n* **1** building for the acting of plays. **2** the —, drama. **the'atrical** *adj* **1** of or for the —(1). **2** (of behaviour, etc) exaggerated; designed for effect.

theft *n* (the act of) stealing.

their(s) *adj & pron* belonging to them: *That is — book. That book is —s.*

them *pron* object(2) form of they: *You can see —.* ⇨ they. **—'selves** *pron*: *They hurt —selves when they fell over.*

theme *n* **1** idea which is the subject of a talk or piece of writing. **2** (music) short tune often repeated or expanded in a longer musical piece.

then *adv & conj* **1** at that time past or future. **2** next; after that; afterwards. **3** in that case: *You say you are ill; — why not see a doctor?* **4** and also: *T— there's my mother, she ought to be invited.*

thence *adv* from there. **'—'forth**, **'—'forward** *adv* from that time onwards.

the'ology *n* study of the nature of God and of the foundations of religious belief. **,theo'logical** *adj*.

'theory *n* **1** explanation of the general principles of an art or science (contrasted with *practice*). **2** view, put forward with reasons, to explain facts or events. **,theo-'retic(al)** *adj* based on —, not on practice or experience.

there *adv* (contrasted with *here*) **1** in, at, to, that place. **2** calling attention: *Look out, —!* **3** (with *appear, seem*, etc): *T— seems to be no escape.* *int* expressing pride, dismay, etc. **'—abouts** *adv* near that place, number, quantity. **'—fore** *adv* for that reason. **'—upon** *adv* then. **—'by** *adv* in that way; by that method.

therm *n* unit of heat. **ther'mo-meter** *n* instrument for measuring temperature.

these *adj & pron* (contrasted with *those*): *Look at — men over here. T— are the tallest.*

'thesis *n* (*pl* 'theses) written essay submitted for a university degree.

they *pron* referring to more than one (person, thing, etc) as the subject(3): *T— can see you.* ⇨ them.

thick *adj* (-er, -est) **1** (opp of thin) of comparatively greater measurement from one side to the other or from the upper surface to the lower surface: *a plank three inches —*; of large diameter: *a — rod of steel.* **2** having a large number of units crowded together: *a — forest* (with trees close together). **3** (of liquids, the atmosphere) that cannot be seen through; not flowing freely: — *soup*; *a — fog*; *air — with dust.* **4** (colloq) unintelligent. —*est* part; part where activity is greatest: *in the — of the fight.* **'—en** *v* make or become —. **'—ly** *adv.* **'—ness** *n* (esp) layer.

'thicket *n* mass of trees, bushes, etc, growing close together.

thief *n* (*pl* thieves) person who steals, esp secretly and without violence. **thieve** *v* steal.

thigh *n* part of the leg above the knee. ⇨ p 29.

'thimble *n* cap (of metal, etc) used to protect the end of the finger when pushing a needle through cloth, etc.

thin *adj* (-ner, -nest) **1** (opp of *thick*) having opposite surfaces close together; of small diameter; (of people) slender. **2** having not much flesh: — *in the face.* **3** (of liquids) watery; without much substance. *v* (-nn-) make or become —. **'—ly** *adv.* **'—ness** *n.*

thing *n* **1** any material object (but not an animal or plant). **2** (*pl*) general conditions: *T—s are getting better.* **3** (*pl* colloq) belongings.

think *v* (*pt & pp* thought) **1** use the mind in order to form an opinion, consider a problem. **2** — highly (well, nothing, etc) of (*sb or sth*), have a high (good, low, etc) opinion of. — better of (*doing sth*), reconsider and give up.

— **sth over**, consider further before doing it, etc.

third adj & n (coming) next after the second in position, time, order, etc; one of three equal parts; ⅓. '**—ly** adv. '**third-'rate** adj of poor quality.

thirst n 1 feeling caused by a desire or need to drink; suffering through —. 2 (fig) strong desire (for knowledge, etc). v have —. '**—y** adj (-ier, -iest) having or causing —. '**—ily** adv.

'**thir'teen** adj & n 13. '**thirty** adj & n 30. '**thirtieth** adj & n 30th; ¹⁄₃₀.

this adj & pron (pl these) (contrasted with that): Look at — man over here. T— man is the tallest.

'**thistle** n wild plant with prickly leaves and yellow, white, or purple flowers. '**—down** n — seed(s).

thong n narrow strip of leather.

'**thorax** n 1 part of the body between the neck and the waist. 2 middle section of an insect's body.

thorn n 1 sharp-pointed growth on the stem of a plant. 2 shrub or bush with —s. '**—y** adj (-ier, -iest) having —s.

'**thorough** adj complete in every way; absolute; detailed. **—ly** adv. **—ness** n. **—bred** n & adj (animal, esp a horse) of pure breed. **—fare** n street or road, esp one much used by traffic.

those adj & pron (contrasted with these): Look at — men over there. T— men are the tallest.

though conj 1 = although. 2 but yet; however.

thought n 1 (power, process, way, of) thinking: lost in —. **take — for**, think about. 2 idea, opinion, intention, formed by thinking. '**—ful** adj 1 full of —; showing —. 2 thinking of, showing — for, the needs of others. '**—fully** adv. '**—less** adj 1 selfish. 2 unthinking; careless. '**—lessly** adv. '**—lessness** n.

'**thousand** n & adj 1000. **—th** n 1000th; ¹⁄₁₀₀₀.

thrash v 1 beat with a stick, a whip, etc. 2 defeat. 3 — **out** (a problem, etc), discuss thoroughly. 4 thresh. '**—ing** n beating.

thread n 1 length of spun cotton, silk, flax, etc, esp for use in sewing or weaving. 2 chain or line (of thought, etc). v 1 put — through

(a needle); put (beads, etc) on a —. 2 make (one's way) through (a crowd of people, etc) by going in and out among them. 3 spiral ridge round a screw. '**—bare** adj (of cloth, etc) worn very thin.

threat n 1 statement of an intention to punish or hurt sb, esp if he does not do as one wishes. 2 sign or warning of coming trouble or danger. '**—en** v 1 use —(s) to: —en sb with sth; — to do sth. 2 give warning of: clouds that —en rain. 3 (of sth unpleasant) seem likely: if danger —ens. **—eningly** adv.

three n & adj 3. '**—pence** n former British coin. '**—penny** adj costing —pence.

thresh v beat the grain out of (wheat, etc); beat wheat, etc.

'**threshold** n stone or plank under a doorway; (fig) entrance; start.

threw ⇨ throw.

thrice adv three times.

thrift n care, economy, in the use of money or goods. '**—y** adj (-ier, -iest).

thrill n (experience causing) excited feeling: —s of pleasure (horror). v 1 feel a — or —s. 2 cause a — or —s in. '**—er** n —ing story, esp a crime story.

thrive v (pt throve, pp 'thriven) succeed; grow strong or healthy.

throat n 1 front part of the neck. 2 passage or pipe in the neck through which food passes to the stomach and air to the lungs.

throb v (-bb-) (of the heart, pulse, etc) beat, esp more rapidly than usual. n a —bing or vibration.

throne n 1 ceremonial chair of a king, queen, bishop, etc. 2 **the T—**, the sovereign.

throng n & v crowd.

'**throttle** v seize (sb) by the throat and stop (his) breathing. n part of a motor-car that controls the flow of petrol, etc, to the engine.

through prep 1 (of places) from end to end or side to side of; entering at one side, on one surface, etc, and coming out at the other. 2 go —, examine; experience. 3 — **the night**, from the beginning to the end of. 4 because of: It happened — your stupidity. adv 1 from end to end, side to side, beginning to end: see the job —. 2 connect by telephone: Can you put me —?

—'out adv & prep in every part (of); from end to end (of).

throve ⇨ thrive.

throw v (pt threw, pp thrown) 1 cause (sth) to go through the air, usu with force, by a movement of the arm or by a machine. 2 put (articles of clothing) on, off, over, etc, quickly or carelessly. 3 move (one's arms, legs, etc) out, up, down, violently. 4 (of a horse) cause the rider to fall to the ground. 5 (with adv) — away, (esp) lose by foolishness or neglect. — oneself into (an activity), take part in with energy. — off, get rid of. — open (eg a competition), make it open to all persons. — out, make (a suggestion), give (a hint) in a casual way. — over, abandon (a plan, a friend). — up, vomit (food); resign from (a position). n —ing or being —n.

thrush n song-bird.

thrust v push suddenly or violently; make a forward stroke with a sword, etc. n act of —ing.

thud v (-dd-) & n (strike, fall, with a) dull sound as of a blow on sth soft.

thug n violent criminal.

thumb n short, thick finger set apart from the others. ⇨ p 29.

thump v strike heavily, esp with the fist(s); (of the heart) beat fast. n (sound of a) heavy blow.

'thunder n 1 loud noise heard after lightning is seen. 2 loud noise like or suggesting —. v 1 it —ed; there was —. 2 make a loud noise like —. —bolt n lightning and crash of —. —storm n storm with — and lightning and (usu) heavy rain. —struck adj amazed.

'Thursday n fifth day of the week.

thus adv in this way; so. — far, to this point.

thwart v obstruct (a person, his plans).

tick¹ n 1 light, regular sound, esp of a clock or watch. 2 small mark (often ✓) put against names, figures, etc, to show that sth is correct. v 1 (of a clock, etc) make —s(1). 2 put a —(2) against.

tick² n small insect that fastens itself on the skin and sucks blood.

'ticket n card, piece of paper, giving the holder the right to travel in a train, bus, etc, or to a seat in a theatre, etc, or showing the price of sth to be sold. v put a — on (esp sth to be sold).

'tickle v 1 excite the nerves of the skin by touching or rubbing lightly, esp at sensitive parts: — sb in the ribs. 2 have an itching feeling (as if being —d): My nose —s. 3 please (one's sense of humour or of taste). n act of tickling sb; sensation of being —d.

tide n 1 regular rise and fall in the level of the sea, caused by the attraction of the moon. 2 (fig) flow or tendency (of opinion, etc). v — over, get over, enable (sb) to get over (a period of difficulty, etc). 'tidal adj the —(s). tidal wave, great wave such as may accompany an earthquake.

'tidings n pl news.

'tidy adj (-ier, -iest) neat, orderly: a — room (person); — habits. v (often — up) make —. 'tidily adv. 'tidiness n.

tie v (pt & pp tied; present p tying: I am tying my shoe-lace) 1 fasten with string, thread, rope, etc: tie up a parcel; tie his legs together. 2 make (a knot). 3 limit the freedom of. 4 (of players, teams) make the same score. n 1 (fig) sth that holds people together: ties of friendship. 2 sth that limits one's freedom of action. 3 equal score in a game, etc. 4 = necktie.

tier n row (esp of seats), shelf, etc, esp one of a number rising in parallel lines.

'tiger n animal of Asia, yellow-skinned with black stripes. ⇨ p 317. 'tigress n female —.

tight adj (-er, -est) 1 fixed or fitting closely. 2 (of knots) not easily unfastened. 3 fully stretched: — ropes. 4 closely or firmly put together so as to occupy the smallest possible space. 5 produced by or needing pressure: a — squeeze; a — fit. 6 (in compounds, as 'air—, 'water-tight, etc) made so that air, water, etc, can neither enter nor escape. adv = —ly. '—en v (often —en up) make or become — (not loose). 'tight-'fisted adj ungenerous. '—s n pl stockings with panties, worn by women acrobats, dancers, etc. '—ly adv. '—ness n.

tile n square or oblong plate(2) of

baked clay for covering roofs, walls, etc.

till[1] ⇨ until.

till[2] *n* drawer in a cash-register.

till[3] *v* cultivate (land). '**—er** *n.*

'**tiller** *n* handle fixed to the rudder of a small boat.

tilt *v* (cause to) have a sloping position: *T— the barrel up* (to empty it); *The table —ed.* *n* 1 sloping position. 2 **(at) full —,** at full speed and with great force.

'**timber** *n* 1 wood prepared for use in a building, etc. 2 beam forming a support (eg in a roof).

time *n* 1 all the days of the past, present and future; passing of all the days, weeks, years, etc, taken as a whole; portion or measurement of —; point of — stated in hours and minutes. 2 (phrases) **in —,** early enough; after a period of — **in the future. in good —,** early. **at one —,** during a period of past —. **from — to —,** occasionally. **at the same —,** (esp) yet; even if that is true. **— and (—) again,** repeatedly. 3 (*pl*) multiplied by. 4 (often *pl*) period of — associated with sth or sb: *in ancient —s; the —(s)* (of the Pharaohs. 5 (music) (measurement of the) rhythmic beats, speed at which music is played. **beat —,** show the rhythm by movements of the hand, etc. *v* 1 choose, arrange, or decide, the — for (sth to happen). 2 measure the — taken by or for (sth). '**—ly** *adj* coming, happening, at the right —, when needed, etc. '**—table** *n* (book or chart with) list of —s, eg arrivals and departures of trains, ships, etc.

'**timid** *adj* easily frightened. **—ly** *adv.* **ti'midity** *n* '**timorous** *adj* = timid.

tin *n* 1 soft, white metal used for coating iron sheets. 2 tin-plate container (*can*) for food, etc, esp one sealed so as to be airtight. *v* (-nn-) esp pack (food, etc) in tins(2).

tinge *v* 1 colour slightly (*with* red, etc). 2 affect slightly. *n* slight colouring or mixture (*of*).

'**tingle** *v & n* (have a) pricking or stinging feeling in the skin.

'**tinker** *v* — *with,* — *away at* (*sth*), (try to) do repairs without expert knowledge.

'**tinkle** *v* (cause to) make a succession of slight ringing sounds (eg of a small bell). *n* such sounds.

tint *n* (esp pale) shade or variety of colour. *v* give a — to.

'**tiny** *adj* (-ier, -iest) very small.

tip[1] *n* 1 pointed or thin end of sth: *the tips of your fingers.* 2 small piece put on the end of sth. '**tiptoe** *v & n* (walk quietly, be, on) the toes: *tiptoe out of the room; on tiptoe.*

tip[2] *v* (-pp-) 1 (often *tip up, over*) (cause to) lean or slant, rise on one side or at one end; (cause to) overturn. 2 empty (the contents of sth) *out* (*of*) or *in(to)* by tipping.

tip[3] *v* (-pp-) 1 touch or strike gently. 2 give a tip(1),(2) to (see the *n* below): *tip the porter five pence.* *n* 1 gift of money to a porter, waiter, etc, for personal services. 2 useful (often secret) information given in confidence. 3 light blow; tap.

'**tipsy** *adj* (-ier, -iest) intoxicated.

'**tiptoe** ⇨ tip[1].

tire[1] *n* ⇨ tyre.

tire[2] *v* make or become weary, in need of rest, or uninterested. '**—d** *adj* weary in body or mind. **—d out,** exhausted. '**—less** *adj* not easily —d; ceaseless: *—less energy.* '**—some** *adj* troublesome.

'**tissue** *n* 1 any fine woven fabric. 2 substance such as skin or muscle, forming part of an animal or plant. 3 soft paper handkerchief. '**tissue-paper** *n* thin soft wrapping paper.

'**tit for 'tat** *phrase* (usu fig) blow[2] in exchange for blow[2].

'**titbit** *n* choice and attractive bit (*of* food, etc).

'**title** *n* 1 name of a book, poem, picture, etc. 2 word used to show a person's rank (eg *Prince*) or occupation (eg *Professor*). 3 (law) right to the possession of property. '**title-deed** *n* document giving sb a —(3). '**title-page** *n* page at the front of a book, giving its —(1), the author's name, etc.

to *prep* 1 in the direction of; towards. 2 *give* (sth) *to* (sb): 3 indicating comparison: *I prefer walking to climbing.* *adv* 1 towards or in the usual or required position, esp a closed position: *Please, push the door to.* 2 **to and fro,** backwards and forwards.

292 toad | toot

toad *n* frog-like animal that lives on land.

toast[1] *n* sliced bread heated till brown and crisp. *v* **1** make —. **2** warm (one's body) before a fire.

toast[2] *v* wish happiness, success, etc, to (sb or sth) with a raised glass of wine. *n* act of —ing; person, etc, —ed: *She is the — of New York.*

to'bacco *n* (plant having) leaves (to be) dried and used for smoking (in pipes, cigarettes, etc). **—nist** *n* shopkeeper who sells —.

to'boggan *n* long, narrow sledge for sporting purposes. *v* go down a snow- or ice-covered slope on a —.

to'day *adv & n* (on) this day; (at) this present period; now.

toe *n* **1** one of the five divisions of the front part of the foot ⇨ p 29; similar part in an animal's foot. **2** part of a sock, shoe, etc, covering the toes. *v* touch, reach, with the toes.

'toffee *n* (piece of) hard, brown sticky sweet.

to'gether *adv* (opposite of *separately*) in company; one with another (at the same time). **— with**, as well as.

toil *v* **1** work hard (*at* a task). **2** move with difficulty (*up, along, through* sth). *n* hard work.

'toilet *n* **1** process of washing, dressing, arranging the hair, etc. **2** (as *adj*) of or for the —: *— soap.* **3** lavatory.

'token *n* sign, evidence, or guarantee (of sth). **in — of**, in order to show.

'tolerate *v* allow or endure without protest. **'tolerable** *adj* **1** that can be —d. **2** fairly good. **'tolerance** *n* quality of tolerating opinions, customs, etc, different from one's own. **'tolerant** *adj* having or showing tolerance. **,tole'ration** *n* tolerance, esp in religious questions.

toll[1] *n* **1** payment required or made for the use of a road, bridge, harbour, etc. **2** take — of, take or destroy a part of. **'toll-bar, 'toll-gate** *n* one at which a —(1) must be paid.

toll[2] *v* **1** (of a bell) ring with slow, regular strokes. **2** cause (a bell) to ring in this way. *n* sound made by the —ing of a bell.

'tomahawk *n* light axe used as a tool and weapon by N American Indians.

to'mato *n* (*pl* to'matoes) (plant with) soft, juicy, red or yellow fruit eaten raw or cooked. ⇨ p 306.

tomb *n* place dug in the ground, cut out of rock, etc, for a dead body.

to'morrow *adv & n* (on the) day after today.

ton *n* **1** measure of weight (2240 lb in Gr Brit, 2000 lb in USA). **2** (colloq) **tons of** (*money*, etc), a great quantity of.

tone *n* **1** sound, esp with reference to its quality: *speak in angry —s.* **2** (contrasted with *stress*) rise or fall of the voice in speaking. **3** shade (of colour), degree (of light). **4** (music) (— or *half-tone*) interval between one note of a scale and the next. *v* **1** give a particular —(3) of sound or colour to. **2** (esp of colours) be in harmony (*with*). **'—less** *adj* dull; lifeless: *a —less voice.*

tongs *n pl* (often *a pair of* —) tool for lifting and holding (a piece of coal, a lump of sugar, etc).

tongue *n* **1** movable organ(1) in the mouth, used in talking, tasting, and licking. **hold one's —**, be silent. **2** language: *our mother —, our native language.* **3** sth like a —: *the — of a bell; —s of flame.*

'tonic *n* sth (esp medicine) that gives renewed strength or (fig) encouragement: *a bottle of —.*

to'night *adv & n* (on) this (coming) night.

'tonnage *n* **1** weight of cargo that can be carried, stated in tons. **2** total —(1) of a country's merchant shipping.

too *adv* also; in addition; moreover; in a higher degree than is wanted: *too big.*

took ⇨ take.

tool *n* **1** implement held in the hand(s) and used by workmen, eg gardeners, carpenters, builders. **2** machine-tool, one operated by power, used in making machinery.

toot *v & n* (make a) short sharp (warning) sound from a whistle, hooter, etc.

some tools

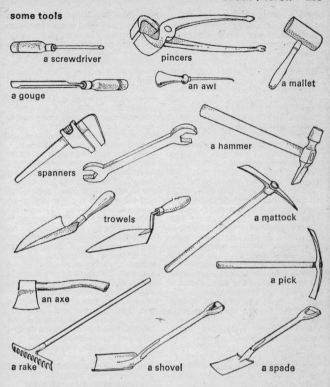

a screwdriver

pincers

a gouge

an awl

a mallet

spanners

a hammer

trowels

a mattock

a pick

an axe

a rake

a shovel

a spade

tooth *n* (*pl* teeth) **1** each of the small white bony structures rooted in the jaws. **fight — and nail**, fight bitterly. **2** tooth-like part, esp of a comb, saw, or rake. **'—ache** *n*.

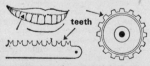

teeth

top¹ *n* **1** highest part or point. **2** utmost degree; fullest capacity. **at the top of one's voice**, as loudly as possible. **3** (as *adj*) of or at the top: *at top speed*. *v* (-pp-) **1** provide a top for; be a top to.

2 reach the top of; be at the top of. **3** cut the top(s) off (eg plants). **'topcoat** *n* overcoat. **'top-'heavy** *adj* too heavy at the top; badly-balanced. **'topmost** *adj* highest.

top² *n* toy that spins and balances on a point. **sleep like a top**, sleep soundly.

'topic *n* subject for discussion. **—al** *adj* of present interest.

'topple *v* (cause to) be unsteady and overturn.

'topsy'turvy *adj* upside-down; in confusion.

torch *n* **1** piece of wood treated with oil, etc, used as a flaming light; (fig) sth that gives enlightenment: *the — of learning*. **2** electric hand-light and battery.

tore ⇨ tear¹.

'**torment** n (cause of) severe suffering. '**torment** v cause — to.

torn ⇨ tear¹.

tor'nado n (pl -es) hurricane; violent whirlwind.

tor'pedo n (pl -es) long self-propelling shell, filled with explosive, discharged to travel below the surface of the sea and aimed at ships. v strike, damage, sink, with a —. **tor'pedo-boat** n small, fast warship from which —es are fired.

'**torrent** n violent rushing stream: rain falling in —s; a — of angry words. **tor'rential** adj of, like, caused by, a —.

'**torrid** adj (of the weather, a country) very hot; tropical.

'**tortoise** n slow-moving four-legged reptile with a hard shell. ⇨ p 233.

'**tortuous** adj full of twists and bends; (fig) not straightforward.

'**torture** v & n (cause) severe pain (to): suffer — from toothache; — sb to make him confess. —r n.

'**Tory** n = Conservative.

toss v 1 (cause to) move restlessly from side to side or up and down. 2 throw up into or through the air. 3 — one's head, jerk it up and back (to suggest contempt, etc). n 1 —ing movement. 2 win (lose) the '—, guess rightly (wrongly) when a coin is —ed up to decide sth.

'**total** adj & n (complete or entire) sum or amount. v (-ll-) find the — of; reach the — of; amount to. —ly adv completely.

'**totali'tarian** adj. — State, one in which only one political party, with complete power, is allowed.

'**totter** v 1 walk with weak, unsteady steps. 2 be almost falling.

touch v 1 (cause to) be in contact with; put (a finger, hand, etc) on or against (3). 2 affect a person or his interests; concern: The sad story —ed our hearts. 3 —down, (of a spacecraft) return to earth by landing on the ground. —(up)on, refer to (a subject, etc). —up, make small changes in (a picture, etc) to improve it. n 1 act or fact of —ing. 2 (sense giving) feeling by —ing: soft to the —. 3 stroke made with a pen, brush, etc. 4 slight quantity, trace (of sth). 5 in — (with),

receiving letters from, meeting, having news of. '**touch-and-go** adj of uncertain outcome. '—ing adj arousing sympathy. prep concerning. '—y adj (-ier, -iest) easily or quickly offended.

tough adj (-er, -est) 1 (of meat) hard to cut or to get one's teeth into. 2 not easily cut, broken, or worn out. 3 strong; able to endure hardships: — soldiers. 4 (of work, etc) difficult. n rough and violent man. '—en v make or become —.

tour n journey out and home again during which various places are visited. v make a — (of). '—ist n person making a — for pleasure.

'**tournament** n series of games between a number of players.

tow v pull (a ship, boat, motor-car, etc) along by a rope or chain. n towing or being towed: (have (take) a boat, etc). in tow, have charge of it, be towing it.

to'ward(s) prep 1 in the direction of; approaching. 2 near. 3 for the purpose of helping. 4 as regards; in relation to.

'**towel** n cloth for drying (oneself) after washing.

'**tower** n tall, strong building; part of a building much taller than the rest, esp as part of a castle or church. v rise to a great height, be very tall, esp in relation to the height of the surroundings.

town n 1 place (bigger than a village) where people live in large numbers. 2 the people of a —. 3 business, shopping, etc, part of a — (contrasted with the suburbs, etc). 4 — hall, building, offices, etc, for local government and public events.

toy n child's plaything. v toy with, handle (sth) without thinking about it; think not very seriously about (sth).

trace v 1 outline; mark out. 2 copy (sth) by drawing on transparent paper the lines, etc, on (a map, design, etc) placed underneath. 3 follow or discover (sb or sth) by observing marks, bits of evidence, etc. n 1 mark, sign, etc, showing that sb or sth has been present, that sth has existed or happened. 2 small, least possible, amount (of). '**tracing** n copy (of a map, etc) made by tracing (2).

track *n* **1** line or series of marks left by a cart, person, animal, etc, in passing along: *cart-tracks*; *the — of a storm.* **on the — of**, in pursuit of. **2** path made by frequent use. **3** set of rails for trains, etc. **4** prepared path for racing. **— events**, athletic events (*running*, etc) for a cinder —. *v* follow (*an animal*, etc), guided by —s(1).

tract[1] *n* stretch or area (*of forest*, farmland, etc).

tract[2] *n* short, printed piece of writing, esp on a moral or religious subject.

'tractable *adj* easily controlled.

'tractor *n* motor-vehicle as used for pulling ploughs.

trade *n* **1** buying, selling, and exchange of goods: *the cotton —.* **— wind**, strong wind blowing always towards the equator from SE and NE. **2** way of making a living, esp a handicraft: *He's a carpenter by —.* **3** the people, organizations, etc, engaged in a —. **— 'union**, organized association of workers in a — or group of —s, formed to protect their interests, improve their conditions, etc. **'—mark**, design, special name, etc, used to distinguish a manufacturer's goods. *v* **1** engage in —(1). **2** — (up)on, take a wrong advantage of, use (sth) in order to get sth. **'—r** *n* merchant. **'—sman** *n* shopkeeper.

tra'dition *n* (handing down from generation to generation of) beliefs, customs, etc; such a belief, etc, handed down from the past. **—al** *adj*.

'traffic *n* **1** movement of people and vehicles along streets and roads. **2** transport business done by a railway, steamship line, etc. **3** trading: *illegal — in drugs.* *v* (*pt & pp* **'trafficked**) — **in**, trade in.

'tragedy *n* **1** play for the theatre, branch of the drama, of a serious and solemn kind, usu with a sad ending. **2** sad event or experience in real life. **'tragic** *adj* of —(1); very sad. **'tragically** *adv*.

trail *n* **1** line, mark(s), traces, footprints, left by sb or sth in passing by: *a — of smoke*; *The storm left a* — *of destruction.* **2** track or scent followed in hunting: *hot on the —*, close behind. **3** path through rough country. *v* **1** pull or be pulled along behind. **2** (of plants) grow *along, over*, etc. **3** walk wearily *along*, etc. **'—er** *n* vehicle (eg a small cart, a caravan(2) —ed(1) by another.

train *v* **1** teach and exercise (a soldier, animal, child) up to a required standard or for a certain purpose: *— children to be good citizens.* **2** cause (a plant) to grow in a certain direction. **3** **— a gun (up)on**, aim it at. *n* **1** (engine and a) number of railway coaches, wagons, etc, joined together. **2** company of persons, animals, carriages, etc, moving in a line. **3** chain or series (*of ideas, events*). **'—er** *n* person who —s(1) (athletes, animals, etc). **'—ing** *n.* **'—ing college**, one for —ing teachers. **in (out of) —ing**, in (not in) good physical condition.

trait *n* distinguishing quality or characteristic.

'traitor *n* person who betrays a friend, is disloyal to his country or to a cause, etc. **—ous** *adj*.

tram *n* (also **—car**) car of an electric railway running (usu) along public roads or streets. **'—line**, **'—way** *n* line of rails for —s.

a tram

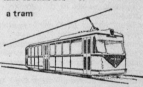

tramp *v* **1** walk with heavy steps. **2** walk (esp a long distance); walk through or over: *— the hills.* *n* **1** sound of heavy footsteps. **2** long walk. **3** person (usu homeless) who walks from place to place and does no regular work. **4** cargo boat that goes to any port for cargo.

'trample *v* tread heavily on; crush under the feet: *— the grass down.*

trance *n* sleep-like condition.

'tranquil *adj* calm; quiet. **—ly** *adv*. **tran'quillity** *n*.

trans- *prefix* across; on or to the other side of: *trans-Atlantic.*

tran'sact v do (business). **—ion** n (—ing of a) piece of business.

tran'scend v be or go beyond or outside the range of (normal experience, etc).

trans'cribe v copy in writing. **trans'cription** n transcribing; sth **—d**.

trans'fer v (-rr-) **1** change position. **2** move or take (sb or sth) *from . . . to*. **3** hand over (property, etc) to. **'transfer** n **—ring**; document **—ring** sb or sth.

trans'fix v pierce (with sth pointed); (fig) cause (sb) to be unable to move, think, etc.

trans'form v change the shape, appearance, quality, or nature of. ,**transfor'mation** n. **—er** n (esp) apparatus that **—s** electric current (from one voltage to another).

trans'fusion n transferring(2), esp of blood from one living person to another.

trans'gress v **1** go beyond (a limit); break (a law, etc). **2** do wrong; sin. **—ion** n. **—or** n wrongdoer.

'transient adj brief (in time).

tran'sistor n **1** tiny electronic device to amplify electric currents. **2** radio set with **—s**.

'transit n (lost, delayed) in **—**, while being taken from one place to another.

tran'sition n change from one condition or set of circumstances to another.

'transitive adj In *'Tom is fighting John'*, the verb is **—**.

trans'late v give the meaning of (sth said or written) in another language. **trans'lation** n act of translating; sth **—d**.

trans'lucent adj allowing light to pass through, but not transparent.

trans'mit v (-tt-) **1** pass or hand on. **2** let through or along: *iron* **—s** *heat*.

trans'parent adj **1** that can be seen through, like clear glass. **2** (fig) unmistakable; undoubted; easily understood.

trans'plant v **1** take up (plants, etc) with their roots and plant them elsewhere. **2** (surgery) transfer living tissue(2) or an organ(1) from one body to another: — *a kidney (heart)*. **'transplant** n sth **—d**; operation(4) to **—sth**: *a kidney (heart)* **—.**

trans'port v carry (persons, goods) from one place to another. **'transport** n **1 —ing**(1). **2** ship for carrying soldiers.

trans'pose v cause (two or more things) to change places. **'transverse** adj lying or placed across.

trap n **1** device for catching animals, etc. **2** plan or trick for making sb say or do sth he does not wish to say or do. v (-pp-) catch in a **—**; capture by a trick. **'—per** n man who **—s** animals for their skins.

trash n worthless thing or writing.

'travel v (-ll-) **1** make (esp long) journeys. **2** move: *Light —s faster than sound*. n **1 —ling. 2** (pl) journeys, esp to other countries. **—ler** n.

'travesty n copy or description that, often on purpose, gives a false or ridiculous idea (of sth or sb). v make or be a **—** of.

trawl v & n (to fish with a) wide-mouthed net pulled along the sea-bottom. **'—er** n boat used in **—ing**.

tray n flat piece of wood, metal, etc, with raised edges, on which to carry or stand light things: *a tea-tray*.

'treacherous adj **1** false or disloyal (to a friend, etc). **2** deceptive; not to be relied on. **'trea,chery** n.

'treacle n thick, sticky liquid produced while sugar is being refined.

tread v (pt. trod, pp 'trodden) **1** walk, put the foot or feet down (on). **2** crush, push in, down, etc, with the feet. **3** make (a path) by walking. n way or sound of walking: *walk with a heavy* **—.**

'treadle n part that drives a machine and is worked by pressure of the foot or feet.

'treason n treachery to one's ruler or government; disloyalty. **—able** adj having the nature of **—.**

'treasure n (store of) gold and silver, jewels, etc) wealth; highly valued object or person. v **1** store *up* for future use; keep; remember. **2** value highly. **—r** n person in charge of money, etc, belonging to a society, etc. **'treasury** n **1** British government department which controls the State's money. **2** place where **—s** are kept. **3** money or funds of a society, organization, etc.

treat v **1** act or behave towards: — sb kindly. **2** consider: — sth as a joke. **3** discuss; deal with. **4** (of a lecture, a book) — of, be about. **5** give medical or surgical care to (sb, a disease). **6** put (a substance) through a process (in manufacture, etc). **7** — sb to sth, supply him with (food, drink, etc) at one's own expense. **8** discuss or arrange terms with. n pleasure, esp sth not often enjoyed. '—ise n book, etc, that deals carefully with a subject. '—ment n (way of) —ing sb or sth.

treaty n agreement made and signed between nations: a trade —.

treble¹ v & adj (make or become) three times as much.

treble² n (boy's voice, instrument, that takes) the highest part in music. adj of or for the —.

tree n **1** large plant from which we get wood. **2** family-tree, diagram showing a family's ancestry.

trek v & n (-kk-) (go on a) long journey.

tremble v shake (with fear, anger, cold, etc); be agitated or worried. n a trembling.

tre'mendous adj very great; enormous.

tremor n shaking or trembling.

trench n ditch dug in the ground (eg for draining off water).

trend n general direction; tendency. v have a certain —.

trepi'lation n alarm.

trespass v — (up)on, go on private land without right or permission; (fig) encroach upon (sb's time, etc). n act of —ing.

tress n portion of hair on the head.

tri- prefix three: triangle.

trial n **1** testing; test: give sth a —, use it to learn whether it is good, useful, etc. on —, being tested. **2** sth or sb troublesome or annoying. **3** inquiry or examination before a judge: on — for theft.

triangle n plane figure with three sides. ⇨ p 253. **tri'angular** adj **1** in the shape of a —. **2** in which three persons, etc, take part.

tribe n racial group, esp one united by language and customs, living as a community under one or more chiefs. '**tribal** adj.

tribu'lation n (cause of) great grief.

tri'bunal n place of judgement; judges with special duties.

tribute n **1** (usu regular) payment which one government or ruler forces another to make. **2** sth done, said, or given to show respect, etc. '**tributary** n & adj (river) flowing into another; (country, ruler, etc) paying —(1) to another.

trice n in a —, in an instant.

trick n **1** sth done in order to deceive, to outwit, sb; sth done in order to make a person appear ridiculous: play a — on sb. **2** action, usu needing skill or practice, done to deceive and amuse people: card —s. v deceive by a —: — sb into believing sth. '—ery n deception; cheating. **-y** adj (-ier, -iest) **1** deceptive. **2** (of work, etc) requiring skill or patience because it is full of hidden difficulties.

trickle v (of liquids) (cause to) flow in drops or in a thin stream. n weak or thin flow.

tricycle n three-wheeled cycle.

tried ⇨ try.

tri'ennial adj lasting for, happening or done every, three years.

trifle n **1** thing, event, of little value or importance. **2** small amount (esp of money). **3** a — (longer, etc), a little. v **1** talk or act lightly, without serious purpose. **2** — with, play with (eg aimlessly with the fingers). '**trifling** adj small and unimportant.

trigger n lever for releasing a spring, esp to fire a pistol, gun, etc.

trigo'nometry n branch of mathematics that deals with the relations between the sides and angles of triangles.

trim adj (-mer, -mest) in good order; neat and tidy. v (-mm-) **1** make —, esp by taking or cutting away uneven or irregular parts: — one's beard. **2** decorate or ornament (a hat, dress, etc). n in — for, prepared for. '—ming n (esp) material (eg lace, ribbon) for —ming dresses or hats.

trinity n group of three. **the T—**, God in three persons.

trio n group of three; (musical composition for a) group of three singers or players.

trip v (-pp-) **1** run with quick light steps. **2** (cause to) stumble; (almost) fall after striking the foot on sth. **3** (often — up) (cause to) make a mistake. n **1** short journey, esp for pleasure. **2** a fall or stumble. '—per *n* sb who takes a —(1).

'**triple** *adj* made up of three parts or persons. *v* make, become, be, three times as much or as many.

'**triplet** *n* one of three children born together of the same mother.

'**tripod** *n* three-legged support (eg for a camera).

trite *adj* (-r, -st) (of ideas, etc) commonplace; not new. '—ly *adv*.

'**triumph** *n* (joy or satisfaction at) success or victory. *v* win a victory *over*; exult *over*. **tri'umphant** *adj* (rejoicing at) having —ed.

'**trivial** *adj* of small value or importance. ,**trivi'ality** *n* — thing, idea, etc.

trod(den) ⇨ tread.

'**trolley** *n* **1** two- or four-wheeled handcart. **2** small, low truck running on rails. **3** connecting wheel between a tramcar or bus (*trolley-bus*) and overhead power lines.

trom'bone *n* large brass musical instrument. ⇨ p 180.

troop *n* **1** group of persons or animals, esp when moving: —*s of children.* **2** unit of cavalry. **3** (*pl*) soldiers. *v* come or go together in a group. '—er *n* soldier in a cavalry regiment. '—ship *n* ship to carry soldiers.

'**trophy** *n* sth kept as a reminder of a victory or success (eg in sport).

'**tropic** *n* **1** certain line of latitude north (**T— of Cancer**) or south (**T— of Capricorn**) of the equator. **2** the —s, area of the world between these lines. —**al** *adj* of, or as of, the —s: —*al weather.*

trot *v* (-tt-) (of horses, etc) go at a pace between a walk and a gallop; (of persons) run with short steps. *n* **1** —ting pace: *at a steady* —. **2** period of —ting: *go for a* —.

'**trouble** *v* **1** cause worry, discomfort, anxiety, or inconvenience to. **2** *May I* — *you (for sth, to do sth)?* Will you please (give me, do sth)? **3** give oneself worry or inconvenience: *Don't* — *about that.* *n* **1** (person or happening causing) worry, anxiety, discomfort, unhappiness, possible punishment, etc. **get into** —, do, have done, sth, bringing, or likely to bring, —. **2** extra work; effort; difficulty. **take** — (*to do sth, with* or *over sth*), use great care. '—**some** *adj* causing —; needing much care.

trough *n* long, open box for animals to feed or drink from.

'**trousers** *n pl* (often *a pair of* —) long outer garment for the legs.

'**trousseau** *n* outfit of clothing, etc, for a woman on marrying.

'**trowel** *n* **1** flat-bladed tool for spreading mortar on bricks, plaster on walls, etc. **2** tool with a curved blade for lifting plants. ⇨ p 293.

troy *n* British system of weights, used for gold and silver, in which 1 pound = 12 ounces.

'**truant** *n* child who stays away from school without good reason. **play** —, **be a** —.

truce *n* (agreement for) the stopping of fighting for a time.

truck *n* **1** open railway wagon for heavy goods (eg coal). **2** porter's barrow. **3** (USA) lorry.

'**truculent** *adj* looking for, desiring, a fight. —**ly** *adv*. '**truculence** *n*.

trudge *v* walk wearily or heavily.

true *adj* (-r, -st) **1** in accordance or agreement with fact. **come** —, (of a hope or dream) become fact, happen. **2** loyal or faithful (*to*). **3** genuine. **4** correct: *a* — *copy.* '**truly** *adv* **1** sincerely. **2** truthfully. **3** certainly; genuinely.

'**trumpet** *n* **1** musical instrument of brass. ⇨ p 180. **blow one's own** —, praise oneself. **2** elephant's cry.

trun'cate *v* shorten by cutting off the top or end.

truncheon *n* short, thick club (eg one used by the police).

'**trundle** *v* (of sth heavy or awkward in shape) roll along.

trunk *n* **1** main stem of a tree. **2** body without head, arms, or legs. **3** large box for holding one's belongings. **4** long nose of an elephant. ⇨ p 317. **5** (as *adj*) — **call**, telephone call on a long-distance line (a *trunk-line*).

trust *n* **1** confidence; strong belief in the goodness, strength, or reliability of sth or sb. **on** —, without proof; on credit(5). **2** person or thing confided in. **3** responsibility: *a position of great* —. **4** (law) property held and managed by one or more persons (*trustees*) for another's benefit. **5** association of business firms to achieve some special object. *v* **1** have —(1) *in.* **2** give (sth) into the care of (sb): — *your affairs to me.* **3** hope.

'**—ful** *adj* ready to — others; not suspicious. '**—ing** *adj* having or showing —(1). '**—worthy** *adj* reliable; dependable.

truth *n* **1** quality or state of being true. **2** that which is true. **3** fact; belief, etc, accepted as true. '**—ful** *adj* **1** (of persons) always telling the —. **2** (of statements) true. '**—fully** *adv*.

try *v* (*pt & pp* tried) **1** attempt to do sth, get sth, etc, in order to learn whether one can do it, etc. **2** try for, make an attempt to get (esp a position). **3** use sth, do sth, as an experiment or test, to see whether it is satisfactory. **try sth on**, put on (eg a coat) to see whether it fits well, etc. **4** inquire into (a case) in a law court. **5** cause annoyance (to); strain: *try sb's patience.* *n* attempt. '**trying** *adj* causing trouble; difficult to endure.

'**tsetse** *n* (in tropical Africa) fly whose bite causes a fatal disease in cattle, etc. ⇨ p 144.

tub *n* **1** large open vessel, usu round and made of wood. **2** (colloq) bath.

tube *n* **1** pipe, esp of glass or rubber. **2** soft metal container with a screw-cap, used for tooth-paste, etc. **3** underground railway (in London). '**tubing** *n* length of —.

tuber *n* swollen, underground root from which a new plant will grow (eg *potato, yam*).

tuberculosis *n* (colloq TB) serious disease affecting various parts of the body's tissues, esp the lungs.

tuck *n* flat stitched-down fold of material in a garment for shorten-ing or ornament. *v* **1** roll, fold, or push (esp part of one's clothing) into a more convenient or secure position. **2** sb up (in), cover warmly by pulling bedclothes over or round, etc.

Tuesday *n* third day of the week.

tuft *n* bunch of hairs, bristles, grass, etc, growing closely, or held firmly, together at one end.

tug *v* (-gg-) pull hard or violently (*at*). *n* **1** sudden or violent pull. **2** small, powerful steamboat for towing ships, etc.

tu'ition *n* (fee for) teaching.

tumble *v & n* fall, esp quickly and violently.

'**tumult** *n* **1** uproar; disturbance. **2** mental excitement. **tu'multu-ous** *adj* disorderly; violent.

tune *n* **1** succession of notes of which a song, hymn, etc, is com-posed. **2** (*sing, play*) **in** —, so that the notes are correct in pitch. *v* **1** adjust (a piano, etc) so that the notes are at the right pitch. **2** — **in**, adjust a radio receiver to get the required programme. '**—ful** *adj* having a pleasing —.

'**tunic** *n* military-style jacket.

'**tunnel** *v* (-ll-) *& n* (make an) underground passage, through a hill, etc, esp for a railway.

'**turban** *n* head-dress formed of a long strip of cloth wound about the head.

'**turbine** *n* engine or motor whose driving-wheel is turned by a strong current of water, steam, or air.

'**turbulent** *adj* violent; uncon-trolled.

turf *n* **1** surface of the soil with grass roots growing in it; piece of this cut out. **2** the —, horse-racing.

'**turkey** *n* large bird used as food. ⇨ p 211.

'**turmoil** *n* noise; confusion.

turn *v* **1** (cause to) move round a point; (cause to) move so as to face in a different direction. **2** (with *adv & prep*) — **down**, reject (an offer, the person making it). — **in**, (colloq) go to bed. — **off (on)**, stop (start) a radio or TV (trans-mission), a tap, etc. — **out**, stop the flow of by —ing a tap; switch off a light; force sb to leave a room, etc; produce (goods); empty (eg drawers, one's pockets, to look for sth); become, develop into: *The day —ed out wet.* — **up**, (of persons) arrive; (of objects) be found, esp by chance. **3** (cause to) change in nature, quality, etc: *His hair is —ing grey.* **4** reach and pass (a certain time, age, etc). **6** (with nouns) — **the corner**, (fig) pass a crisis successfully. — **sb's head**, make him too vain. — **one's hand to anything**, be able to do any kind of job. — **one's stomach**, make one (want to) vomit. *n* **1** —ing movement. **2** change of direction. **3** change in condition. **4** occasion or oppor-tunity for doing sth, esp in one's proper order among others: *wait* (*until it is*) one's —. in —, — and — about, (of two persons) one first and then the other. out of —, before or after the right or regular time. 5 short period of activity: take a — at the oars. 6 act performed by one person or group of persons in an entertainment: *a comic* —. 7 (do sb) a good (bad) —, a kind (an unkind) act. 'turnout *n* act of emptying sth (eg a room) out; that which is moved out; general appearance of a person's equipment. '—over *n* amount of business done (usu within a named period of time). '—stile *n* revolving gate that admits only one person at a time.

'turnip *n* (plant with a) large round root used as a vegetable. ⇨ p 306.

'turpentine *n* oil obtained from certain trees, used for mixing paint.

'turquoise *n* (colour of a) greenish-blue precious stone.

'turret *n* 1 small tower, usu at the corner of a building. 2 steel structure to cover guns in warships, tanks, etc, often able to revolve.

'turtle *n* sea reptile with a soft body protected by a hard shell. ⇨ p 233. turn —, (of a ship) capsize.

tusk *n* long, pointed tooth as in the elephant or walrus. ⇨ pp 247, 317.

'tussle *v & n* (have a) hard fight or struggle (*with*).

'tutor *n* 1 (private) teacher. 2 university teacher. *v* act as — (to sb).

tweak *v & n* pinch and twist.

tweed *n* thick, soft woollen cloth, usu woven of mixed colours.

'tweezers *n pl* small pair of pincers for use with very small things.

twelve *n & adj* 12. twelfth *n & adj* 12th, ½.

'twenty *n & adj* 20. 'twentieth *n & adj* 20th, ⅟₂₀.

twice *adv* two times.

'twiddle *v* twist or turn aimlessly.

twig *n* small branch.

'twilight *n* faint half-light before sunrise or after sunset.

twin *n* either of two children born together of the same mother; (as *adj*) either of two (having) two.

twine *n* thin string. *v* twist; wind.

twinge *n* sudden, sharp pain.

'twinkle *v* shine with an unsteady light. *n* twinkling light.

twirl *v* (cause to) rotate.

twist *v* 1 wind or turn (a number

of threads, etc) one around another. 2 turn the two ends of sth in opposite directions; turn one end of sth. 3 (eg of a road) turn and curve in various directions. *n* —ing or being —ed; —ed place in sth; sth made by —ing.

twitch *n* sudden, quick pull or nervous movement. *v* make a —.

'twitter *v* (of birds) make a succession of soft, short sounds. *n* such sounds.

two *n & adj* 2. '—pence *n* coin worth two pence (2p). '—penny *adj* costing —pence.

ty'coon *n* powerful capitalist.

type *n* 1 person, thing, event, etc, considered as an example of its class or group. 2 class or group considered to have common characteristics. 3 letters, etc, cast in small metal blocks for use in printing. *v* use a —writer. '—writer *n* machine with which one prints letters on paper, by pressing keys with the fingers. '—written *adj* printed with a —writer. 'typist *n* person who —s, esp for a living.

'typhoid *n* (often — *fever*) serious disease which attacks the bowels.

ty'phoon *n* violent storm.

'typical *adj* serving as a type(1). 'typically *adv*. 'typify *v* be a symbol of.

'tyrant *n* cruel or unjust ruler. ty'rannical, 'tyrannous *adj* acting like a —; of a —. 'tyranny *n* cruel and unjust use of power; government by a —.

tyre *n* (in USA tire) band, usu made of rubber, round the rim of a wheel.

'tzetze ⇨ tsetse.

U

'udder *n* part of a cow, goat, etc, from which milk comes. ⇨ p 84.

'ugly *adj* (-ier, -iest) 1 (opp of *beautiful*) unpleasant to look at. 2 threatening (2).

'ulcer *n* open sore filled with pus.

ul'terior *adj* situated beyond; beyond what is first seen or said. — motives, motives other than those expressed.

'ultimate *adj* last; furthest; basic.

,ulti'matum n final demand accompanied by a threat (of war, etc).

ultra- prefix beyond what is reasonable, natural, or usual: *ultramodern*.

'umbrage n take — (at), feel that one has been treated without proper respect, unfairly, etc.

um'brella n folding frame, covered with cloth and held by a stick in the hand to shelter one from the rain or sun.

umpire n person chosen or asked to act as a judge in a dispute or to see that the rules of a game, race, etc, are kept. v act as — in.

un- prefix 1 (before adj, adv) not: *uncertain(ly)*. 2 (before v) do the opposite of; reverse the action of what is indicated by the verb: *undress*; *unscrew*; *untie*. 3 (before n) indicating the absence of: *uncertainty*; *unwillingness*.

u'nanimous adj 1 in complete agreement. 2 all holding the same opinion. —ly adv. ,una'nimity n complete agreement or unity.

unas'suming adj not drawing attention to oneself; modest.

una'wares adv by surprise: *be caught (taken) — by a storm*.

un'balanced adj (esp of a person, his mind) not quite sane.

un'burden v — oneself, get relief by telling one's troubles (*to sb*).

un'called-for adj neither desirable nor necessary.

un'canny adj mysterious; unnatural.

uncle n brother of one's father or mother; husband of one's aunt.

un'couth adj (of persons, their behaviour) awkward; rough; uncultured.

under prep in or to a position lower than; in or covered by; less than. adv in or to a low place. — age, not yet 18 (in Gt Brit); under the required age for sth. — discussion (fire), being discussed (fired at). — orders, having received orders, been ordered (*to do* sth).

under- prefix 1 (before n) worn or placed under or below: *—clothes*; *—carriage* (esp, aircraft's landing gear). 2 (before v) not so much as is reasonable or necessary: *—charge*; *—fed*.

undercurrent n (fig) tendency (of thought or feeling) lying below what is first seen.

,under'cut v offer (goods, services) at a lower price than competitors.

'underdog n weak person in a state of inferiority; person likely to lose (a fight, an argument, etc).

,under'done adj (esp of food) not completely cooked throughout.

,under'go v 1 experience (hardship, suffering). 2 go through (a process).

,under'graduate n university student working for a bachelor's degree.

'underground n & adj (Gt Brit, railway built) below the surface.

'undergrowth n shrubs, bushes, low trees, growing under taller trees.

'under'hand adj & adv deceitful(ly).

,under'lie v be, form, the basis of (a theory, etc); give rise to.

,under'line v draw a line under (a word, etc); (fig) emphasize.

,under'mine v 1 make a hollow under; weaken at the base. 2 weaken gradually: — *sb's authority*.

,under'neath adv & prep under; below.

,under'sell v sell (goods) at a lower price than (competitors).

'undersigned adj the —, the person(s) who signed below.

,under'stand v (pt & pp ,under'stood) 1 know the meaning, nature, explanation, of (sth). make oneself understood, make one's meaning clear. 2 learn (from information received): *I — (that) you are going to resign*. —able adj that can be understood. —ing n 1 power of clear thought. 2 capacity for seeing another person's point of view, etc. 3 reach an —ing (with sb), reach an agreement after realizing his views, feelings, etc. 4 condition: *on this —ing*; *on the —ing that*.

'understudy n person able to, learning to, act in the place of (another).

,under'take v (pt ,under'took, pp ,under'taken) 1 make oneself responsible for: — *a task*; — *to do* sth. 2 start (a piece of work). ,under'taking n 1 work that one has —n to do. 2 promise. 'undertaker n person who —s burials and cremations.

'undertone n low, quiet note, esp talk in —s, with lowered voices.

'undertow n strong current caused by the backward flow of a wave that has broken on the beach.

'underwear n vest, pants, bra, etc.

'underworld n 1 (in Greek, etc, myths(1)) place of the spirits of the dead. 2 section of society that lives by vice and crime.

,under'write v (pt ,under'wrote, pp ,under'written) undertake (an insurance) to bear all or part of a possible loss, eg on ships. —r n.

un'do v (pt un'did, pp un'done) 1 untie, unfasten, loosen (knots, laces, buttons, etc). 2 destroy the result of; bring back the state of affairs that existed before.

un'due adj more than is right: with — haste. un'duly adv.

'undulate v (of surfaces) have wave-like motion or appearance.

un'earth v discover and bring to light; uncover (eg by digging).

un'earthly adj 1 supernatural. 2 mysterious; frightening.

un'easy adj uncomfortable in body or mind; anxious. un'easily adv.

un'erring adj accurate: with — aim.

,unex'ampled adj of which there is no other example that can be compared with it.

un'fold v (esp, fig) make known (one's plans, intentions, etc).

un'founded adj without facts or reasons to support (it): — (ie false) rumours.

un'gainly adj clumsy; ungraceful.

un'governable adj that cannot be kept under control: an — temper.

un'guarded adj (esp of a statement) careless; allowing sth secret to become known.

un'heard-of adj extraordinary.

'unicorn n (in old stories) imaginary horse-like animal with one straight horn in the middle of its forehead.

'uniform adj the same; never varying: a — temperature. n style of dress worn by members of, eg the police, the armed forces. —ly adv. ,uni'formity n.

'unify v 1 form into one; unite. 2 make uniform. ,unifi'cation n.

'union n 1 uniting or being united; joining or being joined. 2 agreement or harmony. 3 group, association, etc, formed by the uniting of persons, smaller groups,

etc: a trade —. the U— Jack, the British flag.

u'nique adj being the only one of its sort; having no like or equal.

'unison n concord; agreement.

'unit n 1 single person, thing, or group regarded as complete in itself. 2 quantity or amount used as a standard of measurement: —s of length (eg yard, metre).

u'nite v 1 make or become one; join. 2 act or work together. —d adj. the U— Kingdom, Great Britain and Northern Ireland.

'unity n the state of being —d; harmony or agreement (of aims, feelings, etc).

'universe n everything that exists everywhere. ,uni'versal adj of or for all; used by, done by, affecting, all. ,uni'versally adv.

,uni'versity n educational institution awarding degrees and engaged in academic research.

un'kempt adj untidy.

un'less conj if not; except when.

,unmis'takable adj about which no mistake is possible; quite clear.

un'nerve v cause to lose self-control, courage, etc.

un'pleasantness n a quarrel; ill will.

,unpre'tentious adj not trying to seem important; modest.

un'principled adj without moral principles.

un'ravel v (-ll-) 1 separate the threads of; pull or become separate. 2 solve (a mystery, etc).

,unre'mitting adj unceasing.

un'rest n (esp) disturbed condition(s): social —:

un'ruly adj not easily controlled.

un'sightly adj ugly.

un'sound adj (esp) of — mind mad.

un'speakable adj that cannot b described in words: —joy.

un'thinkable adj such as one can not have any real idea of, belief in etc; not to be considered.

un'thinking adj thoughtless; don without consideration of effect.

un'til prep & conj (= till) up t (the time when).

un'timely adj coming at a wron or unsuitable time, or too soon.

'unto prep (old use) to.

un'told adj (esp) too much or to many to be measured or counted.

un'utterable adj unspeakable.

un'wieldy adj awkward to move or control because of size or shape.

un'witting adj unknowing; unaware. —ly adj.

up adv & prep 1 to or in an erect or vertical position: *Stand up!* 2 no longer in bed; dressed and ready: *He isn't up yet.* 3 up to, occupied or busy with: *He's up to no good,* doing sth wrong, etc. 4 not up to much, not very good; *don't feel up to (doing) much,* don't feel well enough to do much. 5 What's up? (slang) What's the matter? n ups and downs, (fig) changes of fortune.

up- prefix in an upward direction.

up'braid v scold.

'upbringing n training and education during childhood.

up'heaval n great and sudden change (eg in social conditions).

uphill adj difficult; needing effort: — work. adv (often up'hill) up a slope.

up'hold v (pt & pp up'held) support (a decision, etc).

up'holster v provide (seats, etc) with padding, covering material, etc; provide (a room) with carpets, curtains, etc. —y n.

'upkeep n (cost of) keeping sth in good condition.

'upland n (often pl) high part(s) of a country; (as adj) an — region.

up'lift v influence towards nobler, happier thoughts and feelings.

u'pon prep on.

'upper adj higher. have (get) the — hand, have (get) control (over sb). n part of a shoe or boot above the sole. —most adj & adv highest; on, at, to, the top or surface.

'upright adj 1 erect; placed vertically (at right angles to the ground). 2 honourable in behaviour. adv in an — manner or position. n — support in a structure. —ly adv.

up'rising n revolt.

uproar n outburst of noise and excitement. up'roarious adj noisy; with much loud laughter.

up'root v pull up with the root(s).

up'set v (pt & pp up'set; -tt-) 1 overturn. 2 cause (sb or sth) to be troubled or out of order: — the enemy's plans. 'upset n —ting or being —.

'upshot n result or outcome.

upside-'down adj with the upper side (or top) underneath or at the bottom.

up'stairs adv to or on a higher floor; (as adj, 'upstairs): an — room.

up'stream adv against the current.

'uptake n quick on the —, (colloq) quick to understand.

up-to-'date adj of the present time; of the newest sort.

'upward adj moving or directed up. —(s) adv towards a higher place, etc. —s of, more than.

'urban adj of or in a town. —ize v change from a rural to an — character or condition.

ur'bane adj polite; polished in behaviour. —ly adv. ur'banity n.

'urchin n troublesome boy, esp one playing about in the streets.

urge v 1 push or drive (sth or sb) on, onward, forward. 2 try to persuade (sb) to do sth. 3 press (upon sb) requests and arguments. n strong ambition. '—ncy n need for, importance of, haste or prompt action. '—nt adj needing prompt decision or action; (of a person, his voice, etc) showing that sth is —nt. '—ntly adv.

'urine n waste liquid which is discharged from the body.

urn n 1 large metal container in which tea or coffee, etc, is made or kept warm. 2 vase for the ashes of a person whose body has been cremated.

us pron the object(2) form of *we*: *Can you see us?* ⇨ we.

'usage n 1 way of using sth. 2 sth commonly said or done; general custom or practice.

use v 1 employ for a purpose. 2 use up, come to the end of what one has. 3 behave towards. n 1 purpose for which sth may be employed; work which sth is able to do. 2 using or being used. make use of, use. come into use, begin to be used. go out of use, be no longer used. 3 value; advantage. of no use, worthless. 4 power of using: *lose the use of one's hands.* 5 right to use. used adj no longer new: *a used car.* used to, familiar with, through experience; accustomed to. used to v indicating a constant or frequent action in the past, or the existence of sth in the past: *I used to go to market every day. There used to be a hotel here years ago.*

'useful *adj* helpful; that can be used. **'usefully** *adv.* **'usefulness** *n.* **'useless** *adj* of no use; worthless. **'uselessly** *adv.* **'user** *n* person who uses sth: *telephone users.*

'usher *n* person who shows people to their seats in theatres, etc. *v* show (sb) the way to, take (sb) *into*, (a room, etc): *I was —ed in by the steward.* **,usher'ette** *n* girl or woman —: *a cinema —ette.*

'usual *adj* such as commonly happens; customary: *my — seat.* **—ly** *adv.*

u'surp *v* take (sb's power, authority, position) wrongfully. **—er** *n.*

'usury *n* (practice of) lending money, esp at a rate of interest generally considered to be too high; such high interest. **'usurer** *n.*

u'tensil *n* tool, instrument, etc, esp for use in the home: *kitchen —s* (*pots, pans, brushes,* etc).

u'tility *n* **1** quality of being useful. **2 public utilities,** public services, esp supplying water, gas, electricity, transport. **,utili'tarian** *adj* for use rather than for decoration, etc. **'utilize** *v* make use of (for a special purpose). **,utili'zation** *n.*

'utmost *adj* **1** furthest. **2** greatest: *in the — danger. n* the most that is possible: *enjoy yourself to the —.*

'utter[1] *adj* complete; total. **—ly** *adj.*

'utter[2] *v* **1** make (a sound) with the mouth: *— a cry of pain.* **2** say: *the last words she —ed.* **—ance** *n* way of speaking; sth —ed.

'uttermost *adj* utmost.

V

'vacant *adj* not occupied by anyone; without or not showing signs of thought or interest: *— rooms (looks).* **—ly** *adv.* **'vacancy** *n* empty space; position in business, etc, for which sb is needed.

va'cate *v* give up living in (a house, etc); leave (eg one's seat) unoccupied.

va'cation *n* **1** weeks during which universities and law courts stop work. **2** period of holidays.

'vaccinate *v* protect (sb) against certain diseases, by injecting vaccine (usu into the arm). **,vacci'nation** *n.* **'vaccine** *n* medical substance from the blood of a cow, used in vaccination.

'vacuum *n* space completely empty of substance or air; space in a container from which air has been pumped out. **— cleaner,** apparatus which takes up dirt, dust, etc, by suction. **— flask,** bottle for keeping liquids hot or cold.

'vagabond *adj* habitually wandering; having no fixed living-place. *n* — person. **'vagrant** *adj* & *n* —. **'vagrancy** *n* being —.

vague *adj* (-r, -st) **1** not clear; indistinct. **2** (of persons, their looks, etc) uncertain (*about* needs, intentions, etc). **—ly** *adv.* **—ness** *n.*

vain *adj* **1** without use, value, meaning, or result: *— attempts.* **2** having too high an opinion of one's looks or abilities; conceited. **3** *in* —, without the desired result. **'—ly** *adv.*

'valet *n* manservant who looks after his employer's clothes, etc.

'valiant *adj* brave. **—ly** *adv.*

'valid *adj* **1** (legal) effective because correctly made or done. **2** (of agreements, etc) having force in law: *— for three months.* **3** (of arguments, etc) well based; sound. **—ly** *adv.* **va'lidity** *n.*

va'lise *n* bag for one's clothes, etc during a journey (usu *suitcase*).

'valley *n* stretch of land between hills or mountains, usu with a river flowing through it.

'valour *n* bravery, esp in war.

'value *n* **1** quality of being useful or desirable. **2** worth of sth in money or other goods for which it can be exchanged. **3** what sth considered to be worth. *v* **1** estimate the money — of. **2** have high opinion of. **'valuable** *adj* much —. *n* (often *pl*) sth of much — (eg jewels).

valve *n* **1** mechanical device for controlling the flow of a liquid or gas through a tube, pipe, etc. **2** structure in the heart, allowing the blood to flow in one direction only. **3** vacuum tube used in a radio, etc

van[1] *n* **1** covered or roofed vehicle for delivering goods by road: *the baker's van.* **2** roofed railway wagon.

van[2] *n* **1** front or leading part of an army or fleet in battle. **2** those persons who lead a procession or (fig) a movement. **'vanguard** *n* van of an army.

'vandal *n* person who wilfully destroys public or private property, works of art, etc. **—ism** *n*.

vane *n* **1** arrow, etc, on the top of a building, turned by the wind. **2** sail of a windmill; blade of a propeller.

'vanish *v* **1** disappear suddenly; fade away gradually. **2** go out of existence.

'vanity *n* **1** conceit; having too high an opinion of one's looks, abilities, etc. **2** being worthless, unsatisfying.

'vanquish *v* defeat.

'vapour *n* **1** steam; mist. **2** gas form of a substance which is normally liquid or solid. **'vaporize** *v* (cause to) change into —(2).

'variable, va'riety ⇨ vary.

'varnish *n* (liquid used on wood surfaces, etc, to give a) hard, shiny, transparent coating. *v* put — on.

'vary *v* be, make, or become, different. **'variable** *adj* —ing; that can be changed. **'variance** *n* (esp) **at variance with,** not in agreement with. **'variant** *adj* different or alternative. *n* alternative form (esp of a word, its spelling). **,vari'ation** *n* (degree of) —ing. **'varied** *adj* **1** of different sorts. **2** continually or often changing. **va'riety** *n* **1** quality of not being all the same or not the same at all times. **2** number or group of different things. **'various** *adj* different; several.

vase *n* vessel of glass, pottery, etc, used for ornament, for holding flowers, etc.

'vassal *n* person who, in former times, held land in return for military help to the owner of the land.

vast *adj* (-er, -est) immense; extensive.

vat *n* tank or other large vessel for holding liquids (e g in brewing).

vault[1] *n* **1** arched roof; series of arches forming a roof. **2** under-ground room or cellar, esp for storing wine or valuables. **3** burial chamber. **'—ed** *adj* having, built with, —s(1).

vault[2] *v* jump in a single movement, with the hand(s) resting on sth or with the help of a pole: — (over) *a fence. n* jump made in this way.

vaunt *v & n* boast.

veal *n* flesh of a calf used as food.

veer *v* (esp of wind, (fig) of opinion) change direction.

'vegetable *adj* of, from, relating to, plants or plant life. *n* plant, esp of the sort used for food. ⇨ p 306. **,vege'tarian** *n* person who does not eat meat. **,vege'tation** *n* plants of all kinds; plants growing in a place or area: *tropical vegetation.*

'vehement *adj* (of feelings) strong; eager; (of persons) filled with strong, eager feeling.

'vehicle *n* cart, carriage, van, bus, etc, used on land to transport goods or passengers.

veil *n* **1** covering of fine net or other material to protect or hide a woman's face, or as part of a head-dress. **take the —,** become a nun. **2** sth that hides: *a — of mist. v* put a — over; hide.

vein *n* **1** blood-vessel (tube) along which blood flows back to the heart. **2** one of the vein-like lines in a leaf, etc. **3** crack in rock, filled with ore, etc. **4** mood; state of mind: *in a merry —.*

veld *n* stretch of grass-land of the S African plateau.

ve'locity *n* (of objects) speed.

'velvet *n* **1** cloth wholly or partly made of silk, with thick, soft nap[2] on one side. **2** (as *adj*) made of —; soft like —.

ve'neer *n* **1** thin layer of fine quality wood glued to the surface of cheaper wood (in furniture, etc). **2** (fig) surface appearance (of politeness, etc) covering the true nature. *v* put a —(1) on.

'venerable *adj* deserving respect because of age, character, etc. **'venerate** *v* regard with deep respect. **,vene'ration** *n*.

'vengeance *n* revenge; the return of injury for injury. **take — upon sb,** have one's revenge.

'venom *n* **1** poison of snakes, etc. **2** hate; ill feeling. **—ous** *adj*.

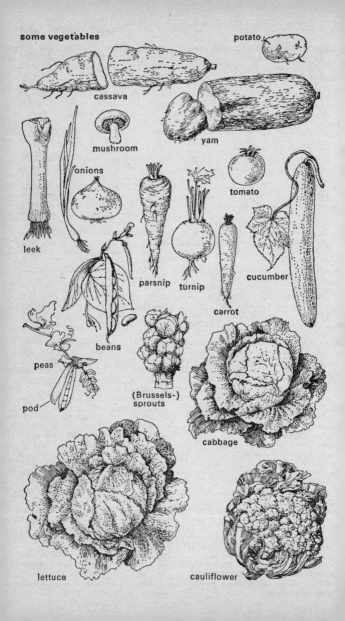

some vegetables

potato

cassava

yam

mushroom

onions

tomato

leek

parsnip   turnip

carrot

cucumber

beans

peas

pod

(Brussels-)
sprouts

cabbage

lettuce   cauliflower

vent n 1 hole serving as an inlet or outlet for air, gas, liquid, etc. 2 (fig) outlet for one's feelings.

'ventilate v 1 cause air to move in and out freely. 2 make (a question) widely known, cause it to be discussed. **,venti'lation** n. **'ventilator** n device for ventilating.

'venture n undertaking in which there is risk. v 1 take the risk of danger or loss; be brave enough (to do sth). 2 dare, go so far as (to say sth, to disagree, etc). —**some** adj ready to take risks; (of acts) risky.

ve'racious adj true; truthful. **ve'racity** n.

ve'randa(h) n roofed and floored open space along the side(s) of a building.

verb n word or phrase indicating what sb or sth does, what state sb or sth is in, what is becoming of sb or sth, etc.

'verbal adj 1 of or in words: — errors. 2 spoken, not written: — messages. 3 of verbs. — **noun**, verb form in -ing used as a noun.

ver'batim adv exactly as spoken or written.

'verdant adj (esp of grass, fields) fresh and green.

'verdict n 1 decision reached by a jury on a question of fact in a lawsuit. 2 decision or opinion given after a test, etc.

verge n 1 edge; border. 2 on the — of doing sth, about to do it. v —**upon**, be near to.

'verger n person who shows people to their seats in an Anglican church.

'verify v 1 test the truth or accuracy of (statements, etc). 2 (of an event, etc) show the truth of (sth said, etc). **,verifi'cation** n.

ver'milion n & adj bright red.

'vermin n 1 wild animals (eg rats) harmful to plants, birds, etc. 2 insects (eg lice) sometimes found on the bodies of human beings or animals. —**ous** adj 1 infected with —(2). 2 caused by —(2).

ver'nacular adj (of a language or word) of the country in question, not foreign: the — languages of Indonesia. n language of a country or district.

versatile adj interested in and clever at many different things. **,versa'tility** n.

verse n 1 (form of) writing arranged in groups of lines with a regular rhythm (and which often rhyme). 2 group of such lines forming a unit in a poem, hymn, etc. 3 one of the short, numbered divisions of a chapter in the Bible.

versed adj — in, experienced in.

'version n 1 translation into another language. 2 person's own account of an event.

'versus prep (Latin) (in law and sport, often written v) against.

'vertical adj upright; at right angles to the earth's surface: a — line. ⇨ horizontal.

very adv to a great extent; to a marked degree: — good (well), excellent(ly). adj this actual one and no other: the — thing I wanted. int — well, all right; I agree.

'vessel n 1 container for liquids (eg a cup, bottle, bucket). 2 ship or large boat.

vest n garment worn on the upper part of the body, next to the skin.

'vestige n trace or sign.

'vestment n garment, esp one worn by a priest in church. **'vestry** n part of a church where —s are kept.

vet n (colloq) veterinary surgeon. v (-tt-) (colloq) examine medically; examine technically.

'veteran n & adj (person) having had long or much experience, esp as a soldier.

'veterinary adj of or concerned with the diseases of animals.

'veto n (pl -es) right to forbid or prevent sth; statement forbidding sth. v use a — against; prohibit.

vex v annoy; distress; trouble. **vex'ation** n being vexed; sth that vexes. **vex'atious** adj annoying.

'via prep (Latin) by way of: travel from London to Paris via Dover.

'viable adj able to exist.

'viaduct n (bridge with arches carrying a) road or railway across a valley or low ground.

vi'brate v 1 (cause to) move quickly and continuously to and fro like the wings of a fly; quiver. 2 (of tightly stretched strings, the voice) throb. **vi'bration** n.

'vicar n (in the Church of England) parish clergyman.

vice¹ n (any particular kind of) evil conduct or immorality.

a vice

vice² n apparatus with strong jaws in which things can be held tightly while being worked upon.

vice- prefix acting for (another); holding rank next below: vice-chairman; vice-admiral.

vice 'versa adv (Latin) the other way round: He can go to her or — (ie or she can go to him).

vi'cinity n nearness; area round about.

'vicious adj 1 of vice, given up to vice. 2 spiteful.

'victim n person, animal, suffering injury, loss, pain, etc, because of cruelty or some force beyond his or its control. **—ize** v make a — of.

'victor n person who conquers or wins: **—y** n success won in battle, contest, etc. **vic'torious** adj having gained a —y (over).

'victual v (-ll-) & n pl (provide eg a ship with) food and drink.

view n 1 sight. **be in —, come into —**, be, come, where (it) can be seen. **on —**, being displayed. 2 sth (to be) looked at, esp a stretch of natural scenery. 3 opinion. **in — of**, considering, taking into account. 4 purpose; intention. **fall in with** (meet) sb's **—s**, agree with his wishes. **with a — to**, with the intention to. v look at; examine; consider. **'—er** n person **—ing** TV programmes.

'vigil n staying awake to keep watch. **—ance** n keeping watch; watchfulness. **—ant** adj watchful.

'vigour n mental or physical energy. **'vigorous** adj energetic; strong.

vile adj (-r, -st) 1 shameful and disgusting. 2 (colloq) bad in quality.

'villa n house in its own garden or grounds, esp one outside a town.

'village n large group of houses, shops, etc, smaller than a town.

'villain n (eg in drama) wicked man. **—ous** adj wicked. **—y** n wicked conduct.

'vindicate v show or prove the truth, justice, etc (of sth that has been attacked or questioned). **,vindi'cation** n.

vin'dictive adj unforgiving; having or showing a desire for revenge.

vine n climbing plant, esp the kind that bears grapes. **'—yard** n area of land planted with grape-vines.

'vinegar n acid liquid used in cooking, for flavouring food or keeping it in good condition.

vi'ola n stringed musical instrument like a violin but bigger.

'violate v 1 break (a treaty, etc); act contrary to (what conscience requires, etc). 2 treat without proper respect. **,vio'lation** n.

'violent adj 1 using, having, showing, great force: — passions. 2 due to great force: a — death. 3 severe: — toothache. **—ly** adv. **'violence** n.

'violet adj & n (having the colour of a) bluish-purple flower.

vio'lin n four-stringed musical instrument played with a bow. ⇨ p 180. **—ist** n player of a —.

,violon'cello ⇨ cello.

'viper n small, poisonous snake.

'virgin n girl or woman who has not experienced intercourse(2). adj 1 pure and untouched: — snow. 2 in the original condition; unused: — soil (forests). **vir'ginity** n.

'virile adj having or showing strength, energy, manly qualities and abilities. **vi'rility** n.

'virtual adj being in fact, though not openly accepted as such: a — defeat. **—ly** adv.

'virtue n 1 (any particular kind of) goodness or excellence (eg patience, chastity). 2 **by (in) — of**, because of. **'virtuous** adj having or showing —.

'virulent adj (of poison) strong; (of ill feeling) bitter.

'virus n poisonous element causing the spread of infectious diseases.

'visa n stamp or signature put on a passport to show that it has been examined by officials of the country which the owner intends to visit or leave.

'visible adj that can be seen; that is in sight. **,visi'bility** n.

'vision n 1 power of seeing or imagining. 2 sth seen, esp in imagination. **—ary** adj 1 existing only in the imagination, not practical: —ary plans. 2 (of persons) having —ary ideas; dreamy.

'visit v go to see (sb), go to (a place) for a time. n act of —ing; time of —ing: pay sb a —; on a short — to Paris. —or n person who —s.

'vista n long, narrow view; (fig) series of events looked back on or forward to.

'visual adj concerned with, used in, seeing. 'visualize v bring (sth) as a picture before the mind.

'vital adj 1 of, connected with, necessary for, living. 2 highest: of —importance. —ly adv. vi'tality n 1 — power; capacity to endure. 2 liveliness; driving force.

'vitamin n sorts of substance, present in certain foods, that are essential to good health.

vi'vacious adj high-spirited; lively. vi'vacity n.

'vivid adj 1 (of colours, etc) intense; very bright. 2 (of descriptions, etc) giving a clear and distinct picture. 3 lively. —ly adv.

viz (Latin; usu read as namely) that is to say.

vo'cabulary n 1 (book containing a) list of words used, usu with definitions or translations. 2 range of words known to or used by a person, a profession, etc.

'vocal adj of, for, with, or using, the voice. —ist n singer.

vo'cation n 1 person's belief that he is called to, and fitted for, certain work, esp religious work. 2 person's trade or profession.

'vodka n Russian alcoholic drink.

vogue n fashion(1).

voice n 1 sounds made when speaking or singing; power of making such sounds. 2 (right to have an) opinion: I have no — in the matter. v put (feelings, etc) into words.

void adj 1 empty. 2 —of, without. 3 (legal) not binding.

'volatile adj 1 (of persons) lively; gay; changeable. 2 (of liquids) that easily change into gas or vapour.

vol'cano n (pl -es) mountain with opening(s) through which gases, lava, ashes, etc, come up. vol'canic adj of, from, like, a —.

vo'lition n (power to) use one's own will when making a decision, choosing, etc.

'volley n hurling or shooting of a number of things together (eg stones, arrows, bullets, or, (fig) oaths, questions); the stones, etc, hurled.

volt n unit of electrical force. —age n electrical force measured in —s.

'voluble adj talking, able to talk, quickly and easily; spoken in this way. 'volubly adv. volu'bility n.

'volume n 1 book, esp one of a set of books. 2 amount of space occupied by a substance, a liquid, or a gas. 3 (of smoke, etc) large mass or amount. 4 (of sound) loudness.

'voluntary adj 1 done or given willingly; doing or ready to do things willingly and freely: — help(ers). 2 carried on, supported, by — work and gifts. 'voluntarily adv.

,volun'teer n 1 person who offers to do sth, esp sth dangerous or without being paid. 2 soldier who voluntarily joins an army. v come forward as a —; offer (to do sth).

'vomit v 1 bring back from the stomach through the mouth. 2 send out in large quantities: factory chimneys —ing smoke.

vo'racious adj greedy; desiring much. vo'racity n.

vote n 1 (right to the) expression of opinion or will, given by persons for or against ,sth, esp by ballot or by the raising of hands. 2 total number of —s (to be) given to a political party: the Labour —. v 1 give a — (for or against); express one's opinion (that . . .) by means of a —. 2 approve by —s. '—r n person with the right to —.

vouch v — for, be responsible for (a person, his honour, etc). '—er n document showing the payment of money or correctness of accounts.

vouch'safe v be kind enough to give (sth) or (to do sth): — a reply; — to help.

vow n solemn promise or undertaking: marriage vows. v make a vow (that . . ., to do sth).

'vowel n any one of the letters a, e, i, o, u or their sounds.

'voyage v & n (make a) journey by ship.

'vulgar adj ill-mannered; displeasing to persons with good taste(5); rough and noisy. vul'garity n — behaviour.

'vulnerable *adj* that can be wounded or damaged; not protected against attack.

'vulture *n* large bird that lives on the flesh of dead animals. ⇨ p 26.

W

wad *n* **1** lump of soft material for keeping things apart or in place, or to stop up a hole. **2** number of bank-notes or other papers rolled up together. *v* (-dd-) put wad(s) or wadding round or into sth. **'wadding** *n* soft material, esp raw cotton, used for packing or stuffing.

wade *v* walk through water; (fig) make one's way with effort (*through* a book, etc).

'wadi *n* rocky water-course in northern Africa, etc, wet only after heavy rain.

waft *v* carry lightly and smoothly through the air.

wag *v* (-gg-) (cause to) move from side to side or up and down: *a dog wagging its tail.* *n* wagging movement.

wage¹ *n* (usu *pl*) payment (usu weekly) made or received for work or services. ⇨ fee, salary.

wage² *v* engage in (war, a campaign).

'wager *v* & *n* bet.

'wagon, 'waggon *n* **1** four-wheeled cart for carrying goods, pulled by horses or oxen. **2** open railway truck (e g for coal).

waif *n* homeless person, esp a child.

wail *v* cry or complain with a loud, usu high, voice; (of the wind) sound like sb who is —ing. *n* —ing cry; complaint.

waist *n* part of the body between the ribs and the hips. ⇨ p 29. **'—coat** *n* close-fitting, buttoning, sleeveless upper garment reaching to the —.

wait *v* **1** stay where one is, delay acting, until sb or sth comes or until sth happens: — *for me*; — *until the rain stops.* — **up**, stay up, not go to bed. **2** —**upon** (**sb**), act as a servant to. — **at table**, serve food, carry away dishes, etc. *n* act or time of —ing. **lie in** — (**for**), be in hiding in order to attack, etc.

'—er (**'—ress**) *n* man (woman) who —s at table in a restaurant, etc.

waive *v* give up, not insist upon (a right, claim, etc).

wake¹ *v* (*pt* woke or —d, *pp* woke or 'woken) **1** (often —up) (cause to) stop sleeping. **2** stir (sb) up; rouse. **'—ful** *adj* unable to sleep; with little sleep: *a —ful night.* **'—n** *v* —.

wake² *n* track left by a ship on water. **in the — of**, following.

walk *v* **1** (of persons) move by putting forward each foot in turn without having both feet off the ground at once; (of animals) move forward at the slowest pace. — **away** (**off**) **with**, carry off, steal. **3** cause to —. *n* **1** journey on foot esp for pleasure or exercise; manner or style of —ing. **2** path for —ing. **'walk-over** *n* (colloq) easy victory.

wall *n* continuous, vertical and strong structure of stone, brick, etc, forming one of the sides of a building, room, etc, or enclosing a garden, town, etc. **with one's back to the —**, fighting where retreat is impossible. *v* close up (e g a window) with a — of bricks.

'wallet *n* folding pocket-book for papers, bank-notes, etc.

'wallow *v* roll about in mud, etc, as a pig does.

'walnut *n* (tree producing) eatable nut in a hard shell; wood of this tree, used for making furniture.

'walrus *n* large sea-animal. ⇨ p 247.

waltz *n* (music for a) dance in which partners go round and round. *v* dance a —.

wan *adj* (of a person, his looks, etc) looking ill and tired; (of light, the sky) pale. **'wanly** *adv*.

wand *n* thin stick or rod, esp the kind used by a fairy or magician.

'wander *v* **1** go from place to place without a special plan; leave the right path or road. **2** allow the thoughts to go from subject to subject. **—er** *n*.

wane *v* **1** (of the moon; cf wax¹) show a smaller bright area (after a *full* moon). **2** become less or weaker: *His influence has —d.* *n* (esp) **on the —**, waning.

want *v* **1** be in need of; require. **2** be —**ing**, be missing; be lacking (*in*). **3** — **for nothing**, have all one needs. *n* **1** lack, shortage

2 need: *in — of money.* '**—ing** *prep* without; in the absence of.

'**wanton** *adj* 1 playful: *— breezes.* 2 uncontrolled; disorderly. 3 serving no purpose; done without good reason: *— damage.* '**—ly** *adv.*

war *n* (period of) fighting between nations or groups: *be at war (with); go to war (against).* *v* (-rr-) fight; make war. '**warfare** *n* making war; condition of being at war; fighting. '**warlike** *adj* ready for war; suggesting war; fond of war. '**warpath** *n* **on the warpath**, ready for, engaged in, a fight or quarrel.

'**warble** *v* (esp of birds) sing, esp with a gentle, trilling note.

ward *n* 1 young person under the guardianship of an older person or of legal authorities. 2 division of a town for purposes of government. 3 division of, separate room in, a building, esp a prison or hospital. *v* — **off**, keep away, avoid (a blow, danger, etc). '**—en** *n* person having authority (eg in a hostel, some colleges). '**—er** ('**—ress**) *n.* man (woman) acting as a guard in a prison.

'**wardrobe** *n* cupboard-like piece of furniture for hanging up clothes.

ware *n* 1 (*pl*) articles offered for sale. 2 (chiefly in compounds) manufactured goods: *silver—; tin—.* '**—house** *n* building for storing goods.

'**warily** *adv* ⇨ wary.

warm *adj* (-er, -est) (between *cool* and *hot*) having sufficient heat to be comfortable to the body; serving to keep the body —; (of behaviour) affectionate, kindly. *v* (often — **up**) make or become —. '**—ly** *adv.* '**warm-'blooded** *adj* (of animals) having — blood (contrasted with reptiles, fish). '**warm-'hearted** *adj* kind and sympathetic. '**—th** *n* state of being —; (fig) excitement.

warn *v* make (sb) aware of possible danger or unpleasantness. '**—ing** *n* that which —s; word(s), happening, etc, which —s.

'**warrant** *n* 1 sth giving right or authority (*for* action, etc). 2 written order giving official authority for sth. *v* be a — for; guarantee (the quality, etc, of goods). '

'**warrior** *n* (liter) fighting man; soldier.

'**wary** *adj* (-ier, -iest) careful; in the habit of looking out for possible trouble: *— of giving offence.* '**warily** *adv.*

was ⇨ be.

wash *v* 1 make clean with or in water or some other liquid. **—(sth) out (off)**, remove by —ing. **— up**, (esp) — dishes, etc, after a meal. 2 (of materials) be capable of being —ed without damage. 3 (of the sea, a river, etc) flow past or against; carry (sth) *away, off,* etc. *n* 1 act of —ing or being —ed. 2 clothing, bed sheets, etc, to be —ed or being —ed; place where these are (sent to be) —ed. 3 swirl of water (eg as made by a ship's propellers). 4 (in compounds) liquid prepared for a special kind of —ing: *mouthwash.* **—ing** *n* = —(2). '**washstand** *n* table with a basin, jug, etc, for —ing oneself (in a bedroom). '**—out** *n* 1 carrying away of earth, rock, etc, by floods. 2 (colloq) useless or unsuccessful person, thing, event, etc. '**—y** *adj* (of colour) pale; (of liquids, etc) thin; watery.

wasp *n* flying insect with a narrow waist and a powerful sting. ⇨ p 144.

waste *adj* 1 (of land) that is not, cannot be, used; no longer of use. 2 useless; thrown away because unwanted: *— paper.* *v* 1 make no use of; use with no good purpose; use more (of sth) than is necessary. 2 destroy growing crops. 3 (cause to) lose strength by degrees. *n* 1 wasting or being —d. **run (go) to —**, be —d. 2 — material. 3 area of — land. '**wastage** *n* amount —d; loss by —. '**—ful** *adj* causing —; using more than is needed.

watch *v* look at; look out *for* (sb or sth expected); be on guard *over.* *n* 1 act of —ing, esp to see that all is well. **keep —**, look out for danger, etc. 2 (in ships) period of duty (four or two hours) for part of the crew. **the middle —**, midnight to 4 am; the men working in such a —. 3 small form of clock for the pocket or worn on the wrist. '**—ful** *adj.* '**—man** *n* man employed to guard a building (eg a bank) against thieves, esp at night. '**—word** *n* password; slogan.

'**water**[1] *n* 1 liquid as in rivers, seas, etc. **under —**, flooded. **will not hold —**, (fig, of a theory, etc) will be seen to be mistaken when tested. **2** state of the tide: *at high (low)* —. **3** (often *pl*) mass of —. **the headwaters of the Nile**, the lakes from which the Nile flows. **4** solution, etc, of a substance in —: '*mineral* —*s*; '*soda-water*. '**water-closet** *n* (colloq **WC**) small room where waste from the body is washed down a drain-pipe by — from a cistern. '**water-colour** *n* **1** (*pl*) paints (to be) mixed with —, not oil. **2** picture painted with water-colours. '**—course** *n* (channel for a) small river. '**—fall** *n* fall of — (esp in a river) from one level to another, esp over a cliff or rocks. '**—front** *n* part of a town beside a river, lake, or harbour. '**—ing-place** *n* (esp) seaside town visited by people on holiday. '**—proof** *adj* which does not let — through. '**—shed** *n* line of high land separating two river systems. '**—tight** *adj* made, fastened, etc, so that — cannot get out or in. '**—y** *adj* of or like —; containing too much —: —*y soup*.

water² *v* **1** put — on or in. **2** give — to (eg horses). **3** (of the eyes and mouth) fill with —; have much liquid.

'**water-buffalo** ⇨ buffalo.

watt *n* unit of electrical power.

wave *v* **1** move or be moved to and fro, up and down, as a flag moves in the wind. **2** cause '(sth)' to move in this way; make a signal to sb by this means: — *sb on*. **3** (of a line or surface, of hair) be in a series of curves like this: ∿; cause to be like this. *n* **1** long raised mass of water, esp on the sea, between two hollows; such a ridge curling over and breaking on the shore, etc. **2** act of waving; waving movement: *a* — *of the hand*. **3** line or shape curved like a — of the sea. **4** steady increase and spreading of sth: *a* — *of anger*. **a heat-** —, period of unusually hot weather. **5** wave-like motion by which heat, light, sound, or electricity travels through space. '**wavy** *adj* (-ier, -iest) having wave-like curves.

'**waver** *v* **1** move uncertainly or unsteadily. **2** hesitate (*between* two opinions, etc). **3** (of troops, etc) become unsteady in attack or defence; show signs of giving way.

wax¹ *n* (esp of the moon; cf wane) show a larger bright area.

wax² *n* **1** soft, yellow substance made by bees and used by them for honeycomb cells. **2** this substance made white and pure, used for making candles, modelling, etc. **3** substance similar to beeswax, eg paraffin wax. '**waxwork** *n* human figure, etc, modelled in wax.

way *n* **1** road, street, path, etc; esp in compounds (*motorway*, *railway*). **2** road, route (to be) used from one place to another: *lose (find) one's way*; *on the way home*. **3** direction: *look this way*. **the wrong way round**, facing in the wrong direction. **4** distance: *a long way from home*. **5** plan; method: *do it in this way*. **ways and means**, (esp) methods of providing money for sth needed. **6** (often *pl*) method of behaving; habit or custom: *British ways of living*. **7** point or detail: *He's clever in some ways*. **8** space or freedom for movement: *Get out of the way*; *Make way for the fire-engine!* **9 by the way**, often used to introduce a remark not connected with the subject of conversation. **by way of**, for the purpose of, in the course of. **in a way**, to some extent. **in a bad way**, in a bad condition, very ill, etc. **in a small way**, on a small scale. **have (get) one's own way**, have, do or get, what one wants. **give way**, break, bend, yield (*under*, *to*). **10** progress: *make one's way home*; *gathe (lose) way*, (of ships) gain (lose speed. **11** (*pl*: also '**slipway** structure of heavy timber dow which a newly built ship slides int the water. '**wayfarer** *n* perso travelling on foot. '**wayside** *ad & n* (of, at, the) side of the road *a wayside inn*.

way'lay *v* (*pt & pp* way'laid) (wai somewhere to) attack or speak t (sb).

'**wayward** *adj* not easily controlle

we used by the speaker or write in referring to himself and others *We can see you*. ⇨ us.

weak *adj* (-er, -est) **1** (opp o *strong*) below the usual standard o strength; easily bent or broken unable to resist attack, hard wear use, etc. **2** (of a solution) having little of a substance in relation to the water, etc: — *lemonade*. **3** (of the senses) below the usual standard: — *sight*. **'—en** *v* make or become —(er). **'—ling** *n* — person or animal. **'weak-'minded** *adj* (esp) easily influenced by others. **'—ness** *n* **1** state of being —. **2** fault of character. **3** have a —ness (for), a special or foolish liking.

weal *n* mark on the skin made by a blow from a stick, whip, etc.

wealth *n* **1** (possession of a) great amount of money, property, etc. **2** great amount or number (of). **'—y** *adj* (-ier, -iest) having —(s).

wean *v* accustom (a baby, a young animal) to food other than its mother's milk.

'weapon *n* sth designed or used for fighting or struggling (eg guns, fists, a strike by workmen).

wear *v* (*pt* wore, *pp* worn) **1** have on the body; be dressed in; bear or show (an expression on the face): —*ing a hat (spectacles, a ring on the finger)*; —*ing a troubled look*. **2** (cause to) become less useful, be in a certain condition, etc, by being used: *This material has worn thin*; *His socks have worn into holes*. **3** (be of a sort to) remain in a certain condition, endure continued use: *Good leather will — for years*. **4** (fig uses with *adv*) **— off**, pass away. **— on**, (of time) pass slowly. **— out**, make or become exhausted: *His patience wore out (was worn out) at last*. *n* **1** use as clothing. **showing signs of —**, no longer new-looking. **the worse for —**, no longer in a good and useful condition. **2** damage or loss of quality from use. **— and tear**, loss in value resulting from normal use. **3** (esp in compound words) things to—(1): **'foot—**, **'under—**.

'weary *adj* (-ier, -iest) **1** tired. **2 — of**, impatient with. **3** causing tiredness. *v* make or become —. **'wearily** *adv*. **'weariness** *n*. **'wearisome** *adj* tiring; long and dull.

'weather *n* conditions of sunshine, temperature, wind, rain, etc (at a particular time). *v* **1** come safely through (a storm, a crisis). **2** become affected by the —: *rocks —ed by water and frost*. **'weather-**

cock (-vane) *n* device, often in the shape of a cock, turning with the wind and showing its direction.

weave *v* (*pt* wove, *pp* 'woven) **1** make (cloth) by crossing threads over and under, by hand or by machine. **2** make (baskets, etc) in a similar way; (fig) compose (a story, etc). *n* style of weaving. **'—r** *n* person who —s.

web *n* **1** network (usu fig): *a web of lies*. **2** sth made of threads by some creatures: *a spider's web*. **3** skin joining the toes of water-birds, bats, and some water animals (eg frogs). **webbed** *adj* having web(3) between the toes. **'web-bing** *n* band of coarse woven material used in belts, etc.

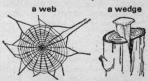

a web   a wedge

wed *v* (-dd-) marry. **'wedding** *n* marriage ceremony.

wedge *n* V-shaped piece, esp of wood or metal, for splitting, separating, or securing sth. *v* fix tightly (as) with a —; keep (sth *open*) with a —.

'wedlock *n* condition of being married.

'Wednesday *n* fourth day of the week.

wee *adj* (Scotland) very small.

weed *n* wild plant growing where it is not wanted (eg in a garden). *v* **1** take —s out of (the ground). **2 — out**, get rid of (what is of lower value). **'—y** *adj* (-ier, -iest) (esp) tall, thin, and weak: —*y young men*.

week *n* **1** period of seven days, esp Saturday midnight to Saturday midnight. **2** the six working days (ie except Sunday). **'—day** *n* any day except Sunday. **'—end** *n* Saturday and Sunday (esp as a period of rest): *a —end visit*. **'—ly** *adj & adv* (happening) once a —, every —; of, for, or lasting, a —. *n* periodical published once a —.

weep *v* (*pt & pp* wept) cry(2).

weigh *v* **1** measure (by means of a scale, etc) how heavy sth is: —

the baby. **2** show a certain measure when put on a scale: *The baby —s ten pounds.* **3** compare, balance, the value or importance of (one thing *with* or *against* another). **— the consequences** (one's words), consider them carefully. **4—with** (sb), have an effect upon, seem important to. **— upon** (sb, his mind), trouble, be heavy on. **5 — anchor**, raise it.

'**weight** *n* **1** force which makes a body want to move towards the centre of the earth. **2** how heavy a body is expressed in a scale (eg in tons, kilograms). **3** piece of metal of a certain —, used in measuring things (*an ounce —*) or in a machine (eg to turn wheels in a clock). **4** (degree of) importance or influence. *v* put a —(3) or —s(3) on; make heavy. '**-y** *adj* (-ier, -iest) very heavy; (fig) important.

weir *n* wall, etc, built across a river to control the flow of water.

weird *adj* (-er, -est) **1** (colloq) hard to understand or explain. **2** unearthly.

'**welcome** *adj* **1** received with, giving, pleasure: *a — rest.* **make sb —**, show him that his coming gives pleasure. **2 You are — to**, It gives me pleasure to (*give, lend, allow*, etc, *you*). *n* words, behaviour, etc, used when sb arrives, when an offer is received, etc. *v* show pleasure or satisfaction at the arrival of sb or sth; greet: *— a suggestion.*

weld *v* join or unite (pieces of metal) by hammering, pressing, etc, together; make (material) *into* sth by doing this. *n* —ed joint. '**-er** *n*.

'**welfare** *n* condition of having good health, a comfortable home, etc.

well¹ *n* **1** hole, usu lined with brick or stone, made in the ground for a water-supply. **2** hole bored for mineral oil. *v* flow *up* or *out* as water flows from a —

well² *adj* ('better, best) **1** in good health: *be* (*look, feel*) —; in a good condition: *Is all — with you?* **2** (it would be) —, to, wise or desirable to. *adv* **1** in a good, right, or satisfactory manner. **2 as — (as)**, in addition (to); also. **3** with good reason: *You may — be surprised.* **4 We may as — (***start***, etc),**

There is no reason why we should not. *n* **wish sb —**, wish him success. *n* **leave — alone**, not change sth already satisfactory. *int* expressing surprise, expectation, acceptance, etc.

well- *prefix* '**well-'being** *n* health and happiness. '**well-'born**, '**well-connected** *adj* of a family with a good social position. '**well-'nigh** *adv* almost. '**well-'timed** *adj* done, said, etc, at a suitable time. '**well-to-'do** *adj* wealthy. '**well-'tried** *adj* (of methods, etc) tested and proved useful.

wend *v* **— one's way** (*home*, etc), go, make one's way.

went ⇨ **go**.

wept ⇨ **weep**.

west *n & adj* direction in which the sun sets. '**-erly** *adj & adv* (of direction) towards the —; (of winds) from the —. '**-ern** *adj* of, in, from, the —. '**-ernize** *v* introduce the civilization of Europe and America into. '**-ward** *adj* towards the —. '**-wards** *adv*.

wet *adj* (-ter, -test) **1** covered or soaked with water. **2** rainy. *n* moisture; rain: *come in out of the wet.* . *v* (-tt-) make wet.

whack *v & n* (strike with a) blow that can be heard.

whale *n* largest sea-animal in existence ⇨ p 247. .

wharf *n* (*pl* —s or '**wharves**) wooden or stone structure at which ships are tied up for (un)loading cargo.

what *adj* (cf which) asking for one or more out of several persons or things: *W— book? W— time? W— authors?* etc. ,—'**ever** *pron & adj* any sort of degree of: *W—ever he says, it doesn't matter.* **no doubt —ever** (,—'**so'ever**), no. doubt at all.

wheat *n* (plant producing) grain from which flour (as used for bread, etc) is made.

wheel *n* circular frame or disc that turns (on a bicycle, car, etc). **at the —**, driving a car, etc; steering a ship. *v* **1** push or pull (sth on —s, eg a barrow). **2** (cause to) turn in a curve or circle. '**-,barrow** *n* small one-wheeled vehicle with two legs for moving small loads. '**-wright** *n* man who makes and repairs —s.

when *adv & conj* at what time?; on what occasion? *adj* at or during the same time. **—'ever** *adv* at every time —.

whence *adv* from which place or cause.

where *adv* **1** in or at what place or position? **2** what place? **3** on or at which: *This is — I found it.* **'—abouts** *adv* in or near what place. *n* place — sb or sth is. **—'as** *conj* taking into consideration that. **'—fore** *conj* why; for which reason. **.—u'pon** *adv* after which; and then. **wher'ever** *adv* in, to, or at, whatever place; at those places —.

whet *v* (-tt-) sharpen (a knife, etc).

whether *conj* (cf if) *I don't know — I can come or not; I don't know — to refuse or accept,* I can't decide which to do.

which *adj* (cf what) *Tell me — books on these shelves you have read.* *pron* **1** *W— things? W— people?* **2** *This river — flows through London is called the Thames* (cf that). **—'ever** *pron & adj* any one or ones (of a limited number, esp of two).

whiff *n* slight breath (of air or smoke); smell: *the — of a cigar.*

while *conj* **1** during the time that; for as long as; at the same time as. **2** although. *n* (period of) time. **once in a —,** occasionally. **worth one's —,** worth the time, effort, etc, needed. *v* **— away the time,** spend the time pleasantly.

whim *n* sudden desire or fancy, often sth unusual or unreasoning.

whimper *v & n* (make a) weak cry of pain or fear or complaint.

whimsical *adj* having whims; odd.

whine *n* low, long-drawn, complaining cry (eg made by a miserable dog). *v* make, say sth with, such a cry.

whip *n* length of cord, strip of leather, fastened to a handle. *v* (-pp-) **1** strike with a —. **2** move or take suddenly: *— out a knife.* **'—ping** *n* beating with a — as a punishment.

whirl *v* **1** (cause to) move quickly round and round. **2** (of the brain, the senses) seem to move in this way. **3** take, be taken, rapidly (off, away, etc) in a car, etc. *n* —ing movement. **'—pool** *n* place where there are —ing currents of water.

'—wind *n* swift, circling movement of air.

whisk *n* **1** small brush for removing dust, flies, etc. **2** light brushing movement (eg of a horse's tail). *v* **1** brush *off, away,* etc, lightly and quickly. **2** take (sb or sth), go, *off, away,* quickly and suddenly.

'whisker *n* **1** (usu *pl*) hair left to grow down the sides of a man's face (cf beard, moustache). **2** one of the long, stiff hairs growing near the mouth of a cat, etc.

'whisky, 'whiskey *n* strong alcoholic drink made from grain.

'whisper *v* speak, say (sth), using only the breath, not the voice. *n* —ing sound; sth —ed.

'whistle *n* **1** (usu high) clear note made by forcing a stream of air through a small opening or by the wind; musical sound made by a bird. **2** instrument for producing such sounds. *v* make a —(1) (eg by blowing through the rounded lips); make a musical series of notes in this way: *— a tune.*

Whit *n* ⇨ Whitsun.

white *adj* (-r, -st) of the colour of the paper that this book is printed on; (of a person's face) pale owing to fear, shock, etc. **the — flag,** symbol of surrender. *n* (esp) the colourless liquid in an egg; — when boiled. **'—wash** *n* mixture of powdered chalk or lime and water, used for coating walls, ceilings, etc. *v* put —wash on; (fig) try to cover up sb's faults and make him appear blameless.

'Whitsun *n* (also **Whit Sunday**) seventh Sunday after Easter. **—tide** *n* — and the three following days.

'whittle *v* (often **— down** or **away**) cut thin slices or strips off (wood); (fig) reduce bit by bit.

whiz(z) *v & n* (make the) sound of sth rushing through the air.

who, whom, whose *pron* referring to a person or persons as the subject(2): *Who can see me? I know who you are. Who did you give it to? To whom did you give it?* (more formal); *Who does this book belong to? Whose book is this?* **who'ever** *pron* any person who; the person who.

whole *adj* **1** **the — truth,** all the truth. **2** undamaged; unbroken:

escape with a — *skin* (ie unhurt). 3 complete; entire: *It rained for three — days.* **a** — number, a number without a fraction. *n* **1** sth complete. **2** all there is of sth: *He lost the — of his money.* **3** (up)on the —, taking everything into consideration. **whole-'hearted(ly)** *adj & adv* (in a manner) showing confidence or enthusiasm. **'—sale** *n* (cf retail) selling of goods in large quantities to shopkeepers, etc, for resale to the public. **'—some** *adj* favourable to health. **'wholly** *adv* completely.

whom, whose ⇨ who.

why *adv* for what reason? *int* (indicating surprise): *Why, look who's here!*

wick *n* (length of) thread through a candle; strip of woven material by which oil is drawn up in a lamp.

'wicked *adj* **1** (of a person, his acts) bad, wrong, immoral. **2** intended to injure: *— rumours.* **—ly** *adv.* **—ness** *n.*

'wicker *n* twigs or canes woven together, usu for baskets or furniture. **—work** *n* things made of —.

'wicket *n* (cricket) three stumps at which the ball is bowled; the stretch of grass between the two —s. **'wicket-,keeper** *n* the player behind the —.

wide *adj* (-r, -st) **1** broad; measuring much from side to side. **2** of great extent: *a man with — interests* (ie in many subjects). **3** — of, far from (what is aimed at or desired): *— of the mark.* *adv* **1** in many directions. **2** fully: *— open; — awake.* **3** —apart, with — space(s) between. **4** far from what is aimed at: *fall —.* **'—n** *v* make or become —(r). **'—spread** *adj* (esp) found, distributed, over a large area. **'—ly** *adv.*

'widow *n* woman whose husband is dead. **—er** *n* man whose wife is dead. *v* make into a —(er).

width *n* **1** quality of being wide. **2** measurement from side to side.

wield *v* hold and use: *— an axe.*

wife *n* (*pl* wives) woman who has a husband.

wig *n* head-covering of false hair.

wild *adj* (-er, -est) **1** (of animals) living in natural conditions; not tamed; (of plants) growing in natural conditions; not cultivated. **2** uncultivated; unsettled: *— and mountainous areas.* **3** violent; angry: *— weather.* **4** done or said without proper thought or care: *— guesses.* *adv* without care or control. *n* the —s, uncultivated and (often) uninhabited areas. **'—ly** *adv.* **'—ness** *n.* **'—fire** *n* (only in) spread like **—fire,** (of news, etc) spread quickly.

'wilderness *n* desert; wild country.

wile *n* trick; cunning behaviour.

'wilful *adj* **1** (of persons) determined to have one's own way. **2** (of bad acts) done on purpose: *— murder.* **—ly** *adv.*

will¹ *v* (I'll = I will) **1** (used in expressing the future tense): *He — come tomorrow.* **2** (used in expressing determination, willingness): *I (we) — come.* ⇨ shall. **3** (used in requests): *W— you come tomorrow?*.

will² *v* (*pt* would) **1** (old use) wish. **2** (expressing wishes): *Would that (I wish that) it were true!* **3** make use of one's mental power in an attempt to do or get sth. ⇨ *(pt & pp —ed)* leave (property, etc) *to* (sb) by means of a will and testament. ⇨ will³(6).

will³ *n* **1** mental power by which a person can direct his thoughts and actions and control those of others. **2** (also **'will-power**) control exercised over oneself. **3** determination; desire or purpose: *do sth with a —; God's — be done.* **4** at will, when and how one pleases. **5 good (ill) —,** kind (unkind) feeling towards others. **6** (often **last — and testament**) statement in writing, saying to whom sb wishes his possessions to go. after his death.

'willing *adj* **1** ready to help, to do what is needed. **2** done, given, etc, readily, without hesitation: *— obedience.* **—ly** *adv.* **—ness** *n.*

wilt *v* (of plants, etc) (cause to) droop, lose freshness.

'wily *adj* (-ier, -iest) cunning.

win *v* (*pt & pp* won; -nn-) **1** get by means of hard work, as the result of competition, etc; do best (in a fight, game, etc). **2** persuade by argument, etc: *win over to one's side.* **3** reach by effort. *n* success in a game, etc. **'winner** *n*

some wild animals

chimpanzee

monkey

baboon

orang-utan

gorilla

trunk

tusk

kangaroo

antlers

antelope

elephant

deer

mane

tiger

lynx

leopard

lion

hippopotamus

bear

water-buffalo

rhinoceros

giraffe

hump

zebra

camel

'**winning** *adj* (esp of looks, behaviour) likely to gain favour: *a winning smile.* '**winnings** *n pl* (esp) money won in gambling.

wince *v & n* (give a) sign of pain (by making a sudden movement).

winch *n* windlass.

wind¹ *n* **1** air blowing along as a result of natural forces: *The — blew my hat off.* **2** breath needed for running, etc: *lose · one's —.* **3** scent carried by —(1). **get** — **of,** (fig) get news of. **4** ·orchestral wind-instruments. *v* (*pt* —ed) cause to be breathless: *The blow —ed me.* '—**fall** *n* fruit blown down by the —; (fig) unexpected piece of good fortune. '**wind-** ,**instrument** *n* bugle, trumpet, etc. '**windmill** *n* mill worked by the —, used for making grain into flour, etc, or pumping up water. '—**pipe** *n* ·passage for air from the throat to the lungs. '—**screen** *n* sheet of glass in front of a driver's seat in a motor-car, etc. '—**y** *adj* (-ier, -iest) with much —.

wind² *v* (*pt & pp* wound) **1** go or move in a curving, circular, or twisting manner. **2** twist (string, etc) into a ball or round or on to sth. **3** turn (a handle); raise (sth) by doing this; tighten the spring (of a clock, etc). **4** — **up,** come or bring to an end. **5 be wound up,** (fig) be tense (with excitement, etc). *n* bend or twist.

'**windlass** *n* machine for lifting or pulling heavy things by means of a handle which winds a chain or rope on to a roller.

'**window** *n* opening in a wall, etc, to let in light and air; framed pane(s) of glass for or in a — opening: *Please shut the —.*

wine *n* alcoholic drink made from the juice of grapes.

wing *n* **1** one of the parts of a bird, insect, aircraft, etc, that helps it to fly. ⇨ p 144. **on the —,** in flight. **2** part of a building, army, etc, stretching out at the side. **3** sides of the stage in a theatre (not seen by the audience).

wink *v* shut and open ·(one's eyes, or, usu, one eye) quickly; do this (with one eye, *at* sb) as a private signal. *n* **1** act of —ing. **2 forty** —**s,** a short sleep.

'**winnow** *v* separate grain from its

dry, outer coverings with a stream of air.

'**winter** *n* season between autumn and spring when (except in the tropics) the climate is usu cold. '**wintry** *adj* of or like —; cold: *a wintry sky.*

wipe *v* **1** clean or dry (sth) by rubbing with cloth, etc. **2** — **off,** remove by wiping. — **out,** clean the inside of; remove (eg a mark, or, (fig) disgrace); destroy completely. — **up,** soak up (liquid)· by wiping. *n* act of wiping.

wire *n* **1** (piece or length of) metal drawn out into the form of thread: *telegraph —s.* **2** (colloq) telegram. *v* **1** fasten (sth) with —. **2** put —(s) into. **3** (colloq) send a telegram to.

'**wireless** *adj* without the use of wires: — *telegraphy.* *n* radio (the more usual word).

wise *adj* (-r, -st) having or showing knowledge, experience, good judgement, prudence, etc. —**ly** *adv.* '**wisdom** *n* **1** quality of being —. **2** — thoughts, sayings, etc.

wish *v* **1** want: *When do you — (me) to leave?* **2** have an unsatisfied desire: *I — I knew* (but I don't); *I — I were· rich.* **3** desire (sth) for (sb); hope (sb) will have (sth): *I — you a pleasant journey.* **4** — **for,** have a desire in one's heart for pray for: *You couldn't — for anything better.* *n* **1** desire; longing **2 with all good —es,** —**ing**(3) you well.

wisp *n* small bundle or twist (o· straw, hair, etc).

'**wistful** *adj* having or showing a· unsatisfied and often vague desire· —**ly** *adv.*

wit *n* **1** intelligence; quickness o· mind. **have one's wits abou·** **one,** be quick to see what is hap·· pening, be ready to· act. **be a·** **one's wits' end,** not know wha· to do or say. **2** (person noted for· clever and humorous expression o· ideas. '**witty** *adj* (-ier, -iest) ful· of humour. '**wittily** *adv.*

witch *n* woman said to use magic· esp for evil purposes. '—**craft** · use of such magic. '**witch** ,**doctor** *n* male —· '—**ery** **1** '—craft. **2** fascination; charm.

with *prep* **1** having, carrying: *a coa·· — four pockets.* **2** indicating wha·

is used: *writing — a pen.* 3 association: *mix one thing — another.* 4 (opposition): *fight (argue) —.* 5 at the same time as; in the same direction as. 6 (support, agreement): *Are you — us or against us?*

with'draw *v* (*pt* with'drew, *pp* with'drawn) 1 pull or draw back. 2 take out, away: *— savings from the bank.* 3 take back (an offer, a statement, etc). 4 move, go, back or away: *— troops.* **—al** *n.*

'wither *v* (often *— up, away*) (cause to) become dry, faded, or dead: *flowers —ed by the heat; our hopes —ed.*

with'hold *v* (*pt & pp* with'held) keep (sth) back; refuse to give.

with'in *adv* inside. *prep* inside; not beyond. **— hearing,** near enough to hear or be heard. **— a (mile) of,** not more than a mile away from.

with'out *prep & adv* 1 (opp of with(1)) not having. 2 (old use) outside.

with'stand *v* (*pt & pp* with'stood) hold out against (pressure, attack).

'witness *n* 1 person who gives evidence, after taking an oath, in a law court; (also **eye-witness**) person who saw an event take place and should, therefore, be able to describe it. 2 what is said about sb or sth. **bear — to,** speak about. 3 person who adds his signature to a paper to show that he has seen it signed by the right person. *v* 1 be a —(3) (*to* an agreement, etc). 2 be a —(1) (*of* an event). 3 give —(2) (in a law court, etc).

'wittingly *adv* knowingly; on purpose.

'witty *adj* ⇨ wit.

wives ⇨ wife.

'wizard *n* magician.

'wizened *adj* (esp of the face) shrivelled; aged (2).

'wobble *v* (cause to) move unsteadily from side to side. 'wobbly *adj.*

woe *n* (cause of) sorrow. 'woeful *adj* sorrowful; causing sorrow.

woke ⇨ wake.

wolf *n.* (*pl* wolves) wild, flesh-eating animal of the dog family, hunting together in large numbers.

'woman *n* (*pl* 'women) adult female human being; female sex. '**—hood** *n* state of being a —; *reach —hood.*

womb *n* part of a female mammal in which her offspring develops before birth.

won ⇨ win.

'wonder *n* feeling caused by sth unusual or surprising; thing or event causing such feeling. *v* 1 feel —(*at*). 2 ask oneself (*about* sth, *who, what, whether,* etc). **—ful** *adj* causing —; remarkable; pleasing.

won't = will not. ⇨ will.

wont *n* what sb is accustomed to doing: *as was his — (custom). adj* **he was — to,** it was his custom to.

woo *v* (*pt & pp* wooed) try to win the love of (a woman), her hand in marriage; try to win (fame, fortune, etc).

wood *n* 1 hard, solid substance a tree-trunk is made of. 2 (often *pl*) area of land covered with growing trees. '**—ed** *adj* with —s(2). '**—en** *adj* made of —; (fig) stiff; clumsy. '**—land** *n* tree-covered land. '**—work** *n* 1 things made of —, esp the —en parts of a building. 2 carpentry. '**—y** *adj* of or like —(1).

wool *n* soft, curly hair of sheep, goats, camels, and some other animals; thread, yarn, cloth, clothing, made from this. '**—len** *adj* made of —. '**—ly** *adj* covered with or like —; *n* (colloq) sweater.

word *n* 1 unit of language made up of one or more letters as spoken, written, or printed. 2 sth said; talk. **have a — with sb,** speak to him. **have —s (with),** quarrel. **take sb at his —,** act on the belief that he means to do what he says. 3 news: *Send me — tomorrow.* 4 promise: *give sb (keep, break) one's —. v* express in —s: *How shall we — it?* '**—ing** *n* choice of —s to express meaning.

wore ⇨ wear.

work *n* 1 use of bodily or mental powers for the purpose of doing or making sth (usu contrasted with play or amusement); use of energy supplied by steam, electricity, etc. **set (get) to —,** begin doing sth. **make short — of sth,** finish it quickly. 2 what a person does to earn a living. **in (out of) —,** having (not having) employment. **at —,** at one's place of employment; busy with one's —. 3 sth (to be) done: *I have a lot of — to do.* 4 things needed or used for — (eg for sewing). **5** sth produced by —: *the — of silversmiths*; '*stone* —. **6** product of the intellect or imagination: —*s of art.* **7** (*pl*) moving parts of a machine (eg a clock); building(s) for manufacturing, etc: *an iron*—*s.* **8** public —*s*, the building of roads, dams, etc, by government authorities. *v* **1** do —. **2** (of a machine, bodily organ, etc) do what it is required or designed to do: *The bell is not* —*ing.* **3** (of a plan, etc) have the result desired. **4** cause to —; set in motion: *It's* —*ed by electricity.* **5** produce, perform: — *a cure*; — *harm.* **6** (cause to) move or go, usu slowly or with difficulty: *This screw has* —*ed loose.* — **off**, get rid of; deal with. — **up**, create by degrees; excite. **7** make or shape by hammering, pressing, etc. **8** make by stitching. '—**able** *adj* that can be —ed; practicable. '**work-bag**, '—**basket**, '—**box** *n* one for holding (esp *needle*—) materials. '—**er** *n* sb who —s, esp sb doing physical work in industry, a factory, etc. '—**man** *n* man who earns a living by physical labour, or in a factory, etc. '—**manlike** *adj* (as) of a good —man. '—**manship** *n* quality as seen in sth made: *poor* —*manship.* '—**shop** *n* room or building where things (esp machines) are made or repaired.

world *n* **1** the earth, its countries and people. **2** persons, etc, connected with a special class of interests: *the* — *of sport.* '—**ly** *adj* **1** material: *my* —*ly goods.* **2** of this —; not spiritual: —*ly pleasures.*

worm *n* small, boneless, limbless, creeping creature of many sorts. ⇨ p 144. *v* (often — **one's way**) go or get slowly (*through, into*).

worn ⇨ wear.

'**worry** *v* (*pt & pp* '**worried**) **1** trouble; give (sb) no peace of mind: — *sb to do sth.* **2** be anxious or uneasy (*about*). *n* **1** cause of anxiety. **2** condition of being troubled.

worse ⇨ bad. — **off**, poorer, less well treated. '—**n** *v* make or become —.

'**worship** *n* **1** (act of) reverence and honour done to God: *place of* —, church or chapel. **2** admiration and respect shown to or felt for

sb or sth: *hero* —. **3 Your (His) W**—, title used to (of) a magistrate or mayor. *v* give — to; attend a church service.

worst ⇨ bad. **get the** — **of it**, be defeated. **if the** — **comes to the** —, if things are as bad as they possibly can be.

worth *adj* **1** having a certain value; of value equal to that of; possessing: *It is* —*five pence*; *He died* — £5,000. **2** giving a satisfactory return or reward for: *The book is well* — *reading.* *n* value; what sb or sth is —: *a dollar's* — *of apples*, as many as a dollar buys. '—**less** *adj.* '**worth-'while** *adj* that is — the time, money, etc, needed.

'**worthy** *adj* (-**ier**, -**iest**) deserving (respect, support, etc): — *of respect*; *a* — *cause.* '**worthily** *adv.*

would (**I'd** = **I would**) **1** ⇨ will[1] and will[2]. **2** (used in conditional statements and questions): *If a car had no brakes there* — *soon be an accident.* — **rather** ⇨ rather.

wouldn't = would not. ⇨ will[1,2].

wound[1] ⇨ wind[2].

wound[2] *n* **1** injury done to the body by cutting, tearing, etc, esp one that is the result of attack. **2** pain given to a person's feelings: *a* — *to his pride.* *v* give a — to.

wove, '**woven** ⇨ weave.

'**wrangle** *v & n* (take part in a) noisy or angry argument.

wrap *v* (-**pp**-) **1** (often — **up**) put (soft material, a shawl, etc) round; cover or roll up (sb or sth) in (soft material, etc). **2** be —**ped up in**, give all one's interest and attention to. *n* extra covering (eg a scarf or rug). '—**per** *n* paper covering for food, a newspaper, book, etc (eg when sent by post). '—**ping** *n* (material for) covering or packing.

wrath *n* (liter) deep anger: strong indignation.

wreath *n* flowers or leaves twisted together in a circle; ring or curving line (*of* smoke, etc).

wreck *n* ruin or destruction, eg of a ship; badly damaged car, building, etc. *v* cause the — of. '—**age** *n* —ing or being —ed; —ed material; fragments: *the* —*age of an aircraft.*

wrench *n* **1** sudden and violent twist or pull. **2** (pain caused by) sad parting or separation. **3** tool for gripping and turning nuts, bolts, etc; spanner. *v* twist or pull violently; injure (eg one's ankle) thus.

wrest *v* take (sth) violently away (*from*): *I —ed the sword from him.*

wrestle *v* struggle (*with* sb) and try to throw him down without hitting him; (fig) struggle *with* (a problem). **—r** *n* person who *—*s (in sport).

wretch *n* **1** very unfortunate and unhappy person. **2** bad person. **'—ed** *adj* **1** feeling very uncomfortable, ill, etc; likely to cause misery. **2** of poor quality.

wriggle *v* twist and turn (the body or a part of it).

wring *v* (*pt & pp* wrung) twist and squeeze tightly; force (esp water) *out* by doing this. **'—er** *n* apparatus with rollers for *—*ing water out of clothes, linen, etc.

wrinkle *n* small fold or line in the skin or on the surface of sth (eg a dress). *v* make or get *—*s in.

wrist *n* joint between the hand and the arm. ⇨ p 29. **'—let** *n* band or ornament for the *—*.

write *v* (*pt* wrote, *pp* 'written) make letters or other symbols on a surface, esp with a pen or pencil on paper. **'—r** *n* sb who *—*s, esp an author or journalist. **'writing** *n* **1** handwriting. **2** (usu *pl*) literary work.

writhe *v* roll about in pain; (fig) suffer in one's mind.

wrong *adj* (opp of *right*) not morally right; incorrect; unjust; unsuitable; out of order; in a bad condition. *adv* in a *—* manner: *You spelt my name —* (cf *—*ly). **go —**, get out of order; fall into bad ways of living. *n* what is morally *—*; evil; injustice; instance of unjust treatment. **in the —**, having done or said sth *—*. *v* do *—* to; judge (sb) unfairly. **'—'doing** *n* doing *—*; sin; crime. **'—ful** *adj* unjust; unlawful. **—fully** *adv*. **'—ly** *adv* (esp with a *pp*): *—ly informed*.

wrote ⇨ write.

wrought (*pp* of *work*; used in) **— iron**, iron shaped by hammering while hot. **— up**, (of a person, his feelings) excited; in a nervous state.

wrung ⇨ wring.

wry *adj* a **— face**, with the features pulled out of shape (to show disgust, disappointment).

X

Xmas *n* (sometimes used, in writing and print only, for) Christmas.

'X-'ray *n* (*pl* 'X-'rays) short wave rays that go through solids and enables doctors to see into the body; photograph taken by this means.

Y

yacht *n* **1** sailing-boat built for racing. **2** small (usu privately owned) ship for pleasure-cruising.

yam *n* tuberous root of a tropical plant used as food. ⇨ p 306.

yard[1] *n* **1** unit of length, 3 feet or 36 inches. **2** pole hung at its centre in front of a mast to support a sail of a ship.

yard[2] *n* (usu unroofed) enclosed space near or round building(s): *a farm—*.

yarn *n* **1** thread prepared for knitting, weaving, etc, esp woollen *—*. **2** (colloq) story; traveller's tale.

yawn *v* **1** open the mouth widely because sleepy, bored, etc. **2** be wide open. *n* act of *—*ing(2).

year *n* time taken for the earth to orbit the sun (365¼ days); period from 1st January to 31 December (365 days); this period starting from any day: *academic (financial) —*; ⇨ leap. **'—ly** *adj & adv* every *—*, once every *—*.

yearn *v* have a strong desire (*for, to do*). **'—ing** *n* longing (*after, for*). **'—ingly** *adv*.

yeast *n* substance used in the making of bread, added to make the dough rise.

yell *v & n* (utter a) loud cry of pain, excitement, etc; say (sth) in a *—*ing voice.

'yellow *n & adj* the colour of gold, egg yolk, butter, etc. **— fever**, tropical disease causing the skin to turn *—*. *v* (cause to) become *—*.

yelp v & n esp of dogs (utter a) short, sharp bark (of pain, anger, excitement).

yes int (opp of no) indicating agreement, consent, etc.

'yesterday n & adv (on the) day before today.

yet adv being by this or that time; up to now, then; so far; at some future time. (cf already.) conj but still; nevertheless.

yew n (wood of an) evergreen tree with dark green leaves.

yield v 1 give as a natural product, as a result or profit. 2 give way, esp to force; surrender. n amount produced: the — per acre. **'—ing** adj easily giving way.

'yogh(o)urt n fermented, creamy food made from milk.

yoke n 1 shaped piece of wood placed across the necks of oxen pulling a plough, etc. 2 throw off the —, rebel, refuse to obey. v 1 put a — on (oxen). 2 **—d to**, united to.

a yoke

yolk n yellow part of an egg.

'yonder adj & adv (that is, that can be seen) over there.

you pron the person(s) addressed: I can see you and you can see me. 2 any person (cf one(2)): You never know who may become your enemy.

young adj (-er, -est) 1 (contrasted with old) not far ahead in life, growth, etc; of recent birth or origin. 2 still near its beginning: The night is yet —. n (of animals) — offspring. **'—ster** n child, esp boy.

your(s) adj belonging to, related to, you: That is your book. That book is yours. **your'self** pron (pl your'selves): You hurt yourself (yourselves) when you fell over.

youth n 1 the state of being young. 2 young persons: the — of the nation; — clubs. 3 young man

(about 15 to 20 years of age). **'—ful** adj (looking) young.

yule n (also **—tide**) Christmas.

Z

zeal n enthusiasm (for). **'—ous** adj having, showing, acting with, —.

'zebra n horse-like wild animal of Africa, with dark stripes. ⇨ p 317.

'zenith n part of the sky directly overhead; (fig) highest point of one's fame, fortune, etc.

'zero n 1 the figure 0; nought. 2 the point between + and — on a scale, esp a thermometer.

zest n 1 great interest or pleasure. 2 pleasing quality or flavour.

'zigzag n line or path that turns first one way and then the other at sharp angles. adv in a —. v (-gg-) go in a —.

a zigzag

a zipper

zinc n white metal used for roofing, coating iron pails, etc.

'zip-,fastener n device as shown above for fastening clothing, etc.

'zodiac n (plan of the) night sky containing the path of the principal planets round the sun divided into twelve equal parts, called the signs of the —, used by astrologers.

zone n 1 belt or band round sth, different in colour, appearance, etc. 2 one of the five parts into which maps of the world are divided by lines parallel to the equator (the tropical, the N & S temperate and the arctic and antarctic —s). 3 area with particular features or purpose.

zoo n zoological gardens.

zo'ology n science of the structure, forms, etc, of animals. **zoo'logical** adj of —. **zoological gardens**, park (usu public) in which many kinds of animals are kept for exhibition. **zo'ologist** n expert in —.

COMMON ABBREVIATIONS

The selection has been made from situations in which you are most likely to meet abbreviated words: language texts, advertisements, newspapers, travel brochures, keeping a bank account, leisure, geography, etc.

A Adult; Association; first class
A1 excellent
AA Automobile Association
AAA Amateur Athletics Association
A-bomb atomic bomb
A-level advance level (examination)
ABC alphabetical (order)
abb., abbr. abbreviation
a.c. alternating current
a/c account
ack(n) acknowledge(d)
ad., advt. advertisement
AD after the birth of Christ
add. additional; address
adj adjective
Adm. Admiral
admin. administration
adv. adverb
AF Air Force
AGM Annual General Meeting
agt. agreement
alt. alternate; altitude
a.m. before midday
amp ampère
anon. anonymous
ans. answer
appro. approval
approx. approximately
appt. appointment
Apr. April
arch. archaic; architectural
arith. arithmetic(al)
arr. arrives (at)
art. article
Assoc. Association
asst. assistant
Aug. August
Av(e) Avenue

b. born; bowled
b & k bathroom and kitchen
B Bachelor; second class
B & B bed and breakfast
BA Bachelor of Arts
bach. bachelor
BBC British Broadcasting
    Corporation
BC before the birth of Christ
BEA British European Airways
bedsit. bed-sitting room
bef. before
bet. between
b.f. bring (brought) forward

Bibl. biblical
b.o., B.O. body odour; box office
BOAC British Overseas Airways
    Corporation
Bor. Borough
br. branch; brother; brown
BR British Rail
Br. Britain; British; Brother
Bros. Brothers
B.Sc. Bachelor of Science
BSI British Standards Institute
BUA British United Airways
BUPA (Gt Brit) private medical
    insurance scheme

c. caught; cent(s); centimetre; cold;
    cubic
c & c carpets and curtains
C Catholic; Centigrade; Century;
    Conservative; third class
cap. capital letter
Cath. Catholic
cc carbon copy; cubic centimetre
Cd Commander
CD Civil Defence; Diplomatic Corps
C of E Church of England
cert. certified; certainty
Cert. Certificate
cf compare
c/f carry (carried) forward
ch. chapter; church
c.h. central heating
c.h.w. constant hot water
chap. chapter
choc. chocolate
CIA (USA) Central Intelligence
    Agency
CID (Gt Brit) Criminal Investigation
    Department
C in C Commander in Chief
cm centimetre
CND Campaign for Nuclear
    Disarmament
Co. Company
C.O. Commanding Officer
c/o care of
c.o.d., C.O.D. cash to be paid on
    delivery
Col. Colonel
colloq. colloquial(ism)
Com. Commissioner;
    Commonwealth; Communist
Cmdr. Commander

comp. compare; compound
concl. conclusion
conf. conference
conj. conjunction; conjunctive
Cons. Conservative; Consul
cons. consonant
cont. continent; continue(d)
Co-op Co-operative
Corp. Corporation
corres. correspondence
CP Command Post; Communist Party
Cpl. Corporal
CS Civil Servant; Civil Service
cu. cubic
cwt hundredweight

d. date; daughter; died
D Department; Doctor; Duchess; Duke; fourth class
D-day date for the start of a major military offensive
DA (USA) District Attorney
dau. daughter
d/bed double bedroom
dbl. double
DDT insecticide
dec. deceased; declension; decrease
Dec. December
def. definite; definition
deg. degree
Dem. Democracy; Democrat
dep. departs; deposit
Dept. Department
diag. diagram
diam. diameter
dict. dictation; dictionary
diff. difference; different
Dip.Ed. Diploma in Education
Dir. Director
disc. discount
div. divided; division; divorced
D.J. disc jockey; dinner jacket
do. the same
dol. dollar(s)
doz. dozen
dr. dram; debit
Dr. Doctor; Drive
dup. duplicate(d)
dz. dozen

E Earth; east(ern); English; Excellent; fifth or lowest class
Ed. editor; edited (by)
EEC European Economic Community (= the Common Market)
e.g. for example
elec. electric(ity)
Emp. Emperor; Empire; Empress
encl. enclosed

ENE east northeast(ern)
Eng. England; English
EP extended play(ing record)
eq. equals
E.R. Queen Elizabeth II
ESE east southeast(ern)
esp. especially
Esq. Esquire
est. established; estimated
e.t.a. estimated time of arrival
etc., &c and the rest
e.t.d. estimated time of departure
eve. (in the) evening
exam. examination
Exc. Excellency
excl. exclamation; exclusive
exec. executive
exp. experiment; express
ext. external; extinct; extract

f. female; feet; foot
F Fahrenheit; Fellow; France; French
f & f, F & F fixtures and fittings
FA Football Association
FAO Food and Agriculture Organisation
FBI (USA) Federal Bureau of Investigation
Feb. February
Fed. Federal; Federation
fem. female; feminine
fig. figurative; figure
fin. financial; finish
fl. floor; fluid
FM Field-Marshal
fol. following
for. foreign
fr. from
Fr Father; France; Franc; French
Fri. Friday
ft. feet; foot
furn. furnished
fut. future
fwd. forward

g. gram(me)
G Guide; Gulf
gal. gallon
GB Great Britain
GCE General Certificate of Education
gdn garden
Gen. General
geog. geography
Ger. German(y)
G.I. (USA) soldier
gm. gram(me)
GMT Greenwich Mean Time (British time)

Gov. Governor
Govt. Government
GP General Practitioner (doctor)
GPO (Gt Brit) General Post Office
gr. grade; group
gt. great
Gt Brit Great Britain

h. height; hour; hundred
H-bomb hydrogen bomb
h. & c. hot and cold water is available
H.E. Her/His Excellency
hf. half
hi-fi high fidelity (sound)
HK Hong Kong
H.M.S.O. Her Majesty's Stationery Office
H of C House of Commons
H of L House of Lords
Hon. Honorary
Hosp. Hospital
H.P. Horse Power; Hire Purchase
H.Q. Headquarters
hr. hour
H.R.H. Her/His Royal Highness
se. house

Island; Italy
.e. that is; in other words
llus. illustrated; illustration
MF International Monetary Fund
mp. imperative; imperfect
n. inch
nc. increase
nc. Incorporated
ncl. include; including; inclusive
nd. industrial; industry
nd. Independent; India(n)
ndef. indefinite
ndiv. individual
nf. inferior; infinitive; information
ns. inches; inspector; insurance
nst. instant(ly)
nst. Institute
nt. interest; interior
nter. intermediate
nterr(og). interrogative
ntro. introduction
nv. invoice
O.U. I owe you
PA International Phonetic Alphabet
Q. intelligence level
s. Island
TA Independent Television Authority
tal. italic

Judge; Junior; Justice
an. January
C Jesus Christ

JP Justice of the Peace (magistrate)
Jnr., Jr., Jun. Junior
Jul. July
Jun. June
juv. juvenile

kg., kilo. kilogram
km. kilometre
k.o. knock out
Kt. Knight
kw. kilowatt

l. late; latitude; left; length; litre
L. Labour; Lake; large size; Latin
lab. laboratory
lang. language
lat. latitude
Lat. Latin
lb. pound(s) (weight)
LEA Local Education Authority
leg. legal
lge. large
l.h. left hand
Lib. Liberal; Liberation
lit. literature; literary
liter. literary
ll. lines
log. logarithm
long. longitude
LP long play(ing record)
£SD (former) British money
LSD drug
Lt. (-Gen.) Lieutenant (-General)
Ltd. Limited
lux. luxury
LV luncheon voucher

m. male; married; masculine; metre; mile; million; minute
M. Master; Member; *Monsieur*, French for *Mr*; Motorway
M.A. Master of Arts
mag. magazine
Maj. Major
Mar. March
masc. masculine
maths mathematics
max. maximum
M.C. Master of Ceremonies
M.D. Doctor of Medicine
med. mediaeval; medical; medium
Messrs. *pl* of *Mr*
mg. milligram(me)
mil. military
min. minimum; minute
M.I.5 (Gt Brit) department controlling State security
misc. miscellaneous
Mlle *Mademoiselle*, French for *Miss*
mm. millimetre
Mme *Madame*, French for *Mrs*

Mon. Monday
MP Member of Parliament (the Commons); Military Police
m.p.g. miles per gallon
m.p.h. miles per hour
Mr, Mrs ⇨ the dictionary
ms(s), MS(S) manuscript(s)
M.Sc. Master of Science
Mt. Mount; mountain
mth. month

n. born; name(d); neuter; noon; north(ern); noun
N North(ern); November
Nat. National; Natural
'NATO North Atlantic Treaty Organisation
nb., N.B. note carefully or in particular
NE northeast(ern)
neg. negative
NHS (Gt Brit) National Health Service
NNE north northeast(ern)
NNW north northwest(ern)
no., No. number
Nov. November
nr. near
NSPCC National Society for the Prevention of Cruelty to Children
N.T. New Testament
NW northwest(ern)
N.Y. New York
N.Z. New Zealand

O. Ocean; Officer; Organisation
OAU Organisation for African Unity
ob. died
OBE Officer/Order of the British Empire
obj. object(ive)
obs. obsolete
occas. occasional(ly)
Oct. October
off. official
O.H.M.S. On Her Majesty's Service
o.k., O.K. ⇨ the dictionary
o.n.o. or nearest offer
opp. opposite
orch. orchestra(l)
O.T. Old Testament
oz. ounce

p. British decimal pence or penny; page; past
P Parking; President; Priest; Prince
p.a. once a year
P.A. Personal Assistant
P.A. system public address system
'Pan'Am Pan American Airways

para. paragraph
Parl. Parliament
part. participle
p.c. per cent
P.C. policeman
pd. paid
P.E. Physical Education
per cent by the hundred
perf. perfect
pers. personal
P.G. paying guest
Ph.D. Doctor of Philosophy
Phil. Philosophy
phon. phonetic(s)
phr. phrase
phys. physical; physics
pl. plural
Pl. Place
plur. plural
p.m. after midday; per month
P.M. Prime Minister
P.O. Personnel Officer; Post Office; Postal Order
poet. poetic; poetical
pop. popular; population
pp. pages; past participle; in place of
pr. pair; per; present; price
Pr. Priest; Prince; Province
prep. preparatory; preposition
Pres. President
priv. private
pro professional; in favour of
prod. product(ion)
Prof Professor
pron. pronoun
Prot. Protestant
pro tem for the time being
PS also
p.t. past tense
P.T. Physical Training; Purchase Tax
PTA Parent Teacher Association
PTO please turn over
pty party
Pvt. private
p.w. per week

Q Queen
qr. quarter
qt. quart; quantity
q.t. quiet
qu. question
Qu. Quarter; Queen
quad quadruplet
quot. quotation
q.v. which see

r. railway; right
R. King; Queen; Rabbi; Republic(an); River; Royal

three R's reading, writing, and arithmetic
R.A. Royal Academy; rear Admiral
RAC Royal Automobile Club
rad. radical; radius
RAF Royal Air Force
R.C. Red Cross; Roman Catholic
Rd. road; round
recd. received
red. reduced
ref. refer(ence); reformation
Reg. Regent
regd. registered
Regt. Regiment
rel. relative; religion
rep. repair; repeat
Rep. Representative; Republic(an)
rept. receipt; report
res. research; reserve; residential; resolution
Rev. Reverend
r.h. right hand
R.I. Religious Instruction
R.I.P. may he/she rest in peace
riv. river
rm. room
RN Royal Navy
RSA Royal Society of Arts
RSPCA Royal Society for the Prevention of Cruelty to Animals
r.s.v.p., R.S.V.P. please reply (to)
Rt. Hon. Right Honourable
Ry railway

s. second; shilling(s); singular; son
S Saint; Sea; Sister; small size; south(ern)
SA South Africa; South America
s.a.e. stamped, addressed envelope
Sat. Saturday
sb. somebody
s.c. self-contained
Sc. Science; Scene
Sch. School
SE southeast(ern)
SEATO South East Asia Treaty Organisation
sec. second; secondary
Sec. Secondary; Secretary
Sen., Sr., Snr. Senior
Sep(t). September
Serg., Sgt. Sergeant
SF science fiction
sgd. signed
sgle bed single bedroom
sh. shilling
sing. singular
sl. slang
Soc. Society
Sol. Solicitor

SOS distress signal for help
Sov. Sovereign
sp. spelling
Sp. Spain; Spanish
sq. square
SRN State Registered Nurse
SSE south southeast(ern)
SSW south southwest(ern)
st. stone (weight)
St. Saint; Strait(s); Street
sta. station
STD (Gt Brit) automatic telephone dialling
str. straight
subj. subject(ive)
subst. substitute
Sun. Sunday
superl. superlative
Supt. Superintendent
s.w. short wave (sound)
SW southwest(ern)
syn. synonym(ous)

t. tense; time
T Temperature; Territory
TB tuberculosis
tel. telegram; telephone
temp. temperature; temporary
Thos. Thomas
Three-D, 3-D three-dimensional
Thurs. Thursday
TNT explosive
trans. translated (by)
Treas. Treasurer
TU Trade Union
TUC (Gt Brit) Trade Union Congress
Tues. Tuesday
TV television

UFO unidentified flying object
UHF ultra high frequency (sound)
UK United Kingdom
UN United Nations
U'NESCO United Nations Educational, Scientific and Cultural Organisation
unfurn. unfurnished
'UNICEF United Nations International Children's (Emergency) Fund
Univ. University
'UNO United Nations Organisation
USA United States of America
USSR Union of Soviet Socialist Republics
usu. usually

v. verb; versus; very; volt; volume
V Victory; Volt; Volume

vac. vacant; vacation; vacuum
vb. verb
V.C. Vice-Chairman; Vice-Chancellor
VD venereal (sexually contagious) disease(s)
veg. vegetable(s)
vet. veteran; veterinary
VHF very high frequency (sound)
VIP very important person
viz. namely
vocab. vocabulary
vol. volume; volunteer
vulg. vulgar
v.v. *vice versa*, the other way round

w. watt; wife; with; woman
W west(ern)
w.c. toilet
wd. word; would
Wed. Wednesday

WHO World Health Organisation
W.I. West Indies
wk. week(ly)
Wm. William
WNE west northeast(ern)
WNW west northwest(ern)
WSE west southeast(ern)
WSW west southwest(ern)
wt. weight

X a kiss; extra; unknown name, thing, etc
Xmas Christmas
X-ray ⇨ the dictionary

y. year
yd. yard
YHA Youth Hostel Association
yr. year, your
yrs. years; yours

Symbols

@	at	£	pound sterling
∵	because	$	dollar
∴	therefore	¥	yen
=	equals	©	copyright
+	plus; and	⇨	see; look at
−	minus; take away; from	*	asterisk
×	multiplied by; times	°	degree
÷	divided by	&, &	and
%	per cent	&c	etc

COLLECTIVE NOUNS

Some nouns in English indicate a group of animals, people or things; they describe the group collectively so that you think of the group as a single object. Here are some examples—there are many more:

a **brood** of (very young) birds
a **clutch** of chickens, etc
a **colony** of insects, eg ants
a **drove** of cattle, etc (moving in a group)
a **flight** of birds
a **flock** of birds; sheep, goats, etc
a **gaggle** of geese
a **galaxy** of stars; (fig) celebrities
a **gang** of buffaloes; thieves; workmen
a **herd** of cattle, elephants, whales, etc
a **host** of angels

a **nest** of hornets; tables
a **pack** of wolves; hounds; cards; (fig) lies
a **plague** of locusts, etc
a **pride** of lions; peacocks
a **school** of fish, dolphins, etc
a **sea** of troubles (fig)
a **shoal** of fish
a **stable** of horses (bred together)
a **string** of beads, pearls, etc; (fig) lies
a **swarm** of bees, wasps, etc
a **team** of horses; players, athletes, etc

IRREGULAR VERBS

The verbs listed are defined in the dictionary

Infinitive	Past tense	Past participle
abide	abode, abided	abode, abided
arise	arose	arisen
awake	awoke	awaked, awoke
be (am, is; are)	was, were	been
bear	bore	borne, born
beat	beat	beaten
become	became	become
befall	befell	befallen
beget	begot	begotten
begin	began	begun
behold	beheld	beheld
bend	bent	bent, bended
bereave	bereaved, bereft	bereaved, bereft
beseech	besought	besought
beset	beset	beset
bestride	bestrode	bestridden, bestrid, bestrode
bet	bet, betted	bet, betted
bid	bade, bid	bidden, bid
bide	bode, bided	bided
bind	bound	bound
bite	bit	bitten, bit
bleed	bled	bled
blend	blended, blent	blended, blent
bless	blessed, blest	blessed, blest
blow	blew	blown
break	broke	broken
breed	bred	bred
bring	brought	brought
broadcast	broadcast, broadcasted	broadcast, broadcasted
browbeat	browbeat	browbeaten
build	built	built
burn	burnt, burned	burnt, burned
burst	burst	burst
buy	bought	bought
cast	cast	cast
catch	caught	caught
chide	chid	chidden, chid
choose	chose	chosen
cleave	clove, cleft	cloven, cleft
cling	clung	clung
clothe	clothed	clothed
come	came	come
cost	cost	cost
creep	crept	crept
crow	crowed	crowed
cut	cut	cut
dare	dared, durst	dared
deal	dealt	dealt
dig	dug	dug
do	did	done
draw	drew	drawn
dream	dreamed, dreamt	dreamed, dreamt
drink	drank	drunk

330

Infinitive	Past tense	Past participle
drive	drove	driven
dwell	dwelt	dwelt
eat	ate	eaten
fall	fell	fallen
feed	fed	fed
feel	felt	felt
fight	fought	fought
find	found	found
flee	fled	fled
fling	flung	flung
fly	flew	flown
forbear	forbore	forborne
forbid	forbade, forbad	forbidden
forecast	forecast, forecasted	forecast, forecasted
foresee	foresaw	foreseen
foretell	foretold	foretold
forget	forgot	forgotten
forgive	forgave	forgiven
forsake	forsook	forsaken
freeze	froze	frozen
get	got	got (USA gotten)
gild	gilded, gilt	gilded
give	gave	given
go	went	gone
grind	ground	ground
grow	grew	grown
hang	hung, hanged	hung, hanged
have (has)	had	had
hear	heard	heard
heave	heaved, hove	heaved, hove
hew	hewed	hewed, hewn
hide	hid	hidden, hid
hit	hit	hit
hold	held	held
hurt	hurt	hurt
inlay	inlaid	inlaid
keep	kept	kept
kneel	knelt	knelt
knit	knitted, knit	knitted, knit
know	knew	known
lay	laid	laid
lead	led	led
lean	leant, leaned	leant, leaned
leap	leapt, leaped	leapt, leaped
learn	learnt, learned	learnt, learned
leave	left	left
lend	lent	lent
let	let	let
lie	lay	lain
light	lighted, lit	lighted, lit
lose	lost	lost
make	made	made
mean	meant	meant
meet	met	met
melt	melted	melted, molten
mislay	mislaid	mislaid
mislead	misled	misled
mistake	mistook	mistaken
misunderstand	misunderstood	misunderstood

Infinitive	Past tense	Past participle
mow	mowed	mown
outbid	outbade, outbid	outbidden, outbid
outdo	outdid	outdone
outgrow	outgrew	outgrown
overcast	overcast	overcast
overcome	overcame	overcome
overdo	overdid	overdone
overdraw	overdrew	overdrawn
overhang	overhung	overhung
overhear	overheard	overheard
override	overrode	overridden
overrun	overran	overrun
oversee	oversaw	overseen
oversleep	overslept	overslept
overtake	overtook	overtaken
overthrow	overthrew	overthrown
partake	partook	partaken
pay	paid	paid
put	put	put
read	read (pronounced red)	read (pronounced red)
relay	relaid	relaid
repay	repaid	repaid
rid	ridded, rid	rid, ridded
ride	rode	ridden
ring	rang, rung	rung
rise	rose	risen
run	ran	run
saw	sawed	sawn, sawed
say	said	said
see	saw	seen
seek	sought	sought
sell	sold	sold
send	sent	sent
set	set	set
sew	sewed	sewn, sewed
shake	shook	shaken
shear	sheared	shorn, sheared
shed	shed	shed
shine	shone	shone
shoe	shod	shod
shoot	shot	shot
show	showed	shown, showed
shred	shredded	shredded
shrink	shrank, shrunk	shrunk, shrunken
shut	shut	shut
sing	sang	sung
sink	sank	sunk, sunken
sit	sat	sat
slay	slew	slain
sleep	slept	slept
slide	slid	slid, slidden
sling	slung	slung
slink	slunk	slunk
slit	slit	slit
smell	smelt, smelled	smelt, smelled
sow	sowed	sown, sowed
speak	spoke	spoken
speed	sped, speeded	sped, speeded
spell	spelt, spelled	spelt, spelled

Infinitive	Past tense	Past participle
spend	spent	spent
spill	spilt, spilled	spilt, spilled
spin	spun, span	spun
spit	spat	spat
split	split	split
spoil	spoilt, spoiled	spoilt, spoiled
spread	spread	spread
spring	sprang	sprung
stand	stood	stood
steal	stole	stolen
stick	stuck	stuck
sting	stung	stung
stink	stank, stunk	stunk
strew	strewed	strewn, strewed
stride	strode	stridden, strid
strike	struck	struck, stricken
string	strung	strung
strive	strove	striven
swear	swore	sworn
sweep	swept	swept
swell	swelled	swollen, swelled
swim	swam	swum
swing	swung	swung
take	took	taken
teach	taught	taught
tear	tore	torn
tell	told	told
think	thought	thought
thrive	throve, thrived	thriven, thrived
throw	threw	thrown
thrust	thrust	thrust
tread	trod	trodden, trod
undergo	underwent	undergone
undersell	undersold	undersold
understand	understood	understood
undertake	undertook	undertaken
underwrite	underwrote	underwritten
undo	undid	undone
upset	upset	upset
wake	woke, waked	waked, woken, woke
waylay	waylaid	waylaid
wear	wore	worn
weave	wove	woven, wove
wed	wedded	wedded, wed
weep	wept	wept
win	won	won
wind	winded, wound	winded, wound
withdraw	withdrew	withdrawn
withhold	withheld	withheld
withstand	withstood	withstood
work	worked	worked
wring	wrung	wrung
write	wrote	written

WRITING NUMBERS

Cardinal		Ordinal	
$\frac{1}{8}$	an eighth, one eighth		
$\frac{1}{4}$	a quarter, one quarter		
$\frac{1}{2}$	a half, one half		
$\frac{3}{4}$	three quarters		
1	one	1st	first
2	two	2nd	second
3	three	3rd	third
4	four	4th	fourth
5	five	5th	fifth
6	six	6th	sixth
7	seven	7th	seventh
8	eight	8th	eighth
9	nine	9th	ninth
10	ten	10th	tenth
11	eleven	11th	eleventh
12	twelve	12th	twelfth
13	thirteen	13th	thirteenth
14	fourteen	14th	fourteenth
15	fifteen	15th	fifteenth
16	sixteen	16th	sixteenth
17	seventeen	17th	seventeenth
18	eighteen	18th	eighteenth
19	nineteen	19th	nineteenth
20	twenty	20th	twentieth
21	twenty-one	21st	twenty-first
30	thirty	30th	thirtieth
40	forty	40th	fortieth
50	fifty	50th	fiftieth
60	sixty	60th	sixtieth
70	seventy	70th	seventieth
80	eighty	80th	eightieth
90	ninety	90th	ninetieth
100	a (one) hundred	100th	a (one) hundredth
1 000	a (one) thousand	1 000th	a (one) thousandth
10 000	ten thousand(s)	10 000th	ten thousandth
100 000	a (one) hundred thousand	100 000th	a (one) hundred thousandth
1 000 000	a (one) million	1 000 000th	a (one) millionth

HIGHER NUMERALS

	USA, France	Gt Brit and other European countries
1 000 000 000	a (one) billion	a (one) thousand millions
1 000 000 000 000	a (one) trillion	a (one) billion
1 000 000 000 000 000	a (one) quadrillion	a (one) thousand billions
1 000 000 000 000 000 000	a (one) quintillion	a (one) trillion

COLLECTIVE NUMBERS

                a dozen =   12
                a score =   20
                a gross ≐   144

ROMAN NUMERALS

I	or i	= 1	XVI	or xvi	=	16
II	or ii	= 2	XIX	or xix	=	19
III	or iii	= 3	XX	or xx	=	20
IV	or iv	= 4	XXI	or xxi	=	21
V	or v	= 5	XXX	or xxx	=	30
VI	or vi	= 6	XL	or xl	=	40
VII	or vii	= 7	L	or l	=	50
VIII	or viii	= 8	LX	or lx	=	60
IX	or ix	= 9	XC	or xc	=	90
X	or x	= 10	C	or c	=	100
XI	or xi	= 11	CD	or cd	=	400
XIV	or xiv	= 14	D	or d	=	500
XV	or xv	= 15	M	or m	=	1 000

MCMLXXXIV or mcmlxxxiv = 1984

DECIMAL (£p) (since 14 February 1971)

£1 = 100 (new) pence

Coins			Notes		
½ (new) penny	½p		one pound	£1
1 (new) penny	1p		five pounds	£5
2 (new) pence	2p		ten pounds	£10
5 (new) pence	5p		twenty pounds	£20
10 (new) pence	10p			
50 (new) pence	50p			

£29·00	twenty-nine pounds
£29·26	twenty-nine pounds 26 (twenty-six (new) pence)
£0·8½ (or 8½p)	eight and a half (new) pence

BRITISH MONETARY SYSTEM

(£. s. d.) (until 14 February 1971)

£1 = 20 shillings = 240 pence

Coins			Notes		
half penny	½d		ten shillings	10s, 10/–
penny	1d		one pound	£1
threepence	3d		five pounds	£5
sixpence	6d		ten pounds	£10
shilling	1s, 1/–			
two shillings (florin)	2s, 2/–			
half-crown half-a-crown	2s 6d, 2/6			

WEIGHTS AND MEASURES

Length

Gt Brit and USA			Metric	
1 inch		=	25·3995	millimetres
12 inches	= 1 foot	=	30·479	centimetres
3 feet	= 1 yard	=	0·9144	metres
22 yards	= 1 chain	=	20·1168	metres
220 yards	= 1 furlong	=	201·168	metres
8 furlongs	= 1 mile	=	1·6093	kilometres
1 760 yards	= 1 mile	=	·6093	kilometres

Avoirdupois weight

Gt Brit and USA			Metric	
16 drams	= 1 ounce	=	28·35	grams
16 ounces	= 1 pound	=	0·454	kilograms
14 pounds	= 1 stone	=	6·356	kilograms
2 stone	= 1 quarter	=	12·7	kilograms
4 quarters	= 1 hundredweight	=	50·8	kilograms
112 pounds	= 1 cwt	=	50·8	kilograms
100 pounds	= 1 short cwt	=	45·4	kilograms
20 cwt	= 1 ton	=	1 016·04	kilograms
2 000 pounds	= 1 short ton	=	0·907	metric ton
2 240 pounds	= 1 long ton	=	1·016	metric ton

Liquid measure

Gt Brit		USA	Metric
4 gills	= 1 pint	= 1·201 pints	= 0·5679 litres
2 pints	= 1 quart	= 1·201 quarts	= 1·1359 litres
4 quarts	= 1 gallon	= 1·201 gallons	= 4·5435 litres

The metric system

Length		Weight	
10 millimetres	= 1 centimetre	10 milligrams	= 1 centigram
100 centimetres	= 1 metre	100 centigrams	= 1 gram
1 000 metres	= 1 kilometre	1 000 grams	= 1 kilogram
		1 000 kilograms	= 1 tonne

CIRCULAR OR ANGULAR MEASUREMENTS

60 seconds	= 1 minute
60 minutes	= 1 degree
90 degrees	= 1 right angle
360 degrees	= 1 circle

TIME

60 seconds	= 1 minute
60 minutes	= 1 hour
24 hours	= 1 day
7 days	= 1 week
4 weeks, or 28 days	= 1 lunar month
13 lunar months and 1 day	
12 calendar months	} = 1 year
365 days	
366 days	= 1 leap year
a.m.	= before noon
p.m.	= between midday and midnight
midday	= 12 o'clock (noon) or 12.00 hrs
midnight	= 12 o'clock (at night) or 24.00 hrs

NUMBER OF DAYS IN THE MONTH

30 days have September,
April, June, and November;
All the rest have 31,
Excepting February alone,
Which has but 28 days clear
And 29 in each leap year.

SPEED

Light travels at 186 300 miles per second
Sound travels at 1 130 feet per second

TEMPERATURE EQUIVALENTS

	Fahrenheit (°F)	Centigrade (°C)
Boiling point	212°	100°
	194°	90°
	176°	80°
	158°	70°
	140°	60°
	122°	50°
	104°	40°
	86°	30°
	68°	20°
	50°	10°
Freezing point	32°	0°
	14°	− 10°
	0°	− 17.8°
Absolute zero	− 459·67°	− 273·15°

To convert Fahrenheit temperature into Centigrade: subtract 32, multiply the number by 5, and then divide it by 9.

To convert Centigrade temperature into Fahrenheit: multiply the number by 9, then divide it by 5, and add 32.

GEOGRAPHICAL NAMES

Column 1 gives the name of the country. Column 2 gives the
adjective which is used to refer to the people or things of that
country, e g Polish meat, the Dutch (people), the English
language. Column 3 gives the noun which is used to refer to
a person or people from that country, e g a Frenchman,
a Filipino, the Swedes.

Country	Adjective	Noun
The 'Argentine	'Argentine	‚Argen'tinian
'Denmark	'Danish	Dane
'England	'English	'Englishman
'Finland	'Finnish	Finn
France	'French	'Frenchman
'Ireland	'Irish	'Irishman
'Netherlands or 'Holland	Dutch	'Dutchman
‚New 'Zealand	‚New 'Zealand	‚New 'Zealander
Paki'stan	‚Paki'stan	‚Paki'stani
'Philippines	'Philippine	‚Fili'pino
'Poland	'Polish	Pole
'Scotland	Scots or 'Scottish	'Scotsman
Spain	'Spanish	'Spaniard
'Sweden	'Swedish	Swede
'Turkey	'Turkish	Turk
United 'Kingdom (of Great Britain and Northern Ireland)	'British	'Briton
Wales	Welsh	'Welshman

Column 1 gives the name of the country. Column 2 gives the
word which is used both as an adjective and as a noun—there
are not two different words as in the above list, e g Brazilian
coffee: the Brazilians; Canadian wheat: the Canadians;
Indian music: the Indians.

Country	Adjective/Noun
Af'ghanistan	'Afghan
Al'bania	Al'banian
Al'geria	Al'gerian
Aus'tralia	Aus'tralian
'Austria	'Austrian

Country	Adjective/Noun
Bar'bados	Bar'badian
'Belgium	'Belgian
Bo'livia	Bo'livian
Bot'swana	of, from Bot'swana
Bra'zil	Bra'zilian
Bul'garia	Bul'garian
'Burma	'Burmese (*sing & pl*)
Bu'rundi	of, from Bu'rundi
Cam'bodia	Cam'bodian
,Came'roon	Came'roonian
'Canada	Ca'nadian
Cey'lon	,Ceylo'nese (*sing & pl*)
Chad	of, from Chad
'Chile	'Chilean
'China	Chi'nese (*sing & pl*)
Co'lombia	Co'lombian
'Congo	,Congo'lese
'Cuba	'Cuban
'Cyprus	'Cypriot
,Czechoslo'vakia	,Czecho'slovak
Da'homey	Da'homeyan
,Ethi'opia	,Ethi'opian
The 'Gambia	'Gambian
'Germany	'German
'Ghana	Gha'naian
Greece	Greek
,Guate'mala	,Guate'malan
'Guinea	'Guinean
Guy'ana	,Guya'nese
'Hungary	Hun'garian
'India	'Indian
,Indo'nesia	,Indo'nesian
I'raq	I'raqi
'Israel	Is'raeli
'Italy	I'talian
'Ivory Coast	of, from the 'Ivory Coast
Ja'maica	Ja'maican
Ja'pan	,Japa'nese (*sing & pl*)
'Jordan	Jor'danian
'Kenya	'Kenyan
Ku'wait	Ku'waiti
'Laos	La'otian
'Lebanon	,Leba'nese
Le'sotho	of, from Le'sotho
Li'beria	Li'berian

Country	Adjective/Noun
'Luxemburg	of, from 'Luxembourg
'Libya	'Libyan
Mada'gascar	,Mala'gasy
Ma'lawi	Ma'lawian
Ma'laysia	Ma'laysian
Mali	of, from 'Mali
'Malta	'Maltese
,Maure'tania	,Maure'tanian
'Mexico	'Mexican
Mon'golia	Mon'golian
Mo'rocco	Mo'roccan
Ne'pal	,Nepa'lese (*sing & pl*)
Ni'geria	Ni'gerian
Norway	Nor'wegian
Paraguay	,Para'guayan
Pe'ru	Pe'ruvian
Portugal	,Portu'guese (*sing & pl*)
Rho'desia	Rho'desian
Ru'mania	Ru'manian
Saudi A'rabia	,Saudi A'rabian
Senegal	,Senega'lese
Si,erra Le'one	Si,erre Le'onean
Singapore	,Singa'porean
So'malia	So'malian
South 'Africa	,South 'African
Su'dan	,Suda'nese (*sing & pl*)
Switzerland	Swiss
Syria	'Syrian
Tanza'nia	,Tanza'nian
Thailand	Thai
To'bago	of, from To'bago
Togoland	,Togo'lese
Trinidad	,Trini'dadian
Tu'nisia	Tu'nisian
Ug'anda	Ug'andan
Union of ,Soviet ,Socialist Re'publics or 'Russia	'Soviet or 'Russian
U,nited ,States of A'merica	A'merican
Vene'zuela	,Vene'zuelan
Yugo'slavia	,Yugo'slavian
Zaire	of, from Zaire
Zambia	'Zambian

EXERCISES

There is a great deal of information available to you in this dictionary and you must learn how to find it, and to find it quickly. These exercises will help you to understand the arrangement of the material in the dictionary. But read HOW TO USE THIS DICTIONARY at the front of this book before you begin.

A Put the following words into alphabetical order: -

1 greatest, brother, visit, hate, opening, steward, machine, umbrella, insect, cutlass

2 zodiac, jungle, membrane, wolves, apple, killer, unnecessary, locust, grumble, uneasy

3 kitchen, instrument, inspiration, jelly, heritage, label, instruct, khaki, jealous, herald

4 unbalanced, unity, undertaken, uncle, uniform, unfold, understudy, unawares, unheard, undertaker

5 misspelled, mischief, mislead, misshapen, misfire, misspelt, mission, miscellaneous, mischievous, misfit

B Looking *only* at the words written at the top of the pages in the dictionary, write down the page numbers on which you would expect to find the following headwords:

fact, green, notice, inside, permit, jungle, expand, whip, quote, serpent

C The words at the top left-hand corner of page 138 are **idea/immemorial**. *Without* looking at the dictionary, write down which of the following headwords you would expect to find on that page:

imp, identical, idea, imagine, idiom, immensely, illusion, ignorant, infant, immediate

D Write down a list of the sub-headwords and idioms that appear in the entries of the following words:

account, black, direct, come, well, bear, nation, solid, fruit, trust

E Look up the following sub-headwords or groups of words and write down the headword of the entry in which they are defined:

abusive, space-flight, persistence, yourselves, great-grandson, on the face of it, safety-pin, slip-knot, see eye to eye, remarkable, worsen, certainty, lead a dog's life, white-elephant, aborigines, in relation to, round-about, figure of speech, make sb welcome, blackberry

F Look up the following words and write down how many meanings are listed in each entry:
bar, paper, run, line, plan, point, give, time, hold, odd

G Write down the headword of the entry in which the following words are explained:
1 leap-year, hostess, myself, could, is, shan't, larvae, invasion, stolen, stiffest
2 was, frozen, doesn't, storeys, funnier, taught, fungi, subnormal, relied, bases
3 ate, angrier, vetoes, vice-admiral, oxen, jail, met, variety, would, dyke

H Using the dictionary, write down the plural forms of the following words:
1 index, cactus, dwarf, elf, man, looker-on, thief, sheep, motto, appendix
2 cargo, wolf, axis, offspring, penny, genus, news, synopsis, crisis, nebula

I Using the dictionary, write down the past participles of the following words:
1 rid, try, catch, fulfil, dig, lie, sew, mean, oversleep, be
2 hear, dispel, clap, shrink, hide, lay, forbid, spread, arise, seek

J Look up the words underlined in the following sentences. Write down whether they are nouns, adjectives, etc and then that part of the entry which explains the word as it is used in the sentence:
1 It's much cooler after a rainstorm.
2 He fell over and grazed his knee.
3 She got the sack for often being late.
4 Ben ran into an old friend at the station.
5 There are hardly any tickets left.
6 Good heavens! Use my bike whenever you want to.
7 Can I count on you to be there by six o'clock?
8 Mary is the daughter-in-law of Mrs Brown.

K Using the dictionary to help you, write down which of the following pairs of words have the same stress patterns:

1 bestial/trivial, abide/weapon, turnip/twitter, festival/festivity, union/unite, blue-blooded/bone-idle, grasshopper/gratitude, instant/insure, book-keeper/worthwhile, aware/baboon

2 harness/harpoon, munitions/gigantic, until/spanner, adequate/gramophone, zebra/yourself, underdog/undergo, blaspheme/cement, about/above, typist/typhoon, inspiration/perspiration

3 understood/undertaker, curtail/yellow, pocket-money/police-station, counteract/counterfeit, benevolence/circumference, tarmac/sunblind, impudent/impulsive, hippopotamus/instantaneous, humiliation/ratification, obligation/locomotion

L With the help of both the entries and the illustrations, describe the similarities and differences (e g *size, shape, use, where found*, etc) between the following:

an ostrich and a penguin; a bus and a coach; a butterfly and a spider; an apple and an orange; a helicopter and a hovercraft; a cello and a guitar; a crocodile and a lizard; an oblong and a triangle; a rake and a spade; an elephant and a lion

M Using the list of COMMON ABBREVIATIONS to help you, write out the following paragraphs in full words and sentences:

1 Dr Wm Smith Jun. M.Sc., OBE worked in the labs at UN H.Q. in N.Y. for 5 yrs bef. he recd. an offer from GB to become a Dir. of BBC TV. He flew str. to London by BOAC with his P.A. approx. 7 wks later to accept the offer.

2 S.c. unfurn. lux. flat on 2nd fl. of lge. hse. in NW Birmingham nr. riv. w. lounge, sgle. bed., b & k; c.h.w. and use of sm. gdn. 5 mins shops & sch. Available fr. end Oct. Rent £35·50 p.m. payable wkly. F & F £1600 o.n.o. View by appt only a.m. on Tues. & Thurs. or eve. on Fri. & fol. Mon. Wm. Brown 73 Southend Dr. Elsington Tel. 123-72560

3 Brian Jones was b. in the Bor. of Camden in 1959. His br. was a Cons. M.P. for a constituency in S. Eng. He recd. 8 O-levels & 3 A-levels bef. leaving his sec. sch. He lived in Fr. for 4 mths bef. going to Univ. to read for a deg. in

Phys. The Univ. mag. was ed. by him and he wrote arts on new pop. EPs and LPs. Sadly he left 2 yrs later ∵ his Prof found him with LSD in his rm. He'd hoped to have m. Susan Wilson, SRN, d. of a Cmdr in the RN, the fol. Sept. and become a res. asst. for a Govt. Dept. on the effects of DDT for the EEC.

N Using the APPENDICES to help you, do the following:

1 Write out in full: ¾, 10 000th, 3rd, 1 000 000 000 000, 21st, ⅛, 19, 20th, 100 000th, 12th

2a Write down the following in Roman numerals: 1942, 18, 730, 1503, 33

b Write down the following in ordinary numbers: XVII, lxii, MCMXCIX, XLVI, lxxiii

3 Write out in full: £30·15, 17½p, £173·75
How many feet are there in 1 chain?
How many pounds are there in 6·356 kilograms?
How many litres are there in 4 pints (Gt Brit)?
How many centimetres are there in 1 kilometre?
How many milligrams are there in 1 gram?
How many seconds are there in a right angle?
How many minutes are there in 1 day?
How many days are there in March?
Convert 100° F into Centigrade

4 What are the people who live in Malaysia called?
What is a man from Ghana called?
Which country does an Afghan come from?
Which country does a Spaniard come from?
What is a man who lives in Japan called?
A Singaporean comes from which country?
In which country would a Soviet town be found?
In which country do the Nepalese live?
What language is spoken in Denmark?
What are the people who live in Switzerland called?

O Letters in words can often be rearranged to make others. For example, from the letters in the word **edited** we can make **tide, it, deed, did**, etc. How many words can you make from the letters in each word below? Use the dictionary to check your spelling; only words listed in the dictionary are to be used

ornament   generation
remonstrate   disappointment

P Here is a crossword puzzle. Make a copy of the pattern on a separate piece of paper and see if you can fill in all the empty squares. The clues for each word are taken from entries in this dictionary so you can check your own answers.

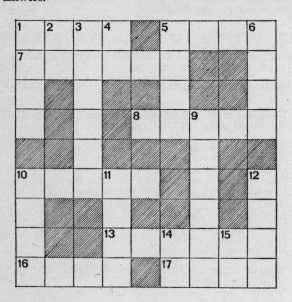

CLUES ACROSS

1 Somebody who writes in verse form
5 Commonest metal from which steel is made
7 Spare or find enough time or money for
8 Short, sharp barks (of pain, anger, excitement)
10 Go into the sea, a river, etc, for swimming
13 Main meal of the day
16 Past tense of **tear**
17 (In fairy-tales) a cruel man-eating giant

CLUES DOWN

1 Past participle of **pay**
2 Made with: *a ring — gold*
3 Result; outcome
4 In the direction of

 5 Unwilling to work
 6 Report or account of what has recently happened
 9 Have a — for, be fond of
10 Superlative form of **good**
11 An animal's skin, esp one used as leather
12 Animal like but larger than a rabbit
14 Stating disagreement or any negative
15 Common abbreviation for *Queen Elizabeth II*